GRAHAM BURGESS achieved the FIDE Master title at the age of twenty following his first place at the international open tournament at Val Thorens, France, in 1988. Since then he has been a regular international competitor, and is the veteran of several chessboard battles with World Championship Candidates. He is the author of twenty highly acclaimed books on chess, and editor of more than two hundred and fifty.

He graduated from the University of Cambridge with a degree in Mathematics in 1989. Since then he has worked as a chess writer, for two years based in Denmark as a club trainer, and later as a commissioning editor in London. Now he is Editorial Director of Gambit Publications Ltd, a chess publishing company founded in 1997. In 1994 he established a new world record for marathon blitz chess playing, scoring a remarkable 87% in 510 games over three days and nights.

In 1997, the first edition of *The Mammoth Book of Chess* won the prestigious British Chess Federation Book of the Year Award.

The Mammoth Book of

CHESS

GRAHAM BURGESS

Foreword by Dr John Nunn

RUNNING PRESS
PHILADELPHIA · LONDON

Constable & Robinson Ltd
3 The Lanchesters
162 Fulham Palace Road
London W6 9ER
www.constablerobinson.com

First edition published in the UK in 1997 by Robinson

This revised and updated edition published by Robinson,
an imprint of Constable & Robinson Ltd, 2009

A copy of the British Library Cataloguing in Publication
Data is available from the British Library

UK ISBN 978-1-84529-931-6

1 3 5 7 9 10 8 6 4 2

9 8 7 6 5 4 3 2 1

Digit on the right indicates the number of this printing

US Library of Congress number: 2008944134
US ISBN 978-0-7624-3726-9

Running Press Book Publishers
2300 Chestnut Street
Philadelphia, PA 19103-4371

Visit us on the web!
www.runningpress.com

Typeset by Graham Burgess
Printed and bound in the EU

CONTENTS

Contents

Part Three: Essential Chess Information

Foreword by John Nunn

The origins of chess are shrouded in mystery. Board games were certainly played by the ancient Egyptians and Romans, but nobody knows the rules of these games or whether they were the ancestors of any games played today. The earliest date to which a definite precursor of chess can be traced is about AD 600. Travelling from India via the Arab world to Europe, chess has exerted its peculiar fascination over a wide range of cultures. This universal appeal, stretching for a span of 1400 years, surely indicates that chess taps some deep-rooted elements of the human mind. Chess almost certainly had its origins in a type of war game, and the sporting or competitive element is still one of its most seductive features. The urge to compete is undoubtedly a fundamental part of the human psyche, and while one may argue as to how much of this urge is a result of upbringing and how much is genetically based, the fact is that it exists and is likely to do so for the foreseeable future.

However, chess does not appeal only to the basic desire to win. It also exerts its pull on another important psychological element, the desire to detect patterns and to impose order on chaos. A human playing chess depends not only on memory and ability to calculate sequences of moves, but also on pattern recognition. This often manifests itself on a subconscious level. Somehow, deep within the brain, all the games of chess one has ever seen have made a mark, and the position on the board at any given moment is compared with all these pre-existing patterns. A close match will result in a sudden "feeling" that one knows what the correct plan should be. A skilled human player will know when to trust these mysterious hunches and when to show a healthy scepticism. Often, when a grandmaster is asked why he played a particular move, he will struggle to explain exactly how he came to a decision. It may appear as though he is trying to keep his secrets to himself, but more often it is simply because he does not himself understand the subconscious processes that led him to play a particular move.

This type of process is one of the highest mental faculties of which human beings are capable. By contrast, purely mechanical reasoning, based on calculation, is less distinctive. Suppose, for example, that a businessman makes decisions about whether to invest money in a particular endeavour purely on the basis of financial calculation. Then he might just as well be replaced by a computer, which would be faster and perform the calculations with less chance of error. A real talent for business goes far beyond routine calculations, into the area of judgement and intuition. Just as in chess, a talented businessman will have a lifetime's experience in his subconscious and this will enable him to make a reasonably accurate decision, even when the information available would result in an "insufficient data" error from a computer. Indeed, his main problem will probably be to try to convince his colleagues of the correctness of his decision. When playing chess, one is alone. There are no colleagues or meetings. One has total authority to implement one's decisions, and conversely one has to accept full responsibility for the consequences, good or bad. This, too, is one of the appeals of chess. There are few areas in life where decisions can be made without consultation and at a moment's notice, and there are few areas where the effects are visible so quickly.

The history of chess is one of very gradual development. The rules have evolved over the centuries but have been more or less static for the past 500 years. For half a millennium, chess knowledge has gradually accumulated, but today's grandmasters still find that much about the game is totally baffling. Now, however, after 1400 years, chess is facing a new challenge from the computer. It is far from clear whether the strongest chess-playing entity on the planet is based on carbon or on silicon. It often seems remarkable to non-chess players that a human has any chance of beating a computer at chess. This arises because of the common misconception that playing chess is all about calculating sequences of moves. The logic then is that since computers are much better at calculating than humans, a computer should normally beat a human. The fallacy here is that, as mentioned above, calculating moves is just one part of playing chess. The mysterious processes of the subconscious are just as important, and these cannot, as yet, be programmed into a machine.

In the 1970s, a human vs computer contest was just a joke, as the poor machines stood no chance at all. Even though they could calculate hundreds of times faster than a human being, the result was a foregone conclusion. At the time, in the artificial intelligence departments of universities all round the world, a great deal of effort was expended on chess programming. The reason was that it was felt that a computer would only play chess successfully when it had been programmed to think like a human being, at least in the limited area of chess. And if it was possible to do it in chess, then why not in other areas of human mental activity? Now, however, the academic interest in chess programming has more or less vanished. Nobody ever succeeded in programming a computer to think like a human being, and all the progress in chess programming has been made by concentrating on what computers do best – calculation. Over the past twenty years the speed of computers has increased enormously and now they can calculate millions of times faster than a human being. What the human does elegantly and with little effort by subconscious pattern recognition, the computer does by "brute force", i.e. by examining millions of possible continuations and finding the right move by an exhaustive analysis probing many moves ahead. Today's computers are so fast that the fact that this method is very inefficient doesn't matter – the computer has megahertz to spare and can afford to waste 99% of its time looking at irrelevant variations that a human would never consider, provided the remaining 1% is spent on the critical lines.

In 1996 the human World Champion, Garry Kasparov, faced the world's leading computer, Deep Blue, in a six-game match. Most commentators imagined that Kasparov would see off the silicon challenge with little difficulty. There was palpable shock when Kasparov lost the first game. Perhaps Kasparov had underestimated the powers of his opponent; in any event, Kasparov played much better in the remaining games and ended up winning by 4-2. However, Kasparov fared less well in the 1997 rematch and the number-cruncher came out ahead by 3½-2½. Since then, the machines have steadily advanced, and Deep Fritz's 4-2 win against Vladimir Kramnik in 2006, in which the then world champion failed to win a single game, indicated that the computers had pushed ahead of the top humans. After this, interest in man-machine contests faded since it was apparent that an interesting contest could only be obtained by handicapping the computer in some way.

The lessons of computer chess may have wider implications. Even though the efforts of computer scientists to make computers think like human beings have not been very successful, perhaps this should not be a cause for regret. In chess, at any rate, computers have achieved their current level of performance precisely by **not** thinking like human beings. The result of this has been a new perspective on chess which has not been provided by 1400 years of human development. Because the processes by which computers select a move are totally different to those employed by humans, computers sometimes come up with an astonishing move which a human would never even consider. Many times in recent years a computer has played a move which the watching humans have dismissed as the result of a programming bug, only for further analysis to reveal the concealed idea behind the move. In other words, the differing perspective of the computer has provided insights which would probably never have been obtained by human analysis. The simple fact is that nobody knows what human beings are missing, and this applies not only to chess.

The limitations of human thought must be there, but little can be said about them because it is impossible to measure the unknown. First of all, our brains are undoubtedly limited by our evolution. Intelligence evolved as a survival characteristic in a world very different from the one we now inhabit. The slow million-year crawl of evolution may have fitted us well for the world in which humanity first appeared, but by comparison the social and technological changes taking place today are lightning-fast. The fact that slightly intelligent apes have developed world-destroying weapons does not imply an ability to manage that same world in a positive way. Moreover, there are probably culturally-based limitations. Human development tends to build gradually from one generation to the next, and only very rarely does it suddenly shoot off at a tangent. Perhaps thousands of years ago there was a fork in the road of knowledge; humanity sped off along one branch, never suspecting that the other existed.

In the absence of any external perspective, we cannot tell how limited our thinking processes are. If we suddenly make contact with extra-terrestrial intelligences, will their thoughts prove to be along utterly different lines to ours, perhaps even to the point of making communication impossible, or will there be enough common ground to make meaningful contact? Nobody can say. However, the progressive development of computers suggests that one day we may be able to create another viewpoint ourselves. Just as the primitive computers of today have shown us new concepts in chess, perhaps one day their successors may show us what we are missing elsewhere. And the first clue will have been provided by a game from sixth-century India.

Symbols and Abbreviations

+	Check	mem	memorial event
++	Double check	wom	women's event
#	Checkmate	Corr.	Correspondence chess
x	Capture	(n)	nth match game
!!	Brilliant move		
!	Good move	GM	Grandmaster
!?	Interesting move	IM	International Master
?!	Dubious move	FM	FIDE Master
?	Bad move		
??	Blunder	FIDE	Fédération Internationale des
Ch	Championship		Echecs (World Chess Federation)
Cht	Team championship	PCA	Professional Chess Association
OL	Olympiad	GMA	Grandmasters Association
Ech	European championship	USCF	United States Chess Federation
Wch	World championship	ECF	English Chess Federation
Z	Zonal event		
IZ	Interzonal event		
Ct	Candidates' event		
jr	junior event		
tt	team tournament		

When a game mentioned is annotated in *The Mammoth Book of the World's Greatest Chess Games*, this is indicated by WGG followed by the game number.

Introduction

Although this is entirely appropriate to be read as a first or second course in chess, it is not a beginners' chess book in the traditional sense. Likewise, although it contains plenty of high-level material and some truly mind-bending chess puzzles, it is not an experts' manual. I have written this book in such a way that it provides inspiration and useful information for everyone with an interest in chess, from total beginners to grandmasters.

The result of this, I hope, is a book that you will refer to and dip into for many years to come; a book you will not outgrow as you become an accomplished player.

Why play chess?
Everyone who plays chess has their own answer to this question, and since you have at least picked this book up off the shelf, the game must have an attraction to you.

To children, chess is a cool way to beat other children (or, better still, adults). Winning at chess is far more satisfying than winning in any more primitive type of battle, and has more street-cred than coming top in a maths test (though that is the sort of thing children who play chess tend to do!).

Parents of chess-playing children delight in the mental training the game provides. Children who excel over the chessboard have an uncanny ability to succeed in other fields too.

For adults playing chess at a high level, the thrill of the game is just as great. Adrenaline flows freely during a tense chess game, and a good win feels better than, well, just about anything.

For adults who play chess at less exulted levels, it is a fun pastime, an enjoyable way to spend time with friends or a way to meet people with similar interests at a club. And yes, everyone gets a kick out of winning, no matter how or who against.

These are mainly the external reasons for playing chess. What is it about the game itself that players like? Simply put, the game is beautiful. For all of the supposed complexity of chess, the geometry is simple and elegant. A well-played game has a certain logical crispness about it. Simply seeing a good move on a board can give chess players pleasure. It is a glorious feeling to play a great game, flowing from start to finish.

A chapter-by-chapter walk-through of this book
I am assuming that readers already know how to play chess and understand chess notation. If you do not know how the pieces move, I recommend that you learn from a friend or relative, face-to-face across a chessboard. This is by far the best way to learn how to play chess. If this is not possible, then

Appendix A, near the end of the book, is the place to start. Then Appendix B explains how chess games are written down, while the next stage in the traditional programme for newcomers to chess is to learn the basic mates: Appendix C.

If you are up to speed with these basics, then the rest of the book beckons. If your main aim is to improve your chess-playing, then proceed to Part One. There you will find tips, examples and positions for solving. Inexperienced players should work through these chapters in turn from the start of the section on delivering mate, while more experienced players can dip in according to taste; the mates in two should provide entertainment, and the combinations a real challenge. I guarantee that no matter how good you are, you will meet your match somewhere in these positions for solving, although for masters this may not be until the tougher combinations.

Seeing tactics is really the key to playing chess successfully, since they are the building blocks from which everything else in chess is made. Therefore, it is especially important to study and understand these early chapters. Once you have got a good feel for the tactical properties of the pieces, it is time to move on to the section on endgames, openings or attack and defence.

The discussion of endgames is quite brief. My aim here was to present a few of the key positions that will be of most use in practice and to explain the basic concepts of endgame play. There are many weighty tomes of detailed analysis of all manner of endgame positions. My experience is that since the exact positions in the endgame manuals will almost never arise in actual play, it is not so much the specifics of the analysis that are important, but rather the concepts. Playing endgames well is about knowing a few key positions well, knowing what to aim for and analysing a great deal at the board.

In the section on openings my aim has been to explain the spirit of each opening and give you some idea of the typical plans and strategies available to both sides. I feel this is far more useful than presenting a lot of detailed analysis. Once you have identified openings that appeal, you will be in a better position to understand detailed monographs on the individual openings, should you decide further study is needed. I have also indicated a great many traps in the openings.

Even if you have no great interest in studying openings, there is much of interest in the openings section. The strategic examples are all highly instructive illustrative games that will repay close examination.

The chapter "Attack and Defence" was a lot of fun to write. Here we see standard sacrifices (sometimes successful, sometimes not) and plenty of examples of creative attacking, defensive and counterattacking chess. It is in attacking play that tactics and strategy come together.

Talking of strategy, you may be wondering where the section on chess strategy has gone. I decided that it was too important a subject to be compartmentalized, and so the discussion of strategy runs throughout the sections on openings, and attack and defence. The glossary also provides a wealth of information on strategic concepts and could very well be read as a course in the basics of chess strategy.

The second part of the book takes a general look at the chess world and is the place to go if you wish to discover more about how you can pursue your interest in chess, whether by playing club or tournament chess, using computers or by getting online. These are exciting times for chess, since the game is so well suited for playing online, and chess data can be transmitted so efficiently in electronic format. For a time in the 1990s, the battle for chessboard supremacy between the strongest human players and the most powerful computers raged, but now the emphasis is more on cooperation between the two. The puzzles chapter allows you, amongst many other things, to test how well you can cooperate with your own computer.

The glossary in the third part of the book is as detailed as I could make it, with just about every significant chess term I could think of defined and discussed. It is worth taking a look at the glossary even if you don't have anything specific you need to look up, since a lot of the entries are entertaining or instructive.

There are many people I should thank for, in one way or another, making this book possible. Firstly, Mark Crean at Robinson Publishing, who first approached me with the idea of a big-value general chess book, and all the other staff at Constable & Robinson deserve thanks, notably Mark's successors, Krystyna Green, Pete Duncan and Duncan Proudfoot. It has been a pleasure to work with such a highly professional publishing company. John Nunn has been a great help; I would like to thank him for his thought-provoking foreword ("I've never before seen a foreword containing Indians, aliens and computers" – Mrs Petra Nunn) and general technical assistance. John also provided plenty of ideas, directly and indirectly, for the content of the book. Indeed, a great many of the people I have met since I first learned how the pieces move thirty-eight years ago have in some way provided ideas for the book or helped clarify what my aims should be. In particular I would like to mention Frederic Friedel, Yasser Seirawan, Jonathan Levitt, Reg Burgess, Andrew Savage, Gary Quillan, Sean Elliott, Tyson Mordue, Natasha Regan, Dr Heather Walton, Niels Højgård, Jakob Bjerre Jensen, Steffen Pedersen, David Norwood and Steve Davis. I should also thank my mother and sister who proof-read some sections of the book. I apologize to anyone I have forgotten to mention.

To conclude, I wish you many years of pleasure using this book, and hope that it provides you with a deep understanding of chess and the people who play it.

Graham Burgess
London 1997
(minor updates to this introduction, 2000 and 2009)

Dedication
This third edition is dedicated to my fiancée, June Mary Stengel.

Introduction to the Second Edition

In this new edition, I have sought to bring the book fully up to date in a number of respects. Firstly, I attended to any typos that had found their way into the first edition. Next, I employed a new automated procedure (developed in 1997) to check all the moves for legality and accuracy of notation, and then ran a computer-check over all the analysis. This threw up a number of points, which led to a good deal of new analysis, and in some cases made it necessary to replace games and positions entirely. For the most part though, the analysis stood up to scrutiny, and remains unchanged, but may now be considered computer-approved.

The next task was to bring the content up to date by addressing developments in the fields of computer chess and online chess. In particular, there is a completely new section in the chapter on Computer Chess, discussing the abilities of the latest generation of chess-playing computer engines. Finally, it was necessary to update any topical content, such as the state of play (or non-play) in the world championship.

Graham Burgess
Bristol, England 2000

Introduction to the Third Edition

Enough time has passed since the first edition of *The Mammoth Book of Chess* that I have now had the experience of players telling me that it was their first book, and even their favourite book, before sitting down at the board – and defeating me. Naturally, I have mixed feelings about this, but I am pleased that this book has made such an impact.

This third edition features a completely new chapter on computer and Internet chess, given how drastically these aspects of chess have changed in the intervening time. I have also added an extra chapter of 60 puzzles which I hope readers will have many hours of pleasure attempting to solve. If they prove too difficult (always an author's main fear when setting puzzle positions), then please view them as additional examples to complement those in the earlier chapters of the book. Naturally, I have also taken the opportunity to update the book in a number of other respects (particularly the opening coverage), but most of the other material remains largely unaltered.

Finally, I would like to thank the staff at Constable & Robinson for their enthusiasm for this project, their generous allocation of an extra 32 pages, and for their patience when some unexpected changes in my personal situation led to a delay in delivering the new text.

Graham Burgess
Woodbury, Minnesota 2009

Frequently Asked Questions

There follow some of the typical questions that chess players get asked by non-players or casual players, with typical answers – or at least my answers.

How far ahead do you look?
Ah, that old chestnut! It varies a lot. In some positions it is possible to look ahead many moves, generally when there is very little material left on the board, or when many of the moves are totally forced. In other positions there is no point calculating – when there are no forcing variations it can be better to think generally about the position and find simple ways to improve it. In some sharp positions where it is not possible to get to the bottom of the tactical variations, chess players will often let their intuition be the main guide in their choice of move.

That isn't the sort of answer you wanted though. In a typical middlegame position (if such a thing exists) with some possibility of sharp tactics, but nothing too forcing or complicated, then a good player will typically look ahead three to five moves by both sides, concentrating solely on the plausible moves – this is where intuition comes in. How many positions this amounts to is hard to judge. Consciously, a player may be aware of looking only at a few dozen positions that arise in the variations he looks at. Subconsciously, hundreds of positions will flash past his mind's eye, but little conscious thought is needed to dismiss those that embody dreadful ideas. Throughout this process, the player will be looking to identify any particularly critical variations that demand more searching analysis.

How do you become a grandmaster?
This is far easier to explain than to do! There are some events (e.g. world junior championship) in which the winner is awarded the title automatically, but most grandmasters gain their title by achieving *grandmaster norms*. These are exceptional results in international events. If a player scores enough points against sufficiently strong opposition, then he achieves a norm. When he has achieved norms equivalent to a total of 24 games, then if his rating is sufficiently high, he is eligible to receive the title. Most grandmasters achieve their title by scoring three norms of 9 to 11 games, but there is nothing to stop a player gaining the title in one 24-round event!

Does chess require a great deal of patience?
No. In appearance the game may look like one in which patience is essential, but the thinking behind it is mostly violent. Each side is trying to destroy the other. This is not a game of peaceful coexistence, where one tries to coexist slightly better than the other. True, once a high level of skill has been reached, some games can reach technical positions, which

become a war of attrition, but even then it is often a slow build-up to a violent finish.

Do the games take a very long time to finish?

Not necessarily. It is entirely possible to play a game of chess in just a few minutes when using a chess clock. When playing for fun (or perhaps for a stake of some sort), one of the standard time limits is five minutes for all the moves – so the game lasts a maximum of ten minutes. Some players prefer even faster time limits – for instance one minute for all the moves. True, the quality of such games is not too good normally! Another way of playing fast games is to use a "lightning buzzer". This makes a noise every ten seconds (or whatever), and the player whose turn it is to move must make his move at that moment. As for tournament chess, there are plenty of quickplay events, in which each player is allotted twenty to forty minutes for all the moves in each game. In standard tournament play each player has two hours for the first forty moves, and an extra hour to reach move sixty. This does not seem slow if you are playing a tense game! It is true, however, that some forms of chess do take a long time. Postal games can take months or even years, while there is the story of one postal game being played at the rate of one move every year.

How can humans hope to play successfully against powerful computers?

Hmm. A few years ago this question would have been "how can computers hope to play successfully against powerful humans?" In purely calculating terms, computers have a huge advantage. Even the primitive chess computers of the mid-1980s were strong enough to see some intricate tactics. However, computers have no real concept of long-term planning, and no intuition. Put a human up against a strong computer in a position with the pieces randomly scattered over the board, with nothing from which the human can take any bearings, and silicon will come out on top. However, such positions don't occur very often in chess games. A skilful human chess-player can guide the play along more intuitively graspable lines, and so give the computer more problems. However, even this is becoming too hard, and as of 2009, even the best players in the world struggle to take many points off the best computers; indeed, this type of match is becoming a rarity. That is not to say that computers comprehensively outclass humans though. Computers still miss ideas that humans see readily, and sometimes choose moves that are obviously bad. A computer working with human guidance will play and analyse far better than either in isolation, and this human-computer cooperation has been one of the major driving forces behind the sharp change in playing style at the top levels of modern chess – see the chapter on Computer Chess for more in this topic.

Why don't more women play chess?

Good question. The reasons generally advanced are social conditioning, or women tending to be less aggressive by nature. I tend to think that most women are much too sensible to persist in playing a board game unless they can become really good at it. Men are perhaps more obsessive. Quite simply, I don't think anyone really knows why chess doesn't appeal to more women, or has even advanced a particularly good explanation.

How come there are so many chess books? What is there to write about?
The market for chess books is substantial since there are many ambitious chess players to whom it is important to be up to date with chess theory, since this gives them an edge over their opponents. If you're spending a lot of time studying chess, there is nothing more annoying than losing a game simply because the opponent is better read. Many books are about openings. Ambitious players tend to specialize in particular ways of starting the game. In a major chess opening, of which there are many, there are hundreds or even thousands of important new master-level games each year. Reading a recent book on the opening in question is the best way to keep up to date. There is also a good market for general books. The understanding of chess strategy does not stand still, and while one could reach a certain level by studying only the games of the "old masters", one would also be missing out on a lot of new dynamic ideas.

Isn't chess getting played out? Don't the top players play most of the game from memory?

This is a common misconception. There are far more possible games of chess than there are particles in the known universe, and the number of possible chess positions, though far fewer, is still astronomical. While it is true that in some openings there are main lines that extend past move twenty, this is not a sign that chess is being played out – just that some of the main highways have been extensively explored. That does not imply that there isn't a great deal of unexplored territory. And once the known territory is left behind, the players are on their own.

I'm just an ordinary social player. How long would it take a grandmaster to beat me?
If you play sensible moves, then no matter how strong your opponent may be, he will not be able to force a quick checkmate. Expect any mistakes to be punished quickly, and to come under pressure if you play passively. Against a grandmaster, a player below club level would be doing well to avoid serious mishaps in the first twenty moves, and could be proud of reaching move thirty alive. In terms of time taken over the moves, a top-class player could play more or less instantly under these circumstances. It is only when the players are evenly matched that the course of the game depends on strategic subtleties or long-term plans.

Can anyone who didn't learn chess when they were a young child hope to become any good?
It depends what you mean by "any good"! Most players who go on to

join the world élite took up the game when they were very young, but it is not unknown for those who started to play chess in their late teens to become good international-level players or grandmasters. However, I'm not aware of anyone who started to play chess as an adult becoming a grandmaster. However, if your ambitions are to reach a good club or county level, then whatever your age, this is an entirely feasible aim. Get hold of a few books, a reasonable chess computer and visit your local club, and don't get too upset if you lose a lot of games to start with. Those who take up chess relatively late in life can often become successful in correspondence chess, since in the slower form of the game, speed of thought is not so critical as when playing against the clock – positional understanding, which can be learnt, and a methodical approach count for a great deal. And you can verify everything with a computer, but check the rules of the individual event if you want to have a clear conscience...

Who is really the World Champion, and what's all this business with FIDE and the PCA, BGN, WCC, etc.? I'm interested in the details.

From 1993 to 2008 it was a rather complicated mess, and there are still some loose ends that could easily become frayed over the next few years. But the good news for chess as a whole is that there is now (as I write in late 2009) a single, undisputed World Champion: Viswanathan Anand from India. But before then...

Garry Kasparov had been the "official" FIDE (Fédération Internationale

des Echecs – World Chess Federation) Champion up to 1993, when he broke away to form a new organization, the PCA (Professional Chess Association). Under the auspices of the PCA, he defended his title against the challenger who had won FIDE's candidates cycle, Nigel Short. Thus the formal legitimacy of both players was obtained by successes in FIDE events. Following the breakaway, FIDE disqualified both players. Under FIDE's rules, Karpov and Timman, the two highest placed men in the candidates' events who had neither been disqualified nor had lost a match to anyone still involved in the cycle, contested the then vacant "official" FIDE World Championship. It did little for the credibility of the FIDE match that both these players had lost matches against Short, who in turn was comfortably defeated by Kasparov. Karpov, who had been FIDE Champion 1975–85, won the match.

Most players tended to accept Kasparov as the real champion, but several factors clouded the issue greatly. Kasparov's organization, the PCA, lost the sponsorship that it had secured from the microprocessor producers Intel. The PCA then ceased operations after just one more title match, Kasparov's successful defence against Anand in 1995. FIDE's own championship was plagued with delays in holding Karpov's next defence, against Kamsky. The match eventually took place in 1996 in Elista, after plans to play in Baghdad had caused outrage around the chess world. FIDE subsequently adopted a knockout format for its world championship, which, while an interesting event in itself, held little credibility as a World Championship. Several key players didn't take part, and the format tended to produce a new champion each year (generally, but not always, from the world's top 20 players), as the statistical probability of even a clearly superior player coming through a whole series of mini-match victorious is extremely small.

Meanwhile Kasparov's attempts to organize a credible world championship had gone further awry. In 1998, Kramnik and Shirov (taking Anand's place, who declined to take part for contractual reasons) were "appointed" to play a match, with the winner to challenge Kasparov. After Shirov unexpectedly beat Kramnik, it proved difficult to find adequate sponsorship for a Kasparov–Shirov match. At the end of 1998, Shirov was left out in the cold, with Kasparov inviting Anand, who had by then established himself as clearly World No. 2, to challenge him directly. Even for this match, sponsorship proved difficult to find. Russia's Vladimir Kramnik was then reappointed challenger, and he unexpectedly defeated Kasparov in a match in London in 2000, largely by stifling Kasparov's creativity with very solid chess.

This was to be Kasparov's last world championship match, as he was granted no rematch.

Various plans and organizations came and went, before Peter Leko qualified through a different cycle again to face Kramnik, and narrowly failed to lift the crown.

Until his retirement in 2005, Kasparov remained the dominant figure in world chess, and no championship that didn't involve him in some capacity was going to have much credibility. Once he was out of the picture, a re-unification plan had a chance to become reality, despite the many aggrieved parties that both world championship cycles had left in their wake, and the obvious difficulties involved in getting two men to sit down to contest a title that they both believed they had already earned, and with FIDE never admitting that their championship had ever been anything other than the "real" one. But the damage to chess as a whole from its highest-profile event being diluted into two rival cycles was evident to all, and the impetus for reunification looked set to sweep all obstacles from its path.

Without going into all the ins-and-outs, Veselin Topalov from Bulgaria won a world championship tournament in 2005. This had been intended as the reunification event, but Kramnik refused to play, still leaving two rival champions. Kramnik and Topalov contested a bitter match in 2006 (so bitter that the reunification process nearly failed), with Kramnik winning eventually. In 2007, the process called for a further world championship tournament, which was won by Anand, ahead of Kramnik. Those of a traditional frame of mind were disappointed that what had generally been a matchplay title had been decided in a tournament. They could finally be content when in 2008, Anand defended his title with a decisive match victory over Kramnik: the line of succession was intact, and the title was reunified to the satisfaction of all. Or most, at any rate.

Delivering Mate

The king is not a very fast moving piece. He can move only one square at a time, and so, even on an open board, has a maximum of only eight squares at his disposal, and at the edge of a board a mere five, while in the corner, he can move to at most three squares.

Checkmate occurs when the king is attacked and there is no way of stopping the attack (whether by taking the attacking piece or putting something in the way), and all of the king's possible flight squares are either attacked by enemy pieces or blocked by "friendly" pieces.

It is not difficult to mate a king. If you have several pieces near your opponent's king, and his defences are not in order, you should expect to find a mate. Likewise, make sure your own king has protection when he needs it – but more on that in the later chapter on attack and defence.

If you are an experienced player, I suggest you skip this introduction and the 25 novice warm-up positions.

To introduce you to a systematic way of thinking about checkmate, let's consider how many squares in the king's field (i.e. the square he is on, and those he might be able to go to) each piece can attack – see the following diagrams.

First, let's consider the most powerful piece, the queen.

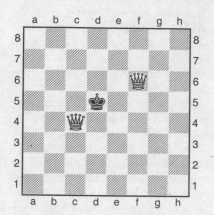

A queen can attack six squares in the king's field (only five if not giving check). This leaves only three to be covered by other pieces.

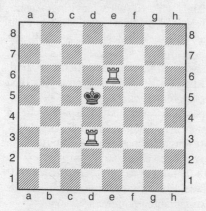

A rook can attack four squares in the king's field, or only three if it is giving check.

A bishop can attack three squares in the king's field (only two if not giving check). All of these squares are of the same colour.

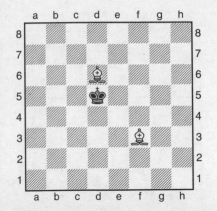

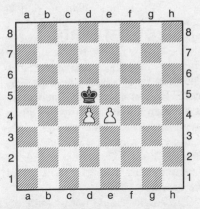

Next we consider the knight, which makes up for its short-range move by moving in a way that no other pieces can.

Let us also not forget that the king itself can also help to deliver mate to his opposite number.

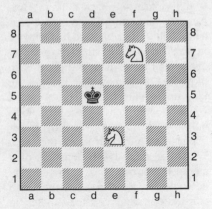

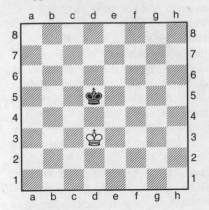

A knight can attack two squares in the king's field. Like the bishop, all the squares are of the same colour, though the colour squares that a knight attacks changes each time it moves.

It is all too easy to forget that the humble pawn can also participate in mating attack. A pawn can attack two squares in the king's field (only one if giving check).

A king can attack three squares in the enemy king's field (and cannot of course give check).

If in each case the above comments are not immediately clear, then I suggest you write down a list of the squares attacked by each white piece in the diagrams. Answers are given on page 33.

One conclusion we can draw immediately is that the queen is a very powerful mating force in itself, and needs only a little help to deliver mate. A single piece attacking a square next to the enemy king is often all the queen needs. If you think of chess as a medieval war game, then this is the equivalent of needing only the most menial spy in the enemy palace – then a state visit by the queen (see page 18) wins the war in itself!

Since the rook attacks squares in a straight line, it can be particularly deadly against a king at the edge of the board.

The knight should not be underestimated. Since it moves in a different way from the other pieces, it is the perfect complement to them. Indeed a queen and knight work together so well that when they are buzzing around a king, there is more often than not a mate.

Two bishops also complement each other well, whether attacking along parallel diagonals or at right angles to each other.

This chapter features a series of positions that test your ability to deliver mate. First, here's a brief look at some standard mating patterns.

Note that in many of the diagrams that follow, only the pieces relevant to the mating idea are shown; in a real game situation there would be plenty of other pieces present.

The Back-rank Mate
This is one of the simplest mating ideas, but a tremendously important one. A rook (a queen is also ideal for the purpose) attacks all the squares along the king's first rank, while a row of pawns prevents the king from advancing to avoid the mate.

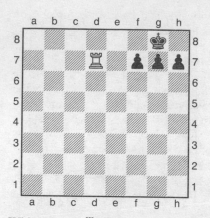

White plays **1 ℤd8#**.

In games between inexperienced players, it is all too common a sight for the player who has been winning to fall victim to a back-ranker. "How can they mate with just a rook?" It is a cruel and bitter blow to lose a game in this way. The simplest way to avoid all risk of a back-ranker is to move one of the pawns in front of the king one square forward. However, I would recommend this precaution only when the game is fully under control and you can spare the time. While the game is still tense, to play any of the moves ...f6, ...g6 and ...h6 not only wastes time, but may also constitute a weakness that invites an attack.

At top level, back-rankers are important too. Not generally as a one-move mating attack, but the value of a complex tactical sequence may hinge on a back-rank trick. (See the glossary entry for Back-rank Mate.)

The back-ranker is also known as the Corridor Mate, though this term also incorporates rare cases (generally in problems) where "friendly" pieces block the king's movement forwards and backwards, or else on both sides.

Smothered Mate

If you thought "friendly" pieces didn't live up to their name in the back-rank mate, here they are positively evil! In a smothered mate, a knight gives check, but this is enough to mate, since all of the king's possible escape squares are occupied.

It is a bit much to expect that the opponent will block off all of his king's escape squares and allow a knight to hop in and give mate, so generally a sacrifice will be necessary. Here is a very simple example to set up a smothered mate:

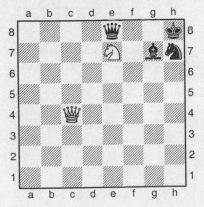

The black king has only the g8-square to which it might flee, so White lures the black queen onto that square: **1 ♕g8+ ♕xg8** (there is no other way to get out of check) and then **2 ♘g6#** finishes off nicely.

The idea of smothered mate is by no means new. The earliest recorded example is from half a millennium ago, in 1497, not long after the queen's powers had been extended:

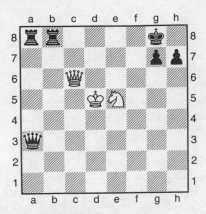

1 ♕e6+ ♔h8

1...♔f8 allows instant mate by either 2 ♕f7# or 2 ♘d7#.

2 ♘f7+ ♔g8 3 ♘h6++

3 ♘d8+ also forces mate – by modern standards an alternative solution is a major flaw in a composition.

3...♔h8 4 ♕g8+! ♖xg8 5 ♘f7#

This position was published by Lucena in his chess manual. It is therefore rather rough on him that in common chess parlance the name Philidor is generally associated with this idea. To compensate for this, a standard, and very important, position in the theory of rook and pawn versus rook, first published by Salvio in 1634 is generally known as the "Lucena Position" (see the chapter on endgames, page 95).

Mate with the Queen

The simplest way to give mate is to put your queen right next to the opponent's king, provided your queen is defended, of course. Then only a few squares need to be denied to the king for it to be mate; none if the king is at the edge of the board. The following are a few examples.

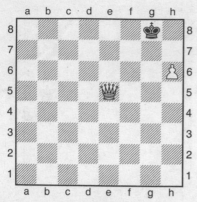

Here a pawn provides the support, and the edge of the board prevents the king from running, so...

1 ♕g7#

Here's another, which should be very familiar.

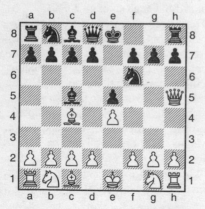

This position has arisen after the moves 1 e4 e5 2 ♗c4 ♗c5 3 ♕h5 (a bad move played millions of times by novices) 3...♘f6 (an even worse move, also unfortunately played millions of times by other novices). Black's last move was a blunder; instead 3...♕e7 gives Black an excellent position. White now plays:

4 ♕xf7#

Here's a more sophisticated idea, often relevant when the king has been dragged out into the open, and the queen is chasing it towards hostile pawns:

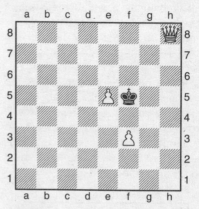

1 ♕f6#

A very economical mate. One pawn covers the two squares the queen cannot reach, while the other pawn defends the queen.

Mate with Several Minor Pieces

Here are some of the most important patterns:

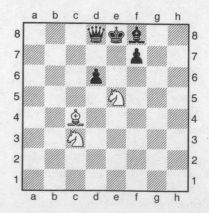

White's minor pieces dive in and mate the king:

1 ♗xf7+ ♔e7 2 ♘d5#

This finish is characteristic of Legall's Mate, which is a drastic tactical method of breaking a pin.

Two knights can suffice to mate a king when he is short of squares:

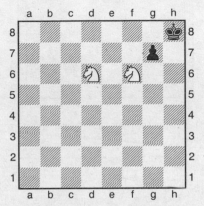

1 ♘f7# finishes off nicely. Note that in general knights are more effective when standing next to each other than when defending one another.

Here are two examples of a pair of bishops delivering mate:

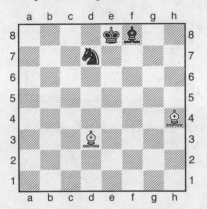

1 ♗g6# is very light compared to some of the mates we have seen. It's very easy to miss such ideas at the board.

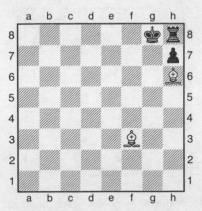

1 ♗d5# is the finish this time.

Now we move on to the positions for solving. The first twenty-five positions are intended as warm-ups for novices, and should not take too long to solve, but don't worry if you get stuck on a few – we all have mental blocks now and then. I have provided some rather generous clues, to some of the positions, in the above diagrams. If all else fails, consider every legal move.

As a rough guide, strong players should solve each position in just a second or two, while ordinary club players should not take long either.

If you have problems solving them, set the position up on a board and concentrate as though you were playing a game.

In the solutions, I note any tactical themes that occur in the positions. These ideas constitute an armoury of checkmating ideas that will help you throughout your chess career.

25 Novice Warm-ups

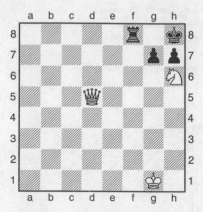

1) White to play and force mate in two moves

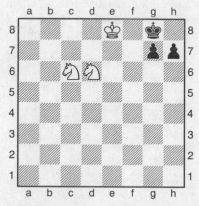

3) White to play and force mate in two moves

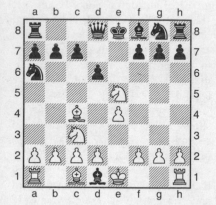

2) White to play and force mate in two moves

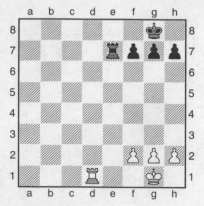

4) White to play and force mate in two moves

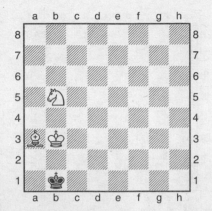

5) White to play and force mate in two moves

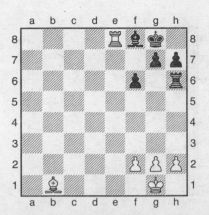

7) White to play and force mate in two moves

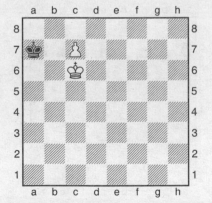

6) White to play and force mate in two moves

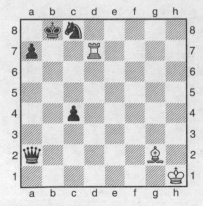

8) White to play and force mate in two moves

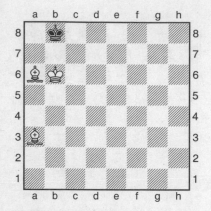

9) White to play and force mate in two moves

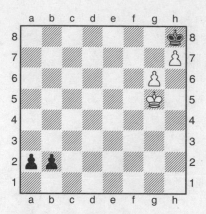

11) White to play and force mate in two moves

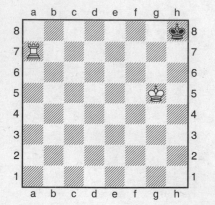

10) White to play and force mate in two moves

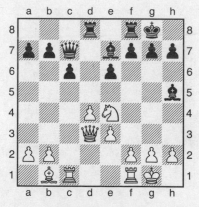

12) White to play and force mate in two moves

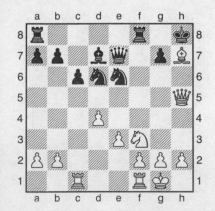

13) White to play and force mate in two moves

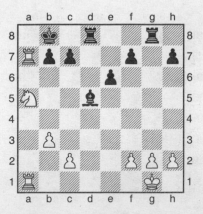

15) White to play and force mate in two moves

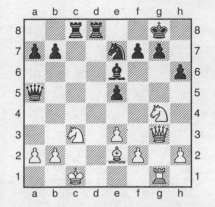

14) White to play and force mate in two moves

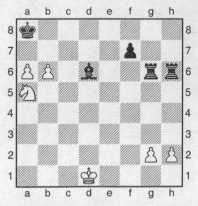

16) White to play and force mate in two moves

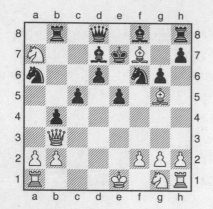

17) White to play and force mate in two moves

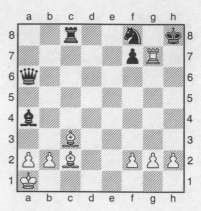

19) White to play and force mate in two moves

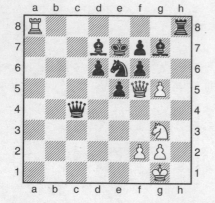

18) White to play and force mate in two moves

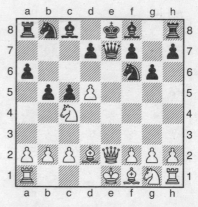

20) White to play and force mate in two moves

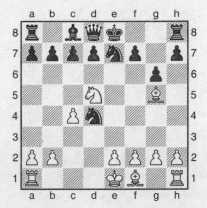

21) White to play and force mate in two moves

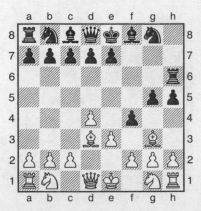

23) White to play and force mate in two moves

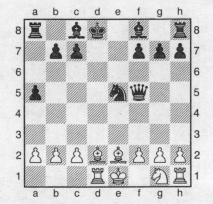

22) White to play and force mate in two moves

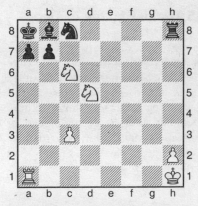

24) White to play and force mate in two moves

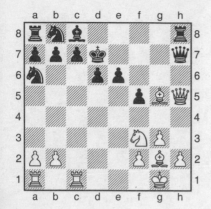

25) White to play and force mate in two moves

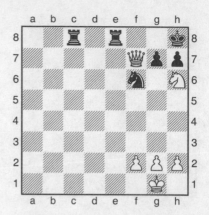

1) White to play and force mate in two moves

25 Trickier Mates in Two

I hope you didn't have too many problems with those positions. Here are twenty-five rather more complex mates in two. The ideas tend to follow on logically from those we have seen, but are more deeply hidden, or combine various ideas. Nevertheless, experienced players should sail through this test as well.

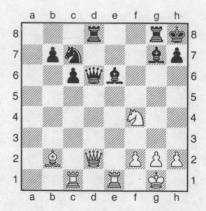

2) White to play and force mate in two moves

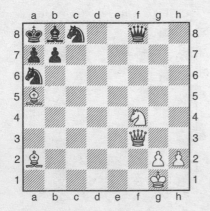

3) White to play and force mate in two moves

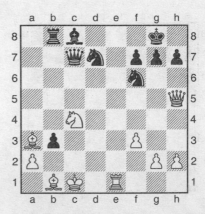

5) White to play and force mate in two moves

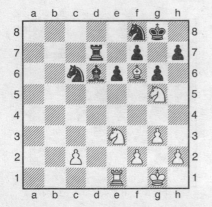

4) White to play and force mate in two moves

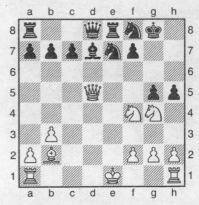

6) White to play and force mate in two moves

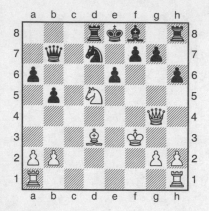

7) White to play and force mate in two moves

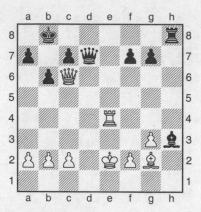

9) White to play and force mate in two moves

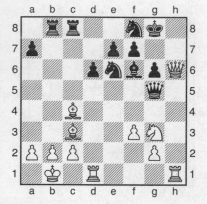

8) White to play and force mate in two moves

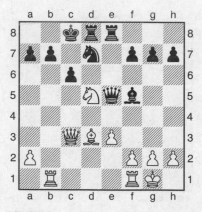

10) White to play and force mate in two moves

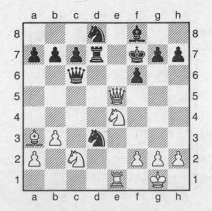

11) White to play and force mate in two moves

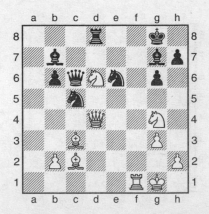

13) White to play and force mate in two moves

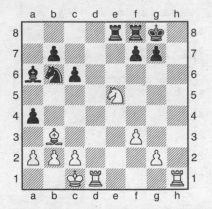

12) White to play and force mate in two moves

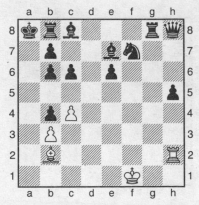

14) White to play and force mate in two moves

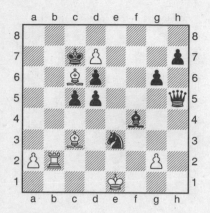

15) White to play and force mate in two moves

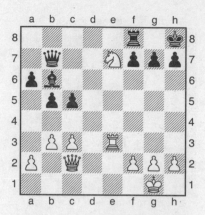

17) White to play and force mate in two moves

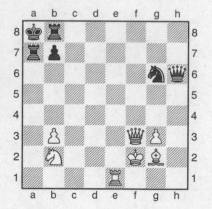

16) White to play and force mate in two moves

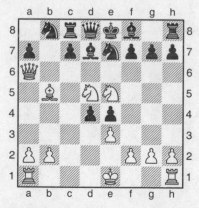

18) White to play and force mate in two moves

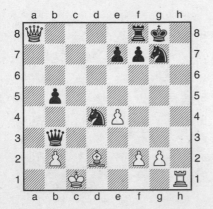

19) White to play and force mate in two moves

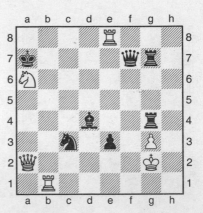

21) White to play and force mate in two moves

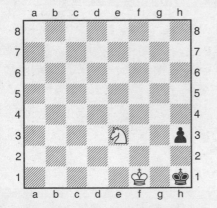

20) White to play and force mate in two moves

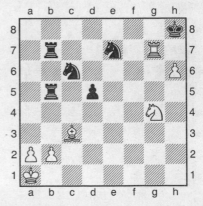

22) White to play and force mate in two moves

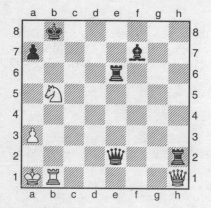

23) White to play and force mate in two moves

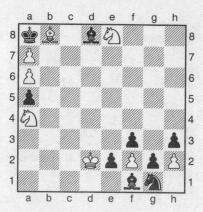

25) White to play and force mate in two moves

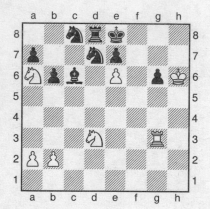

24) White to play and force mate in two moves

Solutions to Delivering Mate

Explanation of diagrams on pages 14–15:

Queens: the f6-queen attacks c6, d4, d6, e5 and e6. The c4-queen attacks c5, c6, d4, d5, e4 and e6.

Rooks: the e6-rook attacks c6, d6, e4 and e5. The d3-rook attacks d4, d5 and d6.

Bishops: the f3-bishop attacks c6, d5 and e4. The d6-bishop attacks c5 and e5.

Knights: the f7-knight attacks d6 and e5. The e3-knight attacks c4 and d5.

Pawns: the e4-pawn attacks d5. The d4-pawn attacks c5 and e5.

King: the white king attacks c4, d4 and e4.

25 Novice Warm-ups – Solutions

1) 1 ♖d8+ ♖e8 2 ♖xe8#
The simple back-rank mate has claimed countless victims. Related ideas can decide games at international level, so look out for them!

2) 1 ♗xf7+ ♔e7 2 ♘d5#
White's minor pieces cooperate very well here. This is the finish of Legall's Mate.

3) 1 ♕g8+ ♖xg8 2 ♘f7#
This is perhaps the simplest mating combination involving a queen sacrifice, but also a beautiful and striking one. It is named Philidor's Legacy, after the great French champion of the eighteenth century, André Danican Philidor, although the idea dates all the way back to Lucena's 1497 manuscript.

4) 1 ♘e7+ ♔h8 2 ♘f7#
A simple mate with two knights. One knight forces the king into the corner, and the other delivers the killer blow.

5) 1 ♘c3+ ♔a1 2 ♗b2#
A typical finish to the mating procedure with bishop and knight versus king. Note that the king must be mated in a corner on which the bishop can cover the corner square, and that White must be careful not to give stalemate.

6) 1 c8♖
1 c8♕ is stalemate, and only a draw!
1...♔a6 2 ♖a8#
Remember to look out for stalemates and that when you promote a pawn you do not have to take a queen. White could also have won here (though not given mate in two) by playing 1 ♔d7 and then 2 c8♕.

7) 1 ♗a2+ ♔h8 2 ♖xf8#
The bishop check forces the king away from the defence of the bishop, so the rook can finish the job with a standard back-ranker.

8) 1 ♖b7+ ♔a8 2 ♖b2#
This is a typical mating finish to a "Windmill" combination, of which

we shall see more in the chapter on tactics. Note that the rook must go to b2 in order to prevent the black queen from taking the bishop.

9) 1 ♗d6+ ♔a8 2 ♗b7#
A typical finish when forcing mate with two bishops against a bare king.

10) 1 ♔g6 ♔g8 2 ♖a8#
A typical finish when mating with rook against a bare king. It is characteristic of the whole procedure for the white king to place itself a "knight's move" away from the black king when the rook controls the line separating them. Then, if after Black's reply the two kings face each other directly, a rook check will force back the sole king or, as here, be checkmate.

11) 1 ♔h6 a1♕
Or 1...b1♕ 2 g7#.
2 g7#
It doesn't matter that Black promotes first – White gives mate! When pawns are racing to promote, it is generally good to have your king in front of the enemy pawns – but only if he slows them down or stops them advancing! Otherwise, he might just encourage them to advance at double speed, with checks or even mate.

12) 1 ♘f6+ and no matter what Black plays, **2 ♕xh7#** follows. Black has left it a little late in playing the defensive move ....♗g6! This is a typical attacking ploy by White in queen's pawn openings.

13) 1 ♗g6+ ♔g8 2 ♕h7#
This is a standard attacking idea,

which may escape a player's attention, especially when this type of situation arises a few moves into a variation. One sees a perpetual check, with the bishop moving between h7 and some other square on the b1–h7 diagonal, forgetting that this "other square" could be g6, preventing the black king from escaping from the mating net.

14) 1 ♘f6+
1 ♘xh6+? ♔f8 2 ♕xg7+ ♔e8 allows the king to sneak out.
1...♔f8 2 ♕xg7#
A simple forced mate, illustrating, if nothing else, the value of an open file towards the opponent's king – and of course the right to move!

15) 1 ♖a8+
1 ♘c6+? bxc6 (and not 1...♗xc6? 2 ♖a8#) permits the king to run out via b7.
1...♔xa8 2 ♘c6#
Rook and knight are very effective at mating kings in corners!

16) 1 ♘c6 and 2 b7# follows. Here we see the vulnerability of the king in the corner, and the power of advancing pawns, even when promotion is not on the cards.

17) 1 ♘c6+ ♗xc6 2 ♕e6#
The knight sacrifice simply diverts the bishop from covering the e6-square. I hope the rather irrational nature of the position did not distract you from this essentially straightforward idea.

18) 1 ♕xf6+ ♗xf6 2 ♘f5#
The thought "if only the queen

weren't there" should have helped you find this move. The queen just needs to vacate f5 in such as way as to avoid disturbing things too much. Then the knight hops in and finishes the job.

19) 1 ♖h7++ ♔g8 2 ♖h8#
This is the end of a so-called "staircase" mate. Everything is done with double checks, so the attacking pieces being *en prise* is irrelevant.

20) 1 ♘d6+ ♔d8 2 ♗a5#
This is the sort of thing that might happen in the early stages of a game, though Black would have had to have been exceedingly incautious. Having said that, I caught a strong county-standard player with something almost as bad in a match once!

21) 1 ♘f6+ ♔f8 2 ♗h6#
A pleasant geometrical mate, and an illustration that it is occasionally even worth sacrificing a whole queen to get rid of a fianchettoed bishop!

22) 1 ♗g5++ ♔e8 2 ♖d8#
A double check forces the king back home to e8, where White gives mate rather economically. This is a simplified version of an idea that we will see in various traps in the chapters on chess openings.

23) 1 ♕xh5+ ♖xh5 2 ♗g6#
Essentially, this is a variation on Fool's Mate, with a decoy of the black rook thrown in. It is also the final sequence of the short game featured in the children's chess book *The Amazing Adventures of Dan the Pawn*! The serious point is, of course, that one must be extremely careful when advancing kingside pawns when undeveloped.

24) 1 ♖xa7+ ♗xa7
Or 1...♘xa7 2 ♘b6#.
2 ♘c7#
This sort of thing should become second nature. The bishop is the only piece stopping ♘c7 being mate, so any means of diverting it must be examined. When one sees that the knight cannot capture on a7, the picture is complete.

25) 1 ♘e5+ dxe5 2 ♖d1#
A surprisingly abrupt finish, until you consider that the black pieces are doing everything but defend in numbers.

25 Trickier Mates in Two – Solutions

1) 1 ♕g8+ ♖xg8
Or 1...♘xg8 2 ♘f7#.
2 ♘f7#
This is of course the simple Philidor's Mate (see page 17), but with the knight also covering g8. It makes no difference here, but I once discovered to my cost in a lightning game that if the rook is on f8 and the knight on f6, there is no mate!

2) 1 ♘g6+
The knight opens the queen's line and diverts the key defensive pawn.
1...hxg6 2 ♕h6#
The clue here was that the black king was extremely short of squares, and so virtually any checks are going to be forcing moves, and should be examined if a mate seems plausible.

3) 1 ♕xb7+ ♔xb7 2 ♗d5#
As we see, having plenty of pieces around a king does not mean that he is defended! Quite the contrary if all they do is box him in.

4) 1 ♘g4 and 2 ♘h6# is unstoppable. This is a fairly typical mating net, and shows a potential problem if a bishop abandons its fianchetto position.

5) 1 ♖e8+ ♘xe8
Or 1...♘f8 2 ♖xf8#.
2 ♕xh7#
A simple piece of diversion, but note the long-range power of the bishops!

6) 1 ♕xf7+ ♔xf7 2 ♘h6#
Black's bunched pieces are worse than useless here, as White's minor pieces cover all the right squares. Of course, in a real game it would be just as good to give mate in three by the simpler 1 ♘h6+ ♔h7 2 ♕xf7+ ♔xh6 3 ♕g7#.

7) 1 ♕xe6+ fxe6
Or 1...♗e7 2 ♕xe7#.
2 ♗g6#
This type of mate is one that Black must look out for in some of the sharper lines of the Sicilian (see page 174) where Black delays his kingside development in favour of pursuing arguably greater strategic aims.

8) 1 ♕h8+ ♗xh8 2 ♖xh8#
This is an X-ray combination. In the start position, White covers the h8-square twice (queen and h1-rook) while Black is also on it twice (king and bishop). Nevertheless, White can sacrifice his queen on this square

with decisive effect since the c3-bishop "X-rays" through the f6-bishop to h8.

9) 1 ♕a8+ ♔xa8 2 ♖e8#
The white queen decoys the black king into a double check that just happens to be mate. It matters not that both checking pieces are attacked; they cannot both be taken at once.

10) 1 ♕xc6+ bxc6
Other possibilities are 1...♕c7 2 ♕xc7# and 1...♔b8 2 ♕xb7#.
2 ♗a6#
This is a fairly standard queen sacrifice to open up an apparently secure queenside. A variation on this theme has a white bishop controlling the h2-b8 diagonal, mate being delivered by the two bishops alone.

11) 1 ♕e8+ ♔xe8
Or 1...♔g8 2 ♕xf8#.
2 ♘d6#
Again, a queen sacrifice lures a king into a double check, which, thanks to the unfortunate disposition of the black pieces, happens to be mate.

12) 1 ♘g6 and 2 ♖h8# follows inevitably. This idea is important in practice, as an important defensive idea is to eliminate a bishop attacking along the a2-g8 diagonal. If the battle is close-fought, the attacker will need to seek ways to keep this bishop alive long enough to help land the decisive blow.

13) 1 ♘h6+
The knight sacrifice diverts the bishop off the long diagonal.

1...&xh6
Instead 1...&h8 2 ♘df7# is a simple
knight mate.
2 ♕h8#

14) **1 &g7** and Black can do nothing
about **2 ♖a2#**. This is, I admit, a
rather unnatural position, but then
the idea embodied in it is a spectacular one. Indeed, the simultaneous
opening of the line for the white
rook, and blocking of lines for the
black queen and g8-rook is the sort
of theme one finds in chess problems. Note that 1 &xh8 not only fails
to force mate in two, but also loses:
Black plays 1...&g5 or 1...♖g1+ 2
&xg1 &c5+ 3 &f1 b5.

15) **1 ♖b7+ &xc6**
Or 1...&d8 2 &f6#.
2 d8♘#

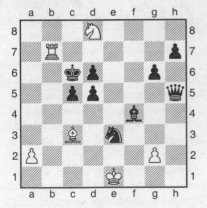

A beautiful finish, which I must admit is based upon the game Runau–
Schmidt, which you can find as a
trap in the Openings section (see
page 171).

16) **1 ♕xb7+**
Whichever rook captures the queen, it

is walking into a pin, and so cannot
parry a check from the white rook.
1...♖bxb7
Or 1...♖axb7 2 ♖a1#.
2 ♖e8#

17) **1 ♕xh7+ &xh7 2 ♖h3#**

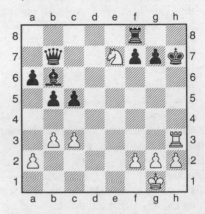

This is quite a standard mating pattern, which often occurs in practice.
It is worth watching out for knight
checks on e7 (or by Black on e2),
since the queen and rook can easily be
in the right positions to give this mate.

18) **1 ♕f6**
A truly spectacular move, threatening mate on f7.
1...gxf6
Otherwise White carries out his
threat: 1...♘xd5 2 ♕xf7# or else
1...&xb5 2 ♕xf7#.
2 ♘xf6#
Another smothered mate. This is
reminiscent of a trick Black can pull
off in the Grünfeld Defence – see the
traps in the Openings section.

19) **1 ♕xf8+ &xf8 2 ♖h8#**
Essentially, this is just a simple back-
ranker, set up by a queen sacrifice.

20) 1 ♘g4

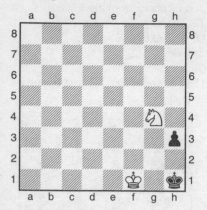

Note that this move carries no threat at all, but puts Black in zugzwang.

1...h2

Black's only legal move sets up a mate in one by denying the black king its only flight square.

2 ♘f2#

21) 1 ♖a8+

1 ♘c7+? is no good since 1...♕xa2+ is check.

1...♔xa8 2 ♘c7#

Double check, and mate. The black king had to be decoyed onto a8 so that when the knight discovered check from the white queen, it also gave check itself.

22) 1 ♘f6 and **2 ♖h7#** follows, unless Black moves his e7-knight, whereupon **2 ♖g8#** is the finish. The battery from the c3-bishop doesn't come into the solution at all here – it was just a red herring. In real games you will also need to decide what is relevant and what isn't!

23) 1 ♕a8+

Decoying the black king into the corner. Instead, 1 ♘xa7+ is not so good, since the king does not have to take the knight: 1...♔c7 and the king walks.

1...♔xa8 2 ♘c7#

24) 1 ♔g7 and no power in the world can prevent **2 ♘c7#**. Black's pieces are just too badly placed.

25) 1 ♔e1

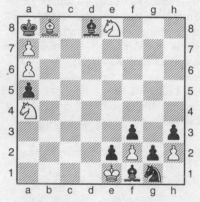

Zugzwang – White does not threaten mate on the move, but Black now has no decent move. I ought to apologize for the somewhat unnatural position, but it was mainly to test whether you were sparing a thought for what the opponent could do, rather than just what you can achieve by force.

1...♗b6

Or 1...♗c7 2 ♘xc7#.

Other bishop moves give White a choice of mates.

2 ♘xb6#

Tactics

In many sports, the word "tactics" refers to the aspects that involve the deepest thought: out-psyching the opponent, or the long-term planning, for instance in pool or snooker. The fact that tactics in chess are the shortest term factors, upon which the medium-term planning and strategy are based, reflects two things: that chess is quite deep, and that it is a game of complete information, in which executing each move is not a problem. If, for instance, pool and snooker were not played using cues and balls, but on a computer that executed the chosen shot exactly as it was intended, then the tactics (e.g. snookering the opponent, safety shots, etc.) would soon become the building-blocks upon which the real strategy of the game was based.

Tactics in chess are the interactions between the pieces that are any deeper than simply capturing material that the opponent has blundered away.

The purpose of this short chapter is to provide an introduction to the main tactical methods that are important in practical chess. The main thing to bear in mind is that it is not so vital to know the precise names of individual tactical devices, but rather to know how to use them to further one's plans at the board and to put them together to produce combinations. That's why this chapter is short, while the next, where we get to the interesting stuff, is long.

Checkmate
This, of course, is the most important tactical device of all!

Destruction
A very simple idea: if a key piece is holding the opponent's position together, it makes sense to remove it, even at a considerable material cost.

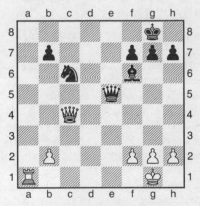

Now 1 ♖a8+ would have no impact: Black could reply 1...♘d8. So White plays 1 ♕xc6!, destroying the knight that is enabling Black to defend against back-rank mates. Then after 1...bxc6 comes 2 ♖a8+, mating.

Another very typical destructive theme is a sacrifice to shatter the pawn cover in front of a king. We shall encounter this many times throughout the book.

Tip: try to visualize what might happen if a particular piece did not exist on the board. If you like what you're seeing, look for ways to destroy the piece in question!

The Fork

This is one of the simplest and most effective tactical devices. One piece directly attacks two or more enemy pieces simultaneously. Typically a knight is effective for this purpose.

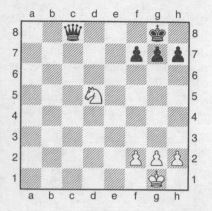

In this very simple example White plays ♘e7+, attacking both king and queen. Black must move his king out of check, so White's next move will be ♘xc8, winning a whole queen.

Between beginners who have reached the level at which they can avoid getting mated in the first few moves, and do not blunder pieces gratuitously, I would reckon that losing material to a knight fork must be the most common single reason for losing a game. The unusual way in which these pesky horses move means that their tricks are often overlooked, even by fairly experienced players.

Forks can also be made by other pieces. Consider the position at the top of the next column. The white b5-pawn is forking the black knights, and the black rook is forking the white king and queen. White wins a knight, but Black a queen for a rook.

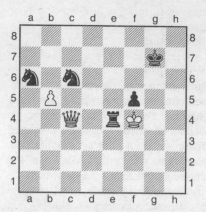

Tip for inexperienced players: if your opponent's knights are at all active, then just before making a move, have a last look to be sure you're not allowing a knight fork. Remember too that for a knight to fork two pieces, they must stand on the same coloured squares.

Double Attack

Whereas in a fork, one piece attacks more than one enemy unit, in a double attack, two or more pieces are responsible for creating the multiple attacks.

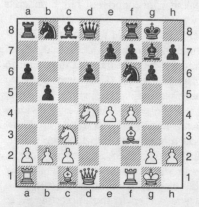

This may come about when a piece

moving to make a discovered attack also makes an attack of its own, as in the diagram.

Here White now plays 10 e5. The pawn attacks the f6-knight directly (an exchange of pawns on e5 would not change this) while, by moving from e4, the pawn has discovered an attack from the f3-bishop onto the black queen's rook. Experienced players would know to look out for this sort of thing.

A double attack can also arise from a piece moving so as to add to or reinforce the action of others.

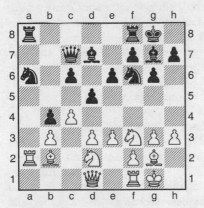

In this position, the move 1 ♕a1 opens up a double attack on the two black knights: suddenly, from being attacked once and defended once, they are both attacked twice, and it turns out there is no way to save them both.

Discovered Attack
This occurs when a piece moves off a line, opening up an attack from a piece that had been behind it. In itself, this is no more difficult to deal with than any normal attack on a piece, except maybe that it is a little

harder to see. The real problem is that the piece that has moved may be able to create some other problem, perhaps giving check and so making it impossible to deal with the discovered attack.

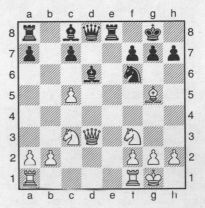

This position comes from a game Ghitescu–Fischer, Leipzig OL 1960. White has just made a horrible blunder by capturing a pawn on c5. Fischer now played 14...♗xh2+ whereupon Ghitescu resigned. After the bishop is taken, the black queen will capture her white counterpart.

Tip: always take note of any potential attacks like this. There may be several pieces in the way, but it is amazing how quickly the rubble can sometimes be cleared.

Discovered Check
This is similar to discovered attack, except that the attack is a check to the king itself. This means that the piece that is moving is free to do pretty much what it likes with complete invulnerability.

In the following diagram Black has carelessly allowed White to give a discovered check from the e1-rook.

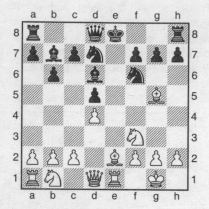

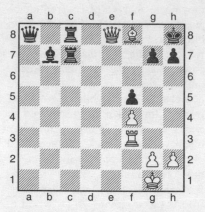

For one move the e2-bishop can go to squares that would normally be unthinkable, since Black must deal with the check. The bishop can do most damage by going to a6, and then taking the b7-bishop: ♗a6+ wins a piece.

Tip: allow a discovered check only if you are absolutely certain it is safe to do so, and if you are able to give a discovered check, be sure to extract the maximum value from it.

Double Check

This is an off-shoot of the discovered check, in which the piece that moves also gives check. Normally there are three possible ways to get out of check, but with two pieces giving check from different directions, there is no way in which both pieces can be taken, or both checks parried, in just one move. Therefore the king must move. This makes the double check into a tremendously potent weapon, frequently devastating.

The next diagram features a characteristic example of a double check crowning a mating attack against the black king:

Black seems to have everything covered, but a double check destroys this illusion:

1 ♗xg7++

This is actually a forced mate in seven!

1...♔xg7

The only legal move.

2 ♖g3+ ♔f6

Or 2...♔h6 3 ♕e6+, etc.

3 ♕e5+ ♔f7 4 ♖g7+ ♔f8 5 ♕f6+ ♔e8 6 ♕e6+ and mate next move.

Tip: calculate any variations involving double checks – however implausible they may seem – with great care.

The Pin

A pin occurs when a piece is attacked (but not necessarily threatened with capture) by an enemy unit, and is preventing or discouraged from moving off the line of attack since this would open up an attack onto a more important piece behind. Often, the pin itself may not cause much damage, but many tactics can spring from it.

In the next diagram there are two pins:

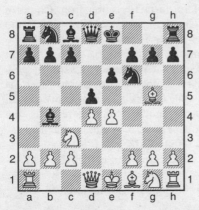

The white bishop on g5 pins the black f6-knight against the queen on d8, while the b4-bishop pins the c3-knight against the white king. The pin against the king is stronger than that against the queen, since sometimes tactical considerations mean that it may be OK to break a pin against a queen, either as a sacrifice, or if there is some reason why the queen cannot be taken.

The pin of the c3-knight creates a threat to capture the e4-pawn – *a pinned piece does not defend* – while White's move ♗g5 enabled him to maintain the central tension a little longer. Thus both these pins can be seen as methods of controlling central squares, and so as good positional moves.

A pin can often give rise to a threat to win material. While a piece is immobilized by a pin, all it takes is for a pawn to attack the piece for it to be in grave danger. In fact, in this precise position, White has the move 5 e5, and it is only thanks to the trick 5...h6 (and then 6 exf6 hxg5 or 6 ♗h4? g5) that Black is not losing a piece. Several methods of breaking

pins are discussed later in this chapter, under the heading "Tactical Defences".

Pins frequently form the basis of simple material-winning combinations.

For instance, in the position in the next diagram, the Welsh player (and pianist) Francis Rayner used a simple trick to gain a pawn and subsequently a surprise victory over the Greek IM Moutousis, at the Novi Sad Olympiad, 1990:

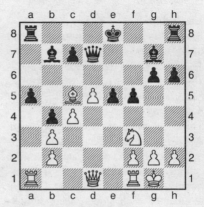

20 ♘xe5! ♗xe5 21 ♖e1
The bishop is pinned against the king, and there is no good way to defend it.

The Skewer
A skewer is a form of pin, but with the added point that the piece creating the attack intends to take either of the enemy pieces. Generally this is because the pieces cannot be defended or the attacking piece is less valuable than those attacked.

In the following position a simple trick based on a skewer helped me to an easy win over the Romanian IM Ilijin at the 1992 Biel Chess Festival:

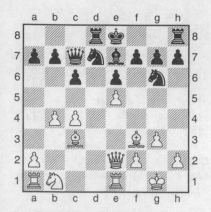

15...♘dxe5!

Black has stolen a pawn in broad daylight, since after 16 ♗xe5 ♕xe5 17 ♕xe5 ♘xe5 18 ♖xe5, Black has 18...♗f6, skewering the white rooks.

The X-ray

This is a much-misunderstood term. An X-ray occurs when a player turns out to be able to use a square, as if he actually controlled it, despite it superficially (i.e. on a simple count of the number of each side's pieces attacking it) appearing to be controlled by the opponent. The phenomenon is best shown by an example:

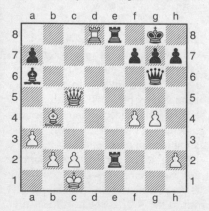

Here, in this position from Chigorin–Znosko-Borovsky, Kiev 1903, the f8-square is attacked twice by White and twice by Black – so it might seem that White cannot sensibly play a piece to the square. However, as soon as Black's e8-rook moves to f8, the white rook on d8 attacks the square too. So, White forces mate:

1 ♕f8+! ♖xf8 2 ♖xf8#

The point here is that f8 was controlled by the white rook "X-raying" through its black counterpart.

Deflection

Also known as distraction, this involves a piece being deflected away from controlling a vital square or line.

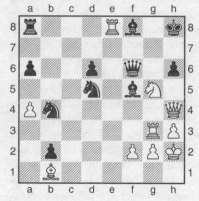

In this position, from the climax of the sensational 20th game from the 1990 World Championship match, between Kasparov and Karpov, Garry Kasparov had a choice of two decisive ways to deflect the black queen. The way he chose was 30 ♕xh6+! ♕xh6 31 ♘f7+ ♚h7 32 ♗xf5+, exploiting the fact that the black queen is no longer covering f7 or f5, to achieve a decisive material gains. One would suppose that such a sequence would be good enough for anyone, but in fact White had better: 30 ♘f7+!, distracting the queen from h6, forces mate in five more moves: 30...♕xf7 31 ♕xh6+ ♔h7 32 ♖xa8 and a prosaic mate follows.

Decoy

Also known as enticement, but not to be confused with deflection, a decoy occurs when a piece is decoyed onto a fatal square or line.

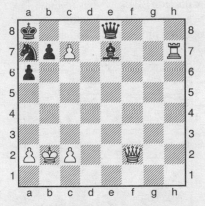

White now makes two decoy sacrifices: 1 ♖xe7! ♕xe7 2 ♕xa7+! ♔xa7 and then underpromotes to fork the two decoyed pieces: 3 c8♘+!, and following 4 ♘xe7, White has an easily won ending.

Overloading

A piece is overloaded if it is performing two vital roles (e.g. defending two pieces, or against a mate threat and stopping a pawn promoting) and so by forcing it to carry out one of these vital functions, it thereby neglects the other. Here is a case in point:

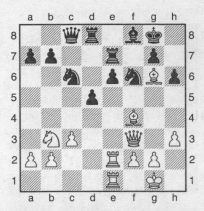

This position, from a game Kharlov–Izkuznykh, Kemerovo 1995, illustrates a common way to win material. The g7-pawn is overloaded, and 20 ♗xh6 exploits this. White wins a pawn, since 20...gxh6 is answered by 21 ♕xf6, now that the knight lacks defence from the pawn.

Square-clearance

This is quite a simple idea. Suppose there is an ideal square for one of your pieces, from which it would have some devastating effect. However, this square is occupied by one of your own pieces.

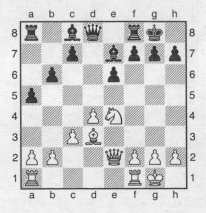

Here is a typical example. If the e4-knight were to spontaneously combust, White would be able to play 1 ♕e4, winning a rook due to the threat of mate on h7. It makes sense then to remove this piece that is in the way by the fastest means possible: exchange it, sacrifice it; somehow dump it to free the square. So, how can White get rid of this knight? The most forcing is 1 ♘f6+ (if you're looking for a forcing move, a check is generally a good option). After 1...♗xf6 2 ♕e4 g6 3 ♕xa8, White is the exchange up.

Line-opening

An extension of the idea of square-clearance, but here it is not a specific square that is needed, but a line. Here is a graphic example:

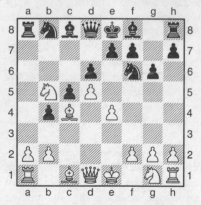

White can now try the very surprising 9 e5 dxe5 10 d6. This sacrifices two pawns to open the diagonals from b3 to f7 and f3 to a8. If Black now plays 10...exd6 (best), then after 11 ♗g5, White is generating some highly potent threats: 12 ♗xf6 (distraction) 12...♕xf6 13 ♘c7+ (fork); 12 ♕f3 (fork/double attack).

Interference

When one forces the opponent's pieces to get in each other's way with catastrophic effect, this is known as interference. (Problemists should note that the term as used by practical players is far more general than the very specific meaning used in problem terminology.) Here is one very simple example, which occurs after the moves 1 e4 c5 2 ♘f3 d6 3 d4 cxd4 4 ♘xd4 ♘f6 5 ♘c3 g6 6 ♗e3 if Black now plays the move 6...♘g4??. This is a well-motivated venture – Black wishes to hunt down White's important bishop – but is a horrible blunder.

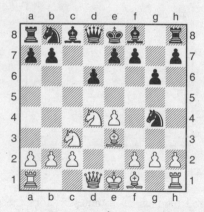

Now the check 7 ♗b5+ brings about a catastrophe for Black. There is no decent way to parry the check. 7...♘c6 is obviously bad in view of simple 8 ♘xc6 bxc6 9 ♗xc6+, while playing either minor piece to d7 loses the g4-knight to 8 ♕xg4: 7...♘d7 interferes with the line of defence from the bishop, while 7...♗d7 is no use either, since the bishop is pinned against the black king.

Another way of interfering with the movement of enemy pieces is to block lines or squares that they may need to use. Here is a typical example:

This is from an old game Tal–Campomanes (the same one who went on to become an extremely controversial FIDE president), after the moves 1 e4 c6 2 d4 d5 3 ♘c3 ♘f6?! 4 e5 ♘fd7. Tal now played 5 e6 fxe6. This pawn sacrifice gives White some chances on the kingside, but the main idea is that the black bishops will have great difficulty making any worthwhile moves. After 6 ♗d3 ♘f6 7 ♘f3 g6 8 h4 c5 9 dxc5 ♘c6 10 ♕e2, Black never got his position in order.

Zwischenzug

This is more of a concept than a precise tactic. The word comes from German, and if you translate it to "in-between move" it ceases to be so strange or frightening. It is a forcing move played before making what appears to be a compulsory move, often a recapture.

Here's an example, from a game Kerchev–Karastoichev, Varna 1965, where Black found an excellent move, illustrating the theme perfectly:

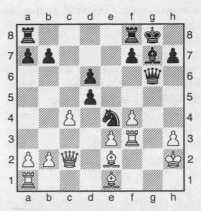

1...♘g5 discovers an attack on the white queen, and hitting the rook on f3. White replied 2 ♕xg6, but rather than recapturing immediately, Black played 2...♘xf3+. Since this is check, White has no time to save his queen, and so after 3 ♗xf3 hxg6, Black had won an exchange (rook for minor piece).

Tactical Defences

Having seen some of the main tactical devices, let us now consider how they might be defended against.

Getting "off prise" by attacking enemy pieces

Suppose one's pieces have been forked, skewered or otherwise seem doomed to be captured. It is often possible to save the day by moving one of the attacked (or potentially attacked) units so as to attack an opposing piece (or ideally give check). If the opponent responds to this counter-threat, then the respite gained may be enough to save the remaining attacked piece.

Here is a miraculous example perpetrated by the computer program

Fritz as Black against Grandmaster Kveinys in a five-minute game at Bonn, 1995:

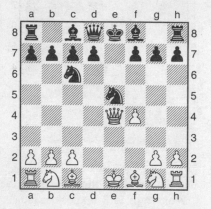

It seems that the e5-knight cannot possibly be saved, but it turns out that Black can generate such activity that White is never able to take the knight:

7...d5 8 ♕e3

8 ♕e2 ♗g4 9 ♘f3 ♗c5! is good for Black, e.g. 10 ♘bd2 0-0 11 fxe5 ♘d4 12 ♕d1 ♖e8 13 ♗d3 ♖xe5+.

8...d4 9 ♕e2

After 9 ♕e4 ♕h4+ 10 g3 ♕g4 11 ♗b5 (else Black plays 11...♗f5 or 11...♕g6, and unravels his pieces easily) 11...♗d7 Black is planning simply to castle, and annihilate White down the centre files.

9...♗b4+ 10 c3 ♗g4 11 ♘f3

11 ♕d2 is met by 11...dxc3!.

11...♗xf3 12 gxf3 dxc3 13 bxc3 ♕h4+ 14 ♕f2 and here 14...♗xc3+! would have won instantly, and rather prettily: 15 ♘xc3 ♕xf3+ 16 ♔e2 ♘fd4+ 17 ♔e3 ♘f5+ 18 ♔e2 ♘cd4+ (now the other knight joins in) 19 ♔e1 ♘c2+ 20 ♔e2 ♘fd4+ and White's queen must drop off. The knight that delivers the killer

blow is the one that has looked doomed from move 7!

Pin-breaking

Pins were made to be broken – except pins against the king, of course. A pin of a knight against a queen by a bishop gives rise to all sorts of tactical ideas that must be taken into account by both sides.

Here's a temporary queen sacrifice:

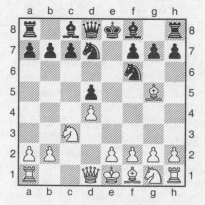

Here we have one of the oldest tricks in the book. If White plays 6 ♘xd5?, hoping to win a pawn thanks to the pin on the f6-knight, he is in for a horrible surprise: 6...♘xd5! 7 ♗xd8 ♗b4+ and now White must put his queen in the way of the check: 8 ♕d2. Then 8...♗xd2+ 9 ♔xd2 ♔xd8 leaves Black a piece up.

True, this is rather a hackneyed trap, but the idea is of great general importance. Consider the opening line 1 d4 d5 2 c4 ♘c6 3 ♘c3 ♘f6 4 ♗g5 ♘e4 5 ♘xe4 dxe4 6 d5. Difficult for Black? Not a bit of it; he plays 6...e6!, with the point that 7 ♗xd8?! ♗b4+ 8 ♕d2 ♗xd2+ 9 ♔xd2 ♘xd8 is at least OK for Black.

Sometimes a direct attack on the enemy queen can be used to break a pin. The following is typical, and used to seem almost magical to me:

1 d4 ♘f6 2 c4 g6 3 ♘c3 ♗g7 4 e4 d6 5 ♗e2 0-0 6 ♗g5 ♘bd7 7 ♕d2 c6 8 ♘f3 e5 9 0-0 exd4 10 ♘xd4 ♘c5 11 f3?

What could be more natural? However, this move, which has been played by at least one grandmaster, is a serious mistake.

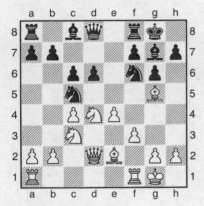

11...♘fxe4!!

Stunning!

12 fxe4

12 ♘xe4 ♘xe4 13 fxe4 ♗xd4+ is similar, while after 12 ♗xd8?? ♘xd2 Black wins a piece.

12...♗xd4+ 13 ♕xd4

13 ♔h1?? loses outright to 13...♗xc3 14 bxc3 ♘xe4.

13...♕xg5

Black has a lovely position. White's e4-pawn is a serious weakness.

Here's another typical situation in the Sicilian Defence, when White has pinned the f6-knight:

1 e4 c5 2 ♘f3 e6 3 d4 cxd4 4 ♘xd4 ♘f6 5 ♘c3 d6 6 ♗g5 ♗e7 7 f4

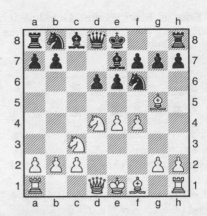

7...h6!

Black needs the white bishop to be undefended.

8 ♗h4 ♘xe4! 9 ♗xe7 ♘xc3 10 ♗xd8 ♘xd1

Black emerges from the skirmish rather well.

Another radical means of breaking a pin involves decoying the enemy king so that the pinned piece can move with check. For example:

1 d4 ♘f6 2 c4 e5 3 d5?!

White should take the pawn.

3...♗c5 4 ♗g5?

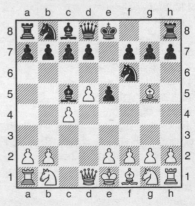

Many years ago I had this position as

Black, and to my eternal shame I missed a very simple combination:

4...♗xf2+! 5 ♔xf2 ♘g4+

Black's next move will be 6...♕xg5, with a material and positional advantage.

Care is needed though – an undefended pinning bishop does not mean there is necessarily a combination. Here's another example where I did something stupid:

1 d4 d5 2 c4 dxc4 3 e4 e5 4 ♗xc4 exd4 5 ♘f3 ♘c6 6 0-0 ♗g4

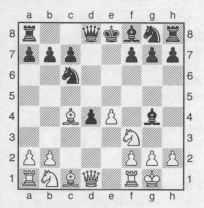

Now White should play 7 ♕b3, with advantage. Instead...

7 ♗xf7+??

Now my opponent played 7...♔d7 and went on to lose, missing that after...

7...♔xf7!

Black wins a piece:

8 ♘g5+ ♕xg5!

The queen defends the g4-bishop, and after 9 ♗xg5 ♗xd1 10 ♖xd1 Black retains an extra piece.

Multiple Tactics

You may be surprised to learn that you have now seen most of the individual

tactics that occur in practice. These are the building blocks of which combinations are built up. Complicated tactical battles and spectacular combinations are based on both sides bombarding each other with a lot of simple tactics. Devices that are complicated in themselves are rarely a factor – bizarre tactics such as a Wurzburg-Plachutta and a Loshinsky Magnet, which you can read about in specialist chess problem literature, just don't crop up in real games. Let's consider a few famous examples:

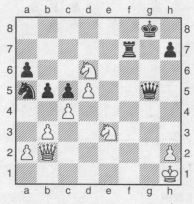

This is a position from Petrosian–Spassky, Moscow Wch (10) 1966 (WGG 56). Petrosian now unleashed the unforgettable move 30 ♕h8+! whereupon Spassky resigned. The queen sacrifice *decoys* the king onto h8 (30...♔xh8), so that then 31 ♘xf7+ is a *fork* of the king and queen.

In the next position, which comes from the pretty game Rosanes–Anderssen, Breslau 1863, Adolf Anderssen, one of the strongest players of the mid-19th century, is a rook down but pulls off a remarkable coup:

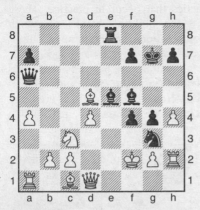

20...♕f1+!
Deflecting the queen away from defending d4.
21 ♕xf1 ♗xd4+ 22 ♗e3 ♖xe3 23 ♔g1 ♖e1# (0-1)

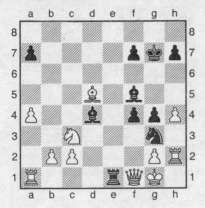

A *discovered check* and a *pin* on the white queen – it adds up to mate.

The next example is from Anderssen–Kieseritzky, London 1851, the so-called "Immortal Game" (for the full game, see page 515, while detailed notes to the whole game can be found in *The Mammoth Book of*

the World's Greatest Chess Games (Game 2).

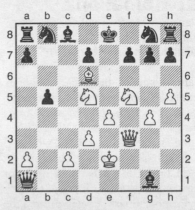

White has already sacrificed heavily. Play continued: **20 e5** (*interfering* with the black queen's defence of g7, and so threatening mate in two: 21 ♘xg7+ ♔d8 22 ♗c7#) **20...♘a6 21 ♘xg7+ ♔d8 22 ♕f6+** (*deflecting* the knight away from covering e7) **22...♘xf6 23 ♗e7# (1-0)**.

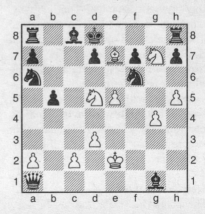

Having familiarized ourselves with the main tactical ideas, it is now time to move on to combinations!

Combinations

What is a Combination?

A combination is a forcing variation, normally with a sacrifice, intended to be to the benefit of the player making the combination.

A combination is not classified as clear or unclear; it is either sound or unsound: it works or it doesn't.

Combinations range from the trivially simple (e.g. a simple piece sacrifice followed by mate in one) to the hideously complicated, with multiple sacrifices by both sides and many long variations. Nevertheless, most combinations you will encounter in chess will be made up of the basic tactical ideas we discussed in the previous chapter. That is why, although it is not so important to know the names of individual tactical devices, it is vital to see how to use and *combine* these tactical building blocks, one with the other.

We start with one of the classics: a simple but highly attractive mating combination. I shall indicate [in square brackets] which specific tactical devices are involved.

Réti – Tartakower
Vienna 1910

1 e4 c6 2 d4 d5 3 ♘c3 dxe4 4 ♘xe4 ♘f6 5 ♕d3 e5?! 6 dxe5 ♕a5+ 7 ♗d2 ♕xe5

It appears that Black's play has worked, and that White must now

defend the e4-knight in some clumsy way. However...
8 0-0-0

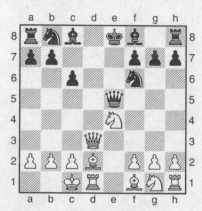

White has a tactical defence! This was not a serious tournament game, so Tartakower light-heartedly took the knight.
8...♘xe4?

8...♕xe4? 9 ♖e1 [pin] wins the queen; 8...♗e7 9 ♘xf6+ ♕xf6 (not 9...♗xf6? 10 ♖e1 [pin]) allows White a pleasant development advantage, but the game would continue.
9 ♕d8+!!

Decoying the black king into a deadly double check.
9...♔xd8 10 ♗g5++ ♔c7

Or 10...♔e8 11 ♖d8#.
11 ♗d8# (1-0)

No fewer than four of the king's possible flight squares are blocked by his own pieces. Shame on them!

The next position shows some deeper ideas.

Peres – Ziatdinov
Netherlands 1994

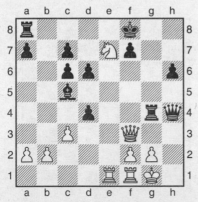

Your first thought on seeing this position from White's side may well be "if that rook weren't there on g4, I could fork his king and queen". The trick is now to make the logical leap and find a way to force a win by bringing about a position where this potential knight fork becomes reality. Remembering that the fork will win queen for knight, a major material sacrifice may well be justified.

1 ♖e4!

[Distraction; pin] This move neatly solves the problem of the black rook! White both attacks the black rook, and pins it against the black queen.

1...♕g5

Black tries to limit the damage to an exchange. 1...♖xe4 2 ♘g6+ [pin; fork] is the main idea behind the sacrifice, and wins for White: 2...♔g7 3 ♘xh4 [decoy] 3...♖xh4 4 ♕g3+ [fork] picks off the h4-rook, while 2...♔e8 3 ♘xh4 ♖xh4 4 ♕xc6+ [fork] eliminates the poor beast in the corner. On the other hand 1...h5 2 ♘g6+ [fork] exploits two pins at once: the black rook may take the

knight, but this opens a line so the white rook can take the queen.

2 ♖xg4 ♕xe7 3 ♕g3 1-0

The threat of ♖g8# forces more material gains.

Many combinations aim neither to give mate nor to win pieces directly, but rather to open the way for a pawn to promote. The following is a good example.

Capablanca – Spielmann
New York 1927 (WGG 22)

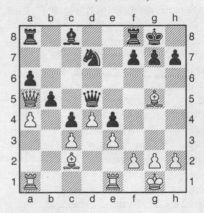

18 axb5!

[Pin] This sacrifice is not especially deep, but demonstrates in clear-cut fashion how the possibility of creating a devastating passed pawn must be borne in mind in even the most innocent-looking positions. Indeed, the task of calculating the sacrifice would be within the capabilities of most experienced players, yet most would simply move the bishop without much thought, oblivious to the existence of something enormously better.

18...♕xg5 19 ♗xe4 ♖b8

19...♖a7 20 b6! [discovered attack]

20...♕xa5 21 bxa7 and White gains material.

20 bxa6 ♖b5 21 ♕c7!

Now Black can only thrash around a little; the a-pawn is not to be stopped.

21...♘b6 22 a7 ♗h3 23 ♖eb1 ♖xb1+ 24 ♖xb1 f5 25 ♗f3 f4 26 exf4 1-0

Exchanging Combinations

Knaak – Christiansen
Thessaloniki OL 1988

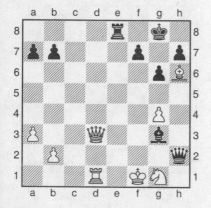

When ahead on material, but under attack, the ideal thing to do is exchange off the opponent's main attacking pieces. Knaak finds a neat way to do so.

25 ♕e2!

[Double attack; distraction]

25...♕xe2+

Black must allow the queens to come off, since White mates in the case of 25...♖xe2 26 ♖d8+ ♖e8 27 ♖xe8#.

26 ♘xe2 ♗e5 27 b4 b5 28 ♖d7 ♖a8 29 ♘d4 a6 30 ♘c6 ♗f6 31 g5 ♗b2 32 ♘e7+ ♔h8 33 ♘d5 a5 34 bxa5 1-0

The Windmill

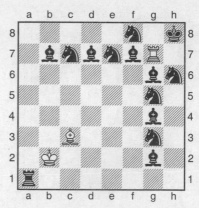

Here is a very silly position, constructed by Matsukevich for the purpose of illustrating the tactical theme of "The Windmill". Watch how all of Black's pieces drop off.

1 ♖xg6+ ♔h7 2 ♖g7+ ♔h8 3 ♖xg5+ ♔h7 4 ♖g7+ ♔h8 5 ♖xf7+ ♔g8 6 ♖g7+ ♔h8 7 ♖xe7+ ♔g8 8 ♖g7+ ♔h8 9 ♖xg4+ ♔h7 10 ♖g7+ ♔h8 11 ♖xg3+ ♔h7 12 ♖g7+ ♔h8 13 ♖xd7+ ♔g8 14 ♖g7+ ♔h8 15 ♖xc7+ ♔g8 16 ♖g7+ ♔h8 17 ♖xb7+ ♔g8 18 ♖g7+ ♔h8 19 ♖xg2+ ♔h7 20 ♖g7+ ♔h8 21 ♔xa1 and now Black must lose one of his knights. Note that in this example White had a great deal of choice as to the order in which he took the black pieces. The point of this is to show that if you can set up a windmill, then it may not matter how much material you are down. The theme (in more sensible form) crops up frequently in practice.

Here is a simple example, in which White is heavily behind on material, but sees a chance to set up a windmill, and invests his queen.

Krejčik – Leitgeib
Vienna 1951

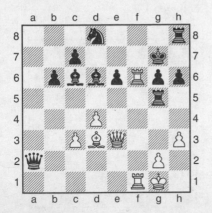

27 ♕xg5
[Destruction]
27...hxg5 28 ♖xg6+ ♔h7 29 ♖xe6+
♔g7 30 ♖g6+ ♔h7 31 ♖xd6+ ♔g7
32 ♖g6+ ♔h7 33 ♖xc6+ ♔g7 34
♖g6+ ♔h7 35 ♖xb6+ ♔g7 36 ♖g6+
♔h7 37 ♖a6+ 1-0
White will be a rook up.

Bishop and rook is the normal team
in a windmill, but not the only one.

Alekhine – Fletcher
London simultaneous 1928

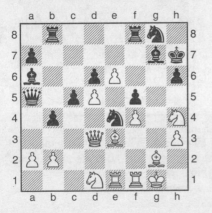

Here we have Alexander Alekhine,
newly crowned world champion,
with his queen and rook skewered.
Mr Fletcher may have thought it was
his lucky day. Well, in a sense it was,
for his game has gone down for pos-
terity.
35 ♕xe4! fxe4
Perhaps in taking the queen, Fletcher
hoped the game would end in perpetual check. However, he had no
good option: 35...♘e7 and 35...♗xf1
36 ♖xf1 ♘e7 both leave Black material down and doomed to lose.
**36 ♗xe4+ ♔h8 37 ♘g6+ ♔h7 38
♘xf8++ ♔h8 39 ♘g6+ ♔h7**

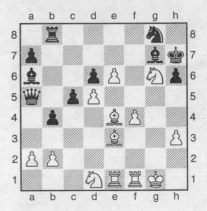

Now what?
40 ♘e5+! ♔h8 41 ♘f7# (1-0)

Find the Combination

There's nothing like practical experience for sharpening your skill at
finding combinations. I'll leave it to
you to decide whether you want to
tackle these positions strictly as exercises, or whether you take a peek at
the solutions.

You are not necessarily expected

to look for a forced mate in each case, but rather a sound combination that gets the best possible result from the position.

The positions are not grouped according to theme, since at the board you will receive no such assistance. However, I have divided them into two groups according to difficulty: medium and tough. Reckon yourself to be of good club standard if you can solve most of the medium ones, even if you have to think long and hard. If you are new to chess, consider any position solved correctly to be an achievement. And strong players should find these positions a lot of fun!

Medium Difficulty

1)
Mikenas – Flohr
Folkestone OL 1933

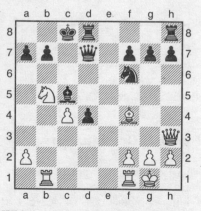

White smashes the black king's defences.

2)
Dietrich – Kindl
Böblingen 1988

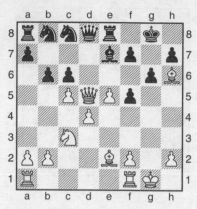

White now wins with a simple combination.

3)
Nezhmetdinov – Zagorovsky
Russian Cht (Gorky) 1963

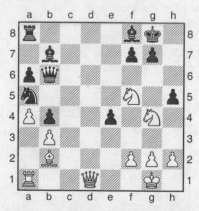

How does White (to play) take full advantage of Black's weakened kingside?

4)
Hort – Byrne
Varna OL 1962

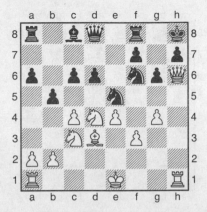

How does White, who has launched a standard attack up the h-file, crash through?

6)
Bisguier – Larsen
Zagreb 1965

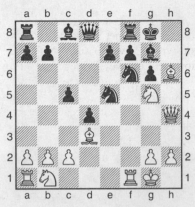

White is nearing the climax of a standard hack-attack against the fianchetto set-up. The finish is spectacular. White to play.

5)
Kirillov – Gaidarov
USSR 1978

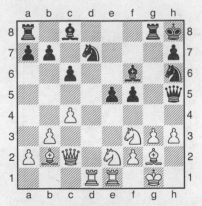

Here White finds a way to exploit the black king's shortage of flight squares.

7)
Sarapu – Browne
Skopje OL 1972

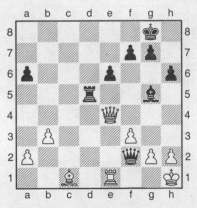

This fairly innocent-looking position conceals a way for Black, who is to play, to wreak havoc.

8)
Erbis – Kempf
W. Germany 1954

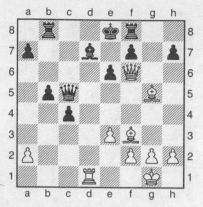

White, substantially behind in material, can force an instant win.

10)
Zaverbny – Gumelis
Belgium 1953

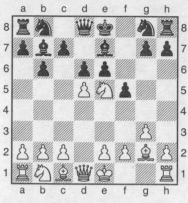

It looks as if White must retreat, but he has a spectacular move.

9)
Mattison – Wright
Bromley 1924

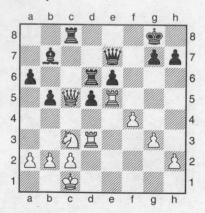

White can win material in a surprising way.

11)
Kupfer – Janig
E. Germany 1988

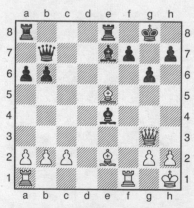

This position looks innocent enough, but how safe is Black's king? White to play.

12)
Troinov – Popov
Bulgaria 1962

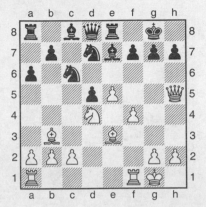

Black's king is not very well defended; how does White smash through?

13)
Ed. Lasker – Ayala
New York 1947

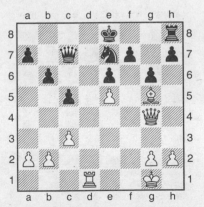

Black's uncastled king turns out to be his undoing, even at this relatively late stage of the game. White to play.

14)
Mishto – Kloza
Poland 1955

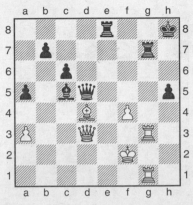

White, to play, finds an idea that, while not especially deep, is highly "visual".

15)
Serebrjanik – Atanasiadis
Belgrade 1991

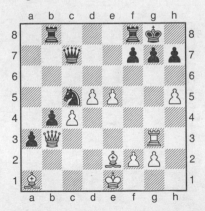

A position where you might find the key move out of sheer desperation! That doesn't matter, as long as you do actually play it. White to play.

16)
Khmelnitsky – Kabiatansky
USSR 1989

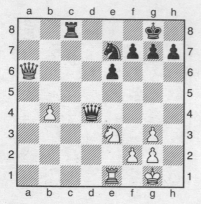

Should White be trying to make something of the passed b-pawn – or is there a far more dramatic continuation?

18)
Benko – Oney
Budapest 1949

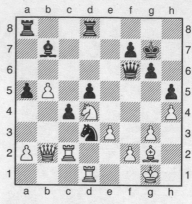

Black's position looks as solid as a rock – but appearances can be deceptive. White to play.

17)
Urusov – Kalinovsky
St Petersburg 1880

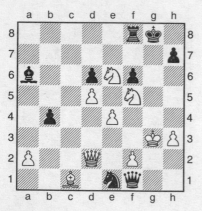

Black has some extremely powerful threats, but it is White to play, and he has some active pieces – yet how to coordinate them?

19)
Wirthensohn – Lin Ta
Novi Sad OL 1990

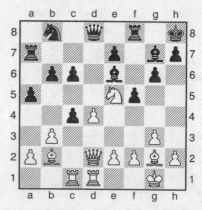

In a quiet-looking position, Black has just innocently captured on c4 – not something he's likely to do again in a hurry! White to play.

20)
Reshevsky – Ivanović
Skopje 1976

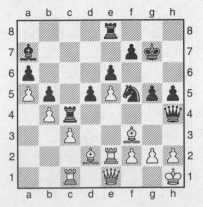

Black, to play, has a standard mating idea at his disposal.

22)
Kosikov – Privanov
USSR 1977

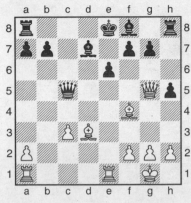

White, to play, takes full advantage of Black's backward development.

21)
Bogoljubow – Anon.
1935

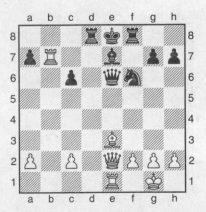

At a glance, it is not even clear that White, to play, can regain the sacrificed piece. In fact, he can do so with a lot of interest!

23)
Luchkovsky – Gridnev
Corr. 1976

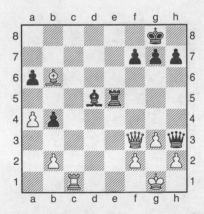

The position looks desperate for White, but he has an astonishing winning move.

24)
Kataev – Markov
USSR 1977

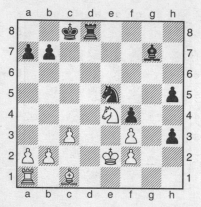

The position looks fairly quiet, but Black has a stunning resource...

26)
Krivonosov – Grants
USSR 1976

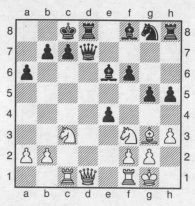

White launches a surprise attack against the black king.

25)
Kirillov – Suetin
USSR 1961

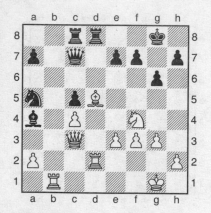

White finds a powerful move to punch home his advantage.

27)
Mudrov – Khenkin
USSR 1958

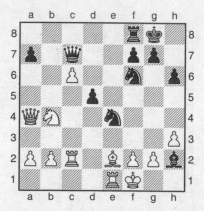

White's position looks quite solid, but his pieces prove oddly powerless. Black to play and win.

28)
Smirin – Beliavsky
USSR Ch (Odessa) 1989

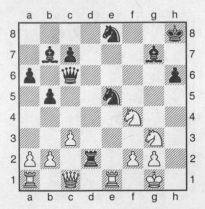

The time has come for Black to put the white king out of his misery.

30)
Scholtz – Lorenz
Corr. 1964

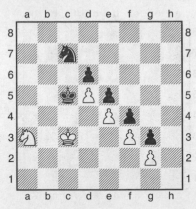

A dead draw? Or can Black start a chain reaction?

29)
Rubtsova – Milovanović
1st wom Corr. Wch

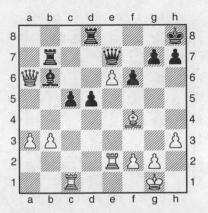

White rounds off the game with a spectacular tactical coup.

31)
Gaidarov – Vitolinš
Riga 1978

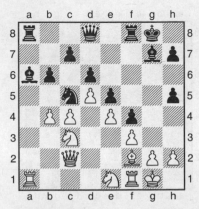

Must Black, to play, retreat his attacked knight?

32)
Sapi – Barczay
Szolnok 1963

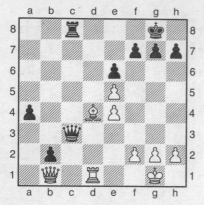

Both back ranks are weak, but if you know an important endgame principle, you should find a win for Black.

34)
Antoshin – Rabar
Baku 1964

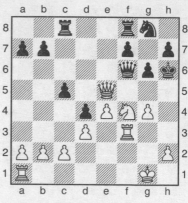

Surely White, to play, must be able to win on the spot?!

33)
Vasiliev – Burliaev
USSR 1974

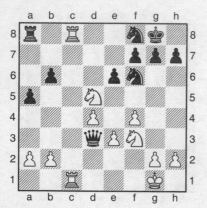

What is White up to? Some horse-play, no doubt! White to play.

35)
Ulybin – Krapivin
Naberezhnye Chelny 1988

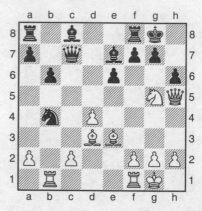

How did White, to play, round off his attack?

36)
Bunis – Krasenkov
Bulgaria 1988

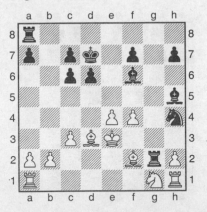

Black is extremely active here, but how does he actually finish the game off?

38)
Fischer – Miagmasuren
Sousse IZ 1967

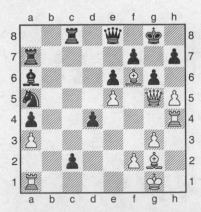

It might seem as though Black's queenside play has broken through just in time to save his king, but in fact White can force mate – how?

37)
Zso. Polgar – Peng Zhaoqin
Thessaloniki wom OL 1988

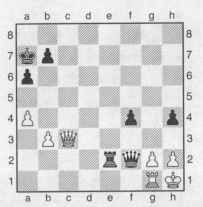

In a critical game from the 1988 Women's Olympiad, Black finds a neat way to finish off her renowned opponent.

39)
Capablanca – Fonaroff
New York 1918

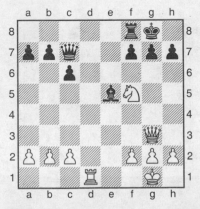

White to play and win. The combination involves a knight fork – but where and how?

40)
Wahls – Bjarnason
Malmö 1985

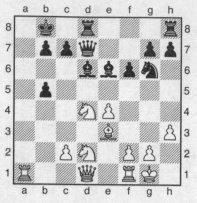

White wins with one of the most brilliant combinations of the 1980s.

42)
Brodsky – Tregubov
Wijk aan Zee 1995

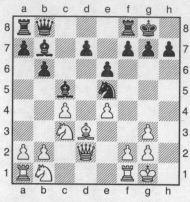

It's hard to believe Black can have a forced win on the spot here. Nevertheless, that's what you are asked to find.

41)
Karpov – Csom
Bad Lauterberg 1977

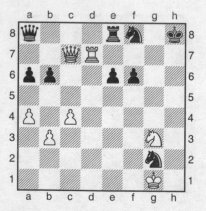

White to play, and pull off a gigantic swindle!

43)
Buječić – Tringov
Belgrade 1988

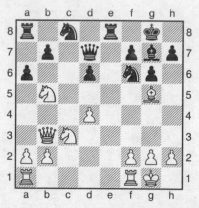

It appears at first glance that White must retreat his knight from b5. However, he has a devastating trick.

44)
Vidoniak – Fluerasu
Romania 1993

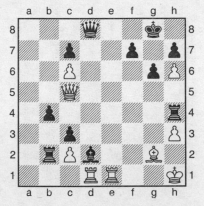

Whose king is safer? Whose pieces are better coordinated? White's next move answers both these questions.

46)
Ståhlberg – Keres
Bad Nauheim 1936

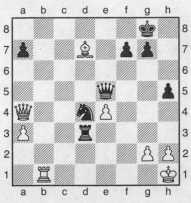

Black is obviously doing well, but how does he most simply round off the game?

45)
Brynell – Z. Almasi
Malmö 1994

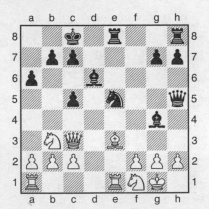

Anyone who thinks they cannot get mated with a knight on f1 should look closely at this position! Black to play.

47)
Kranz – Gretarsson
Schaan 1996

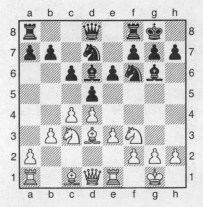

Should White now play **10 e4**?

48)
Perlasco – Grassi
Como 1907

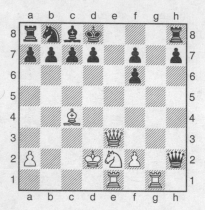

Black unsuspectingly played the move **14...Ξe8??**. It is hard to see the danger here. After all, what harm could a discovered check by the e2-knight do?

Tough Positions

These positions do not necessarily involve deeper ideas that those we saw in the previous section, but are more complicated in terms of length of the variations, number of sub-variations, or the ferocity with which the victim can cause trouble.

You will need a clear head, and plenty of time to solve these positions.

1)
Shirov – Malaniuk
Moscow GMA 1989

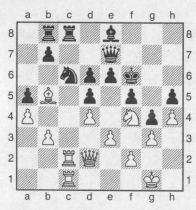

Here, most players as White would be trying to find ways to regain their pawn with some advantage, but Shirov finds an altogether more dynamic approach.

2)
Winsnes – Krasenkov
Stockholm Rilton Cup 1989/90

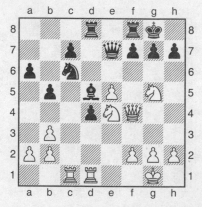

Here a young Swedish player downs a Russian GM with a stunning array of sacrifices. White to play.

3)
Lukin – Timoshchenko
Moscow 1979

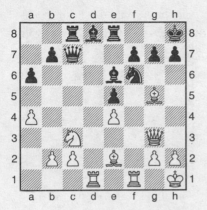

White spots a fatal flaw in Black's fairly normal-looking Sicilian position.

5)
Tal – Miller
Los Angeles 1988

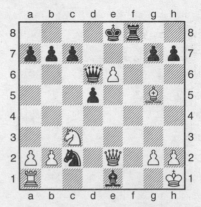

Here a complicated combination, as much defence as attack, brings White victory. Consider yourself a tactical genius if you can solve it. White to play.

4)
Averbakh – Bondarevsky
USSR Ch (Moscow) 1951

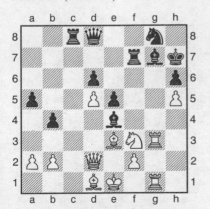

Here Black played 26...♕e7. Your task is to find White's spectacular combination in reply to the alternative 26...♘f6?.

6)
Dvoirys – Eingorn
Lvov 1990

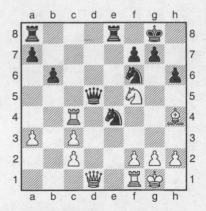

It appears that Black has things under control, but a great move goes some way towards shattering the illusion. White to play.

7)

Kasparian – Manvelian
Erevan 1939

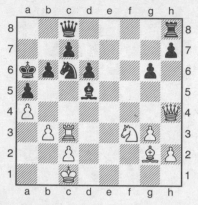

Kasparian, arguably the greatest composer of chess positions ever, was also a strong player; here he uncorks a fabulous combination. White to play.

8)

Petrosian – Simagin
Moscow 1956

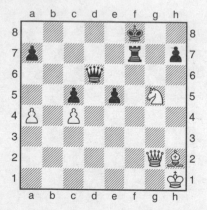

It looks as though there is a hard struggle ahead, but White has a clever trick.

9)

Zhuravlev – Koskin
Gorky 1963

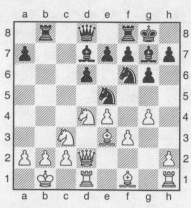

If you recognize this as a Dragon Sicilian (page 176), you will already be trying to find a spectacular, though standard combination on the a1–h8 long diagonal. Black to play.

10)

Ishchenko – Petrovsky
USSR 1976

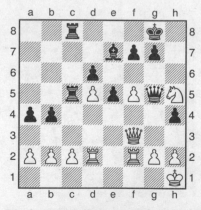

Black must pull together a number of tactical threads to highlight the shortcomings of White's position.

11)
Rausis – Gofshtein
Sofia 1988

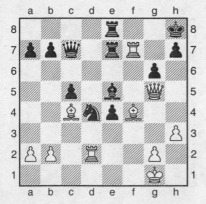

White uncorks one of the most sensational moves I have ever seen, though it does not clearly win.

13)
Tal – Koblencs
Latvia 1976

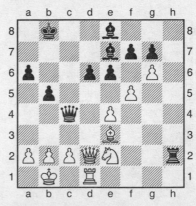

Mikhail Tal often played magical games, but this one was fantastic even by his standards. White to play.

12)
Calderin – Sariego
Manzanillo 1991

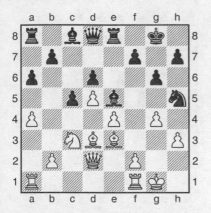

A normal-looking position from the Modern Benoni (page 235); surely Black, to play, does not have to retreat?

14)
Krylenko – Siniavskaya
Leningrad girls 1984

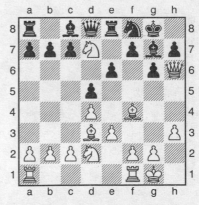

Black has just played an ill-advised *zwischenzug*, 12...♗f6-g7?. How does White take advantage, in spectacular fashion?

15)
Ruban – Miles
Belgrade GMA 1988

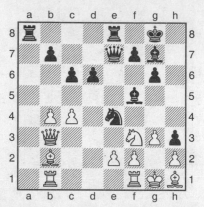

It may seem incredible that Black can have a forced win here, but the white king's shortage of squares is your clue. Black to play.

17)
Tal – Karev
Glazunovka 1972

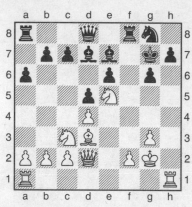

Here Tal has a large positional advantage, which he punches home by a spectacular combination, eventually culminating in a windmill. White to play.

16)
Rotlewi – Rubinstein
Lodz 1907/8

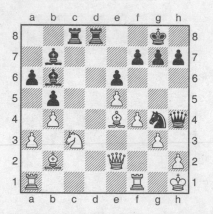

This is one of the most famous combinations of all time. Can you find Rubinstein's incredible route to victory? Black to play.

18)
Dreev – de Firmian
Biel 1995

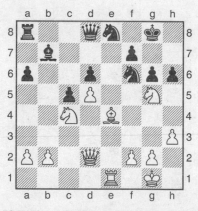

If White, to play, must retreat, then he is certainly no better. So...?

19)
Bereziuk – Joecks
Erfurt 1993

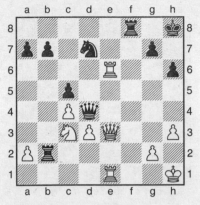

White finds an impressive and complicated winning combination.

21)
Karić – Justin
Yugoslavia 1987

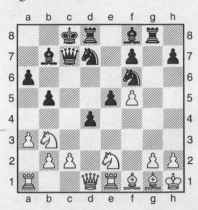

Surely White can't be in danger, with so many pieces around his king, and so few black ones attacking? But *are* White's pieces actually defending? Black to play.

20)
Shutzman – Sharm
Philadelphia 1994

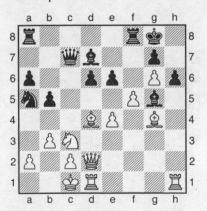

Must White play 1 ♗e3 ♗xe3 2 ♕xe3, when 2...♖ae8 sets up a very robust defence? Or does he have a brilliant sacrificial forced win?

22)
J. Gonzales – Pogorelov
Berga 1995

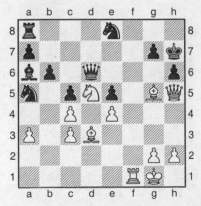

It's clear that White, to play, should do something brutal here. So, which pieces to sacrifice, and where?

23)
Shteinikov – Yashkov
USSR 1988

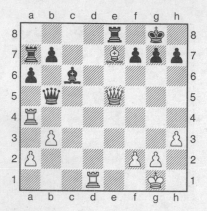

White has been enjoying some initiative, but the queen exchange that has just been offered would clearly kill White's attacking chances. He found an impressive solution.

24)
Boleslavsky – Ufimtsev
Omsk 1944

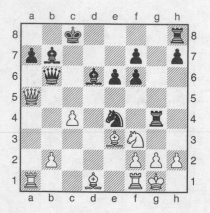

Who is really attacking here? Must Black, to play, exchange queens? Black finds a surprising answer.

25)
Burgess – Rendboe
Odense, Frem–Sydøstfyn 1991

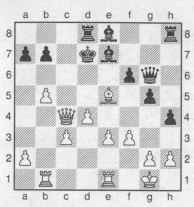

In time-trouble I bottled out and took a draw by repetition (26 ♕c7+ ♔e6 27 ♕c4+ ♔d7 28 ♕c7+ ♔e6 29 ♕c4+ ½-½). Was I right, or was there anything better?

26)
Barczay – Pokojowczyk
Subotica 1981

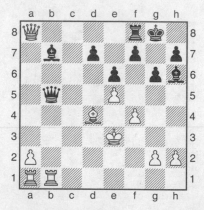

Black now played a spectacular combination with **21...♗xf4+!**. This is certainly best, but does it win, draw, or fail against best defence?

Solutions to Combinations

Medium Difficulty – Solutions

1)
1 ♘xa7+
1 ♕a3?? is too clever by half: Black wins after 1...♕xb5!.
1...♗xa7 2 ♕a3 b6 3 ♖xb6 and White wins (3...♗xb6 4 ♕a8#).

2)
17 ♕xf7+! ♔xf7 18 ♗c4+ ♖d5 19 ♘xd5 b5 20 ♗b3 1-0

3)
24 ♘f6+! gxf6 25 ♕xh5 ♖d8
25...e3 can also be met by 26 ♕g4+. Now Nezhmetdinov played **26 ♖e1 ♖d2 27 ♕g4+ ♔h7 28 ♕h4+** (and went on to win), missing a quicker win by 26 ♕g4+! ♔h7 27 ♕h4+ ♔g6 (27...♔g8 28 ♗xf6 wins) 28 g4, mating.

4)
1 ♘xc6!
White's only task here is to remove the f6-knight – it does not matter how much material it costs!
1...♘xd3+
1...♘xc6 2 ♘d5 ♕a5+ 3 b4.
2 ♔d2 1-0
2...♕e8 3 ♘d5.

5)
1 ♖xd7!
Now Black is overwhelmed by sheer horsepower. 1 ♘f4 is fairly strong, but not so decisive.

1...♗xd7 2 ♘xe5 ♗e8 3 ♘f4 ♕g5 4 ♘e6 ♕h5 5 ♘d7! ♗g7 6 ♘xg7 ♖xg7 7 ♗xg7+ 1-0

6)
1 ♖xf6! ♗h8 (sad)
1...♗xf6 2 ♗g7!! is the key variation – you must know this idea if you are going to play for attacks like this! 1...exf6 2 ♗xg7 forces mate.
2 ♖f1 ♖e8 3 ♗f8!? ♗f6 4 ♖xf6 exf6 5 ♕h6! ♖xf8 6 ♕h7# (1-0)

7)
1...♗h4 0-1
Since 2 g3 ♗xg3 3 hxg3 ♖h5+ wins everything, while 2 ♖g1 ♕xg1+ 3 ♔xg1 ♖d1+ mates.

8)
1 ♗c6! 1-0
Black will be mated: 1...♕xc6 2 ♕e7# or 1...♗xc6 2 ♖d8+ ♖xd8 3 ♕xd8#.

9)
1 ♘xd5!
A sacrifice on a very well defended square, but Black has no adequate reply.
1...♕d7
Or 1...♖xc5 2 ♘xe7+ and 3 ♖xc5; 1...♖xc5 2 ♘xe7+ and 3 ♖xc5; 1...exd5 2 ♕xc8+ ♗xc8 3 ♖xe7.
2 ♘e7+ 1-0
2...♕xe7 allows 3 ♕xd6.

10)
1 ♘f7!!

Once seen, this idea is never forgotten. John Emms, in the days before he was a grandmaster, once allowed a similar idea, leading to a horrible loss against Zurab Azmaiparashvili.

1...♔xf7 2 dxe6+ followed by 3 ♗xb7 wins for White.

11)

1 ♖xf7! ♔xf7

1...♗xg2+ is a desperate measure, but insufficient since after 2 ♕xg2 ♕xg2+ 3 ♔xg2 ♔xf7 4 ♗c4+ ♔f8 5 ♖f1+ White wins material.

2 ♗c4+ ♗d5 3 ♕f3+! ♔e6 4 ♖e1

White makes full use of the doubly pinned bishop on d5.

4...♗b4 5 ♕h3+ ♔e7 6 ♕xh7+ ♔d8 7 ♗c7+ 1-0

7...♕xc7 8 ♖xe8+.

12)

1 ♕xf7+!

A surprisingly common sacrifice in such positions; the key features are the knight on d4, bishop on b3, and no black pieces covering d5, e6 or f7. Instead after 1 ♗xd5? ♘dxe5 suddenly Black's position is working.

1...♔xf7 2 ♗xd5+ ♔g6

2...♔f8 3 ♘e6+ wins heavy material; after his actual move, White can force mate.

3 f5+ ♔h5 4 ♗f3+ ♔h4 5 g3+

5 ♘e2 is a quicker mate.

5...♔h3 6 ♗g2+ ♔g4 7 ♖f4+ 1-0

7...♔h5 8 ♗f3+ ♔h6 (8...♔g5 9 ♖e4#) 9 ♖h4#.

13)

1 ♕a4+ ♕c6

1...♘c6 2 ♕xc6+! ♕xc6 3 ♖d8#; 1...♔f8 2 ♗h6+ ♔g8 3 ♕e8#.

2 ♖d8+!!

A spectacular decoy!

2...♔xd8 3 ♕xc6

White wins.

14)

1 ♕h7+!!

This is actually a forced mate in seven. It is curious that the pinned bishop on d4 is able to play a vital role.

1...♔xh7 2 ♖xg7+ ♔h8

2...♔h6 3 ♖1g6#.

3 ♖g8++ ♔h7 4 ♖1g7+ ♔h6 5 ♖g6+ ♔h7 6 ♖8g7+ ♔h8 7 ♖h6# (1-0)

15)

1 ♖xg7+!!

With this sacrifice, White is able to open two diagonals simultaneously.

1...♔xg7

1...♔h8 2 ♕f3! ♕d8 3 e6.

2 ♕g3+ ♔h8 3 e6+ 1-0

3...f6 4 ♕xc7 b3, Black's last gasp attempt, can be refuted in many ways, most simply by 5 h6, with mate to follow shortly.

16)

1 ♘f5!! 1-0

A very unusual back-rank combination! White manages to exploit the drawbacks to the positions of all of Black's pieces simultaneously. The lines are: 1...♘xf5 2 ♕xc8+; 1...♕xb4 2 ♘xe7+ ♕xe7 3 ♕xc8+; 1...exf5 2 ♕xc8+! ♘xc8 3 ♖e8#.

17)

1 ♕g5+!!

It's forced mate from the three minor pieces.

1...fxg5 2 ♘h6+ 1-0

2...♔h8 3 ♗b2+ and mate next move.

18)
1 ♖xd3! cxd3 2 ♘e6+!
The point – the black queen is inadequately defended.
2...fxe6 3 ♖c7+ 1-0
With loss of the black queen and king to follow.

19)
1 d5!!
Suddenly White has a deadly mating attack.
1...cxd5
1...♗f7 2 ♕h6! is annihilating: 2...♘xh6 3 ♘xf7++ ♔g8 4 ♘xh6#; 2...♗f6 3 dxc6 gives White an overwhelming game; 2...♔g8 3 ♕xg7+!! ♔xg7 4 ♘g4+ and ♘h6 will be mate.
2 ♘xg6+! 1-0
2...hxg6 3 ♕h6+ ♔g8 4 ♕xg7#.

20)
1...♕xh2+! 2 ♔xh2 ♖h4+ 3 ♔g1 ♘g3! 0-1
No force on Earth can prevent 4...♖h1#.

21)
1 ♗c5!
Did White's back rank intuitively put you off this move?
1...♕xe2 2 ♖xe7+!
The point. The e1-rook "X-rays" through the black queen to e7. White must avoid 2 ♖xe2?? ♖d1+, of course.
2...♕xe7 3 ♖xe7# (1-0)

22)
1 ♖xe6+! ♗xe6
1...fxe6 2 ♗g6# highlights a drawback of Black's earlier move ...h5.
2 ♗b5+

This is an "X-ray" move – the white queen bishop defends the bishop "through" the black queen.
1-0
2...♗d7 3 ♖e1+ ♕e7 (3...♗e7? 4 ♕xc5) 4 ♗xd7+ is overwhelming for White.

23)
1 g4!!
White simultaneously threatens ♖c8+, mating, and to capture the black queen. 1 ♖d1? is the only other move to meet the immediate threat, but it gives Black time for 1...h6 or 1...♕e6, with a large plus in either case.
1-0
1...♕xf3 2 ♖c8+ ♖e8 3 ♖xe8#.

24)
1...♖d1! 0-1
There is no sensible way for White to stop Black's h3-pawn promoting, e.g. 2 ♔xd1 h2 and 3...h1♕.

25)
1 ♘e6!
It's a knockout! This tactical idea is worth committing to memory, since it crops up in practice quite often. Note how weak Black's kingside has become without a bishop on the dark squares.
1...fxe6 2 ♗xe6+ ♔f8 3 ♕h8# (1-0)

26)
1 ♘a4! ♔b8
1...♕e7 2 ♗xc7.
2 ♖xc7! ♕xd1 3 ♖c8++! ♔a7
3...♔xc8 4 ♘b6#.
4 ♗b8+ ♔a8 5 ♘b6# (1-0)

27)
1...♕b6!

A forced mate, no less!

2 &f3 ♕xf2+! 3 ♖xf2 ♘g3# (0-1)

28)

1...♖xf2! 2 ♔xf2 ♘d3+! 3 ♘xd3 ♕xg2+ 4 ♔e3 ♘d6!

A piece for two rooks down, Black calmly brings his least active piece into the hunt.

5 ♖f1

5 b3 ♕xg3+ 6 ♔d2 ♕g2+; 5 ♕d1 is best met by 5...&f6 with the horrible threat of ...&g5+.

5...♘c4+ 6 ♔f4 ♕d5 7 ♔g4 &c8+ 8 ♔h4 ♕d8+ 9 ♔h5 ♕e8+ 10 ♔h4 ♕e7+ 11 ♔h5 ♘e3 0-1

For detailed notes to this game, see *The Mammoth Book of the World's Greatest Chess Games* (no. 84).

29)

1 &d6!! ♖xd6

1...♖xd6 2 ♕b7.

2 ♕xb7! ♕xb7 3 e7

This pawn is worth a whole queen.

3...♕xe7 4 ♖xe7 h6 5 ♖ce1 &d8 6 ♖7e6 ♖d7 7 ♖c6 1-0

30)

1...♘xd5+! 0-1

2 exd5 e4 will give Black a new queen after either 3 fxe4 f3 or 3 ♘c4 exf3 4 ♘d2 f2 5 ♔d3 f3.

31)

The answer is, "No".

1...&xc4! 0-1

Since after 2 ♖xa8 ♕xa8 3 bxc5 Black has 3...♕a6! winning a whole rook, rather than just an exchange, on f1.

32)

1...♕xd4! 2 ♖xd4 ♖c1+ 3 ♖d1 ♖xb1

4 ♖xb1 a3 0-1

The key idea is that two connected passed pawns on the sixth rank over-power a rook; here one of them is even further advanced. After 5 ♖d1 g5 6 ♖d8+ ♔g7 7 ♖b8 a2 a pawn queens.

33)

1 ♘e5! 1-0

Instead 1 ♘e7+ ♔h8 2 ♘e5 ♕xe3+ 3 ♔h1 is no good since simply 3...g6, for instance, relieves the mate.

After 1 ♘e5 either the black queen drops or Black is mated: 1...♕d2 2 ♘e7+ ♔h8 3 ♘xf7#; 1...♖xc8 2 ♘e7+ ♔h8 3 ♘xf7#.

34)

1 ♘e6!! 1-0

White leaves all three of his active pieces *en prise* – but Black, of course, can only take one of them: 1...♕xf3 2 ♕g5#; 1...♕xe6 2 ♖h3#; 1...♕xe5 2 ♖h3+ ♕h5 3 g5#.

35)

1 &h7+! ♔h8 2 &e4

White attacks both a8 and f7.

2...♕xg5 3 &xg5 ♘d5

Now a simple sacrifice finishes the game.

4 &xh6 g6 5 ♕h4 ♔g8 6 &xd5 1-0

36)

1...♘f5+!

A striking line-opening idea.

2 exf5 ♖e8+ 3 &e4 d5 4 ♖f1 ♖xe4+ 5 ♔d2 &h4 0-1

White is losing a lot of material.

37)

36...h3! 37 ♕g7

37 gxh3 ♕xh2#; 37 ♕f3 hxg2+ 38

♕xg2 ♕e3 and White cannot avoid a killing check on the long diagonal: 39 ♕f1 ♖f2 or 39 ♕d5 ♖d2.

37...f3

Now g2 collapses, so...

0-1

38)

1 ♕h6 ♕f8

1...c1♕+ 2 ♖xc1 ♖xc1+ 3 ♔h2! and then Black will be mated as in the game.

2 ♕xh7+!! ♔xh7 3 hxg6++ ♔xg6

3...♔g8 4 ♖h8#.

4 ♗e4# (1-0)

39)

1 ♘h6+ ♔h8 2 ♕xe5!

2 ♘xf7+? would be a blunder in view of 2...♕xf7 3 ♕xe5 ♕xf2+ 4 ♔h1 ♕f1+ 5 ♖xf1 ♖xf1#.

2...♕xe5 3 ♘xf7+! 1-0

White will be a piece up, since 3...♖xf7 4 ♖d8+ forces mate.

40)

1 ♖a8+! ♔xa8 2 ♕a1+ ♔b8 3 ♕a7+!! 1-0

It is difficult to know when best to resign as the victim of a spectacular combination – which is one good reason for the nineteenth-century tradition of announcing a mate.

The finish would have been 3...♔xa7 4 ♘c6++ ♔a8 (4...♔a6 5 ♖a1+ and mate next move) 5 ♖a1+ ♗a3 6 ♖xa3#.

41)

49 ♘f5!! 1-0

White threatens 50 ♖h7+ ♘xh7 51 ♕g7#.

After 49...exf5 there would follow 50 ♕h2+ ♔g8 51 ♕g3+ (putting knights in the way changes nothing) 51...♔h8 52 ♕g7#.

A tragedy for Csom, who had been clearly winning before blundering into this horrible trap.

42)

15...♘f3+! 16 gxf3 ♕xg3+ 17 ♔h1 ♕h3+ 18 ♔g1

Black now for some reason decided to repeat a couple of moves.

18...♕g3+ 19 ♔h1 ♕h3+ 20 ♔g1 f5 0-1

Black intends ...♖f6-g6 (or -h6); White's only defence against this is to give up his queen for the rook.

Black also had the move 20...♗d6, which would win the white queen for just a bishop.

43)

18 ♗xf6! ♗xf6?!

18...axb5 19 ♗xg7 ♔xg7 20 ♘xb5 is relatively best, though miserable for Black.

19 ♘d5 ♗d8

A rather ungainly retreat, but otherwise White would simply put a knight into c7 and bag an exchange. With this bishop move, Black may still have hoped that White would have to retreat, whereupon he could fight back.

20 ♘bc7! 1-0

White can play this anyway, since the bishop is tied to defending against a knight fork on f6!

44)

1 ♕g5!! ♖d4

Or: 1...♕xg5 2 ♖e8#; 1...♗xg5 2 ♖xd8+ ♗xd8 3 ♖e8#; 1...♕f8 2 ♕xh4 ♗xe1 3 ♖xe1 ♖xc2 4 ♕f6 intending ♖e8, diverting the black

queen from the defence of g7.
2 ♕f6!!

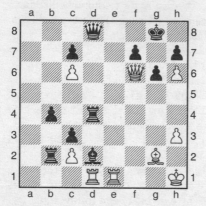

White again exploits the fact that the black queen must cover the e8-square, and threatens both ♕xd4 and, of course, ♕g7#.

1-0

2...♗xh6 3 ♕xd8+ ♖xd8 4 ♖xd8+ gives White a decisive material advantage.

45)
1...♘f3+! 2 gxf3
2 ♔h1 ♗xh2 forces mate.
2...♗xf3 3 ♘bd2
3 ♘g3 ♕h3 and 4...♕g2#.
3...♗xh2+! 0-1
4 ♘xh2 ♕g6+ and all it is in White's power to do, is decide on what move number ...♕g2# is to happen.

46)
27...♘f3!! 0-1
Black threatens 28...♕xh2#, while 28 gxf3 (28 g3 ♖d2 doesn't help either) 28...♖d2 forces mate.

47)
No! This move loses on the spot to **10...♗b4! 0-1**

48)
It turns out that White has a combination along similar lines to, but more complex than, the Réti–Tartakower example that we saw at the start of the combinations chapter (page 52):
15 ♕xe8+!! ♔xe8 16 ♘d4+ ♔f8 17 ♖e8+ ♔xe8 18 ♖g8+ ♔e7 19 ♘f5# (1-0)

Tough Positions – Solutions

1)
37 e4!! dxe4
Or 37...fxe4 38 ♘xh5+ ♗xh5 39 ♕g5+ ♔f7 40 ♕xh5+.
38 d5
38 ♘xh5+ ♔g6 is not bad for Black with his pawns united.
38...♘e5 39 ♖xc8 ♖xc8
39...♘f3+ 40 ♔g2 ♘xd2 41 ♖xb8 ♗xb5 42 axb5 is likewise very good for White in view of his active pieces.
40 ♖xc8 ♘f3+ 41 ♔g2 ♘xd2 42 ♖xe8 ♕c7 43 dxe6 and White won.

2)
19 ♖xc6!
19 ♘f6+ gxf6 20 ♘xh7 ♖xe5! 21 ♘xf6+ ♔g7 22 ♕g5+ ♘g6 23 ♘h5+ ♔h7 24 ♘f6+ ♔g7 is only a draw.
19...♗xc6 20 ♘f6+! gxf6 21 ♘xh7! ♔xh7?
21...fxe5 22 ♘f6+ ♔xf6 23 ♕xf6 ♖d6 24 ♕xe5 ♖e8 25 ♕f5 presents White with some technical obstacles.
22 ♕h4+ ♔g7 23 ♕g4+ ♔h8 24 ♖d3 ♗e4 25 ♖h3+ ♗h7 26 ♕f5 1-0
Krasenkov was so impressed by this, that he annotated the game himself!

3)
1 ♖xd8! ♕xd8
1...♖cxd8 2 ♖xf6!; 1...♖exd8 2 ♖xf6!.
2 ♕h4! (Black is helpless) **2...♗c4**
2...♖g8 fails to 3 ♖xf6!; 2...♕b6 3 ♗xf6 will leave White material up: 3...gxf6 (3...♕xb2 4 ♗xe5) 4 ♕xf6+ ♔g8 5 ♖g5+ ♔h8 (5...♔f8 6 ♕h6+ followed by 7 ♘d5(+) wins) 6 ♕xe5+ ♔g8 7 ♖g5+ ♔h8 8 ♕f6+ ♔g8 9 ♘d5.
3 ♖xf6 ♗xe2 4 ♖h6! f6 5 ♗xf6 gxf6 6 ♖xh7+ ♔g8 7 ♕h6 ♖c7 8 ♖g6+ ♔f8 9 ♖h8+ ♔e7 10 ♘d5+ 1-0

4)
26...♘f6 fails to:
27 ♗xh6!! ♖xh6 28 ♕xh6+! ♔xh6 29 ♖g6+ ♔xg6
29...♔h7 30 ♘g5+ ♔h8 31 ♘xf7+ ♔h7 32 ♖h6#.
30 ♖xg6+ ♔xh5
30...♔h7 31 ♘g5+ ♔h8 32 ♘xf7+ ♔h7 33 ♘xd8 gives White an extra piece.
31 ♘xe5+ ♘g4
31...♔h4 32 ♖h6+ ♔g5 33 ♘xf7+ ♔f5 34 ♘xd8 ♖xd8 35 ♗c2+ ♔e5 36 f4+ wins the knight.
32 ♗xg4+ ♔h4 33 ♖h6+ ♔g5 34 ♘xf7+ ♔xg4 35 ♘xd8
White should win the rook ending.

5)
1 ♘b5!
Not 1 ♖xe1? ♘xe1 2 ♕xe1 ♕e5!.
1...♕e5!
1...♕c6 2 ♖d1 threatens ♖xd5, to which Black has no adequate response.
2 h4!!
I imagine this move could be found by considering what Black's threats are. ...♕xe2 is not a threat in view of

♘c7#, so the moves to be worried about were ...♕xg5, ...♘xa1 and ...c6. Tal's move solves the back-rank problem and so threatens ♕xe5.
2...♕g3
2...♕xe2 3 ♘xc7#; 2...♘xa1 is met by 3 ♕xe5.
3 ♖d1! ♖f2
3...c6 4 ♖d3 ♕b8 5 ♖f3! overpowers the black king.
4 ♖xf2! ♗xf2
4...♕xf2 allows 5 ♘xc7+ ♔f8 6 e7+ and 8 e8♕, winning.
5 ♖xd5!
Black has no decent defence against the threat of ♖d8#.

6)
1 ♘e7+! ♖xe7 2 ♕xd5 ♘xd5 3 ♗xe7 ♘d2
3...f5 is a far better try, since 4 ♗d6!? (4 f3? ♘d2 5 ♖d4 ♘xf1 6 ♖xd5 ♘e3 permits the knight to escape) 4...♖d8 (4...♘d2 5 ♖d4) 5 ♗e5 ♘d2 (5...♖e8 6 f4 ♘d2 7 ♖d4 ♘xf1 8 ♖xd5 ♘e3 9 ♖d7) 6 ♖d4 ♘xf1 7 c4 ♖e8 gives Black some drawing chances after either 8 ♖xd5 ♘d2 9 ♖xd2 ♖xe5 or 8 cxd5 ♖xe5 9 ♔xf1 ♔f7.
4 ♖d4 ♘xf1 5 ♖xd5 ♖e8 6 ♖d7 ♘d2 7 ♖xa7
White has two extra pawns – a decisive advantage.

7)
1 ♖xc6! ♗xc6
1...g5 2 ♕d4 changes nothing.
2 ♕c4+ ♔b7 3 ♕xc6+!! ♔xc6 4 ♘e5++ ♔c5 5 ♘d3+ ♔d4 6 ♔d2 1-0
Whatever Black plays, there follows 7 c3#. Kasparian was clearly an absolute perfectionist when it came to

chess tactics, but even so I am surprised he did not even include this finish in a selection of 100 of his best games!

8)
1 ♕a8+
1 ♘xf7 ♕d1+ draws on the spot, since Black can keep checking on h5, f3 and d1, e.g. 2 ♕g1 ♕f3+ 3 ♔g2 ♕d1+ 4 ♗g1 ♕h5+ 5 ♔h2 ♕f3+ 6 ♔g2 ♕h5+ 7 ♗h2 ♕d1+.
1...♔g7
1...♔e7 2 ♕xa7+ ♔f6 3 ♘e4+.
2 ♗xe5+!
2 ♕h8+ ♔g6 (2...♔xh8 3 ♘xf7+) 3 ♘xf7 ♕d1+ leaves Black in no danger of losing.
2...♕xe5 3 ♕h8+!! ♔xh8
3...♔g6 is not an option with the black queen *en prise* on e5.
4 ♘xf7+ 1-0
A once-in-a-lifetime combination, one might think. However, in 1966 Petrosian played an almost identical combination in a critical world championship game against Spassky (page 50). He must hardly have believed his eyes!

9)
1...♘xf3! 2 ♘xf3 ♘xe4 3 ♘xe4
This loses, but letting Black take on c3 would be abject.
3...♖xb2+ 4 ♔c1 ♖b1+! 5 ♔xb1 ♕b8+
Forcing mate.
6 ♔c1 ♕b2# (0-1)

10)
1...e4! 2 ♕xe4
Else 2...e3 will fork the white rooks.
2...♖xc2!
2...♕xh5 3 ♖xe7 ♖xc2 4 h3 is far

less clear.
0-1
3 ♕xc2 ♖xc2 4 ♖xc2 ♕xh5 picks off the loose knight, while 3 ♖xc2 ♕c1+ (the black rook on c8 X-rays through to support the queen on c1) 4 ♖xc1 ♖xc1+ forces mate.

11)
1 ♗e6!! ♘c6?
After 1...♘f5? 2 ♖xe7 White also wins simply.
    However, 1...♘xe6! is best; then 2 ♗xe5+ ♔g8 3 ♕f6 ♕xe5 4 ♕xe5 ♖xf7 (4...♔xf7 5 ♕xe4 is similar) 5 ♕xe4 leaves White with a great deal of work to do, if it is indeed possible for him to win.
2 ♖d7 ♖xd7 3 ♖xd7 ♕b8 4 ♖xh7+ 1-0

12)
1...♕h4!
White's rash advance has opened up his own king for Black to launch a winning attack.
2 gxh5
2 ♔g2 ♗xg4 is completely hopeless for White.
2...♗h2+! 3 ♔xh2
3 ♔h1 ♕xh3 4 f3 ♗f4+ 5 ♔g1 ♗xe3+ 6 ♕xe3 ♕g3+ 7 ♔h1 ♖e5 wins.
3...♕xh3+ 4 ♔g1 ♕g4+ 5 ♔h1
5 ♔h2 ♖e5.
5...♕f3+ 6 ♔h2
6 ♔g1 ♗h3 and mate next move.
6...♖e5 0-1

13)
1 f6!!
Incredible; it is the white pawns that will decide the game!
1...♖xe2

After 1...gxf6 2 g7 ♖g2, 3 ♖g1 wins quite simply, but 3 ♗g5 ♖xg5 4 ♕xg5 as given in some sources, is not so clear after 4...fxg5 5 g8♕ ♕c8.

1...♗xf6 2 ♕xd6+ picks up the h2-rook: 2...♕c7 3 ♕xc7+ ♔xc7 4 ♗f4+.

1...♗f8 2 fxg7 ♗xg7 3 ♕xd6+ and again the h2-rook drops.

2 fxg7! ♖xd2 3 ♗xd2

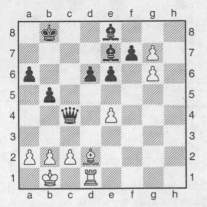

An astonishing position; Black, to play, is almost a full queen up, with loose white pieces to attack, yet is utterly powerless to stop White promoting.

3...♕e2

3...♕c8 4 g8♕ fxg6 5 ♗b4 is hopeless for Black.

4 ♔c1 1-0

14)

13 ♕xg7+!! ♔xg7 14 ♗e5+ ♔h6 15 ♘f6 ♘d7 16 ♘g4+ ♔h5 17 ♗g7!

Cutting off the king's retreat. Well done if you saw this far.

17...♖g8?

Black can put up far more resistance with 17...g5 18 ♘e5 ♘xe5 19 dxe5 f5 20 exf6 e5, when White must play

very accurately: 21 g4+! (better than 21 f7 ♖f8) 21...♔h4 22 ♘f3+ ♔xh3 23 ♘xg5+ ♔xg4 24 ♘xh7 and now:

a) 24...♕f3 25 ♗g6 and 26 ♗h5+ followed by 27 f7.

b) 24...♔h3 25 f3 (25 f7?! ♕h4) 25...♕g3 26 f7 ♗h3 27 ♖f2 ♕e7 28 fxe8♕ ♖xe8 29 ♖h2 ♕xg7 30 ♔h1 and White will emerge material up.

c) 24...♖g8 25 ♔h2 and the white rook(s) will come to the g- and/or h-files with decisive effect.

18 ♘f6+!

Forcing mate in six more moves.

18...♘xf6

18...♕xf6 19 g4+! ♔h4 20 ♔g2 ♖xg7 21 f4 and ♘f3# cannot be prevented.

19 ♗e2+ ♔g5

19...♔h4 20 ♘f3+ ♔h5 21 ♘e5+ ♔g5 22 ♘xf7+ ♔h4 23 g3+ ♔xh3 24 ♘g5#.

20 ♘f3+

20 f4+ ♔h4 21 ♔h2 forces mate a move more quickly.

20...♔h5 21 ♘e5+ ♔h4 22 g3+ ♔xh3 23 ♗xf6

Or 23 ♗f3 and 24 ♗g2#.

23...♕xf6 24 ♗g4# (1-0)

15)

1...♘xf2!! 2 ♖xf2

2 ♔xf2 ♕xe2+ 3 ♔g1 ♗c2 wins – the white queen is also out of flight squares!

2...♗xb1 3 ♗xg7

Otherwise White remains material down.

3...♔xg7 4 ♕xb1 ♕f6!

Now Black threatens ...♖a1.

5 ♘d2

After 5 ♖f1 ♖xe2 Black stomps all over the white position, while in the event of 5 ♕d3 ♖a1+ 6 ♖f1 ♖xf1+ 7

♔xf1 ♖a8 the second rook appearing at a1 will end White's resistance.

5...♕d4!

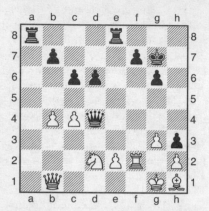

Renewing the threat of ...♖a1, while pinning the white rook.

6 ♕d3

6 ♘b3 is relatively best.

6...♖a1+ 0-1

7 ♘f1 ♖xf1+ 8 ♔xf1 ♕a1+ and mate next move.

---

16)

1...♖xc3!!

1...♗xe4+ 2 ♘xe4 ♕xh2+ 3 ♕xh2 ♘xh2 is by no means a clear win.

2 gxh4

2 ♗xb7 ♖xg3 is a straightforward win. 2 ♗xc3 ♗xe4+ and ...♕xh2 will soon be mate.

2...♖d2!! 3 ♕xd2

There is nothing else.

3...♗xe4+ 4 ♕g2 ♖h3! 0-1

Whatever White does, ...♖xh2 will be mate. See WGG 11 for detailed notes to this game.

---

17)

17 ♖xh7+! ♔xh7 18 ♗xg6+ ♔g7 19 ♖h1 ♖f6 20 ♕g5!

An incredible queen sacrifice, just to remove the rook from f6!

20...♖xf2+

20...♔f8 21 ♖h7 threatens 22 ♗f7, and forces Black to transpose to the game by 21...♖xf2+ since 21...♗e8 22 ♗f5! wins for White – who now wants to keep his queen!

21 ♔xf2 ♗xg5?! 22 ♖h7+ ♔f8

22...♔f6 allows 23 ♖f7#.

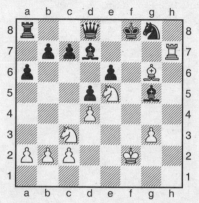

The scene is set; the windmill's blades are about to turn.

23 ♖f7+ ♔e8 24 ♖xd7+ ♔f8 25 ♖f7+ ♔e8 26 ♖xc7+ ♔f8 27 ♖f7+ ♔e8 28 ♖xb7+ ♔f8 29 ♖f7+ ♔e8

Well, that bit was easy. Now what?

30 ♖h7+ ♔f8 31 ♘d7+ ♕xd7 32 ♖xd7

So, all that was to win two pawns?

I find that for a combination of such splendour to achieve such a modest (though sufficient) goal makes the achievement more impressive, suggesting that it was only small errors by the opponent that allowed the combination, rather than some crashing blunder allowing a mating combination.

After that piece of chessboard magic Tal of course went on to win from this position.

18)

1 ♘xf7! ♔xf7 2 ♕xh6 ♘g7

The most interesting line is 2...♘e4 3 ♕h7+ ♘g7 (3...♔f8 4 ♖xe4 wins) 4 ♖xe4 ♗c8 (not 4...♕f6 5 ♖e6!).

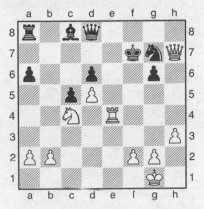

Now White must avoid the "flashy" move:

a) 5 ♖e8?! ♕xe8 (5...♕xe8? 6 ♘xd6+) 6 ♕g8+ ♔e7 (6...♔d7 7 ♕xg7+ ♕e7? 8 ♘b6+) 7 ♕xg7+ is only a draw.

b) 5 ♖f4+ ♗f5 6 g4 ♕g8 (6...♕g5 7 ♘xd6+) 7 ♕h6 is very good for White.

3 ♗xg6+ ♔g8 4 ♖e6! ♗xd5

4...♘xe6 5 dxe6 and ♗f7+ wins.

5 ♖xd6 ♗xc4

5...♕e7 6 ♖xd5 wins since 6...♘xd5 7 ♕h7+ ♔f8 8 ♕h8# is the end.

6 ♖xd8+ ♖xd8 7 ♕h4

White has gained a decisive material advantage.

19)

1 ♖xh6+! gxh6

1...♔g8 2 ♕e6+ ♖f7 3 ♖h8+ ♔xh8 4 ♕xf7 is hopeless for Black, since 4...♕xc3 5 ♖e8+ ♔h7 6 ♕h5# is mate.

2 ♕xh6+ ♔g8 3 ♘d5! ♘e5

Black has a number of other moves:

a) 3...♕g7 4 ♘e7+ ♔f7 5 ♕h5+ ♔f6 6 ♕f5#.

b) 3...♖b6 4 ♘e7+ ♔f7 5 ♕h7+ ♕g7 6 ♕h5+ ♖g6 7 ♕d5+ ♔e8 8 ♘c6+ is a catastrophe for Black.

c) 3...♕xg2 4 ♘e7+ ♔f7 5 ♕h7+ ♕g7 (5...♖g7 6 ♕h5+ and mate next move; 5...♔f6 6 ♔xg2 is now safe for White) 6 ♕h5+ ♖g6 7 ♕d5+ ♔e8 8 ♘c6+ is a recurring theme.

d) 3...♕xd3 is perhaps the best defensive try, but still 4 ♘e7+ ♔f7 5 ♕e6+ ♔g7 (5...♔e8 6 ♘c6#) 6 ♕g4+ ♔h7 is good for White.

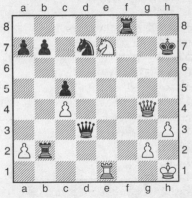

Here White has the clever 7 ♘f5! ♕xf5 8 ♖e7+ ♕f7 (8...♔h6 9 ♕g7+ ♔h5 10 g4+) 9 ♕xd7, and he will end up with queen vs two rooks, but with a few extra pawns and a safe king. This is enough to win.

4 ♘e7+ ♔f7 5 ♘f5! ♕c3 6 ♖f1! 1-0

6...♔e8 7 ♕e6+ ♔d8 8 ♕e7+ mops up, while 6...♖e8 7 ♕g7+ ♔e6 8 ♘d4+ forces mate.

20)

1 ♕xg5! hxg5

Black has nothing better, e.g. 1...e5 is met by 2 ♘d5.

2 ♖h7

White threatens mate in two, so Black's choice is limited.

2...♖f7

Black is mated in the event of either 2...♗e8 3 ♖dh1 ♗xg6 4 ♖h8+ ♔f7 5 fxe6+ ♔e8 6 ♖xf8+ ♔xf8 7 ♖h8+ ♔e7 8 ♘d5# or 2...♖xf5 3 exf5 ♗e8 4 ♖dh1 ♔f8 5 ♘d5! exd5 6 ♖h8+ ♔e7 7 f6+ ♔d8 8 ♖xe8+ ♔xe8 9 ♖h8#.

3 ♖dh1

3 ♖h8+! ♔xh8 4 gxf7, with ♖h1 to follow, mates a few moves more quickly.

3...♔f8 4 f6! ♖xf6

Or 4...♔e8 5 ♖h8+ ♖f8 6 ♖xf8+ ♔xf8 7 ♖h8#; 4...gxf6 5 ♖xf7+ ♔g8 6 ♗xf6 with ♖h8# to follow.

5 ♗xf6 gxf6 6 ♖h8+ ♔g7 7 ♖1h7+ ♔xg6 8 ♗h5# (1-0)

21)

1...♖xg2! 2 ♗xg2

Yes, and now what?

2...♕c6!!

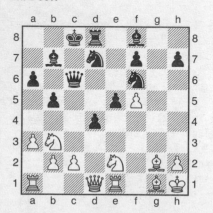

3 ♘f4

3 ♗xc6 ♗xc6# is what might have been called "diagonalization" by Dr Nunn on the 1970s television series

The Master Game, had it not been edited out.

3...exf4 4 ♕d2

4 ♗xc6 ♗xc6+ still forces mate.

4...f3 5 ♗xd4 fxg2+ 0-1

One can understand that White wished to see no more.

22)

1 ♘f6+?!

This was the move played in the game, but it is not the right answer!

1 ♖f6! is stronger, and wins conclusively in all lines:

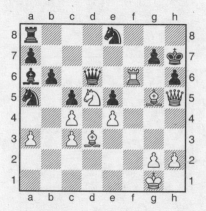

a) 1...gxf6 2 ♕xh6+ ♔g8 3 ♕g6+ ♔h8 4 ♘xf6.

b) 1...♘xf6 2 ♘xf6+ ♔h8 (or 2...gxf6 3 ♕f7+ ♔h8 4 ♗xf6+) 3 ♗xh6 ♕xf6 4 ♗g5+.

c) 1...♕d7 2 ♖xh6+ gxh6 3 ♕xh6+ ♔g8 4 ♘e7+ ♕xe7 5 ♗xe7.

1...♘xf6

1...gxf6 2 ♕xh6+ ♔g8 3 ♗xf6 and Black must part with his queen.

2 ♖xf6 ♕xd3??

2...♕d7 is better:

a) 3 ♕g6+ ♔g8 (3...♔h8 4 ♖f7) 4 ♗xh6 ♖f8 5 ♖xf8+ ♔xf8.

b) 3 ♖f7 ♕e6! 4 ♗f6 ♖g8 is not at all clear.

3 ♖xh6+ 1-0
3...gxh6 4 ♕f7+ ♔h8 5 ♗f6#.

23)
38 ♕xg7+!!
The g7-square is a standard place for a sacrifice, but a whole queen is something special, particularly when the mate is far from trivial. In fact, it's forced mate in a further 9 moves.
38...♔xg7 39 ♖g4+ ♔h6
39...♔h8 40 ♗f6#; even 39...♕g5 does not stop the mate: 40 ♖xg5+ ♔h6 41 ♖d6+ f6 42 ♖xf6+ ♔xg5 43 f4+ ♔h5 44 g4+ ♔h4 45 ♔h2 h5 46 ♖f5+ ♖xe7 47 ♖xh5#.
40 ♖d6+ f6
40...♔h5 41 ♖h4#.
41 ♖xf6+ ♔h5

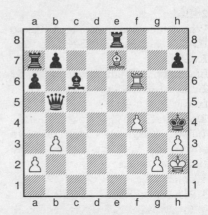

44...h5 45 g3#; 44...♔h5 45 g4+ ♔h4 46 ♖h6#; 44...♕g5 45 ♖h6#; 44...♖xe7 45 ♖h6+ ♕h5 46 g3#.

A queen, rook and bishop sacrificed to give mate – impressive!

24)
20...♖hg8!
20...♕xa5 21 ♖xa5 is marginally favourable for White, since Black's queenside is loose.
21 ♘e1
21 ♗xb6 ♖xg2+ 22 ♔h1 ♖xh2+ (22...♘xf2+ also mates next move) 23 ♘xh2 ♘xf2#.
21...♖xg2+! 22 ♘xg2 ♘d2!

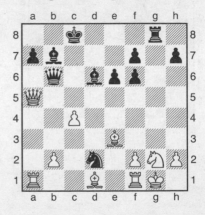

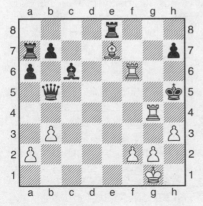

42 ♖h4+!!
42 ♖g7 also wins, but the beautiful move played forces mate.
42...♔g5
42...♔xh4 43 ♖h6#.
43 f4+ ♔xh4 44 ♔h2 1-0
Now that White has covered the g3-square, which was neglected by the move 43 f4+, there is no adequate defence to the threatened mate with ♖h6:

23 ♕d5

Pure desperation in face of 23 ♗xb6 ♖xg2+ 24 ♔h1 ♖xh2++ 25 ♔g1 ♖h1#.

23...♗xd5 24 cxd5 ♕xb2 25 ♗xd2 ♕xa1 26 ♗f3 ♗xh2+ 0-1

25)

26 b6! is a great example of pawn power, and would have given White excellent chances:

a) 26...fxe5 27 ♕c7+ ♔e6 28 ♕xd8 ♗xd8 29 bxa7 ♗c6 30 a8♕.

b) 26...axb6 27 ♖xb6 ♗f7 28 ♕b5+ ♔c8 29 ♖c6+ mates.

c) 26...a6 27 ♕d5+ ♔c8 28 ♕e6+ and then:

c1) 28...♖d7 29 ♕c4+ ♔d8 30 ♗c7+ ♔c8 31 ♕xa6! bxa6 32 b7+ ♔xc7 33 b8♕+ ♔c6 34 ♕b6+ ♔d5 35 c4+ ♔xc4 36 ♕b3#.

c2) 28...♗d7 29 ♕xe7 fxe5 30 ♕xe5 ♕c6 and, with four pawns for the piece, White should eventually win.

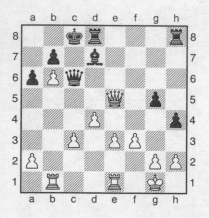

26)

It is good enough to draw the game: **22 ♔xf4 ♕d3 23 ♕xb7 f6**

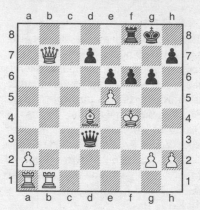

Unnatural positions like this are hard to assess and even harder to play, so it is not surprising that in the game White now erred with 24 ♖d1?? and got bulldozed as follows: 24...g5+ 25 ♔g4 h5+ 26 ♔xh5 ♕h7+ 27 ♔g4 fxe5 28 g3 ♕f5+ 29 ♔h5 ♕h3+ 30 ♔g6 ♕h7+ 0-1.

Instead White should have gone in for:

24 exf6 ♕xd4+ 25 ♔g3

Not 25 ♔f3? ♖xf6+ 26 ♔g3 ♕e3+, when White must give up his queen to avoid mate.

25...♕e3+ 26 ♕f3 ♕g5+ 27 ♕g4

27 ♔f2 ♖xf6 is good for Black.

Now Black can only give checks, and White has no way to avoid them; for example, 27...♕e3+ 28 ♔h4 ♕h6+ 29 ♔g3 ♕e3+ 30 ♕f3 ♕g5+ 31 ♔h3 ♕h6+ 32 ♔g4 ♕h5+ 33 ♔g3 ♕g5+.

Endgames

In this short chapter I am looking mainly to explain some of the key endgame principles, and pass on some of the genuinely essential knowledge. There are some enormous tomes of endgame theory in print, and I suggest you consult these for further details. There are also detailed definitions of some endgame terms in the glossary, and examples of endgame play throughout the book.

One point I'd like to make is that the myth of the endgame being about effortless technique and memorizing a mass of theory, is pure nonsense. Playing the endgame well involves a great deal of hard work and calculation at the board. It is worth knowing some key positions from which to take bearings, but these are at best background knowledge, except in some very simplified positions.

King and Pawn vs King

This endgame is absolutely fundamental. All chess-players must know and understand it so well that they can quickly assess any position without difficulty. This is because many endgames can simplify down to king and pawn vs king.

In many positions the assessment depends on possession of the **opposition**, which is a way in which kings fight for position, and is a term defined in the glossary.

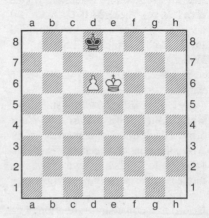

This is one of the fundamental positions, of great importance.

If White is to play, he wins:
1 d7 ♔c7 2 ♔e7
The pawn queens next move.

On the other hand, if Black is to play, then the game is a draw after **1...♔e8** as we are about to see.

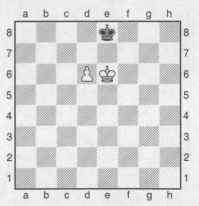

In the previous position, both sides benefited from it being their turn to move. Here the opposite is the case:

if Black is to play he loses, since after 1...♔d8 we have the position we have just seen, whereas White can only draw if he is to move:

a) 1 ♔d5 ♔d7 2 ♔c5 ♔d8! (the only move; 2...♔c8? 3 ♔c6 ♔d8 4 d7 ♔e7 5 ♔c7 wins for White) 3 ♔c6 ♔c8 achieves nothing for White.

b) 1 ♔e5 ♔d7 2 ♔d5 ♔d8! 3 ♔e6 ♔e8.

c) 1 d7+ ♔d8 2 ♔d6 is stalemate, while other king moves by White allow Black to take the pawn.

A situation in which it is a disadvantage for either side to have the move is called a *reciprocal zugzwang*.

Now let's consider a situation with the pawn further back.

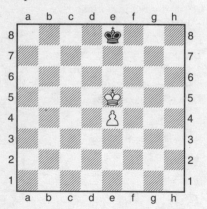

This is another key position. The player with the pawn generally does best to keep his king in front of the pawn, but this alone is not enough to guarantee victory when the pawn has not crossed the half-way line.

1...♔e7! (the only move to draw) **2 ♔d5 ♔d7!** (again Black has no choice: 2...♔e8? allows 3 ♔e6 ♔d8 4 ♔f7 and the pawn waltzes through

to queen) **3 e5** (3 ♔d4 ♔e6 is obviously no way for White to make progress) **3...♔e7!**. Now the presence of the pawn on e5 means that White cannot keep the opposition, so he must either go backward or settle for **4 e6 ♔e8!**, when we have a familiar drawn position.

The rook's pawn is a special case.

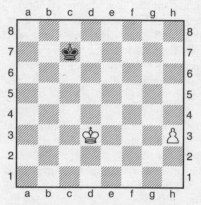

Here the defender's drawing chances are far better. The opposition is not so vital; provided the defending king can place himself in front of the pawn the game is drawn.

1 ♔e4 ♔d6 2 ♔f5 ♔e7 3 ♔g6 ♔f8 4 ♔h7

4 h4 ♔g8 5 h5 ♔h8 6 h6 ♔g8 7 h7+ ♔h8 8 ♔h6 is stalemate.

4...♔f7 5 h4 ♔f8

If there were an "i"-file to the right of the h-file, this would of course be a very simple win. But there is no such thing, and the position is drawn.

6 h5

6 ♔g6 ♔g8 7 h5 ♔h8 8 h6 is no better.

6...♔f7 7 h6 ♔f8 8 ♔h8

8 ♔g6 ♔g8 9 h7+ ♔h8 is a draw we have seen before.

8...♔f7 9 h7
9 ♔h7 ♔f8 just repeats.
9...♔f8

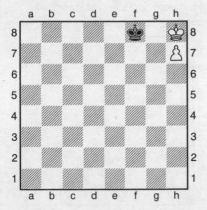

Now it is White who is stalemated. Even keeping the black king away from the queening square isn't necessarily enough with a rook's pawn!

When there are several pawns, there are some interesting effects possible.

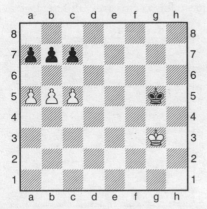

This is another idea that every chess player should know. Three pawns can actually batter their way through against three pawns opposing them like this.

1 b6! cxb6

1...axb6 2 c6! bxc6 3 a6 is similar.
2 a6! bxa6
2...bxc5 3 axb7 and a queen appears.
3 c6 and White's pawn promotes.

Clearly such a cascade of pawn sacrifices only works when the attacking pawns are far advanced, and there are no enemy pieces to stop them promoting once they are past the enemy pawns.

Now we move on to endings with major pieces.

Queen vs Pawn

This is an important ending, which often arises in practice.

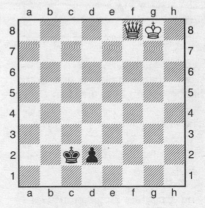

This is a typical sort of position that might arise from a king and pawn ending in which White has narrowly won the race to promote. Is the position, with White to play, a win or a draw? Can Black be prevented from promoting? Firstly, if the pawn is any further back than its seventh rank, then the queen wins without difficulty. But surprisingly, when the pawn has reached its seventh rank, the result depends on which file the pawn is on. If it is on the b-, d-, e-, or g-file, then the following method is effective.

1 ♕c5+

White must operate with queen checks.

1...♔b2 2 ♕b4+ ♔c2 3 ♕c4+ ♔b2 4 ♕d3

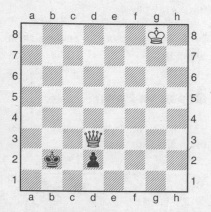

A critical point. The queen attacks the pawn from behind at a time when it has no support from the king.

4...♔c1

The only square.

5 ♕c3+!

Forcing the black king in front of the pawn.

5...♔d1

Now the white king can make a step towards the pawn.

6 ♔f7 ♔e2

Now the checking procedure starts again.

7 ♕e5+ ♔f2 8 ♕f4+ ♔e2 9 ♕e4+ ♔f1 10 ♕d3+ ♔e1 11 ♕e3+ ♔d1 12 ♔e6 ♔c2

And once more.

13 ♕c5+ ♔b1 14 ♕b4+ ♔c2 15 ♕c4+ ♔b2 16 ♕d3 ♔c1 17 ♕c3+ ♔d1 18 ♔d5 ♔e2 19 ♕e5+ ♔f1 20

♕f4+ ♔e2 21 ♕e4+ ♔f2 22 ♕d3 ♔e1 23 ♕e3+ ♔d1 24 ♔c4

White moves in for the kill.

24...♔c2 25 ♕c3+ ♔d1 26 ♔d3

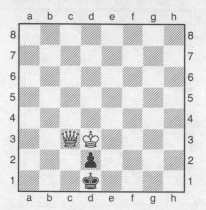

The pawn no longer seems such a threat! White mates in trivial fashion. Although it takes a while, this is a very simple procedure to remember.

However, with a bishop's (c- or f-) pawn things are totally different.

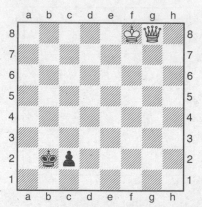

White may begin as normal.

1 ♕g7+ ♔b1

Not 1...♔b3??, as this allows 2 ♕a1, when White permanently stops the pawn.

2 ♕b7+ ♔a2 3 ♕d5+ ♔b2 4 ♕d4+ ♔b1 5 ♕b4+ ♔a2 6 ♕c3 ♔b1 7 ♕b3+

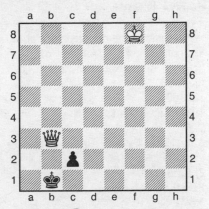

At this critical moment, Black need not go in front of the pawn. Instead...

7...♔a1!

Now if White takes the pawn it is stalemate. Since Black is threatening to promote, White gains no respite to bring in his king, so the game is drawn.

With a rook's (a- or h-) pawn, the king *can* be forced in front of the pawn.

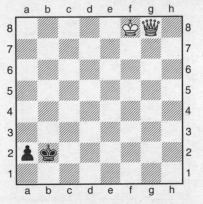

However, so long as he only plays into the corner when forced to do so by a queen check, the enemy king will have no time to approach. Thus:

1 ♕g7+ ♔b1

Again, the queen must on no account be allowed to get in front of the pawn.

2 ♕g1+ ♔b2 3 ♕d4+ ♔b1 4 ♕b4+ ♔a1

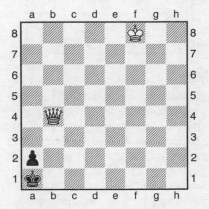

Already we see the problem. The white king cannot approach, since Black would be stalemated. There is no way around this problem, and the game is drawn.

Rook vs Pawn(s)

Rook vs pawn is often far harder to judge. In the most famous position of this type, the Saavedra Position (see page 527), the pawn even wins, but this is an exception. The rook is nothing like so agile as the queen, so a far-advanced pawn supported by its king will tend to draw against a lone rook. If the attacking king is too far away, all the rook can do is sacrifice itself for the pawn. The diagram shows one helpful trick.

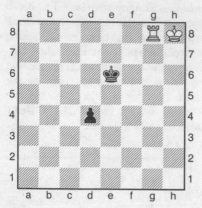

1 ♖g5!

By placing itself on the fifth rank, the rook cuts off the king from its pawn, and also prevents the pawn from advancing, since **1...d3 2 ♖g3! d2 3 ♖d3** rounds up the pawn in the nick of time. Thus after ♖g5, Black will just have to shuffle his king. White will then bring his king back into the action at his leisure, winning easily.

You may well have heard the idea that "two connected passed pawns on the sixth rank are stronger than a rook". The next diagram illustrates what is meant.

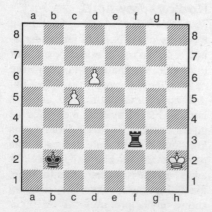

However, remember that this is a very specific instance, and that in almost all cases a rook is far stronger than two pawns.

1 c6

White sets up the dreaded formation. The black king is too far away to help, so it's between the pawns and the rook.

1...♖d3

1...♖c3 is similar.

2 c7

2 d7, with 3 c7 to follow, is just as effective.

2...♖c3

Else the c-pawn promotes.

3 d7

One or other of the pawns will now queen. The best Black can do is **3...♖xc7 4 d8♕**, with rook vs queen; although not trivial, this is a loss for the rook.

Rook and Pawn vs Rook

This is another fundamental ending, since so many other endings can simplify to it. Let's start with a key drawing procedure.

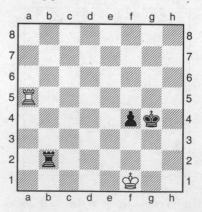

Here we see White employing a standard drawing method, attributed to Philidor. This position looks fairly dangerous for White, with the black king and pawn both able to advance to their sixth rank, putting the white king in danger. However, White has a reliable drawing method.

1 ♖a3!

The key is to put the rook on the third rank, so that the black king is unable to lead the charge; the pawn must go first, which in turn allows White another simple defensive idea.

1...f3

There's little else for Black to try. If the rook retreats, the white king can come to the second rank, while if Black shuffles, White can do the same (e.g. ♖a3-c3-a3). 1...♖h2 2 ♖b3 ♖h3 3 ♖xh3 ♔xh3 4 ♔f2 ♔g4 5 ♔g2 is a drawn pawn ending.

2 ♖a8!

Yes, to the very end of the board. White's defence is to be based on a barrage of checks to the black king. In almost all such instances, it pays for the checking piece to be as far from the enemy king as possible.

2...♔g3 3 ♖g8+ ♔f4 4 ♖f8+

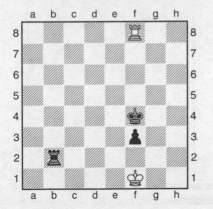

White will keep checking the black king, which, following the pawn's advance to f3, has no accessible shelter. In such instances, the standard way for a king to evade the checks is by advancing towards the rook, but this will not be effective here, since after, e.g., **4...♔e4 5 ♖e8+ ♔d5 6 ♖d8+ ♔e6** (not that Black has any threats with his king here) White can win the f3-pawn by **7 ♖f8 ♖b3 8 ♔f2**.

If the defender cannot get his king in front of the pawn, then a position such as the following can arise:

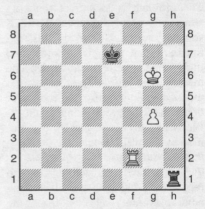

Here we see that the black king is cut off from the area in front of the pawn by the white rook standing on the f-file. This factor constitutes a major advantage for White, since his king can shepherd the pawn up to the seventh rank without difficulty:

1 g5 ♖g1 2 ♔h6 ♖h1+ 3 ♔g7 ♖g1 4 g6 ♖h1 5 ♔g8 ♖g1 6 g7 ♖h1

We have now arrived at the famous so-called Lucena Position. White has a little trick to get the pawn through. This is the best-known endgame position. Even players with no other endgame knowledge tend to know this one.

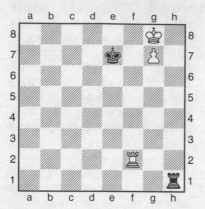

The problem is to extract the king from in front of the pawn. There is some choice in how to do this, but the important thing is to know and understand a method that works. The black pieces are doing quite a good job of preventing this: the rook prevents the king from going to the h-file, while access to the f-file is denied by the black king.

7 ♖e2+ ♔d7

7...♔f6 allows the white king to reach the f-file with the black king now preventing checks from the black rook: 8 ♔f8 and the pawn queens.

    7...♔d6 8 ♖e4 ♔d5 9 ♖f4 ♔e5 10 ♖f2 and the black king does not have time to get back to e7 to prevent ♔f8.

8 ♖e4!

The reason why the rook needs to go to the fourth rank will become clear shortly. 8 ♔f7 allows a barrage of rook checks: 8...♖f1+ 9 ♔g6 ♖g1+ 10 ♔f6 ♖f1+.

8...♔d8

There isn't much for Black to do.

8...♖f1 9 ♔h7 leads to a similar finish.

9 ♔f7 ♖f1+ 10 ♔g6 ♖g1+ 11 ♔f6 ♖f1+

11...♖g2 allows White time for 12 ♖e5 and bringing the rook to g5.

12 ♔g5 ♖g1+ 13 ♖g4

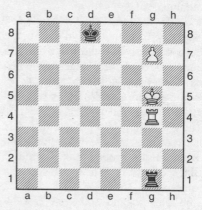

The rook turns out to be ideally placed to stop the checks. The pawn queens shortly.

We now consider the main defensive method when the king is cut off:

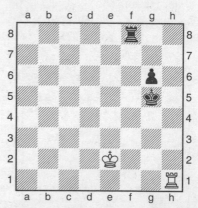

Here we see that the king being cut off does not mean automatic loss. If the pawn is not very far advanced, then the rook can defend by checking from in front of the pawn:

1 ♖g1+ ♔h5 2 ♖h1+ ♔g4 3 ♖g1+ ♔h5 4 ♖h1+ ♔g5 5 ♖g1+ ♔h6 6 ♖h1+ ♔g7 7 ♖g1

It is impossible for Black to make progress. Let us consider one attempt:

7...♖f5 8 ♔e3 ♔f6 9 ♔e4 ♖g5 10 ♖f1+ ♖f5

10...♔g7 11 ♖f4 and the white king gets in front of the pawn, via f3.

11 ♖xf5+ gxf5+ 12 ♔f4

As we have seen, this is a simple drawn king and pawn vs king position.

It would be wholly inappropriate to go into great detail in a non-specialist work, but this method suffices to draw when the rank on which the pawn stands (viewed from its own side of the board) plus the number of files by which the king is cut off is five or less.

Rooks and Passed Pawns

One of the best known endgame principles is that rooks belong behind passed pawns, whether of the same colour or the opponent's. This is largely an extension of the idea that rooks are most effective when active, and are relatively feeble when passive. As an aside, regarding rook activity in general, I recall veteran IM and trainer Bob Wade once being asked how one could judge whether a rook was really active or not. His reply: "It should be attacking something just about every move."

Here we see a rook behind an outside passed pawn of its own colour.

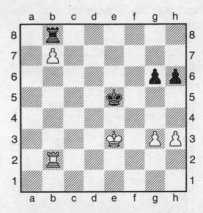

This is a very favourable arrangement for White – so much that the position is very easy to win. The black rook has no freedom of movement, whereas the white one has plenty. White can win this ending very much as though it were just a king and pawn ending in which he has as many tempo moves as he likes (and the ability to use the rook actively, and the possibility of bringing the king to c7 with decisive effect). If Black moves his king to c7 and takes the pawn with his rook, then after the rook exchange White will win the pawn ending with ease since the black king will be so far from the action.

1 ♖b5+ ♔d6 2 ♔e4 ♔c6 3 ♖b3 ♔d6

Or 3...♖xb7 4 ♖xb7 ♔xb7 5 ♔e5 followed by ♔f6, and taking pawns; 3...♖e8+ 4 ♔d4 ♖b8 5 ♔e5 and White has made obvious progress.

4 ♔d4 ♔c6

4...♔e6 5 ♔c5 and the king will support the b-pawn: 5...♔d7 6 ♔b6 ♔d6 7 ♔a7 wins the rook for the pawn.

5 ♔e5

Black is helpless against the white king decimating his kingside.

Next, a practical example with a defending rook profiting from being behind the enemy passed pawn.

Glek – Lobron
Bern 1994

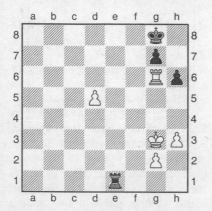

Here the active position of the black rook, behind White's passed pawn, allowed him to save the game without much difficulty.

51...♖d1 52 ♖d6 ♔f7 53 ♔f4 ♖f1+ 54 ♔e5 ♖e1+ 55 ♔d4 ♖g1
Now the rook turns its attention to the kingside pawns. White did not have to allow this, of course, but there was no other way for him to try to make progress.

56 g4 ♖g3 57 ♖e6 ♖xh3 58 ♖e4 ♖h1 59 d6 ♔f6 60 ♔d5 ♖d1+ 61 ♔c6 ♖c1+ 62 ♔b7 ♖b1+ 63 ♔c7 ♖c1+ 64 ♔d8 ♖d1 65 d7 g6
Lobron has defended very alertly. Although he will shortly be obliged to give up his rook for the d-pawn, Black will be able to create a passed pawn of his own. This is a standard theme in rook endings, but he will delay sacrificing his rook as long as possible, so as to gain as much time as possible in the race to come.

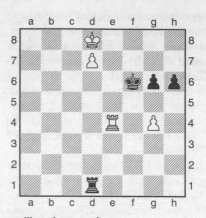

66 ♖c4 ♔g5 67 ♔c7
67 ♔e7!? h5 68 ♖c1 ♖xd6+ is also a draw.
67...h5 68 ♖c6
Threatening 69 ♖d6
68...♖xd7+ 69 ♔xd7 h4
There is no point letting White have the g6-pawn just yet.
70 ♔e6 h3 71 ♔f7 ♔xg4 72 ♖xg6+ ♔f3 73 ♖h6 ½-½
All White can do is sacrifice his rook for Black's h-pawn.

However, just because a rook is in front of a passed pawn it should not be considered harmless.

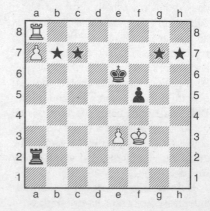

Here we see a standard idea. Black has no way to prevent White from winning immediately by means of a small trick. The immediate threat is ♖e8+ followed by a8♕. It seems that **1...♔f7** solves this problem, but then comes **2 ♖h8** when **2...♖xa7** loses the rook to the through check **3 ♖h7+**. In order to avoid this trick, the black king would need to stand on one of the highlighted squares or else have some pawn shelter from checks.

Outside Passed Pawns

A passed pawn far distant from the main theatre of action is very useful in diverting the enemy forces from the part of the board where you wish to operate in earnest.

Dreev – Lerner
Simferopol 1988

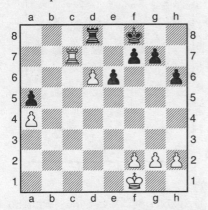

This is an excellent example of the value of an outside passed pawn in rook endings. If you find it surprising that White might win this position, study the moves especially carefully.

45 ♖c6

White wishes to exchange his d6-pawn for Black's a5-pawn. 45 ♖a7? ♖xd6 46 ♖xa5 ♖d2 is far less good for White, since his king's freedom is limited by the active black rook.

45...♔e8

45...♖b8 46 ♖a6 ♔e8 47 ♖xa5 ♔d7 48 ♖a7+ ♔xd6 49 ♖xf7 gives Black no hope.

46 ♖a6 ♔d7 47 ♖xa5 ♔xd6 48 ♖a7 ♖f8?!

48...♖d7 might be a better try.

49 a5 ♔c6 50 h4 g5 51 h5 g4 52 ♔e2 f5 53 a6 ♖b8 54 ♖h7 ♖b2+ 55 ♔e3 ♖a2 56 ♖xh6 ♔d6 57 ♖g6 ♖xa6

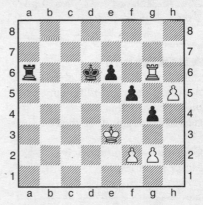

White has managed to convert his previous advantage to a clear plus on the kingside.

58 h6 ♖a1 59 ♔f4 ♖g1 60 ♖g8 ♖xg2 61 h7 ♖xf2+ 62 ♔g3 ♖f3+ 63 ♔g2 ♖h3 64 h8♕ ♖xh8 65 ♖xh8

Black's pawns are not far-advanced, and the white king is well placed. Therefore it is a fairly simple matter for White to mop up.

However, as Chris Ward explains in his book *Endgame Play*, inexperienced players might expect the pawns to have a chance here. Not so!

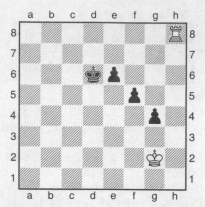

**65...♔e5 66 ♔g3 ♔e4 67 ♖h1 ♔e5
68 ♖e1+ ♔f6 69 ♔f4 ♔f7 70 ♖a1
♔f6 71 ♖a6 ♔f7 72 ♔e5 ♔g6 73
♖xe6+ ♔g5 74 ♖e8 1-0**

A Bad Bishop

A bishop obstructed by many pawns
on its own colour squares can be a
catastrophic liability in the endgame.

Cherniak – Bogdanovich
Moscow Ch 1989

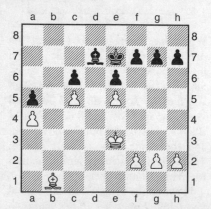

This is a fairly extreme case of a bad
bishop ending. The black bishop is
obstructed by several pawns fixed on
squares on its own colour. In the
following play we see White striving
to find a way to open up the position
in order to penetrate with his king on
Black's hopeless dark squares.

Black's bishop may be viewed as
canned meat; it may help the can keep
its shape, but is helpless against an
opponent with a can opener!

27 ♗e4

27 ♗xh7? would be a horrible mistake since 27...g6 28 h4 ♔f8 29 h5
♔g7 30 hxg6 fxg6 traps and wins the
bishop.

27...♔f8 28 ♔d4 g6 29 ♔e3

Time is not of the essence here.
Black's move ...g6 has given the white
king a possible entry square on h6, so
the change of track is logical.

**29...♔g7 30 ♔f4 h6 31 h4 ♗e8 32
♗d3 ♗d7 33 ♗a6 ♔h7 34 ♔g4
♔g7 35 ♗d3 ♗c8 36 f4 ♗d7 37 h5**

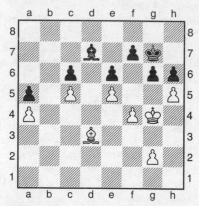

37...♗c8

37...gxh5+ 38 ♔xh5 allows White to
make progress.

**38 ♔h4 ♗d7 39 ♗e4 ♗e8 40 ♗f3
♗d7 41 g4 ♗e8 42 g5 ♗d7 43 hxg6
fxg6 44 gxh6+ ♔xh6 45 ♗e4 ♗e8
46 ♗d3 ♗d7 47 ♗a6 ♔g7 48 ♔g5**

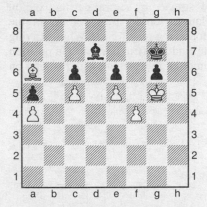

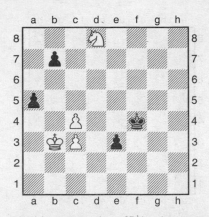

Now Black will be zugzwanged out of one of his pawns, and so the rest will follow.

48...♔f7 49 ♗d3 ♗c8 50 ♗xg6+ ♔e7 51 ♗e4 ♗b7 52 ♔g6 ♗a8 53 ♗g2 ♗b7 54 ♗f3 ♗a8 55 ♗g4 ♗b7 56 ♗xe6! ♔xe6 57 f5+ 1-0

After 57...♔xe5 (57...♔e7 58 ♔g7; 57...♔d7 58 f6 ♗a6 59 f7 ♔e7 60 ♔g7) 58 f6 Black is powerless to stop the pawn.

An Odd Geometrical Effect

If a king is moving between squares on the same diagonal, there is a single shortest route for its journey. In other cases, it has a choice of routes that take the same number of moves. For instance there are seven routes from e1 to e4 that take three moves. (You may, as an exercise, count the number of king routes from e1 to e8 that take seven moves if you wish.)

This point is easily forgotten in the heat of battle...

Bronstein – Botvinnik
Moscow Wch (6) 1951

Black's e-pawn is sufficiently strong to rule out any winning chances for White. It seems White has a number of safe ways to play, but for one fatal moment, Bronstein apparently forgot that kings do not have to travel in straight lines...

57 ♔c2??

This was not a time-trouble blunder – Bronstein had plenty of time to think. He just forgot that for the black king to travel from f4 to f2 did not have to involve it going via f3. One naturally assumes that the black king will stay next to its pawn. Instead after 57 ♘e6+ ♔f3 (57...♔g3 is met by 58 ♘d4) White has two ways to draw: 58 c5 e2 59 ♘d4+ ♔f2 60 ♘xe2 ♔xe2 61 ♔a4 ♔d3 62 ♔xa5 ♔xc3 63 ♔b6 ♔c4 64 ♔xb7 ♔xc5 or 58 ♘d4+ ♔f2 59 ♔a4! e2 60 ♘c2 e1♕ 61 ♘xe1 ♔xe1 62 ♔xa5 ♔d2 63 ♔b4 b6.

57...♔g3 0-1

57...♔f3 58 ♘f7 e2 59 ♘e5+ was clearly the line Bronstein envisaged.

Instead after 57...♔g3 he resigned since the pawn cannot be stopped. This awful oversight haunted Bronstein for decades.

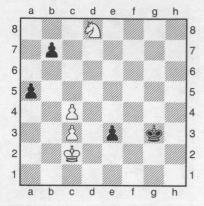

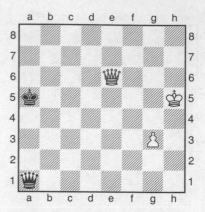

These are the sad possibilities:

a) 58 ♘e6 e2 59 ♘d4 is not check.

b) 58 ♘f7 e2 59 ♘e5 again is not the saving knight check that White needed.

c) 58 ♔d1 ♔f2 59 ♘e6 e2+ and the pawn promotes.

d) 58 ♔d3 ♔f2 59 ♘e6 e2 60 ♘f4 e1♕ and White cannot play 61 ♘d3+.

A tragedy for Bronstein, and an unexpected windfall for Botvinnik, who went on to retain his title by drawing the match.

Queen and Pawn vs Queen

This is another important ending, with a reputation for being deadly dull, with long checking sequences during which the position hardly changes. It is also a fiendishly difficult ending to understand, even though it is one for which computer databases have already provided definitive analysis.

The following example illustrates some important themes.

Botvinnik – Minev
Amsterdam OL 1954

This is an instructive queen ending.

57...♕h8+

Or 57...♕h1+ 58 ♔g5.

58 ♔g6 ♕c3 59 g4 ♕d2 60 g5 ♕d4 61 ♕f5+ ♔a4 62 ♔h5 ♕h8+ 63 ♔g4 ♕h1 64 ♕f4+ ♔a5 65 ♕e5+ ♔a4 66 g6 ♕d1+ 67 ♔g5 ♕d8+ 68 ♔f5 ♕c8+ 69 ♔f4 ♕c1+ 70 ♕e3 ♕c7+ 71 ♕e5 ♕c1+ 72 ♔f5 ♕c8+ 73 ♔g5 ♕d8+ 74 ♕f6!

After 74 ♔h6? ♕h4+ 75 ♔g7, 75...♕h3? was given by Botvinnik, but 75...♔a3 is a draw, the computer database informs us!

74...♕d5+ 75 ♕f5 ♕d8+ 76 ♔h5 ♕e8

76...♕h8+ 77 ♔g4 ♕g7 78 ♕f7 ♕c3 79 g7! gets the pawn through, since 79...♕d4+ 80 ♕f4 pins the black queen to the king.

77 ♕f4+? ♔a5? 78 ♕d2+ ♔a4 79 ♕d4+ ♔a5 80 ♔g5 ♕e7+ 81 ♔f5! ♕f8+ 82 ♔e4 ♕h6 83 ♕e5+ ♔a4 84 g7 ♕h1+ 85 ♔d4 ♕d1+ 86 ♔c5 ♕c1+ 87 ♔d6

87 ♔d5 ♕c8 only slows down the winning process, despite Botvinnik's opinion that "the white king doesn't stand too well, whereas Black's king is well placed".

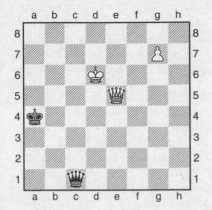

87...♕d2+

After 87...♕a3+, 88 ♔d5 gets a "!" from Botvinnik, though it is not the quickest, which is 88 ♔c7 ♕c1+ 89 ♔b8 ♕b1+ 90 ♔c8 ♕c2+ 91 ♕c7.

88 ♔e6 ♕a2+ 89 ♔d5 ♕e2+ 90 ♔d6 ♕h2+ 91 ♔c5! 1-0

No matter how Black plays, a cross-check will force off the queens.

Breaking the Fortress

A fortress is a position in which one side holds a draw despite being substantially down on material due to some feature of the position preventing any progress from being made.

The most striking examples occur when a queen faces a rook, but the rook is well placed and supported by pawns. There may be no way for the queen to force any progress or to gain useful support from other pieces. Typically the attacking king will be cut off along rank and file by the rook, and so is denied any opportunities to penetrate the defences. Breaking a near-fortress can require considerable imagination and skill.

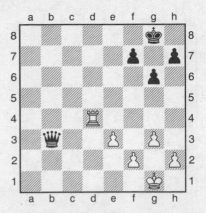

The diagram position could have arisen in Troianescu–Botvinnik, Budapest 1952. White does not have a fortress, but it is close – Black must play extremely accurately to win. The following variation is Botvinnik's analysis.

1...♔f8 2 h4 ♔e7 3 ♔g2 f5 4 ♔g1 h6 5 ♔g2 ♔e6 6 ♔g1 ♔e5 7 ♔g2 g5 8 hxg5 hxg5

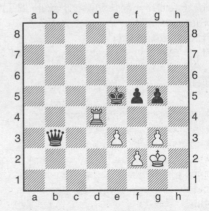

White has problems finding moves.

9 ♔g1

9 ♔f1 ♕b1+ 10 ♔e2 ♕b5+ 11 ♔e1 ♕a6 and the queen penetrates to f1.

9...♕c2 10 ♔g2 ♕c3 11 ♔f1

11 ♖d8 ♕c6+ 12 ♔g1 ♔e4 13 ♔g2

f4 14 gxf4 gxf4 15 exf4 ♕g6+ 16 ♔f1 ♔f3 and White will soon be mated.

11...♕a1+ 12 ♔g2

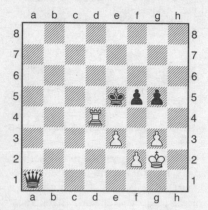

12...♕xd4!

Did you see this coming? The winning method involves reaching a winning king and pawn ending with level material.

13 exd4+

13 f4+ ♔e4 14 exd4 g4! wins for Black.

13...♔xd4 14 ♔f1!

The best try. Passive play, viz. 14 ♔h3 ♔e4 15 ♔g2 ♔d3, does not help:

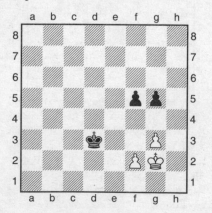

a) 16 ♔h1 ♔d2! 17 ♔h2 ♔d1! wins: 18 ♔h3 ♔e2; 18 ♔g2 ♔e1; 18 ♔g1 ♔e2; or 18 ♔h1 f4.

b) 16 ♔f1 ♔d2 17 ♔g2 ♔e1 18 ♔g1 ♔e2 19 ♔g2 f4 20 g4 (20 gxf4 gxf4 21 f3 ♔e3 22 ♔g1 ♔xf3 23 ♔f1 is a familiar position, where the opposition does not save White) 20...♔e1 21 ♔g1 f3 and f2 drops.

14...♔d3 15 ♔e1 f4 16 g4 ♔c2!

16...f3? 17 ♔d1 ♔e4 18 ♔d2 ♔f4 19 ♔d3 ♔xg4 20 ♔e3 picks off the f3-pawn, with a draw.

17 ♔e2 ♔c1!

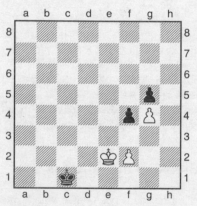

18 ♔d3

18 ♔e1 f3 19 ♔f1 ♔d1 20 ♔g1 ♔e1, etc.

18...♔d1 19 ♔e4 ♔e2 20 f3 ♔f2 21 ♔f5 ♔xf3 22 ♔xg5 ♔e3

Black promotes first, and will win the queen vs pawn ending since White has a knight's pawn.

The Active King

A common feature of the endings we have looked at is the king, normally a feeble stay-at-home piece in the middlegame, becoming an important fighting unit. This is because there is little danger, with substantially reduced force, of the king being subject to a mating attack in the ending. The king is particularly adept in holding back pawns, or in decimating a cluster of pawns. Strong players will begin activating their king at the earliest feasible point in an endgame, and will bear this in mind during the late middlegame.

The next example provides a simply superb example of a number of important endgame themes: passed pawns, rook activity, king activity and an admirable avoidance of materialism when the initiative is at stake.

Capablanca – Tartakower
New York 1924 (WGG 21)

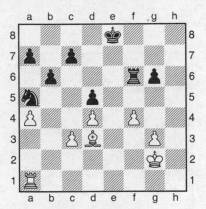

How would you assess this ending? It may seem that the c3-pawn is a serious weakness, but it turns out that the g6-pawn is just as easily attacked. Moreover, it is far easier for White to create a passed pawn on the kingside than it is for Black on the queenside. Thus White should play very actively, rather than try to defend his queenside.

29 ℤh1 ♚f8 30 ℤh7 ℤc6 31 g4 ♘c4 32 g5

"Threatening ℤh6 followed by f5, and against it there is nothing to be done." (Alekhine)

32...♘e3+ 33 ♚f3 ♘f5

"Or 33...♘d1 34 ℤh6 ♚f7 35 f5 ℤxc3 36 fxg6+ ♚g8 37 ♚e2 ♘b2 38 ♗f5 with an easy win." (Alekhine)

34 ♗xf5

Capablanca sees a rook ending as the simplest way to win. His rook is very active, he has a passed pawn, and he has foreseen a superb way to introduce his king into the thick of battle.

34...gxf5

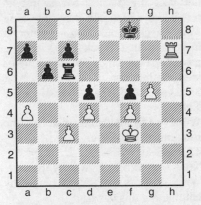

Glancing at this position superficially, we see that White is about to lose a pawn. A deeper look shows that White has in fact made enormous progress.

35 ♚g3!

"Decisive! White sacrifices material in order to obtain the classical position with king on f6, pawn on g6 and rook on h7, whereupon the pawns tumble like ripe apples." (Alekhine)

35...ℤxc3+ 36 ♚h4 ℤf3 37 g6!

A memorable move, making way for the king.

37...🖤xf4+ 38 🖤g5 🖤e4 39 🖤f6!

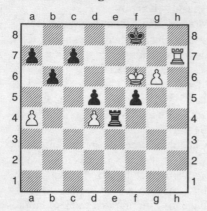

1)

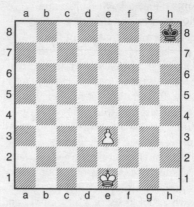

Again highly instructive. White does not take the black f-pawn; instead this pawn will shield the white king from checks. It does not matter at this point that Black has a mobile passed pawn, since White's threats are so immediate.

39...🖤g8 40 🖤g7+ 🖤h8 41 🖤xc7 🖤e8

White was threatening mate, so the rook must go passive.

42 🖤xf5

Now that Black is wholly passive, White kills off any counterplay by eliminating this pawn.

42...🖤e4 43 🖤f6 🖤f4+ 44 🖤e5 🖤g4 45 g7+ 🖤g8

45...🖤xg7 46 🖤xg7 🖤xg7 47 🖤xd5 🖤f6 48 🖤c6 is a trivially won king and pawn ending.

46 🖤xa7 🖤g1 47 🖤xd5 🖤c1 48 🖤d6 🖤c2 49 d5 🖤c1 50 🖤c7 🖤a1 51 🖤c6 🖤xa4 52 d6 1-0

Endgame Challenges

Now it is your turn to analyse some tricky endings!

Put to use the examples we saw at the start of the chapter to work out a method by which White, to play, wins this ending.

2)

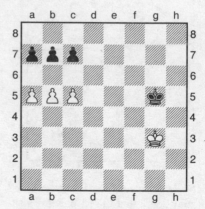

Black is to play, and you know from earlier in the chapter what White is threatening. Which of these moves do you play?

a) 1...a6;
b) 1...b6;
c) 1...c6;
d) 1...🖤f5.

3)
Pomar – Cuadras
Olot 1974

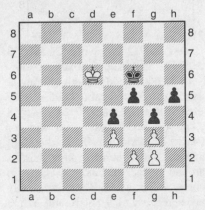

A more complicated pawn avalanche. How does Black, to play, sneak a pawn through?

4)
T. Horvath – Angantysson
Reykjavik 1982

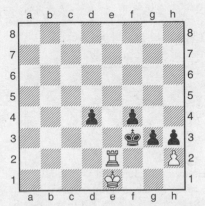

White seems to be powerless against the black pawns, but nevertheless there is a way to draw. Can you find it?

5)
Anand – Karpov
Monte Carlo Amber blindfold 1994

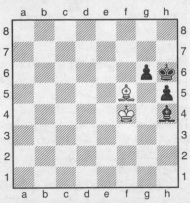

Black's dark-squared bishop is the 'wrong' bishop for his h-pawn; after 1...gxf5 2 ♔xf5 White can draw as long as his king can get in front of the h-pawn. How does Black (to play) nevertheless win?

Solutions to Endgame Challenges

1)
1 ♔d2

1 ♔f2? ♔g7 2 ♔g3 ♔f7! draws for Black: 3 ♔f3 (3 ♔f4 ♔f6; 3 ♔g4 ♔g6) 3...♔e7! and now White cannot keep the opposition since the e3-pawn obstructs the king. 4 e4 (4 ♔e4 ♔e6; 4 ♔f4 ♔f6; 4 ♔g4 ♔e6 5 ♔f4 ♔f6) 4...♔e6 5 ♔f4 ♔f6.

1...♔g7 2 ♔c3 ♔f6

2...♔f7 3 ♔d4 ♔f6 (3...♔e6 4 ♔e4) and by comparison with the line following 1 ♔f2, White now has the move 4 ♔d5 winning easily.

3 ♔d4 ♔e6

Else White plays 4 ♔e5, and wins quite easily.

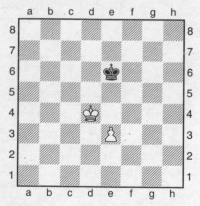

4 ♔e4

White has the opposition, and this is enough to win, even with the pawn only on the third rank. Instead 4 e4? ♔d6 draws, as we have seen.

4...♔d6 5 ♔f5 ♔e7 6 ♔e5 ♔d7 7 ♔f6 ♔e8 8 e4 ♔f8 9 ♔e6 ♔e8 10 e5 ♔d8 11 ♔f7 ♔d7 12 e6+, etc.

2)
a) 1...a6? 2 c6! wins: 2...axb5 3 cxb7; 2...b6 3 bxa6; 2...bxc6 3 bxa6.

b) 1...b6 is good enough to draw: 2 axb6 axb6 3 cxb6 cxb6 4 ♔f3 ♔f5 5 ♔e3 ♔e5 6 ♔d3 ♔d5 7 ♔c3 ♔c5 8 ♔b2! (8 ♔b3? ♔xb5 is a win for Black) 8...♔xb5 (if Black does not take the pawn, the white king shuffles around on a2, b2 and c2, ready to come to b3 when Black eventually takes the pawn) 9 ♔b3! and White seizes the opposition, and draws.

c) 1...c6? loses to 2 a6, sneaking a pawn through to queen.

d) **1...♔f5!** is best, and wins for Black. **2 b6** (else the black king will walk over and take the white pawns: 2 a6 bxa6 3 bxa6 ♔e5; 2 c6 bxc6 3 bxc6 ♔e5) **2...cxb6 3 axb6** (3 a6 bxa6 4 c6 ♔e6 5 c7 ♔d7 stops the pawn in the nick of time) **3...axb6** (3...a5? loses to 4 c6) **4 cxb6**

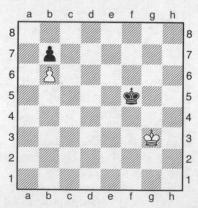

4...♔e4 (any one of the shortest routes to b6 will suffice) **5 ♔f2 ♔d4**

6 ♔e2 ♔c5 7 ♔d3 ♔xb6 8 ♔c4 (the white king needs to be on b4 at this point) **8...♔a5**.

Black can force his pawn through to promotion.

3)
1...f4! 2 ♔d5
Otherwise:

a) 2 gxf4 h4 and the h-pawn makes a touch-down on h1.

b) 2 exf4 h4! 3 gxh4 (else Black has a choice of ways to promote) 3...g3 4 fxg3 e3 wins.

2...h4!
This move makes a very strong visual impression. Who said pawns were boring pieces?

3 ♔xe4 f3!

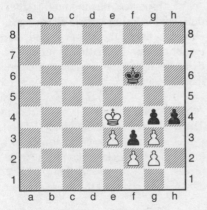

The familiar idea – the g-pawn is diverted to allow the h-pawn through to become a queen.

4 gxf3 h3 0-1
White's own pawn on f3 prevents his king from stopping the black pawn.

4)
1 ♔f1!
What on earth is White up to? This doesn't activate the king!

1...d3
1...g2+ 2 ♔g1 draws, since 2...♔xe2 is immediate stalemate.

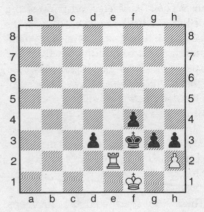

2 ♖f2+! ½-½
2...gxf2 is stalemate, while after 2...♔e3 3 hxg3 fxg3 4 ♖f8 White draws by checking the black king from behind.

A marvellous and resourceful finish by Horvath.

5)
1...♗g3+!
Black gains a tempo, since White must eliminate the f-pawn.

2 ♔e4 gxf5+ 3 ♔xf5
It now transpires that Black can shut out the white king.

3...♗b8! 4 ♔e4 h4 5 ♔f3 h3 6 ♔f2 ♗h2! 0-1
Black will simply bring up his king.

Chess Openings

In the following four large chapters of the book I provide details of all the main chess openings. For many of the openings I have also cited some traps and illustrative games, showing typical strategic and tactical themes from the opening. These games can also be studied for enjoyment and for general chess instruction in strategy and tactics.

The openings are divided into four sections.

Open Games

These are the traditional openings starting 1 e4 e5. More than a century ago, this was by far the most common way to start a game. It remains popular amongst chess enthusiasts, but is no longer anything like so dominant. Amongst young juniors and social players, however, most games are still begun this way, and for this reason I have gone into particular detail in this section to explain the various options for both sides, especially in the old-fashioned King's Gambit and Evans Gambit.

Semi-open Games

These are openings in which White's 1 e4 is not met by the symmetrical 1...e5. The most popular opening in this section – and indeed the most popular chess opening overall – is the Sicilian Defence, 1...c5. In this section, and the following two, rather than give an exhaustive summary of the options for both sides, I have provided a lot of game examples which I hope will provide inspiration and ideas. There is plenty of literature available if you want to look deeper into these openings. After all, if you want to play the Najdorf Poisoned Pawn, you will need more detailed information than I could possibly supply in this book!

Closed Games

Essentially, this means queen's pawn openings: White opens 1 d4. The word "closed" makes them sound rather dull, but this is unjustified. Black has a choice between the classical and uncompromising 1...d5, and a variety of dynamic openings, including the Indian defences.

Flank Openings

These are openings in which White makes no immediate effort to occupy the centre, but seeks to control it with pieces, and attack anything Black erects in the centre of the board.

Before moving on to a discussion of specifics, here are a few general thoughts on opening play. Note that I propose a few principles rather than provide a whole list of outmoded opening dos and don'ts. I feel that such a list inhibits creativity in the opening, and encourages beginners to play like automatons, almost never deviating from the Giuoco Piano (the chess equivalent of "Chopsticks" on the piano). Moreover, what is a beginner to think when he compares the games of top grandmasters with the cast-iron "rules" of opening play, and sees how breakable they are?

Strong players will not always adhere to the standard principles – but they will have a reason if they do not. Indeed the real sign of a great player is the willingness to go against tradition, and play strictly in accordance with the requirements of the specific position, whether this means sacrificing material, accepting apparently horrific weaknesses, or whatever.

How to Survive the Opening

1) Make only as many pawn moves as are necessary to develop your pieces
Pushing pawns is great fun. I used to love to crush my opponents against the wall with a huge pawn phalanx. However, it's not so much fun when the opponent's pieces start to checkmate your denuded king. Two pawn moves (your d- and e-pawns) is plenty to get your forces mobilized.

2) Put all your pieces on active squares as soon as possible
They should have plenty of scope for further movement. Note **all** your pieces – not just one or two. One piece on its own doesn't constitute an attacking force.

3) Arrange your pieces and pawns so that your pieces are not exposed to attack

Obviously there is no point putting your pieces on squares where your opponent can immediately drive them back. Your pawns can help in this respect, by controlling some key squares.

4) Do not waste any time
Any move that does nothing to increase the activity of your pieces should be regarded with suspicion. Naturally, you should respond to direct threats.

What Constitutes a "Good" Opening

To have much appeal to over-the-board players, an opening must have the following qualities:

1) It must not lose by force
No one likes to gamble on the opponent not having memorized the winning continuations.

2) It should not involve too much simplification
An overly simplified position gives little scope for outplaying the opponent.

3) It should be reasonably promising
For White this means some hope of preserving an advantage; for Black, either equality or at worst just a small disadvantage, with some counterplay. Whether a player's priority is equality or counterplay depends on his temperament.

Open Games

Belgrade Gambit (1 e4 e5 2 ♘f3 ♘c6 3 ♘c3 ♘f6 4 d4 exd4 5 ♘d5)
See the Four Knights Opening.

Bishop's Opening (1 e4 e5 2 ♗c4)

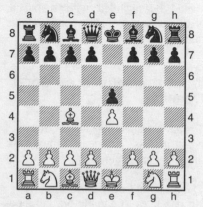

This is a sensible, generally solid opening for White, against which Black has difficulties generating quick counterplay. White often follows up with d3 and simple development, but aggressive plans with f4 at some point are possible too. The Bishop's Opening is frequently used by those who would like to play the standard Italian Game, 1 e4 e5 2 ♘f3 ♘c6 3 ♗c4, but wish to avoid the Petroff Defence, 2...♘f6.

Strategic Example
Zlochevsky – Tsarev
Moscow Ch 1989

1 e4 e5 2 ♗c4 ♘f6 3 d3 c6 4 ♘f3 d5 5 ♗b3

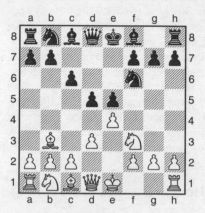

In this line of the Bishop's Opening, at a glance it seems that Black ought to have no problems. However, he has taken on considerable obligations in the centre.

5...♘bd7 6 0-0 ♗d6 7 exd5!?
White decides to play with his pieces against Black's pawn centre. 7 ♘c3 dxe4 8 ♘g5 0-0 9 ♘cxe4 ♘c5 is less awkward for Black.

7...cxd5 8 ♘c3 d4
8...♘b6 misplaces the knight; then 9 ♖e1 gives Black a headache on the e-file.

9 ♘g5! 0-0
9...dxc3 10 ♘xf7 is hopeless for Black since after taking the h8-rook, the knight's escape route is already secure.

10 ♘ce4 ♘c5 11 ♘xc5 ♗xc5
Both black bishops are having problems finding employment, while both of White's are about to become fiendishly active.

12 f4 exf4 13 ♗xf4 h6?

This is more than Black's fragile position can take. I suspect Tsarev realized he was playing with fire, but hoped to bluff White out of sacrificing on f7. 13...♗g4 14 ♕e1 ♗h5 15 ♕h4 ♗g6 16 ♗e5 is not exactly pleasant for Black either.

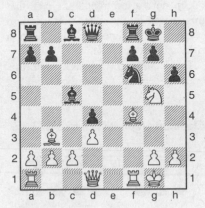

14 ♘xf7! ♖xf7 15 ♗e5
Black's forces are in no fit state to defend against the kingside threats.
15...♗e7 16 ♗xf6 ♗xf6 17 ♕h5 ♕c7 18 ♖ae1 ♔f8 19 ♖xf6! 1-0
19...gxf6 20 ♕xh6+ ♖g7 21 ♕h8+.

Centre Game (1 e4 e5 2 d4 exd4 3 ♕xd4)

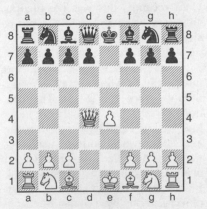

The main problem with this old opening is that White's queen is rather too exposed in the middle of the board. Black should gain fully equal play without much difficulty. The natural continuation is 3...♘c6, whereupon 4 ♕e3 is the most interesting. In recent years, White has started to use 3 ♘f3 as an anti-Petroff move-order ploy. Then 3...♘c6 is a Scotch, while 3...♘f6 is a sideline of the Petroff: 1 e4 e5 2 ♘f3 ♘f6 3 d4 exd4, sidestepping the more popular 3...♘xe4.

Damiano Defence (1 e4 e5 2 ♘f3 f6)

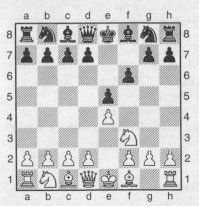

History has been cruel on Damiano. This is not the sort of opening that anyone would want named after themselves, as we are about to see...

Trap: 1 e4 e5 2 ♘f3 f6?
This move is not a good way to defend the e5-pawn. Greco analysed it as bad for Black as long ago as 1620.
3 ♘xe5! fxe5
3...♕e7 4 ♘f3 ♕xe4+ 5 ♗e2 is simply very good for White.
4 ♕h5+ ♔e7
4...g6 5 ♕xe5+ wins the rook.

5 ♕xe5+ ♔f7 6 ♗c4+ d5 7 ♗xd5+ ♔g6

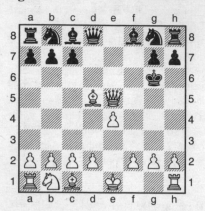

Now the key move:
8 h4! h5

8...h6 9 ♗xb7! is similar, while 8...♗d6 allows 9 h5+ ♔h6 10 d4+ g5 11 hxg6+ ♔xg6 12 ♕h5+ ♔f6 (12...♔g7 13 ♕f7#) 13 ♕g5#.
9 ♗xb7!!
White wins the a8-rook, since **9...♗xb7 10 ♕f5+ ♔h6 11 d4+ g5 12 ♕f7** forces a speedy mate.

Danish Gambit (1 e4 e5 2 d4 exd4 3 c3)

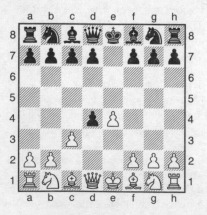

This is one of the more notoriously wild gambits. White generally intends to offer a second pawn, viz. 3...dxc3 4 ♗c4 cxb2 5 ♗xb2, but Black has one line that has dented its appeal substantially: 5...d5 6 ♗xd5 ♘f6 7 ♗xf7+ ♔xf7 8 ♕xd8 ♗b4+, regaining the queen with a level ending. Given that this simple reply exists, few modern players are inclined to play such a risky gambit as White.

Incidentally, in Denmark itself, this opening is called the Nordic Gambit.

Elephant Gambit (1 e4 e5 2 ♘f3 d5)

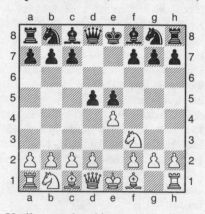

Until recently, this was regarded as simply a bad way to lose a pawn, since after 3 exd5, Black has no good way to keep the material balance. 3...♕xd5 4 ♘c3 costs Black too much time, while 3...e4 4 ♕e2 doesn't work for Black. The best hope for Black is the unlikely looking 3...♗d6, aiming to mobilize the kingside pawn majority. I can't believe this for Black, but it has been analysed extensively by the English FM Jonathan Rogers and the German player and publisher Stefan Bücker.

Evans Gambit (1 e4 e5 2 ♘f3 ♘c6 3 ♗c4 ♗c5 4 b4)

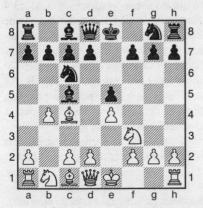

It is virtually impossible to discuss the Evans Gambit without using the word "swashbuckling". The Welsh sea captain Evans invented this gambit in the 1830s, and it rapidly became one of the most popular openings of the nineteenth century.

The idea of White's fourth move is to deflect the bishop from c5, and follow up with c3 and a quick d4. White hopes to catch the black king in the centre and put his development and open lines to use to finish the game with a whirlwind attack.

For decades, players with Black tried various ways to hang on to the extra pawn – some reasonable, some bad, but White would always get some sort of attacking chances.

The first world champion, Wilhelm Steinitz, had some particularly awkward ideas against the Evans; witness the mess in the following diagram, which arose in the game Chigorin–Steinitz, Havana Wch (17) 1889.

Not one of Black's pieces is functioning well. His queen and c8-bishop are particular embarrassments.

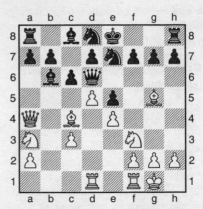

Play continued 12...♕b8 13 ♗xe7 ♔xe7 14 d6+ ♔f8 15 ♕b4 f6 16 ♗b3 g6 17 ♘c4 ♔g7 18 a4 ♘f7 19 ♘xb6 axb6 20 ♗xf7 ♔xf7 21 ♘xe5+!, with an overwhelming game for White, although Chigorin contrived somehow to let Steinitz off with a draw.

However, the second world champion, Emanuel Lasker, dealt a blow to the Evans with a modern idea: returning the pawn under favourable circumstances. The basic plan is to play 4...♗xb4 5 c3 ♗a5 6 0-0 d6 7 d4 ♗b6.

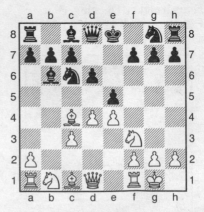

White can now regain the pawn, but has difficulty maintaining any sort of initiative. For instance, 8 dxe5 dxe5 9

♕b3 (9 ♕xd8+ ♘xd8 10 ♘xe5 offers White little too) 9...♕f6! (a key part of the plan) 10 ♗g5 ♕g6 11 ♗d5 ♘ge7 12 ♗xe7 ♔xe7 13 ♗xc6 ♕xc6 14 ♘xe5 ♕e6 is obviously very acceptable for Black.

White can vary his move order to try to avoid this problem, and the modern revival of the Evans has seen (after 4...♗xb4 5 c3 ♗a5), 6 d4 rising to the fore. Then 6...d6 can be met by 7 ♕b3, while after 6...exd4, 7 0-0 ♘ge7 8 cxd4 d5! 9 exd5 ♘xd5 is a line that retains its solid reputation, but 7 ♕b3 is under active investigation.

The Evans attracted renewed attention after Kasparov played it successfully a couple of times in the 1990s (most notably a famous victory over Anand), and it also gels with the modern trend towards the (re-)investigation of openings with a significant material imbalance. Nigel Short and Alexander Morozevich are among the players to watch for new ideas in the Evans.

Four Knights Opening (1 e4 e5 2 ♘f3 ♘c6 3 ♘c3 ♘f6)

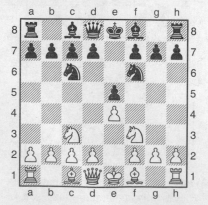

This old opening has a reputation for leading to drawish chess. Both sides develop methodically, with little imbalance in the position. In the late 1980s and early 1990s the Four Knights was rejuvenated by the English grandmasters Nigel Short, John Nunn and Murray Chandler, and became quite fashionable for a while. As an aside, one of the positive practical features of the Four Knights is that it can be played against the Petroff: 1 e4 e5 2 ♘f3 ♘f6 3 ♘c3, when Black's best move is 3...♘c6.

Play may continue 4 d4, when after 4...exd4 5 ♘xd4, a variation of the Scotch Opening is reached. However, there are two sharp alternatives: 4...♗b4 5 ♘xe5 ♘xe4 6 ♕g4! ♘xc3 7 ♕xg7 ♖f8 8 a3 leads to a chaotic, messy position.

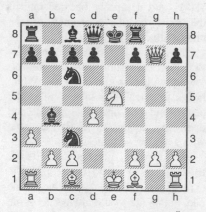

Then in the event of 8...♘xd4 (8...♗a5 is safer) 9 axb4 ♘xc2+, the white king goes on the rampage: 10 ♔d2 ♘xa1 11 ♔xc3. White has a dangerous attack, e.g. 11...a5 12 ♗c4 ♕e7 13 ♖e1 d5 (13...axb4+ 14 ♔d2!) 14 ♗b5+ c6 15 ♘xc6 ♕e1+ 16 ♗d2 bxc6 17 ♗xc6+ ♗d7 18 ♗xd7+ ♔xd7 19 ♗xe1 was good for White in the game Evers–Schitze,

Corr. 1986 – an incredible variation. The other interesting possibility is for White: 4...exd4 5 ♘d5, the Belgrade Gambit, which looks crazy, but is quite dangerous.

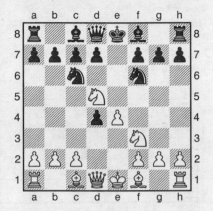

Unfortunately for White, Black has a good, simple response: 5...♗e7, when 6 ♗c4 ♘xe4 7 ♘xd4 0-0 8 ♘b5 ♗c5 9 0-0 ♘xf2 10 ♕h5 ♘e5! is good for Black, while 6 ♗f4 d6 7 ♘xd4 0-0 8 ♘b5 ♘xd5 9 exd5 ♘e5 is absolutely OK for Black.

However, let's take a look at the really sharp stuff: 5...♘xe4 6 ♕e2 f5 7 ♘g5 d3! 8 cxd3 ♘d4 9 ♕h5+ (John Nunn pointed out the resource 9 ♘xe4 ♘xe2 10 ♗g5 ♘f4!!, winning for Black) 9...g6 10 ♕h4 c6 11 dxe4 cxd5 12 exd5 and now:

a) 12...♘c2+ 13 ♔d1 ♘xa1 14 ♕d4 ♖g8 15 d6 ♗xd6 16 ♗c4 is the sort of attack White is looking for.

b) 12...♗g7! 13 ♕g3 0-0 is absolutely fine for Black.

c) 12...♕a5+ 13 ♔d1 ♕xd5 14 ♗c4 ♕xc4 15 ♖e1+ ♗e7 16 ♖xe7+ ♔xe7 17 ♘e4+ ♔e6 18 ♕f6+ ♔d5 19 ♘c3+ ♔c5 is a position where one wonders whether it's a king-hunt or a king-walk.

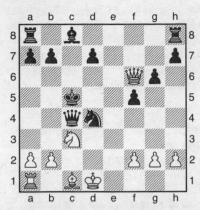

In fact, the main question is whether White can make a draw or not, e.g. 20 b4+ ♕xb4 21 ♕e5+ ♔c4 22 ♗d2 (22 ♕d5+ ♔d3!) 22...d6 23 ♕xh8 ♕b2 24 ♖c1 ♔d3 25 ♘b1 f4 (forced) 26 f3 ♗d7 27 ♕xa8 ♘e2 and White's king turns out to be the one in more danger!

Returning to the mainstream Four Knights, the normal fourth move for White is 4 ♗b5, which puts pressure on the e5-pawn by threatening to remove the c6-knight. Black has two good answers: the symmetrical 4...♗b4 and Rubinstein's counterattacking thrust 4...♘d4. Note that 4...♗c5 allows White the trick 5 0-0 0-0 6 ♘xe5 ♘xe5 7 d4 ♗d6 8 f4 ♘c6 9 e5, when White will regain the piece with some advantage.

After 4...♘d4, there is a "drawing line": 5 ♘xd4 exd4 6 e5 dxc3 7 exf6 ♕xf6 8 dxc3 ♕e5+ 9 ♕e2, but if White wishes to play for a win there is 5 ♗a4 ♗c5 6 ♘xe5 0-0, although this can give Black quite dangerous play for the pawn.

The classical main line is the so-called Metger Unpin: 4...♗b4 5 0-0

0-0 6 d3 d6 7 ♗g5 ♗xc3 8 bxc3 ♕e7 9 ♖e1 ♘d8 10 d4 ♘e6. By this knight manoeuvre, Black frees himself from the irritating pin. A tense, strategic battle results, in which Black has his fair share of the chances.

Trap: Four Knights, Rubinstein Defence
Mordue – Menadue
County Match 1986

1 e4 ♘f6 2 ♘c3 e5 3 ♘f3 ♘c6 4 ♗b5 ♘d4
This is Rubinstein's well-known equalizing line in the Four Knights Opening. Recent investigations, notably by Nunn, had livened the line up slightly, but not greatly dented its reputation.
5 ♘xe5
5 ♗a4 is better.
5...♕e7 6 f4 ♘xb5 7 ♘xb5 d6

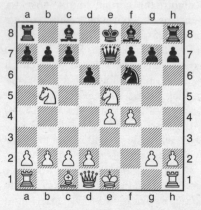

Now White should drop the knight back to f3, when Black obviously has no problems. However...
8 ♘d3?? ♗g4! 0-1
White's queen is lost. This occurred on a high board of a county match!

Trap: Four Knights, queen trap
Rysan – Drtina
Slovakian Cht 1993/4

1 e4 e5 2 ♘f3 ♘f6 3 ♘c3 ♘c6 4 ♗c4 ♘xe4!
This is the most logical way for Black to play.
5 ♘xe4 d5 6 ♕e2 dxc4 7 ♕xc4 ♗e6 8 ♕a4 f6 9 d3 a6

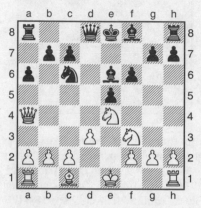

This position is quite good for Black, and he also has a little threat...
10 ♘c3??
While this deals with the immediate threat of 10...b5, it allows Black to force it through next move. Instead 10 ♘g3 would keep him alive, since 10...♗b4+ 11 c3 is no problem for White.
10...♗b4
Now 11...b5 will win material.
0-1

Trap: Four Knights
Atanasov – Gerasimov
Bulgarian Corr. Ch 1967

1 e4 e5 2 ♘f3 ♘c6 3 ♘c3 ♘f6 4 ♗b5 ♘d4 5 ♗c4 ♗c5 6 ♘xe5 ♕e7

7 f4?!

7 ♘f3 can be met by 7...d5!?.

7...d6

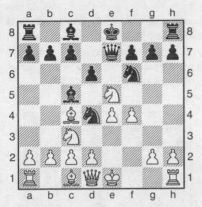

8 ♘xf7?

Instead White should choose 8 ♘f3 ♘xe4 (8...d5 is playable) 9 ♘d5 ♕d8 (9...♘c3+ 10 ♘xe7 ♘xd1 11 ♘d5):

a) 10 ♘xd4 is met by 10...♗xd4 11 ♕e2 0-0.

b) 10 b4 ♗g4 11 h4 (what else?) 11...c6 12 bxc5 cxd5 13 ♗xd5 ♘f6 is fairly good for Black.

c) 10 c3 is really quite OK for White: 10...♘xf3+ 11 ♕xf3 0-0 (11...♘f2 12 ♖f1 ♗g4 13 ♕g3 and Black's pieces are in a mess) 12 d4 ♖e8 13 0-0.

8...♘xe4

8...♗g4 is possibly stronger.

9 ♘e2?

9 0-0? ♘e2++ 10 ♔h1 ♘4g3+ 11 hxg3 ♘xg3+ 12 ♔h2 ♕h4#. 9 ♔f1! ♖f8 10 ♘xe4 ♕xe4 11 d3 ♕g6 is maybe only a little better for Black.

9...♘f3+

9...♕h4+ 10 ♘g3 ♘xg3 is also a wipe-out.

10 gxf3

10 ♔f1 ♕h4! is annihilation.

10...♗f2+ 11 ♔f1 ♗h3# (0-1)

Giuoco Piano (1 e4 e5 2 ♘f3 ♘c6 3 ♗c4 ♗c5)

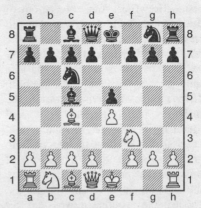

This is the first opening that most players learn, and in some books and by many teachers it is shown to beginners as an example of ideal opening play: put a pawn in the centre, develop a knight and then a bishop, etc. I beg to differ. If the only experience of chess that beginners get is playing either side of a symmetrical opening, then they will develop little feeling for dynamism and imbalance in chess.

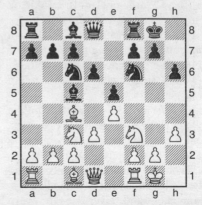

Snooker champion Steve Davis cites this opening as one reason why he lost interest in chess as a teenager. Playing against his father, the position on the previous page would always tend to result. He writes: "Once we're out of the opening we find ourselves in positions where neither of us can find a plan – and they don't tend to be very exciting positions either.... This is a fairly typical position for us. We both advance the h-pawn to stop the bishop coming to pin the knight. But there isn't really a lot happening here, is there? I mean, we've both got the same position." The result of this was that he didn't enjoy playing the opening at all: "...it's boring.... we just play routine moves and get into the same type of position with either colour."

And the reason for this? "Well, this was recommended as the strongest way to start the game. Who were we to question the word of experts? We continued in our own little world of chess, game after game following a similar pattern, never experimenting, and not really improving, until snooker appeared on the horizon."

Chris Ward, one of Britain's top players and most successful junior coaches, commented that it was not uncommon for young players to have this same opening, as both colours, in every single game of a six-round tournament.

Conclusion: if you're teaching a player, suggest some other openings, and if you're learning, do yourself a favour and try out something else.

That said, what about the opening itself? It can actually be handled dynamically, and give rise to sharp gambits or tense strategic manoeuvring. For a start, 4 b4 constitutes the Evans Gambit, discussed above.

One of the oldest gambits in the whole of chess is the Greco Attack, named after the Italian player/analyst who was active in the early seventeenth century. It runs 4 c3 ♘f6 5 d4 exd4 6 cxd4 ♗b4+ 7 ♘c3?! (after 7 ♗d2 ♗xd2+ 8 ♘bxd2 d5! White will have active piece-play in return for an isolated d-pawn) 7...♘xe4 8 0-0.

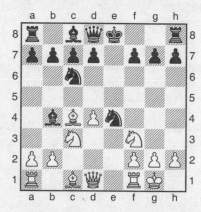

It works quite well except against the strong move 8...♗xc3!. Then the best chance for White is the idea of the Danish player Møller: 9 d5, when the main line is 9...♗f6 10 ♖e1 ♘e7 11 ♖xe4 d6 12 ♗g5 ♗xg5 13 ♘xg5. There is no good reason for either side to deviate from this sequence. Black then has a choice: 13...0-0 is safe, and tends to lead to a forced draw: 14 ♘xh7 ♔xh7 15 ♕h5+ ♔g8 16 ♖h4 f5 17 ♕h7+ (or 17 ♗e2) 17...♔f7 18 ♖h6 ♖g8 19 ♖e1 ♕f8 20 ♗b5 ♖h8 21 ♕xh8 gxh6 22 ♕h7+ ♔f6 23 ♖xe7 ♕xe7 24 ♕xh6+ with a perpetual check. Only Black has ways to deviate. The other move, 13...h6 is more ambitious, and has been regarded as good for Black, but perhaps an "unclear" evaluation is more in order in

view of the line 14 &b5+ &d7 15
We2 &xb5 16 Wxb5+ Wd7 17
Wxb7.

The whole line with 4 c3 followed
by 5 d4 is unpopular in modern-day
international chess. I would like to
mention that at lower club level, 4 c3
&f6 5 d4 exd4 6 e5 may prove
highly effective. Black then needs to
find the counter-thrust 6...d5! to gain
a satisfactory position.

The modern treatment of the
Giuoco Piano involves a slower,
rather more circumspect approach.
Typically play proceeds 4 d3 or 4 c3
&f6 and then 5 d3 d6 6 0-0, developing quietly, or 5 b4 &b6 6 d3 d6 7
a4, gaining queenside territory.

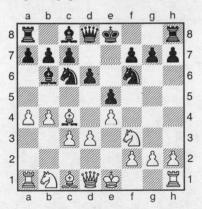

There are plenty of subtleties in these
lines, including various move-orders;
either side may delay castling, while
Black may play ...a6 to allow the
bishop to drop back to a7, or he may
delay ...d6 in the hope of playing
...d7-d5, etc. Play is often along lines
reminiscent of the Spanish, with
White slowly building up to a d3-d4
advance, and manoeuvring his
queen's knight via d2 and f1 to e3 or
g3.

Trap: Giuoco Piano
Vasiliev – Shabanov
USSR 1989

**1 e4 e5 2 &f3 &c6 3 &c4 &c5 4 0-0
&f6 5 d4!? &xd4**
Instead 5...exd4 6 e5 d5 7 exf6 dxc4 8
&e1+ is the sharp and unclear Max
Lange Attack, but 5...&xd4?! 6 &xe5
&e6 (6...0-0? 7 &e3 wins) 7 &xe6
fxe6 8 &d3 is quite good for White.
6 &xd4 &xd4 7 &g5
7 f4 is an alternative.
7...h6 8 &h4

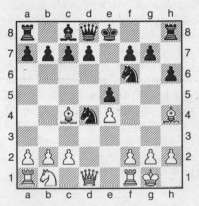

8...g5!? 9 f4! &e6?
After 9...gxf4? 10 &xf4 exf4 11
Wxd4 White wins the knight on f6.
9...d5! keeps the game unclear.
**10 &xe6 dxe6 11 Wxd8+ &xd8 12
fxg5 &xe4 13 g6+ &e8 14 &xf7
&g5 15 &xg5 hxg5 16 &c3 &g8 17
&b5 &xg6 18 &af1 1-0**

Göring Gambit (1 e4 e5 2 &f3 &c6
3 d4 exd4 4 c3)

This off-shoot of the Scotch Opening has ideas in common with the
Danish Gambit. It is quite dangerous,
and can lead to great complications.

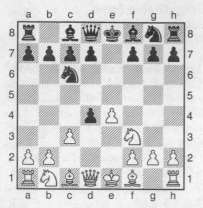

However, as in many such gambits, Black has a sensible, equalizing response: 4...d5 5 exd5 ♕xd5 6 cxd4 ♗g4 7 ♗e2 ♗b4+ 8 ♘c3 ♗xf3 9 ♗xf3 ♕c4, as introduced by Capablanca, is very irritating for White, and has virtually banished the Göring from tournament play: why take all the risk of playing a speculative gambit just to be dumped in this position?

Hungarian Defence (1 e4 e5 2 ♘f3 ♘c6 3 ♗c4 ♗e7)

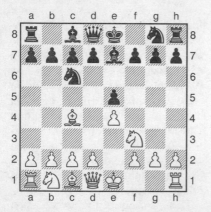

This is a very passive response to the Italian Game. White has no trouble keeping an advantage after 3 d4.

Italian Game (1 e4 e5 2 ♘f3 ♘c6 3 ♗c4)

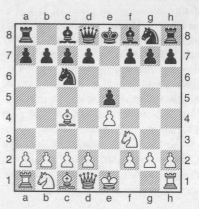

Play now branches off into either the Two Knights (3...♘f6), the Giuoco Piano (3...♗c5) or, occasionally, the Hungarian Defence (3...♗e7).

Trap: The "Oh My God!" Trap

1 e4 e5 2 ♘f3 ♘c6 3 ♗c4 ♘d4?

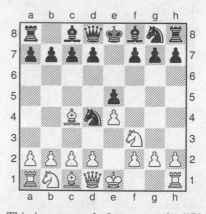

This is apparently known as the "Oh My God!" Trap since to have the full effect, Black is meant to make some such anguished comment to make White think he has simply blundered the e5-pawn. This is of course profoundly unethical, and I hope readers of this book do not try it. It is not a very good trap to try, since if White does not walk into the snare, Black will be at a considerable disadvantage.

4 ♘xe5??

White gullibly takes the pawn. These three alternatives all give White a substantial development advantage: 4 c3 ♘xf3+ 5 ♕xf3, 4 0-0 or 4 ♘xd4.

4...♕g5!

Already White is quite lost. It's incredible, but true!

5 ♘xf7

5 ♗xf7+ ♔e7 does not help; 6 d3 ♕xe5 gives White only two pawns for the piece. 5 c3 ♕xg2 6 ♖f1 ♕xe4+ 7 ♗e2 ♘c2+ wins the white queen.

5...♕xg2 6 ♖f1 ♕xe4+ 7 ♗e2 ♘f3# (0-1)

King's Gambit (1 e4 e5 2 f4)

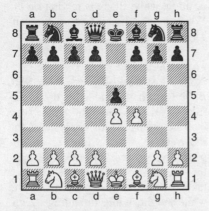

The King's Gambit was far and away the most popular opening of the nineteenth century, and to this day retains its appeal to fearless attackers.

One indication of its former dominance over other openings is that in *The Chess-Player's Handbook*, published in 1847, Howard Staunton (not someone particularly noted as an exponent of gambit systems) devotes 109 pages to the King's Gambit, of 343 in total covering all openings.

At a glance, the King's Gambit looks like a reckless adventure: White exposes his king and allows Black to establish a pawn on f4, which White has no guarantee of regaining. The point, though, is that if White can maintain the initiative, these problems will just not matter. Maybe the white king will be checked; it can move, so be it. One check is not an attack. White envisages that after 2...exf4 he will gain a free hand in the centre and open up the f-file to land a big attack on the f7-square and thus the black king. If Black hangs on to the f4-pawn to keep the f-file blocked, then this commits him to further weakening pawn moves (...g5) or some odd piece placements (e.g. king's knight on h5 or g6). However, in the supposedly scientific era of chess, starting with Steinitz and Lasker et al., such gambits became far less fashionable. Steinitz's view, that an attack was only justified when an advantage had been secured, and that an advantage could only be secured when the opponent had gone wrong, became prevalent. Since 1...e5 does not look like a fatal error, White should not therefore be launching an attack! In the first quarter of the twentieth century, the new "hypermodernism" became central to chess thought, with such players as Nimzowitsch and Réti leading the way. The King's Gambit did not fit in with their way of thinking either: there is no scope here for controlling the centre from afar!

Some modern players have been returning to the King's Gambit. Notably the English grandmasters, Mark Hebden and in particular Joe Gallagher, have revitalized it. Gallagher's book, *Winning With the King's Gambit*, proved extremely popular, suggesting that a lot of club players find the gambit attractive. While teenagers, Judit and Zsofia Polgar also contributed greatly to the modern popularity of the King's Gambit, and in particular the King's Bishop's Gambit, 2...exf4 3 ♗c4.

A systematic look at the main variations is called for. First of all, I shall discuss Black accepting the gambit, 2...exf4, since this is the most critical response. The normal move is then 3 ♘f3, the King's Knight's Gambit.

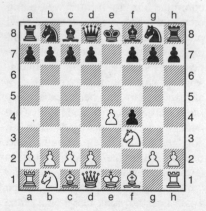

White has two main ideas in mind: to play d4 and ♗xf4, dominating the centre, and to attack f7 with ♗c4 and 0-0. Black's most straightforward reply is 3...g5 (and then 4 h4 g4 5 ♘e5,

the Kieseritzky, is critical), but there are plenty of others:

Cunningham Defence
3...♗e7 is an old and flexible move. Black develops and may continue with an irritating check on h4. One line is then 4 ♘c3 ♗h4+ (4...♘f6 5 e5 ♘g4 6 d4 is quite good for White) 5 ♔e2 d5 6 ♘xd5 ♘f6 7 ♘xf6+ ♕xf6 8 d4 ♗g4.

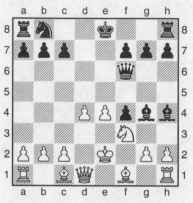

White has several advantages in this position, while Black is relying on the White king's discomfort to compensate.

Fischer Defence
After a loss against Spassky in 1960, Bobby Fischer decided to try to refute the King's Gambit. Some time later he published his analysis of the move 3...d6, which aims for an improved version of the lines following the immediate 3...g5. The d-pawn takes away the e5-square from the white knight, while intending 4...g5, when after 5 h4 g4, the knight will have to find another square. The main line is 4 d4 g5 5 h4 g4 6 ♘g1 (and not 6 ♘g5 f6!).

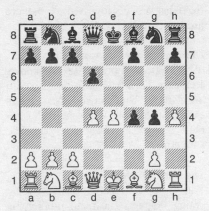

This rather odd position offers White good attacking prospects.

Modern Defence
Here Black hopes to kill White's initiative by returning the pawn immediately, with quick development and early castling, viz. 3...d5 4 exd5 ♘f6.

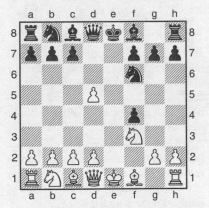

Here Hebden and Gallagher have used the move 5 ♗c4 to good effect, e.g. 5...♘xd5 (5...♗d6 is not good, since the d5-pawn is more valuable than the one on f4) 6 0-0 ♗e7 7 d4 0-0 8 ♗xd5 ♕xd5 9 ♗xf4 c5?! 10 ♘c3 ♕c4 11 ♕e1 ♗f6 12 ♗d6 ♗xd4+ 13 ♔h1 ♖d8 14 ♘e4 f5?! 15 ♕h4 ♘c6 16

♘e5! is a beautiful trap with which Gallagher has caught two grandmasters.

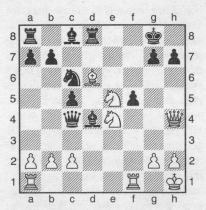

On move 6, Black does better to play 6...♗e6, so as to recapture with the bishop. Then 7 ♗b3 ♗e7 8 c4 ♘b6 9 d4 ♘xc4 10 ♗xf4, an interesting pawn sacrifice, is the preference of Hebden and Gallagher.

Miscellaneous third moves for Black
a) 3...♘c6 can transpose to a Vienna Gambit after 4 ♘c3, though 4 d4 is a very interesting alternative.

b) 3...h6, the Becker Defence, can be met by 4 b3!? seeking to discourage ...g5.

c) 3...♘f6 4 e5 ♘h5, the Schallop Defence, looks eccentric, but is not too bad. White can play 5 d4 d5 6 c4, when 6...g5 7 g4! is good for White, since 7...♗xg4 8 ♖g1 opens lines to White's advantage.

d) 3...♘e7 was played by Seirawan against Spassky, but he soon regretted it after 4 d4 d5 5 ♘c3 dxe4 6 ♘xe4 ♘g6 7 h4 ♕e7 8 ♔f2! ♗g4 (not 8...♕xe4? 9 ♗b5+ and 10 ♖e1) 9 h5 ♘h4 (9...♗xh5 10 ♖xh5 ♕xe4 11 ♗c4 gives White a lot of threats) 10

♗xf4 ♘c6 11 ♗b5 0-0-0 12 ♗xc6 bxc6 13 ♛d3, launching a decisive attack.

e) 3...f5, although a mirror-image of the sort of move Black would try in the Queen's Gambit Accepted, is here rather silly, though White must be alert: 4 e5 g5 5 d4 g4 6 ♗xf4! gxf3 7 ♛xf3 ♛h4+ 8 g3 ♛g4 9 ♛e3 gives White an enormous attack for the piece.

f) 3...h5, Wagenbach's Defence, is the sort of odd move that gets discussed in the *Myers Openings Bulletin* and other specialist "weird openings" publications. The main idea is to play 4 d4 g5 5 ♗c4 h4, physically preventing White from breaking up the kingside by playing 6 h4.

The Kieseritzky Gambit

Now we move on to the most critical line of the King's Gambit. After 3 ♘f3 Black defends his pawn with 3...g5, with some ideas of kicking the f3-knight with a later ...g4. Now 4 ♗c4 g4 5 0-0 gxf3 6 ♛xf3 is the notorious Muzio Gambit, reputed to be a draw with best play. The Kieseritzky continues instead 4 h4 g4 5 ♘e5.

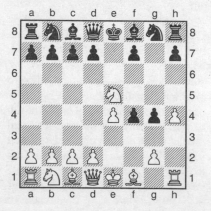

Note that White's fourth move was not just to break up Black's kingside pawns; the h4-pawn prevents ...♛h4+ and guards the g5-square. Black has many responses, but 5...♘f6 is considered best. Then 6 d4 d6 7 ♘d3 ♘xe4 8 ♗xf4 ♛e7 9 ♗e2 is Gallagher's interesting suggestion. White hopes to exploit Black's shattered kingside structure.

The King's Bishop's Gambit

This, 3 ♗c4, was often played by the young Polgars. The main problem is 3...♘f6 4 ♘c3 c6.

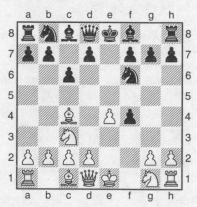

Black prepares ...d5, which should yield good play.

Black can decline the King's Gambit in various ways:

Falkbeer Countergambit

Here Black tries to seize the initiative by refusing the gambit and offering a pawn sacrifice of his own: 2...d5 3 exd5. Falkbeer's original idea, 3...e4, is now considered suspect due to 4 d3, so attention has shifted to Nimzowitsch's 3...c6, though this is hardly a typical Nimzowitsch move.

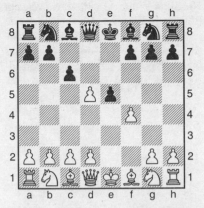

One important line then is 4 ♘c3 exf4 5 ♘f3 ♗d6 6 d4 ♘e7 7 dxc6 ♘bxc6. This play has a very modern look to it – both sides going for development rather than material gain. Black's active pieces compensate for his suspect pawn structure.

Classical Defence

2...♗c5 is a sensible move, one of a number that exploit the fact that White is not threatening 3 fxe5, since there would then come the deadly check 3...♕h4+.

Stefan Bücker's peculiar idea 3 ♕h5 is an imaginative way to use the bishop's position on c5, but then the gambit 3...♘f6 4 ♕xe5+ ♗e7 and the natural 3...♘c6 4 fxe5 g6 are good replies.

After 3 ♘f3 d6, White can choose between the ambitious 4 c3, angling for d4, and the sensible 4 ♘c3, reaching a fairly standard sort of position. I should also mention that after 4 c3 f5!? 5 fxe5 dxe5 6 d4 exd4 7 ♗c4! fxe4, Gallagher prefers 8 ♘xd4 to the greedy 8 ♘g5 ♘f6 9 ♘f7 ♕e7 10 ♘xh8, which allows Black strong threats.

Two odd ideas

One unusual reply to the King's Gambit is the Nordwalde Variation, analysed extensively by Stefan Bücker: 2...♕f6, with the cheeky plan of 3...♕xf4. It is nothing like as bad as it looks, but my advice is "don't try this at home!" For example, after 3 ♘c3 ♕xf4 4 4 ♘f3 d6 5 d4 ♕g4 6 dxe5 ♘c6 Black is surviving, but Bücker draws attention to 4 d4!. Really, such lines are fascinating to analyse and demonstrate the almost inexhaustibility of chess, but should not be used in key games! Bücker himself only became interested in the line when he had problems finding a concrete refutation.

Another idea was analysed by German GM Matthias Wahls: 2...♘c6 3 ♘f3 f5.

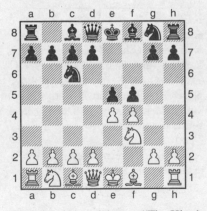

The title of his article was "The King's Gambit Finally Refuted!", though surely this was a tongue in cheek reference to Fischer's earlier claim. In his magazine *Kaissiber*, Stefan Bücker gives five counter-arguments, e.g. 4 ♗c4 exf4 (4...fxe4 5 ♘xe5) 5 d3 ♘f6 6 ♗xf4 fxe4 7 dxe4 ♕e7 8 ♘c3 with good play.

Trap: King's Gambit, Schallop Defence

1 e4 e5 2 f4 exf4 3 ♘f3 ♘f6 4 e5 ♘h5

This is the Schallop Defence. With an undefended knight stuck on h5, Black must be very wary.

5 d4 d6 6 ♕e2

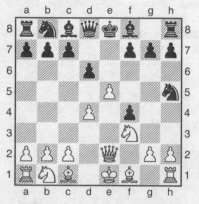

6...♗e7?

6...d5 is viable, as possibly also is 6...♕e7, but 6...dxe5 7 ♕xe5+ (7 ♘xe5 ♕h4+ 8 g3 ♘xg3 9 hxg3 ♕xh1 10 ♘g6+ ♗e6 11 ♘xh8 is not too clear) 7...♕e7 8 ♗e2 offers White pleasant play.

7 exd6

After Black recaptures, 8 ♕b5+ picks off the h5-knight.

Strategic Example
Bird – Anon.
London 1886

1 e4 e5 2 f4 exf4 3 ♘f3 g5 4 ♘c3 g4 5 ♘e5 ♕h4+ 6 g3 fxg3 7 ♕xg4 g2+ 8 ♕xh4 gxh1♕ 9 ♕h5 ♗e7

9...♘h6 seems sensible.

10 ♘xf7 ♘f6??

10...♗h4+ 11 ♕xh4 ♔xf7 keeps Black alive.

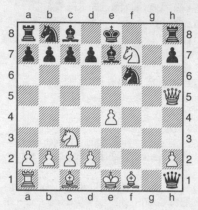

Now White can force a smothered mate.

11 ♘d6++! ♔d8 12 ♕e8+! ♖xe8 13 ♘f7# (1-0)

Strategic Example
Teschner – Anon.
Southsea 1951

1 e4 e5 2 f4 exf4 3 ♘f3 ♗e7 4 ♗c4 ♘f6 5 ♘c3?!

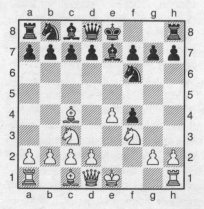

Now Black decides to employ a standard exchanging manoeuvre. It is a good idea, but leads to complications.

5...♘xe4! 6 ♗xf7+

6 ♘xe4 d5 was the masterplan.

6...♔xf7

6...♔f8?! leaves White with excellent attacking chances.

7 ♘e5+ ♔e6?

7...♔g8 is good for Black.

8 ♕g4+ ♔xe5 9 d4+ ♔xd4?

9...♔d6; 9...♔f6.

10 ♗e3+! 1-0

Black wished to see neither 10...fxe3 11 ♕xe4+ ♔c5 12 ♕d5+ ♔b6 13 ♕b5# nor 10...♔xe3 11 ♕e2+ ♔d4 12 ♕xe4+ ♔c5 13 ♕d5+ ♔b6 14 ♕b5#, while 10...♔e5 (best) 11 ♗xf4+ ♔f6 12 ♗xc7 ♘g5 13 ♗xd8 should be winning for White – but Black may as well have played on.

Latvian Gambit (1 e4 e5 2 ♘f3 f5)

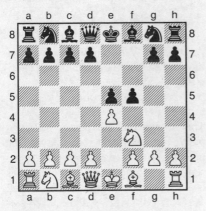

If the King's Gambit is risky for White, then surely this is suicide for Black? Well, the first thing to note is that the line given in some books as a refutation of the Latvian, 3 ♗c4, is probably nothing of the sort, since after 3...fxe4 4 ♘xe5, the move 4...d5 may be rather good for Black, while

even the standard move 4...♕g5 is not utterly clearly bad.

White should prefer the sensible 3 ♘xe5 ♕f6 4 d4 d6 5 ♘c4 fxe4, when he has a choice of several pleasant options. 6 ♗e2 is one good idea, preventing the black queen from settling on g6 and maintaining the b1-knight's flexibility.

Petroff Defence (1 e4 e5 2 ♘f3 ♘f6)

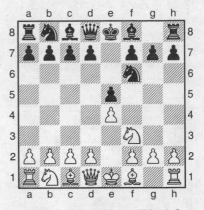

A safe and extremely sensible defence. At club level it suffers a little due to its reputation for being excessively dull, but at international level it often leads to exciting play as White tries to prove an advantage.

The first point to note is that after 3 ♘xe5, Black should avoid 3...♘xe4?!, since then 4 ♕e2 wins material (if the black knight moves, 5 ♘c6+ is a rude awakening). There are two main lines:

3 ♘xe5 d6 4 ♘f3 ♘xe4 5 d4 d5. Here Black will strive to show that the knight is well placed on e4, and generates activity. On the other hand, White will try to prove that the knight's position is unstable – if White can force the knight to retreat to f6, he will be

two tempi up (one in addition to the one White starts with). In practice, White generally can make the knight retreat, but at some structural cost (e.g. having to play c4), which tends to balance things out. These lines are very solid for Black, and in recent top-level practice White has often tried 5 ♘c3 ♘xc3 6 dxc3 followed by kingside aggression. This may not be objectively preferable, but at least leads to more unbalanced play.

3 d4 ♘xe4 4 ♗d3 d5 5 ♘xe5 is a similar line (only White's knight is differently placed) and also very solid for Black. Black chooses between the solid and symmetrical 5...♗d6, and the more aggressive 5...♘d7.

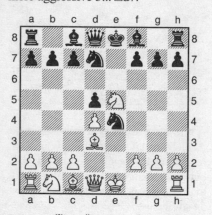

Then 6 ♕e2 ♘xe5 7 ♗xe4 dxe4 8 ♕xe4 ♗e6 is reckoned to give Black good compensation for the pawn, however White recaptures the knight. The critical line is 6 ♘xd7 ♗xd7 7 0-0 ♕h4 8 c4 0-0-0 9 c5, when both sides will attack the enemy king. Very exciting stuff, but if White wishes to avoid anything sharp, then there is the line 3 ♘xe5 d6 4 ♘f3 ♘xe4 5 ♕e2 ♕e7 6 d3, when queens come off, and a draw is in prospect.

Trap: Petroff, bad play
Lawrence – Stafford
Corr. 1950

1 e4 e5 2 ♘f3 ♘f6 3 ♘xe5 ♘c6?
Some players just seem to like being a pawn down! Perhaps they feel it encourages the opponent to be careless...
4 ♘xc6 dxc6 5 e5
5 d3 simply leaves White a pawn up.
5...♘e4

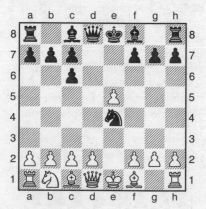

Amazingly, White now has a plausible way to lose the game on the spot!
6 d3??
6 d4 is again quite good enough.
6...♗c5 0-1
This shows that no matter how stupidly the opponent has played the opening, it can be catastrophic to assume "anything wins"! White loses heavy material: 7 dxe4 ♗xf2+ 8 ♔e2 ♗g4+, 7 d4 ♘xf2! 8 ♔xf2 ♗xd4+ or 7 ♗e3 ♗xe3 8 fxe3 ♕h4+ 9 g3 ♘xg3.

Trap: Petroff 3...♘xe4?!

1 e4 e5 2 ♘f3 ♘f6 3 ♘xe5 ♘xe4?!
Not disastrous yet, but 3...d6 4 ♘f3 ♘xe4 is certainly far more reliable.
4 ♕e2

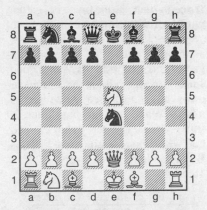

4...♘f6??

Black overlooks a simple idea. He has to play 4...♕e7 5 ♕xe4 d6, hoping for compensation for a pawn in the play following 6 d4.

5 ♘c6+ wins the black queen. Interestingly enough, this occurred in a game between future grandmasters Nigel Short and David Norwood – aged 10 and 6 respectively!

Philidor Defence (1 e4 e5 2 ♘f3 d6)

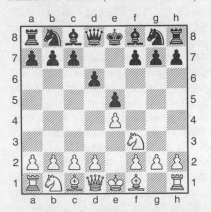

This opening has a consistent following at club level and has gained some recent popularity in international chess, but with Black often using a different move-order entirely (see below).

Philidor's original concept was that pawns should not be obstructed, and therefore knights should not be placed in front of pawns. Therefore he envisaged a quick ...f5 by Black, forming a kingside pawn phalanx. However, the variation 3 d4 f5 is a little too loosening, so the Philidor in modern practice is a more passive beast than its inventor intended, with 3 d4 being met by 3...exd4, 3...♘d7 or 3...♘f6, and Black generally playing to equalize the position. With the last two of these moves, Black is aiming for the position after 3...♘f6 4 ♘c3 ♘bd7, when 5 ♗c4 ♗e7 6 0-0 0-0 leads to a tough strategic struggle, while 5 g4!? is a recently popular way to stir up immediate chaos, in line with several other g4 thrusts that have been tried out in other openings. However, both moves have a drawback: 3...♘d7 4 ♗c4 gives Black problems with f7, while Black struggles to equalize in the open position after 3...♘f6 4 dxe5 (see below).

In modern play, this line is more often reached via a Pirc move-order: 1 e4 d6 2 d4 ♘f6 3 ♘c3 and now 3...e5 (intending 4 ♘f3 ♘bd7 and considering 4 dxe5 dxe5 5 ♕xd8+ ♔xd8 6 ♗c4 ♗e6 acceptable) or the less common 3...♘bd7, intending 4 ♘f3 e5, but 4 f4 is a more aggressive reply.

Strategic Example
Sammalvuo – J. Johansson
Swedish League 1995/6

1 e4 e5 2 ♘f3 d6 3 d4 ♘f6 4 dxe5 ♘xe4 5 ♕d5 ♘c5 6 ♗g5 ♕d7 7 exd6 ♗xd6 8 ♘c3 0-0 9 0-0-0 ♘c6 10 ♗e3

This is interesting, but 10 ♘b5! is a clearer route to an advantage, at least.
10...♕e7 11 ♕h5 ♗e6 12 ♘g5 ♗f5 13 ♘d5 ♕d8 14 ♘f4 ♕e8

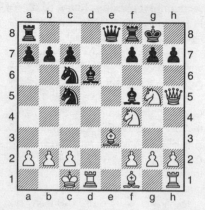

Now White tries to force matters, but his own position has its defects too.
15 ♗xc5 ♗xf4+

This is best, although 15...♗xc5 16 ♗d3 (16 g4 ♕e5 keeps Black afloat) is very interesting too:

a) 16...♕e5 17 ♘g6!! ♗xg6 18 ♗xg6 ♕f4+ 19 ♔b1 h6 20 ♗xf7+ ♖xf7 (20...♔h8 21 h4!?) 21 ♘xf7 is at least quite good for White.

b) 16...♗d6 17 ♗xf5 ♗xf4+ 18 ♔b1 h6.

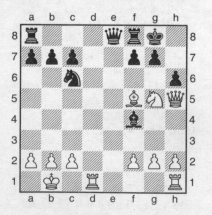

It seems that Black must be getting wiped off the board here, but it is not so clear. 19 ♖he1 is probably best, assuring White of a large middle-game plus. 19 ♘h7 is quite good, since 19...g6, although simultaneously attacking three white pieces, allows White a clear plus after 20 ♘f6+ ♔h8 21 ♘xe8 gxh5 22 ♘f6, but with opposite-coloured bishops, Black can hope to survive.

16 ♔b1

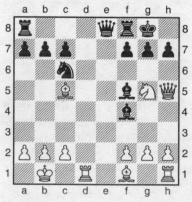

16...♕e5

16...♗g6!? 17 ♕g4 (17 ♕h4? ♕e5! 18 ♗xf8 ♗xg5 is very good for Black) 17...♕e5 (17...♗d6 18 ♗xd6 cxd6 is also a reasonable try; although his d6-pawn is chronically weak, Black can hope for some play against the white king) 18 ♗xf8 ♖xf8 is actually quite OK for Black:

a) 19 ♘h3 ♗h5 (19...♘b4!?) 20 ♕xf4 ♗xd1 is about equal.

b) 19 ♘f3? allows 19...♗xc2+! 20 ♔xc2 ♕e4+ 21 ♗d3 (21 ♔b3? ♘a5+ and a bishop check next move picks off the white queen) 21...♘b4+ 22 ♔b1 ♘xd3 forces White to surrender a rook for the d3-knight, whereupon he will be a pawn down.

c) 19 h4 ♗f5 – see the note to Black's 18th move below.

17 ♗xf8 ♖xf8

17...♗g6?! is now met by 18 ♕e2! (18 ♕g4 ♖xf8 is the previous note), when Black does not have so many tricks.

18 h4

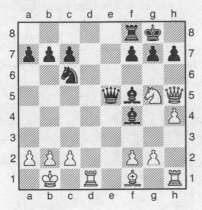

18...♘b4??

This oversight costs Black the game immediately. Instead 18...♗g6 is absolutely fine for Black: 19 ♕g4 (19 ♕f3? ♘d4; 19 ♕e2 ♘d4 20 ♕xe5 ♗xc2+ – see line "b") and then:

a) 19...♘b4 may not be quite adequate: 20 ♗d3 ♗xd3 (20...♘xd3 21 cxd3 ♖d8 gives Black some compensation) 21 cxd3 ♕d5 22 ♕xf4 (22 b3? ♕c6) 22...♕xa2+ 23 ♔c1 ♕a1+ 24 ♔d2 ♕xb2+ 25 ♔e1 ♘xd3+ (25...♖e8+ 26 ♘e4 ♘xd3+ 27 ♖xd3 ♕b1+ 28 ♔e2 ♕xh1 and now 29 ♕e5! is the clearest win for White) 26 ♖xd3 ♕b1+ 27 ♔e2 ♕xh1 28 ♘xf7! wins for White.

b) 19...♗f5 20 ♕e2 (20 ♕h5 ♗g6 repeats) 20...♘d4 21 ♕xe5 ♗xc2+ 22 ♔a1 ♗xe5 and it is hard to see White creating winning chances.

19 ♕xf7+!! 1-0

19...♖xf7 20 ♖d8+ ♖f8 21 ♗c4+

♘d5 22 ♗xd5+ ♕xd5 23 ♖xd5 leaves White a clear exchange up.

Ponziani Opening (1 e4 e5 2 ♘f3 ♘c6 3 c3)

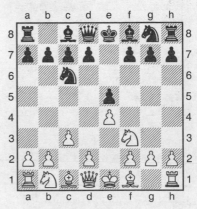

This is a relic from a bygone age, popular neither at top level nor at club level. 3...♘f6 4 d4 ♘xe4 5 d5 ♘e7 6 ♘xe5 ♘g6 is a good, sensible response, while the obscure 3...d5 4 ♕a4 could take players unaware if they have not studied the line.

Portuguese Opening (1 e4 e5 2 ♗b5)

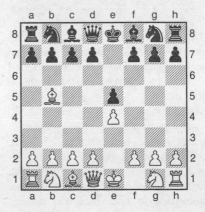

This looks like simply a Ruy Lopez where White has forgotten about the knight moves, but there is some logic. White may be able to find a better follow-up than ♘f3; maybe d3 and f4. Nevertheless Black has a choice of good answers. The most popular is 2...c6 3 ♗a4 ♘f6, when the miniature Vescovi–I.Sokolov, Malmö 1995 has become quite famous: 4 ♕e2 (4 ♘c3 is better) 4...♗c5 5 ♘f3 d5 6 exd5 0-0 7 ♘xe5 ♖e8 8 c3 ♗xf2+ 9 ♔f1 ♗g4 10 ♕xf2 ♖xe5 11 ♔g1 ♕e7 0-1. 12 h3 would be met by the annihilating 12...♗xh3.

Ruy Lopez (Spanish) (1 e4 e5 2 ♘f3 ♘c6 3 ♗b5)

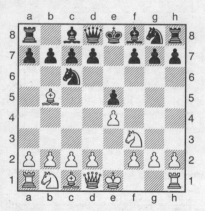

This is one of the oldest and most famous of chess openings. It has so many systems and sub-variations, and such strategic diversity that I cannot do the opening justice in the limited amount of space available here.

The bishop move puts pressure on the c6-knight, and so on the e5-pawn. Although as yet there is no threat to win the pawn, there will be shortly, and Black generally has to weaken his queenside to kick back the bishop.

Generally he starts this immediately with 3...a6, but there are several alternatives:

Steinitz Defence

This (3...d6) is the forerunner to the more modern Deferred Steinitz Defence (3...a6 4 ♗a4 d6), which is discussed later.

Schliemann Defence

This is a spirited gambit response, 3...f5, that is played at grandmaster level now and then.

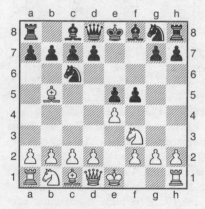

It is one of those openings that inspires fanaticism in its adherents, and can lead to some bizarre and intricate play. The argument is that, by comparison with the Latvian Gambit, the moves ♗b5 and ...♘c6 improve Black's chances considerably since an exchange on c6 would suit Black well in a gambit scenario, where development is all-important. White's best response is considered to be 4 ♘c3, continuing with development. Then after 4...fxe4 (4...♘d4 5 exf5 c6 6 ♘xe5! is John Nunn's dangerous piece sacrifice) 5 ♘xe4, Black has a choice between 5...♘f6, which might be just about viable, and the more exciting 5...d5 6 ♘xe5 dxe4 7 ♘xc6 ♕g5.

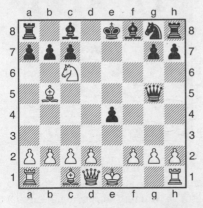

It's amazing that this position is not a wipe-out for one side or the other, but in fact the main line is 8 ♕e2 ♘f6 9 f4 ♕xf4 10 ♘e5+ c6 11 d4 ♕h4+ 12 g3 ♕h3 13 ♗c4 ♗e6 14 ♗g5, with a relatively quiet position, where Black will have some difficulty making sure his piece activity is enough to compensate for the weak isolated e-pawn.

I should now move on, without further ado, to the next variation, but cannot help expanding on the move 4...♘d4. This variation was a favourite of a friend of mine at university, who shall remain anonymous. At the British Championship in 1989, each night he would analyse some new idea in the lines following the knight move, and whenever he had something that looked like it might work, he would wake everyone up to analyse the new move. This happened at about ten-minute intervals through the whole of one night, each idea taking the bleary-eyed and none-too-amused impromptu analysis team a few seconds to refute. Therefore the 4...♘d4 line of the

Schliemann occupies a very special place in my memory!

Berlin Defence
In this ancient line, Black simply develops by 3...♘f6. After prolonged neglect, it has become very popular in the new millennium, following its use by Kramnik to infuriate Kasparov in their 2000 match. The main line is 4 0-0, when the sharp 4...♗c5 5 c3 0-0 6 d4 ♗b6 7 ♗g5 h6 8 ♗h4 d6 9 ♗xc6 bxc6 10 ♘bd2 is pleasant for White, but the dull-looking 4...♘xe4 5 d4 ♘d6 6 ♗xc6 dxc6 7 dxe5 ♘f5 8 ♕xd8+ ♔xd8 is the surprising basis for the new-found popularity.

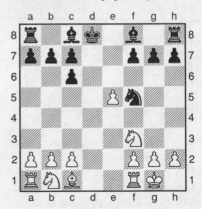

It seems that Black faces a difficult ending, due to White's kingside pawn majority and the crippled black queenside. However, the pawn is a little too far advanced on e5 (Black has more squares for manoeuvring his pieces), and this makes it hard for White to claim much advantage; some players even use this line as a winning attempt for Black! White's most promising approaches are based on sharp concrete play, treating the position as a middlegame rather than an ending.

Bird Defence

The 19th century English master Bird had a number of eccentric ideas in the opening, and his 3...♘d4 does not disappoint. Nevertheless, the move is not bad, and enjoyed some popularity at top level in the late 1980s. 4 ♘xd4 exd4 5 ♗c4, preventing 5...♗c5 due to 6 ♗xf7+ ♚xf7 7 ♕h5+, is a good response. A critical line runs 5...♘f6 6 0-0 ♘xe4 7 ♗xf7+ ♚xf7 8 ♕h5+ g6 9 ♕d5+ ♚g7 10 ♕xe4 ♕f6 11 d3.

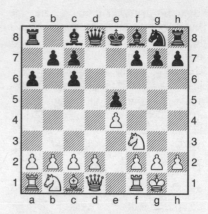

White now threatens the e5-pawn in earnest, but is thinking in the long term of winning an ending. Consider the following position:

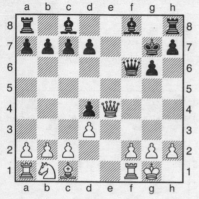

White retains some winning chances in view of his superior structure.

The normal reply is 3...a6. White generally drops the bishop back to a4, but there is an alternative:

The Exchange Variation

Here White plays 4 ♗xc6 dxc6. Then 5 ♘xe5 is dubious due to 5...♕d4, regaining the pawn, while 5 d4 is too simplifying. Fischer's move 5 0-0 breathed new life into the Exchange Variation in the 1960s, and although it has never become really popular, it is a reliable weapon used by many players. It retains a largely unjustified reputation for leading to dull play.

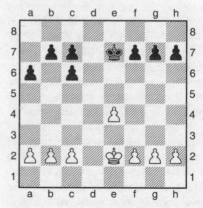

This ending, which could be reached if Black were naïvely to agree to mass exchanges, is easily won for White. He will create a passed pawn on the kingside, whereas Black will be unable to do so on the queenside. However, if Black keeps the pieces on the board, and activates his bishops, he should have a good share of the play.

After the normal **3...a6 4 ♗a4** there are plenty of ideas for Black:

Norwegian Variation

This is a somewhat eccentric and dubious idea, by which Black hunts down the Spanish bishop: 4...b5 5 ♗b3 ♞a5. It has its logic, but few players, except a few excessively patriotic Norwegians, including Simen Agdestein, have much stomach for the black position after 6 0-0 d6 7 d4 ♞xb3 8 axb3 f6 9 ♞c3. Anand–Timman, Linares 1993 was a particularly grisly example: 9...♗b7 10 ♞h4 ♕d7 11 ♞d5 ♕f7 12 c4 c6 13 ♞e3 ♞e7 14 d5 cxd5 15 cxd5 g6 16 ♗d2 f5 17 ♖c1 ♖c8 18 ♖xc8+ ♗xc8 19 exf5 gxf5 20 ♗b4 f4 21 ♗xd6 fxe3 22 fxe3 ♕g7 23 ♕c2 ♗d7 24 ♕c7 ♕g5 25 ♞f3 ♕xe3+ 26 ♔h1 ♗g7 27 ♖e1 ♕f4 28 ♗xe7 ♔xe7 29 ♞xe5 1-0.

Deferred Steinitz Variation

4...d6 is a fairly unpopular though quite respectable move, occasionally used by leading grandmasters such as Yusupov, Lautier and Short. In their day Capablanca and Keres used it to good effect.

In reply 5 d4 has the drawback that 5...b5 6 ♗b3 ♞xd4 7 ♞xd4 exd4 makes it difficult for White to regain the pawn in a satisfactory way (see the Noah's Ark Trap later in this section!), while 5 c4 (to discourage ...b5) leaves the d4-square weak.

5 0-0 can be met by the irritating 5...♗g4, and then 6 c3 ♕f6 or 6 h3 h5, with sharp play. 5 ♗xc6+ bxc6 6 d4 exd4 gives Black decent prospects too – White has a little more space, but Black's position is solid and has some dynamic potential.

The critical move is therefore 5 c3, preparing to build a pawn centre, but this allows Black a very sharp reply.

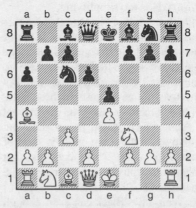

Then 5...f5 is the aggressive *Siesta Variation*. Anand showed some good preparation in his 1994 candidates match against Yusupov, seizing a big advantage: 6 exf5 ♗xf5 7 0-0 ♗d3 8 ♖e1 ♗e7 9 ♗c2 ♗xc2 10 ♕xc2 ♞f6 11 d4 0-0 12 d5! e4 13 ♞g5 ♞e5 14 ♞e6 ♕d7 15 ♞d2! e3 16 ♖xe3.

Black can fall back upon 5...♗d7, but this allows White the initiative.

One of the difficulties in discussing the Ruy Lopez is that there are so many alternatives at every move.

After 1 e4 e5 2 ♞f3 ♞c6 3 ♗b5 a6 4 ♗a4 ♞f6, White has the following:

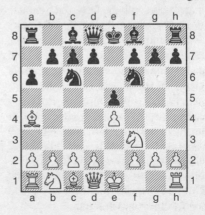

a) 5 d4 is too simplifying.

b) 5 d3 d6 6 c3 is a subtle idea that has been used by John Nunn. It seems that when White later plays d3-d4 he will have lost a tempo compared to main lines where d2-d4 is played, but this may not be the case. In those lines, White generally plays h3 to prevent ...♗g4, which would be an annoying move when the pawn on d4 is short of protection. The "big idea" is that White may thus be able to execute the manoeuvre ♘bd2-f1-g3 (in some of the main lines Black can exert enough pressure on e4 to prevent this) and play the pawn to d4 without a real loss of tempo. Psychologically 5 d3 is of value against those looking to play the Open Variation, or the Marshall.

c) 5 ♕e2 will tend to come to the same thing as 5 0-0 followed by 6 ♕e2, but has the advantage of preventing 5...♘xe4.

d) 5 0-0 is the most common move, when Black normally chooses between 5...♘xe4 (the Open Variation) and 5...♗e7 (Closed), while there are a few other moves. The *Møller Defence*, 5...♗c5 is similar to the Neo-Arkhangelsk, whereas 5...d6 has much in common with the Deferred Steinitz.

The *Neo-Arkhangelsk* (5...b5 6 ♗b3 ♗c5) and *Arkhangelsk Variation*, 5...b5 6 ♗b3 ♗b7, are closely related and the most important of the unusual ideas for Black here. The latter leads to very sharp play in many lines and calls for specialist knowledge. One of the main lines is 7 ♖e1 ♗c5 8 c3 d6 9 d4 ♗b6 10 ♗e3 0-0 11 ♘bd2 h6 12 h3, while 7 c3 ♘xe4 8 d4 ♘a5 is altogether sharper and more chaotic. The Neo-Arkhangelsk is less wild, and more popular at top level.

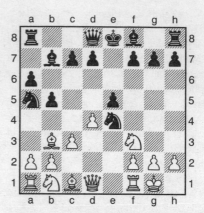

Then 9 ♘xe5 ♘xb3 10 ♕xb3 ♘d6 11 ♖e1 is critical; 9 ♗c2 exd4 10 ♗xe4 ♗xe4 11 ♖e1 d5 12 b4 ♘c4 13 ♘xd4 c5 14 bxc5 ♗xc5 15 f3 0-0 16 fxe4 dxe4 is a deeply analysed sacrifice.

The *Open Spanish* (5 0-0 ♘xe4) is a very popular line that featured prominently in the Karpov–Korchnoi world championship matches in 1978 and 1981 and played a decisive role in the 1995 Kasparov–Anand match. The main line continues 6 d4 b5 (6...exd4 7 ♖e1 d5 is not completely clear) 7 ♗b3 d5 (Black returns the pawn to gain a foothold in the centre) 8 dxe5 ♗e6.

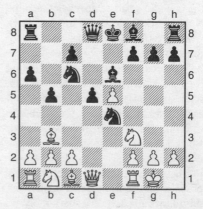

One of the most exciting lines is then 9 ♘bd2 ♘c5 10 c3 d4 11 ♘g5.

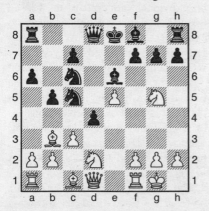

This move, Igor Zaitsev's idea, was first played by Karpov against Korchnoi in 1978. The idea is that if Black takes the knight, 11...♕xg5, then 12 ♕f3 regains the material (12...0-0-0 being the main line then). However, some apparently reasonable methods were found for Black, so it was quite a surprise when Kasparov successfully used this as his main weapon against Anand in 1995. Anand abandoned the Open Spanish for the remainder of the match after he had been mauled in the line 11...dxc3 12 ♘xe6 fxe6 13 bxc3 ♕d3 14 ♗c2 (Tal's suggestion back in 1978) 14...♕xc3 15 ♘b3 (Kasparov's new input, but perhaps Tal envisaged it). Naturally, further surprises awaited Black in other lines after the piece sacrifice (such as 11...♗d5 12 ♘xf7!), and this whole line remains critical.

The traditional main line is 9 c3, when some lines have been analysed in extraordinary depth over the years.

After 9...♗c5 (9...♗e7 is a major alternative – see page 140) 10 ♘bd2 0-0 11 ♗c2 Black must decide how to resolve the attack on his e4-knight.

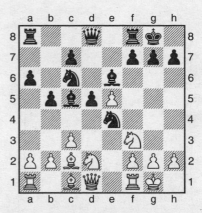

11...♗f5 was played by Korchnoi a few times in 1978, but eventually Karpov managed to gain clear pluses in a few games. The main line is now 12 ♘b3 ♗g6 13 ♘fd4 ♗xd4 and then 14 cxd4 a5 15 ♗e3 a4 16 ♘d2 f6 17 f4!? or 14 ♘xd4 ♕d7 15 f4 ♘xd4 16 cxd4 f6 17 ♗e3, though these lines ought to be viable for Black.

11...f5 is a very old move, which has been resurrected with some success by the ever-imaginative grandmaster from Sarajevo, Ivan Sokolov. After 12 ♘b3 ♗a7 13 ♘fd4 ♘xd4 14 ♘xd4 ♗xd4, the combinative line 15 cxd4 f4 16 f3 ♘g3 17 hxg3 fxg3 18 ♕d3 ♗f5 19 ♕xf5 ♖xf5 20 ♗xf5 ♕h4 21 ♗h3 ♕xd4+ 22 ♔h1 ♕xe5 (called La Grande Variante) is very sharp and messy. However, White has instead Bogoljubow's move 15 ♕xd4, which offers White at least a little advantage.

11...♘xf2 is the Dilworth Attack, which generally leads to endgames that are unbalanced and difficult for both sides to handle. The main line runs 12 ♖xf2 f6 13 exf6 ♗xf2+ 14 ♔xf2 ♕xf6 15 ♘f1 ♘e5 16 ♗e3 ♖ae8 17 ♗c5 ♘xf3 18 gxf3 ♖f7.

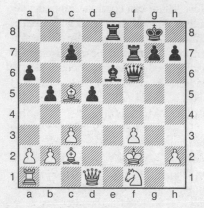

The fact that Yusupov has more than survived as Black in top-level games suggests that Dilworth's idea has been unjustly neglected.

The other main reply to 9 c3 is 9...♗e7, which leads to marginally calmer play. Play tends to continue 10 ♗e3 ♕d7 11 ♘bd2 ♖d8 12 ♖e1 0-0 13 ♗c2.

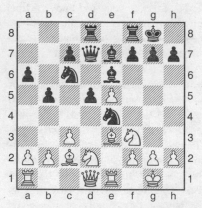

The simplifying 13...♘xd2 14 ♗xd2 ♗f5 is probably Black's most secure continuation.

The Closed Spanish
This is one of the main battlegrounds of modern chess, with variations to suit players of almost all temperaments. Whole books have been written on individual variations of the Closed Spanish, and many variations analysed extremely deeply, yet its mysteries remained as unsolved today as they were when Ruy Lopez first introduced 3 ♗b5 in the sixteenth century. The Closed Spanish is as good a test of a player's strategic understanding as there is; little wonder that Kasparov, Karpov and Fischer seemed able to run rings around top-class opponents in this opening.

The main line runs 5 0-0 ♗e7 6 ♖e1 b5 7 ♗b3. Each of these moves is readily understandable in terms of threats to both sides' e-pawns.

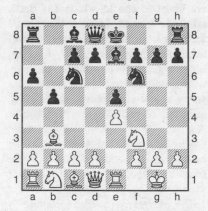

This is a major decision point for Black: does he wish to play the *Marshall Attack*? If so, his next move is 7...0-0, and if White plays 8 c3, he continues with 8...d5 9 exd5 ♘xd5 10 ♘xe5 ♘xe5 11 ♖xe5.

To the uninitiated, it may appear that Black has just been careless and lost a pawn. However, the pawn sacrifice has denuded White's kingside of its defenders and given Black a lead in development.

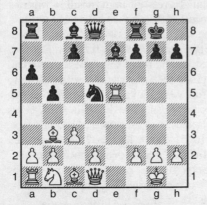

Note that White's eighth move, the purpose of which was to build up in the centre with d4, is now of little use. Black will put everything into a massive kingside attack, which has been analysed in great depth without any clear verdict. If you wish to play either side of the Marshall Attack, a good deal of expertise is essential.

White can avoid these complications with 8 a4, which Kasparov used to good effect against Short in 1993.

If Black does not wish to try the Marshall, then he continues 7...d6 8 c3 (preparing d4) 8...0-0.

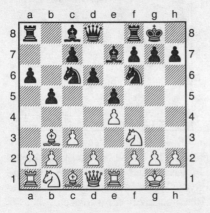

Now White can continue immediately with 9 d4, but then 9...&g4 makes it difficult for him to maintain the central tension. There will be a full-blooded battle whether the game continues 10 d5 &a5 11 &c2 c6 12 h3 or 10 &e3 exd4 11 cxd4 &a5 12 &c2 &c4 13 &c1 c5 14 b3 &b6.

The main line is 9 h3, preventing the annoying ...&g4 and preparing to play d4 in such a way that White will be able to maintain the tension for a prolonged period, so making it difficult for Black to find counterplay.

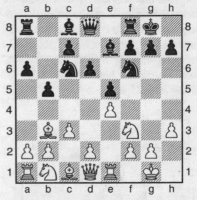

John Nunn explained the essence of this position with his usual clarity to me as follows: White wants to play d4, followed by &bd2, &f1 and &g3. Then he would have an excellent position: e4 is firmly supported, both bishops can hope to find employment on good diagonals and the two knights are aiming menacingly at the black king.

Most of Black's defences are based on hindering White in his attempts to regroup the queen's knight, either by initiating central activity, queenside play or by direct pressure against the e4-pawn.

After 9...a5, Patrick Wolff's idea 10 d4 a4 11 ♗c2 ♗d7 12 ♗d3 ♕b8 13 ♘a3 b4 14 ♘c4 gives White attractive queenside play.

9...♗e6 is an unusual move. After 10 d4 ♗xb3 11 axb3 exd4 12 cxd4 it is not easy for Black to find reasonable play, e.g. 12...♘b4 13 d5 c5 14 dxc6 d5 15 e5 ♘e4 16 ♘c3 with central pressure or 12...d5 13 e5 ♘e4 14 ♘c3 f5 15 exf6 ♘xf6 16 ♗g5, when Black's pieces are clumsily placed.

9...♘d7 was played several times by Karpov in the 1990 world championship match, but Kasparov eventually caused it severe damage in the eighteenth game: 10 d4 ♗f6 11 a4 ♗b7 12 ♘a3 exd4 13 cxd4 ♘b6 14 ♗f4 bxa4 15 ♗xa4 ♘xa4 16 ♕xa4 a5 17 ♗d2 ♖e8 18 d5 ♘b4 19 ♗xb4 axb4 20 ♕xb4 ♖b8 21 ♕c4.

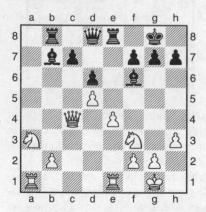

Nothing at all works for Black here. He can take the b2-pawn, but then the c7-pawn will be too weak.

The Smyslov Variation, 9...h6, has some features in common with the Zaitsev Variation, but is virtually a loss of tempo, since Black can manage without preventing ♘g5. White can build up a pleasant position without much difficulty.

The *Breyer Defence*, 9...♘b8, is a very major and subtle line. The idea is to regroup the knight to d7, with ...♗b7 to follow. Black keeps his pawns flexible, puts pressure on e4, and in many cases has ideas of executing a ...d5 advance. 10 d4 ♘bd7 11 ♘bd2 ♗b7 12 ♗c2 (note that Black's tempo-loss is illusory, as the pressure on e4 forces White to move his bishop anyway if he is to untangle his pieces) 12...♖e8 13 ♘f1 ♗f8 14 ♘g3 g6 15 a4 c5 16 d5 c4 17 ♗g5 h6 18 ♗e3 ♘c5 19 ♕d2 h5 20 ♗g5 ♗e7 21 ♗h6 is a typical line, when White may retain a slight pull.

The *Chigorin Defence*, 9...♘a5 10 ♗c2 c5 (10...d5!? is a gambit alternative, in the spirit of the Marshall Attack), was once very popular, but is now considered to give White a little too much freedom. It is still very solid. After 11 d4 Black has a choice.

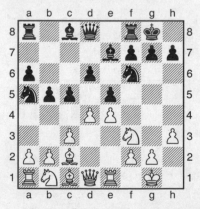

11...♗b7 12 ♘bd2 cxd4 13 cxd4 exd4 14 ♘xd4 ♖e8 15 ♘f1 ♗f8 16 ♘g3 gives White a structural edge, but Black's activity compensates.

11...♘d7 is Keres's move, with some ideas of ...♗f6; 12 ♘bd2 cxd4 13 cxd4 ♘c6 14 ♘b3 should give White a modest edge.

After 11...♕c7, White should also maintain the tension, e.g. 12 ♘bd2 cxd4 (12...♖d8 and 12...♗d7 are both met by 13 ♘f1) 13 cxd4 ♘c6 14 ♘b3 a5 15 ♗e3 a4 16 ♘bd2 ♘b4 17 ♗b1 ♗d7 18 a3 ♘c6 19 ♗d3 ♘a5 20 ♖c1 ♕b8 21 ♕e2 ♖e8 22 ♖c2, doubling on the c-file, offers White a plus.

The Zaitsev Variation, 9...♗b7 10 d4 ♖e8, is the main line of the Closed Spanish, and in many ways the main line of the whole opening. It is named after Igor Zaitsev, a long-term member of Anatoly Karpov's analytical team. Karpov played this line for many years, on the whole successfully, despite a few losses to Kasparov in critical world championship games.

It has the practical drawback that White can repeat the position by 11 ♘g5 ♖f8 12 ♘f3, when Black must either acquiesce to a draw, or choose a different line of the Closed Spanish.

If White is seeking an advantage, then the best line is 11 ♘bd2 ♗f8 12 a4 (variations where White closes the centre at an early stage with d5 are in general a little less critical) 12...h6 13 ♗c2 and now Black's main attempt for counterplay is 13...exd4 14 cxd4 ♘b4 15 ♗b1 c5 16 d5 ♘d7 17 ♖a3, when Black has a major decision. 17...c4, seeking to use the d3-square as a knight outpost, is viable, though it constitutes a pawn sacrifice in many lines. The most ambitious move is 17...f5, seeking to destroy White's

pawn-centre completely. Then the critical lines are 18 ♖ae3 ♘f6 19 ♘h2 ♕d7, 18 exf5 ♘f6 19 ♘e4 ♗xd5 and 18 ♘h2 ♘f6 19 ♖f3 (or 19 g4!?), leading to very sharp play.

Trap: Spanish, Noah's Ark Trap

1 e4 e5 2 ♘f3 ♘c6 3 ♗b5 a6 4 ♗a4
One well-known way for White to get a lost position in the Spanish (Ruy Lopez) is to fall into the ancient Noah's Ark Trap. This is more a concept than a precise sequence of moves. The following is an example:
4...d6 5 d4
This is a little too committal.
5...b5 6 ♗b3 ♘xd4 7 ♘xd4 exd4

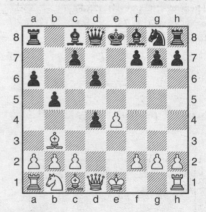

8 ♕xd4??
8 ♗d5 followed by 9 ♕xd4 would be safe enough, while 8 c3 is a reasonable gambit.
8...c5
Now there is no way for White to save the b3-bishop.
9 ♕d5 ♗e6 10 ♕c6+ ♗d7 11 ♕d5 c4
And that is that. The queenside pawns, which White hopes to prove weakened by their advance in this opening, have wrought terrible revenge.

Scotch Gambit (1 e4 e5 2 ♘f3 ♘c6 3 d4 exd4 4 ♗c4)

This variant of the Scotch Opening is not reckoned to trouble Black, and has virtually disappeared from use. After 4...♗c5 5 0-0 (5 c3 ♘f6! reaches a line of the Giuoco Piano, Greco Attack) 5...d6 6 c3 ♗g4 7 ♕b3 ♘a5 8 ♗xf7+ ♔f8 Black has little to fear.

Scotch Opening (1 e4 e5 2 ♘f3 ♘c6 3 d4 exd4 4 ♘xd4)

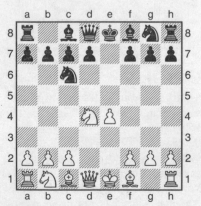

For many years the Scotch was largely neglected, considered too simplifying and committal for modern tastes.

However, Garry Kasparov's espousal of the Scotch in the 1990s as one of his more important occasional weapons made it fashionable again.

An offbeat idea for Black is to play 4...♕h4, which can be met by the dangerous pawn sacrifice 5 ♘b5.

A major option for Black is 4...♗c5, when rather than the messy 5 ♘f5 d5 6 ♘xg7+ ♔f8 7 ♘h5 ♕h4 8 ♘g3 ♘f6, White can play the sharp 5 ♗e3 ♕f6 6 c3 ♘ge7 7 ♗c4 or Kasparov's 5 ♘xc6 ♕f6 6 ♕d2 dxc6 7 ♘c3 ♗e6, when 8 ♘a4!? ♖d8 9 ♗d3 ♗d4 10 0-0 seeks a structural edge.

The main line is 4...♘f6, when White has a choice:

The *Scotch Four Knights* normally continues 5 ♘c3 ♗b4 6 ♘xc6 bxc6 7 ♗d3 d5 8 exd5 cxd5 9 0-0 0-0.

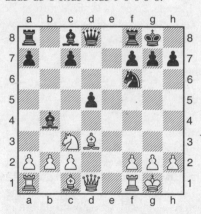

Here some such continuation as 10 ♗g5 c6 11 ♘e2 h6 12 ♗h4 ♗d6 holds few terrors for Black.

The main line of the Scotch is sharper, and runs 5 ♘xc6 bxc6 6 e5 ♕e7 7 ♕e2 ♘d5 8 c4 ♗a6 (8...♘b6 is a main line too) 9 b3. The idea used in Kasparov–Anand, New York PCA Wch (8) 1995 worked well for Black: 9...g5!? (this odd move has the points of preventing f4 by White, and preparing both ...♗g7 and ...♘f4) 10 ♗a3 d6 (10...♕xa3!? 11 ♘xa3 ♗b4+ works tactically, but Black still has a poor pawn-structure) 11 exd6 ♕xe2+ 12 ♗xe2 ♗g7!.

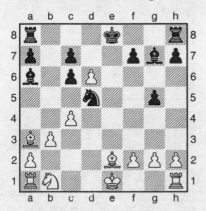

13 cxd5 ♗xe2 14 ♔xe2 ♗xa1 15 ♖c1 0-0-0!. The game was later drawn, with White needing to find some accurate moves.

Two Knights Defence (1 e4 e5 2 ♘f3 ♘c6 3 ♗c4 ♘f6)

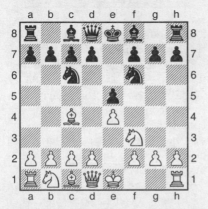

This is one of the oldest openings, and, after the Giuoco Piano, one of the first that beginners tend to learn. Black's play is more counterattacking in nature than the symmetrical 3...♗c5.

The Two Knights is by no means a simple system. Some of its lines lead to bizarre tactical complications, of the sort that correspondence players spend years trying to work out.

White's most forcing and popular reply is the crude 4 ♘g5. Steinitz roundly condemned the move, but Fischer, Karpov, Short and Anand number among those who have played it, and indeed there is a growing sense in modern chess that White should keep the advantage here. Black generally replies 4...d5 to prevent a piece from landing on f7, but there is an alternative:

The Wilkes-Barre (or *Traxler*) *Countergambit* consists of playing the astonishing 4...♗c5, allowing f7 to drop off in return for counterplay against f2. Grandmasters Shirov and Beliavsky have both played the move with success.

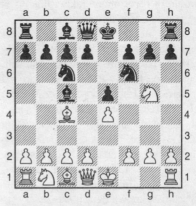

Rather than enter the maze after 5 ♘xf7 ♗xf2+, White generally seeks a stable plus with 5 ♗xf7+ ♔e7 6 ♗d5.

Returning to 4...d5, most chess players have experienced the position after 5 exd5 as one colour or the other.

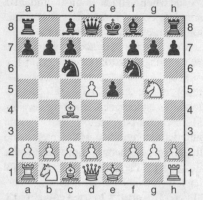

The most obvious reply, 5...♘xd5, is fraught with danger. The *Fegatello* (or *Fried Liver*) *Attack*, 6 ♘xf7 ♔xf7 7 ♕f3+ forces the black king into the middle of the board, while the simple 6 d4 intending 0-0 and a straightforward attack, is considered even more convincing. Attempts have been made in correspondence chess to defend these variations as Black, but I wouldn't recommend taking this up as a mainstay of your repertoire!

Two variations, the *Fritz*, 5...♘d4 and the *Ulvestad*, 5...b5, are closely related. This seems a strange comment, but the best reply to 5...b5 is reckoned to be 6 ♗f1 (the bishop is less effective elsewhere, while 6 dxc6 bxc4 and 6 ♗xb5 ♕xd5 are OK for Black) when 6...♘d4 7 c3 follows. After 5...♘d4, the normal continuation, oddly enough, is 6 c3 b5 7 ♗f1, again with the position in the following diagram. Some specialist knowledge is necessary to play either side of these lines with confidence against a player who is familiar with their subtleties.

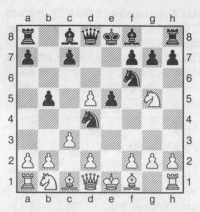

The normal continuation for Black is 5...♘a5 6 ♗b5+ c6 7 dxc6 bxc6.

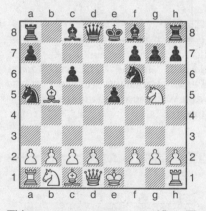

This amounts to a pawn sacrifice. The standard line used to be 8 ♗e2 h6 9 ♘f3 (9 ♘h3!? was revived by Fischer) 9...e4 10 ♘e5 ♗d6 11 d4 exd3 12 ♘xd3 ♕c7, when Black may have enough compensation. 8 ♕f3 ♖b8 was considered too risky for White, but this has been reassessed in recent practice, along with 8 ♗d3!?, which is the latest fashion.

Returning to White's fourth move, 4 d3 leads to quiet manoeuvring, while the highly visual line 4 d4 exd4 5 0-0 ♘xe4 (5...♗c5 6 e5 d5 7 exf6 is the

Max Lange Attack) 6 ♖e1 d5 7 ♗xd5 (7 ♘c3?! is the *Canal Variation* – see page 398) 7...♕xd5 8 ♘c3 ♕a5 9 ♘xe4 ♗e6 should be fine for Black on general grounds, with 10 ♘eg5 0-0-0 11 ♘xe6 fxe6 12 ♖xe6 ♗d6 a likely continuation.

Trap: Two Knights, 4 d3 d5?!
Tagansky – Glazkov
Moscow 1975

1 e4 e5 2 ♘f3 ♘c6 3 ♗c4 ♘f6 4 d3
This move aims to take the fun out of Black playing the Two Knights Defence.
4...d5?!
The most ambitious reply, generally dismissed as over-ambitious. Black normally chooses 4...♗e7 or 4...♗c5.
5 exd5 ♘xd5 6 0-0 ♗c5!?
Rather than the tried, tested and rejected 6...♗g4 7 ♖e1 ♗e7 (7...f6? 8 ♘xe5! ♗xd1 9 ♘xc6+) 8 h3 ♗h5 9 g4 ♗g6 10 ♘xe5.
7 ♖e1 0-0 8 ♘xe5

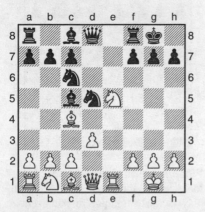

8...♕h4
Instead, 8...♘xe5 9 ♖xe5 doesn't work for Black:

a) 9...♕h4 10 ♕f3 should be good enough to win. Note that White must avoid 10 ♖xd5?? ♕xf2+ 11 ♔h1 ♗g4, when Black wins, and 10 ♗xd5 ♗xf2+ 11 ♔h1 ♗g4 12 ♖e2 ♖ae8, which is OK for Black.

b) 9...♗xf2+ 10 ♔xf2 ♕f6+ 11 ♕f3 ♕xe5 12 ♗xd5 is very good for White.
9 ♖f1??
9 ♕d2! works quite nicely, denying Black compensation.
9...♘xe5 10 ♗xd5 ♗g4?
10...♘g4! wins far more convincingly, e.g. 11 ♗f4 ♘xf2 12 ♕f3 ♗g4.
11 ♕d2 ♖ad8 12 ♘c3 ♖xd5 13 ♘xd5 ♘f3+ 14 gxf3 ♗d6 15 h3 ♗h2+ 0-1

Trap: Two Knights, queen trap
Moskvitin – Rozin
Biriusinsk 1969

1 e4 e5 2 ♘f3 ♘c6 3 ♗c4 ♘f6 4 ♘g5 d5 5 exd5 ♘a5 6 ♗b5+ c6 7 dxc6 bxc6 8 ♗e2 h6 9 ♘f3 e4 10 ♘e5 ♕d4 11 f4 ♗c5 12 ♖f1

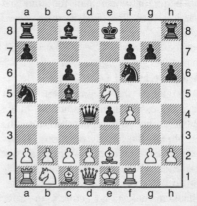

12...♘d5??

12...0-0 is met by 13 c3 followed by b4. 12...♛d8 is necessary.

13 c3! 1-0
Who would have thought that the queen would be trapped mid-board?

Vienna Gambit (1 e4 e5 2 ♘c3 ♘c6 3 f4)

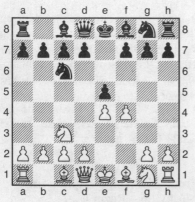

This is an off-shoot of the Vienna Game, in which White argues that the moves ♘c3 and ...♘c6 give him an improved version of the King's Gambit. The evaluation depends on various subtleties, and my feeling is that it is no better or worse than the standard version, but the play is even more violent.

Vienna Game (1 e4 e5 2 ♘c3)
At a glance, the Vienna Game seems less aggressive than the standard move 2 ♘f3, since White poses no immediate threat, but simply develops. However, the point is that White has not surrendered the option of playing f2-f4, in the style of the King's Gambit. Black must respond actively in order to avoid all the problems of facing the

King's Gambit, with few of the consolations.

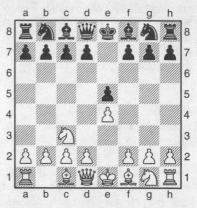

For instance, 2...♝c5 is well met by 3 f4. Black normally responds 2...♘c6, challenging White to play 3 f4, or 2...♘f6, when 3 f4 can be met by the classical central thrust 3...d5, refusing the pawn and securing, Black intends, good active play. All in all, 2...♘f6 is Black's most reliable move.

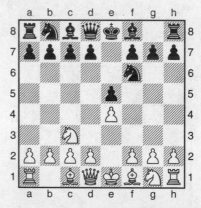

White now has several moves. 3 ♝c4 looks innocent enough, and indeed the play is fairly tranquil in the event of 3...♘c6 4 d3, though White can hope to exert some pressure thanks to his extra tempo. The critical reply is

3...♘xe4, a typical temporary sacrifice. White's only try for advantage is then 4 ♕h5 ♘d6 5 ♗b3 ♘c6 6 ♘b5 g6 7 ♕f3 f5 8 ♕d5 ♕e7 9 ♘xc7+ ♚d8 10 ♘xa8.

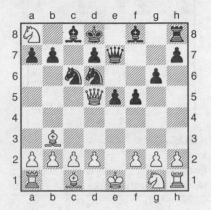

This is effectively an exchange sacrifice since the knight will not escape. Analysis has shown that Black is OK in this line, but the verdict is always going to be open to question in view of the complexity of the variations.

Another possibility for White is 3 g3, aiming for a harmonious development of his forces.

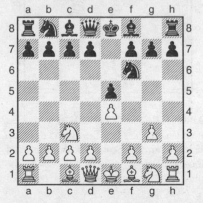

However, it is not especially forcing or aggressive. Black must be wary of responding too actively; after 3...d5 4 exd5 ♘xd5 5 ♗g2 ♘xc3 6 bxc3, Black is under some pressure and must play with extreme caution. It is better for Black to get on with developing his pieces, putting the bishop on c5 and launching a crude kingside attack should White be careless with respect to his king's safety.

The move most consistent with the Vienna is 3 f4, when, as already observed, Black responds 3...d5 (instead 3...exf4? 4 e5 is very bad indeed for Black). Then 4 fxe5 ♘xe4 arrives at a critical position, in which White has been unable to prove any advantage.

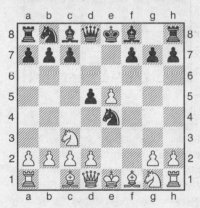

Here one line is 5 ♘f3 ♗e7 6 ♕e2 ♘xc3 (6...♘g5 has been played by Karpov) 7 dxc3 c5 8 ♗f4 ♘c6 9 0-0-0 ♗e6, which is interesting, but should be OK for Black.

Trap: Vienna 3...♘a5?
Schelkonogov – Morozenko
Krasny Luch 1989

1 e4 c5 2 ♘c3 ♘c6
2...♗c5 3 ♘a4 ♗xf2+?! very nearly works for Black (3...♗e7 is better

though): 4 ♔xf2 ♕h4+ 5 ♔e3 ♕f4+
6 ♔d3 d5 7 ♕e1! dxe4+?! (7...♗d7 is
a better try) 8 ♔c3 e3 9 ♘b3 ♗e6+ 10
♔a3 and Black has no follow-up.

3 ♗c4 ♘a5?

This waste of time is severely punished. Black should instead develop
his pieces. 3...♗c5 is normal, e.g. 4
♕g4 is met by 4...♘f8! (but not
4...♕f6?!, which is extremely dubious in view of 5 ♘d5! ♕xf2+ 6
♔d1). 3...♘f6 is sensible too.

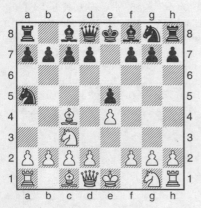

4 ♗xf7+!

With an extra move, as compared to
the line just mentioned where it is
Black who sacrifices on f2, it is no
surprise that this is strong.

4...♔xf7 5 ♕h5+ ♔e6

5...g6 6 ♕xe5 forks the loose h8-
rook and the rather silly-looking
knight on a5.

6 ♕f5+ ♔d6 7 d4! ♘c6

Everything else loses: 7...♕f6 8
dxe5+ ♕xe5 9 ♗f4; 7...exd4 8 ♗f4+
♔e7 9 ♘d5+ ♔e8 10 ♘xc7+;
7...♕e8 8 dxe5+ ♔c6 9 e6.

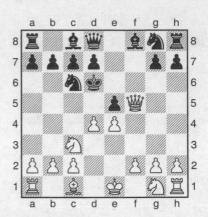

8 dxe5+ ♔c5

8...♔e7 9 ♗g5+; 8...♘xe5 9 ♗f4
♕f6 10 ♗xe5+ ♕xe5 11 0-0-0+
wins the black queen.

9 ♗e3+ ♔b4

9...♔c4 10 ♕f7+ d5 11 exd6+.

**10 a3+ ♔a5 11 e6+ d5 12 exd5
♘ce7 13 b4+ 1-0**

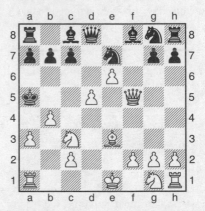

Mate follows shortly. Black paid a
heavy price for his failure to develop
rapidly enough and for his lack of
attention to the centre.

Semi-open Games

In this group of openings Black responds to White's opening move 1 e4 with some reply other than the symmetrical 1...e5. Black's main options are to challenge the e4-pawn directly, hinder White in establishing a second central pawn on d5, or allow White to occupy the centre, preparing to counterattack in hypermodern fashion.

Alekhine Defence (1 e4 ♘f6)

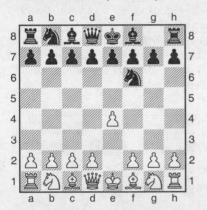

This is an opening for those who do not find the Najdorf and Sveshnikov Sicilians enough like living on the edge. From the outset, both sides are posed with awkward problems, and must find original solutions or suffer catastrophe. The critical lines are the megalomaniac *Four Pawns Attack* (2 e5 ♘d5 3 d4 d6 4 c4 ♘b6 5 f4) and the *Modern* (2 e5 ♘d5 3 d4 d6 4 ♘f3), which aims for a nagging edge. Other systems include the unusual *Chase Variation* (2 e5 ♘d5 3 c4 ♘b6 4 c5 ♘d5), the solid but dangerous

Exchange Variation (2 e5 ♘d5 3 d4 d6 4 c4 ♘b6 5 exd6) and the dull 2 ♘c3, which tends to be popular with club players; the most interesting answer is 2...d5 3 e5 ♘e4.

I can recommend the Alekhine Defence to ambitious players who are willing to specialize. If you are wondering about the rights and wrongs of Black's many knight moves, Black claims that they have provoked White's pawns into becoming overextended, so the time is well spent.

A majority of the world champions have played the Alekhine Defence, but never as more than an occasional weapon.

Trap: Pin-breaking; ....♗g4? met by ♗xf7+

1 e4 ♘f6 2 e5 ♘d5 3 d4 d6 4 ♘f3 g6 5 ♗c4 ♘b6 6 ♗b3

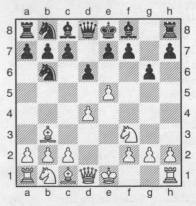

This is a perfectly normal position in

the Alekhine Defence, but one that illustrates the care that must be exercised when pinning knights.

6...♝g4? 7 ♝xf7+ ♚xf7 8 ♞g5+
White's next move will be 9 ♛xg4, regaining the piece with an extra pawn and an overwhelming position. This ♝xf7+ trick crops up frequently in many openings as a reply to an incautious ...♝g4 pin.

Trap: ♝xf7+ sacrifice
Rozentalis – Yermolinsky
Moscow OL 1994

1 e4 ♞f6 2 ♞c3 d5 3 exd5 ♞xd5 4 ♝c4 c6 5 ♛f3 ♞f6 6 h3 ♞bd7 7 ♛e2 g6 8 ♞f3

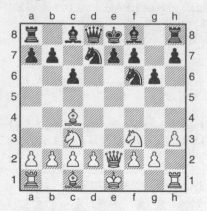

With this standard developing move, White sets a simple but easily overlooked trap.

It would take just one incautious move for the trap to be sprung, viz. 8...♝g7?? 9 ♝xf7+ would be catastrophe for Black, since after 9...♚xf7 10 ♞g5+ ♚e8 (10...♚g8 11 ♛e6+ ♚f8 12 ♛f7#; 10...♚f8 11 ♞e6+ picks off the queen directly) 11 ♞e6 ♛a5 12 ♞xg7+ ♚f7 13 ♞e6 White

emerges with an extra pawn, while Black's position is shattered.

However, Yermolinsky was alert:
8...♞b6
Black needs to cover the e6-square, so uses his c8-bishop for the purpose.
9 ♝b3 ♝g7 10 0-0 0-0 and a fairly normal position resulted. Black has avoided the trap, but had to place his knight on b6 a little earlier than he might have liked.

Trap: Alekhine, loose pieces
Chachalev – Ayupbergenov
Volgograd 1994

1 e4 ♞f6 2 e5 ♞d5 3 d4 d6 4 ♞f3 dxe5 5 ♞xe5 g6 6 ♝c4 c6 7 ♛f3 ♝e6 8 ♞c3 ♞d7 9 0-0 ♝g7 10 ♜e1 0-0

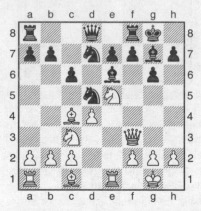

In this perfectly normal position Black has no great threat, but unfortunately White now gives him one!
11 ♝d2??
Surprisingly catastrophic.
11...♞xe5 12 dxe5 ♞xc3 0-1
Black wins a piece due to the loose bishops on c4 and d2.

Trap: Alekhine, bizarre queen trap de Firmian – Rohde
USA Ch (Long Beach) 1989

1 e4 ♘f6 2 e5 ♘d5 3 d4 d6 4 ♘f3 dxe5 5 ♘xe5 ♘d7

This is a highly ambitious and precarious line for Black, introduced by Bulgarian players in the early 1960s.

6 ♘xf7 ♔xf7 7 ♕h5+ ♔e6 8 c4 ♘5f6 9 d5+ ♔d6 10 ♕f7 ♘e5 11 ♗f4

White now threatens c5, so Black has no choice.

11...c5 12 ♘c3 a6

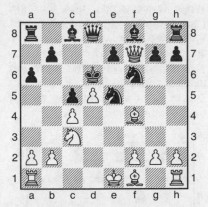

This chaotic mess is actually a critical theoretical position. When this line became fashionable around the beginning of the 1990s, three high-rated players fell victim to the same trap, even though it was already known, and recorded in theoretical works.

13 0-0-0??

13 b4 is the main line, when 13...♕b6 is rather unclear.

13...g6!

Now Black is winning, since White has no decent way to meet the threatened ...♗h6, diverting the f4-bishop and so freeing the e5-knight to take the white queen.

14 ♗xe5+

14 ♖e1 ♗h6 is no better for White.

14...♔xe5 15 d6 ♗h6+ 16 ♔c2

16 ♔b1 ♕f8! 17 ♖d5+ ♘xd5 18 ♕xd5+ ♔f6 19 ♘e4+ ♔g7 20 ♕e5+ ♔f7 21 dxe7 ♕xe7 22 ♘d6+ ♕xd6 (forced, but quite sufficient to win) 23 ♕xd6 ♗f5+ 0-1 Elburg–Krantz, Corr. 1990; a rook will come to d8 next move with decisive effect.

16...♕e8 17 ♖d5+ ♘xd5 18 ♕xd5+ ♔f6

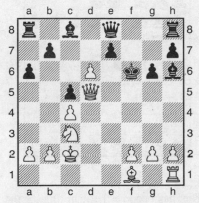

19 ♘e4+

19 ♗d3 exd6 20 ♕xd6+ ♔f7 21 ♘e4 ♕c6 22 ♕e5 ♖d8 0-1 Rozentalis–A.Sokolov, Bern 1992 – Black intends ...♗f5 and then ...♖xd3.

19...♔g7 20 ♕e5+ ♔f7

Not 20...♔g8?? 21 ♘f6+.

21 ♗d3

21 dxe7 ♕a4+ wins easily for Black.

21...♗f5

Black even has a choice at this point: 21...♗g7 22 ♕f4+ ♔g8 23 ♖e1 ♕f8 24 ♕g5 exd6 25 ♕d5+ ♕f7 26 ♘xd6 ♕xd5 27 ♖e8+ ♗f8 28 cxd5 c4 29 ♗xc4 b5 30 ♗b3 ♔g7! (not 30...♗f5+?? 31 ♘xf5 ♖xe8 32 d6+) 31 ♘xc8 ♗c5 32 ♖e7+ ♔h6 0-1 Rublevsky–Hauchard, Oakham 1992.

22 g4 ♗xe4 23 ♗xe4 e6 24 ♖e1 ♕a4+ 25 ♔d3 ♖he8 26 h4 0-1

Strategic Example
Topalov – Carlsen
Morelia/Linares 2008

1 e4 ♘f6 2 e5 ♘d5 3 d4 d6 4 ♘f3 dxe5 5 ♘xe5

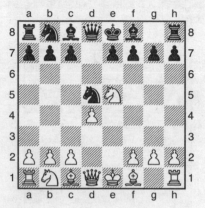

5...c6

This has become the main line of the Alekhine in modern practice, and leads to positions a little like some from the Caro-Kann or Scandinavian. This move has made the Alekhine a "respectable" opening in the eyes of some players who previously felt it was rather dubious, with Nigel Short even using it, after roundly condemning the opening for years. 5...c6 came to the world's attention after excellent pioneering work by Tony Miles.

5...g6 was the main line for much of the 1990s, but is a little less flexible, as Black may find it useful to play a set-up with ...e6 instead, and in this line the move ...c6 normally proves necessary in any case. 6 ♗c4 c6 7 0-0 ♗g7 8 ♖e1 0-0 9 ♗b3 ♗e6 10 ♘d2 ♘d7 is

a typical continuation. 6 c4 is also a good reply, when Black may not equalize after 6...♘b6 7 ♘c3 ♗g7 8 ♗e3 c5 9 dxc5. However, 5...g6 allows White no more than a small plus, and a player well versed in its subtleties should find it a reliable choice. A study of the games of Latvian GM Kengis will provide many ideas for how Black can generate counterplay.

6 ♗d3

6 ♗c4 ♘d7 7 ♘f3 and now 7...♘7f6 intending ...♗g4 and ...e6 gives Black more comfortable development, and White fewer targets, than the older lines with ...g6 already played. 7...♘7b6 8 ♗b3 ♗g4 is also quite viable; note that 9 h3 can be met by 9...♗h5, which would be impossible together with ...g6.

6 c4 is now comfortably met by 6...♘b4, threatening ...♕xd4.

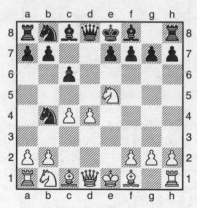

In the Alekhine, Black must be open-minded and avoid playing by routine, such as automatically dropping the knight back to its normal square, b6.

6 ♗e2 has been preferred by some top-level players lately, but is rather cautious. 6...♗f5 7 g4 (7 0-0 ♘d7 8 ♘f3 e6 9 c4 ♘5f6 10 ♘c3 and it is

hard for either side to find targets in the opponent's position) 7...♗e6 8 c4 (8 f4 f6 9 ♘d3 ♗f7 10 0-0 ♘a6 gives White at least as many problems as Black) 8...♘b6 9 b3 f6 and White had to sacrifice a pawn in Kasparov–Short, Moscow rpd 2002.

6...♘d7 7 ♘xd7

7 0-0 ♘xe5 8 dxe5 ♗e6 9 ♘d2 g6 10 ♘f3 ♗g7 11 h3 ♘b4 12 ♗e4 ♗c4 was quite acceptable for Black in Adams–Short, London 2008.

7 ♘f3 ♘7f6 8 h3 prevents ...♗g4 but allows another standard idea: 8...♘b4 9 ♗c4 (9 ♗e2 ♗f5 10 ♘a3 e6 gives White little) 9...♗f5 10 ♘a3 e6 11 c3 ♘bd5 12 ♘c2 ♗e7 led to a draw in Adams–Carlsen, Moscow 2007, albeit only a blitz game.

7...♗xd7 8 0-0 g6 9 ♘d2

9 ♖e1 ♗g7 10 c3 0-0 11 ♗g5 is another way to play the position, adopting a fairly active stance.

9...♗g7 10 ♘f3 0-0 11 ♖e1?!

11 c3 is much better (when 11...♕c7 12 ♖e1 c5 is one possibility), as this prevents the little trick that Black now pulls off.

11...♗g4! 12 c3?! c5!

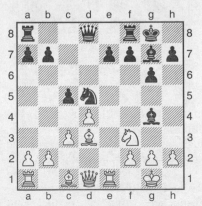

13 ♗e4?!

L.B.Hansen points out that Topalov should have bailed out by 13 dxc5 (best, even though it walks right into the teeth of Black's idea) 13...♘xc3! 14 bxc3 ♗xc3 15 ♗h6! ♗xe1 16 ♗xf8 ♔xf8 17 ♗e4!.

13...cxd4 14 cxd4 e6

Black now has a dream position: a clear plus as Black without having taken any major risks.

15 ♕b3?! ♗xf3 16 ♗xf3 ♗xd4 17 ♗xd5 ♕xd5 18 ♕xd5 exd5 19 ♖d1 ♗g7 20 ♔f1

After 20 ♖xd5 ♖fd8 21 ♖xd8+ ♖xd8 22 ♗e3 ♗xb2 23 ♖b1 b6! Black keeps an extra pawn.

20...♖fd8 21 ♗g5 ♖d7 22 ♖d2 h6 23 ♗e3 d4 24 ♖d3 ♖c8 25 ♗d2 ♖c2 26 ♖b1 ♖e7 27 a4 f5 28 b3 ♖ec7 29 ♗e1 ♔f7 30 ♖d2 ♖c1 31 ♖xc1 ♖xc1 32 ♔e2 ♖b1 33 ♖d3 ♔e6 34 h4 ♔d5 35 ♗d2 ♔e4 36 ♗g3 f4! 37 ♖d3

37 ♖xg6? allows 37...d3#.

37...♔e5 38 f3+ ♔d5 39 ♗e1 ♗d6 40 ♗d2 g5 41 hxg5 hxg5 42 ♗e1 g4! 43 fxg4 ♔e4! 44 g5 0-1

There follows 44...♖xe1+! 45 ♔xe1 ♔xd3. This game showed how effective a surprising choice of opening variation can be. Even as a teenager, Magnus Carlsen is very shrewd in chess psychology.

Strategic Example
Dhar – Mohota
Calcutta 1996

1 e4 ♘f6 2 e5 ♘d5 3 d4 d6 4 c4 ♘b6 5 ♘f3 ♗g4 6 ♗e2 dxe5 7 ♘xe5 ♗xe2 8 ♕xe2 ♕xd4 9 0-0 ♘8d7 10 ♘xd7 ♘xd7?! (10...♕xd7 is better) 11 ♘c3 c6 12 ♖d1 ♕e5 13 ♕f3 e6 14 ♗f4 ♕f5

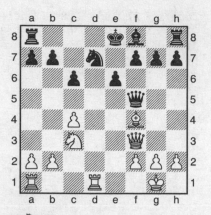

15 ♘b5!

An excellent way to exploit Black's backward development.

15...♖c8

15...cxb5 16 ♖xd7 ♗c5 (16...♔xd7 17 ♕xb7+ ♔e8 18 ♕xa8+ removes most of Black's queenside) 17 ♖xb7 0-0 18 ♖xb5 gives White a solid extra pawn.

16 ♘c7+ ♔d8

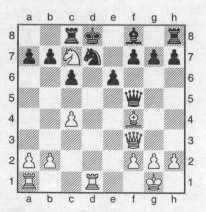

17 g4!

The point is to deny the black king a safe route to the kingside. "What route to the kingside?" you may exclaim. Well, if you have been calculating a sacrifice on d7, you will have seen one. After 17 ♖xd7+ ♔xd7, 18 g4! is just as good, but 18 ♕d1+ ♔e7 19 ♕d6+ ♔f6 leads White absolutely nowhere.

17...♕c5

17...♕g6 18 ♖xd7+ ♔xd7 19 ♕d1+ ♔e7 20 ♕d6+ ♔f6 21 ♕d4+ ♔e7 22 ♗d6+ ♔d7 23 ♗e5+ ♔e7 24 ♕d6#.

18 ♖xd7+ ♔xd7 19 ♖d1+ ♔e7 20 ♕d3 1-0

The threat to win the black queen is quite enough, but White also has mating ideas with g5 followed by ♕d7#.

Strategic Example

J. Fries Nielsen – C. Hansen

Esbjerg Vesterhavs 1981

1 e4 ♘f6 2 e5 ♘d5 3 d4 d6 4 ♗c4 ♘b6 5 ♗b3 ♗f5 6 ♘f3 e6 7 0-0 ♗e7 8 a4 dxe5 9 ♘xe5 ♘6d7?

This move needlessly invites what turns out to be a very strong sacrifice on f7. 9...0-0 would be wholly appropriate.

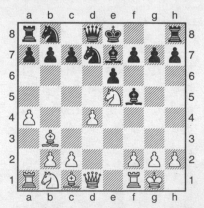

10 ♘xf7 ♔xf7 11 ♕f3

From here to the end of the game, no one, including powerful analysis

engines, has come up with any significant improvements for Black.
11...♔e8 12 ♕xb7 ♘b6 13 a5 ♕c8 14 ♕f3 ♘d5 15 c4 ♖f8
If only Black could have castled...
16 cxd5 ♗xb1 17 ♕e2 ♗f5 18 dxe6

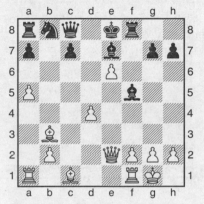

The upshot is a position with three pawns for the piece, but what pawns! The e6-pawn especially is right in Black's face, while the a5-pawn restricts Black's queenside options.
18...♕b7 19 ♗a4+ ♔d8 20 d5 ♕b4 21 ♗d2 ♕d4 22 ♗c3 ♕d3 23 ♕e5 ♕e4 24 ♕xg7 ♕g4 25 d6 cxd6 26 a6!

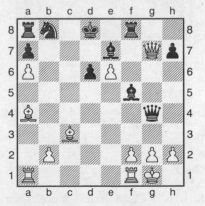

Clearing a5 for the bishop.

26...♕xg7 27 ♗a5+ ♔c8 28 ♖ac1+ ♘c6 29 ♖xc6+ ♔b8 30 ♗c7+ ♔c8 31 ♗xd6+ ♔d8 and 1-0
In view of 32 ♗c7+ ♔c8 33 ♗e5+ ♔d8 34 ♖d1+ ♗d6 35 ♖dxd6+ ♔e7 36 ♖c7#. A beautiful game.

Caro-Kann Defence (1 e4 c6, with 2 d4 d5 to follow)

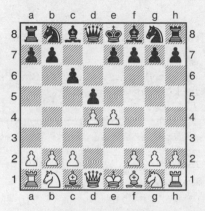

A very solid defence, with plenty of sharp variations for those looking for them. Compared to the French, Black does not block in his queen's bishop, but the drawback is that, apart from supporting ...d5, the move ...c6 is not terribly useful. The *Advance Variation* (3 e5) has gained enormous popularity in recent decades, with 3...♗f5 (3...c5 also has enthusiastic adherents) first being met with the aggressive 4 ♘c3, preparing 5 g4 and a pawn-storm, but more lately, flexible play such as 4 ♗e3 has proved highly venomous. The *Panov Attack*, 3 exd5 cxd5 4 c4, has many adherents amongst classically-inclined players. The *main line* of the Caro-Kann runs 3 ♘c3 dxe4 4 ♘xe4, when Black has a number of ways to counter White's spatial plus:

4...♘f6, which counterattacks at the cost of structure; 4...♘d7 intending 5...♘gf6 and methodical exchanges; and 4...♗f5 5 ♘g3 ♗g6, aiming for "full-employment" of the black pieces.

The Caro-Kann has been a favourite of a number of world champions, most notably Karpov in recent decades, though Kasparov played it occasionally as a junior.

Trap: Caro-Kann with 5...exf6 (...♕e7+, ...♕b4+)

1 e4 c6 2 d4 d5 3 ♘c3 dxe4 4 ♘xe4 ♘f6 5 ♘xf6+ exf6 6 ♗c4?! ♕e7+!

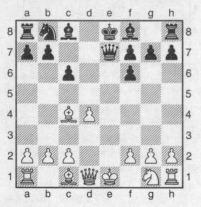

This is a good equalizing idea.
7 ♗e3??

7 ♕e2 ♗e6 8 ♗xe6 ♕xe6 9 ♕xe6+ fxe6 leads to an extremely boring endgame where Black has nothing to fear, while 7 ♗e2 is obviously a concession. Thus White, having played the apparently aggressive move 6 ♗c4, may be tempted into a fatal mistake. Of course, 7 ♘e2?? ♕b4+ is just as bad.
7...♕b4+
Black wins a piece for nothing.

I am aware of one grandmaster coming very close to losing a piece in this fashion (the same theme, but in a slightly different setting). It is not so easy to see the idea, since "normally" in the opening there would be some way to parry the check while defending the bishop, but with White's queen's knight no longer extant, there is no way to save the bishop.

Trap: Caro-Kann, loose pieces
Nilsson – Dahl Pedersen
Copenhagen Politiken Cup 1996

1 e4 c6 2 c4 d5 3 exd5 cxd5 4 cxd5 ♘f6 5 ♗b5+ ♗d7 6 ♗c4 ♕c7

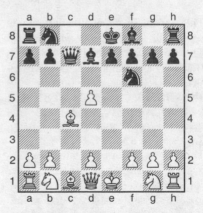

In this fairly innocent-looking position, White finds a self-destruct.
7 ♕b3?? b5
Yes, that is a loose bishop on c1! Unfortunately there are no tricks to save White.
8 ♘a3
Other ways to drop a piece are 8 ♗xb5 ♕xc1+ and 8 d6 ♕xc4.
8...bxc4 9 ♘xc4 ♘xd5 10 ♘e2 ♘c6 11 d4 e6 0-1

Trap: Caro-Kann, queen win
Nunn – Ki. Georgiev
Linares 1988

1 e4 c6 2 d4 d5 3 ♘c3 dxe4 4 ♘xe4 ♘d7 5 ♘g5

This is one of the main lines of the Caro-Kann, although it was practically unknown before the late 1980s. For quite a while the various knight sacrifices on e6 or f7 claimed victim after victim.

5...h6? 6 ♘e6! ♕a5+

6...fxe6 7 ♕h5+ mates.

7 ♗d2 ♕b6 8 ♗d3 fxe6??

This allows a not especially deep sequence that wins material – rather surprising given that both players are top-class grandmasters. Black should get on with his development, and accept that he is somewhat worse.

9 ♕h5+ ♔d8 10 ♗a5

Although Georgiev rather unsportingly played on, he of course lost in the end. Perhaps he envisaged that by doing this he would stop the game being quoted around the world in chess magazines. He was unlucky: many magazines cited the game as ending at move 10!

Trap: Caro-Kann, checkmate in the Fantasy Variation
Tartakower – Anon.
Paris 1932

1 e4 c6 2 d4 d5 3 f3

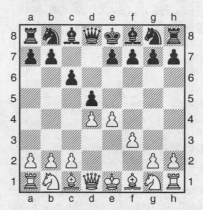

This is the unusual Fantasy Variation – a rather under-rated system against the Caro-Kann. The move looks strange since it weakens the white kingside, but by keeping the central tension, White challenges Black to start forcing matters in the centre.

Black's next few moves are very natural, but lead to disaster.

3...dxe4

This looks the most natural. Instead, 3...e6 4 ♘c3 ♘f6 5 e5 ♘fd7 6 f4 c5 transposes to one of the main lines of the French Defence (1 e4 e6 2 d4 d5 3 ♘c3 ♘f6 4 e5 ♘fd7 5 f4 c5).

4 fxe4 e5

A logical central thrust.

5 ♘f3

Not 5 dxe5? ♕h4+ when the white king must go walkies.

5...exd4?!

This is asking too much from the position. If White now had to recapture on d4, there would be no problem.

However, White can play a strong gambit. Instead, 5...♗e6 is normal, and quite OK for Black.

6 ♗c4

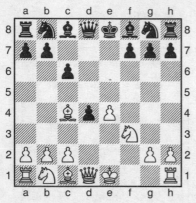

There is now considerable pressure building up on f7, and the position is already very dangerous for Black, so it is easy to understand that with his next move he should try to catch up in development by getting a piece out with check. However, it turns out already to be too late for this approach.

6...♗b4+?

Black would have a chance of surviving with 6...♗e7, but this is also far from easy for Black.

7 c3!

Now Black is really in trouble. Unfortunately for him, White's lead in development is such that further tactics and sacrifices are possible in answer to Black's ambitious bishop move.

7...dxc3 8 ♗xf7+! ♔xf7

8...♔e7 9 ♕b3 cxb2+ 10 ♕xb4+ ♔xf7 allows White an enormous attack, as in Gallagher–Sathe, London 1985. Indeed, Gallagher has snared several victims in this line.

9 ♕xd8 cxb2+ 10 ♔e2 bxa1♕

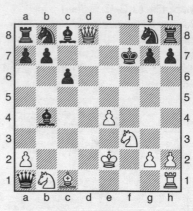

Black regains the queen and so is a rook and knight up. However, his material plus is of no help since it is White to play and he now has a forced mate.

11 ♘g5+ ♔g6 12 ♕e8+

In the later game Tatai–Mariotti, Reggio Emilia 1967/8, Black elected to resign at this point. Mariotti was probably left wishing that he had studied Tartakower's games!

12...♔h6 13 ♘e6+ g5 14 ♗xg5# (1-0)

Next a typical and thematic example of play in one of the main lines of the Caro-Kann. Black's manoeuvring is highly instructive.

Strategic Example
Timman – Portisch
Antwerp Ct (2) 1989

1 e4 c6 2 d4 d5 3 ♘d2 dxe4 4 ♘xe4 ♗f5 5 ♘g3 ♗g6 6 h4 h6 7 ♘f3 ♘d7 8 h5 ♗h7 9 ♗d3 ♗xd3 10 ♕xd3 e6 11 ♗f4

After 11 ♗d2, 11...♕c7 comes to the same thing, but the transposition is not compulsory for Black.

11...♕a5+ 12 ♗d2 ♕c7

12...♗b4 is the latest fashion, encouraging White to advance his c-pawn, and so loosen his queenside.

13 0-0-0 ♘gf6 14 ♘e4 0-0-0 15 g3

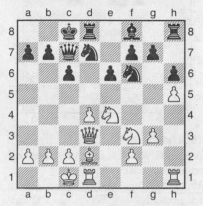

There is nothing organically wrong with Black's position, but he is short of space. His main task is to exchange off the right pieces to avoid a nagging disadvantage.

15...♘xe4 16 ♕xe4 ♗e7 17 ♔b1 ♖he8 18 ♕e2 ♗f8 19 ♗c1 ♗d6

19...e5 20 dxe5 ♘xe5 21 ♗f4 is very good for White.

20 ♖he1 ♕a5

Black now causes White some inconvenience by attacking the h5-pawn.

21 ♘d2 ♘f6 22 g4

Now Black has gained more scope for his bishop.

22...♗c7 23 ♘b3 ♕d5 24 f3

24 c4 ♕g2 25 ♖g1 ♕e4+ is quite satisfactory for Black.

24...♗g3!? 25 ♖g1 ♕d6

Black has established a firm grip on the dark squares, which White decides he must challenge vigorously.

26 ♘d2! ♕c7 27 ♘c4 ♘d5 28 ♘e5 ♗xe5 29 dxe5

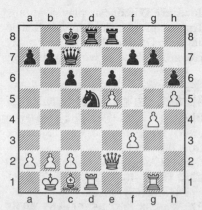

The latest exchange has left Black with a knight versus White's bishop. There are several reasons for supposing that Black should be OK here:

1) the pawn structure is symmetrical;

2) White's bishop is slightly "bad" since the e5-pawn is fixed on a dark square;

3) Black is excellently poised to control the open d-file.

29...♕b6

Not just a cheap threat, since White has no particularly ideal way to prevent ...♘c3+.

30 ♗d2 ♖d7

Black hastens to get counterplay on the d-file. Note that given a little free time, White could make progress on the kingside by playing g5.

31 c4 ♕a6

Black keeps his knight on its central post for a long as possible, given its nuisance value.

32 ♖ge1 ♘b6 33 b3 ♖ed8 34 ♗b4 ♖xd1+ 35 ♖xd1 ♖xd1+ 36 ♕xd1

It is well known that queen and knight work together well, so the exchange of all the rooks is welcome for Black.

36...♘d7 37 ♗d6

Timman plays it safe. 37 ♕d6?! ♕b6 38 ♕e7 is extremely risky, and at any rate gives White no winning chances:

a) 38...♘xe5 39 ♗d6 (39 ♕f8+ ♕d8 40 ♕xg7 ♕d1+ 41 ♔b2 ♘d3+ 42 ♔a3 ♕c1+ 43 ♔a4 b6 wins for Black) 39...♕g1+ 40 ♔b2 ♕d4+ is a draw; White has no way to escape from the checks.

b) 38...♕g1+ is possible too: 39 ♔b2 ♕d4+ 40 ♔a3 (40 ♗c3 ♕f2+ and 41...♕xf3) 40...c5.

37...♕a5 38 ♕e2 b5 39 cxb5 ♕xb5 40 ♕e3

The exchange of queens certainly would not offer White winning chances, viz. 40 ♕xb5 cxb5 41 ♔c2 ♔b7 42 ♔d3 ♔c6 43 ♔d4.

40...♔b7 41 ♕f4 ♕d3+ 42 ♔b2 ♕e2+ 43 ♔a3 ♕a6+ ½-½

Strategic Example
V. Ragozin – Boleslavsky
Sverdlovsk 1942

1 e4 c6 2 d4 d5 3 ♘c3 dxe4 4 ♘xe4 ♘f6 5 ♘xf6+ exf6 6 ♗c4?! ♗d6?!

As we saw in the traps, 6...♕e7+! is a good solid move here.

7 ♕e2+ ♗e7 8 ♘f3 0-0 9 0-0 ♗d6 10 ♖e1 ♗g4 11 ♕e4!

White has managed to secure the initiative.

11...♗h5

11...f5 12 ♕d3 ♗xf3 13 ♕xf3 ♕h4 14 g3 (14 ♗xf7+!? is an interesting sacrifice) 14...♕xd4 15 ♗d3 g6 16 ♗h6 ♖d8 17 ♖ad1 gives White a strong attack for the sacrificed pawn.

12 ♘h4 ♘d7 13 ♕f5 ♘b6 14 ♕xh5 ♘xc4

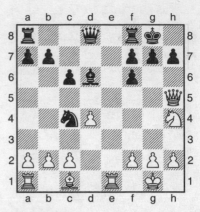

15 ♗h6!?

A wonderful attacking idea, but with an unclear assessment.

15...♕d7?

15...gxh6 is best; White has a variety of ways to regain the piece, but no clear win that I can detect: 16 ♘f5 ♗f4 17 h4; 16 b3 ♘b6 17 ♘f5 ♗f4 18 ♖e4 ♗g5 19 f4 wins back the piece; 16 ♕xh6 can be answered by 16...♖e8 or 16...♕a5.

16 ♗xg7 ♔xg7 17 ♘f5+ ♔h8 18 ♖e4 ♗xh2+ 19 ♔h1!

Instead 19 ♔xh2 ♘d6 enables Black to limp on.

1-0

19...♘d6 20 ♘xd6 ♕xd6 21 ♖h4 forces mate.

French Defence (1 e4 e6, with 2 d4 d5 to follow)

Although apparently a quiet choice, the French is a controversial opening, popular with fighters who like to create board-wide chaos. Black accepts certain difficulties from the start: a spatial inferiority and often problems developing the c8-bishop.

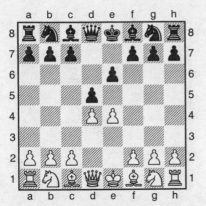

Some find the French dull; others regard it as the sharpest and most cutthroat of openings. It *is* an opening of great diversity: the *Exchange Variation* (3 exd5 exd5) is indeed sleep-inducing, whereas the *Winawer* (3 ♘c3 ♗b4) can lead to extremely messy situations, for example the Poisoned Pawn (4 e5 c5 5 a3 ♗xc3+ 6 bxc3 ♘e7 7 ♕g4 ♕c7), not to be confused with the variation of the Sicilian Najdorf. After 3 ♘c3, the quieter option is 3...♘f6, when 4 e5 ♘fd7 5 f4 is the most popular choice if White wants to force the pace, while 4 ♗g5 is more traditional, when 4...♗e7 is the solid *Classical* and 4...♗b4 the counterattacking *McCutcheon*.

White's other options on move three are:

The *Tarrasch* (3 ♘d2) gives Black a choice between the simplifying 3...c5, the sharp 3...♘f6, and a host of minor options besides.

In the *Advance Variation* (3 e5, with 3...c5 4 c3 normally to follow) White will generally try to attack on the kingside, while looking for ways to frustrate Black's queenside counterplay.

Trap: **French, trapped pieces**
I. Ivanov – Gausel
Gausdal 1993/4

1 e4 e6 2 d4 d5 3 e5 c5 4 c3 ♘c6 5 ♘f3 ♗d7 6 a3 c4 7 ♗f4 ♘a5 8 ♘bd2 ♘e7 9 ♗e2 ♘c8 10 0-0 ♘b6 11 ♖e1 ♗e7

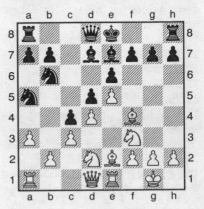

It looks as though Black has just played a straightforward developing move, but there was a darker intention...

12 a4??
Fiddling while the kingside pieces burn.

12...g5 0-1
If the bishop moves, then 13...g4 wins the f3-knight.

Throughout this book you will see many disasters occurring on the f7-square. Here is another...

Trap: **French Tarrasch, ♗xf7+**
Keres – Botvinnik
USSR Ch (Moscow) 1955

1 e4 e6 2 d4 d5 3 ♘d2 ♘c6 4 c3 e5 5 exd5 ♕xd5 6 ♘gf3 ♗g4 7 ♗c4 ♗xf3 8 ♕b3

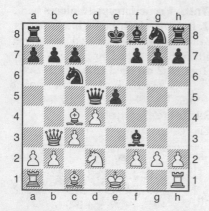

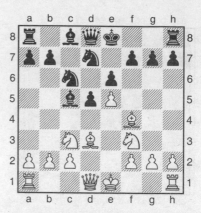

Black is already in some trouble here.

8...♘a5? 9 ♕a4+ ♕d7 10 ♗xf7+!

White wins a pawn and keeps a great position. Black has no chance of saving the game.

10...♔d8 11 ♕xd7+ ♔xd7 12 ♘f3 exd4 13 ♘xd4 c5 14 ♘f3 ♔e7 15 ♗d5 ♘f6 16 ♗g5 h6 17 ♗xf6+ ♔xf6 18 0-0-0 ♗d6 19 g3 ♖he8 20 ♘d2 ♗f8 21 ♘e4+ ♔f5 22 f3 ♖ed8 23 h4 ♘c6 24 h5 ♗e7 25 ♖he1 ♘e5 26 ♘f2 g5 27 hxg6 1-0

In view of the space disadvantage Black suffers in the French and the fact that White tends to establish a pawn on e5, Black must be very wary of castling kingside too early, as this may present White with a ready-made attack. Here is an extreme case, where White lands the ♗xh7+ sacrifice immediately.

Trap: French, early ...0-0? met by ♗xh7+!

1 e4 e6 2 d4 d5 3 ♘c3 ♘f6 4 e5 ♘fd7 5 ♘f3 c5 6 dxc5 ♘c6 7 ♗f4 ♗xc5 8 ♗d3

This is a fairly normal-looking position from the French Defence, but if Black now innocently castles, White can seize total control of the game.

8...0-0? 9 ♗xh7+!

This is a standard sacrificial idea that we encounter many times throughout the book. As an aside, spotting when "stock" sacrifices might work is still an area where strong human players can sometimes outdo computers.

For further details on the ♗xh7+ sacrifice, see the chapter "Attack and Defence", later in this book.

9...♔xh7 10 ♘g5+ ♔g6

10...♔g8 11 ♕h5 wins trivially.

11 ♕d3+

11 ♕g4 is the other routine follow-up to the sacrifice, but is far less convincing in this instance in view of 11...♘dxe5. Note that instead 11...f5? 12 ♕g3 transposes to the analysis of 12 ♕g3 in the note to White's 12th move on the next page, in which Black avoids serious trouble by the skin of his teeth.

11...f5

Otherwise mate follows instantly, with the white queen penetrating to the h7-square.

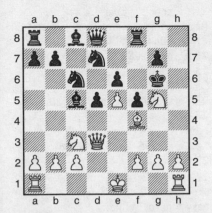

12 ♘xe6

12 ♕g3 is OK, but 12...♗xf2+!? 13 ♔xf2 ♘dxc5 14 ♘xe6+ ♘g4+ (Black's idea in sacrificing the bishop) 15 ♕xg4+ fxg4 16 ♘xd8 ♖xf4+ leads, miraculously, to an unclear ending.

12...♘dxe5

Other moves allow White a material advantage and an on-going attack.

13 ♕g3+

13 ♘xf8+ ♕xf8 is messy.

13...♘g4 14 ♘xd8 ♗xf2+

Black has found another miracle save, but remains worse.

15 ♕xf2 ♘xf2 16 ♔xf2 ♖xd8

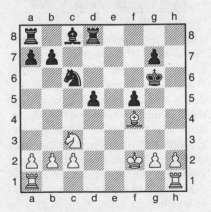

White has a large advantage here. Material is level, but White's pieces are far better placed and will have little trouble attacking Black's weak pawns and exposed king.

Strategic Example
Tiulin – Riabov
Corr. 1929–30

1 e4 e6 2 d4 d5 3 ♘c3 ♗b4 4 e5 c5 5 ♗d2 ♘c6 6 ♘b5 ♗xd2+ 7 ♕xd2 ♘xd4 8 ♘d6+ ♔f8 9 0-0-0 f6

9...♘h6 is safer.

10 f4 ♘c6 11 ♘f3 ♘h6 12 ♕c3 b6 13 ♗b5 ♗d7 14 ♖he1 f5 15 ♗xc6 ♗xc6 16 b4!

A startling way to make inroads into Black's sensitive dark squares.

16...♗d7 17 bxc5 ♕c7

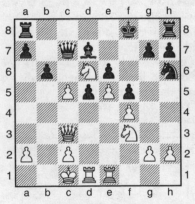

In this position it seems that Black has everything in order: he will recapture on c5 and begin to take over the initiative, still a pawn up. As so often is the case, a sacrifice radically alters the picture.

18 ♖xd5!! exd5

If Black does not accept, he is worse.

19 e6

A critical moment has arisen, with a major choice for Black. However, it seems that there is no way out of his problems.

19...♖e8

Or:

a) 19...♗e8 20 e7+ ♔g8 21 ♕e5 ♘f7 (21...♕xc5 22 ♘g5) 22 ♘xf7 ♕xe5 23 ♘7xe5 bxc5 and despite his extra exchange Black is still in some trouble due to his lack of development, e.g. 24 c4 d4 (24...dxc4 25 ♖d1 with ♖d8 to follow) 25 ♘d3 ♖c8 26 ♖e5.

b) 19...♗xe6 20 ♖xe6 ♘f7 (20...♘g4 21 h3 ♘f6? 22 ♖xf6+ gxf6 23 ♕xf6+ ♔g8 24 ♕e6+ ♔f8 25 ♘e5 forces mate) 21 ♕e3 threatens mate in two by 22 ♖e8+; Black has no satisfactory continuation, e.g. 21...♘xd6 (21...♕d7 22 c6 ♕d8 23 ♘xf7 ♔xf7 24 ♘g5+ ♔f8 25 ♕e5 is overwhelming) 22 cxd6 ♕c5 23 ♘d4 threatening 24 ♖f6+! gxf6 25 ♕e7+ ♔g8 26 ♘xf5.

c) 19...♘g4 20 exd7 ♕xd7 21 ♘d4 and the white knights walk all over the black position.

20 e7+! ♔g8 21 ♕e5

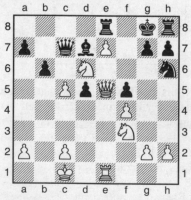

21...♕c6

21...♕xc5 22 ♘xe8 ♗xe8 23 ♘g5 (threatening 24 ♕e6+) 23...♕c6? 24 ♘e6 costs Black his king or queen.

22 ♘xe8 ♗xe8 23 ♘d4

23 ♘g5 ♘g4 is less clear.

23...♕f6

23...♕xc5 24 ♘xf5 and g7 collapses.

24 c6

Now White's pawns decide.

24...♕xe5 25 ♖xe5 ♔f7 26 c7 ♗d7 27 ♘b5 1-0

27...♗xb5 28 e8♕+ ♖xe8 29 ♖xe8 ♗d7 30 c8♕ ♗xc8 31 ♖xc8 is an easy win for White.

Modern Defence (1 e4 g6, generally followed by 2 d4 ♗g7)

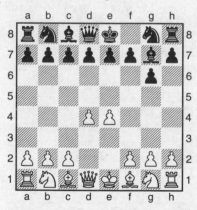

This is closely related to the Pirc Defence, with Black sharply counterattacking the white pawn centre, but Black hopes to benefit from delaying ...♘f6 (the knight is not exposed and there is more pressure on d4). In return, White has more flexibility, and can play c4. Moreover, there are lines in which White attacks on the kingside (including the moves ♗e3, ♕d2, and ♗h6 when the knight moves from g8) in which the position of the bishop on g7 actually loses Black time. Thus some specialists prefer move-orders with 2...d6, sometimes followed by 3...c6, with transpositions to the Pirc always in mind.

White can play most of the same systems that he can against the Pirc, but has a few extra options in view of the fact that Black has not attacked e4. Most notably, White can play 3 c4, reaching a position more akin to a queen's pawn opening; indeed Black can transpose to a King's Indian with a quick ...♘f6 if he so desires.

Trap: Modern 4 ♗c4 ♘d7??

1 e4 g6 2 d4 ♗g7 3 ♘f3 d6 4 ♗c4

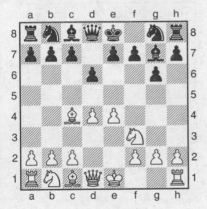

White develops actively, and sets a little trap for the unwary.

4...♘d7??

This move is rather passive, but it is a little surprising that it can be so catastrophic! Dave Norwood admits to having played this move once, immediately realizing it lost on the spot, and then suffering a nerve-racking wait while the opponent contemplated his reply. Fortunately

for Dave, his opponent missed the devastating...

5 ♗xf7+! ♔xf7

5...♔f8, though abject, would be a lesser evil.

6 ♘g5+ ♔e8 7 ♘e6 wins the black queen.

The knight on d7 commits two crimes: it removes Black's protection of the e6-square, and it robs the queen of her flight square.

Trap: Modern/Caro-Kann, piece win
Unzicker – Telljohann
Münster 1994

1 e4 g6 2 d4 ♗g7 3 ♘c3 c6 4 ♘f3 d5

This position can also arise via the Caro-Kann: 1 e4 c6 2 d4 d5 3 ♘c3 g6 4 ♘f3 ♗g7.

5 h3 ♘f6 6 ♗d3 dxe4 7 ♘xe4 ♘xe4 8 ♗xe4 ♘d7 9 0-0 0-0

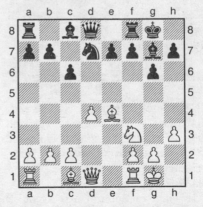

This is a very ordinary position, where White enjoys a slight edge due to his greater space. Surely no grandmaster could lose it in two moves?!

10 ♗e3
Not a great move, since the bishop is not needed here, but hardly catastrophic.
10...♕c7
Now for something horrible...
11 ♕d2?? f5 0-1
Black wins a piece since 12 ♗d3 f4 traps the e3-bishop.

Trap: Modern, disaster on c7
Burgess – S. James
Newport 1986

1 d4 g6 2 e4 ♗g7 3 c4 d6 4 ♘c3 ♘c6 5 ♗e3 e5 6 ♘ge2 f5 7 exf5 gxf5 8 f4 exd4 9 ♘xd4

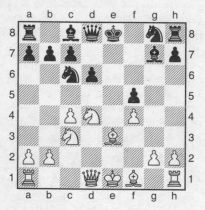

In positions like this, it is quite easy for Black to be careless, and find both of White's knights attacking the c7-square, with no adequate means of defending it.
9...♕e7??
The point of this move is to attack the e3-bishop, but unfortunately White can defend it while simultaneously gaining time on the black queen.
10 ♘d5 ♕f7 11 ♘b5 1-0

The c7-pawn is dropping off, together with Black's position. My opponent, who had played international chess for Wales, saw little point in playing on two pawns down with his king on the run.

Trap: Modern Defence, Austrian Attack

1 e4 g6 2 d4 d6 3 ♘c3 c6 4 ♗e3 ♗g7 5 f4 ♕b6 6 ♖b1 e5 7 ♘f3

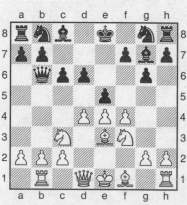

Here's a trap that isn't totally clear. Black's next move is risky, but the lines are messy.
7...♗g4 8 fxe5 dxe5 9 ♗c4 exd4
9...♗f6 is an odd move, but with its logic, hindering ♘g5 ideas.
10 ♗xf7+ ♔f8
10...♔xf7 11 ♘g5+ ♔e8 12 ♕xg4 ♘e7 is quite nice for White, but not game over.
11 ♗f2
This position is not especially clear but White has very dangerous attacking chances, e.g.:
11...♕c7
11...♕a5 12 ♗xg8 dxc3 13 b4 is quite good for White.

12 &xg8 dxc3 13 &b3 cxb2 14 0-0
Black's king will suffer a nomadic existence.

Strategic Example
Wikman – Uimonen
Corr.

1 e4 d6 2 d4 g6
This is one of a number of ways for Black to play the Pirc/Modern, each with their set of pros and cons.
3 f4 &g7 4 &f3 &f6 5 e5
White decides to try to take advantage of Black's delay in developing his king's knight. Instead 5 &c3 would be a normal Pirc, Austrian Attack.
5...&fd7
5...&d5 6 c4 &b6 is a transposition to a variation of the Alekhine Defence, Four Pawns Attack.
6 &c4

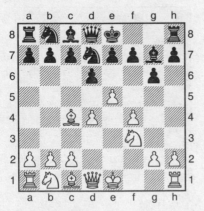

White develops his bishop to an active square, and incidentally threatens to start a few tactics. However, Black is able to walk into the "trap".
6...c5
Risky, but logical. White's centre

will crumble. 6...&b6 is again reminiscent of the Alekhine Defence, and should be OK for Black.
7 &xf7+!?
7 &g5 0-0 (7...e6 8 d5 &b6 9 &b5+) 8 &xf7 &xf7 9 e6 &b6 10 exf7+ &f8 gives Black some compensation for the exchange, while 7 exd6 0-0!? is quite attractive for Black.
7...&xf7 8 e6+ &xe6?
The king should instead retreat, when things would be not at all clear: 8...&g8 9 exd7 &xd7; 8...&e8 9 exd7+ &xd7 or 8...&f8 9 exd7 and then either 9...&xd7 or 9...&xd7.
9 &g5+ &f6
9...&d5?? 10 &f3+ &c4 11 &b3+ &xd4 12 &e3#; 9...&f5? 10 &c3 intends to use both knights to weave a mating net around the black king, e.g. 10...e6 11 &ce4 h5 12 &d3 forces mate.
10 dxc5 &xc5
Otherwise:

a) 10...h6? 11 &d5! forces mate in remarkably short order.

b) 10...&a5+? 11 &d2 wins since the queen has no decent square.

c) 10...dxc5? 11 &d5.

d) 10...&g8? also loses: 11 &d4+ &f5 (11...&e5 12 0-0 &f5 13 cxd6! and Black's position crumbles) 12 g4+ &xg4 13 &d3 with the devastating threat of &h3#.

e) 10...&f8!? 11 &d4+ (11 &d5 is less clear) 11...e5 12 &d5 &e8 13 0-0 wins: 13...&xc5 (13...&g7 14 &e6+ &g8 15 &c7+ &f7 16 &xf7+ &xf7 17 fxe5+ forces a decisive gain of material) 14 fxe5++ &g7 and now 15 exd6 gives White overwhelming threats, and is better than 15 &f7+ &g8 16 &e7+ &e6.
11 &d4+ e5 12 fxe5+ dxe5 13 0-0+

&f5 14 &xc5 h6 15 &e4+ &e6 16 &bc3 &xe4 17 &xe4 &a6
17...&d4+ 18 &xd4 exd4 19 &c5+ is hopeless for Black.
18 &c4+ &d5 19 &e2 &c6 20 b3
Planning 21 &a3, with 22 &g4+ next.
20...b5 21 c3 &b6+ 22 &e3 &c6 23 &g4+ &e7 24 &ad1 &hd8 25 &h4+ &e8 26 &xd8+ &xd8 27 &xh6 &c5 28 &xg7 &e6 29 &f6 1-0

Strategic Example
Semkov – Kr. Georgiev
Plovdiv 1988

1 d4 g6 2 c4 d6 3 &c3 &g7 4 e4 e5 5 &ge2 &c6 6 &e3 &h6 7 f3 f5 8 d5 &e7 9 &d2 &f7 10 0-0-0 f4 11 &f2 g5 12 h3 h5 13 &b1 &g6 14 c5 g4?

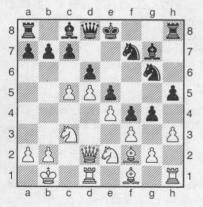

With White's king safely tucked away on the queenside, this type of play by Black is far less dangerous than if the king is on g1.
15 hxg4 hxg4 16 &xh8+ &xh8 17 &b5!
Black cannot defend his queenside.
17...a6 18 &a5! &d7
The king is not the best piece to use to try to hold a position together!

19 c6+ bxc6 20 dxc6+ &xc6 21 &xc7!

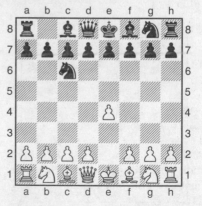

21...&d7 22 &b6 &b7 23 &c1 &b8 24 &xa8 &xa8 25 &c7+ &e6 26 &a4 &f8 27 &b3+ d5 28 &c5 &d7 29 &xb7 1-0
An absolute slaughter!

Nimzowitsch Defence (1 e4 &c6)

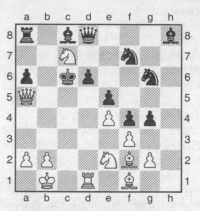

A very rare choice, practised by a few free spirits. 2 d4 d5 can follow, when 3 &c3 is considered promising for White, but there is plenty of unexplored territory here, and many players prefer the simple 2 &f3, when it is hard to find a better reply than 2...e5.

Trap: Nimzowitsch Defence, under-promotion
Runau – Schmidt
W. Germany 1972

1 e4 ♘c6 2 d4 d5 3 exd5 ♛xd5 4 ♘f3 ♗g4 5 ♗e2 0-0-0 6 c4 ♛h5 7 d5!?
Now Black embarks on a disastrous pawn-grabbing mission.
7...♗xf3 8 ♗xf3 ♛e5+
8...♛h4 might be OK.
9 ♗e3 ♛xb2 10 0-0

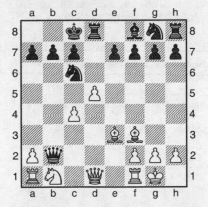

10...♛xa1?
10...♘e5 is the last chance for Black to stay in the game; White's compensation is highly dangerous, but at least it isn't a forced win.
11 dxc6!!
A brilliant idea; White's bishops, rook and far-advanced pawn will hunt down the black king.
11...♖xd1
11...b6 12 ♛a4 wins without a fight.
12 cxb7+ ♔b8 13 ♖xd1 c6 14 ♗xc6 ♔c7
Or 14...♛b2 15 ♗f4+ e5 16 ♗xe5+ ♛xe5 17 ♖d8+ ♔c7 18 b8♛+.
15 ♖d7+ ♔xc6 16 b8♘# (1-0)
Instead 16 b8♛ ♔xd7 is only a draw.

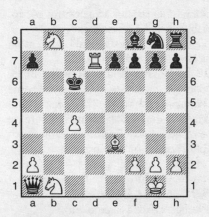

An astonishing final position!

Pirc Defence (1 e4 d6, generally followed by 2 d4 ♘f6)

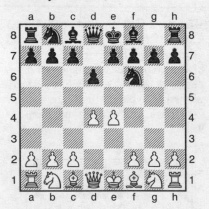

Black will continue his development with a king's fianchetto, putting piece pressure on White's centre before committing himself to a pawn thrust (normally ...c5 or ...e5). White has simple schemes such as the *Classical* (3 ♘c3 g6 4 ♘f3 ♗g7 5 ♗e2) in which Black must try to avoid a slight disadvantage, and aggressive systems such as the *Austrian Attack*, 3 ♘c3 g6 4 f4 ♗g7 5 ♘f3, with the aim of swamping Black, but allowing far more counterplay. More "surgical" attacking lines have been popular recently, such as 3 ♘c3 g6 4 ♗e3, often followed by ♕d2 and ♗h6.

Note that two lines in which Black does not fianchetto have enjoyed some popularity: the *Czech System* 3 ♘c3 c6, intending 4...♕a5, with pressure on e4; and 3 ♘c3 e5, offering White simplifications, or a transposition to the Philidor Defence with 4 ♘f3 (previously normally reached via 1 e4 e5 2 ♘f3 d6 3 d4 ♘f6 4 ♘c3; in this sequence 4 dxe5 is a problem).

Trap: a standard trick in the Pirc
Stangl – Azmaiparashvili
Tilburg 1994

1 d4 d6 2 ♘f3 g6 3 e4 ♗g7 4 ♘c3 ♘f6 5 ♗f4 c6 6 ♕d2 ♕a5 7 h3 ♘bd7 8 0-0-0 b5

8...0-0 could well be suggested here, but GM Azmaiparashvili evidently wanted to avoid castling into a kingside attack. Out of the frying pan...

9 e5

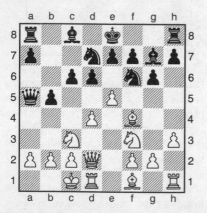

Black is already in trouble here, but his next move allows a very attractive, though standard idea.

9...b4?

9...dxe5 10 dxe5 ♘h5 11 ♗h2 threatens 12 g4.

10 exf6! bxc3 11 ♕xc3!

11 fxg7 cxd2+ 12 ♗xd2 ♕xd2+ lets Black off the hook.

11...♕f5

11...♕xc3 12 fxg7! is the key point. Azmaiparashvili is regarded as a leading expert on the Pirc/Modern Defence, so he must have felt rather sick about allowing this.

12 fxg7 ♕xf4+ 13 ♔b1 ♖g8 14 ♕xc6 ♖b8 15 ♗b5 ♔d8 16 ♖d3 ♕f5 17 ♖c3 ♕xb5 18 ♕c7+ 1-0

Scandinavian Defence (1 e4 d5)

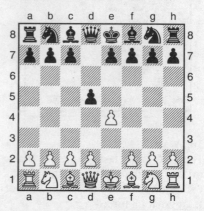

Also known as the Centre Counter. After 2 exd5 ♕xd5, White gains time on the black queen by 3 ♘c3 and can try to put his development advantage to use, while Black will seek to demonstrate his queen's nuisance value after either 3...♕a5 or 3...♕d6. Alternatively, 2 exd5 ♘f6 is a fashionable line. Then 3 d4 is the normal move, when Black regains the pawn and a battle between White's mobile pawns and Black's nimble minor pieces will ensue. In recent years, Black has often been using 2...♘f6 as a gambit, meeting 3 c4 with 3...e6, the *Icelandic Gambit* (instead of the definitely sound 3...c6, which White normally declines), and 3 d4 with the outrageous and ambitious 3...♗g4 (see page 405, where 3 ♘f3 is discussed too).

Trap: Scandinavian, Caro-Kann theme
de Firmian – Owen
Las Vegas 1995

1 e4 d5 2 exd5 ♕xd5 3 ♘c3 ♕a5 4 d4 ♘f6 5 ♘f3 ♗f5 6 ♗d2 c6 7 ♘e4 ♕c7 8 ♘xf6+ gxf6 9 g3 e6 10 ♗g2 ♘d7 11 0-0 ♗e4 12 ♖e1

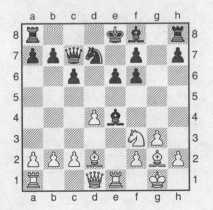

12...f5?
Black decides to maintain his bishop on e4, but there is a tactical flaw. The idea seen in this game is also relevant to the 3 ♘c3 dxe4 4 ♘xe4 ♘f6 5 ♘xf6+ gxf6 line of the Caro-Kann.
13 ♘g5! ♗xg2? 14 ♖xe6+! ♗e7
14...fxe6 15 ♕h5+ ♔d8 16 ♘xe6+ wins the queen.
15 ♕h5 ♖f8 16 ♔xg2
16 ♖ae1 is also very strong.

16...♘f6 17 ♖xf6 ♗xf6 18 ♘xh7 0-0-0 19 ♘xf8 1-0
19...♖xf8 20 ♕xf5+ picks up the bishop.

Strategic Example
Dimitrov – Rivera
Lalin 1994

1 e4 d5 2 exd5 ♘f6 3 d4 ♗g4
This is an interesting gambit which Rivera had analysed with the Portuguese players Damaso and Galego.
4 f3
Otherwise Black is comfortable.
4...♗f5 5 c4 e6 6 dxe6
6 ♕b3 exd5 7 ♕xb7 ♘bd7 looks like reasonable compensation for Black.
6...♘c6 7 exf7+?!
This move is a bit too greedy and opens lines for Black.
7...♔xf7 8 ♗e3 ♗b4+ 9 ♔f2
One attractive possibility is 9 ♘c3 ♖e8 10 ♔f2 ♖xe3 11 ♔xe3 ♘xd4 (11...♗c2!? might be better) 12 ♕xd4 ♕e7+ 13 ♔f4?? (White must play 13 ♔d2) 13...♘h5+ 14 ♔xf5 ♕e6+ 15 ♔g5 ♗e7+ 16 ♔xh5 ♕g6#.
9...♖e8 10 ♘e2
For 10 ♘c3 see the previous note.

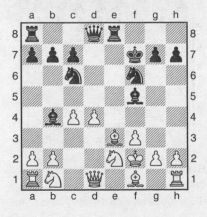

**10...♖xe3!! 11 ♔xe3 ♕e7+ 12 ♔f2
♖e8 13 ♕c1 ♘xd4!! 14 ♘xd4**
14 ♘bc3 is wiped out by 14...♗c5!.
14...♗e1+
Although a highly eye-catching move,
this is one slight blot on an otherwise
outstanding attacking performance.
Instead 14...♕e5 wins on the spot:

  a) 15 g3 ♗h3 forces mate.

  b) 15 ♘e2 ♕c5+ 16 ♔g3 ♗e1+ 17
♕xe1 ♘e4+ 18 fxe4 ♕e3+ 19 ♔h4
♖xe4+ 20 g4 ♖xg4+ 21 ♔h5 ♕g5#.

  c) 15 ♗e2 ♕xd4+ 16 ♔f1 ♘g4
forces mate: 17 fxg4 ♗c5 18 ♕e1
♕f4+.

  d) 15 ♘b3 ♗c5+ 16 ♘xc5 ♕d4+
mates.

  e) 15 ♘xf5 ♗c5+ wins trivially.

  f) 15 g4 ♘xg4+ forces mate.

  g) 15 h3 ♕xd4+ 16 ♔g3 ♗d6+ 17
f4 ♖e3+ with mate to follow.
15 ♔g1 ♕c5! 16 ♕d1 ♗c2!! 0-1
17 ♘a3 ♗xd1 18 ♖xd1 would allow
White to limp on, but he evidently
didn't feel like it.

Sicilian Defence (1 e4 c5)

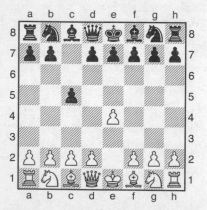

This is by far the most popular single
chess opening. To many players, the

Sicilian is a way of life; they would
not consider playing anything else after 1 e4.

Black avoids symmetrical positions
in an attempt to generate counterchances, while preparing to take
White's pawn if it comes to d4, and so
ensuring that White will not dominate
the centre completely.

White's most critical response is to
play 2 ♘f3 followed by 3 d4. White
will then argue that his advantage in
development outweighs Black's strategic advantage of having more pawns
on the central files.

Sicilian: White avoids the main lines (Anti-Sicilian Systems)

Although in top-level chess, the main
line (2 ♘f3 followed by 3 d4) occurs
in the majority of games, at club
level, White very often prefers a
simpler system against the Sicilian.
There are many possible reasons for
this, most importantly that it is so
difficult to keep up with the ever-
changing theory of the main lines;
besides many players feel that it is
psychologically annoying for Black
not to get a chance to play his favourite Najdorf, Dragon, or whatever. Also, some of these Anti-
Sicilian systems are not at all bad.

The *c3 Sicilian* (2 c3) is an attempt to
set up a big pawn centre. It is a popular choice at all levels of play. White's
intended follow-up is 3 d4, when
White will be able to recapture with
the c-pawn if Black exchanges pawns
on d4, thus denying Black his characteristic central pawn majority.

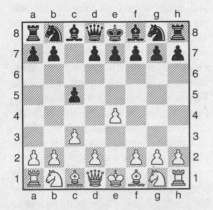

Black can exploit the cumbersome nature of the move by immediately attacking the e4-pawn, with 2...♘f6 or 2...d5, and indeed these are the most popular replies. The c3 Sicilian gives Black plenty of scope for early disasters if he is too ambitious, but in the main lines Black seems able to deny White the slight edge he is seeking.

2 ♘c3 traditionally implied that White intended the *Closed Sicilian* (3 g3 and a slow kingside build-up) or the *Grand Prix Attack* (when 3 f4, ♘f3 and ♗c4 or ♗b5 follows). However, in recent years, White has added 3 ♘f3 and d4, reaching an Open Sicilian, to his arsenal, so Black's choice of 2nd move must take all these possibilities into account. For instance, Najdorf players' only option is 2...d6, whereupon the Grand Prix Attack option has a good deal more venom (compared to 2 ♘c3 ♘c6 3 f4 g6 4 ♘f3 ♗g7, when both 5 ♗b5 ♘d4! and 5 ♗c4 e6 6 f5 ♘ge7! are unconvincing for White). Black can also play 2 ♘c3 ♘c6 3 ♘f3 e5, with a different type of game entirely, while 2 ♘c3 ♘c6 3 ♘f3 ♘f6 4 ♗b5 is a way to avoid a Sveshnikov.

The *Morra Gambit* (2 d4 cxd4 3 c3) is a club-players' favourite. It is lively and speculative. There are myriad pitfalls if Black is unprepared, but it is not too dangerous otherwise.

The *Moscow* (2 ♘f3 d6 3 ♗b5+) and *Rossolimo* (2 ♘f3 ♘c6 3 ♗b5) are logical systems that have gained in popularity as White has become weary of facing the main lines, such as the Najdorf and especially the Sveshnikov. Imaginative play by either player can breathe fire into both these ♗b5 lines.

The antidote to 2 f4 is 2...d5 3 exd5 ♘f6!. The *Wing Gambit* (2 b4) is a bit too reckless; Black should take the pawn. However, 2 a3 has gained some attention as a way to prepare this, while 2 ♘a3 is the latest anti-Sicilian.

Main Line Sicilians (2 ♘f3 followed by 3 d4 cxd4 4 ♘xd4)

The *Kan* (2...e6, 4...a6) gives Black interesting possibilities. He maintains total flexibility, but as yet puts no pressure on the centre, so White may develop as he pleases. 5 ♗d3 is a good answer, with c4 and ♘c3 to follow in most cases, but the straightforward 5 ♘c3 is very popular too.

The *Kalashnikov* (2...♘c6, 4...e5 5 ♘b5 d6) weakens d5, and even lets White nail down the square with 6 c4. Black has counterplay with his pieces, and the pawn-breaks ...f5 and ...b5.

The *Pelikan* (2...♘c6, 4...♘f6 5 ♘c3 e5 6 ♘db5 d6) and its main line, the *Sveshnikov* (7 ♗g5 a6 8 ♘a3 b5), was shocking to previous generations, but is nowadays considered very solid. It is one of the most important openings of all in the new millennium.

The *Taimanov* (2...e6, 4...♞c6) can transpose to the Scheveningen (having avoided the Keres Attack) after a subsequent ...d6 and ...♞f6, while Black can also leave the pawn on d7 and seek piece play. White can reply 5 ♞b5 d6 6 c4, with a variety of Maroczy Bind, but 5 ♞c3 is most common.

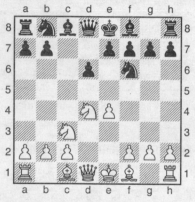

This diagram, after the moves 2...d6 3 d4 cxd4 4 ♞xd4 ♞f6 5 ♞c3 shows a key position: 5...g6 is the Dragon, 5...a6 is the Najdorf, 5...e6 is the Scheveningen, and 5...♞c6 (the Classical) 6 ♝g5 is the Richter-Rauzer.

The *Dragon* (2...d6, 4...♞f6 5 ♞c3 g6) is one of the most cut-throat lines, with play frequently degenerating into a race for the opponent's king. Specialist knowledge is paramount.

The *Najdorf* (2...d6, 4...♞f6 5 ♞c3 a6, preparing 6...e5, which White often discourages with 6 ♝c4 or 6 ♝g5) is one of the best-known opening lines,

and a favourite with many of the top players. It is entirely uncompromising, and frequently leads to chaotic complications. The notorious *Poisoned Pawn* arises after 6 ♝g5 e6 7 f4 ♛b6, with current theory suggesting that the b2-pawn is not too heavily laced with arsenic, though it is suicide to enter this line without specialist knowledge. The main line nowadays is 6 ♝e3 with f3, leading to the *English Attack*.

The *Richter-Rauzer* (2...♞c6, 4...♞f6 5 ♞c3 d6 6 ♝g5) was a hot favourite with many of the top players of the 1990s, who played it enthusiastically with either colour, but it occurs less often now. It is less chaotic than the Najdorf, but just as uncompromising.

The *Scheveningen* (2...d6, 4...♞f6 5 ♞c3 e6) was for many years a popular work-horse of tournament players. However, the *Keres Attack* (6 g4!) has caused many players to adjust their move-order, playing the Najdorf, not fearing the line 6 ♝g5, and returning to a Scheveningen after 6 ♝e2 e6 or 6 ♝e3 e6 (rather than the true Najdorf, with 6...e5).

The *Sozin Attack* (2...♞c6, 4...♞f6 5 ♞c3 d6 6 ♝c4), a Fischer favourite, is an extremely direct attacking line. White is looking to land a quick sacrifice, typically on e6, though in an offshoot called the Velimirović Attack, White often sacrifices a knight on f5.

Trap: Sicilian Dragon, 6...♞g4??

1 e4 c5 2 ♞f3 d6 3 d4 cxd4 4 ♞xd4 ♞f6 5 ♞c3 g6 6 ♝e3

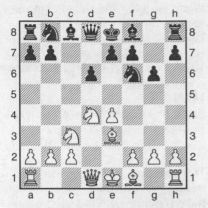

This is a normal position in the Sicilian Dragon.

6...♘g4??

It is natural to molest the important e3-bishop, but the move just happens to be disastrous.

7 ♗b5+ ♗d7

7...♘c6 8 ♘xc6 bxc6 9 ♗xc6+ and White wins material, as he does in the event of 7...♘d7 8 ♕xg4.

8 ♕xg4

White has won a piece in broad daylight.

Trap: Sicilian Wing Gambit
Shirazi – Peters
USA Ch (Berkeley) 1984

1 e4 c5 2 b4

Although one of the all-time greats, Paul Keres, tried ideas related to this gambit a few times in his youth, few modern masters would touch it, but it is better than this "game" suggests!

2...cxb4 3 a3 d5

A logical reply to White's dodgy gambit, denying White the central dominance he is hoping for.

4 exd5 ♕xd5

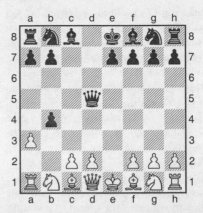

Now, in a moderately well-known position, White falls into a trap of his own making.

5 axb4?? ♕e5+ 0-1

Even the resourceful Shirazi cannot conjure up any tricks if he starts without a whole rook!

Trap: Morra Gambit 6...♘f6

1 e4 c5 2 d4 cxd4 3 c3 dxc3 4 ♘xc3

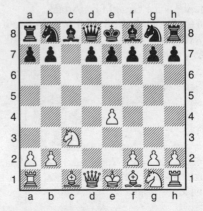

This is the basic position of the Morra Gambit. It is a dangerous system, full of traps for Black, though objectively speaking Black has some excellent defences, if he knows what to do.

4...♘c6 5 ♘f3 d6 6 ♗c4 ♘f6?!

This move is the most natural on the board, but it is highly suspect, and leaves Black struggling to survive.

7 e5! ♘xe5??

7...♘d7 is probably best, while 7...♘g4 8 e6 is not totally clearly good for White either.

8 ♘xe5 dxe5?

Black is going down in any case, with just two pawns for a piece, but this move loses the queen to a simple piece of deflection.

9 ♗xf7+ ♚xf7 10 ♕xd8

White is a queen to the good.

Trap: Sicilian, trapped pieces
Pessi – Helmer
Odorheiu Secuiesc 1993

1 e4 g6 2 ♘c3 ♗g7 3 f4 c5

The game has now transposed from a Modern to a line of the Sicilian Defence – the Grand Prix Attack.

4 ♘f3 ♘c6 5 ♗b5 d6 6 ♗xc6+ bxc6 7 d3 ♖b8 8 0-0 ♘h6 9 ♕e1 0-0 10 f5

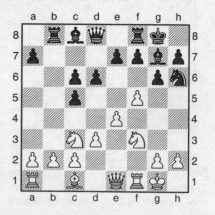

White is going for a crude kingside hack.

10...e6??

10...gxf5 might be playable, while 10...♚h8 11 ♕h4 ♘g8 12 ♘g5 ♘h6 isn't too clear.

11 f6! 1-0

Black loses a piece, since 11...♕xf6 12 ♗g5 traps the queen.

Trap: Sicilian, odd piece win
Demeny – Giurumia
Baile Herculane 1996

1 e4 c5 2 ♘c3 d6 3 d4 cxd4 4 ♕xd4

Rather an odd idea by White: 2 ♘c3 suggested a Closed Sicilian, but she now goes for a type of Open.

4...♘c6 5 ♗b5 ♗d7 6 ♗xc6 ♗xc6 7 ♗g5

The idea is to damage Black's kingside pawn formation by taking the knight if it moves to f6, and meanwhile to prevent ...e6. However, there is a flaw. 7 ♘f3 would seem more sensible, with ♗g5 then to follow.

7...h6

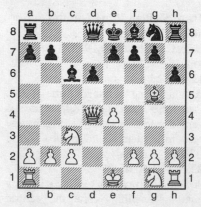

8 ♗h4??

This loses a piece in a simple but

most surprising way.

8...e5 0-1

9 ♗xd8 exd4 leaves two white pieces attacked.

Trap: Closed Sicilian ...♗h3 trick

P. Rasmussen – Brøndum

Copenhagen Open 1995

1 e4 c5 2 ♘c3 d6 3 ♘f3 a6 4 g3 g6 5 ♗g2 ♗g7 6 d3 ♘c6 7 ♗e3 e5 8 ♕d2 ♘d4

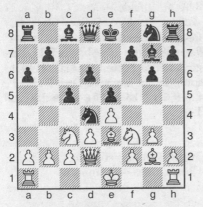

This move carries a threat that anyone who wishes to play this set-up as White absolutely must be aware of, since it is not obvious.

9 ♘d5?? ♗h3! 0-1

Amazingly, White loses material – but he should play on. After 10 ♘xd4 (not 10 ♗xd4 ♗xg2; nor 10 0-0 ♘xf3+ 11 ♗xf3 ♗xf1) 10...♗xg2 11 ♗g5 White can hope for compensation for a pawn, but 11...♕b8!? (11...f6? 12 ♘e6; 11...♘f6 12 ♖g1 ♗xe4 13 dxe4; 11...♗f6 12 ♘xf6+ ♘xf6 13 ♖g1 ♗xe4 14 dxe4) 12 ♖g1 cxd4 13 ♖xg2 h6 forces the win of two pieces for a rook: 14 ♘b6 hxg5 15 ♘xa8.

Trap: Sicilian, Nimzowitsch Variation – 5...b6? 6 e6!

1 e4 c5 2 ♘f3 ♘f6 3 e5 ♘d5 4 ♘c3 ♘xc3 5 dxc3

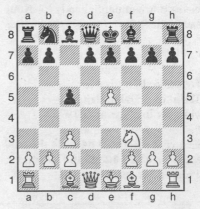

This position does not seem to hold much danger for Black, but White's lead in development and abundance of open lines mean that he must be careful.

5...b6?

White can now exploit the vulnerability of a8 and f7. This is far from obvious, as shown by the fact that Nimzowitsch played this move and even failed to see the problem when annotating the game, describing 5...b6 as "a concept of hypermodern boldness". Had he not been one of the originators of hypermodernism, he might have been sued for libel!

6 e6! dxe6

6...fxe6 7 ♘e5 threatens both 8 ♕f3 and 8 ♕h5+.

7 ♕xd8+

Simplest. After 7 ♗b5+ ♗d7 8 ♘e5, 8...♗c8 9 ♘xd7 ♘xd7 10 ♕f3 gives Black very serious problems with the d7-knight, especially since the queen is currently tied to the defence of the a8-rook, while 8...♕c7 9 ♗xd7+ ♘xd7 10 ♘xf7 is very good for White too.

7...♔xd8 8 ♘e5 ♔e8 9 ♗b5+ ♗d7 10 ♘xd7 ♘xd7 11 ♗f4 "and White is close to winning already" – Nunn and Gallagher, in *Beating the Sicilian 3*.

Trap: Sicilian disaster
Tiviakov – Dzhandzhgava
Moscow Intel qualifier 1995

1 e4 c5 2 ♘f3 b6 3 d4 cxd4 4 ♘xd4 ♗b7 5 ♘c3 d6 6 ♗g5 ♘d7 7 ♘d5

7 ♘db5!? is interesting too.

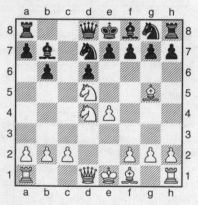

Black is already under considerable pressure here, having chosen a rather suspect line of the Sicilian.

7...h6??

This is far more than his position can take. 7...a6 was played in Mikhal-chishin–Psakhis, USSR 1978. Then:

a) 8 ♗b5?! axb5 (8...♗xd5 9 ♗xd7+ ♕xd7 10 exd5) 9 ♘xb5 gives Black a choice between 9...f6, 9...♘df6 and 9...♗xd5 10 ♘xd6+ exd6 11 ♗xd8, which is not too clear.

b) 8 ♕f3 ♕c8 9 ♘f5? (9 0-0-0 should be quite good for White) 9...g6 (9...e6 10 ♘de7 ♕c7! 11 ♘xg8 exf5 12 ♕xf5 ♕c5 and a subsequent ...♖xg8 will leave Black a piece up) 10 ♘dxe7 ♗xe7 11 ♘g7+ (11 ♗xe7? gxf5) 11...♔d8 (11...♔f8 12 ♘e6+) 12 ♕xf7 ♘c5 makes it not so easy for White to justify his play.

8 ♘e6!

8 ♘b5 is good too, but Tiviakov's actual move is annihilating.

8...hxg5

8...♕b8 9 ♘dc7+ ♕xc7 10 ♘xc7+ ♔d8 11 ♘xa8 hxg5 gives Black only three pieces versus rook and queen.

9 ♘xd8 ♔xd8 10 ♗b5 ♘e5 11 ♕d4 e6 12 ♘c3 ♘f6 13 a4 ♖h4 14 f3 ♘h5 15 a5 ♘g3 16 ♖g1 ♖xh2 17 0-0-0 ♔c7 18 axb6+ axb6 19 ♘a4 1-0

Trap: Sicilian Pelikan
Chelekhsaev – Filimonov
Saratov 1989

1 e4 c5 2 ♘f3 ♘c6 3 d4 cxd4 4 ♘xd4 ♘f6 5 ♘c3 e5 6 ♘db5 d6 7 a4 a6 8 ♘a3 ♗e6 9 ♗g5 ♕b6!?

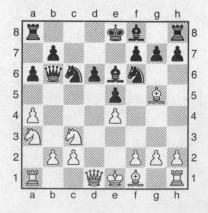

10 ♗xf6?

Perhaps White played this move mechanically, assuming that Black must recapture. If so, this was a fatal lapse. Instead 10 b3? is answered by 10...♕b4, but 10 ♖b1 ♕b4 11 ♗xf6 gxf6 is necessary.

10...♕xb2! 11 ♘d5

11 ♘e2 can be met by 11...gxf6 or the more interesting 11...d5!?.

11...♗xd5 12 exd5 ♕c3+ 0-1

Trap: Sicilian Kan ♘xe6, ♕h5+

1 e4 c5 2 ♘f3 e6 3 d4 cxd4 4 ♘xd4 a6 5 ♗e3 ♘f6 6 ♗d3 d5?! 7 e5

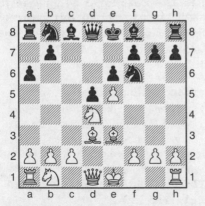

7...♘fd7?

7...♘g8 is a necessity; that Black falls so far behind in development is sufficient reason for condemning Black's play. If he tries to keep the knight active, the punishment is far more severe. 7...♘e4 is also vaguely feasible.

8 ♘xe6 fxe6

8...♗b4+ 9 c3 fxe6 10 ♕h5+ ♔f8 11 cxb4 is also horrid for Black.

9 ♕h5+ ♔e7

9...g6? 10 ♗xg6+ hxg6 11 ♕xg6+

♔e7 12 ♗g5+ wins the lot.

10 ♗g5+ ♘f6 11 0-0

White will regain the piece, having rendered Black's position utterly chaotic. Note that 11 exf6+ gxf6 12 ♗xf6+ ♔xf6 13 ♕h4+ ♔g7 14 ♕xd8 ♗b4+ 15 c3 is roughly level.

Trap: Sicilian; unusual material win
McShane – R. Phillips
British League (4NCL) 1996

1 e4 c5 2 ♘f3 g6 3 d4 ♗g7 4 dxc5 ♕a5+ 5 c3 ♕xc5 6 ♗e3 ♕c7 7 ♕a4

An imaginative plan from the then very young Luke McShane. It clearly made an impact on those who saw the game live, as one of Luke's teammates recently caught another victim in the same way (G.Wall-G.Pinter, British League (4NCL) 2008/9).

7...♘f6 8 ♘a3 ♘c6 9 ♘b5

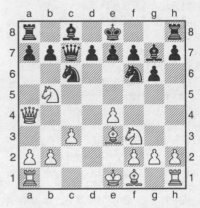

Now Black must be very careful.

9...♕b8?

This looks quite normal. Black intends to push White's pieces backwards with ...a6, but he never gets the chance. 9...♕d8 10 0-0-0 makes it difficult for Black to unravel, but at least it is a fight.

10 ♗b6!!

A horrible surprise for Black. There is no way of avoiding serious material losses.

10...axb6

Otherwise ♗c7 wins the queen or ♘c7+ picks up a whole exchange.

11 ♕xa8 ♕xa8 12 ♘c7+ and White went on to win.

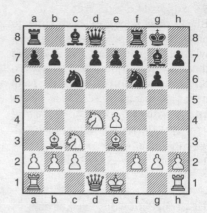

Trap: Accelerated Dragon; disaster on f7 and e6
Palac – Ostojić
Belgrade 1988

1 e4 c5 2 ♘f3 ♘c6

2...d6 3 d4 cxd4 4 ♘xd4 ♘f6 5 ♘c3 g6 is the normal Dragon. Note that White cannot play c4, while for Black there is no longer a possibility of playing ...d5 in one move.

3 d4 cxd4 4 ♘xd4 g6

This is the Accelerated Dragon, one of the most logically motivated of all Sicilian lines.

5 ♘c3

5 c4 is the main alternative, aiming to punish Black's move-order by putting a clamp on the centre. It is probably the best line against the Accelerated Dragon, but the play tends to be fairly slow and positional, and not to the taste of many Open Sicilian players.

5...♗g7 6 ♗e3 ♘f6 7 ♗c4 0-0 8 ♗b3

Now Black can re-enter normal Dragon lines by playing 8...d6, but will more frequently look for an alternative, often based on executing the ...d5 advance as a temporary pawn sacrifice.

8...♘a5?

This move, however, can certainly not be recommended. Nevertheless, it is played quite often, including two games where grandmasters had the black pieces.

9 e5 ♘e8 10 ♗xf7+!! ♔xf7

10...♖xf7 11 ♘e6 wins the black queen.

11 ♘e6!! ♔xe6

11...dxe6 12 ♕xd8 once occurred in a game Fischer–Reshevsky. Fischer was very young at the time – but already strong enough for it to be an insult for Reshevsky to play on!

12 ♕d5+ ♔f5 13 g4+ ♔xg4 14 ♖g1+ ♔h5 15 ♕g2 1-0

It will be mate next move.

Trap: Sicilian, neglecting development
Smirin – Afek
Israeli Ch 1992

1 e4 c5 2 ♘f3 ♘c6 3 ♗b5 ♕b6 4 ♘c3 ♘d4

This attempt to avoid normal channels proves unfortunate. 4...e6 would be more conservative.

5 ♘xd4 cxd4 6 ♘d5 ♕d8

Black now hopes to have time to push back White's advanced pieces with his pawns (...e6 and ...a6) and then to develop normally. However, Smirin is too alert to allow this, and manages to make use of his pieces on the fifth rank. Perhaps 6...♕c5 7 c3 e6 8 cxd4 ♕d6 was a lesser evil, with just a small advantage for White.

7 ♕h5!

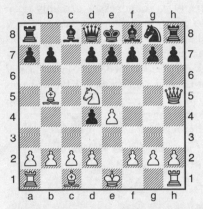

The threat is 8 ♕e5, which Black cannot prevent by ...d6, due to the pin from the b5-bishop.

7...a6??

This move does not address the problem. 7...♘f6 was necessary, but after 8 ♘xf6+ gxf6 Black will have long-term problems with his damaged and inflexible pawn structure. Now it is carnage.

8 ♕e5!

"The end; the rest is history" said my electronic chum Fritz 4.

8...f6

8...e6 9 ♘c7+ ♔e7 10 ♘xa8 axb5 11 ♕xb5 and the knight escapes without difficulty.

9 ♘c7+ ♔f7 10 ♕d5+ 1-0

White's next move will be 11 ♘(x)e6, with utter devastation.

Trap: Sicilian, Najdorf-Sozin, disaster on the long diagonal
Soltis – Browne
New York 1970

1 e4 c5 2 ♘f3 d6 3 d4 cxd4 4 ♘xd4 ♘f6 5 ♘c3 a6 6 ♗c4 e6 7 ♗b3 b5 8 0-0 ♗e7 9 ♕f3

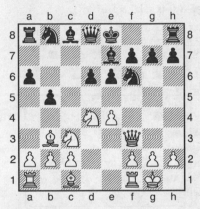

Now Black must be careful.

9...♗d7?

Of course Browne would have seen White's idea of e4-e5, but thought his resources were adequate.

10 e5! dxe5 11 ♘xe6!

11 ♕xa8 exd4 will give Black good compensation.

11...e4

Suicide, but if Black takes the knight, then he will simply be an exchange down.

12 ♘xg7+ ♔f8 13 ♘xe4 ♗c6

The pin on the e4-knight is Black's last-gasp attempt, but with his king so exposed, White has no difficulty finding a win.

14 ♗h6 ♗xe4 15 ♘h5+ 1-0

After 15...♔g8, 16 ♘xf6+ ♗xf6 17 ♕xe4 is simply too humiliating for Black.

Trap: Taimanov Sicilian, ♘d5 pseudo-sacrifice
Karklins – Sandrin
USA 1990

1 e4 c5 2 ♘f3 ♘c6 3 d4 cxd4 4 ♘xd4 e6 5 ♘c3 ♕c7 6 g3 a6 7 ♗g2 b5 8 0-0 ♗b7 9 ♖e1

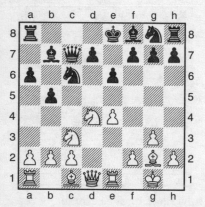

Black has been setting himself up for a devastating ♘d5. He now really had to attend to this threat, but alas...
9...d6? 10 a4
There's no harm in loosening Black's queenside first. 10 ♘d5 ♕b8 would be more acceptable here.
10...b4 11 ♘d5 exd5?
11...♕b8 12 ♘b6!? is good for White, but the game would not be over by any means.
12 ♘xc6
Perhaps Black thought White's intention was the suspect piece sacrifice 12 exd5+ ♘ce7. However, matters are far simpler than that.
12...dxe4 13 ♗xe4 ♘e7 14 ♕f3! f5

15 ♗d5 1-0
Black is helpless, while White can win material virtually how he pleases.

Strategic Example
Burgess – C. Jacobsen
Glamsbjerg tt 1992

1 e4 c5 2 d4 cxd4 3 c3 dxc3 4 ♘xc3
This is the Morra Gambit. Objectively its soundness is certainly open to question, but in practice it is very dangerous. This game is a typical example.
4...e6 5 ♘f3 ♘c6 6 ♗c4 ♗c5 7 0-0 a6 8 ♗f4 ♘ge7 9 e5 0-0 10 ♘e4

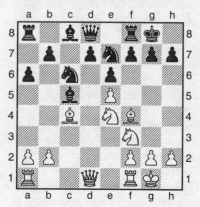

10...♗a7?
This move gives White far too much leeway. Instead 10...♘g6 is sensible, when after 11 ♗g3 ♗e7 Black is not in such danger.
11 ♗g5
Direct attacking play is called for.
11...♕c7
The attempt to solve Black's problems tactically by 11...♘xe5 12 ♘xe5 f6 is doomed to failure since White has too much development:

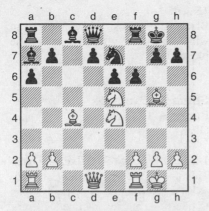

White would blast through with the energetic 13 ♗xf6! gxf6 14 ♗xe6+! dxe6 (14...♔g7 15 ♕g4+) 15 ♘xf6+ ♔g7 (15...♖xf6 16 ♕xd8+; 15...♔h8 16 ♘f7+) 16 ♘h5+ ♔g8 17 ♕g4+ ♘g6 18 ♘xg6 and White wins.

12 ♘f6+! gxf6

12...♔h8 is a more resilient defence.

13 ♗xf6 ♘f5

13...h6!?; 13...♘d4 14 ♘xd4 ♕xc4 15 ♕g4+ ♘g6 16 ♕g5 followed by ♕h6 forces mate.

14 ♘d4!

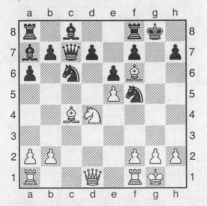

14...h6

14...♘xe5 15 ♘xf5 exf5 16 ♕h5 ♗d4 (16...♕d6 17 ♕h6 ♕xf6 18

♕xf6 ♘xc4 is hardly adequate with the black king so exposed) 17 ♕g5+ ♘g6 18 ♗xd4 is very good for White since 18...♕xc4 19 ♕f6 forces Black to part with his queen.

15 ♘xf5 ♘xe5

15...exf5 16 ♕h5, with ♕xh6 to follow, forces mate.

16 ♕g4+

I couldn't resist this flashy move, but 16 ♘xh6+ ♔h7 17 ♕h5 forces mate a good deal quicker.

16...♘xg4

Black plays ball. Instead 16...♘g6 17 ♕h5 would be prosaic.

17 ♘e7+ ♔h7 18 ♗d3# (1-0)

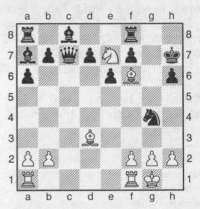

Simple stuff, but my team captain really liked it!

Strategic Example
Zlochevsky – Yuferov
USSR Central Chess Club Ch 1989

1 e4 c5 2 ♘f3 ♘c6 3 ♗b5

This variation, the Rossolimo, is not the most aggressive against the Sicilian, but it is a well-founded system, which is favoured by several young ex-Soviet grandmasters.

3...♛b6 4 ♗xc6 ♛xc6 5 ♘c3 b5 6 0-0 b4 7 ♘d5 e6

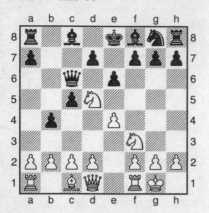

Now, if you were White here, would you automatically look for where to retreat the knight? If so, you would allow Black to justify his play so far. Play uncompromising chess!

8 ♖e1!

Black will have to work a little harder if he wishes to remove the irritating knight.

8...♛b7

Now Black does threaten to take the knight.

9 d4

Again, White finds a way to maintain his knight in the centre, but this time far less clear-cut.

9...♘e7?!

9...exd5 10 exd5+ ♚d8 11 dxc5 ♗xc5 gives White some attacking chances, but nothing too definite. Black ought to have gone in for this line.

10 dxc5 ♘xd5 11 exd5 ♗xc5 12 ♘g5 h6 13 ♘e4 ♗e7 14 dxe6

14 d6 doesn't really cramp Black, and just blocks White's lines of attack.

14...dxe6 15 ♘d6+ ♗xd6 16 ♛xd6

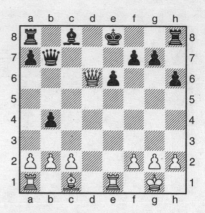

It is far from easy for Black to complete his development.

16...a5 17 a3

White wishes to break open the queenside.

17...♖a6 18 ♛g3 g5

18...0-0? 19 ♗xh6 is horrible.

19 ♗d2 ♛d5

Black rests his hopes on centralization, but to no avail.

20 ♖ad1 ♛c5 21 ♗e3 ♛c6 22 ♛e5 0-0

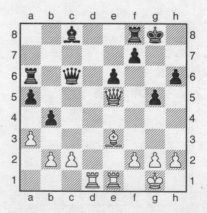

Finally castled, but hardly into safety due to the weakening ...g5 that he had to play.

23 ♗xg5! ♗b7

23...hxg5 24 ♕xg5+ ♔h7 25 ♖d4 e5
26 ♖h4+ wins material.

24 f3 ♔h7

24...hxg5 25 ♕xg5+ ♔h7 is a good
deal more robust now, since 26 ♖d4
can be answered by 26...♕b6.

25 ♖d4 ♖g8

25...hxg5 should be compared with
the previous note.

**26 ♖h4 ♖g6 27 ♖xh6+ ♖xh6 28
♗xh6 f6**

28...♔xh6 29 ♕f6+ ♔h7 30 ♖e5
wins.

**29 ♕xf6 ♕d7 30 ♗f4 bxa3 31 ♗e5
a2 32 ♕h8+ ♔g6 33 ♕g8+ 1-0**

It will be mate: 33...♔h5 34 g4+
♔h4 35 ♕h8+ ♕h7 36 ♕xh7+ ♔g5
37 h4#.

Next we see a standard pawn sacrifice by White to break Black's apparent grip on the centre, and an
imaginative counter from Black.

Strategic Example
Dreev – Lputian
USSR Ch First League (Simferopol)
1988

**1 e4 c5 2 ♘f3 ♘c6 3 ♗b5 g6 4 0-0
♗g7 5 c3 e5**

The idea of this move is to hinder
White's intended d4 advance. However, the move weakens Black's position sufficiently for White to play
the move as a gambit.

**6 d4 cxd4 7 cxd4 exd4 8 ♗f4 ♘ge7
9 ♗d6 0-0 10 ♘bd2 a6 11 ♗c4 b5
12 ♗d5 ♗b7 13 ♘b3**

Black is under very considerable
pressure here. If he does not play the
following exchange sacrifice, then he
would simply be worse after White
recaptures the pawn.

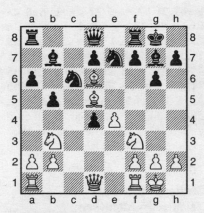

13...♘xd5!?

13...♖e8 unpins the knight, but allows 14 ♗xf7+ ♔xf7 15 ♘c5 with
ideas of ♘g5+ and ♕b3.

14 ♗xf8 ♕xf8 15 exd5 ♘b4 16 a3

16 ♘fxd4 is an alternative.

16...♘xd5 17 ♘a5

White reckons that the best way to
get winning chances is by removing
one of Black's bishops.

17...♕b8

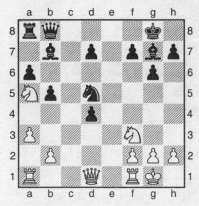

18 ♕d2

18 ♘xb7 ♕xb7 19 ♘xd4?! ♘f4 and
Black wins the b2-pawn, keeping
two healthy pawns for the exchange.

18...♘b6 19 ♘xb7 ♘c4 20 ♕d3

♛xb7 21 b3 ♞a5 22 ♜ad1 ♞c6 23
♜fe1 ♛b8 24 h4 ♛d6 25 b4 ♛d5 26
♜c1 ♝f8 27 ♛e4 ♛xe4 28 ♜xe4 a5
29 bxa5 ♜xa5 30 ♞e5 ♞xe5 31
♜xe5 ♝xa3 32 ♜b1 ♚f8 33 g3 h5
34 ♚f1 ♝e7 35 ♜d5 ♚e8 36 ♜dxb5
♜xb5 37 ♜xb5 ♝f6 38 ♚e2 ♚e7
This ending presents no great dangers to either side. The game finished
as a draw 18 moves later.

Strategic Example
Negulescu – Moldovan
Olanesti 1996

**1 e4 c5 2 ♞f3 e6 3 b3 b6 4 ♝b2
♝b7 5 ♞c3 a6 6 ♛e2 d6**
It seems that White is aiming for a
very quiet, closed game, but as we
shall see, his moves so far have by no
means committed him to forego attacking options.
**7 d4 cxd4 8 ♞xd4 ♞f6 9 0-0-0 ♛c7
10 g4 ♝e7 11 g5 ♞fd7 12 ♜g1 0-0
13 ♛h5**

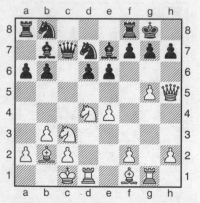

Now Black must watch out for ♜d3-
h3 or ♜g3-h3, but these are not
White's only ideas.
13...♜c8

13...b5 (to stop ♝c4) 14 ♜d3 ♜c8 15
♜h3 ♞f8 16 ♝d3 b4 17 ♞ce2 is
good for White: 17...♛a5 18 ♞f5!
exf5 19 exf5 or 17...♞bd7 18 g6!!
fxg6 19 ♞xe6! with a strong attack.
14 ♝c4! ♞f8?
This walks into a horrible trick.
14...g6 15 ♛h6 ♞c5 (15...♞e5 16
♞xe6 fxe6 17 ♝xe6+ ♚h8 18 ♝xc8;
15...♝f8 16 ♞xe6) 16 ♞cb5! is not
too bright for Black either, so
14...♞c5!? was the move to try.

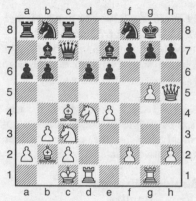

15 ♞f5! ♞c6
15...exf5?? 16 ♛xf7+ ♚h8 17
♛g8#; 15...b5 16 ♞xb5! axb5 17
♛h6! forces mate. 15...♞g6 is relatively best, although 16 ♞xg7 picks
off a pawn for nothing, and threatens
17 ♞xe6 to boot.
16 ♞b5! 1-0
16...axb5 17 ♛h6! gxh6 (17...♝xg5+
18 ♜xg5 f6 19 ♜xg7+ ♚h8 20 ♝xf6
mates brutally) 18 ♞xh6#.

Strategic Example
Krivonogov – Galliamova
USSR jr Ch (Pinsk) 1989

1 e4 c5 2 ♞f3 ♞c6 3 d4 cxd4 4

♘xd4 ♘f6 5 ♘c3 d6 6 ♗c4 e6 7 ♗e3 ♗e7 8 ♕e2

This is the Velimirović Attack.

8...0-0 9 0-0-0 a6 10 g4?!

This somewhat reckless move involves a speculative pawn sacrifice.

10...♘e5 11 ♗b3

Allowing Black to take the bishop would not make any sense of White's play.

11...♘fxg4

11...♘exg4 would make it far harder for White to justify the pawn sacrifice.

12 f4

The e3-bishop is not such a fundamental player in White's attacking designs, so he is willing to part with it, considering there is gain of tempi involved.

12...♘xe3 13 ♕xe3 ♘c6

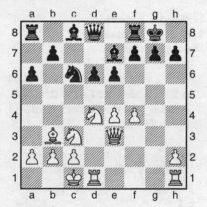

14 ♘f3

The knight, on the other hand, avoids exchange, for several reasons: firstly, White needs a reasonable number of pieces to launch an attack; e4-e5 is now an idea; and as we shall see, the knight has a bright future on g5.

14...♘a5

14...♕a5!? 15 ♖hg1 is also quite dangerous.

15 ♖hg1 ♘xb3+ 16 axb3 ♗d7?!

With this move, things start to become trickier for Black. Instead she could try 16...♕a5 17 ♘g5 (or 17 ♕d4 g6) 17...f6.

17 e5 ♗c6

17...d5 18 f5 ♔h8 is not too clear.

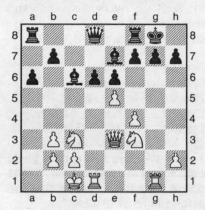

18 ♘g5! ♕c7?

This walks into an attractive sacrificial idea. 18...♗xg5 is necessary, though 19 ♖xd6 offers White good play.

19 ♘xh7! dxe5

19...♔xh7 20 ♖xg7+ ♔xg7 21 ♖g1+ and mates; 19...♖fd8 20 ♖xg7+, etc.

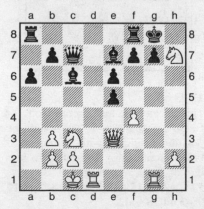

20 ♘xf8?

White has a forced mate with 20 ♖xg7+! ♔xg7 21 ♖g1+.

20...exf4

20...♗xf8 would have kept the game going, although Black does not have compensation for the exchange.

21 ♘xe6! fxe6

21...fxe3 lets White keep an extra rook.

22 ♕xe6+ ♔f8 23 ♖xg7! 1-0

Strategic Example
Ermolinsky – Tukmakov
USSR Ch 1st League (Simferopol) 1988

1 e4 c5 2 ♘f3 d6 3 d4 cxd4 4 ♘xd4 ♘f6 5 ♘c3 ♘c6 6 ♗g5 e6 7 ♕d2 ♗e7 8 0-0-0 0-0 9 ♘b3 a6 10 ♗xf6 gxf6 11 f4 b5 12 f5 ♔h8

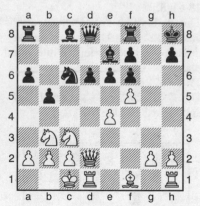

13 g3 b4

This is an essential preparation for Black's next move. 13...e5 would be positional suicide with White's c3-knight controlling, and ready to hop into d5, at any moment.

14 ♘e2 e5 15 g4 a5 16 ♕h6 ♖g8 17 ♘g3 a4 18 ♘d2

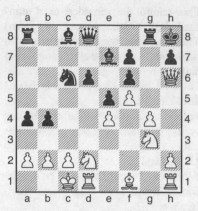

Now Black seizes the initiative with a sequence of crisp pawn thrusts.

18...b3! 19 axb3 d5! 20 exd5 a3! 21 ♔b1 axb2 22 ♗b5 ♘d4 23 ♗a4 ♕c7 24 ♘c4 ♖xa4! 25 ♖xd4 ♖a8 26 ♖dd1? ♖xg4 27 d6 ♕a7 28 ♔xb2 ♖xc4 0-1

Strategic Example
Yanovsky – Golubenko
Moscow Ch 1989

1 e4 c5 2 ♘f3 d6 3 d4 cxd4 4 ♘xd4 ♘f6 5 ♘c3 a6 6 ♗c4 e6 7 ♗b3 ♗e7 8 ♗e3 0-0 9 g4 d5 10 exd5 ♘xd5 11 ♘xd5 exd5

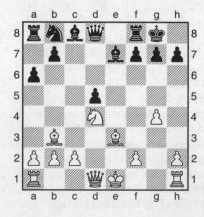

This cannot be regarded as a standard IQP (isolated queen's pawn) position, since the kingside situation rules out a drawn-out manoeuvring battle.

12 ♕f3 ♘c6 13 h3 ♕a5+ 14 c3 ♗a3!

This is a standard tactical theme, but very hard to see if you're not familiar with it.

15 ♘xc6

White must avoid 15 0-0-0?? ♕xc3+ and 15 bxa3? ♕xc3+.

15...bxc6

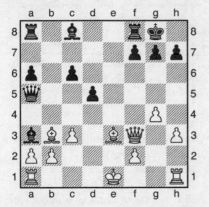

16 ♖b1

16 bxa3? ♕xc3+ 17 ♔e2 ♕b2+ 18 ♔d3 (18 ♗d2 ♖e8+ 19 ♔d3 a5 is no better) 18...a5 and the threat of 19...♗a6+ gives Black a strong attack, while 19 ♗c2 d4 20 ♗xd4 ♗a6+ is devastating.

16...♗xb2??

Black should simply settle for dropping the bishop back to d6 or e7. He would then have disrupted any plans White may have had for castling queenside.

The move played looks strong, but has a surprising defect.

17 ♖xb2 ♕xc3+ 18 ♖d2 d4

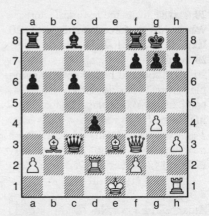

Now White has a cunning resource.

19 0-0!

By unpinning his rook, White makes the e3-bishop invulnerable.

19...♗xg4

19...dxe3 20 ♕xf7+! ♖xf7 21 ♖d8# is the key point.

20 hxg4 dxe3 21 ♕xe3 1-0

Strategic Example
Donchev – Ermenkov
Bulgarian Ch (Sofia) 1988

1 e4 c5 2 ♘f3 d6 3 d4

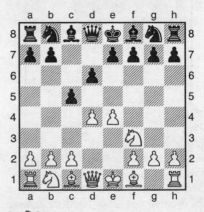

3...♘f6

This is a little move-order subtlety, varying from the normal 3...cxd4. It is employed by some Sicilian players to avoid White recapturing on d4 with his queen, rather than playing the normal 4 ♘xd4 ♘f6 5 ♘c3. After 4 ♕xd4 White has ideas of playing c4 if appropriate, e.g. after 4...♘c6 5 ♗b5. This is not such a troublesome line for Black, but play tends to be rather slower than most Sicilian players would like.

4 ♘c3

4 dxc5 ♘xe4 5 cxd6 ♘xd6 is quite satisfactory for Black.

4...cxd4 5 ♘xd4

5 ♕xd4 would make no sense at all here, since White is unable to set up a bind by playing c4, so will just lose time with his queen.

5...e6

This is the basic position of the Scheveningen Variation – a popular choice. Black erects a "small centre" and maintains maximum flexibility with his queenside development.

6 g4

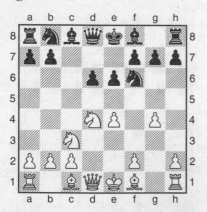

This move is named the Keres Attack in honour of the great Estonian grandmaster.

6...h6

This is the normal reply, though 6...♘c6 7 g5 ♘d7 is a major alternative.

7 ♗g2

White avoids the heavy theoretical lines after 7 h4 ♘c6 8 ♖g1 h5.

7...♘c6 8 ♘xc6 bxc6 9 e5 ♘d5 10 exd6 ♗xd6 11 ♘e4

White is still trying to force the pace, but this is a risky way to do so, and gets White into trouble.

11...♗a6

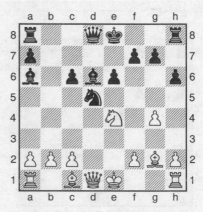

Black seizes a chance to keep the white king in the centre.

12 b3

Aiming to play c4, but the move has drawbacks of its own.

12...♗e5

12...0-0 is a good solid move; then 13 ♘xd6 ♕xd6 14 c4? bumps into 14...♕e5+, while 13 c4 can be well met by 13...♗e5 or 13...♗b4+!?.

13 ♗d2

13 ♖b1 hands the initiative fully to Black, so White sacrifices the exchange.

13...♗xa1

Black sees no reason not to grab the material.

14 ♕xa1 0-0 15 c4

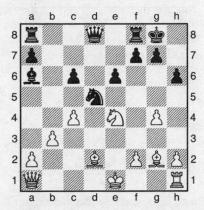

This position must be winning for Black. However, a remarkable turnabout occurs during the next few moves.

15...f5?!

This gives White chances. Black had two better moves:

15...♘e7 is quite safe, since 16 ♗xh6 gxh6 17 ♘f6+ ♔h8 18 ♘d7+ f6 (18...♔g8 19 ♘f6+ repeats) 19 ♘xf6 (19 ♘xf8 ♕xf8 is a win for Black) 19...e5 wins for Black, e.g. 20 ♕xe5? ♘g6.

15...♕h4 is even possible, since after 16 cxd5 ♕xg4 17 ♘g3 exd5 Black has a rook and two pawns versus White's two minor pieces, and he also has attacking chances against the white king.

16 ♘c5 ♘f4

Black was probably relying on this idea when he played his risky fifteenth move.

17 ♖g1!

White finds his best chance; the g-file may prove a happy hunting ground for the white rook. 17 ♗xf4 ♕a5+ clears things up nicely for Black.

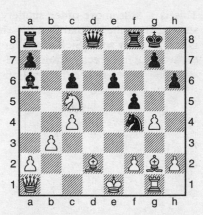

17...♘d3+

17...♘xg2+ 18 ♖xg2 ♗c8 (after 18...♕b6 19 ♘xe6 ♖f7 20 gxf5 ♕b7 21 ♗xh6 White smashes through on g7) 19 gxf5 ♕e7 20 fxe6 (better than 20 ♗xh6 exf5+ 21 ♔f1 ♖f7, when White has run out of steam) gives Black little comfort:

a) 20...♗xc6 21 ♖xg7+ ♕xg7 22 ♕xg7+ ♔xg7 23 ♘xe6+ ♔g6 24 ♘xf8+ ♖xf8 reaches an ending with bishop and five pawns versus rook and three; White should have winning chances.

b) 20...♖f6 21 ♗c3 ♖f7 22 ♖g6 ♗xe6 23 ♘xe6 ♕h4 and Black grovels on.

18 ♘xd3 ♕xd3 19 ♗xc6

White is not just grabbing a stray pawn; he is opening the g-file for a shock counterattack!

19...♖ad8?

19...♖ac8? 20 ♗xh6 is also good for White, but Black should play 19...♗xc4! 20 bxc4 ♖ab8 21 ♗b5 ♕e4+ (or 21...a6), when a draw is the most likely outcome.

20 ♗xh6!

Suddenly the whole of White's position makes sense.

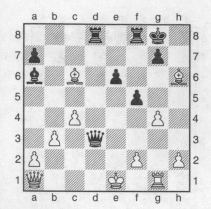

20...Ⴜd4
20...Ⴜf7 21 gxf5 e5 is the best try at holding things together.
21 gxf5 Ⴜxf5 22 Ⴜxg7+ ⵠh8 23 Ⴜg3 Ⴜe5+ 24 ⵠe3
White's plan is now to play the bishop to e2 via f3, whereupon Black will be finished.
24...ⵠh7 25 ⵠf3 Ⴜxc4
Pure desperation.
26 bxc4 Ⴔxc4 27 Ⴔxe5 Ⴔf1+ 28 ⵠd2 Ⴔd3+ 29 ⵠc1 1-0

Next a game where the pawn formations become symmetrical, and by alert play White seizes a powerful initiative.

Strategic Example
Van der Wiel – Klinger
Belgrade GMA 1988

1 e4 c5 2 ᣵf3 e6 3 d4 cxd4 4 ᣵxd4 a6 5 ⵠd3 ᣵf6 6 0-0 Ⴔc7 7 Ⴔe2 ⵠd6 8 ⵠh1
8 f4 is a more standard move.
8...ᣵc6
8...ⵠxh2 walks the bishop into a trap.
9 ᣵxc6 dxc6 10 f4

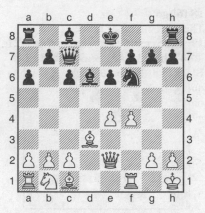

Black is in some danger here due to his lack of development.
10...ᣵd7?!
10...e5 11 f5 is good for White, but gives Black more survival chances.
11 e5 ⵠe7 12 ⵠe3 b5 13 ᣵd2 ⵠb7 14 c4!
White has ideas of playing c5, with a hideous grip on d6; ...c5 is ruled out by the pressure on b5.
14...ᣵc5 15 ⵠxc5! ⵠxc5 16 ᣵe4 Ⴔb6
Now White can embark upon the final attack, but 16...ⵠe7 17 c5 is too horrible to contemplate.
17 f5! ⵠc8

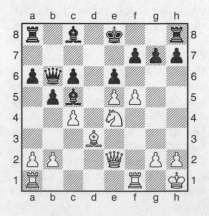

18 f6! g6

There are no other moves.

19 cxb5 cxb5 20 ♘xc5 ♕xc5 21 ♗e4 ♖b8 22 ♖ac1 ♕a7 23 ♕d2 1-0

Black will be mated when the white queen lands on d8 (following ♖fd1), on e7 (if Black plays ...♗d7) or on g7 (if Black castles).

Strategic Example
Ivanchuk – Kramnik

Monte Carlo 5th Amber Rapid 1996

1 e4 c5 2 ♘f3 ♘c6 3 d4 cxd4 4 ♘xd4 ♘f6 5 ♘c3 d6 6 ♗g5 e6 7 ♕d2 a6 8 0-0-0 h6 9 ♗e3 ♘xd4 10 ♕xd4 ♕c7 11 f4 b5 12 a4 bxa4 13 ♕xa4+ ♗d7 14 ♗b5

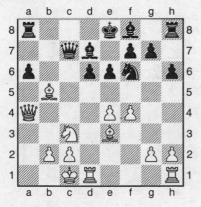

White makes good use of the pin on the a-file. Rather than having to retreat his queen, White has instead found an active move, and so keeps the initiative.

14...♕b7 15 ♗xd7+ ♕xd7 16 ♖d4 ♗e7 17 ♖hd1 0-0 18 e5 ♕xa4 19 ♖xa4 ♘e8 20 ♘b5

For the second time White uses the pin, and the knight proves remarkably effective here.

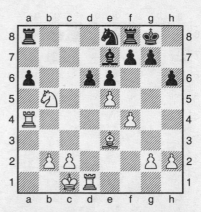

20...d5 21 f5 exf5 22 ♖xd5 ♗g5 23 ♗xg5 hxg5 24 c4 g6 25 c5 f4 26 c6 ♘g7 27 ♘d6 ♘e6 28 ♖da5 f6

Kramnik desperately tries to open the f-file to get the rook behind his passed pawns, but it is all too slow. 28...g4 carries no real punch without support from behind.

29 exf6 ♖xf6 30 ♖xa6 ♖af8 31 ♘e4 ♖6f7 32 h3 f3 33 gxf3 ♖xf3 34 ♖a8 ♖f1+ 35 ♔d2 1-0

Strategic Example
Chiburdanidze – Hoffmann

Lugano 1989

1 e4 c5 2 ♘f3 e6 3 ♘c3 a6 4 d4 cxd4 5 ♘xd4 ♕c7 6 g3 b5 7 ♗g2 ♗b7 8 0-0 d6 9 ♖e1 ♘d7 10 a4!

A standard idea for White in Open Sicilian positions where Black has played ...b5, but is not fully developed.

10...bxa4

10...b4 should be met by the straightforward 11 ♘a2, intending c3, since 11 ♘d5!? exd5 12 exd5+ is probably too speculative.

11 ♖xa4

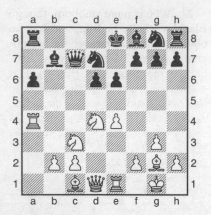

11...♘gf6

11...♘b6 12 ♖a2 ♘f6 13 ♘b3 ♘c4 14 ♗f1 intends ♕d4 and ♘a5 after the black knight moves – Black's position is difficult.

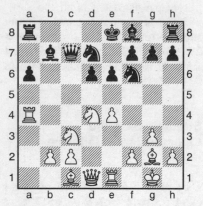

12 ♘d5!

This is a standard sacrificial idea when Black's king is caught in the centre. Here it is by no means calculable, but the fact that both her rooks are active may have helped Chiburdanidze to believe in the sacrifice.

12...exd5 13 exd5+ ♔d8

Chiburdanidze felt that this was too ambitious, and that 13...♘e5 14 f4

♘d7 is better, but that White would then be substantially better in any case.

14 ♘c6+ ♗xc6 15 dxc6 ♘b6

15...♘c5 16 ♖c4 ♘e6 17 f4 g6 18 g4 gives White good play.

16 ♖d4! d5

16...♘c8 is a more passive idea, which allows White to infiltrate via the a-file: 17 ♗d2 ♖b8 18 ♖a4.

17 c4! ♕xc6

17...♗c5 18 cxd5 ♗xd4 (18...♖e8 19 ♗f4) 19 ♕xd4 ♖e8 20 ♖xe8+ wins:

a) 20...♘xe8 21 ♗f4 ♘d6 (or 21...♕a7 22 d6, etc.) 22 ♕xg7 with some very painful threats.

b) 20...♔xe8 21 d6 ♕a7 22 c7 ♖c8 23 ♕e5+ ♔f8 24 ♕e7+ ♔g8 25 ♕d8+ ♘e8.

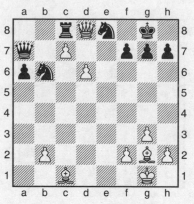

Now White has the wonderful trick 26 ♕xc8!! (26 d7? ♖xd8 27 cxd8♕ ♕xd7 is only quite good for White) 26...♘xc8 27 d7, winning.

18 cxd5 ♕c5 19 d6

Where should the rook go?

19...♖b8

After 19...♖c8, White can prove an advantage with vigorous play: 20 d7 ♘fxd7 21 ♗h3 ♕b5 (21...♖c7) 22 ♗g5+, and now:

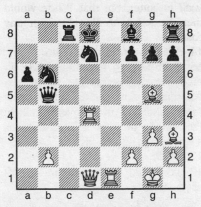

a) 22...f6 23 ♖e6 ♔c7 24 ♗f4+ ♘e5 25 ♕c2+ and White wins: 25...♕c5 26 ♕e4 ♔b8 27 ♗g2 ♕c7 28 ♖c4; 25...♔b7 26 ♖xb6+ ♔xb6 27 ♕xc8; or 25...♗c5 26 ♗f1.

b) 22...♔c7 23 ♗f4+ ♔d8 24 ♖e3 leaves Black with no decent defence to ♖b3 and ♖xb6 after the queen moves.
20 ♗f4 ♘bd7 21 ♕d2

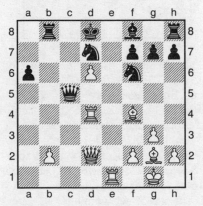

21...h6?
21...♖c8? is met by the killer 22 ♖c4! ♕b6 (22...♕xc4? 23 ♕a5+; 22...♕b5 23 ♖xc8+ ♔xc8 24 ♖c1+ ♔b8 25 ♕c3) 23 ♖xc8+ ♔xc8 24 ♖c1+ ♔d8 (24...♔b8? 25 ♖c6) 25 ♕c3 winning back heavy material.

21...♕b6 is more stubborn, though Black is wholly tied up, and has no obvious plan for unravelling his position. After 22 ♖c4 it is very difficult to see even what Black's next move should be. White's threat is to triple her major pieces on the c-file, and 22...♕xb2 23 ♕a5+ ♕b6 24 ♗d2 is extremely awkward for Black.
22 ♖c1 ♕b6 23 ♕c3
Now White is winning.
23...♘e8 24 ♕c7+! ♘xc7 25 dxc7+ ♔e8 26 ♖e4+ ♗e7 27 cxb8♕+ ♘xb8 28 ♖c8+ ♔d7 29 ♗h3+ 1-0

Strategic Example
Anand – Epishin
Belgrade GMA 1988

1 e4 c5 2 ♘f3 ♘c6 3 d4 cxd4 4 ♘xd4 ♕b6 5 ♘b3 ♘f6 6 ♘c3 e6 7 ♗d3 ♗e7 8 0-0 0-0 9 ♗e3 ♕c7

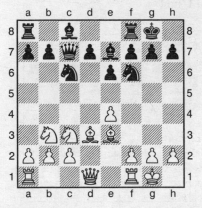

Why has Black moved his queen twice only for it to end up on c7? After all, there are some Sicilian lines where White voluntarily drops the knight back to b3. The point is that the knight is less active on b3, and generally when it retreats there "voluntarily" in some lines it is because Black is threatening to exchange it off in a favourable way. Black's preparation for a favourable exchange on d4 may not constitute the most efficient development of his pieces. There are lines, for instance, in which Black has played ...♗d7, and then after White plays ♘b3, the best plan for Black is to redeploy the bishop on b7, "undeveloping" it via c8. This gives rise to some strange subtleties in these Sicilian lines, as both players battle to lose fewer tempi than the opponent in reaching their target positions.

10 f4 d6 11 ♕f3

The queen moves into an attacking position on the kingside.

11...a6

Black makes the standard pawn move to launch his queenside counterplay.

12 ♘d4

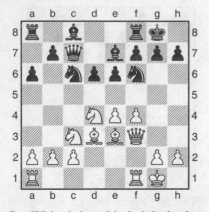

So, White brings his knight back to d4, reckoning he needs it if his attack is to have much force. He does so at a loss of two tempi (♘d4-b3-d4), whereas Black lost only one tempo

with his queen (...♕d8-b6-c7, rather than ...♕d8-c7). Has the opening therefore been a total success for Black? Not necessarily, since White has been able to play his bishop directly to the aggressive square d3, whereas in some variations it must move there via a stop-over on e2. In the Sicilian there is no such thing as a free tempo!

12...♗d7

12...b5 could be answered by 13 e5!?.

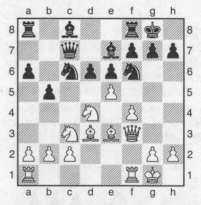

Then White wins in the event of 13...♗b7? 14 exf6 ♘xd4 15 ♕h3, but Black can play 13...♘xd4 14 ♗xd4 (14 ♕xa8 dxe5 is not too clear) 14...dxe5 (but not 14...♗b7?, when 15 ♕h3 dxe5 16 fxe5 wins a piece, e.g. 16...♗c5 17 ♗xc5 ♕xc5+ 18 ♔h1 ♕xe5 19 ♖xf6) 15 fxe5 ♗c5 16 ♗xc5 ♕xc5+ 17 ♔h1 ♘d5 18 ♘xd5 exd5, when White is better, but the game is not over.

13 ♔h1 b5 14 a3 ♖ab8

Anand now chooses a direct way to start an attack.

15 ♘xc6 ♗xc6 16 ♕h3

White threatens 17 e5, winning on the spot.

16...g6 17 f5

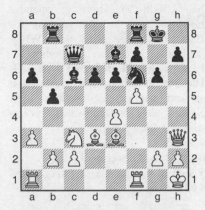

Note that White's exchange on c6 has taken the bishop's eye off the f5-square.

17...b4

With hindsight 17...exf5 18 exf5 b4 would appear more logical.

18 axb4 exf5

18...♖xb4 19 fxe6 ♖xb2 20 ♗d4 is very good for White.

19 b5!

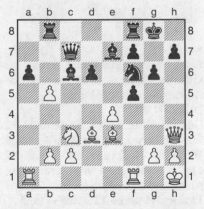

Clogging up Black's queenside play.

19...axb5 20 exf5 b4 21 ♘e2 ♖a8 22 ♖xa8 ♗xa8 23 ♗d4

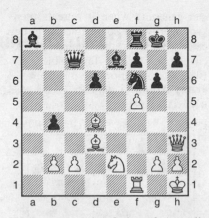

Here we see the fruits of Anand's calm, logical attacking play. Black has no meaningful activity or counterplay and can do little more than await the execution.

23...♕d8 24 ♘f4 ♗c6 25 ♕h6 ♕a8 26 ♗c4! 1-0

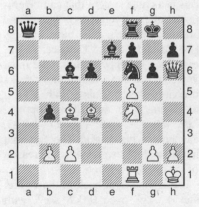

The only defence against White simply taking three times on g6 is to play 26...d5, but then it takes only a simple sacrifice to smash through on that square: 27 fxg6 fxg6 28 ♘xg6 hxg6 29 ♕xg6+ ♔h8 30 ♗d3 with mate to follow very shortly.

Queen's Pawn Openings

Barry Attack (1 d4 ♘f6 2 ♘f3 g6 3 ♘c3 d5 4 ♗f4)

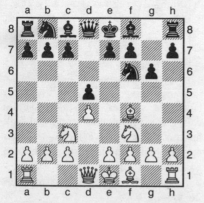

This is a crude system that can be employed to avoid the King's Indian and Grünfeld. White's third move intends 4 e4, reaching a Pirc Defence, so unless Black is happy with this he must play 3...d5. White's fourth move seeks to control the e5-square, with a view to playing ♘e5 and, if appropriate, ♗e2 (after e3, of course), h4-h5, launching a big attack. The fact that this attack looks so naïve is the reason for the opening's name!

Black should hit back in the centre, after 4...♗g7 5 e3 0-0 6 ♗e2, with 6...c5 7 dxc5 ♘bd7 (7...♕a5 is also quite all right) when White doesn't have much in the way of attacking chances.

Trap: Barry Attack, ♖xh7 idea
Pallau – de Kolste
London OL 1927

1 ♘f3 ♘f6 2 d4 g6 3 ♘c3 d5 4 ♗f4
The now infamous Barry Attack is not an exclusively modern idea: players were getting cheap points with it in the 1920s too!
4...♘h5
Black should develop: 4...♗g7.
5 ♗e5 f6 6 ♗g3 ♘xg3 7 hxg3 ♗g7 8 e3 c6 9 ♗d3

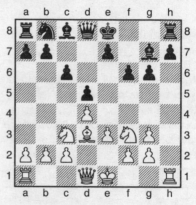

9...e5?
Black misses the threat, which is virtually identical to that in Euwe–Alekhine (a Grünfeld trap).
10 ♖xh7! ♔f7
Otherwise 10...e4 11 ♖xg7 exd3 12 ♘h4 is very good for White, while 10...♖xh7 11 ♗xg6+ ♔f8 12 ♗xh7 e4 13 ♘h4 gives him two extra pawns and a good position.
11 ♗xg6+! ♔xg6 12 ♘xe5+! fxe5
12...♔xh7 13 ♕h5+ ♔g8 14 ♕f7+ ♔h7 15 0-0-0 and ♖h1 will bring about a speedy mate.
13 ♕h5+ ♔f6 14 ♕xe5+ ♔f7 15 ♕xg7+ ♔e6 16 ♕e5# (1-0)

Benko Gambit (1 d4 ♘f6 2 c4 c5 3 d5 b5)

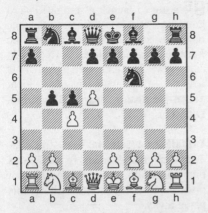

Black will answer 4 cxb5 with 4...a6. and follow up with ...g6, ...♗g7, ...d6, ...0-0, and bringing the major pieces to the a- and b-files. This is a real gambit; Black cannot expect to regain the pawn.

The Benko Gambit embodies some weighty strategic concepts. For the pawn Black gets a little bit of development, but his main compensation is in terms of positional pluses. White's queenside will come under intense pressure, while the black pawn structure presents no obvious targets for White to attack. The most vulnerable spot is e7, and it takes enormous effort to blast a way through to that.

From White's viewpoint, the worst thing about his position is that if he exchanges off a lot of pieces (standard procedure when material up), this can often serve only to intensify Black's pressure; moreover, some of the pawn-down endings are good for *Black*.

White has a variety of systems against the gambit. In general terms, he can refuse to win a pawn, accept but then mix things up immediately, or take the pawn and seek to consolidate.

Quiet ways of declining the pawn include 4 a4, 4 ♘f3 and 4 ♘d2, while 4 ♗g5 is more adventurous.

The *Zaitsev* line, 4 cxb5 a6 5 ♘c3 axb5 6 e4 b4 7 ♘b5 is extremely tricky and tactical. I once wrote a booklet on the crazy lines following 7...d6 8 ♗c4. Black can play either 8...♘bd7 9 ♘f3 g6 (9...♘b6 is OK too) 10 e5 ♘xe5 11 ♘xe5 dxe5 12 d6 exd6 13 ♗g5 ♖b8 14 ♕a4 ♗d7 15 ♗xf6 ♕xf6 16 ♘c7+ ♚d8 17 ♕a5 ♕h4!, when the game should end in perpetual check by the white knight, or enter the real complications: 8...g6 9 e5 dxe5 10 d6 exd6 11 ♗g5 ♖a5 12 ♘f3 h6 13 ♘xe5 hxg5 14 ♘xf7 ♕e7+ 15 ♔f1 ♖xb5 16 ♘xh8, etc.

A very popular line is 4 cxb5 a6 5 f3, looking to build a solid centre. There may follow 5...axb5 6 e4 ♕a5+ 7 ♗d2 b4 8 ♘a3, with ♘c4 next.

The quiet way to accept the gambit is 4 cxb5 a6 5 e3, but Black has some very sharp responses based on the move ...e6, smashing open the centre.

The main line is 4 cxb5 a6 5 bxa6 g6 6 ♘c3 ♗xa6 and then either 7 e4 ♗xf1 8 ♔xf1, building a centre at the cost of castling rights, or the quieter 7 g3. Then 7...d6 8 ♗g2 ♗g7 9 ♘f3 ♘bd7 10 ♖b1!? is an important idea, as White is in time to meet 10...♘b6 with 11 b3, preventing ...♗c4.

**Trap: Benko, elastic band
Kholovsky – Khomenko
Corr. 1988**

1 d4 ♘f6 2 c4 c5 3 d5 b5 4 cxb5 a6 5 bxa6 g6 6 g3 ♗g7 7 ♗g2 d6 8 ♘f3 ♕a5+ 9 ♘c3?!
9 ♗d2 is normal and sensible.
9...♘e4 10 ♗d2 ♘xc3

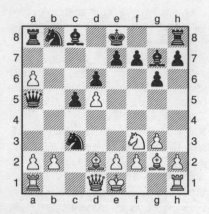

11 ♕c2??

This is White's idea, but there is something horribly wrong with it. Instead 11 bxc3 ♗xc3 12 0-0 keeps White in the game.

11...♕a4! 0-1

Black keeps an extra piece with this "elastic band" move. This is a standard trap, which has claimed several victims in similar positions.

Blackmar-Diemer Gambit (1 d4 d5 2 e4?! dxe4 3 ♘c3 ♘f6 4 f3)

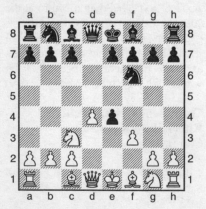

This is a somewhat rustic and no doubt unsound gambit, but it should

not be underestimated. White gets a move and an open file for a pawn, and is looking to launch a straightforward kingside attack. Accurate defence ought to see Black through, but he must be extremely alert.

Trap: Halosar Trap (Blackmar-Diemer)

1 d4 d5 2 e4?! dxe4 3 ♘c3 ♘f6 4 f3
The Blackmar-Diemer is dangerous but unsound. There is insufficient positional justification for giving this pawn away.

4...exf3 5 ♕xf3?!
5 ♘xf3 is more normal.

5...♕xd4 6 ♗e3 ♕b4?!
6...♕g4 is better.

7 0-0-0

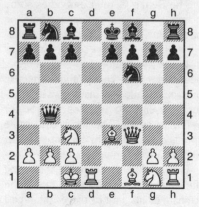

7...♗g4?
Black's idea was that White would not be able to castle because of this move, but White has an astonishing reply.

8 ♘b5!!
White is threatening ♘xc7#, while the queen cannot take the knight since 9 ♗xb5 would be check. Thus there is no choice:

8...♘a6 9 ♕xb7 ♕e4 10 ♕xa6

10 ♕xe4 ♘xe4 11 ♖d4 is quite good for White.

10...♕xe3+

10...♗xd1 11 ♔xd1 ♖d8+ 12 ♗d2 is winning for White, e.g. 12...♘g4 13 ♘xc7+ ♔d7 14 ♕xa7.

11 ♔b1 ♕c5 12 ♘f3

Although White has some advantage, Black has avoided instant loss.

Blumenfeld Gambit (1 d4 ♘f6 2 c4 e6 3 ♘f3 c5 4 d5 b5)

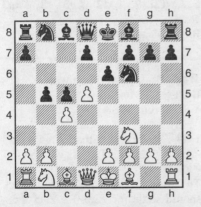

This gambit aims to exploit the fact that White has played ♘f3 rather than ♘c3. Despite the superficial similarity with the Benko, the themes are wholly different; here Black is aiming for central control in such lines as 5 dxe6 fxe6 6 cxb5 ♗b7, with ...d5 most likely to follow soon. The tough positional move 5 ♗g5 is more stable, and should be enough for a normal edge, but the Blumenfeld is certainly playable.

Bogo-Indian Defence (1 d4 ♘f6 2 c4 e6 3 ♘f3 ♗b4+)

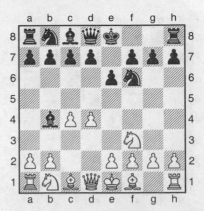

This is an opening with a reputation for being deadly dull. It was phenomenally popular in the late 1980s, but is less in vogue now as more players are choosing ♘c3 as White on the third move, avoiding it altogether.

White has three moves in response:

4 ♘c3 transposes to a line of the Nimzo-Indian.

4 ♘bd2 aims to gain the bishop pair in the event of such lines as 4...b6 5 a3 ♗xd2+ 6 ♗xd2. However, it is difficult for White to gain much initiative then.

4 ♗d2 is the main line. Black has a choice between the solid 4...a5, the unambitious 4...♗xd2+, the audacious 4...c5 (far better than it looks) and the normal move, 4...♕e7, when play tends to continue 5 g3 0-0 6 ♗g2 ♘c6 7 ♘c3 ♗xc3 8 ♗xc3 ♘e4 9 ♖c1, with chances for both sides.

Budapest Defence (1 d4 ♘f6 2 c4 e5)

This surprising gambit is actually quite respectable. It was first played, in Budapest, in 1916.

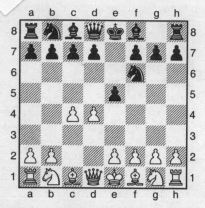

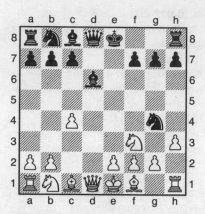

After 3 dxe5 Black will lose time with his knight, but will argue that the move c4 is of little value in the open position that results, and can even be a tactical liability. The main line is 3...♘g4, when White should probably not hang on to the pawn, but aim for a positional edge instead.

Black has an interesting off-shoot in the *Fajarowicz*, 3...♘e4, but I doubt its viability against 4 a3, preventing 4...♗b4+.

Trap: Budapest 4 ♘f3 d6

1 d4 ♘f6 2 c4 e5 3 dxe5 ♘g4 4 ♘f3 d6?!
This is a dubious off-shoot from the normal Budapest Defence. Black can choose the natural 4...♗c5 5 e3 ♘c6 (Black can often seek kingside play in the typical middlegames), while 4...♘c6 is not quite so bad as the next trap might suggest.
5 exd6 ♗xd6 6 h3??
This is a really horrible move, forcing Black to execute his only threat in the position. It has occurred in practice, but I won't name names.

6...♘xf2! 7 ♔xf2 ♗g3+ 8 ♔xg3 ♕xd1
Black is a queen to the good.

Trap: Budapest, pawn win
Burgess – Moisan
Val Thorens 1988

1 d4 ♘f6 2 c4 e5 3 dxe5 ♘g4 4 ♘f3 ♘c6 5 ♗g5 ♗e7 6 ♗xe7 ♕xe7 7 ♘c3 ♕c5?!
This move is too ambitious. Black should settle for 7...0-0 8 ♘d5 ♕d8, with chances of equality.
8 e3 ♘gxe5 9 ♘d5

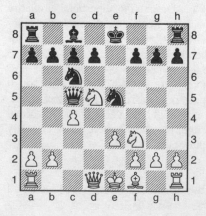

9...0-0??

Black follows a recommendation by Borik, but there is a big hole in it.

10 ♘xe5

Borik does not mention this move, giving only the insipid 10 ♕d2? ♘xf3+ 11 gxf3 ♘e7!.

10...♘xe5 11 b4! ♕d6 12 c5

White wins an important pawn for nothing. Black resigned a few moves later.

Trap: Budapest 4 ♗f4

1 d4 ♘f6 2 c4 e5 3 dxe5 ♘g4 4 ♗f4 ♗b4+ 5 ♘d2 ♘c6 6 ♘f3 ♕e7!

Black now regains his pawn and has a little trick to narrow down White's options.

7 a3 ♘gxe5

7...♗xd2+ turns out not to be necessary here.

8 ♘xe5 ♘xe5

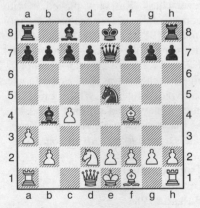

9 axb4??

White should instead play 9 e3, with some chances of a modest edge.

9...♘d3#

Some strong players have fallen for this mate, including one of Britain's top players, though again I shall not embarrass anyone by naming them.

Strategic Example
Sarmiento – Aristizabal
Bogota 1996

1 d4 ♘f6 2 c4 e5 3 dxe5 ♘e4 4 ♕d4

This move is highly ambitious; 4 a3 is more methodical.

4...♘c5 5 ♘f3 ♘c6 6 ♕d1 d6 7 ♗f4 ♗f5 8 exd6 ♕f6 9 ♘c3 0-0-0

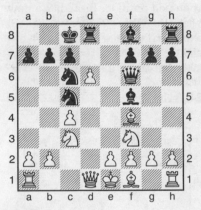

10 ♗g5

10 ♘d5 is an unsuccessful attempt to refute Black's play: 10...♕xb2 11 dxc7 ♖xd5 12 cxd5 ♘b4 (12...♘d3+ 13 exd3 ♗b4+ 14 ♘d2 ♖e8+ 15 ♗e2 ♘d4 is awkward for White) 13 ♖c1 ♘c2+ 14 ♖xc2 ♗xc2 15 ♕c1 ♘d3+ (15...♕xa2 is also extremely interesting) 16 exd3 ♗b4+ 17 ♔e2 ♖e8+ 18 ♘e5 ♖xe5+ 19 ♔f3 ♕xc1 20 ♗xc1 ♗d1+ is at least quite good for Black.

10...♕e6 11 ♗xd8 ♘d3+ 12 ♔d2

12 ♕xd3 ♗xd3 13 ♗xc7 gives White a fair amount of material for the queen.

12...♘xf2 13 ♕a4 ♗xd6 14 ♗g5

♖d8 15 ♘d5 f6 16 ♗e3 ♗b4+ 17 ♔c1 ♖xd5

Since the game continuation should only be a draw, Black could consider 17...♘xh1, even though it doesn't really seem in the spirit of the position.

18 ♗xf2 ♖c5 19 e4 ♕xe4 20 ♗xc5 ♗xc5 21 ♘d2 ♗e3 22 ♕b3 ♘d4 23 ♕c3

23 ♕d3 might be possible.

23...♘c2 24 ♖b1

24 b3 ♘xa1 25 ♔b2 ♗xd2 26 ♕xd2 is an odd position; Black has a draw with 26...♕b1+ 27 ♔c3 ♘xb3 28 axb3 ♕a1+ 29 ♕b2 (29 ♔b4 a5+ and the king march becomes a kamikaze mission) 29...♕e1+ 30 ♕d2 ♕a1+, etc.

24...♘b4

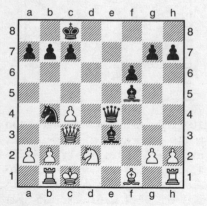

25 ♖a1??

25 ♔d1 ♗xd2 26 ♔xd2 is far better, appearing to draw:

a) 26...♕xb1 27 ♕xb4 ♕c2+ 28 ♔e1 ♕c1+ 29 ♔f2 ♕f4+ is a perpetual.

b) 26...♘xa2 27 ♕a3 and here too, neither side should avoid a draw by perpetual check.

25...♘xa2+ 0-1

Catalan Opening (1 d4 ♘f6 2 c4 e6 3 g3)

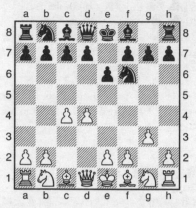

This is a fairly sedate opening, with White aiming for persistent pressure against the black queenside. The play can become exciting if Black continues 3...d5 4 ♘f3 dxc4, and plays to hold on to the pawn, though it is generally White who has more of the fun.

The Catalan is often used in top-level chess. Kasparov played it with considerable success against Korchnoi in their 1983 Candidates' match, while in many of the Karpov–Korchnoi and Karpov–Kasparov world championship matches it was used as a safe way to avoid danger as White, especially after a player had suffered a bad loss as Black in the previous game. Kramnik is a notable modern aficionado.

Trap: Catalan
Dimitrov – Bunis
Bulgaria 1988

1 ♘f3 ♘f6 2 c4 e6 3 d4 d5 4 g3
In the Catalan, White aims for pressure on the long h1-a8 diagonal.
4...b6 5 ♗g2 ♗b7 6 0-0 ♗e7 7 ♘e5 0-0 8 ♘c3 c6 9 e4

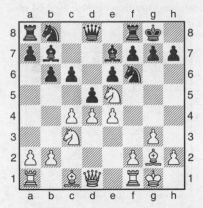

Now Black must be extremely careful.

9...♘bd7?

Oh dear! Now White wins a pawn in a very neat way.

10 ♘xc6! ♗xc6 11 exd5 exd5 12 cxd5 ♗b7 13 d6 ♗xg2 14 dxe7 ♕xe7 15 ♔xg2

Now it's "just" a matter of converting the extra pawn to a full point. In fact, Dimitrov failed to do so, but that is not our concern right now.

Czech Benoni (1 d4 ♘f6 2 c4 c5 3 d5 e5)

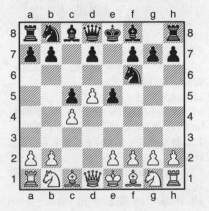

This is a rather passive system, in which Black sets up a solid defensive wall. There are some active ideas at Black's disposal, for instance a kingside advance, except that White will normally advance in that area himself. A positional aim for Black is to exchange dark-squared bishops with ...♗e7 and ...♗g5.

Dutch Defence (1 d4 f5)

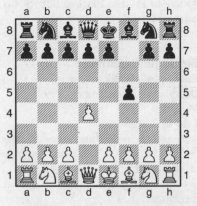

The Dutch is a much maligned opening which became very popular in the 1990s, thank to the successes of top ex-Soviet players such as Malaniuk, Bareev and Mikhail Gurevich. White has all manner of unusual attempts to exploit the weakening of Black's kingside, but Black's resources seem just about adequate. Examples are the *Staunton Gambit* (2 e4), 2 ♘c3 ♘f6 3 ♗g5, 2 ♗g5, and the *Korchnoi Gambit* (2 h3 intending 2...d5 3 g4)

However, it is still the main lines with a king's fianchetto by White that are most popular. After 2 g3 ♘f6 3 ♗g2 Black has two popular options:

The *Stonewall*, 3...e6 with ...d5 to follow, became very popular in the

1980s due to the efforts of Agdestein and Short, who showed that Black's king's bishop belonged on d6, and that Black could also seek queenside play.

The *Leningrad*, 3...g6 with ...♗g7 and normally ...d6 to follow, is the exciting way to play the Dutch. Black aims for dynamic play on the long diagonal with some ideas of storming the kingside when the time is right. White will aim to keep the battle firmly focused around the centre, with a view to making Black suffer for his weakness on e6.

Strategic Example
Zazhogin – Kalikshtein
USSR jr Ch (Simferopol) 1990

1 d4 f5 2 ♗g5

An enterprising line against the Dutch Defence. White plans to chop off the black knight if it should come out to f6, damaging Black's pawn formation.

2...h6 3 ♗h4

3 ♗f4 is also an interesting move, first played by the author in 1988 – one point is 3...♘f6 4 ♘c3 d6?! 5 e4! fxe4 6 ♘xe4 when 6...♘xe4 7 ♕h5+ ♔d7 8 ♕f5+ regains the piece with advantage.

3...c5 4 e3

4 e4 is even sharper, and also good for White.

4...♕b6 5 ♘c3 cxd4 6 exd4 g5 7 ♕h5+ ♔d8 8 ♗xg5

This is an incredible position to occur after only eight moves of the game. Black has moved just pawns, queen and king, while White has busily been getting his pieces *en prise*!

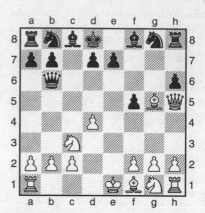

8...♕xb2

8...♘f6 9 ♗xf6 is no good for Black. **9 ♔d2 ♕xa1 10 ♕f7 ♕xf1 11 ♕xf8+ ♔c7 12 ♘d5+ ♔c6 13 ♕xc8+ ♔xd5**

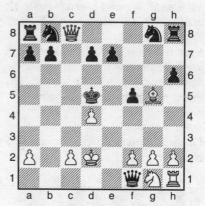

14 ♘e2! ♕xf2

14...♕xh1 allows mate: 15 ♘f4+ ♔xd4 16 ♕c3+ ♔e4 17 f3#.

15 ♗e3

15 ♕c5+ ♔e6 16 d5+ ♔f7 17 ♕xf2 hxg5 is at least quite good for White.

15...♕xg2 16 ♕xb7+ ♘c6 17 ♖g1 ♕f3

17...♕e4 walks into 18 ♘c3+, while 17...♕xg1 18 ♕xd7+ forces mate.

18 ♕b3+ (18 ♖f1! wins on the spot)

18...♔d6 19 ♗f4+ ♕xf4+ 20 ♘xf4
♘f6 21 ♔c1 a5 22 ♕b6 ♖ab8 23
♕c5+ ♔c7 24 ♕xf5 ♖b6 25 d5
♖hb8 26 dxc6! ♖b1+ 27 ♔d2 ♖xg1
28 ♕e5+ d6 29 ♕xe7+ ♔xc6 30
♕xf6 ♖f1 31 ♕c3+ ♔b7 32 ♕g7+
♔a6 33 ♕d4 ♖bb1 34 ♕xd6+ ♔b5
35 ♘d3 a4 36 c4+ ♔a5 37 ♕c7+ 1-0

Strategic Example
Timman – Speelman
London Ct (5) 1989

1 d4 f5 2 g3 ♘f6 3 ♗g2 g6 4 ♘h3
A good idea against the Leningrad
Dutch, since the knight may find a
good home on f4, eyeing e6.
**4...♗g7 5 0-0 0-0 6 c4 ♘c6 7 ♘c3
e6!?**
Imaginative play by Speelman.
White is ready to seize upon the
weakness of e6, so Speelman sees no
point in being cooperative! 7...d6
would be the standard continuation.
8 d5 ♘e5 9 b3
9 ♕b3!? is interesting.
9...♘f7
From here the knight reinforces the
dark squares on the kingside.
10 ♗a3 ♖e8 11 ♖c1 e5 12 d6

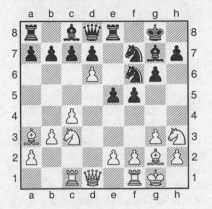

12...c6!?
Black decides to tolerate a pawn
wedged on d6, rather than allow the
centre to become open. This is a
highly committal course of action,
about which Black's queen's bishop
is unlikely to be very appreciative.
13 b4 b6 14 e4?!
After 14 ♘b5!? ♖b8 15 ♘c7 ♖f8 16
c5 ♘e8 Black removes the invader,
but meanwhile White has supported
his d6-pawn.
**14...fxe4 15 ♘xe4 ♘xe4 16 ♗xe4
♕f6! 17 b5**
17 c5 ♗a6 gives Black play.
**17...♗b7 18 ♕d3 ♕e6 19 ♔g2 ♖ab8
20 f3 c5**

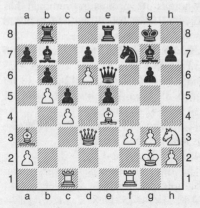

Now the d6-pawn has become rather
a weakness.
**21 ♖fd1 ♗xe4 22 fxe4 a6 23 bxa6
♖a8 24 ♖c2 ♖xa6 25 ♗c1 ♖ea8 26
a3 h6?!**
26...♗h6 27 ♗xh6 ♘xh6 28 ♘g5
♕f6 29 h4 ♖xa3 30 ♕d5+ ♔g7 31
♖f1 (31 ♖f2 ♖a2) 31...♖xg3+ 32
♔xg3 ♕xf1 33 ♕xe5+ (33 ♕xa8
♕d3+) 33...♕f6 leaves White struggling for a draw.
**27 ♘f2 ♖c8 28 ♕e2 ♖c6?! 29 ♖d5
♖xd6 30 ♘d1**

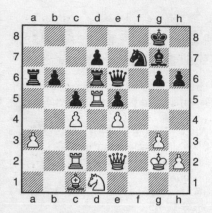

Winning the d6-pawn has not really been of much use for Black; the pawn was doomed in any case, whereas its premature removal has opened lines for White and exposed some of Black's weaknesses.

30...h5 31 ♘c3 ♗h6 32 ♗xh6 ♘xh6 33 ♖xd6 ♖xd6 34 ♖d2 ♕c6 35 ♘d5 ♔g7 36 ♕f3 ♖a8 37 ♖f2 ♖b8 38 h3 ♕e6 39 ♕e3 ♘g8 40 ♕g5 ♕d6 41 a4 ♖a8 42 ♘xb6 ♖a6

42...♕xb6? 43 ♕xe5+ ♘f6 44 ♕e7+ is best avoided by Black.

43 ♘d5 ♖xa4 ½-½

The final position is not very clear. Sample possibilities: 44 ♘e3 (or 44 ♕d8 ♖xc4 45 ♕e8 ♖xe4 46 ♖f7+ ♔h8 47 ♖xd7 ♖e2+!?) 44...♘h6 (44...♘e7? 45 g4! hxg4 46 ♘xg4) 45 g4 hxg4 46 h4 ♖a3 47 h5 g3 48 ♘f5+ ♘xf5 49 ♖xf5 ♖a2+ 50 ♔xg3 ♖a8 (not 50...♕d3+?? 51 ♖f3 ♕xe4 52 h6+ ♔g8 53 ♕d8+ ♔h7 54 ♖f7+ ♔xh6 55 ♕f8+ ♔g5 56 ♕e7+ ♔h5 57 ♖h7#) 51 ♔g2 with a kind of equilibrium. White's surprising king advance at the end of this line is based on the point that White must not allow the black queen to become active with check.

Dzindzi-Indian Defence (1 d4 ♘f6 2 c4 e6 3 ♘f3 a6)

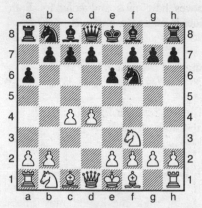

This is an oddity from the 1980s, not much seen any more. The ideas are similar to the Blumenfeld Gambit, e.g. 4 ♘c3 c5 5 d5 b5, but the big problem is that 6 e4 b4 7 e5 is good for White.

There is another form of Dzindzi-Indian, worked out by Spanish players, 1 d4 ♘f6 2 c4 c5 3 d5 a6:

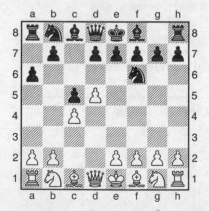

Now Black will meet 4 ♘c3 with 4...b5 when 5 cxb5 axb5 transposes to the Zaitsev line of the Benko. After 4 a4, Black will seek a form of Benoni where he benefits from having the moves ...a6 and a4 inserted so early. This is an awkward choice, since these moves have pros and cons for both sides in many Benoni lines.

Englund Gambit (1 d4 e5)

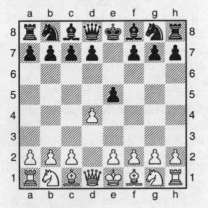

This is an extremely odd gambit, which should not be completely underestimated. In one of the main lines there is a devious trap, but only weak players have fallen into it.

Trap: Englund Gambit

1 d4 e5 2 dxe5 ♘c6 3 ♘f3 ♕e7 4 ♗f4
4 ♘c3 and 4 ♕d5 are good moves too.
4...♕b4+ 5 ♗d2
5 ♘bd2?? ♕xf4 is a simpler pitfall that has claimed some victims.
5...♕xb2 6 ♗c3??
Natural, maybe, but a horrible mistake. 6 ♘c3 ♗b4 7 ♖b1 ♕a3 8 ♖b3 ♕a5 9 a3 is quite difficult for Black.
6...♗b4 7 ♕d2
7 ♗xb4 ♘xb4! wins – this is even better than 7...♕xa1, though this does not give White sufficient compensation for the exchange.

7...♗xc3 8 ♕xc3
8 ♘xc3 ♕xa1+ gives Black a whole extra rook.
8...♕c1#

Grünfeld Defence (1 d4 ♘f6 2 c4 g6 3 ♘c3 d5)

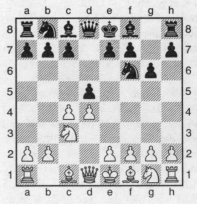

This is one of the most important chess openings, and one that shows in pure form the idea that a large pawn centre can either be a target or a deadly battering ram.

The main battleground is the *Exchange Variation*, 4 cxd5 ♘xd5 5 e4 ♘xc3 6 bxc3 ♗g7. Then White has a choice. In the *Classical Exchange*,

White plays 7 ♗c4 followed by ♘e2, the reason for this development being to evade a ...♗g4 pin; this ambitious line has regained much of its former popularity in the new millennium. The *Modern Exchange*, 7 ♘f3, only became popular in the early 1980s, when it was seen that the ...♗g4 pin could be handled. The most critical line is 7...c5 8 ♖b1 (an odd-looking move, stepping off the g7-bishop's diagonal and putting pressure on b7) 8...0-0 9 ♗e2 cxd4 10 cxd4 ♕a5+ 11 ♗d2 ♕xa2. White is reckoned to have very potent compensation for the pawn.

There are plenty of other dangerous systems against the Grünfeld. The *Russian Variation*, 4 ♘f3 ♗g7 5 ♕b3 dxc4 6 ♕xc4 also gives White a big centre, but here Black will aim for play against the white queen as well as the d4-pawn.

The 4 ♗f4 system can lead to sharp play in lines such as 4...♗g7 5 e3 c5 6 dxc5 ♕a5 7 ♖c1 (7 ♕a4+ is another try of a calmer nature) 7...♘e4 8 cxd5 ♘xc3 9 ♕d2 ♕xa2 10 bxc3 ♕a5.

White may also employ an early king's fianchetto, viz. 1 d4 ♘f6 2 c4 g6 3 g3 ♗g7 4 ♗g2 0-0 5 ♘f3 d5, but note that this also commits White to a fianchetto system against the King's Indian (Black does not have to play ...d5). While the lines with ...d5, cxd5 ♘xd5 are playable for Black, a more solid option is to play ...c6 followed by ...d5. This can be deadly dull.

For the player wanting a line that is not totally anaemic but leads to non-chaotic positions against the Grünfeld, I suggest 4 ♘f3 ♗g7 5 ♗g5, putting pressure on d5, and so encouraging 5...♘e4. Then after 6 cxd5 ♘xg5 7 ♘xg5 e6, Black will

regain the pawn, but White has chances with either the ambitious 8 ♕d2 exd5 9 ♕e3+ ♔f8 10 ♕f4, or the sedate 8 ♘f3 exd5 and launching a queenside minority attack. Note that one of the most often recommended lines for Black in this system, 7...c6 8 ♕b3 e6 9 dxc6 ♘xc6 10 ♘f3 ♘xd4?! 11 ♘xd4 ♗xd4, is flawed, since 12 0-0-0 gives White a huge advantage. (I got to play this once in the British Championship!)

Trap: Grünfeld, loose pieces
Schirm – Lücke
Bundesliga 1992/3

1 ♘f3 g6 2 d4 ♘f6 3 c4 ♗g7 4 ♘c3 d5 5 ♗g5 dxc4 6 e3
6 e4 is more of a move.
6...♗e6 7 ♘e5 ♘d5

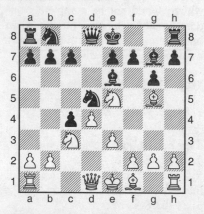

White's passive play has given him some problems here, since it is harder than he realizes to regain the pawn conveniently.

8 ♗xc4??
8 ♘xc4 gives Black a development advantage, though was, of course, a far lesser evil.

8...♘xc3 9 bxc3 ♗xc4 10 ♘xc4 ♕d5

Oops! Loose pieces again.

11 ♕g4

A last-ditch attempt.

11...f6 0-1

Black gives his king a square while attacking the bishop once more, and avoiding the highly embarrassing 11...♕xc4?? 12 ♕c8#.

Trap: Grünfeld, ♖xh7 catastrophe
Euwe – Alekhine

Groningen Wch (14) 1935

1 d4 ♘f6 2 c4 g6 3 ♘c3 d5 4 ♗f4 ♘h5?! 5 ♗e5!

5 ♘xd5?! ♘xf4 6 ♘xf4 e5 is good for Black, who threatens 7...♗b4+.

5...f6

5...♗g7? 6 ♗xg7 ♘xg7 7 ♘xd5 now wins a pawn in safety.

6 ♗g3 ♘xg3 7 hxg3 c6 8 e3 ♗g7 9 ♗d3

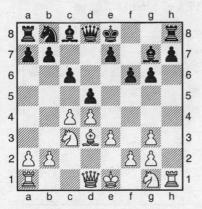

Now Alekhine's sense of danger failed him completely.

9...0-0??

9...♔f7 is not so bad for Black, while 9...f5 is fairly solid too.

10 ♖xh7

Since 10...♔xh7 11 ♕h5+ ♔g8 12 ♗xg6 ♖e8 13 ♗xe8 is completely hopeless for Black. White has won a pawn for nothing.

Alekhine played **10...f5** and eventually resigned on move 41.

Trap: Grünfeld, spectacular idea with ...♕f3!!
Kuchta – Honfi

Corr. 1956

1 d4 ♘f6 2 c4 g6 3 ♘c3 d5 4 cxd5 ♘xd5 5 e4 ♘xc3 6 bxc3 ♗g7 7 ♗c4 c5 8 ♘e2 ♘c6 9 ♗e3 cxd4

The main line continues 9...0-0.

10 cxd4 ♕a5+

This is reckoned to be rather a suspect line of the Grünfeld for Black, but there is at least one sensational idea in it.

11 ♗d2 ♕a3 12 ♖b1 0-0 13 d5?

13 0-0 ♗g4 14 d5 b5 15 ♗c1 is the theoretical main line, which is meant to be good for White.

13...♘e5

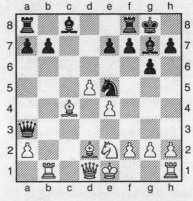

14 ♗b4?

This attempt to trap the queen is fatal

for White, but otherwise he is in some difficulties anyway.

14...♕f3!!

The queen does have a square! 14...♕h3 also rescues the queen, but does not win the e4-pawn.

15 0-0

15 gxf3 ♘xf3+ 16 ♔f1 ♗h3# is the point, of course.

15...♕xe4 16 ♗b5 ♖d8 17 ♘c3 ♕h4 18 ♗e2 ♗f5

Black has a good extra pawn, and so is in a position to win.

Strategic Example
Tabatadze – Neverov
Barnaul 1988

1 d4 ♘f6 2 c4 g6 3 ♘c3 d5 4 e3 ♗g7 5 ♘f3 0-0 6 ♗e2 c6 7 b3

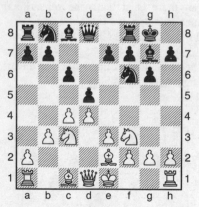

This is not one of White's more ambitious choices against the Grünfeld, and Black quickly takes over the initiative.

7...♘e4 8 ♗b2

8 ♘xe4 dxe4 9 ♘d2 does not tie Black down to defending the e4-pawn, since he can counterattack with 9...c5 or 9...e5.

8...♗g4 9 0-0 ♘d7 10 ♘xe4 dxe4 11 ♘g5 ♗f5

Now Black threatens to drive the white knight back to h3, whereupon ...♗xh3 would shatter the defences of the white king.

12 g4 e5 13 ♘h3 ♗e6 14 d5

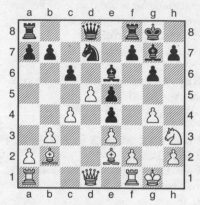

Has Black just blundered a piece? Well, no; he has a shockingly brutal attacking scheme in mind...

14...cxd5 15 cxd5 ♗xg4 16 ♗xg4 f5 17 ♗e2 ♕h4 18 ♔g2 g5

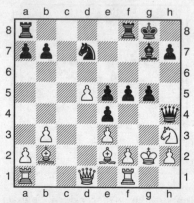

19 ♗b5 ♖f7 20 ♘g1 f4 21 ♗xd7 f3+ 22 ♔h1 ♖xd7

How to avoid being mated? White does not solve this problem at all.

23 ᐠe2?

23 ᐠxf3 exf3 24 ♕xf3 e4 25 ♕e2 ♗xb2 26 ♕xb2 ♖xd5 27 ♕f6 is not at all bad for White. 23 h3 and 23 ♖c1 ♖ad8 are possible too.

23...♖d6! 24 ᐠg1 ♖h6 25 h3 ♕g4 0-1

Strategic Example

Roitman – Goncharov

USSR Central Chess Club Corr. Ch 1988

1 d4 ᐠf6 2 c4 g6 3 ᐠc3 d5 4 ᐠf3 ♗g7 5 ♗g5

White puts pressure on d5 by attacking the knight that supports the pawn. Black has a tactical answer.

5...ᐠe4

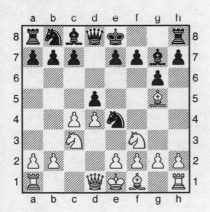

6 ♕c1

The main line is 6 cxd5 ᐠxg5 7 ᐠxg5 e6, when Black regains the pawn.

6...c5

6...ᐠxg5 7 ♕xg5 dxc4 allows White's idea to come to fruition, but this cannot offer White much nevertheless. Black has the bishop pair, and White's queen is exposed.

7 ♗h6 ♗xd4 8 e3

8 ᐠxd4 cxd4 9 ᐠxd5 is hard to believe for White, but note that 9...e6? (9...♗e6 is rather more sensible) 10 ♕f4! seems to win for White, viz.: 10...exd5 (10...f5 11 ᐠc7+; 10...ᐠd6 11 ♗g5) 11 ♕e5+ ♔d7 12 ♕xd5+ ᐠd6 13 c5.

8...♗xc3+ 9 bxc3 ♕a5 10 cxd5 ♖g8

A little cowardly maybe? 10...ᐠxc3 was possible, e.g. 11 ♕d2 ♕a3 12 ♗g7 ᐠe4.

11 ᐠg5 ᐠxc3 12 ♕d2 b5

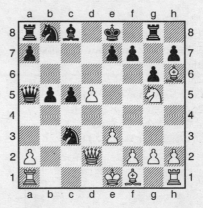

13 d6

13 ♗xb5+ ♕xb5 14 ♕xc3 leaves White with problems castling.

13...ᐠc6 14 dxe7 ♔xe7 15 ♖c1 b4

Now pandemonium breaks out, if it hasn't already!

16 ᐠxf7 ♗e6

16...♔xf7? 17 ♗c4+ ♗e6 18 ♕d7+ is a disaster for Black, but instead 16...ᐠe4!? looks good.

17 ᐠd6 ♕xa2 18 ♗g5+ ♔d7 19 ♖c2 ♕d5 20 ᐠb7 ᐠd4 21 exd4

21 ᐠxc5+ ♕xc5 22 ♗f6 is one hell-raising idea.

21...cxd4 22 ♗a6

This is hardly what you might call ordinary development!

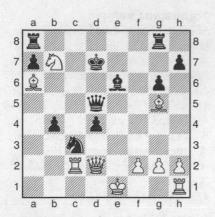

22...♗h3

22...♗f5 is perhaps too mundane for a game like this, but appears sensible.

23 ♖g1 ♖ge8+ 24 ♗e3 ♖xe3+ 25 fxe3 ♖e8 26 ♘c5+ ♔d6

26...♕xc5 allows White to try 27 ♗b5+ ♕xb5 28 ♕xd4+.

27 ♘d3 ♖xe3+ 28 ♔f1

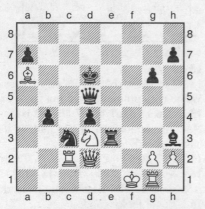

Now White has almost – after a fashion – consolidated.

28...♗d7

28...♗f5 looks like Black's last chance: 29 ♘xb4 ♕c5 30 ♘d3 ♕b6 31 ♗c4 ♘b1.

29 ♕f2 ♔e7 30 ♕h4+ g5 31 ♕xh7+

♔d8 32 ♔f2 ½-½

Now 32...♘e4+ 33 ♔f1 ♘c3 repeats, but 32 ♕h8+ seems to leave Black in trouble, so why was a draw agreed? An incredible game in all its phases.

Strategic Example
Zlochevsky – Krasenkov
Moscow Ch 1989

1 d4 ♘f6 2 c4 g6 3 ♘c3 d5 4 ♗f4 ♗g7 5 e3 c5 6 dxc5 ♕a5 7 ♖c1 dxc4 8 ♗xc4 0-0 9 ♘e2 ♕xc5

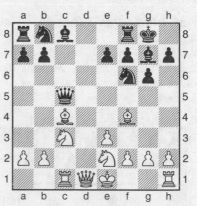

10 ♕b3 ♘c6 11 ♘b5 ♕h5 12 ♘c7

12 ♘g3!? is more critical.

12...♖b8!

12...♕a5+ 13 ♕c3 ♕xc3+ 14 ♘xc3 ♖b8 15 ♘7d5 ♖a8 16 ♘xf6+ (16 ♘c7 ♖b8 17 ♘7d5 could be a forced draw, since 17...♘xd5 18 ♘xd5 e5 19 ♗g5 can only favour White; 16 0-0!? is suggested by Gagarin and Gorelov, e.g. 16...♗f5 17 ♖fd1) 16...♗xf6 17 ♔e2 ♗f5 18 ♖hd1 ♖ac8 gave rise to a level ending in Barlov–Gulko, New York 1988.

13 ♗xf7+ ♖xf7 14 ♖xc6 ♕a5+ 15 ♘c3

White has won a pawn, but the board is on fire!

15...②e4

15...e5 16 ☒xf6 ♗xf6 17 ②d5 ♗e6 18 ♗g3 is good for Black too.

16 ②d5 ②xc3!

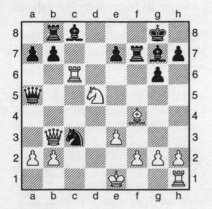

17 ②xe7+?

This is the decisive mistake, oddly because it results in the f7-rook no longer being pinned. 17 ②xc3? is no better: 17...bxc6 18 ♗xb8 (18 ♕xb8 ♗xc3+ 19 bxc3 ♕xc3+ 20 ☖e2 ♕c4+ is good for Black) 18...e6! with the horrible threat of ...☒b7 and then ...☒xb2, e.g. 19 ♗g3 ☒b7 20 ♕c2 ☒xb2 21 ♕xb2 ♗xc3+.

17 ☒xc3 was essential, though Black retains excellent prospects after either 17...♗xc3+ 18 ♕xc3 (18 bxc3 ♗e6 19 ♗xb8 ♗xd5 20 ♕b4 ♕xa2 21 0-0 ♗c4 and Black wins material) 18...♕xd5 19 ♗xb8 ♗h3 or 17...♗e6 18 ♗xb8 ♗xd5 19 ♕a3 ♗xc3+ 20 ♕xc3 ♕b5.

17...☖f8 18 ☒xc3 ♗xc3+ 19 bxc3 ☒xf4! 20 exf4 ☖xe7 21 0-0 ♗e6 22 ☒e1 ♕b6 23 ♕d5 ☖f7 24 ♕g5 ☒d8 25 ♕h4 ☖g8 26 h3 ♗xa2 27 f5 ♗f7 28 ☒e7 ☒d1+ 29 ☖h2 ♕d6+ 30 f4 ♕c5 31 ☒e1 ☒xe1 32 ♕xe1 ♕xf5 33 ♕e3 a5 34 ♕d4 ♗d5 35 ♕a4 ♕e4 0-1

Strategic Example
Fedorowicz – Shamkovich
New York 1981

1 d4 ②f6 2 c4 g6 3 ②c3 d5 4 ②f3 ♗g7 5 cxd5 ②xd5 6 e4 ②xc3 7 bxc3 c5 8 ♗e3 ♗g4 9 ☒c1 ♕a5 10 ♕d2 ♗xf3 11 gxf3 ②d7 12 d5

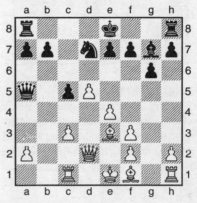

The pawn advance to d5 is one of the main strategic aims for White in the Exchange Grünfeld.

Now Black cannot afford to allow White to establish a massive pawn centre with 13 c4.

12...b5 13 f4

White has in mind the advance e5, shutting out the black bishop. 13 c4 b4 threatens 14...♗c3.

13...☒d8

13...0-0 14 c4 b4 15 e5 makes it hard for Black to secure counterplay.

14 c4 b4 15 e5 e6 16 ♗h3

16 dxe6? ②xe5; 16 d6 ②xe5! 17 fxe5 ♗xe5 gives Black three pawns and a lot of play for the sacrificed piece.

16...g5!!

Highly thematic – Black attacks the white centre with all the devices at his disposal.

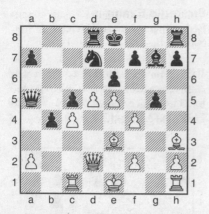

17 ♖g1 gxf4 18 ♖xg7 ♘xe5!

Before recapturing the piece, Black extracts the full benefit from the threat of ...♘f3+. 18...fxe3 19 ♕xe3 is not clear, e.g. 19...b3+ 20 ♔f1 b2 21 dxe6 bxc1♕+ 22 ♕xc1 ♘xe5 23 exf7+ looks good for White.

19 ♔e2

Instead 19 ♔f1 allows Black to get a little mileage out of the loose h3-bishop: 19...♕a3 (19...fxe3 20 ♕xe3 is more awkward) 20 ♗g2 fxe3 21 ♕xe3 ♕xe3 should win for Black.

There is an important alternative in 19 ♗g2 fxe3 20 ♕xe3 b3+ 21 ♔f1, with the following position:

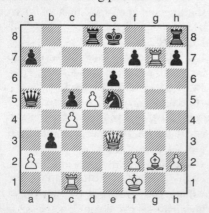

Shamkovich's play in this game was great, but he made a major slip in his analysis of this position. His line went 21...♘xc4? 22 ♖xc4? (the only move given in Shamkovich's notes) 22...bxa2, winning for Black. However, instead of 22 ♖xc4?, 22 ♕f4! is best, when 22...♘d6 23 dxe6 wins for White, surprisingly enough, e.g.:

a) 23...fxe6 24 ♗c6+.

b) 23...♖f8 is met by 24 ♗c6+ ♔e7 25 ♕g5+ ♔xe6 26 ♖e1+.

c) 23...♕b5+ 24 ♔g1.

d) 23...bxa2 walks into 24 exf7+ ♔f8 25 ♖g8+ ♖xg8 26 fxg8♕++ ♔xg8 27 ♗d5+ ♔g7 28 ♕g5+ ♔f8 29 ♕g8+ ♔e7 30 ♕g7+ ♔e8 31 ♗c6+ winning a lot of black pieces.

e) 23...b2 24 exf7+ ♔f8 25 ♖g8+ is similar to the line following 23...bxa2.

However, Black has an enormous improvement from the diagram: 21...b2!, e.g. 22 ♖d1 ♘xc4 23 ♕f4 ♘d6 24 dxe6 ♕b5+ 25 ♔g1 b1♕.

19...fxe3 20 ♕b2

20 ♕xe3 ♕xa2+ 21 ♔f1 ♕a3 is quite good for Black.

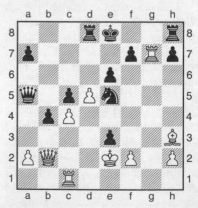

20...♖xd5!!

A spectacular sacrifice to open a line

for the queen toward the white king.
21 cxd5 ♕b5+ 22 ♔xe3
Otherwise White is mated.
22...♕d3+ 23 ♔f4 f6! 24 ♕b3
24 ♖g3 ♘g6+ 25 ♖xg6 e5+; 24 ♗g2
♘g6+ 25 ♖xg6 e5+ 26 ♔g4 ♕xg6+
27 ♔f3 ♕d3+ 28 ♔g4 ♖g8+ is another possibility.
24...♘g6+ 25 ♖xg6
Or 25 ♔g4 h5#.
25...e5+ 26 ♔g4 h5+ 27 ♔h4 ♕e4+!
0-1
Mate is forced: 28 ♔g3 h4#; 28 ♖g4
hxg4+; 28 ♗g4 hxg4+ 29 ♔g3
♖h3#.

Strategic Example
Khenkin – Neverov
Barnaul 1988

1 d4 ♘f6 2 c4 g6 3 ♘c3 d5 4 cxd5
♘xd5 5 e4 ♘xc3 6 bxc3 ♗g7

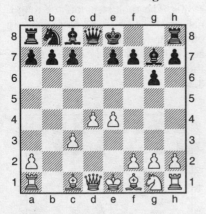

In the Exchange Variation of the
Grünfeld Defence, White sets up a
big centre, hoping to stifle Black,
who in turn will chip away at the
white central pawns, aiming to show
them to be weak.
7 ♕a4+ ♗d7 8 ♕a3

White wishes to hinder Black's standard thrust ...c5. However, this manoeuvre loses quite a lot of time.
8...b6 9 ♘f3 c5 10 dxc5 0-0
Black's pawn sacrifice is motivated
by White's lack of development and
the fact that White's once-proud
pawn centre is now a collection of
rubble.
11 ♗c4
11 cxb6 axb6 12 ♕xa8 (otherwise
Black just has very strong pressure)
12...♗xc3+ 13 ♗d2 ♗xa1 gives
Black very comfortable play.
11...♗c6 12 0-0 ♗xe4 13 ♘g5 ♗d5
14 ♖d1

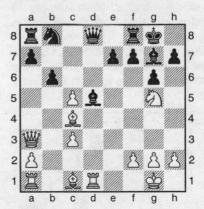

14...♗xc4!
Many players have almost a mental
block about giving up their queen,
even for a great deal of material.
Neverov correctly perceives that the
white queen will struggle against his
rook and bishop.
15 ♖xd8 ♖xd8 16 ♗e3 ♘c6 17 ♘f3
b5 18 h4 b4 19 ♕a4 ♗xc3 20 ♖c1
♗d5 21 ♕a6 ♖ac8
Now Black is really in control. There
is no looseness in his position for the
white queen to attack. In such situations a queen can be quite helpless.

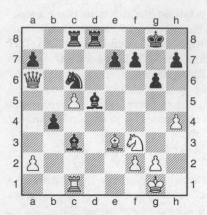

22 h5 ♘b8 23 ♕e2

23 ♕xa7 ♘c6 and Black will pick off the white a2-pawn, turning his b4-pawn into a monstrous passed pawn.

23...a5 24 ♘g5 ♘c6 25 ♖d1 ♗f6 26 f4 a4 27 ♔f2 b3 28 axb3 axb3 29 ♕g4 b2 30 hxg6 hxg6 31 ♕h4

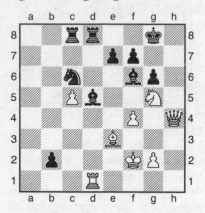

At last, White's queen has created a threat: 32 ♕h7+ ♔f8 33 ♖xd5 and 34 ♕xf7#. However, in the meantime Black has established a pawn on the brink of promotion, and has no trouble repulsing cheap threats.

31...♗a2 32 ♖h1 ♖b8 33 f5 b1♕ 34 ♕h7+ ♔f8 35 ♖xb1 ♖xb1 36 fxg6

♘e5 **37 gxf7 ♘xf7?**

Presumably the players were in time trouble by now. 37...♖b2+ would leave White entirely without hope.

38 ♘xf7?

38 ♘e6+ gives White some chances to survive after either 38...♔xe6 39 ♕xb1 or 38...♔e8 39 ♕g8+ ♔d7 40 ♘xd8.

38...♖b2+ 39 ♔f3 ♗xf7 40 g4 ♗d5+ 41 ♔g3 ♗e5+ 42 ♔f4 ♖g2+ 0-1

Strategic Example
Epishin – Khenkin
Barnaul 1988

1 d4 ♘f6 2 c4 g6 3 ♘c3 d5 4 ♘f3 ♗g7 5 cxd5 ♘xd5 6 e4 ♘xc3 7 bxc3 c5 8 ♖b1

This odd-looking rook move has been causing major headaches for Grünfeld players since the early 1980s. The rook steps off the diagonal of the g7-bishop, puts pressure on b7, and can often later swing into action laterally via a square on the b-file.

8...0-0 9 ♗e2

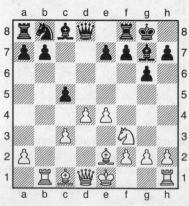

9...♕a5

Black tries to punish the rook move by grabbing a loose pawn.

10 0-0 ♕xa2

The c3-pawn is an even less tasty morsel.

11 ♗g5 ♕e6 12 ♕d3 b6 13 d5 ♕d6

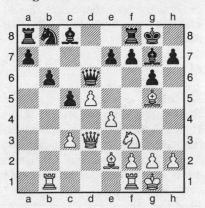

14 e5!?

White must play vigorously, lest Black consolidate.

14...♗xe5 15 ♘xe5 ♕xe5 16 ♕d2

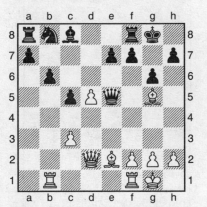

White has made great strategic gains at the cost of two pawns. He is ahead in development and has eliminated Black's key dark-squared bishop. I can hear sceptical readers: "Yes, but White's hardly going to be able to

play ♕g7#, and it is two pawns." You may have a point!

16...♕d6 17 ♕e3 ♖e8 18 ♗f3 ♘d7 19 ♖fe1 ♘f6 20 c4 ♗f5 21 ♖a1 a6 22 h3 h5

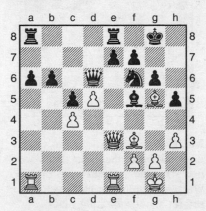

It is remarkable how quickly White now builds up a crushing attack.

23 ♗f4 ♕d7 24 ♗e5 ♔h7 25 ♕f4 ♖g8 26 ♕g5 ♘e8?

26...♖a7 would keep Black alive.

27 ♗f4

All White has done, effectively, is swap around his queen and bishop, and the game is over!

27...♖f8 28 ♖xe7 ♕d8 29 ♕h6+ ♔g8 30 ♗e5 1-0

Mate is forced.

Strategic Example
Flear – Ftačnik
Belgrade GMA 1988

1 d4 ♘f6 2 c4 g6 3 ♘c3 d5 4 ♘f3 ♗g7 5 ♕b3 dxc4 6 ♕xc4 0-0 7 e4 ♘a6

This is known as the Prins Variation.

8 ♗g5

8 ♗e2 is more normal, less ambitious, but more promising.

8...h6 9 ♗h4 c5 10 d5

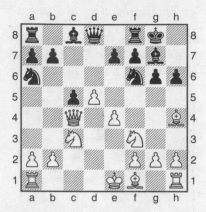

10...b5!

A wonderfully thematic pawn sacrifice. If Black meekly sits around, White will complete his development and set about squashing Black.

11 ♘xb5

After 11 ♕xb5 ♖b8 12 ♕e2 ♖xb2! 13 ♕xb2 ♘xe4 14 ♖c1 ♕a5 15 ♗xe7 ♖e8 16 d6 ♘xd6 17 ♕d2 ♖xe7+ 18 ♗e2 Black has 18...♘c4 19 ♕d3 ♘b4 20 ♕xc4 ♗a6 winning brutally, e.g. 21 ♕h4 ♗xc3+ 22 ♖xc3 ♖xe2+ is a wipe-out.

11...♕a5+ 12 ♘d2 ♖b8!?

Highly aggressive. 12...♘xe4 has apparently been analysed to a draw!

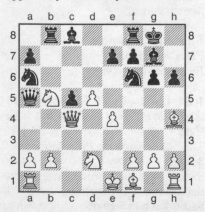

13 0-0-0?

13 ♖d1 ♘b4 14 a3 ♖xb5! 15 f3 ♖b6 gave Black a strong attack in Panchenko – Sideif-Zade, USSR 1980.

13 ♗g3 ♘xe4 14 ♕xe4 ♖xb5 15 ♗xb5 ♕xb5 16 ♕e2 (16 ♗e5 ♗xe5 17 ♕xe5 ♘b4) 16...♕xb2 17 0-0 ♘b4 is the theoretical line, but Black's compensation is clearly excellent.

13...♘g4!

The threat is 14...♘e5.

14 ♕b3

14 ♗g3 would be met by 14...♗d7! 15 ♗xb8 ♖xb8 – this is no position for half-measures! Any move that doesn't activate a piece or generate a threat should be regarded with extreme suspicion.

14...c4!

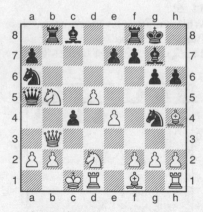

15 ♗xc4 ♗d7 16 a4 ♖fc8 17 ♔b1 ♘c5 18 ♕a3 ♕xa4 19 b3 ♗xb5! 0-1
20 bxa4 ♗xc4+ 21 ♔c1 ♗b2+ 22 ♕xb2 ♘d3+ and after all his sacrifices, Black emerges with a substantial material advantage and a mating attack. I must admit that this incredible game almost inspired me to take up the Grünfeld. But then I remembered all the drawing lines that are at

White's disposal and the mass of theory Black needs to know to play it at international level.

King's Indian Defence (1 d4 ♘f6 2 c4 g6 3 ♘c3 ♗g7)

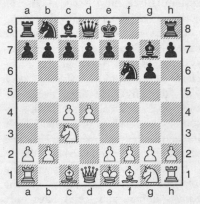

This, to me, is real chess. The King's Indian is a cross between all-out warfare and a fairyland where incredible sacrifices and sensational brilliancies are possible.

In the first moves of the game, Black allows White to set up a big centre. He will soon strike back, either to demolish the centre, or more normally to fix the centre having secured enough of a foothold for him to be able to start attacking on one of the wings. The traditional way to do this is by playing ...e5, and inducing White, by some means or another, to make the d5 advance. Then Black's natural plan will be to play on the kingside with ...f5. If White has castled kingside and supports his e4-pawn with f3, then Black will be able to launch a massive attack with ...f4, ...g5, etc. The pawn structure would be something like this:

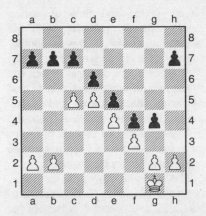

Meanwhile White will be attacking on the queenside, hoping to break through and "turn right" in time to prevent the reinforcements from arriving to finish off the white king. Time is of the essence, and there are many tricks for speeding up one's own attack and delaying the opponent's.

It is not always like this though. The King's Indian evolved greatly during the 1980s and 1990s, and some more subtle ideas have gained prominence. There tends to be more piece play and more jockeying for position in modern King's Indian games than when the pioneers first experimented with this opening in the 1940s. The attacks still come though!

You may be wondering why Black puts the bishop on g7 only to bury it behind a wall of blocked pawns. I tend to view it as air-support, if we use the military analogy of the pawns being the ground forces. In the first place, White would be under no great pressure to resolve the central tension if the e5-pawn were not backed up by the g7-bishop. Then, after d5 has been played, it would be very natural to meet the ...f5 advance by exchanging on f5 (exf5) and then answering ...gxf5 with f4. However, with the bishop sitting on g7, this is double-edged, since it presents the bishop with an excellent diagonal. When the structure with white pawns on f3 and e4 facing Black's on e5 and f4 has arisen, there are ways to activate the g7-bishop: it can be brought to h4, or go to h6 so that a ...g3 pawn sacrifice can open a line for the bishop.

The main alternative plan for Black, instead of basing his play on ...e5, is to play ...c5, and continue in Benoni (or sometimes Benko) fashion, with the g7-bishop glaring ominously down the long diagonal.

Here are the main systems of the King's Indian:

The *Classical* (4 e4 d6 5 ♘f3 0-0 6 ♗e2) is the main line of the opening, and tends to lead to the scenario I have been discussing. It incorporates, among others, the *Petrosian System* (6...e5 7 d5), the *Gligorić System* (6...e5 7 ♗e3) the *Glek System* (6...e5 7 0-0 ♘a6), the *Fluid System* (6...e5 7 0-0 ♘bd7) and the *Classical Main Line* (6...e5 7 0-0 ♘c6 8 d5 ♘e7) as seen in the diagram.

The *Sämisch* (4 e4 d6 5 f3) is a subtle blockading system, and a critical challenge to the King's Indian.

The *Averbakh* (4 e4 d6 5 ♗e2 0-0 6 ♗g5) is a very flexible line for White.

The *Four Pawns Attack* (4 e4 d6 5 f4) is White's most overtly aggressive system. Black must either choose an early ...c5 or prepare ...e5 with ...♘a6.

Otherwise, White can omit the move e4. There are many harmless systems of this type, but the *Fianchetto Variation* (4 g3 0-0 5 ♗g2 d6 6 ♘f3, though White often avoids an early ♘c3), is a real test of Black's resources; so much so that some King's Indian players reply with the Grünfeld ideas ...d5 or ...c6 followed by ...d5.

In various books, I have written a total of about 1000 pages on the King's Indian, and feel I have only scraped the surface. Obviously I cannot encapsulate the opening here, but hope the following examples inspire you to take up the opening yourself.

Trap: King's Indian, Averbakh

1 d4 ♘f6 2 c4 g6 3 ♘c3 ♗g7 4 e4 d6 5 ♗e2 0-0 6 ♗g5

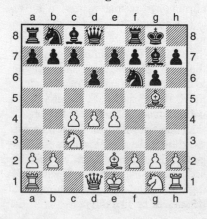

This is the Averbakh Variation, which prevents Black from playing the standard move ...e5, as we now see...

6...e5?? 7 dxe5 dxe5 8 ♕xd8 ♖xd8 9 ♗xf6

9 ♘d5 is also strong, though Black could try to claim that 9...♘xd5 10 ♗xd8 ♘b4 is an exchange sacrifice.

9...♗xf6 10 ♘d5 ♘d7 11 ♘xc7

White is a clear pawn up.

Strategic Example
Zita – Bronstein
Prague–Moscow 1946

This was a great pioneering game that popularized the King's Indian.

1 c4 e5 2 ♘c3 ♘f6 3 ♘f3 d6 4 d4 ♘bd7 5 g3 g6 6 ♗g2 ♗g7 7 0-0 0-0 8 b3 c6 9 ♗b2 ♖e8 10 e4 exd4 11 ♘xd4 ♕b6 12 ♕d2

12 ♘a4 is more to the point.

12...♘c5 13 ♖fe1 a5

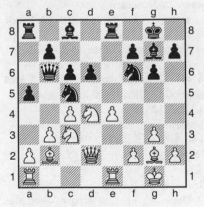

14 ♖ab1 a4 15 ♗a1

15 bxa4 was Reuben Fine's suggestion, but then 15...♕a6!? looks quite good for Black. 15...♕c7 is possible too, but 15...♘xa4? 16 ♘xa4 ♖xa4 17 ♘f5 is very good for White.

15...axb3 16 axb3 ♘g4

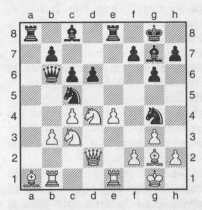

Nowadays, it would be readily seen that Black's dark-square strategy is about to reach a crescendo, with a1, b3, d2 and f2 the main targets. But in 1946 this was all very new.

17 h3

With hindsight, this is asking to be hit in the face.

17...♖xa1!

It is often well worthwhile sacrificing a rook for the opponent's dark-squared bishop on general grounds in King's Indian positions. Here there are specific reasons too! Instead 17...♘e5 is OK, but far less incisive.

18 ♖xa1

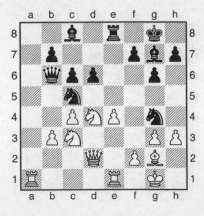

18...᷾xf2!!

This shattering blow gives Black a winning position.

19 ᷾e3

Capturing the knight is hopeless: 19 ♕xf2 ᷾d3; 19 ♔xf2 ᷾xb3.

19...᷾xh3+

Black has two pawns for the exchange and an all-powerful dark-squared bishop. This constitutes an overwhelming plus.

20 ♔h2 ᷾f2 21 ᷿f3 ᷾cxe4 22 ♕f4 ᷾g4+ 23 ♔h1 f5 24 ᷾xe4 ᷿xe4 25 ♕xd6 ᷿xd4 26 ♕b8 ᷿d8 27 ᷿a8 ᷿e5 28 ♕a7 ♕b4 29 ♕g1 ♕f8 30 ᷿h3 ♕h6 0-1

Strategic Example

Kan – Boleslavsky

USSR Ch (Moscow) 1952

1 d4 ᷾f6 2 c4 g6 3 ᷾f3 ᷿g7 4 g3 0-0 5 ᷿g2 d6 6 0-0 ᷾bd7 7 ♕c2 e5 8 ᷿d1 ᷿e8 9 ᷾c3 c6 10 e4 exd4 11 ᷾xd4

11 ᷿xd4 is too crude a way to exert pressure on d6: 11...♕c7 12 ᷿f4 ᷾e5 13 ᷿ad1 ᷿g4 is very pleasant for Black.

11...♕e7

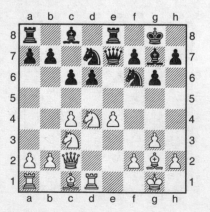

12 h3?

This is a move White often plays in positions of this type. Indeed it is very natural to cover the g4-square, but the move has potential drawbacks, as we shall see.

12 ᷿f4 is normal, when Black must be precise: 12...᷾e5 (12...᷾c5? allows a standard trick: 13 ᷾xc6! bxc6 14 ᷿xd6 with a decisive advantage) 13 b3 ᷾fd7 (the stock manoeuvre is best here) 14 ᷿d2 ᷾c5 15 h3 a5 16 ᷿ad1. Shamkovich argued that Black was suffering here, but Boleslavsky understood that Black could create counterplay by 16...a4 17 ᷿e3 (17 ᷾de2 f5 18 ᷿xd6 fxe4 19 ᷾xe4 ᷿f5) 17...♕c7 18 f4 axb3 19 axb3 ᷾ed7 20 ᷿f2 ᷾a6.

12...᷾c5 13 f3

Now the problem with 12 h3 is revealed: by ganging up on e4, Black has forced White to leave the g3-pawn unprotected.

Instead 13 ᷾b3 ᷾cxe4 14 ᷾xe4 ᷾xe4 15 ᷿e1 ᷿f5 16 g4 ᷾c5! keeps an extra pawn, while 13 ᷿e1 d5! 14 cxd5 ᷾xd5 15 ᷾xd5 cxd5 16 e5 ᷾e4! 17 ᷿xe4 dxe4 18 ᷿xe4 ᷿xh3 is good for Black (Boleslavsky).

13...a5 14 g4

Preventing ...᷾h5.

14...᷾fd7 15 ᷿b1?!

Development is better: 15 b3 ᷾e5 16 ᷿f4.

15...᷾e5 16 b3 f5!

A thematic idea to smash open the kingside.

17 exf5?!

17 ᷿e3 fxe4 18 fxe4 is positionally a failure for White, but 17 f4 must be answered sacrificially: 17...fxg4! 18 fxe5 dxe5 19 ᷾de2 gxh3 with three pawns and an attack for the piece.

17...gxf5

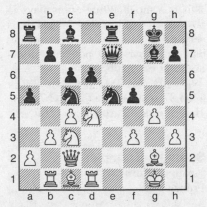

18 gxf5

18 ②xf5 ②xf5 19 ♕xf5 ♖f8 20 ♕g5 ♕xg5 21 ②xg5 ②xf3+ 22 ②xf3 ♖xf3 23 ②e2 ②e4 will give Black a winning ending.

18...②ed3!

A great combination, pinpointing the deficiencies of White's position.

19 ♖xd3?

19 ②de2 ②xf5 is also horrible, but 19 ②ce2 ②e1 20 ♕d2 (20 ♖xe1 ②xd4+) 20...②xg2 21 ②xg2 is not so hopeless for White.

19...②xd3 20 ♕xd3 ♕e1+

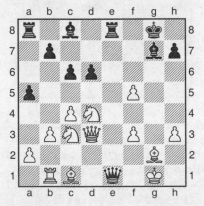

21 ②f1

21 ②h2 ♕e5+ wins the d4-knight.

21...♕g3+ 22 ②h1 ♖e1 23 ②e3

23 ②f4 ♕xh3+ 24 ②h2 ②e5 is terminal.

23...♕xh3+ 24 ②g1 ♕g3+ 25 ②h1 ♕h4+!

25...②e5 26 ②g1 allows White to resist.

26 ②g2 ♖xe3 27 ♕xe3 ②xd4 28 ♕e8+ ②g7 29 f6+

29 ②e4 ②xf5 30 ♕xa8 ♕h3#.

29...②xf6 30 ♕e4 ♕g5+ 0-1

Strategic Example
Neverov – Asanov
Barnaul 1988

1 d4 ②f6 2 c4 g6 3 ②c3 ②g7 4 e4 d6 5 ②f3 0-0 6 ②e2 e5 7 0-0 ②a6 8 ♖b1 exd4 9 ②xd4 ♖e8 10 f3 c6 11 b4

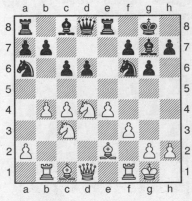

11...②h5?!

Black decentralizes rather prematurely. Better ideas are 11...②c7 and 11...②xb4 12 ♖xb4 c5.

12 g4 ♕f6

12...♕b6? 13 ②e3 ②f4 14 ②f5 is rotten for Black.

13 ②e3 ②f4 14 ②h1 d5

14...②c7 is a better try.

15 cxd5 ♘xd5 16 ♘xd5 cxd5 17 ♘b5

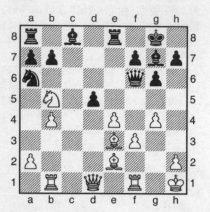

Black's tactical sequence has "worked" in as much as he has not shed any material, but the upshot is that he has highlighted and amplified his lack of development.

17...♕e6 18 ♗d4 dxe4 19 ♗xg7 ♔xg7 20 ♘d6 ♗e7

20...♖d8 loses to 21 ♘f5+.

21 ♗c4 ♕f6 22 fxe4

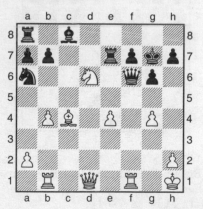

The traditional weakness of f7 is Black's undoing.

22...♗xg4 23 ♕d3! ♗e2

23...♕e5 24 ♖xf7+ ♖xf7 25 ♘xf7 ♕f6 26 ♖f1 ♕b2 (Black must not

allow the white queen to give a check on the long diagonal) 27 ♕e3 with the devastating threat of ♕h6+.

24 ♕g3

The key idea is to retain the monstrous horse on d6.

24...♗xf1 25 ♖xf1 ♕e5 26 ♖xf7+ ♔h8 27 ♕xe5+ ♖xe5 28 ♖xb7 1-0

Half of Black's army is *en prise*.

Strategic Example
Kozlov – Neverov
Frunze 1988

1 d4 ♘f6 2 c4 d6 3 ♘c3 e5 4 ♘f3 ♘bd7 5 e4 g6 6 ♗e2 ♗g7 7 0-0 0-0 8 ♕c2 c6 9 ♖d1 ♕e7 10 d5 c5 11 ♗g5 h6 12 ♗h4 a6 13 ♘d2 h5 14 ♗g5 ♕e8 15 ♖ab1 ♘h7 16 ♗e3 f5 17 f3 f4 18 ♗f2 g5 19 b4 b6 20 a4 ♕g6 21 a5 cxb4 22 axb6 a5 23 ♘b5 g4

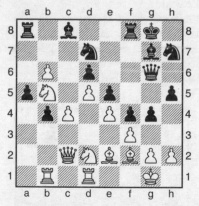

A typical King's Indian position has arisen. Black is getting murdered on the queenside but there's a chance of the white king getting garrotted too!

24 ♔h1 g3 25 ♗g1 h4 26 h3 ♘c5 27 ♗f1 ♘g5 28 ♘b3 ♘cxe4 29 b7

29 fxe4 f3 is messy.

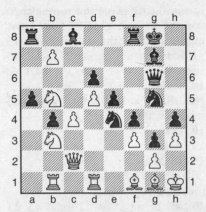

What follows in the next few moves is total mayhem, surely played in desperate mutual time-trouble. In such a situation, decisions are based on pure instinct, with the personalities of the players a major factor.

29...♗xh3

29...♗xb7 might well be objectively forced, but would have been less of a shocking move to face at the board.

30 fxe4

White should just play 30 bxa8♕.

30...♗xg2+ 31 ♔xg2 ♖ab8 32 ♘xd6 ♕xd6 33 ♗c5 ♕h6 34 ♗xf8 h3 35 ♔g1

Instead 35 ♗f1 is more resilient.

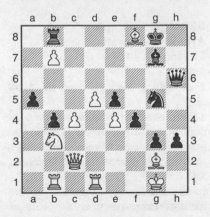

35...hxg2

35...f3 wins on the spot.

36 ♕xg2 ♖xf8 37 ♖d3 a4 38 ♘d2 ♕b6+ 39 ♔f1 b3 40 ♘f3? ♖xe4 41 d6 ♘xd6 42 ♘g5 ♘f7

42...♖xc4 is very strong.

43 c5 ♕xc5 44 ♘xf7 ♔xf7 45 ♖d7+ ♔g6 46 ♖bd1 ♗f6 47 ♕e2 f3 48 ♕xf3 ♗e7 49 ♔g2 ♖xf3 50 ♔xf3 ♕f2+ 51 ♔g4 ♕f4+ 52 ♔h3 ♕h4+ 53 ♔g2 ♕h2+ 54 ♔f3 ♔f5 0-1

Strategic Example
Aseev – Yurtaev
Barnaul 1988

1 d4 ♘f6 2 c4 g6 3 ♘f3 ♗g7 4 g3 0-0 5 ♗g2 d6 6 0-0 ♘bd7 7 ♘c3 e5 8 e4 exd4 9 ♘xd4 ♖e8 10 h3 ♘c5 11 ♖e1 ♗d7 12 ♖b1 ♕c8 13 ♔h2

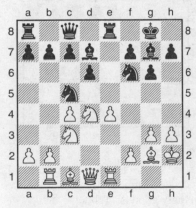

Leonid Yurtaev, one of the hardest of King's Indian hard men, weighs in with an audacious rook manoeuvre.

13...♖e5

Now where is that rook headed?

14 b4! ♘e6

14...♖h5 15 bxc5! ♗xh3 16 ♕xh5! ♘g4+ (or else 16...♘xh5 17 ♗xh3; 16...gxh5 17 ♗xh3 ♘g4+ 18 ♗xg4

♕xg4 19 f3!? ♕d7 20 ♘ce2!? dxc5
21 ♘f5) 17 ♕xg4 ♗xg4 18 ♘d5
gives White good chances of victory
– analysis by Aseev.

15 ♘de2

White avoids exchanges to highlight
the traffic jam in Black's position.
However, the simple 15 ♘f3 looks
good.

15...♕d8

15...♘f8 16 ♕d3 ♖h5 17 ♘f4 ♘g4+
18 ♔g1 ♘e5 19 ♕f1 is given by
Aseev, e.g. 19...♗e6 or 19...♘c6 20
b5. 15...♘g5!? is also interesting.

16 f4 ♖h5 17 ♗f3 ♖h6

Instead 17...♖xh3+ 18 ♔xh3 ♘g5++
achieves nothing after 19 ♔g2.

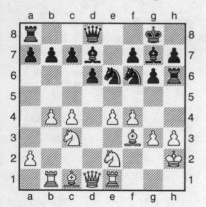

18 ♔g2?!

18 f5!? ♘f8 19 g4 is more critical,
and was claimed by Aseev to be extremely good for White:

a) 19...♖xg4+ 20 ♗xg4 ♕h4 21
♔g2 is the only line given by Aseev.

b) 19...♘e8 20 ♔g2 ♕h4 21 ♖h1
and White should win.

c) 19...♖h4 is harder to refute; e.g.,
20 ♔g3 (20 ♗g5 ♘xg4+; 20 ♕d2 h6)
20...h6 21 e5 ♘xg4 22 hxg4 (22
♗xg4 ♗xe5+ 23 ♔f2 gxf5; but not 22
f6? ♖xh3+) 22...♗xe5+ 23 ♗f4 gxf5

is not exactly clear! But probably 20
♔g2 h5 21 ♗g5 hxg4 22 hxg4 (how
to assess 22 ♗xh4 gxf3+ 23 ♔xf3
gxf5 is anyone's guess) 22...♖h8 favours White.

18...♘h5!

Now Black is able to justify his odd
rook position.

19 ♖h1

19 e5!?.

19...f5 20 ♕d3

20 exf5 gxf5 21 ♗xb7 wins a pawn
but frees the h6-rook.

**20...a5 21 a3 axb4 22 axb4 c5 23
bxc5 ♘xc5 24 ♕xd6 fxe4 25 ♘xe4
♘xe4 26 ♕d5+**

26 ♗xe4?? ♖xh3+.

**26...♖h8 27 ♕xe4 ♗c6 28 ♕e3 ♕d7
29 ♗b2 ♖e8 30 ♕f2 ♗xb2 31 ♖xb2
♘f6 ½-½**

The position looks a little precarious
for White, and this, together with the
tournament situation, was enough to
encourage Aseev to accept Yurtaev's
well-timed draw offer. However, 32
♘d4 ♘e4 33 ♕g1!! is good for
White – the queen is headed for a1,
aiming at the black king down the
long diagonal.

Strategic Example
Arbakov – Muratov
Moscow Ch 1989

**1 c4 ♘f6 2 ♘c3 g6 3 e4 d6 4 d4
♗g7**

This move-order to reach a King's Indian is suitable if White is happy to
play an English Opening, and wishes
to avoid a standard Grünfeld Defence.

5 f3

In this, the Sämisch Variation, White
fortifies his e-pawn at the cost of

sluggish development and a marginal weakening of his dark squares.

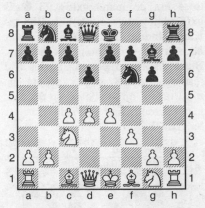

5...♘c6

Black would normally castle here: 5...0-0 6 ♗e3 (6 ♗g5 is another story) and then choose between the surprisingly good pawn sacrifice 6...c5, the more traditional 6...e5 and the sharp and chaotic 6...♘c6, which is similar to the line seen here.

5...a6 6 ♗e3 ♘c6 is another way of implementing Black's idea in this game.

6 ♗e3

6 d5 ♘e5 7 f4 is the critical test of Black's idea, since here, without White's bishop on e3, the knight would hit air if it went to g4.

6...a6

This looks like rather an odd plan. Black's play can only be understood by considering how White might play over the next few moves. The most natural square for White's king's knight is e2 (since f3 has been denied it), and ideally, White would like to play ♗d3 before blocking in the bishop by playing ♘ge2. However, when White plays ♗d3, he is momentarily neglecting the d4-square,

and this allows Black a chance to play ...e5 and meet d5 with ...♘d4 (this is why the knight went to c6), and has time to cement the knight on d4 by playing ...c5 (and if White takes *en passant*, time to bring a second pawn to c5). With a beautifully centralized and well-supported knight Black is rarely in trouble. There is an even deadlier point to Black's play revealed if White tries to maintain the central tension: 7 ♗d3 e5 8 ♘ge2 is met by 8...♘g4!.

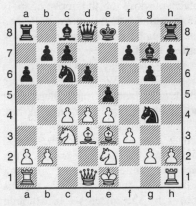

If White takes the knight, 9 fxg4, then 9...exd4 regains the piece with a big structural advantage.

So the first gain made by playing the knight to c6 is that White needs to block in his king's bishop by playing ♘ge2. Thereafter Black will keep a close eye on the e2-knight, and the instant it moves, will play ...e5, and after d5 will drop the knight into d4. This often involves a pawn sacrifice, but Black can expect good compensation, especially if White has to exchange his e3-bishop.

The second natural question to ask about Black's play is why he is playing ...a6 and (next move) ...♖b8.

OK, perhaps ...b5 might be an idea in some positions, but surely there are more relevant matters? These moves have another purpose. In the sequence of moves we are envisaging at some point after the white knight moves from e2, viz. ...e5, d5 ♘d4, Black will follow up with ...c5 to reinforce the knight, whereupon White may take *en passant* on c6. The recapture ...bxc6 will open the b-file and *voilà!* the rook is on an open file, staring at the loose b2-pawn. The other purpose of the move ...a6 is more mundane: the pawn will then no longer be *en prise* after the rook moves to b8.

Thus the play can resemble a waiting game: White avoids moving the knight from e2, and Black does not want to play ...e5 while White has d4 well defended. Black's useful moves that do not disturb the central situation are ...0-0, ...♖e8 and ...♗d7, whereas White is scraping around a little more: there are ♕d2, various moves by the queen's rook (though this has its committal side) and pawn advances on either flank. Thus the main lines involve White either launching an attack on a wing without solving the problem of his king's bishop, or else moving the knight from e2 and getting embroiled in a battle in the centre. We see the latter course of action in the featured game.

7 ♘ge2 ♖b8 8 ♘c1 e5

As explained above, it is a fundamental part of Black's plan to play this move as soon as White leaves d4 slightly less well supported.

9 d5

9 ♘b3 exd4 10 ♘xd4 is obviously

inefficient from White's viewpoint – the manoeuvre ♘g1-e2-c1-b3-d4 does not compare well with ♘g1-e2/f3-d4, which is often seen in the King's Indian. True, while White has been losing two tempi for nothing, Black has been playing moves like ...a6 and ...♖b8, which are not the most useful on the board, so this line is not actually bad for White.

9...♘d4

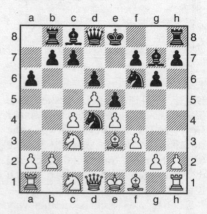

Again, Black absolutely *must* play this move – otherwise his play has been pointless, and White can make quick progress with a queenside onslaught.

10 ♘b3

10 ♗xd4 exd4 11 ♕xd4 wins a pawn, but for excellent compensation – Black's g7-bishop is unopposed on the dark squares. For example, 11...0-0 12 ♕d2 c5 13 a4 ♘h5 14 g4 (else ...f5 gives Black good play) 14...♕h4+ 15 ♔d1 (an exchange of queens would not kill Black's compensation) 15...♘f6 16 ♕e1 ♕xe1+! 17 ♔xe1 ♘d7 18 ♗e2 ♘e5 19 ♖g1 f5! 20 exf5 gxf5 21 g5 ♗d7 22 ♔d2 b5! 23 axb5 axb5 24 cxb5.

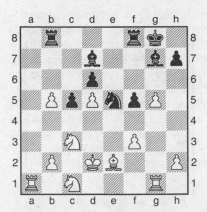

24...♗xb5! 25 ♘xb5 ♖xb5 26 ♗xb5 ♘xf3+ 27 ♔c2 ♘xg1 should have led to a win for Black in Korchnoi–Kasparov, Leningrad simul. 1975. Note that it was Korchnoi giving the simultaneous, and Kasparov was twelve years old! Yet just eight years later, it was this same Kasparov who stopped Korchnoi in his bid to become the official challenger to the world championship for the third time in a row.

10...c5

Black naturally maintains his centralized knight.

11 dxc6

Otherwise the d4-knight will remain a permanent nuisance for White – until he decides to take it, whereupon a protected passed pawn on d4 will be an even more permanent nuisance.

11...bxc6!

11...♘xc6 is not Black's idea at all, since he would then have too many weaknesses. Nevertheless in some related positions the knight recapture is viable, generally when White has played the knight from c1 back to e2 again, which "reconstipates" White's kingside development.

12 ♘xd4

Once again, 12 ♗xd4 exd4 13 ♕xd4 0-0 gives Black superb compensation.

12...exd4

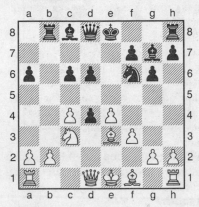

13 ♕xd4!

13 ♗xd4 is worse, due to some diabolical tactics: 13...♖xb2 14 ♘b5 (14 ♕c1 would keep White in the game) 14...♘xe4!! 15 ♗xb2 (15 ♗xg7 ♕a5+ 16 ♘c3 ♘xc3 is a wipe-out) 15...♕a5+ 16 ♘c3 ♗xc3+ 17 ♗xc3 ♕xc3+ 18 ♔e2 ♗e6! and White resigned in a game Platonov–Shamkovich, USSR Ch (Leningrad) 1971, since 19...♗xc4+ is threatened, while 19 fxe4 ♗g4+ costs White his queen. This is precisely the sort of spectacular tactical sequence of which White must beware in the Sämisch if the position opens up before his development is completed.

13...♖xb2

Now the game blows up in a mess of tactics. 13...0-0 14 ♕d2 ♕a5 is suggested by a Russian analyst called Gagarin (no, not the cosmonaut!) as a sane way to achieve compensation for the pawn.

14 0-0-0!

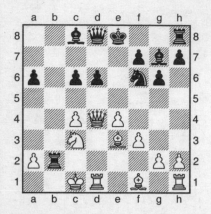

White makes good use of the castling move – two black units are threatened.

14...罩b7

This is a new move. It may be hard to believe, but this position had been seen before: 14...分h5 was played in Gelpke–Tarjan, London 1983; then 15 e5! 罩b7 16 分e4 0-0 17 分xd6 罩e7 18 f4 f6 19 c5 豐a5 was analysed by the American GM Tarjan, and assessed as "unclear". Very often, "unclear" is just a lazy assessment, but in this case it is very hard to do much better. Believe me, I've tried!

15 豐xd6 分d7 16 奧d4 奧xd4 17 罩xd4 豐a5 18 含c2

Of the two kings, White's is rather the safer – not least because he has somewhere to run.

18...c5 19 罩d5 罩b6 20 罩e5+ 含d8

20...分xe5 21 豐xe5+ costs Black the h8-rook.

21 豐e7+ 含c7 22 罩d5 豐a3

The time has come for decisive action. White plays a combination, having mapped out an escape route for his king.

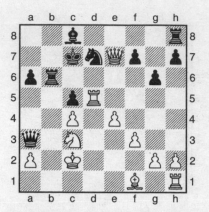

23 罩xd7+ 奧xd7 24 分d5+ 含c6 25 分xb6 豐xa2+ 26 含c1 豐a1+ 27 含d2 豐b2+ 28 含e1 豐c3+ 29 含f2 豐d4+ 30 含g3 含xb6 31 奧e2

Now White threatens 32 罩d1.

31...罩e8 32 罩b1+ 含c7 33 豐xf7 豐d6+ 34 含f2 罩f8 35 豐d5 奧c6 36 豐xd6+ 含xd6 37 罩a1 罩a8 38 奧d1

The ending offers Black no hope.

38...含c7 39 奧a4! 奧xa4 40 罩xa4 含b6 41 含e3 罩d8 42 e5 罩d1 43 f4 h5 44 罩a2 罩d4 45 罩d2 1-0

London System (1 d4 分f6 2 分f3 e6 3 奧f4 or 1 d4 分f6 2 分f3 g6 3 奧f4, etc.)

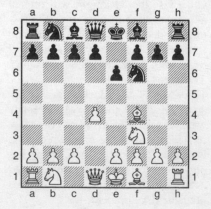

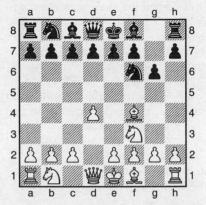

This is a quiet opening, often used to avoid opening theory. The main danger for White is that the bishop will be driven to h2 and remain out of play. There are two main dangers for Black: he may become impatient that White has played such an "insipid" opening and try to force matters in the centre, with generally catastrophic results; or he may forget about the bishop on h2 and allow some horrible tactic on the h2–b8 diagonal. 2 ♗f4 is an alternative move-order, with some subtle points.

Modern Benoni (1 d4 ♘f6 2 c4 c5 3 d5 e6 4 ♘c3 exd5 5 cxd5 d6)

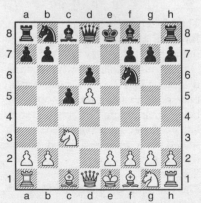

The Modern Benoni is a dynamic system, closely related to some King's Indian lines. However, it lacks flexibility: Black is already committed to a specific pawn structure and this helps White choose a plan. Black must seek vigorous counterplay by pressure on the e-file, by advancing his queenside pawns (...b5 being a major goal), and generally seeking active piece-play wherever he can find it. It is an opening that rarely leads to drawish simplifications and provides both players with a variety of ready-made plans – the primary battle is in the implementation of them.

A very potent plan for White is to advance both his e- and f-pawns, launching a pawn-storm similar to that seen in the King's Indian Four Pawns Attack. In the Benoni version, White can make his play more potent by throwing in a bishop check on b5. Some Benoni players are so unhappy to face this, that they only adopt the Benoni when White's knight is already committed to f3, using a move-order like 1 d4 ♘f6 2 c4 e6, meeting 3 ♘f3 with 3...c5 4 d5 exd5 5 cxd5 d6, and after 3 ♘c3 playing, e.g., a Nimzo-Indian. Alternative move-order tricks are to play the Benoni via a King's Indian move-order, or to delay ...e6 (or at least ...exd5) using a sequence like 1 d4 ♘f6 2 c4 c5 3 d5 g6 4 ♘c3 ♗g7 5 e4 d6 with ...0-0 and ...e6 to follow. However, these move-orders also have their problems, as in the King's Indian White need not meet ...c5 with d5, while in the Benoni with ...e6 delayed, White can tailor his response to make dxe6 a potent reply, or else arrange to meet ...exd5 with exd5 in a situation where this is unpleasant for Black.

From the diagram position, the main pawn-storm systems start 6 e4 g6 7 f4 ♗g7, when 8 ♘f3 is the regular *Four Pawns Attack*, which merges with the King's Indian version, while 8 e5 is the aggressive but ineffective *Mikenas Attack*, but 8 ♗b5+ is the feared *Taimanov Attack* (see Strategic Example).

White often plays an early ♘f3, either because of move-order constraints, or because he simply prefers a more classical set-up. The most classical line is 6 e4 g6 7 ♘f3 ♗g7 8 ♗e2 0-0 9 0-0, with 9...♖e8 10 ♘d2 ♘bd7 a possible follow-up. This has lost much of its popularity due to 7...a6!? 8 a4 ♗g4 9 ♗e2 ♗xf3 10 ♗xf3 ♘bd7 11 0-0 ♗g7, when Black stabilizes the position in a pleasant way; e.g., 12 ♗f4 ♕e7 13 ♖e1 0-0, with ...h5 and ...♘h7 a common idea. The *Modern Classical* features e4, ♗d3, ♘f3 and h3; the main question is in what order. 6 e4 g6 7 h3 ♗g7 8 ♘f3 0-0 9 ♗d3 is one way that avoids the ...♗g4 idea. Then Black struggles to find good counterplay unless he opts for the tactical blow 9...b5, which is a fine aggressive move in itself, but it has also been analysed to endgame positions where Black is fighting for no more than a draw.

There are many other lines for White against the Benoni, many with some real sting. 6 ♘f3 g6 7 ♘d2 ♗g7 8 ♘c4 is the *Knight's Tour*, immediately attacking the weakness on d6, which Black often just sacrifices for activity. Lines with ♗g5 or ♗f4 are also potent, with many possible move-orders and follow-ups. Some King's Indian systems transpose very naturally to a Benoni, making lines

with f3 and the *Fianchetto Benoni* (6 ♘f3 g6 7 g3 ♗g7 8 ♗g2 0-0 9 0-0) particularly important, with the latter often leading to astonishingly cut-throat positions after 9...a6 10 a4 ♘bd7 11 ♘d2 ♖e8 12 ♘c4 ♘e5 13 ♘a3 ♘h5, with Black willing to make large material sacrifices to further his kingside initiative.

Strategic Example
I. Sokolov – Topalov
Wijk aan Zee 1996

1 d4 ♘f6 2 c4 e6 3 ♘c3 c5 4 d5 exd5 5 cxd5 d6 6 e4 g6 7 f4 ♗g7 8 ♗b5+

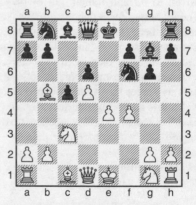

The Modern Benoni was an absolute favourite of counterattacking players in the 1970s and early 1980s, but this "killer" move, played with destructive effect by Kasparov, caused many players to abandon the Benoni. This being such a painful decision, some hardened Benoni players became obsessed with finding a good answer for Black...

8...♘bd7

The conventional line goes 8...♘fd7, with Black struggling to achieve an acceptable Four Pawns-type position in lines like 9 a4 0-0 10 ♘f3 ♘a6 (simply 10...♘f6 will leave Black a tempo down compared to a regular Four Pawns, a dangerous enough line as it is) 11 0-0 ♘b4 12 ♖e1 a6 13 ♗f1.

Interposing the queen's knight is far riskier, as it is a piece sacrifice in fact. It is also a lot more ambitious, because if Black can reply with this natural move, then the bishop check is not a very logical idea at all.

9 e5 dxe5 10 fxe5 ♘h5 11 e6 ♕h4+
The other main line is 11...fxe6 12 dxe6 0-0 13 ♘f3 ♗d4. This was played for the first time by Hodgson against Mestel in the critical game of the 1983 British Championship. One crazy line runs 14 ♕b3 ♕e7 15 ♗e3 ♘e5 16 ♘xe5 ♗xe3 17 ♘d5 ♗f2+?! 18 ♔e2 ♕xe6 19 ♘c7 ♕xb3 20 axb3 ♖b8 21 ♖xa7 ♗g3 22 ♗c4+ ♔g7 23 hxg3 ♘xg3+ 24 ♔e3 ♘xh1 25 ♘c6 bxc6 26 ♘e6++, which is probably about equal. White has improvements near the start of this line, however.

12 g3 ♘xg3 13 hxg3 ♕xh1 14 ♗e3
This is considered more powerful than 14 exd7+.

14...♗xc3+ 15 bxc3 a6
After many years of analysis and practical testing, this has emerged as the critical line for 8...♘bd7.

16 exd7+ ♗xd7 17 ♗xd7+ ♔xd7 18 ♕b3!?
Sokolov described this as "A novelty that might bother Black for quite a while." And indeed it did, as it was proclaimed for several years as the move that buried 8...♘bd7.

18...b5 19 0-0-0 ♖he8
19...♖ac8 20 d6 c4 21 ♕c2 ♖he8 22 ♕f2 gives White a large advantage – analysis by Sokolov.

20 ♗xc5

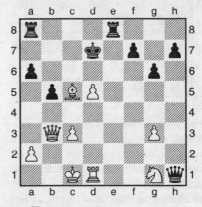

20...♖ac8?!
Now White can target the a6-pawn. 20...♕g2! is the move that has resurrected this whole line (which is now looking rather solid for Black, as White's alternatives on move 18 generally lead to a murky ending where White is running out of pawns fast; e.g., 18 ♕g4+ f5 19 ♕f3 ♕xf3 20 ♘xf3 ♖he8 21 ♔f2 ♖e4 and now 22 ♘g5 ♖c4 or 22 ♗xc5 ♖c8 23 ♗d4 ♔d6). Black's plan is to prevent the g1-knight from developing. 21 d6 ♖e6 22 ♘h3 ♕xh3 23 ♕d5 ♖b8 24

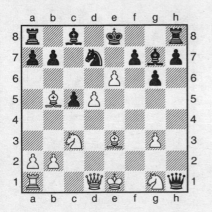

♗a7 ♕h6+ followed by ...♕f8 is at least OK for Black.

21 ♗d4 ♕g2 22 ♕a3! ♕xg3 23 ♕xa6 ♖xc3+ 24 ♔b2 ♖cc8 25 ♕xb5+ ♔d6 26 ♔a1! ♕a3 27 ♗b2 ♕c5 28 ♕a6+ ♔d7 29 ♕a4+ 1-0

Nimzo-Indian Defence (1 d4 ♘f6 2 c4 e6 3 ♘c3 ♗b4)

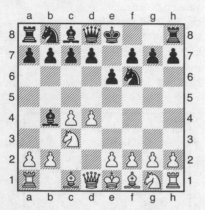

The Nimzo-Indian was Aron Nimzo-witsch's brainchild. His idea was to inflict doubled c-pawns on White and then use his famous procedure, re-strain, blockade, destroy. In the blocked positions that result, Black hopes that his knights will be at least the equal of White's bishop pair.

The Nimzo-Indian brings about some of the most truly thematic chess-board struggles: bishop vs knight, structure vs dynamism and force against elasticity.

The main systems for White are:

The *Sämisch* (4 a3) loses time to force an exchange on c3, doubling White's pawns. However, it is not a totally bad idea, since this clarifies the situation so White can aim for central domination.

The *Leningrad* (4 ♗g5) leads to obscure play after 4...h6 5 ♗h4 c5.

Kasparov has popularized the idea of playing 4 ♘f3 and meeting 4...c5 with 5 g3. However, this lost some of its popularity in the late 1980s when good methods, based on central counterplay, were found for Black.

The *Rubinstein Variation* (4 e3) is logical and unpretentious. White simply prepares to develop, and will challenge the b4-bishop as and when appropriate. It leads to rich battles, and fairly normal positions.

The most popular line is the *Clas-sical* (4 ♕c2). Here White avoids doubled c-pawns at the cost of some time. Black will then either need to preserve his bishop from exchange, or argue that his lead in development compensates for White's bishop pair.

Trap: Nimzo-Indian, loose pieces
Sämisch – Capablanca
Karlsbad 1929

1 d4 ♘f6 2 c4 e6 3 ♘c3 ♗b4 4 a3 ♗xc3+ 5 bxc3 d6 6 f3 c5 7 e4 ♘c6 8 ♗e3 b6 9 ♗d3

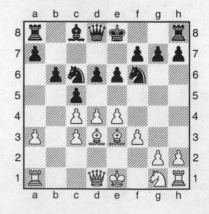

In this fairly normal Nimzo-Indian position, White has a big centre, but Black hopes to show White's structure to be inflexible and weak. Capablanca presumably forgot to think about short-term tactics, planning a war of attrition.

9...♗a6?? 10 ♕a4

Normally, such a move would only leave the queen misplaced.

10...♗b7 11 d5

Black is now losing a piece. Capablanca could have resigned here, but instead dragged out the game to move 67.

Old Indian Defence (1 d4 ♘f6 2 c4 d6 3 ♘c3 ♘bd7 4 ♘f3 e5)

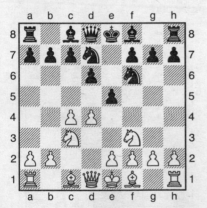

The name "Old Indian" is used to cover quite a variety of systems with ...d6 against 1 d4, but the one shown in the diagram is the most important. White's normal response is 5 e4, when lines similar to a King's Indian can arise, but with Black's bishop on e7 instead of g7. This changes the strategy for both sides considerably, as Black has less counterplay in the centre but a more solid kingside structure.

Polish Defence (1 d4 b5)

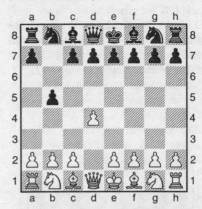

This is a rather odd opening, staking out some space on the queenside, but allowing White a central preponderance. The most logical response is 2 e4 ♗b7 3 ♗d3, followed by very solid development, supporting the d4-pawn with c3 when it is attacked by ...c5.

Queen's Gambit (1 d4 d5 2 c4)

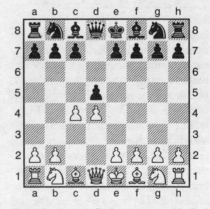

This is one of the most classical openings. White offers a safe gambit to start the battle to remove Black's central presence. The play varies greatly from wild, obscure gambit play to sedate minority attacks.

Black has a number of responses.

The *Chigorin* (2...♞c6) is an anarchic attempt to obtain piece play. The assessment is volatile, but it is currently looking playable for Black.

The *Albin Countergambit* (2...e5) is a sharp but unconvincing attempt to seize the initiative.

The **Orthodox Queen's Gambit** (2...e6 3 ♞c3) is the starting point for a number of systems.

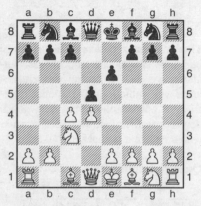

The *Tarrasch Defence* (3...c5) is a controversial line. Black is likely to receive an isolated pawn after 4 cxd5 exd5 (4...cxd4 is the very dangerous, but probably suspect *Hennig-Schara Gambit*) 5 ♞f3 ♞c6 6 g3. Black must play with the utmost activity to avoid coming under great pressure.

After 3...c6, play can transpose to the Semi-Slav following 4 ♞f3 ♞f6, but White can deviate with the sharp *Marshall Gambit* (4 e4 dxe4 5 ♞xe4 ♝b4+ 6 ♝d2 ♛xd4), while after 4 ♞f3 Black can try 4...dxc4 5 a4 ♝b4 6 e3 b5, the *Abrahams* or *Noteboom*.

The *Exchange Variation* has two main forms: 3...♞f6 4 cxd5 exd5 and 3...♝e7 4 cxd5 exd5. White has a

choice of plans: a minority attack is suggested by the pawn structure, but a central advance is possible, with kingside space-gaining an option too.

The main line continues 3...♞f6 4 ♝g5 ♝e7 5 e3 when Black's main choices are:

The *Classical Defence* (5...0-0 6 ♞f3 ♞bd7) is the old way of handling the position. It remains viable but is too passive for modern tastes.

5...h6 6 ♝h4 (6 ♝xf6 leads to interesting play too) 6...0-0 7 ♞f3 with a choice between the *Lasker Defence* (7...♞e4) and the *Tartakower Defence* (7...b6).

The **Queen's Gambit Accepted** (2...dxc4) can lead to interesting piece play.

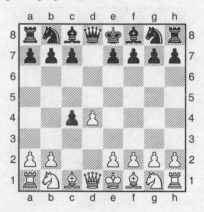

White can choose between ambitious lines such as 3 e4, and 3 ♞f3 ♞f6 4 ♞c3, intending 5 e4 but allowing Black to cling on to the c4-pawn, and more sedate lines including 3 e3 and the main line, 3 ♞f3 ♞f6 4 e3, in which he regains the pawn and then sets about trying to advance his central majority. Black should generally not rush to give White an IQP here.

The **Slav Defence** (2...c6) is a solid line with counterattacking potential.

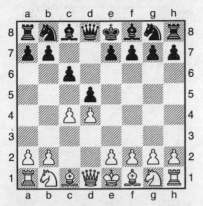

From a practical angle, the *Exchange Variation* (3 cxd5 cxd5) is a nuisance for Black. Black must play accurately to maintain equality and has few winning chances unless White is too ambitious (although some move-order tricks like 4 ♘c3 e5!? are possible). Whether to accept that as Black you can be faced by such a line is as much a question of your approach to chess as anything else. Some players relish the challenge of trying to outplay opponents from an equal position, while for others it is a reason for avoiding the Slav altogether.

The main line continues 3 ♘f3 ♘f6 4 ♘c3, when Black can try the odd-looking 4...a6, intending to stabilize the queenside with ...b5, without giving up his central foothold. Alternatively, 4...e6 is the Semi-Slav, but the main line of the "pure" Slav is 4...dxc4. Then after 5 e4 b5 White does not get enough attack for the lost pawn, so he generally chooses between the tame 5 e3 and the normal 5 a4, after which White intends 6 e4, followed by 7 ♗xc4.

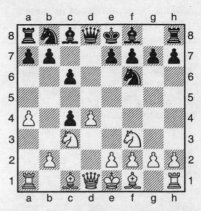

Black can play the *Smyslov Variation*, 5...♘a6, seeking counterplay by bringing the knight to b4 (6 e4 ♗g4 7 ♗xc4 ♘b4), though this doesn't have much bite.

The *Steiner Variation*, 5...♗g4, is more popular, since 6 e4 can then be met by the interesting 6...e5, so White does better to try 6 ♘e5 ♗h5, with sharp play.

The main line is 5...♗f5, the *Czech Variation*, which prevents 6 e4 directly. Then 6 e3 leads to moderately quiet play after 6...e6 7 ♗xc4 ♗b4. White's most ambitious line is 6 ♘e5, intending f3 and e4. The critical line for most of the 1990s was 6...e6 7 f3 ♗b4, when 8 e4 ♗xe4 9 fxe4 ♘xe4 is a complex piece sacrifice. However, it started to become clear that this line favoured White, so attention turned back to the older 6...♘bd7, which was revitalized with a lot of new ideas, notably by Morozevich, such as 7 ♘xc4 ♕c7 8 g3 e5 9 dxe5 ♘xe5 10 ♗f4 ♘fd7 11 ♗g2 g5!?.

The **Semi-Slav Defence** (2...c6 3 ♘f3 ♘f6 4 ♘c3 e6) is an off-shoot of the Slav that can also arise via the

Orthodox (e.g., 1 d4 d5 2 c4 e6 3 ♘c3 c6 4 ♘f3 ♘f6).

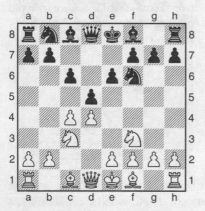

There are three especially complex systems that can arise from the Semi-Slav. The *Anti-Meran Gambit* features 5 ♗g5 dxc4 6 e4 b5. The main line is then 7 e5 h6 8 ♗h4 g5 9 ♘xg5 hxg5 10 ♗xg5 ♘bd7, which leads to colossal tactical complications. The *Anti-Moscow Variation* is 5 ♗g5 h6 6 ♗h4!? dxc4 7 e4 g5 8 ♗g3 b5; its chaotic and dynamic nature make it popular among the 21st century's top GMs. The *Meran System* is 5 e3 ♘bd7 6 ♗d3 dxc4 7 ♗xc4 b5 with Black making progress on the queenside, while White will go through the centre. Although slightly less tactically sharp than the Anti-Meran and Anti-Moscow, it leads to very deep strategy.

Trap: Slav, loose piece
Farago – Bliumberg
Budapest 1994

1 d4 d5 2 c4 dxc4 3 ♘f3 c6
The Slav move-order would be 1 d4 d5 2 c4 c6 3 ♘f3 dxc4.

4 e3 ♗e6

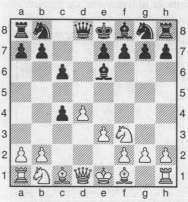

Black has just played a greedy move, which White seeks to punish.
5 ♘g5?? ♕a5+ 0-1
It's very embarrassing for a grandmaster to miss such a simple move!

Trap: Albin Countergambit

1 d4 d5 2 c4 e5 3 dxe5 d4 4 e3?
This natural move allows a nasty trick. 4 ♘f3 is normal, and best.
4...♗b4+ 5 ♗d2
5 ♘d2 dxe3 6 fxe3 damages White's pawns, but is not a disaster.
5...dxe3!

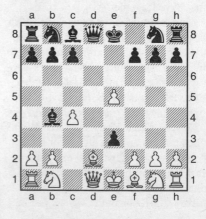

6 ♗xb4??

White is oblivious to the danger. He should instead simply recapture the pawn and accept a bad pawn structure.

6...exf2+ 7 ♔e2

7 ♔xf2 is no good due to 7...♕xd1.

7...fxg1♘+!!

7...♗g4+? is met by 8 ♘f3, while 7...fxg1♕ 8 ♕xd8+ ♔xd8 9 ♖xg1 is not bad for White.

8 ♔e1

8 ♖xg1 ♗g4+ wins the queen, now that the g1-knight no longer exists.

8...♕h4+ 9 ♔d2

Instead 9 g3 ♕e4+ picks off the h1-rook.

The position after 9 ♔d2 is hopeless for White, e.g. **9...♘c6 10 ♗c3 ♗g4** and 11...0-0-0+.

Trap: Cambridge Springs

1 d4 d5 2 c4 e6 3 ♘c3 ♘f6 4 ♗g5 ♘bd7 5 e3 c6 6 ♘f3 ♕a5

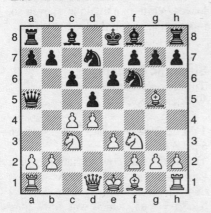

This is the Cambridge Springs Variation of the Orthodox Queen's Gambit Declined. Black has ideas of ...dxc4, ...♘e4 and ...♗b4, putting pressure on White's position. White should reply with 7 ♘d2 or perhaps 7 cxd5 ♘xd5 8 ♕d2, but must avoid a few traps; for example:

7 ♗d3? dxc4 8 ♗xc4 ♘e4 9 ♗f4 ♘xc3 10 bxc3 ♕xc3+

Black has a clear extra pawn.

Strategic Example
Garcia Palermo – Gelfand
Oakham 1988

1 d4 ♘f6 2 c4 e6 3 ♘f3 d5 4 ♘c3 dxc4 5 ♕a4+ ♘bd7?! 6 e4 c5 7 d5 exd5 8 e5 d4? 9 exf6 dxc3 10 ♗xc4 ♕xf6 11 ♗g5 ♕c6 12 0-0-0!

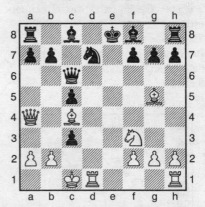

This brilliant move gives White an enormous advantage.

12...♗e7

Or:

a) 12...cxb2+ 13 ♔xb2 (13 ♔b1!?) 13...♗e7 14 ♖he1 f6 15 ♗b5 ♕b6 (15...♕c7 16 ♗f4) 16 ♔c1 fxg5 17 ♗xd7+ ♔f8 18 ♖xe7! ♔xe7 19 ♕e4+ ♔d8 20 ♗f5+ ♔c7 21 ♕e5+ ♔c6 22 ♖d6+ ♔b5 23 ♕b2+ 1-0 Taimanov–Polugaevsky, USSR 1960.

b) 12...♕xa4 is no better in view of 13 ♖he1+ ♗e7 14 ♖xe7+ ♔f8 15

♖xf7+ ♔g8 (15...♔e8 16 ♖e1+ ♘e5 17 ♖xe5+ ♗e6 18 ♗xe6) 16 ♖fxd7+ ♕xc4 17 ♖d8+ ♔f7 18 ♘e5+ regaining the queen, having picked up an extra piece along the way.

13 ♕xc6 bxc6 14 ♗xe7 cxb2+ 15 ♔xb2 ♗xe7 16 ♖he1+ ♔d8 17 ♘e5 ♔c7 18 ♘xd7 ♗xd7 19 ♖e7 ♖ad8 20 ♗xf7 ♖hf8 21 f3 1-0

Trap: Queen's Gambit Accepted
Illescas – Sadler
Linares Z 1995

1 d4 d5 2 c4 dxc4 3 e4 ♘c6 4 ♗e3 ♘f6 5 ♘c3 e5 6 d5 ♘a5 7 ♘f3

7 ♕a4+ c6 8 b4 cxb3 9 axb3 is interesting.

7...♗d6

Better than 7...a6?! 8 ♘xe5, Kamsky–Salov, Sanghi Nagar Ct (5) 1995.

8 ♕a4+

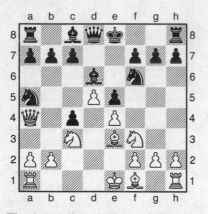

The immediate impact of Illescas's loss in this game suggested that this move itself fell into a trap. However, this is not so; his error came later.

8...♗d7!?

8...c6 9 dxc6 ♘xc6 10 ♗xc4 is good for White.

9 ♕xa5

Otherwise White is simply a pawn down.

9...a6!

This is Sadler's idea: the white queen is short of squares.

10 ♘b1?

Other moves:

a) 10 ♗xc4 b6 11 ♕xa6 ♖xa6 12 ♗xa6 was played in Karpov–Lautier, Monaco 5th Amber rpd 1996, but only Black seemed to have any winning chances – a draw was the result.

b) 10 b4 b6 11 ♕a3 a5 12 ♕c1 axb4 13 ♘e2 ♘xe4! 14 ♕xc4 f5 gives Black good play.

c) 10 ♘a4 is suggested as best by René Mayer in the Spanish magazine *Jaque*. He has a point: this move is the only way to cover the b6-square. 10...♘xe4 (10...b6 11 ♘xb6 cxb6 12 ♗xb6 ♕e7 13 a3 ♘xe4 14 ♗xc4 is extremely good for White) 11 ♗xc4 b5 12 ♗d3 ♕e7 13 a3 is unclear.

10...♘xe4 11 ♔d1 c3! 0-1

12 b4 b6 13 ♕a3 a5 14 ♕c1 axb4 leaves White in a total mess; even so, most players would have battled on.

Strategic Example
Topalov – Kramnik
Wijk aan Zee 2008

1 d4 d5 2 c4 c6 3 ♘f3 ♘f6 4 ♘c3 e6 5 ♗g5 h6

This is the Moscow Variation, which is now a good deal more popular than the Botvinnik System, 5...dxc4 6 e4 b5 7 e5, which was for a long time the dominant line here. There is no very clear reason for the switch from one move to the other in this line of the Semi-Slav, but the fact that Botvinnik System theory has been worked out in phenomenal detail is surely relevant. Anyone playing 5...dxc4 has to be willing to accept that the game may be decided by the quality of preparation in a very forcing line such as 5...dxc4 6 e4 b5 7 e5 h6 8 ♗h4 g5 9 ♘xg5 hxg5 10 ♗xg5 ♘bd7 11 exf6 ♗b7 12 g3 c5 13 d5 ♕b6 14 ♗g2 0-0-0 15 0-0 b4 16 ♖b1 ♕a6 17 dxe6 ♗xg2 18 e7.

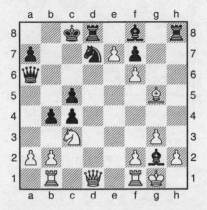

This is just one of many such lines where chaotic tactics play the leading role. While the Moscow Variation can also lead to exceptionally complex positions, there is generally a lot more scope for over-the-board creativity, and the structure remains more fluid, providing greater strategic variety.

6 ♗h4

In the days when the Moscow was just a rare sideline, 6 ♗xf6 ♕xf6 was the normal continuation, with a general presumption that White's greater freedom should provide him with some advantage. Closer examination in the 1990s overturned this notion, with Black finding ways to stabilize the position, and then seek to open

lines for his bishops, particularly in some apparently risky set-ups with ...g6. The text-move's status was initially that of a somewhat reckless and marginal gambit, but as Black's most obvious replies were mown down one by one, it became clear that White's amorphous compensation was in fact of a highly sturdy nature.

6...dxc4 7 e4 g5

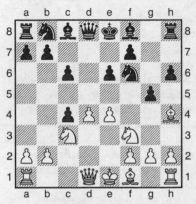

This is the key difference from the Botvinnik System. White is making a true pawn sacrifice, and will not win material back with a temporary sacrifice on g5.

8 ♗g3 b5 9 ♗e2

This calm move is considered best. After 9 ♘e5, 9...h5 10 h4 g4 11 ♗e2 ♗b7 12 0-0 ♘bd7 was shown by Anand to be an accurate move-order for Black. 13 ♕c2 ♘xe5 14 ♗xe5 ♗g7 15 ♖ad1 0-0 16 ♗g3 ♘d7 17 f3 c5! and Black went on to win in Aronian–Anand, Mexico City Wch 2007.

9...♗b7

The Anti-Moscow received a huge boost when 9...b4 10 ♘a4 ♘xe4 11 ♗e5 ♘f6 12 ♘c5! was shown to be extremely dangerous for Black.

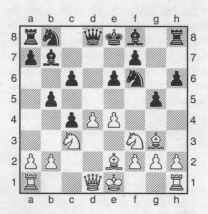

10 0-0

After a fair amount of investigation of the alternatives, this move has become established as the main line. It is the most flexible move unless White wants to play h4, but once White had given up on finding a viable way to implement this idea, the case for castling became clear.

a) 10 h4 has fallen somewhat from grace after 10...b4 11 ♘a4 ♘xe4 12 ♗e5 ♖g8 13 ♕c2 c5 14 ♗xc4 g4 15 ♗b5+ ♘d7 turned out well for Black in I.Sokolov–Dreev, Dos Hermanas 2001.

b) 10 e5 reduces White's options, and is thus easier to handle:

b1) 10...♘h5 was played in a top-level game when the Anti-Moscow Variation was largely virgin territory (Kramnik–Anand, Belgrade 1997). Anand then analysed 11 ♘xg5 ♘xg3 12 ♘xf7 ♔xf7 13 fxg3 ♔g8 (another idea is 13...♔e8) 14 0-0 ♘d7 15 ♗g4 (15 ♗xc4 bxc4 16 ♕g4+ ♗g7 17 ♕xe6+ ♔h7 is only a draw since 18 ♖f7? is met by 18...♖f8!) 15...♕e7 16 ♕c2 as most likely favouring White, but there are many complex variations possible here.

b2) 10...♘d5 has been preferred in practice, when 11 h4 g4 12 ♘d2 h5 13 ♘de4 ♘d7 leads to a more conventional gambit position, where White may have enough resources to keep the game sharp and unclear.

10...♘bd7 11 ♘e5 ♗g7

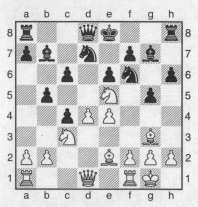

12 ♘xf7!?

This was Topalov's extraordinary idea, prepared in great detail in 2005 for use against Kramnik in particular, but in their 2006 match, Kramnik did not allow this line. It is by no means clear whether the sacrifice is good, or even adequate, but until Topalov is challenged to repeat it against a fully prepared opponent, it is very hard to say for sure. Facing it over the board, it is no surprise that Kramnik soon stumbled.

12 ♘xd7 ♘xd7 13 ♗d6 a6 had been played previously, with Black seeming to survive in the most critical lines, but with plenty of scope for new ideas remaining:

a) 14 ♗h5 ♗f8! 15 ♗xf8 ♖xf8 16 e5 ♕b6 17 b3 0-0-0 18 bxc4 ♘xe5 19 c5 ♕a5 20 ♘e4 and now 20...♘c4!? was Anand's improvement over Kramnik–Anand, Mexico

City Wch 2007, a critical game that he drew with some difficulty.

b) 14 a4 e5!.

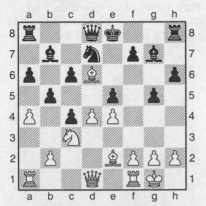

15 ♗g4 (15 d5 c5 16 b4 ♕b6! leads to equality; 15 ♖e1 ♕f6 16 ♗a3 is Kramnik's latest try) 15...exd4 16 e5 c5! (16...dxc3? 17 e6) 17 ♗f3 (17 ♖e1 ♘xe5 18 ♗xe5 0-0 and the pawns counterbalance the piece) 17...♘xe5! 18 ♗xb7 ♕xd6 19 ♗xa8 0-0 was shown in a computer game to be (probably!) OK for Black.

12...♔xf7 13 e5

13 f4 had been played in two obscure Romanian correspondence games.

13...♘d5

Topalov now activates his forces to the maximum before seeking to force matters, and will tailor his play according to Black's set-up.

14 ♘e4 ♔e7 15 ♘d6 ♕b6 16 ♗g4 ♖af8 17 ♕c2 ♕xd4?

Now Black falls into deep trouble. 17...♖hg8 is the critical line:

a) 18 a4? ♗a8 19 ♖fe1 ♘c7 didn't look vigorous enough to justify White's sacrifice in the game Timman–Ljubojevic, Wijk aan Zee 2008 (which was played the day after our main game).

b) 18 ♖ad1 c5 19 ♕g6 ♘c7 20 ♘xb7 cxd4 21 ♕e4 d3 (21...♘d5!?) 22 ♖xd3 cxd3 23 ♕b4+ ♘c5 24 ♘xc5 a5 25 ♕a3 ♖d8 (Bromberger–Sandipan, Zurich 2009) 26 ♘xd3+ b4 27 ♕b3 and the game remains undecided.

c) 18 ♕g6 ♘c7 19 ♕e4 ♗a8 20 f4 ♔d8 and White is yet to prove the strength of his attack.

18 ♕g6! ♕xg4 19 ♕xg7+ ♔d8 20 ♘xb7+ ♔c8 21 a4!

Opening lines on the queenside while keeping options open for the b7-knight; it doesn't have to move yet.

21...b4 22 ♖ac1

Threatening 23 ♖xc4! ♕xc4 24 ♘d6+.

22...c3 23 bxc3 b3!? 24 c4! ♖fg8 25 ♘d6+ ♔c7 26 ♕f7 ♖f8

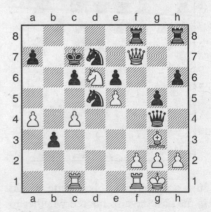

27 cxd5?

Kasparov claimed 27 h3! ♖xf7 28 hxg4 ♘f4 29 ♘xf7 ♘e2+ 30 ♔h2 ♘xc1 31 ♖xc1 ♖b8 to be winning for White when watching the game live on PlayChess.com.

27...♖xf7 28 ♖xc6+ ♔b8 29 ♘xf7 ♖e8?

Now Kasparov indicated 29...♕e2!, with the point 30 ♘xh8 ♕xf1+! 31 ♔xf1 b2 32 ♖xe6 b1♕+.

30 ♘d6 ♖h8 31 ♖c4! ♕e2 32 dxe6
♘b6 33 ♖b4 ♔a8 34 e7 ♘d5 35
♖xb3 ♘xe7 36 ♖fb1 ♘d5 37 h3 h5
38 ♘f7 ♖c8 39 e6! a6 40 ♘xg5 h4
41 ♗d6! ♖g8 42 ♖3b2 ♕d3 43 e7
♘f6 44 ♗e5! ♘d7 45 ♘e6 1-0

This game is an excellent example of
the modern tendency to make long-
term sacrifices for the initiative,
backed up by deep preparation.

Strategic Example
Vokač – Cvetković
Trnava 1988

1 d4 ♘f6 2 c4 e6 3 ♘f3 d5 4 ♘c3
♘bd7 5 ♗g5 c6 6 ♕c2 h6

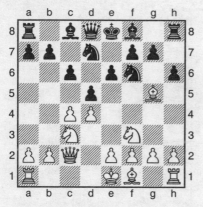

In a position like this, White would
in the past have wondered whether to
exchange on f6, and if not, then
where the bishop should retreat.

7 cxd5

However, against Portisch in 1986, in
a similar position, Kasparov introduced this piece sacrifice idea.

7...hxg5

7...exd5 allows White to choose the
more active retreat 8 ♗f4 since there
is no danger of it getting hit by a
knight coming to d5.

8 dxe6 fxe6 9 ♘xg5

White has only two pawns for the
piece, but the black king will have a
rough time.

9...♔e7 10 e4 ♘h7 11 ♘f3 ♔f7 12
h4 ♗b4 13 ♗c4 ♘hf8 14 ♖h3

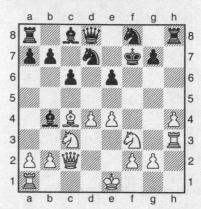

14...♔g8 15 a3 ♗xc3+ 16 ♕xc3
♖h6 17 0-0-0 b5 18 ♗b3 b4 19
♕xb4 ♖b8 20 ♕c3 ♕b6 21 ♘g5
♕xb3 22 ♕xb3 ♖xb3 23 ♖xb3
♖xh4 24 g3 ♖h2 25 f4 ♗a6 26 ♖c3
♗b7 27 ♖d2 ♖h1+ 28 ♔c2 ♖g1 29
♖h2 a5 30 a4 ♖a1 31 g4 ♘f6 32
♖ch3 ♘g6 33 f5 ♘xg4 34 fxg6
♘xh2 35 ♖b3! ♖xa4 36 ♖xb7 ♔f8
37 ♘xe6+ ♔e8 38 ♘xg7+ 1-0

Strategic Example
Magerramov – Oll
Klaipeda 1988

1 d4 d5 2 c4 c6 3 ♘f3 ♘f6 4 ♘c3 e6
5 ♗g5 dxc4 6 e4 b5

This is the Semi-Slav Anti-Meran
Gambit (a.k.a. Botvinnik System), one
of the sharpest opening lines. Black
hangs on to the c-pawn, establishing a
big queenside majority, but White now
gains ground on the kingside.

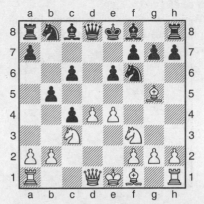

7 e5 h6 8 **♗h4** g5 9 **♘xg5** hxg5 10 **♗xg5 ♘bd7** 11 g3 **♕a5** 12 exf6 b4 13 **♘e4 ♗a6** 14 **♕f3** 0-0-0?! 15 **♗e2 ♘b6**?! 16 **♗e3 ♗b7** 17 0-0 c5 18 dxc5 **♘a4** 19 **♗xc4 ♘xb2**

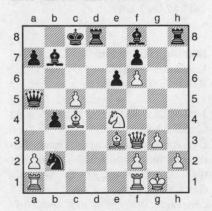

Now White decided it was time to launch the final attack, and invests some heavy material to open up the black king.

20 c6 **♗xc6** 21 **♖ac1 ♔b7** 22 **♗xe6!** fxe6 23 **♖xc6! ♔xc6** 24 **♖c1+ ♔d7** 25 f7 **♘d3** 26 **♘f6+ ♔d6** 27 **♘e8+ ♔e7** 28 **♗g5+ ♔xg5** 29 **♖c7+** 1-0

Black decided not to allow 29...♖d7 30 ♖xd7+ ♔xd7 31 ♕b7+ ♔d8 32 ♕c7# to appear on the board.

Strategic Example
Chiburdanidze – Peng Zhaoqin
Belgrade wom 1996

1 d4 d5 2 c4 c6 3 **♘f3 ♘f6** 4 e3 **♗f5** 5 **♘c3** e6 6 **♘h4 ♗g4** 7 **♕b3 ♕b6** 8 h3 **♗f5** 9 g4 **♗g6** 10 **♘xg6** hxg6 11 **♗g2 ♘a6** 12 **♗d2 ♗e7** 13 c5 **♕xb3** 14 axb3

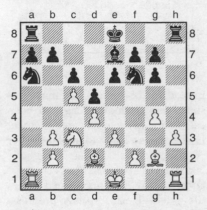

White has quite a pleasant grip on the position, and can exert some queenside pressure, though it's hard to believe that Black should be in great danger of losing. Let's see how the former women's world champion turns the screws.

14...**♘c7** 15 b4 a6 16 **♔e2 ♖c8** 17 f3 **♘d7** 18 f4 f5 19 g5!

White signals her intention to break things open with h4-h5 at some point.

19...**♘b5** 20 **♗f3 ♔f7** 21 **♗e1 ♘b8** 22 **♗f2 ♖h7** 23 h4 **♖ch8** 24 **♔d3 ♗d8** 25 **♔c2 ♗c7** 26 **♗e2 ♖c8** 27 **♔b3 ♘a7**

Foisor suggests that it would be better to play 27...♖ch8; we shall soon see why.

28 **♖h2 ♗d8** 29 **♖ah1 ♗e7**

Now a big surprise.

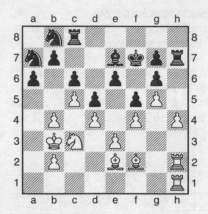

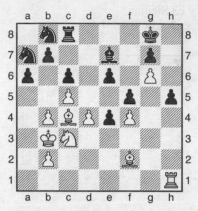

30 e4!?

Instead 30 h5 (which we may presume was the move Peng had been calculating at each plausible moment in the game) leads to nothing after 30...♖ch8.

30...dxe4

Otherwise White breaks open the e-file and will make speedy progress. 30...fxe4 31 h5 ♖ch8 32 hxg6+ ♔xg6 33 ♖xh7 ♖xh7 34 ♖xh7 ♔xh7 35 ♗g4 is similar.

31 h5 ♖xh5?!

31...♖ch8 32 hxg6+ ♔xg6 33 ♖xh7 ♖xh7 34 ♖xh7 ♔xh7 35 ♗c4 is White's marvellous idea, regaining the pawn and, with d5 soon to follow, making some major inroads. 31...gxh5 looks best: 32 g6+ (32 ♗xh5+ ♔f8 and now what does White play?) 32...♔xg6 33 ♗xh5+ ♖xh5 34 ♖xh5 is not too clear.

32 ♖xh5! gxh5 33 g6+ ♔g8?

33...♔e8 34 ♗c4 ♔d7 35 ♘a4 ♗d8 36 ♖xh5 ♗c7 37 ♖h7 ♖g8 38 ♗h4, intending ♗f6, is good for White in view of Black's hopelessly placed knights.

34 ♗c4

Now the game is decided.

34...♖e8 35 ♗xe6+ ♔f8 36 ♖xh5 ♗f6 37 ♗xf5 ♘b5 38 ♘xb5 axb5 39 ♖h8+ ♔e7 40 ♖xe8+ ♔xe8 41 ♗xe4 ♔e7 42 ♗f5 ♘a6 43 d5 cxd5 44 ♗c8 ♘c7 45 f5 ♔e8 46 ♗xb7 ♔d7 47 ♔c2 1-0

Strategic Example
Kaidanov – Hulak
Belgrade GMA 1988

1 c4 ♘f6 2 ♘c3 c5 3 ♘f3 e6 4 e3 ♘c6 5 d4 d5

By transposition, the game has reached the Symmetrical Variation of the Tarrasch Defence to the Queen's Gambit (1 d4 d5 2 c4 e6 3 ♘c3 c5 4 e3 ♘c6 5 ♘f3 ♘f6 is the "standard" move-order). Clearly, this is a position that can be reached by many move-orders.

6 cxd5 exd5

6...♘xd5 leads instead to a line of the Semi-Tarrasch, when 7 ♗d3 (or 7 ♗c4) 7...cxd4 8 exd4 often follows – this is another position, referred to as "The IQP Position", which can be reached from many openings, notably the Caro-Kann Panov Attack and the c3 Sicilian.

7 ♗e2 ♗d6 8 0-0 0-0

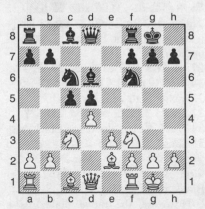

9 ♘b5

This move looks a little odd, but White is planning to exchange on c5, leaving Black with an isolated pawn on d5. He therefore wants to establish a solid base on the blockading square d4.

9...♗e7 10 dxc5 ♗xc5 11 b3 ♕e7 12 ♗b2 ♖d8 13 ♖c1 ♘e4

White certainly has a firm grip on d4, but Black in exchange has seized the e4-square, which may become the springboard for a kingside attack.

14 ♘bd4 ♖d6!?

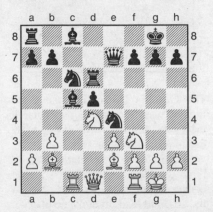

Black wastes no time bringing his pieces over to attack the white king. There's really no point being too subtle about it – it is Black's most logical plan.

15 ♘xc6

15 ♖xc5 ♘xc5 16 ♗a3 is a critical test of Black's play:

a) 16...b6 17 ♘xc6 ♖xc6 18 b4 ♘e4 19 b5 (19 ♕xd5?! ♗b7) 19...♕xa3 20 ♕xd5 is quite good for White, e.g. 20...♘c3 21 ♕xc6 ♘xe2+ 22 ♔h1 ♖b8 23 ♕c7 ♖a8 24 ♕d8+ ♕f8 25 ♕d2 a6 26 ♕xe2 axb5 – White's pawns are a little better.

b) 16...♖g6 was claimed to be good for Black by Rudolf Marić, but this may not be clear after 17 ♗d3 (and not 17 ♕c2 ♘xd4 18 exd4 ♕e4! 19 ♕xc5 ♗h3, which wins for Black).

15...bxc6 16 b4

16 ♖xc5!? ♘xc5 17 ♗a3 ♘e4 18 ♗xd6 ♕xd6 19 ♕c2 is certainly safe for White, and possibly mildly advantageous.

16...♗b6

16...♗xb4?! 17 ♕d4 ♖f6 18 ♖xc6 is good for White.

17 ♘e5 ♗b7

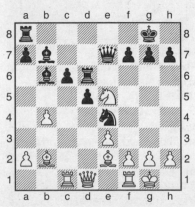

Not the bishop's dream square, but it is necessary to hold c6 while preparing the big attack with ...♖h6 and ...♗c7.

18 ♗d3 ♖e6!

White must give ground in the centre.

19 ♗xe4 dxe4 20 ♘c4 ♖d8

20...♕xb4 21 ♕g4 gives White a large share of the initiative.

21 ♕g4 f5!

21...♖g6 22 ♕f4 makes it difficult for Black to generate threats.

22 ♕xf5 ♖d5

Black is funnelling both rooks towards the white king.

23 ♕g4 ♗c7

Black now threatens 24...♖g6 and 25...♗xh2+.

24 f4 exf3 25 ♕xf3 c5

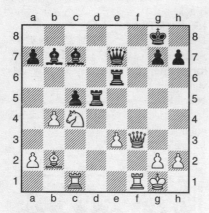

Black even succeeds in bringing his inactive bishop into the attack.

26 ♔h1

26 e4 ♖xe4 doesn't help White.

26...cxb4

26...♖h6 27 h3 ♖d2 is less powerful:

a) 28 ♕f8+ ♕xf8 29 ♖xf8+ ♔xf8 30 ♘xd2 ♖xh3+ 31 ♔g1 ♖g3 32 ♖f1+ ♔g8 33 ♖f2 cxb4 is good for Black (this is better than 33...♖xe3

34 ♘f1).

b) 28 e4 ♗xe4 29 ♕f8+ ♕xf8 30 ♖xf8+ ♔xf8 31 ♘xd2 ♖xh3+ 32 ♔g1 ♗xg2 33 ♖xc5 (33 ♔xg2 ♖h2+ is very good for Black) 33...♗d6 is unclear.

27 e4 ♖d8 28 ♘e3 ♗xe4 29 ♕g4 h5 30 ♕h3 ♗b6 31 ♘f5 ♕g5 32 ♘g3

32 ♘xg7 ♖g6 wins for Black.

32...♗d5 33 ♖f5 ♕d2 34 ♖xh5??

34 ♖cf1 ♖e1 is good for Black, e.g. 35 ♗xg7 ♖e6 or 35 ♖xh5 ♗xg2+ 36 ♕xg2 ♕xg2+ 37 ♔xg2 ♖d2+ 38 ♔h3 ♖xf1 39 ♘xf1 ♖xb2 gives Black a won ending.

However, the move played is a blunder, losing on the spot.

34...♕xc1+ 0-1

Queen's Indian Defence (1 d4 ♘f6 2 c4 e6 3 ♘f3 b6)

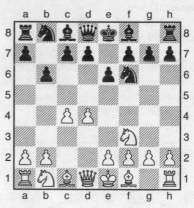

The Queen's Indian, like the Bogo-Indian, was tremendously popular in the 1980s, but has suffered due to the rise to prominence of 3 ♘c3.

White has three main systems. Firstly, 4 ♘c3 ♗b4 5 ♗g5 is a cross between the Queen's and Nimzo-Indians, and leads to dynamic play.

The traditional main line is 4 g3, starting a battle for control of the long diagonal. The most popular reply is 4...♗a6, causing White some inconvenience on the queenside. After 4...♗b7, one interesting possibility is Polugaevsky's pawn sacrifice 5 ♗g2 ♗e7 6 0-0 0-0 7 d5 exd5 8 ♘h4.

The line introduced by Petrosian, 4 a3, was viewed as a dull attempt for a slight edge, until Kasparov made it into a deadly winning weapon. The idea is simple: prevent ...♗b4, play ♘c3 and dominate the centre. Given the chance, White will block out the b7-bishop by playing d5, followed by e4. Thus Black normally replies 4...♗b7 5 ♘c3 d5, when after 6 cxd5 Black generally prefers the counter-play he gets after 6...♘xd5 rather than the static position following 6...exd5.

Trap: Queen's Indian, piece win
Christiansen – Karpov
Wijk aan Zee 1993

1 d4 ♘f6 2 c4 e6 3 ♘f3 b6 4 a3 ♗a6 5 ♕c2 ♗b7 6 ♘c3 c5 7 e4 cxd4 8 ♘xd4 ♘c6 9 ♘xc6 ♗xc6 10 ♗f4 ♘h5 11 ♗e3

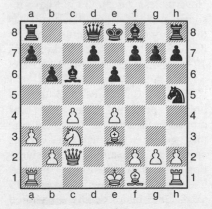

This seems like a fairly quiet position. Neither side threatens anything too drastic. White has a little more space, but Black's position is solid. Like Capablanca against Sämisch (Nimzo-Indian trap), Karpov forgot for one catastrophic moment that this did not mean that tactics were impossible.

11...♗d6??
11...♕b8 would be a rather better way to establish a grip on the f4-square, as indeed Karpov later played with success.

12 ♕d1
Two pieces attacked, and no way to save them. Oh dear.

1-0
The remarkable thing is that Karpov went on to win his mini-match against Christiansen after this initial set-back.

Queen's Pawn Opening (1 d4)

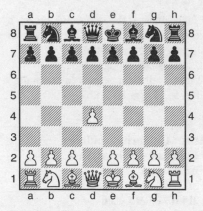

This name is given to a whole group of minor openings that start 1 d4, but do not reach standard openings, generally due to quiet play by White, often by holding back with the move c4.

Trap: Queen's Pawn, double attack
Maiwald – Bockius
Bad Wörishofen 1994

1 d4 ♘f6 2 ♘f3 e6 3 g3 b6 4 ♗g2 ♗b7 5 0-0 ♗e7 6 ♗g5 d6 7 ♕d3

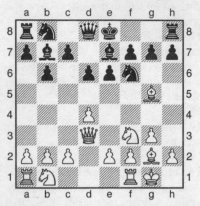

A cheeky but not illogical idea. Maiwald prevents castling, and begins a fight for control of e4.

7...0-0??

Black misses the idea, which is a very standard one, but generally in slightly different settings.

8 ♗xf6 ♗xf6 9 ♘g5! 1-0

White will win a whole exchange after 9...♗xg5 10 ♗xb7.

Trap: Chigorin avoidance
Langeweg – Dückstein
Zurich 1975

1 d4 d5 2 ♘f3 ♘c6

Black indicates his willingness to play a Chigorin Defence (1 d4 d5 2 c4 ♘c6), but with White unable to play the critical 3 ♘c3 or 3 cxd5.

3 ♗f4

A sensible move, controlling e5 and refusing to allow the position to become messy. In time, White hopes to show that the c6-knight is misplaced.

3...♗g4

The most consistent reply.

4 e3 e6 5 c4

White could develop and then think about playing this. Now Black becomes active.

5...♗b4+ 6 ♘bd2 ♘f6

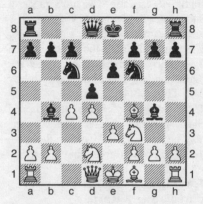

7 cxd5?

7 a3 ♗xd2+ 8 ♕xd2 isn't so bad for White, while 7 ♗g5 targets the f6-knight, but doesn't feel right.

7...♘e4 0-1

White has no way to defend d2. Nevertheless, he should not have resigned just yet, since Black still has to find one very difficult move: 8 dxc6 ♘xd2 (8...♗xd2+ 9 ♔e2 ♕d5 10 ♕a4; 8...♕d5? 9 ♕a4) 9 ♔e2 and now 9...♕d5 10 ♕a4 ♗xf3+ 11 gxf3 ♕xf3+ 12 ♔d3 ♕e4+ 13 ♔e2 is only a perpetual. This line was quoted by analysts as best play, and this game was cited in various sources as an example of a resignation in a drawn position. However, 9...b5! is very strong: 10 a3 ♕d5 11 axb4 ♘xf3 and a deadly discovered

check will follow; 10 h3 ♕d5 11
hxg4? ♕c4+ 12 ♔e1 ♘xf3#; or 10
♕c2 ♕d5 11 e4 ♘xe4 with an excellent position for Black.

Strategic Example
Plaskett – K. Arkell
London 1991

**1 ♘f3 ♘f6 2 d4 e6 3 e3 c5 4 ♗d3
b6 5 0-0 ♗b7 6 c4 ♗e7 7 ♘c3 cxd4
8 exd4 d5 9 cxd5 ♘xd5**
Here we have an IQP position, but
one in which Black has been able to
fianchetto his queen's bishop earlier
than normal.
10 ♘e5

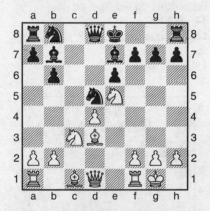

Black must attend to the threat of 11
♗b5+.
10...0-0 11 ♕g4
This highly aggressive thrust is very
much in Plaskett's style.
11...♘f6 12 ♕h4
Black now has a very plausible losing move. Arkell played it.
12...♘c6?
12...♘bd7 is quite all right, while
12...♘e4 may well be playable too.
    Now events develop by force.
13 ♗g5

Threatening, of course, 14 ♗xf6.
13...g6
13...h6 14 ♗xf6 ♗xf6 (14...gxf6 15
♕xh6 f5 16 ♘xc6 ♗xc6 17 ♗xf5
exf5 18 ♕xc6 ♕xd4 is awful for
Black) 15 ♕e4 wins a piece, e.g.
15...g6 16 ♘xc6 ♕d6 17 ♕f3 ♗g7
18 ♗e4 f5 19 ♘e7+.

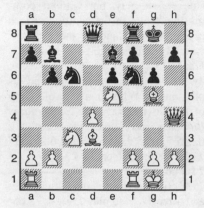

14 ♗a6!
This is the sort of move a good computer will find in a split second, but
humans will struggle over, unless
they're looking for it. The point is
that Black's bishops are both overloaded defending knights, and it just
so happens that a white knight landing on c6 will fork d8 and e7.
14...h6
14...♘xe5 15 dxe5 ♗xa6 16 exf6 and
♕h6 mates. 14...♗xa6 15 ♘xc6 followed by taking on e7 and c6.
15 ♗xh6 ♘d5 16 ♕h3 ♘xc3
16...♗xa6 17 ♘xc6 wins White a lot
of material.
**17 ♗xb7 ♘e2+ 18 ♔h1 ♘cxd4 19
♗xf8 ♗xf8 20 ♗xa8 ♕xa8**
A loss of two exchanges is too much
even for Keith Arkell.
**21 ♕e3 ♕d5 22 ♖ae1 ♗d6 23 f4 g5
24 ♖xe2 1-0**

Strategic Example
Galliamova – Akopian
Oakham 1990

1 ♘f3 ♘f6 2 g3 g6 3 ♗g2 ♗g7 4 d4 0-0 5 0-0 d6 6 a4

This odd move hopes to gain space, and limit Black's scope for queenside counterplay, but without committing White in the centre so much as the more standard move 6 c4, which is a Fianchetto King's Indian.

6...a5

Two alternatives were analysed as pleasant for White in a very old copy of the Soviet magazine *Shakhmatny Biulleten* (no longer in existence): 6...c5 7 dxc5 dxc5 8 a5 and 6...♘bd7 7 a5 e5 8 dxe5 dxe5 9 ♘c3.

7 b3 c6

7...♘c6 is possible, intending ...e5, and after dxe5, to play ...♘g4. 7...e5! 8 dxe5 dxe5 9 ♗a3 (9 ♗b2 e4 10 ♕xd8 ♖xd8 11 ♘g5 ♗f5 12 ♘a3 h6 13 ♘h3 ♘c6 is fine for Black) 9...e4! 10 ♗xf8 ♕xf8 11 ♘d4 e3! gives Black excellent compensation according to analysis in the same issue of *Shakhmatny Biulleten*.

8 ♗b2

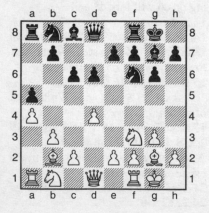

8...♘bd7

8...d5 is a good way to stodge things up, and ought to be fairly equal. When White's play has been so quiet, Black can afford to lose a little time (i.e. by using two moves rather than one to advance the d-pawn from d7 to d5), especially to make the b2-bishop look silly. However, Akopian, as the substantially higher rated player, would have been looking to win this game, and so felt it necessary to keep more dynamism in the position. However, White possesses most of this dynamism.

9 ♘bd2 ♕c7 10 e4 e5 11 dxe5 dxe5 12 ♖e1 ♖d8 13 ♘c4 ♘e8

Preventing an invasion on d6.

14 ♕e2 b6

14...f6, intending ...♘f8 and ...♗e6, has been suggested.

15 ♖ad1 ♗a6

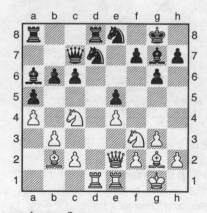

16 ♗h3!? ♘f8

16...f6 seems both necessary and sufficient: 17 ♗e6+ (17 ♖xd7 ♖xd7 18 ♗xd7 ♕xd7) 17...♔h8 18 ♗a3 appears to put Black under severe pressure, but 18...♘f8, with ...b5 to follow, looks rather good.

17 ♖xd8 ♖xd8 18 ♗xe5!

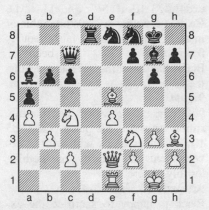

This move initiates tremendous complications, but the girl from Kazan had everything worked out.

18...♗xe5 19 ♘fxe5 b5

After this, Akopian gets blown out of the water, but otherwise he is just worse. White now exploits the deficiencies of Black's queenside set-up.

20 ♘xa5! ♖a8

The a6-bishop needs to be defended. 20...♕xa5 21 ♘xc6 ♕b6 22 ♘xd8 ♕xd8 23 axb5 gives White rook and four pawns for two knights.

21 ♘exc6

Alisa keeps on eating.

21...bxa4 22 ♕d2 ♗b5

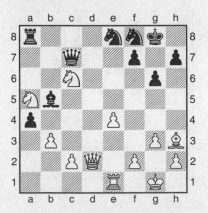

Crunch time. Can White rescue her knights?

23 ♘d4!

Though not the only way, this is the neatest solution.

23...♗d7

23...♖xa5 24 b4, forcing the rook away from the defence of the bishop, is the very nice point; 23...♕xa5 24 ♕xa5 ♖xa5 25 b4 is similar.

24 ♗xd7 ♘xd7 25 b4

25 ♘c4, with ♖a1 to follow, is simpler.

25...♘e5 26 f4 ♘c4 27 ♕c3

This returns a pawn to simplify the position. Instead 27 ♘xc4 ♕xc4 leaves White having to cope with the a-pawn's nuisance value.

27...♘xa5 28 ♕xc7 ♘xc7 29 bxa5 ♖xa5 30 ♔f2 ♔f8 31 ♔e3 ♔e8 32 ♖a1 ♔d7 33 ♔d3

33 ♘b3?? loses to 33...axb3! 34 ♖xa5 b2.

33...a3 34 c3 ♘a6 35 ♘c2 ♘c5+ 36 ♔e3 a2 37 ♘b4 ♖a3 38 ♖xa2 ♖xc3+ 39 ♔d4 ♖c1 40 ♖a7+ ♔e8 41 ♖a8+ ♔d7 42 ♘d5

White has emerged with only one extra pawn, but her active king and much better coordinated pieces seal Black's fate.

42...♘b7 43 ♘f6+ ♔e6 44 ♘xh7 ♘d6 45 ♘g5+ ♔e7 46 ♖a7+ ♔f8 47 ♔d5 ♖d1+ 48 ♔c6 ♔e8 49 e5 ♘c8 50 ♖xf7 1-0

Strategic Example
Velikov – Dorfman
Palma de Mallorca GMA 1989

1 ♘f3 g6 2 g3 ♗g7 3 d4

Otherwise Black may seize control of the centre, viz. 3 ♗g2 e5 4 d3 d5.

For Black to occupy the centre is not necessarily a good thing, but he is certainly not overextended here, and he retains a great deal of flexibility with his piece placement. White will have to work hard to make any real dent in Black's centre.

3...c5

Having threatened an occupation of the centre, Black reverts to the role of sniper.

4 c3 b6?!

Now if White continues routinely, Black's bishop will proceed to b7, neutralizing White's kingside fianchetto. However, his move does have the drawback of losing a pawn.

5 dxc5

5 ♗g2 ♗b7 6 0-0 ♘f6 is quite satisfactory for Black.

5...bxc5

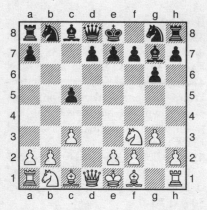

Rather amusingly, Dave Norwood once, in the game Galliamova–Norwood, Prestwich 1990, played this line accidentally with Black, not realizing that he was losing a pawn!

6 ♕d5 ♘c6 7 ♕xc5 ♘f6

7...♗b7 was analysed by Dorfman as not providing compensation: 8 ♗g2 ♘d4 (8...♖c8 9 ♕b5 ♗a8 10 0-0) 9 cxd4 ♖c8 10 ♕g5!? ♗h6 11 ♕xh6 ♘xh6 12 ♗xh6 gives White a lot of material for the queen.

8 ♗g2 ♗a6

Black has irritating pressure against the e2-pawn.

9 ♘d4

9 0-0 might be worth considering, simply returning the pawn. 9 ♕e3 d5 10 0-0 leaves Black with a lot of development and activity, but nothing terribly concrete.

9...♘xd4 10 ♕xd4 0-0!

Black is happy to sacrifice the exchange here, which is just as well, since 10...d5?? drops the bishop to 11 ♕a4+, while 10...♖c8 11 ♕xa7 causes disruption.

11 ♗xa8

11 ♕d1 d5 again gives Black development as compensation; 11 ♕a4 is an interesting alternative, looking to win the exchange in improved circumstances – then 11...♕b6 12 ♗xa8 does not bring the black queen to an active position on the long diagonal. Nevertheless, White faces an arduous defensive task.

11...♕xa8 12 f3

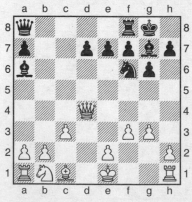

12...e5!

Having sacrificed so much material, Black's task is clear: to open the position at all cost.

13 ♕d1

13 ♕d6 ♕b7 14 ♗g5 e4 15 ♗xf6 ♗xf6 16 ♕xf6 ♕xb2 and now 17 0-0? ♗xe2 wins for Black: 18 ♖f2 (or 18 ♖e1 ♗xf3) 18...e3! 19 ♖xe2 ♕xe2 20 ♘a3 ♕f2+ 21 ♔h1 e2, while 17 ♕xa6 ♕c1+ 18 ♔f2 ♕xh1 (Dorfman) should give Black at least a draw, since White has problems developing his queenside pieces.

13...e4 14 ♔f2

14 0-0 exf3 15 exf3 (15 ♖xf3?! ♖e8) 15...♗xf1 16 ♕xf1 ♖e8 (Dorfman) gives Black good play for the pawn.

14...♖e8 15 ♖e1 ♕c6

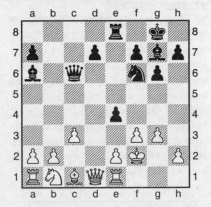

The queen begins a journey to h3 – after all, Black has invested a lot for control of the light squares, so he may as well use them!

16 ♘a3

16 ♗g5 looks fairly good. Then 16...exf3 17 exf3 ♕c5+ 18 ♗e3 ♖xe3 19 ♖xe3 ♘d5 20 ♕e1 ♗h6 21 f4 g5 is given by Dorfman, but after 22 b4 ♕b6 23 ♔f3 it isn't clear how Black is to proceed.

On the other hand, 16 ♗e3 exf3 17

exf3 ♘g4+!! 18 fxg4 ♗b7 19 ♖g1 (19 ♔e2? ♕g2+ 20 ♔d3 ♗e4+ 21 ♔c4 d5+ wins for Black; 19 ♖e2 ♕f3+ 20 ♔e1 ♖xe3 21 ♖xe3 ♕xe3+ 22 ♕e2 ♕c1+ 23 ♔f2 and again White has problems with his queenside pieces) 19...♕f6+ 20 ♗f4 ♕b6+ is a draw.

16...♕e6 17 ♘c2

17 ♔g2? exf3+ 18 ♔xf3 ♕e4+ and Black mates.

17...♕h3 18 ♔g1 ♖e5 19 ♗f4!

Apart from this move, there are many ways for White to get into very hot water:

a) 19 ♕d6? exf3 wins.

b) 19 ♘e3 ♖h5 20 ♘g2 ♕xh2+ 21 ♔f2 ♖f5 threatens mate in two, and 22 ♗f4 c3+ makes good use of the various pins: 23 ♔xe3 ♕xg2.

c) 19 g4 ♘xg4! 20 fxg4 ♕xg4+ 21 ♔h1 (21 ♔f2 ♖f5+ 22 ♗f4 e3+! 23 ♘xe3 ♖xf4#) 21...e3 22 ♘d4 (22 ♖f1 ♖h5 is a forced mate, e.g. 23 ♘xe3 ♖xh2+ 24 ♔xh2 ♗e5+ 25 ♖f4 ♗xf4+ 26 ♔h1 ♕h3+ 27 ♔g1 ♕h2+ 28 ♔f1 ♗g3 and mate next move) 22...♗b7+ 23 ♘f3 ♖h5 24 ♗xe3 ♗e5 forces mate.

19...♖d5!

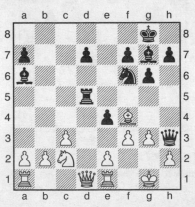

A cunning move, disrupting White's defence, which might otherwise hang by a thread.

20 ♘d4

20 ♕c1 ♖h5 21 g4 exf3 22 exf3 ♕xf3 (since the white queen no longer defends this pawn) 23 gxh5 ♗b7 and now 24 ♖e8+ (24 ♘e3 ♘g4 mates) 24...♘xe8 25 ♘e1 (25 ♕d2? ♘f6 is no good for White; 25 ♕f1 ♕h1+ 26 ♔f2 ♕e4 27 ♕c1 allows Black to take an immediate draw or try for more with 27...♘f6) 25...♕h1+ 26 ♔f2 ♘f6 (with the threat of 27...♘g4+ 28 ♔e2 ♕e4+ 29 ♔f1 ♕c4+ 30 ♕c5+) 27 ♔e2 (threatening to unravel, e.g. 28 ♕e3) 27...♘xh5 looks quite attractive for Black.

20...♖h5 21 g4 ♘d5 22 ♕b3

22 ♕c1? ♘xf4 23 ♕xf4 ♗e5 24 ♕e4 ♕xh2+ 25 ♔f1 ♗g3 forces mate; 22 ♗g3? ♘e3 wins.

22...♘xf4 23 ♕b8+ ♗c8!

23...♗f8 24 ♕xf4 is no use to Black.

24 ♕xc8+ ♗f8 25 ♔f2

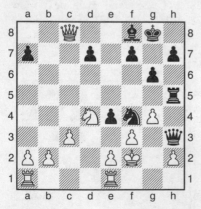

25...♖e5

Instead 25...♘d5! is decisive:

a) 26 ♖h1 e3+ 27 ♔e1 ♕g2 28 ♖f1 ♖xh2.

b) 26 ♖g1 ♕h4+ 27 ♖g3 ♕xh2+ 28 ♖g2 e3+! (even stronger than 28...♕h4+) 29 ♔f1 ♕h1+ 30 ♖g1 ♕h4 31 ♖g2 ♘f4 32 gxh5 ♕h3 forces mate.

c) 26 ♕b8 e3+ 27 ♔g1 d6 28 gxh5 ♘f4.

26 ♔e3 exf3+ 27 ♔xf4

27 ♔d2 f2 wins for Black.

27...d6 28 e4

White is mated in the event of 28 ♘xf3 g5+ 29 ♘xg5 ♕e3#.

28...f2 29 ♘f3 fxe1♕ 30 ♖xe1 h5

30...g5+ and 30...♖e6 are more methodical.

31 ♘xe5

31 ♖g1 is a sturdier defence, when Black would resort to 31...♖e6.

31...dxe5+ 32 ♔g5

32 ♔xe5 ♕xh2+ 33 ♔d5 ♕d2+ and 34...♕xe1, winning.

32...♔g7

It is always very satisfying to see a king participating in a mating attack against its opposite number.

33 ♕d7 ♕xg4+ 0-1

Velikov was rather a spoilsport to resign at this point; would it have been so much effort to allow a pretty mate, viz. 34 ♕xg4 ♗e7#?

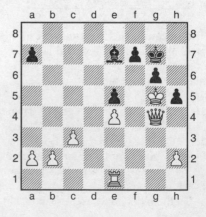

Schmid Benoni (1 d4 c5 2 d5 e5)

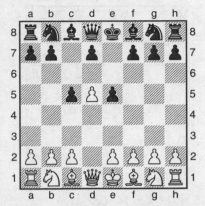

This is similar to the Czech Benoni, but White has not played c4, and can rely more on piece-play, while Black can play the exchanging manoeuvre ...♗e7-g5 more quickly. One very interesting line is 3 e4 d6 4 ♘c3 ♗e7 5 ♘f3 ♗g4 6 h3 ♗xf3 7 ♕xf3 ♗g5 8 ♗xg5 ♕xg5 9 ♘b5 ♕d8 10 ♕g4 ♔f8 11 ♘xd6 ♘f6 12 ♕c8 ♕xc8 13 ♘xc8 ♘xe4. The term "Schmid Benoni" is also used to refer to other Benoni structures without an early c4.

Snake Benoni (1 d4 ♘f6 2 c4 c5 3 d5 e6 4 ♘c3 exd5 5 cxd5 ♗d6)

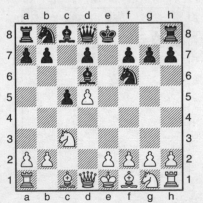

This is a highly eccentric opening that attained some notoriety in the 1980s. The idea of putting the bishop on c7 has some points, and bemused players for quite a while, but eventually things calmed down and the Snake stopped being so much fun for Black. Most notably, White can play 6 g3 with ♗g2 to follow. The king's knight retains the option of going to h3 and then to f4. This also makes the plan of playing d6 when Black drops the bishop back to c7 a better idea.

Torre Attack (1 d4 ♘f6 2 ♘f3 e6 3 ♗g5 or 1 d4 ♘f6 2 ♘f3 g6 3 ♗g5)

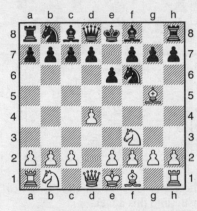

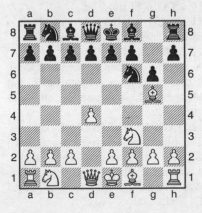

The Torre Attack is a simple opening, which largely avoids complex theory. The version against 2...e6 has rather the more bite, and can lead to some good attacks.

Strategic Example
G. Mohr – Anand
Belgrade GMA 1988

1 d4 d5 2 ♘f3 ♘f6 3 ♗g5 e6
3...♘e4 is a good active move.
4 e3 c5 5 ♘bd2 ♘bd7 6 c3 ♗e7 7 ♗d3 b6 8 ♘e5 ♗b7 9 f4 0-0?!

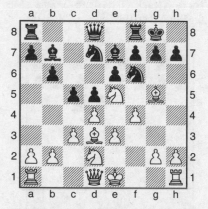

There was no real need for Black to castle into this attack.
10 ♕f3 h6 11 h4! ♘e8
11...hxg5? 12 hxg5 brings about a catastrophe for Black on the h-file.
12 ♗xh6!?
A sacrifice to open up the black king. It cannot be analysed to a finish, but Mohr must have intuitively felt it was good value.
12...gxh6 13 ♕h5 f5 14 g4 ♘g7
The older engines liked 14...♖f6 15 ♖g1 ♘g7 16 gxf5 exf5, but 17 0-0-0, threatening ♖xg7+, is good for White; e.g., 17...♗f8 18 ♗xf5 ♖xf5 19 ♕xf5 ♘xe5 20 dxe5.

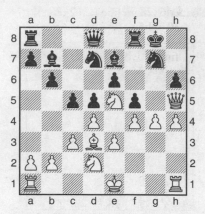

15 ♕xh6 ♖f6 16 ♘g6 ♖xg6
16...♔f7 17 h5 fxg4 18 ♖g1 threatens 19 ♖xg4 and 19 ♘f3.
17 ♕xg6 ♘f8 18 ♕h6 fxg4 19 0-0-0 ♘f5
19...♕e8!? 20 ♖dg1 ♕h5 21 ♕xh5 ♘xh5 22 ♖xg4+ ♔f7 23 ♘f3 gives White the chances.
20 ♕h5 ♘xe3 21 ♖de1 cxd4 22 ♖xe3!
22 cxd4 ♕c7+ 23 ♔b1 ♕xf4 24 ♖hf1 ♘xf1 25 ♖xf1 is only a draw.
22...dxe3 23 ♕xg4+ ♔f7 24 ♕h5+ ♔f6 25 ♕e5+ ♔f7 26 ♕h5+ ♔f6 27 ♘f3!

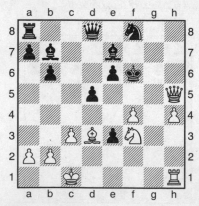

Black is helpless.

27...♗d6 28 ♕h6+ ♔e7 29 ♕g7+ ♔e8 30 ♗b5+ ♘d7 31 ♘g5 ♕e7 32 ♕g8+ 1-0

The finish would be 32...♕f8 33 ♕g6+ ♔d8 34 ♘xe6+.

Trompowsky Attack (1 d4 ♘f6 2 ♗g5)

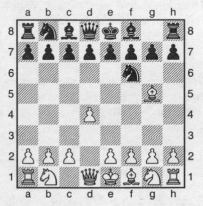

The Trompowsky became quite fashionable, especially in Britain, in the 1990s following its extensive use by Julian Hodgson and, on occasion, Michael Adams. It is a tricky opening, easily underestimated and difficult for Black to handle.

If Black allows it, White will double Black's pawns by taking on f6 and then play with his knights against Black's inflexible position. If Black plays 2...♘e4, then the fun starts. 3 ♗h4 leads to interesting play after 3...c5 4 f3 g5 5 fxe4 gxh4. The odd move 3 h4 is not at all bad, but the main line is 3 ♗f4. Then 3...d5 is a solid move, when White can try 4 f3 ♘f6 5 e4 dxe4 6 ♘c3, which is a Blackmar-Diemer Gambit with an extra tempo. 3...c5 is a more dynamic answer. After 4 d5, Black plays 4...♕b6, intending to take on b2 given

the chance, while after 4 f3 there is 4...♕a5+ 5 c3 ♘f6 6 d5 ♕b6.

Trap: Trompowsky, discovered attack
Landenbergue – M. Röder
Bern 1993

1 d4 ♘f6 2 ♗g5 ♘e4 3 ♗f4 c5 4 f3 ♘f6 5 dxc5 ♘a6 6 e4 ♘xc5 7 ♘c3 d6 8 ♕d2 ♗d7

The next two and a half moves could well be considered a "help-cheapo": both sides seemingly cooperate to allow White to land a big cheapo!

9 0-0-0 ♕a5 10 ♔b1

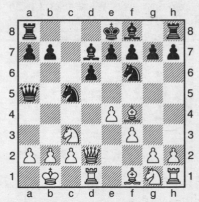

Now Black, an experienced IM, should have heard alarm bells ringing. But no...

10...♖d8?? 11 ♘d5! 1-0

This wins the black queen, since 11...♕xd2 12 ♘c7# mates the suicidal black king.

Trap: Trompowsky, knight invasion
Gant – Kauschmann
Berlin 1988

1 d4 ♘f6 2 ♗g5 ♘e4 3 h4

The "h4 Tromp" has, as Joe Gallagher puts it in his marvellous book *Beating the Anti-King's Indians*, "been the subject of much ridicule and laughter over the years." Still, some very strong players have practised the move with success, so perhaps in this game the player with White did not feel so obliged to check each move so carefully as one normally would when playing an experimental opening.

3...d5

White's main idea behind his odd h-pawn advance is that 3...♘xg5 4 hxg5 (or the same exchange at some later point) gives White useful h-file pressure, and ideas of throwing in g6 as a disruptive pawn sacrifice.

4 ♘d2 ♕d6

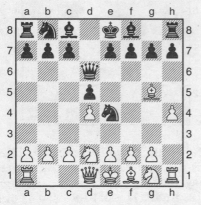

This move is not unknown in Torre Attack positions where Black has kicked back the bishop to h4 with ...♘e4. There are some ideas of an irritating queen check on b4. Here there is another idea too...

5 c3?

5 ♘xe4 dxe4 followed by taking precautions against ...♕b4+ would give White an entirely reasonable position. Presumably he was still hoping for ...♘xg5.

5...♘g3! 0-1

White's resignation is certainly premature, since Black is only winning a pawn, and although White's development is chaotic, he still has quite a lot of it. I could imagine Julian Hodgson swindling something out of the position after 6 ♖h2 f6 7 ♗e3 ♘xe2 8 ♘gf3 ♘g1!?.

Trap: Trompowsky, pawn promotion
Terentiev – Gallagher
Liechtenstein 1990

1 d4 ♘f6

The thematic precursor to this game was the line 1...d5 2 c4 c6 3 ♘f3 ♘f6 4 e3 ♗f5 5 ♕b3 ♕b6 6 cxd5 ♕xb3 7 axb3 ♗xb1? (7...cxd5 8 ♘c3 is mildly troublesome for Black) 8 dxc6 ♗e4?? (8...♘xc6 9 ♖xb1 gives White an extra pawn, as in a game Schlechter–Perlis, Karlsbad 1911) 9 ♖xa7!! ♖xa7 10 c7 Komolstev–Arianov, Alma-Ata 1964.

2 ♗g5 ♘e4 3 ♗f4 c5 4 c3 ♕b6 5 ♕b3?!

5 ♘d2 should be played, but Black has no problems.

5...cxd4! 6 ♕xb6 axb6 7 ♗xb8?!

7 cxd4 ♘c6 is pleasant for Black.

7...dxc3 8 ♗e5??

8 ♘xc3 ♘xc3 9 ♖c1 ♖xb8 10 ♖xc3 restricts the damage to a pawn.

8...♖xa2!!

White could now have resigned, but didn't. After 9 ♖xa2 c2 the pawn promotes either on b1 or c1. There is no particular strategic basis for this; it's just a tactic that works.

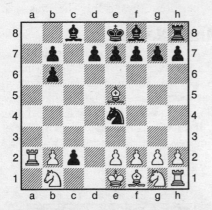

Note that if White's b1-knight were not on the board at all, the pawn could be stopped easily. This was very alert play by Joe Gallagher, but it would have been even more impressive if the idea had been entirely original.

Veresov Opening (1 d4 ♘f6 2 ♘c3 d5 3 ♗g5)

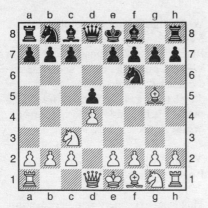

1 d4 d5 2 ♘c3 ♘f6 3 ♗g5 is another possible move-order. Unlike its mirror image, the Spanish (Ruy Lopez), the Veresov has never been a very popular opening, but has a fairly consistent

following. It is a tricky opening, favoured by maverick players who are not put off by the idea that blocking the c-pawn is a bad thing. One may view it as a kind of reversed Chigorin Queen's Gambit, but the nature of the play is more akin to various 1 e4 openings. Indeed, 3...e6 4 e4 transposes to a French Defence.

Black's most reliable independent answer to the Veresov is 3...♘bd7, when White's most natural continuation is 4 f3, to build a centre with e4. However, Black has a good answer to this in 4...c6 5 e4 dxe4 6 fxe4 e5! 7 dxe5 ♛a5, as played by Tal.

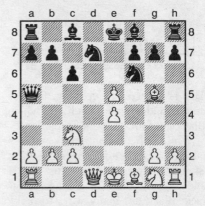

Now 8 exf6 ♛xg5 9 fxg7 ♗xg7 gives Black tremendous compensation for the pawn, so White has nothing better than 8 ♗xf6 gxf6 9 e6 fxe6, but then White cannot even play the natural 10 ♗c4 because of the trick 10...♛a3!.

Given that 4 f3 is ineffective, White will normally opt for 4 ♘f3, but this removes much of the sting from the opening. There might then follow 4...g6 (4...e6 5 e4 is again a French) 5 e3 ♗g7 6 ♗d3 0-0 7 0-0 c5 8 ♖e1, which holds no particular terrors for Black.

Flank Openings and Miscellaneous Systems

Bird's Opening (1 f4)

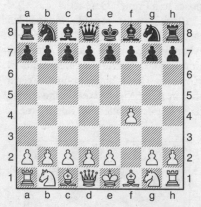

This is a very rare opening, far less common than the Dutch, in which Black goes for the same formation.

White often continues with a queen's fianchetto or else with a Stonewall formation (pawns on d4 and e3) and aims for a kingside attack. Black has many ways to reply, but 1...d5 followed by a king's fianchetto is certainly logical.

Trap: From's Gambit

1 f4 e5
This is From's Gambit, which, if accepted, leaves White facing a whole barrage of tricks and traps.
2 fxe5
2 e4 refusing the pawn, and instead offering one of White's own, transposes to the King's Gambit.

2...d6 3 exd6 ♗xd6
Black now threatens mate in three moves by 4...♕h4+ 5 g3 ♗xg3+ 6 hxg3 ♕xg3#.
4 ♘f3 g5

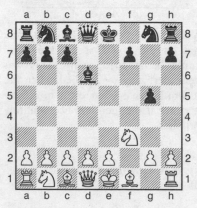

White must be very careful here.
5 e4?
Black can now cause mayhem in White's kingside. 5 d4 and 5 g3 are the normal, viable moves.
5...g4 6 e5 gxf3 7 exd6 ♕h4+ 8 g3 ♕e4+ 9 ♔f2 ♕d4+ 10 ♔xf3 ♗g4+
White's queen is lost.

English Opening (1 c4)

This is an extremely popular opening; it is the third most common first move, after 1 e4 and 1 d4. There are transpositional possibilities to queen's pawn openings, but also plenty of lines of independent significance.

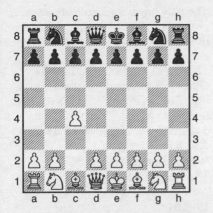

1...e5 is called the *Reversed Sicilian*. Black needs to exercise caution in playing ...d5, since some reversed *Open* Sicilians can be very dangerous for Black, though a reversed Classical Dragon is quite solid. Often a reversed *Closed* Sicilian results, e.g. 2 ♘c3 ♘c6 3 g3 (3 ♘f3 ♘f6 is the Four Knights, a major line leading to intricate play) 3...g6 4 ♗g2 ♗g7 5 d3 d6 6 ♘f3 ♘f6 7 0-0 0-0 8 ♖b1 a5 9 a3. Black will play on the kingside and in the centre, while White will aim to make progress on the queenside.

The *Symmetrical English* (1...c5) can lead to quiet play, but lines with an early d4 or ...d5 can be lively, while there are many gambit ideas and strategically deep options throughout this complex. As normal in symmetrical openings, it is often hard to assess whether it is best for Black to maintain or break the symmetry; for instance, 1 c4 c5 2 ♘c3 (2 ♘f3 intending a quick d4 leads to completely different play) ♘c6 3 g3 g6 4 ♗g2 ♗g7 5 ♘f3 ♘f6 (5...e6 and 5...e5 are other ideas) 6 0-0 0-0 7 a3 (7 d4 breaks the symmetry and may be better) 7...a6 (7...d5 has scored well in practice) 8 ♖b1 ♖b8 9

b4 cxb4 10 axb4 b5 11 cxb5 axb5 12 d4 d5 13 ♗f4 was long considered good for White, but after 13...♖b6 14 ♘e5 ♗f5 15 ♖b3 ♘e4 it is not so easy for *White* to find a useful move.

If Black plays 1...♘f6, then after 2 ♘c3, White has some subtleties if Black is looking to transpose to a defence based on ...e6 or ...g6. After 2...e6 there is 3 e4, when 3...c5 4 e5 ♘g8 5 ♘f3 ♘c6 6 d4 cxd4 7 ♘xd4 ♘xe5 8 ♘db5 a6 9 ♘d6+ ♗xd6 10 ♕xd6 gives White interesting gambit play. Meanwhile, if Black is seeking a Grünfeld, then 2...g6 may not achieve its goal, as White can angle for a King's Indian by playing 3 e4. Thus, Grünfeld fans generally play 2...d5 3 cxd5 ♘xd5, but the fact that White has not played d4 gives him some additional options. If Black wants to defend a QGD, then 1...e6 followed by 2...d5 is a good option. Slav players *can* choose 1...c6, but they must be ready for the Caro-Kann line that results after 2 e4.

Clearly Black has plenty of leeway in how he responds to White's somewhat slow opening move, and just about everything has been tried. For instance, 1...g5 has the argument that this is better than the Grob (1 g4) is for White, since the move 1 c4 lessens White's ability to shore up the a1-h8 diagonal, as c3 is no longer possible. Food for thought perhaps!

Strategic Example
Aseev – Smirin
USSR Ch 1st League (Klaipeda) 1988

1 d4 ♘f6 2 c4 c5 3 ♘f3
Although this is technically classified as a line of the English Opening (1

c4 c5 2 ♘f3 ♘f6 3 d4), in practice it more often arises (as here) when White avoids a Benko or Benoni.

3...cxd4 4 ♘xd4

Black can play this position quietly, but given that White would be happy in that case, Black often prefers the following sharp gambit.

4...e5 5 ♘b5

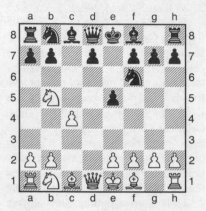

5...d5

5...♗c5 6 ♗e3 (6 ♘d6+?! ♔e7) is difficult for Black, as the weakness of d6 outweighs the damage to White's pawn structure.

6 cxd5 ♗c5 7 ♘5c3 0-0 8 h3 ♗f5 9 e3 ♗g6 10 g4 e4 11 ♗g2 ♘a6 12 g5

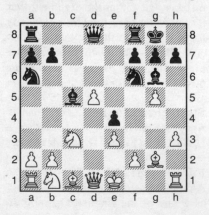

The play has been extremely uncompromising. White has played ambitiously and now hopes to destroy the e4-pawn.

12...♘b4 13 gxf6 ♘d3+ 14 ♔d2

Other destinations for the king (14 ♔e2; 14 ♔f1) come into consideration.

14...♕xf6 15 ♖f1 ♖fe8 16 a3 b5 17 ♖a2 h5

With a cunning plan.

18 ♘xb5? ♕g5

Now things are tricky for White.

19 ♗h1

19 ♖g1 ♘xf2 20 ♕e2 gives White more of a fighting chance.

19...♘xf2!

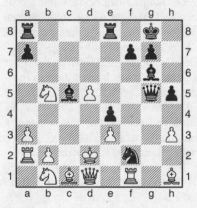

Suddenly Black is winning!

20 ♕e2

20 ♖xf2 ♕xe3+ 21 ♔c2 ♕xf2+, and then 22...e3(+), is devastating.

20...♘xh1 21 ♖xh1 ♕xd5+ 22 ♔c2 ♕xa2 23 ♘1c3 ♕e6 24 ♘c7 ♕f5 25 ♔b1 ♕f3 26 ♕e1 ♖ac8 27 ♘xe8 ♖xe8 28 h4 ♖d8 29 ♖f1 ♕h3 30 ♖h1 ♕d7 31 ♔a1 ♖b8 32 ♕g3 ♗d6 33 ♕g5 ♕f5 34 ♕g1 ♗e5 35 ♘e2 f6 36 ♘d4 ♗xd4 37 exd4 ♖b3 38 d5 ♔h7 39 ♕xa7 ♕xd5 40 ♖g1 ♗f7 41 ♔b1 ♖d3 0-1

Strategic Example
Krasenkov – Kozlov
USSR Central Chess Club Ch 1989

1 ♘f3 ♘f6 2 c4 c5 3 ♘c3 d5
Black is clearly looking for Grünfeld-like play with this move. However, White does not oblige and delays playing his pawn to d4.
4 cxd5 ♘xd5 5 g3 ♘xc3 6 bxc3 g6 7 ♕a4+ ♘d7 8 ♗g2 ♗g7 9 d4 0-0 10 0-0 a6 11 ♕a3 ♕c7 12 ♖d1 e5 13 ♗e3 c4 14 ♖ab1 ♖e8 15 dxe5 ♘xe5 16 ♗f4 ♗f5 17 ♘xe5 ♖xb1 18 ♖d7 ♕b6 19 ♗d5 ♗f8? 20 ♘xf7 ♗e4

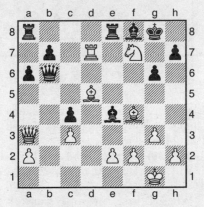

21 ♘h6++?!
21 ♗xc4! is very strong, since then 21...♗xa3 loses to 22 ♘g5+.
21...♔h8 22 ♘f7+ ♔g8 23 ♘h6++? ♔h8 24 ♘f7+ ♔g8 ½-½

Strategic Example
I. Sokolov – Tseshkovsky
Wijk aan Zee 1989

1 c4 e5 2 g3 d6 3 ♗g2 g6 4 e3 ♗g7 5 ♘e2
White's unassuming set-up must not be underestimated. If Black replies unimaginatively, then White will seize firm control of the centre and queenside.

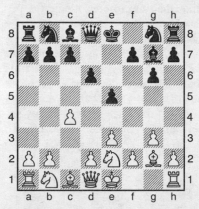

5...h5
This type of h-pawn advance is quite a useful ploy against this kingside formation, particularly since the knight is not on f3. If White's knight had gone to f3, then the right pawn to lead a kingside push by Black would be the f-pawn, a later advance to f4 being a useful way to open attacking lines. However, with the knight on e2, the move ...f5 would lack punch for two reasons: White has the f4-square well covered, so ...f4 would be harder to arrange; moreover, White could play f4 at any time, when a static black pawn on f5 would only get in the way of Black's pieces.
6 d4
Classically responding to Black's activity on the wing with a thrust in the centre. 6 h4 would be rather a concession since Black is in a better position to make use of the g4-square than White is to benefit from the weakness of g5.
6...h4 7 ♘bc3 ♘h6 8 e4 ♗g4 9 ♕d3

♘d7 10 d5 ♘c5 11 ♕e3 h3 12 ♗f1
White has obviously lost a lot of
time, but this will not matter if he
finds the time to consolidate the position with f3.

12...f5

12...a5 13 f3 ♗d7 is quite pleasant
for White, e.g. 14 ♘g1 ♘g8 (this
looks like an undevelopment contest,
but 14...♕c8 15 ♕f2 f5 16 ♗e3 fxe4
17 ♗xc5 dxc5 18 ♘xe4 is hardly acceptable for Black) 15 ♕f2 ♗h6 16
♗xh6 ♖xh6 17 0-0-0.

13 f3

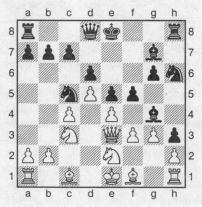

13...fxe4

13...♗h5? 14 b4 pushes Black back,
with a large advantage for White.
However, Tseshkovsky's piece sacrifice ruins that little scheme.

14 fxg4?

14 fxe4? allows Black's pieces plenty
of squares on the kingside, and makes
it easy for him to hold on to the h3-
pawn. 14 ♘xe4 is correct.

14...♘xg4 15 ♕g1 ♕f6

The tragedy for White here is that all
he needs to do to cover the d3-square
is to move his knight from e2 – but it
doesn't have a square!

16 ♘d1

16 ♘b5 ♘d3+ 17 ♔d2 ♗h6+
(17...♕f3 18 ♘xc7+ ♔d7 19 ♘xa8
♗h6+ 20 ♘f4 exf4 21 ♕xa7 ♘c5 is
also quite good) 18 ♘f4 (18 ♔c3 is
answered by 18...♘xc1 with ...♗e3
to follow) 18...exf4 19 ♗xd3 fxg3+
wins for Black.

16...♘d3+ 17 ♔d2 ♕f3

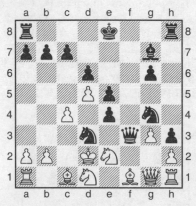

Black has many threats, including
simply walking a knight into f2 and
taking the h1-rook!

18 a3 ♗h6+ 19 ♔c2 ♘b4+! 0-1

It will be mate next move: 20 axb4
♕d3#.

When I first saw this game, it
made quite a strong impression on
me. In a number of games as Black I
raced pawns to h3, to the horror of
team-mates, who thought (and
asked) "won't the pawn just get
rounded up eventually?" The truth is
that the pawn will only become a serious weakness if Black does not
make full use of the tactical opportunities that should arise from the
displacement of the white pieces.
Indeed, I remember being quite
smug when, in one game, the h3-
pawn did drop off sometime around
move 40, but by then I had more

than enough initiative on the other side of the board to compensate.

Strategic Example
Karpov – Hjartarson
Seattle Ct (2) 1989

1 c4 e5 2 g3 ♘f6 3 ♗g2 d5 4 cxd5 ♘xd5 5 ♘c3 ♘b6 6 ♘f3 ♘c6 7 0-0 ♗e7 8 a3 ♗e6 9 b4 0-0

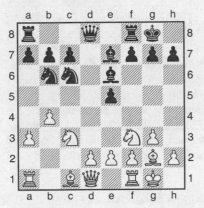

10 ♖b1 f6 11 d3 ♕d7 12 ♘e4 ♘d5 13 ♕c2 b6 14 ♗b2 ♖ac8 15 ♖bc1 ♘d4 16 ♗xd4 exd4 17 ♕c6

17 ♘xd4 ♘xb4 regains the pawn, with a good position.

17...♕xc6 18 ♖xc6 ♗d7

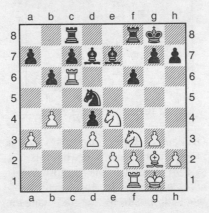

Now Karpov plays what can only be described as a "text-book" exchange sacrifice.

19 ♘xd4! ♗xc6 20 ♘xc6 ♖ce8 21 ♖c1

White already has one pawn for the exchange, but more significantly all of his pieces are active, whereas Black's rooks, which have no access to open lines, are rather impotent.

21...f5 22 ♘d2 ♘f6 23 ♘xa7

Two pawns, and still no activity on Black's part.

23...♗d6 24 e3 c5 25 ♘c4 ♗b8 26 ♘c6 b5 27 ♘4a5 cxb4 28 axb4 ♘d7 29 d4 g5 30 ♘xb8

White exchanges an active knight for a bishop that was preventing his rook from invading on the seventh rank – a good trade.

30...♖xb8 31 ♖c7 ♘f6 32 ♘c6 ♖b6 33 ♘e7+ ♔h8 34 ♘xf5

A third pawn signals the end for Black unless he can do something drastic.

34...♖a6 35 ♖c1 ♖a2 36 h3 ♖b2

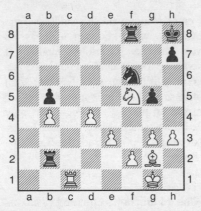

Karpov has seen that he can afford to let Black have the b-pawn; his centre pawns cannot be stopped.

37 e4 ♖xb4 38 g4

This frees the e-pawn from the duty of covering the knight.

38...h5 39 e5 hxg4

Hjartarson tries a desperate piece sacrifice.

40 exf6 gxh3 41 &xh3 &xf6 42 &c8+ &h7 43 &c7+ &g6 44 &g7+ &h5 45 f3 1-0

The mate threat will win yet more material.

Grob's Opening (1 g4)

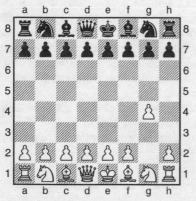

I can't recommend this odd opening, but it is worth knowing it exists, so you can take it seriously enough if someone tries it against you. 1...d5 is a good sensible answer. If White then plays 2 &g2, there is no point getting mixed up in 2....&xg4 3 c4; just play 2...c6 and after White defends his g-pawn, play 3...e5 and develop normally.

King's Fianchetto Opening (1 g3)

This is a very flexible opening, also known as the Benko Opening. It is mainly a transpositional tool.

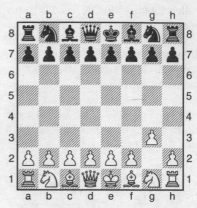

It can lead to a King's Indian Attack, Réti, English, or even a form of Bird's Opening. Another possibility is a g3 line of a king's pawn opening, e.g. 1...g6 2 &g2 &g7 3 e4 can result in a Closed Sicilian (if Black plays ...c5 soon) or a g3 Pirc/Modern.

King's Indian Attack (1 &f3, 2 g3, 3 &g2, 4 0-0, 5 d3, 6 &bd2, 7 e4)

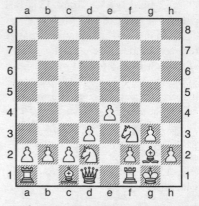

Of course, Black also plays seven moves in the mean time, but this is a system White can play against virtually anything. In the section on blocked positions in the chapter called "Attack and Defence", I present the game example Martin–Burgess, which shows King's Indian Attack ideas used by Black.

White will look to attack on the kingside, having established a firm grip on at least part of the centre.

Meštrović Opening (1 ♘c3)

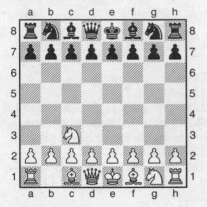

This is a sensible move, probably no worse than the standard ones, though a little lacking in flexibility. However, it has never gained much popularity. The problem is that White cannot effectively enter queen's pawn openings with his c-pawn blocked, whereas in a king's pawn opening Black can tailor his play to the fact that the knight is committed to c3. For instance, after 1...♘f6, 2 d4 d5 is a Veresov, while 2 e4 e5 is a Vienna (Black may also choose 2...d5) – neither of these are especially difficult openings for Black.

Trap: Meštrović Opening, double attack

1 ♘c3 d5 2 e4 dxe4 3 ♘xe4 e5 4 ♗c4

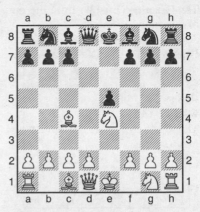

It is now easy for Black to be caught napping. White's unusual opening has given him a lead in development.
4...♗e7?
Very natural; very hopeless.
5 ♕h5!
Black will lose at least a pawn, with a severely damaged position. This is a trap that has caught a few victims.

Nimzowitsch-Larsen Attack (1 b3)

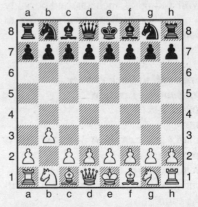

This is not actually bad, of course, but Black can erect a solid centre, aiming to block out the fianchettoed queen's bishop. White can hardly hope for an advantage.

Réti Opening (1 ♘f3)

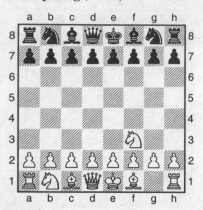

This is quite a major opening. Play can transpose to lines of the Queen's Gambit, but play can proceed along independent lines. After 1...d5 2 c4 Black should probably avoid 2...d4, since 3 e3 gives White good chances of an advantage, while 2...dxc4 is a little compromising too. Therefore, Black generally plays 2...c6 or 2...e6. In the true Réti, White will continue with a king's fianchetto, and possibly a queen's fianchetto too, and aim to control the centre from afar.

Trap: Réti, back ranker
Andonov – Lputian
Sochi 1987

1 ♘f3 d5 2 c4 dxc4 3 ♕a4+ ♗d7 4 ♕xc4 e6 5 d4 b5 6 ♕c2 ♘a6 7 a3
White does not wish to allow ...♘b4 but it is not clear whether it is worth the time.
7...c5 8 dxc5 ♘xc5 9 ♗e3
White's problems start with this move, which places the bishop on an unnatural square.
9...♖c8 10 ♘bd2 ♘f6 11 g3 ♕c7

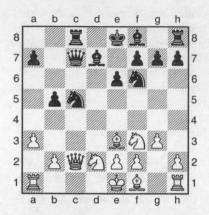

Black has a threat.
12 ♗d4??
12 ♗g2?? loses to 12...♘d3+ but 12 ♖d1 ♘g4 is good for Black, though not an instant catastrophe for White.
12...♘d3+ 0-1
The white queen is lost in view of the line 13 ♕xd3 ♕c1+ 14 ♖xc1 ♖xc1#.

Strategic Example
Taimanov – Kaidanov
Belgrade GMA 1988

1 ♘f3 d5 2 b3 ♘f6 3 ♗b2 e6 4 c4

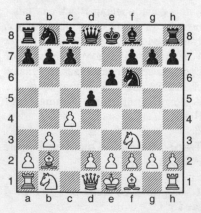

White has employed a relatively quiet "flank opening". This move begins the sniping at Black's centre. The danger in playing a flank opening is that if your sniping misses the target, the opponent will put his pieces in the centre, say "thank you very much", and smash you flat!

4...c5 5 e3 ♞c6 6 cxd5

6 ♗e2 d4 makes the b2-bishop look rather silly.

6...exd5 7 ♗b5 ♗d6 8 ♞e5 0-0!?

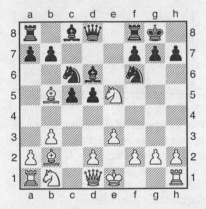

A very sharp challenge to White's strategy. Objectively, this move's merits are not utterly clear, but psychologically it is a direct hit, since White is not looking for a sharp game.

9 ♞xc6 bxc6 10 ♗e2?!

Now White is seriously behind in development. 10 ♗xc6 ♖b8 will lead to White's adventurous bishop being sidelined somewhere around a4, giving Black attacking prospects on the kingside, but nothing too definite for the pawn.

10...♖e8 11 0-0 ♖b8

Now Black is contemplating the strong positional move ...c4, but also has far more evil intentions.

12 d3 ♖b4!

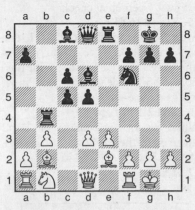

13 ♞d2

13 g3 ♗h3 14 ♖e1 should be better for Black, who can even go on the rampage by 14...♞g4 15 a3 ♞xe3 (15...♛g5 16 ♗f3) 16 fxe3 ♛g5 (Black intends ...♗xg3) 17 ♔h1 ♖h4 18 ♖g1 ♛xe3 19 gxh4 ♛xe2.

13...♖h4 14 g3

14 ♞f3 ♖h6 followed by ...♞g4 gives Black a very strong attack.

14...♞g4 15 ♗xg4

Or:

a) 15 gxh4 ♛xh4 16 ♞f3 ♛h3 is horrible for White.

b) Instead, White had to try 15 ♞f3 ♖xh2 (15...♖h3 is better, e.g. 16 ♖e1 ♞xh2) 16 ♞xh2 ♞xh2, with a crucial decision for White:

b1) 17 ♖e1 does not appear at all adequate in view of 17...♛g5! 18 ♔xh2 ♛h4+ 19 ♔g1 ♗xg3 20 fxg3 ♛xg3+ 21 ♔h1 ♖e6 22 ♗h5 ♖h6 23 ♛e2 ♗g4 24 ♛g2 ♗f3 and in view of the two pins, Black wins.

b2) 17 ♔xh2! (sometimes the simple move is best; White's tempo gain in the line we have just seen was not much use to him) 17...♛h4+ 18 ♔g2 ♛h3+ 19 ♔g1 ♗xg3 20 fxg3 ♛xg3+

21 ♔h1 and Black has no more than a draw by perpetual check.

15...♗xg4 16 f3

After the more resilient 16 ♕e1, one idea for Black is 16...♖e6!? 17 f4 (the only move) 17...♖h3, with possible ...h5-h4 ideas, and good prospects on the e- and h-files.

16...♖xh2!! 17 fxg4

White cannot contemplate 17 ♔xh2 since mate then follows: 17...♕h4+ 18 ♔g1 ♕xg3+ 19 ♔h1 ♕h2#.

17...♖xe3

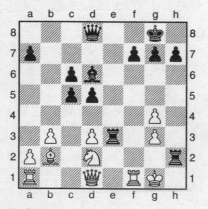

18 ♗f6!?

The best way to go down; 18 ♘f3 ♖xb2 and 18 ♖f3 ♖ee2 are both hopeless for White.

18...♖h3!! 19 ♖f3

19 ♗xd8 ♖exg3+ 20 ♔f2 ♖h2+ 21 ♔e1 ♖e3+ 22 ♕e2 ♖exe2+ 23 ♔d1 ♖xd2+ erases White from the board.

19...♖xg3+ 20 ♔h1 gxf6 21 ♖xg3 ♗xg3 22 ♘f3 ♕d7 0-1

Apparently after the game, Kaidanov became known as "the new Morphy". But only briefly, since in the next round, he was beaten in spectacular fashion by Hulak, as we saw in the illustrative games for the Queen's Gambit.

Réti-Smyslov Opening (1 ♘f3 ♘f6 2 g3 g6 3 b4)

An idiosyncratic anti-King's Indian system, used over many years by Smyslov.

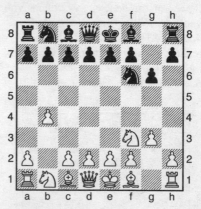

White opposes Black on the long darksquare diagonal and stakes out some space on the queenside. It is difficult for Black to generate much counterplay, but then again White isn't generating a lot of play himself.

Saragossa Opening (1 c3)

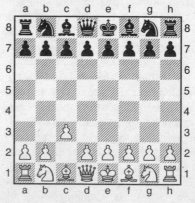

There's not much to say about this move, except its name! It generally transposes to some other slow system, though I should mention that 1...c5 2 d4 (2 e4 is a c3 Sicilian) 2...cxd4 3 cxd4 d5 is a normal Exchange Slav, and 1...e5 2 d4 exd4 3 cxd4 d5 a regular Exchange Queen's Gambit. 1...d5 is a sensible reply, when White will probably go for 2 d4 and possible transposition to a Torre Attack or London System. King's Indian players will probably choose 1...♘f6 followed by 2...g6, since 1...g6 2 e4 ♗g7 3 d4 ♘f6 4 ♗d3 gives White a decent, though dull, line of the Modern.

Sokolsky Opening (1 b4)

This is one of the better known of the weird openings.

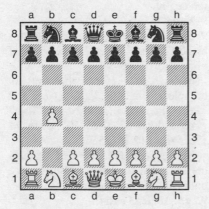

White seizes space and prepares to fianchetto. Black does well to build a centre, e.g. 1...d5 2 ♗b2 ♕d6

followed by 3...e5, while 1...e5 2 ♗b2 ♗xb4 3 ♗xe5 ♘f6 is a line where Black must play actively to make use of his development advantage, since he has ceded White a central pawn majority.

Trap: Sokolsky, disaster on f7
M. Vokač – Bazant
Czech Ch (Turnov) 1996

1 b4 d5 2 ♗b2 ♘d7 3 ♘f3 ♘gf6 4 e3 g6 5 c4 dxc4 6 ♗xc4

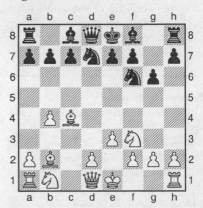

When White has opened 1 b4, Black tends not to expect instant tactics. However, care is needed in any position.

6...♗g7?? 7 ♗xf7+! 1-0
After 7...♔xf7 8 ♘g5+ ♔e8 (8...♔f8 9 ♘e6+ also picks up the queen; 8...♔g8 9 ♕b3+ mates) 9 ♘e6 the queen is trapped.

Attack and Defence

General Attacking Methods: Pieces Swarming Around the Enemy King

One of the key ideas in chess is that for an attack to have much chance of succeeding, the attacker must have more pieces in the vicinity of the enemy king than there are pieces defending. The idea is not at all deep, yet in practice many doomed attacks are launched due to players ignoring this principle. Here are some examples of how it should be done.

Keres – Botvinnik
USSR Ch (Moscow/Leningrad) 1941

1 d4 ♘f6 2 c4 e6 3 ♘c3 ♗b4 4 ♕c2 d5 5 cxd5 exd5 6 ♗g5 h6
6...c5 was played in the game Lebedev–Botvinnik, Moscow 1941. This time Botvinnik first kicks the bishop slightly out of play.

7 ♗h4 c5

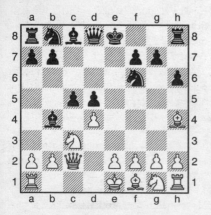

8 0-0-0?
This plan, which had previously been played with success by Mikenas against Botvinnik (Moscow 1940), is too committal, and allows Black a strong attack. Kasparov adopted instead 8 dxc5 to considerable effect at the end of the 1980s and into the 1990s.

8...♗xc3
This is an improvement over 8...0-0, which had been Botvinnik's choice against Mikenas. Instead Black hastens to attack the white king; his own is safe enough for the time being in the centre.

9 ♕xc3
9 ♗xf6 is better, exchanging this bishop before it gets kicked out of play. Then:

a) 9...♗xb2+ is possible but not too clear, e.g. 10 ♔xb2 (10 ♕xb2 ♕xf6 11 dxc5 ♕xf2 12 ♕xg7 ♕xc5+ 13 ♔b2 ♖f8) 10...♕xf6 11 ♕xc5 ♘a6 12 ♕xd5.

b) 9...♕xf6 10 ♕xc3 ♘c6 "retains the initiative for Black" (Botvinnik), but is not too bad for White.

9...g5! 10 ♗g3 cxd4!
Opening more lines. The less effective 10...♘e4 was played by Simagin against Belavenets in late 1940.

11 ♕xd4 ♘c6 12 ♕a4 ♗f5
White has the bishop-pair and an isolated pawn to target. However, this is of no relevance since half of his pieces are undeveloped and mating nets are already forming around his king.

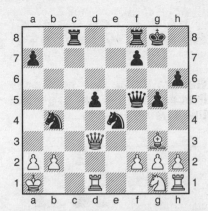

13 e3 ♖c8 14 ♗d3

14 ♘e2 a6 15 ♘c3 b5 16 ♕xa6 b4 17 e4 (Botvinnik mentioned that 17 ♗b5 ♗d7 was good for Black) 17...♗xe4 (17...♘xe4? 18 ♖xd5; 17...bxc3 18 exf5) 18 ♗b5 0-0 19 ♗xc6 bxc3 20 f3 cxb2+ 21 ♔xb2 ♕e7 22 ♕b5 (22 fxe4 ♕b4+ 23 ♔c2 ♕c5+ regains the piece with a decisive attack) 22...♘h5 will remove the bishop, one way or another, from the h2–b8 diagonal, whereupon the move ...♖b8 will be devastating.

14...♕d7

Threatening to win White's queen.

15 ♔b1 ♗xd3+ 16 ♖xd3 ♕f5

The d3-rook is in a horrible pin.

17 e4 ♘xe4 18 ♔a1 0-0

Castling is now appropriate, since it unpins the c6-knight and the threat of a discovery against the d3-rook is now real since there will be no saving ♖e3+.

19 ♖d1

Now for a really good move.

19...b5!

To gain d4 for the knight.

20 ♕xb5 ♘d4

Black has two octopuses!

21 ♕d3 ♘c2+ 22 ♔b1 ♘b4 0-1

White will lose at least a whole queen. A horrible loss for Keres, and one that was doubtless a severe blow to his confidence, since at the time Botvinnik and Keres were regarded as the men most likely to replace Alekhine as world champion.

Karpov – Hübner
Tilburg 1982

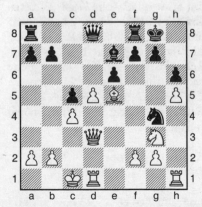

This is an interesting position for analysis. Does White have enough attack?

17 ♗xg7!? ♔xg7 18 ♕e2

Now the game continued 18...♗g5+

19 ♔b1 ♘f6 20 dxe6 ♕c8 21 e7 ♖e8 22 ♖d6 ♕g4 23 ♕e5 ♔g8 24 ♖e1 ♘d7 25 ♖xd7 ♕xd7 26 ♘f5 f6 27 ♕d5+ ♕xd5 28 cxd5 and White soon won.

The critical line was **18...♘f6 19 dxe6 ♕c7 20 ♘f5+ ♔h7 21 g3** (with advantage – Karpov) **21...fxe6**:

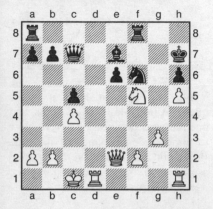

Then V.Iskov pointed out that after 22 ♕xe6, Black repulses the attack by 22...♖ae8 intending 23...♗d8. White can also try **22 ♘h4 ♘g8 23 ♕xe6 ♖xf2 24 ♖d7**, when 24...♕b6 25 ♕e4+ ♔g7 26 ♖xb7 (26 ♖xe7+ ♘xe7 27 ♕xe7+ ♔g8 and Black is doing well) 26...♕f6 27 ♖e1 looks pretty unclear. Instead after 24...♕c6 25 ♖xe7+ ♘xe7 26 ♕xe7+ ♔g8 27 ♖e1 ♖af8 it's not clear how White should continue.

Kamsky – Karpov
Elista FIDE Wch (10) 1996

1 d4 ♘f6 2 c4 e6 3 ♘f3 b6 4 a3 ♗b7 5 ♘c3 d5 6 cxd5 ♘xd5 7 ♗d2 ♘d7 8 ♕c2 c5 9 ♘xd5 exd5 10 dxc5 bxc5 11 e3 ♗e7 12 ♗d3 g6 13 h4 ♕b6 14 h5 ♗f6 15 ♖b1 ♖c8 16 ♕a4 ♗c6 17 ♕g4

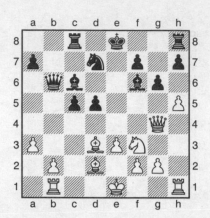

After some rather direct opening play, Kamsky has staked everything on a kingside offensive.

17...♗b5

17...♕b3!? is an attempt to disrupt White's communication.

18 ♗c2 a5

A rather odd-looking move from Karpov.

19 hxg6 hxg6 20 ♖xh8+ ♗xh8 21 ♘g5 ♗f6 22 a4 ♗c6 23 ♔f1 ♔e7 24 e4 ♕a6+ 25 ♔g1 ♘e5 26 ♕f4 d4 27 ♘h7 ♗h8 28 ♕h4+ f6 29 f4 ♘d7 30 ♖e1

Threatening 31 e5. The immediate 30 e5 allows 30...♕e2.

30...♕c4

30...d3!? is best met by 31 ♗d1 with ideas of ♗c3 and e5.

31 ♗b1 ♔d6

31...♖b8 32 e5 (32 b4!? axb4 33 e5) 32...♖xb2 33 exf6++ ♔d8 (33...♔d6 34 f5! ♔c7 35 fxg6) 34 f7+ ♔c8 35 ♘g5 leaves Black without a decent defence: 35...♗f6 (35...♗g7 36 ♘e6) 36 ♕g4 ♗g7 (36...♔b7 37 ♗e4) 37 ♖e8+ ♔c7 (37...♔b7 38 ♗e4) 38 ♗xa5+ ♔b7 39 ♗e4 ♗xe4 40 ♘xe4 with too many threats.

32 e5+

32 ♘xf6!? with 33 e5+ to follow, is also interesting.

32...fxe5 33 fxe5+ ♘xe5?!

33...♗xe5!? looks reasonable for Black.

34 ♗f4 ♕d5?

34...♕e6 35 ♘g5 ♕e7 36 ♗xg6 ♖f8 (or 36...♗d5 37 ♗e4) 37 ♗e4 is very good for White.

35 ♗e4 ♕e6 36 ♘g5 ♕e7 37 ♗xc6 ♔xc6 38 ♗xe5 ♗xe5 39 ♕e4+ ♔d6 40 ♕xg6+ ♔c7 41 ♘e6+ ♔d6 42 ♘f4+

It doesn't particularly matter, but 42 ♘xd4+ is even clearer: 42...♕f6 43 ♘b5+ ♔e6 44 ♕g4+ ♕f5 45 ♖xe5+ ♔xe5 46 ♕xf5+ ♔xf5 47 ♘d6+.

42...♕f6 43 ♕xf6+ ♗xf6 44 ♖e6+ ♔d7 45 ♖xf6 ♖b8 46 ♘d3 c4 47 ♘e5+ ♔e7 48 ♖f4 ♖xb2 49 ♘xc4 ♖b4 50 ♖xd4 ♖xa4 51 ♔f2 ♖a2+ 52 ♔f3 a4 53 ♘e3 ♔e6 54 ♔e4 ♖a1 55 g4 ♔e7 56 ♖d5 ♔f6 57 ♖a5 ♔g6 58 ♔f4 ♔f7 59 ♖a6 1-0

Here's yet another blood-curdling example...

Dragomaretsky – Arbakov
Moscow Ch 1989

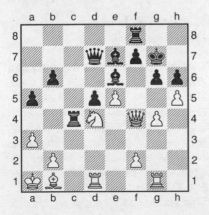

It is clear at a glance that both sides have designs on the opponent's king, and it is a case of who can make the most of their chances.

28...♕a4! 29 hxg6!

White cannot afford to play a defensive move: 29 ♕e3? ♗c5 30 ♘xe6+ fxe6 31 ♕d3 ♖xg4 halts White's kingside play completely.

29...♕xa3 30 ♕f6+ ♔g8 31 b3 ♕b4 32 gxf7+ ♗xf7

32...♖xf7 33 ♕g6+ ♔f8 34 ♕xh6+ ♔g8 35 ♕g6+ ♔f8 36 ♘xe6+ ♔e7 37 ♕g5+ ♔xe6 38 ♗f5+ ♖xf5 and White wins.

33 ♖g3! ♗c1!

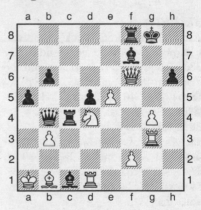

The only try. Black threatens mate in two, and none of the obvious defensive moves are of any use.

34 ♘b5!!

34 ♕d6 ♖c5 35 ♘c2 ♕f4 is not at all clear.

34...♕xb5

34...♗e8 35 ♕e6+ ♔g7 36 g5! ♗xg5 and now 37 ♖xd5 should be adequate to win (but not 37 ♖xg5+? when 37...hxg5 38 ♖g1 ♖h4! refutes White's idea).

35 g5! ♖a4+ 36 ♗a2 ♖xa2+ 37 ♔b1!

This must have been a difficult move to see in advance. Black must now be inventive just to stay in the game.

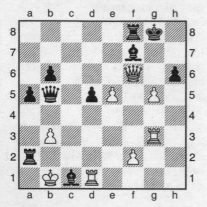

37...♖b2+
After 37...h5 38 g6, Black's best is to transpose to the next note by 38...♖b2+ 39 ♔xc1. He would be mated in the event of 38...♗e8?? 39 ♕e6+ ♔g7 40 ♕e7+ ♗f7 41 ♕f6+ ♔h6 42 gxf7+ ♔h7 43 ♕g7#.

38 ♔xc1 ♖c8+?
38...♖xb3? 39 gxh6+ ♖xg3 40 h7+! ♔xh7 41 ♖h1+ mates. 38...h5 39 g6 ♕c5+ 40 ♔b2 ♗e8 is less clear.

39 ♔xb2 ♕e2+ 40 ♔a3
Sanctuary!

40...♕xd1 41 gxh6+ ♔f8 42 ♖g8+! 1-0

The most vulnerable squares when a king is castled kingside are f2 (or f7) and h2 (or h7). Between them is g2 (or g7), which, if the other squares are well fortified, may be a good invasion point too.

Here is an example in which White has fortified both f2 and h2 (including the "ultimate" defensive manoeuvre of putting a knight on f1), but falls foul of a sacrifice on g2.

Serper – Ivanchuk
Frunze 1988

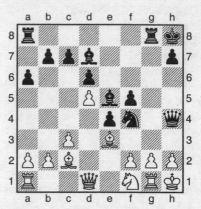

24...♘xg2! 25 ♖xg2 ♖xg2 26 ♔xg2 f4!
Black will have queen, rook, two bishops and a rampant f-pawn in the attack – more than enough to mate one king.

27 ♗d4 ♗g4 28 ♗xe5+ dxe5 0-1
White is completely defenceless, and will lose his queen or be mated in short order.

Next, a simple example of a kingside attack in the opening itself, which ought to have been parried:

K. Blom – N. Jensen
Copenhagen 1938

1 e4 e6 2 d4 d5 3 ♘c3 dxe4 4 ♘xe4 ♗d6?!
Not a good start by Black. The bishop doesn't belong on d6 since it does little to defend the kingside from here, while it makes little sense to let White have the bishop pair whenever he so chooses.

5 ♗d3 ♘e7
This was the idea, but it isn't worth

it. 5...♘f6 6 ♗g5 is good for White.

6 ♗g5

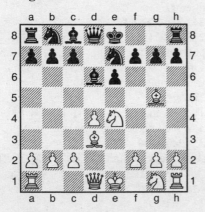

6...0-0?!

6...h6 is answered by 7 ♕h5. 6...♘d7 avoids immediate tactics, but White will soon take on d6 and develop normally, with a clear plus.

7 ♘f6+!?

This sort of brutal sacrifice is only possible when the opponent has developed carelessly.

7...gxf6

7...♔h8 8 ♕h5 h6 9 ♗xh6 is a wipe-out.

8 ♗xf6

Despite appearances, Black is not totally lost here.

8...♕d7??

8...♗b4+ was the only way to prevent mate without losing the queen. 9 c3 (9 ♔f1 ♕d5 10 c4 ♕a5) 9...♕d5 10 cxb4 ♘g6 11 ♘f3 ♘d7 12 ♗g5 and now Black can choose between 12...a5 and 12...e5.

9 ♗xh7+ 1-0

In view of 9...♔xh7 10 ♕h5+ ♔g8 11 ♕h8#.

Next the finish to an incredible game that deserves to be far better known.

Vaganian – Planinc
Hastings 1974/5

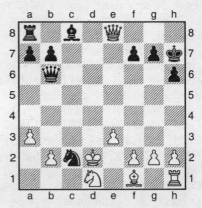

19...♗f5!! 20 ♕xa8 ♕d6+ 21 ♔c1?

21 ♔c3 is more resilient, but 21...♕e5+! 22 ♔d2 ♕d5+ 23 ♔c3 ♕a5+ should lead to a win for Black.

21...♘a1!

22 ♕xb7?

This drops the queen. Instead:

a) 22 b4? gets mated: 22...♘b3+ 23 ♔b2 ♕d2+ 24 ♔xb3 ♕c2#.

b) 22 e4? ♗xe4 23 ♗c4 is not an improvement for White: 23...♕c5 24 ♘c3 (24 ♘e3 ♘b3+ 25 ♔d1 ♕d4+ mates) 24...♕xc4 25 ♕d8 ♘b3+ 26 ♔d1 ♘d4 gives Black decisive threats.

c) 22 ♗c4 ♛c6 wins the bishop, while keeping an attack: 23 ♘c3 ♛xc4 24 ♛d8 (otherwise 24...♘b3+ 25 ♔d1 ♛d3+ is terminal) 24...♘b3+ 25 ♔d1 ♛g4+ and now:

c1) 26 f3? ♛xg2 wins.

c2) 26 ♘e2 ♛xg2 27 ♖g1 ♛e4 28 ♔e1 (only move) 28...♛b1+ 29 ♛d1 ♛xb2 and White is fast running out of pawns, while his king is still exposed.

c3) 26 ♔e1 ♛xg2 27 ♖f1 (27 ♛d5 ♛xd5 28 ♘xd5 ♗e4 wins material) 27...♗h3 28 ♛d3+ allows White to limp on.

22...♛c7+ 0-1

23 ♛xc7 ♘b3# is the stunning point.

Richtrova – Zsu. Polgar
Thessaloniki wom OL 1988

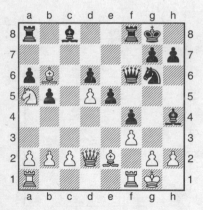

Black now employs a standard attacking ploy, which often crops up when Black has a pawn on f4, and White's kingside has been weakened by the advance f2-f3.

20...♗g3! 21 ♗d3

21 hxg3 fxg3 followed by bringing the queen to h2 gives Black a devastating attack, e.g. 22 ♖fc1 ♛h4 23 ♗d1 ♘f4 24 ♗e3 ♛h2+ 25 ♔f1

♘xg2 26 ♗g1 ♛h1! and White has no good answer to Black's many threats.

21...♛h4 22 h3

22 hxg3 fxg3 is of course no improvement for White, e.g. 23 ♖fd1 ♘f4 24 ♘c6 ♛h2+ 25 ♔f1 ♗h3 with carnage to follow.

22...♛g5

The queen has done her job on h4; now the knight needs the square.

23 ♘c6 ♘h4

Now Black is threatening 24...♗xh3, since 25 gxh3 ♗e1+ picks up the white queen.

24 ♔h1

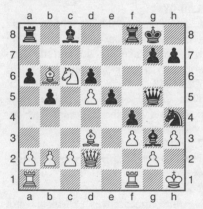

The white king side-steps one problem only to walk straight into another.

24...♘xg2! 25 ♛xg2 ♛h4 26 ♔g1 ♗xh3 27 ♛h1

27 ♛e2 ♖f6.

27...♖f6

The rook is making its way to h6, and there's not much White can do about it!

28 ♗d8 ♖xd8 29 ♘xd8 ♖h6 30 ♘e6 ♛e7 0-1

Throughout this example the main problem wasn't that White was under-developed, or even a general lack of space. The problem was a lack of space in the region of her king, leading us to the general principle that the king is safest on the wing where one controls the most space. Note "controls" – this is not an argument for advancing pawns in front of your own king!

Bashkov – Kiselev
Naberezhnye Chelny 1988

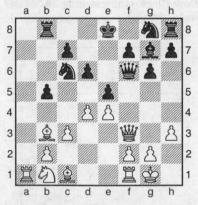

Here Black's king is marooned in the centre, and his development is rather backward. White must keep the pressure on in order to prevent Black from curing these problems.

13 ♕g3!

Now Black must respond to the threat of 14 ♗g5, winning the queen.

13...exd4

Other moves are very passive, but this loses by force.

14 ♗g5

14 ♗d5 is even better.

14...♕e5 15 ♗d5

Gaining time by hitting the loose knight on c6, and cutting off the black queen from sanctuary on c5.

15...♔d7

Necessary to give the queen the e8-square. Still, a royal divorce seems imminent.

16 f4 ♕e8 17 ♕g4+ f5 18 exf5 ♕e3+ 19 ♔h1 h5 20 ♗e6+ ♔e8 21 ♕d1 ♕g3 22 ♗xg8

22 ♖f3 ♕g4 23 hxg4 hxg4+ 24 ♔g1 is quite good enough too.

22...♘e5 23 ♕e1 ♕xe1 24 ♖xe1 dxc3 25 f6 1-0

Before we move on to some specific attacking themes, here are two games in which Capablanca, arguably the most naturally-talented chess player of all time, turns unpromising-looking positions into attacks.

Capablanca – Zubarev
Moscow 1925

1 d4 d5 2 c4 e6 3 ♘f3 dxc4 4 e4 c5 5 d5 exd5 6 exd5 ♘f6 7 ♗xc4 ♗d6 8 0-0 0-0 9 ♗g5 ♗g4 10 ♘c3 ♘bd7 11 ♘e4 ♕c7 12 ♗xf6 ♘xf6 13 ♘xf6+ gxf6 14 h3 ♗h5 15 ♖e1 ♖fe8 16 ♕b3 a6 17 a4 ♗g6 18 ♗d3 ♕d7

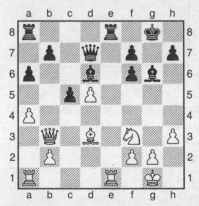

Capablanca has not obtained too much from the opening – his passed pawn is more of a weakness than a strength, and he has only the slight weakness of Black's kingside to work against.

19 ♘d2!

Thus this knight manoeuvre.

19...♖e7 20 ♗xg6 fxg6

20...hxg6? loses: 21 ♘e4 ♔g7 22 ♕f3 f5 23 ♘xc5! ♗xc5 24 ♕c3+ ♔g8 25 ♕xc5 ♖xe1+ 26 ♖xe1 ♕xa4 27 ♕e7 ♕a5 28 d6.

21 ♘e4 ♔g7 22 ♕c3

22 ♘xd6 ♕xd6 23 ♖xe7+ ♕xe7 24 d6 is more promising.

22...♗e5 23 ♕xc5 ♗xb2

23...♖ae8! is a good alternative, e.g. 24 ♖e2 ♗xb2 25 ♖xb2 ♖xe4 26 a5. Then again, the move played is perfectly all right, even though it allows White a few tricks.

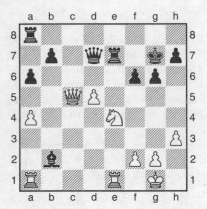

24 ♘g5!? ♖ae8 25 ♘e6+ ♔f7 26 ♖ab1 ♗e5 27 ♕c4 ♖c8 28 ♕b3 ♗b8?

Black wavers at the critical moment. 28...♖c3 was essential:

a) 29 ♕xb7 ♕xb7 30 ♖xb7 ♖xb7 31 ♘d8+ ♔f8 32 ♘xb7 ♖d3 regains the pawn with a draw in prospect.

b) 29 ♕a2 b5 30 ♕d2 ♖c4 and here 31 ♕h6 wins according to Golombek, but then 31...♕xd5 looks quite OK:

32 ♖bd1 and now whether Black opts for the simple 32...♕xe6 or the fancy 32...♖e4, White has nothing more than a draw by perpetual check.

29 g3 ♕d6 30 ♘f4 ♖ce8

30...♖xe1+ 31 ♖xe1 ♖e8 32 ♖e6 ♖xe6 33 dxe6+ ♔f8 34 ♕xb7 ♕c7 35 ♕xc7 ♗xc7 36 ♘d5 paralyses Black completely, since his king will be unable to approach the e6-pawn. White will simply bring up his king and win at a stroll.

31 ♖e6 ♕d7 32 ♖xe7+ ♔xe7 33 ♕xb7 ♗xf4

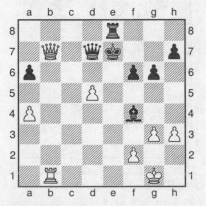

34 ♖e1+!

34 gxf4 ♕xb7 35 ♖xb7+ ♔d6 would give Black very reasonable drawing chances.

34...♗e5 35 d6+ ♔e6 36 ♕b3+ ♔f5 37 ♕d3+ ♔g5 38 ♕e3+ ♔f5 39 ♕e4+ ♔e6 40 ♕c4+ ♔xd6 41 ♖d1+ ♔e7 42 ♖xd7+ ♔xd7 43 ♕xa6 1-0

Capablanca – Znosko-Borovsky
St Petersburg 1913

1 d4 e6 2 e4 d5 3 ♘c3 ♘f6 4 ♗g5 ♗b4 5 exd5 ♕xd5 6 ♗xf6 ♗xc3+ 7 bxc3 gxf6 8 ♘f3 b6 9 ♕d2 ♗b7 10

&e2 &d7 11 c4 &f5 12 0-0-0 0-0-0
13 &e3 &hg8 14 g3 &h5 15 &d3!
&b8 16 &hd1 &f5

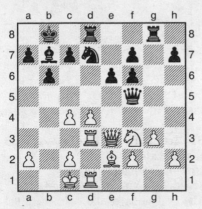

17 &h4

Capablanca was not one to be constrained by dogma about not putting a knight on the edge of the board, though as he relates some contemporary commentators provided knee-jerk criticisms, probably since Capablanca lost the game in the end: "This move has been criticized because it puts the Knight out of the way for a few moves. But by forcing ...&g5 White gains a very important move with f4, which not only consolidates his position, but also drives the Queen away, putting it out of the game for the moment. Certainly the Queen is far more valuable than the Knight, to say nothing of the time gained and the freedom of action obtained thereby for White's more important forces." (From *Chess Fundamentals*, 1921).

17...&g5 18 f4 &g7 19 &f3 &ge8 20 &xb7 &xb7 21 c5! c6 22 &f3 &f8 23 &d2?!

23 &b3.

23...bxc5 24 &c4 &b6 25 &a5+ &a8

26 dxc5 &d5 27 &d4 &c8 28 c4?!

28 &c4!.

28...e5! 29 &g1 e4 30 cxd5 exd3 31 d6 &e2 32 d7 &c2+ 33 &b1 &b8+ 34 &b3 &e7

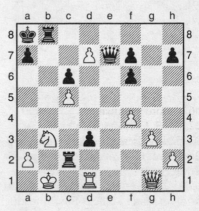

35 &xd3

Annotating this game, one of his rare losses, Capablanca claimed that 35 &d4! &xh2 (35...&xc5? 36 d8&) 36 &xd3! &d8 37 &a6 (37 &f3 may be better) was very good for White. However, while this may well be the case in the event of 37...&e4+ 38 &a1 &b8 39 &b1 and 37...&b8 38 &xc6 when "White will have at least a draw" (Capablanca), 37...&e6! leads to an odd position where it is difficult for either side to do very much, e.g. 38 g4 f5 or 38 &d3 f5 39 &d2.

35...&e2 36 &d4 &d8 37 &a4 &e4 38 &a6 &b8! 39 &c1

39 &d4 &h1+ mates.

39...&xd7 40 &d4 &e1+ 0-1

The &xh7+ Sacrifice

One of the most common sacrificial methods to open up the black king's defences (assuming it has castled kingside) is a bishop sacrifice on h7.

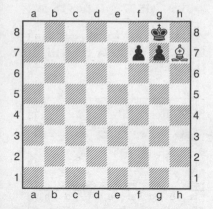

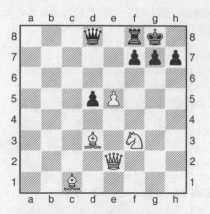

Assuming the king takes the bishop, there are four main follow-ups for White.

1) ♘g5+ with the white queen ready to come to the h-file if the king drops back to g8.

2) The white queen and rook quickly coming to the h-file.

3) A queen check on some square, forking the king and some other piece, regaining the sacrificed material.

4) A further bishop sacrifice on g7, completely destroying the black king's pawn cover – this is covered in the next part of this chapter.

A few points about the sacrifice, especially if the aim is to force mate:

- it is useful to have some way to deny a black knight access to f6 – or else to be able to remove it from there;
- the presence of a black rook on f8, and some piece on e7 can help White by blocking the king's flight squares.

The importance of this second point is shown graphically in the so-called Greco Mate:

Now our thematic line runs:
1 ♗xh7+ ♔xh7 2 ♘g5+ ♔g8
The evaluation of the line where the king comes out into the open, 2...♔g6 3 ♕g4 (or 3 ♕d3+) 3...f5, depends on the specifics of the position.
3 ♕h5 ♖e8
To give the king a flight square.
4 ♕xf7+ ♔h8 5 ♕h5+ ♔g8 6 ♕h7+ ♔f8 7 ♕h8+ ♔e7 8 ♕xg7#

The rook now denies the king a square.

With this in mind, let's take a look at the ♗xh7+ sacrifice in some practical examples.

Barva – Kis
Hajduboszormeny 1995

1 d4 ♘f6 2 ♘f3 d5 3 ♗f4 e6 4 e3 c5 5 c3 ♘bd7 6 ♘bd2 ♗e7 7 ♗d3 b6 8 ♕e2 ♗b7 9 a4 a6 10 h3 0-0

Black is the first to castle. White has carefully been delaying doing so himself, since he may need to be able to throw in the kitchen sink when he launches a kingside attack.

11 ♘e5 ♘xe5 12 dxe5 ♘d7 13 ♕g4 ♖e8 14 ♘f3

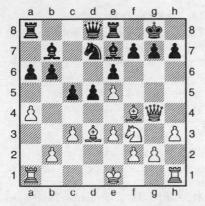

White is amassing a powerful attacking force, but has no instant threats.

14...♗f8??

Oh dear! Mr Kis has forgotten the basics, it seems.

15 ♗xh7+! 1-0

15...♔xh7 16 ♕h5+ ♔g8 17 ♘g5 is about as straightforward as these attacks come.

Tempone – Flores
San Luis 1995

1 e4 e6 2 ♘f3 d5 3 ♘c3 ♘f6 4 e5 ♘fd7 5 d4 c5 6 dxc5 ♗xc5 7 ♗d3 ♘c6 8 ♗f4 ♕b6 9 0-0-0 0-0

It's astonishing that someone who plays the French Defence at international level can be oblivious to the danger – or else underestimate it so.

10 ♗xh7+! ♔h8

Black chooses to decline the sacrifice, since 10...♔xh7 11 ♘g5+ ♔g6 12 ♕d3+ f5 13 ♘xe6 (13 exf6+ ♔xf6 14 ♖ae1 is interesting too) 13...♘cxe5 14 ♘xf8+ ♗xf8 15 ♕g3+ ♘g4 (15...♔f6? 16 ♘xd5+) 16 h3 would leave White the exchange up with a good position.

However, with his king's pawn-cover so badly damaged, Black's days are numbered, and White now wins in straightforward fashion.

11 ♗d3 ♕xb2 12 ♘b5 ♕b4 13 ♘fd4 g6 14 c3 ♕a5 15 ♖e1 a6 16 ♘xc6 bxc6 17 ♘d6 ♕xc3 18 ♖c1 ♕a5 19 ♕g4 ♗xd6 20 exd6 ♖e8? 21 ♗xg6! fxg6 22 ♕xg6 1-0

Makovetsky – Khavanov
Novgorod 1995

1 e4 e6 2 d4 d5 3 ♘c3 ♘f6 4 e5 ♘fd7 5 f4 c5 6 ♘f3 ♕b6 7 ♘a4 ♕a5+ 8 c3 c4 9 b4 cxb3 10 axb3 ♕c7 11 c4 ♗b4+ 12 ♔f2 ♘b6 13

♗d3 ♗d7 14 ♘xb6 ♛xb6 15 ♗d2
♘c6 16 ♔e3

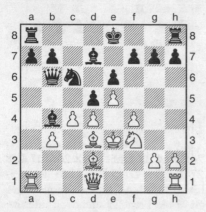

Here, after an unusual opening, it is fairly understandable that Black now castles into a ♗xh7+ sacrifice, since White cannot play it immediately. However, he can prepare it with some forcing moves.

16...0-0 17 c5

17 ♗xh7+? ♔xh7 18 ♘g5+ ♔g8 19 ♗xb4 (19 ♛h5 ♛xd4+) 19...♛xb4 20 ♛h5 (20 ♛d3 g6) 20...♛xb3+ and the queen defends on the b1–h7 diagonal.

17...♛c7 18 ♗xb4 ♘xb4 19 ♗xh7+!
♔xh7 20 ♘g5+

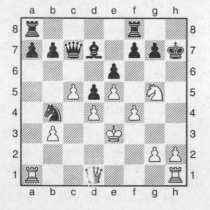

20...♔g6

After 20...♔g8 the standard procedure 21 ♛h5 ♖fe8 22 ♛xf7+ ♔h8 23 ♛h5+ ♔g8 24 ♛h7+ ♔f8 25 ♛h8+ ♔e7 26 ♛xg7+ ♔d8 27 ♘f7+ ♔c8 28 ♘d6+ ♔b8 29 ♘xe8 gives White a decisive material advantage.

21 ♛g4 f5

21...f6 22 ♘xe6+ would have been trivial, but now what?

22 ♛h4!

Instead after 22 ♛g3 ♛c6 23 ♘xe6+ ♔f7 24 ♘xf8 ♔xf8 the game is still a fight.

22...♖h8 23 ♛g3

The point of luring the rook to h8 is that now White is threatening mate in five by 24 ♘xe6+ ♔f7 25 ♛xg7+, etc. Thus Black is hard-pressed to save both his king and queen; indeed he can only do so at the cost of a rook.

23...♔h6 24 ♘f7+ ♔h7 25 ♛h4+
♔g6 26 ♘xh8+ ♖xh8 27 ♛xh8

Resignation would be quite in order here.

27...♘c2+ 28 ♔f2 ♘xd4 29 b4 b6
30 ♛f8 a5 31 ♖hd1 axb4 32 ♖xd4
1-0

De Jong – Plijter
Corr. 1994

1 e4 e5 2 ♘f3 ♘f6 3 ♘xe5 d6 4 ♘f3
♘xe4 5 d4 d5 6 ♗d3 ♗d6 7 0-0 0-0
8 c4 c6 9 cxd5 cxd5 10 ♘c3 ♘xc3
11 bxc3 ♗g4 12 ♖b1 ♘d7 13 h3
♗h5 14 ♖b5

The point of this move is not just to put pressure on the d5-pawn, but White intends that the rook will eventually find some action on the kingside.

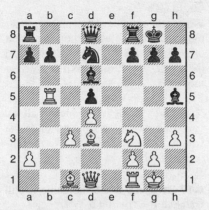

As we are about to see, White has the pawn-break c3-c4, so the d5-pawn is by no means an immovable obstacle.

14...♘b6 15 c4 ♗xf3 16 ♕xf3 dxc4 17 ♗c2

At the cost of a pawn, White has queen, rook and two bishops bearing down on the black king. Still, if Black can survive...

17...♕d7 18 a4 ♖fe8

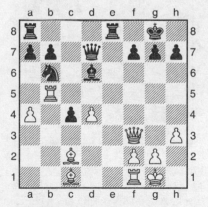

19 ♗f5 ♕c6?

19...♕c7 is more robust: 20 a5 ♕c6 works better now that the b5-rook is unprotected, e.g. 21 ♗xh7+ ♔xh7 22 ♕h5+ ♔g8 23 axb6 axb6 gives

Black an extra pawn, while White's pieces are no longer coordinating.

20 ♗xh7+! ♔xh7

20...♔f8 might be a better try, but Black is in trouble, e.g. 21 ♕h5 with the crude plan of ♖f5, ♗g6, etc.

21 ♕xf7

Now White is clearly well on top.

21...♗e5

A sad necessity.

22 ♖xe5 ♖xe5 23 dxe5 ♕d5

23...♘xa4 24 ♖d1 (threatening ♖d4) 24...♕e4 25 ♕h5+ ♔g8 26 ♖d7 ♖f8 27 ♖xg7+ ♔xg7 28 ♗h6+ is decisive.

24 ♕h5+ ♔g8 25 ♖d1 ♕a5 26 ♗h6 1-0

In view of 26...gxh6 27 ♕g6+ ♔h8 (27...♔f8 28 e6) 28 ♕xh6+ ♔g8 29 ♕g6+ ♔h8 30 ♕f6+ followed by ♖d4.

Rausis – Steingrimsson
Gausdal Peer Gynt 1995

1 e4 c5 2 c3 ♘f6 3 e5 ♘d5 4 ♘f3 e6 5 ♗c4 d6 6 0-0 dxe5 7 ♘xe5 ♗d6 8 d4 0-0 9 ♖e1 ♕c7 10 ♕e2 cxd4 11 cxd4 ♘c6 12 ♘f3 ♘ce7 13 ♘c3 ♘xc3 14 bxc3 b6 15 ♗d3 ♗b7

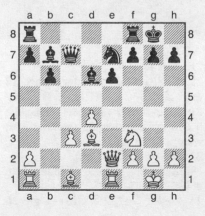

16 ♗xh7+

This sacrifice is unclear. It is a reasonable way to open up the black king and, Rausis presumably reckoned, the only way to keep the initiative.

16...♔xh7 17 ♘g5+ ♔g6

As normal, the king must come out into the open.

18 ♕g4?!

18 h4 is a better idea, threatening 19 h5+. In response, 18...♗f4 19 ♕d3+ ♘f5 20 g4 allows White to regain the piece, but both kings are then exposed, e.g. 20...♖h8 21 gxf5+ exf5 22 ♘f3.

18...f5 19 ♕h4

19 ♖xe6+ ♖f6 20 ♕h3 ♖xe6 21 ♘xe6 dissipates White's initiative.

19...♗d5 20 ♕h7+ ♔f6 21 c4

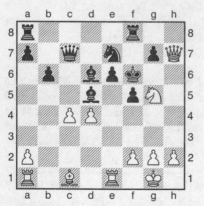

21...♕xc4?

21...♖h8! refutes the attack since 22 cxd5 ♗xh2+ 23 ♔h1 (23 ♔f1 ♕c4+ 24 ♖e2 ♖xh7) 23...♗f4 pins the queen while providing the king with g5 as a flight square.

22 ♕h5 g6 23 ♕h4 ♖h8

23...♔g7 looks like an immediate draw: 24 ♕h7+ ♔f6 25 ♕h4 ♔g7.

24 ♘e4+ ♔g7 25 ♕f6+ ♔g8 26

♘xd6 ♖f8

White is now easily winning, with plenty of choice about how to finish off, so there is little point following the game any further. White won on move 40.

Next an example of an unclear attack launched by White, in the midst of which a strong ♗xh7+ idea appeared.

Kotronias – Djurhuus
Gausdal International 1995

1 e4 c5 2 ♘f3 d6 3 d4 cxd4 4 ♘xd4 ♘f6 5 ♘c3 a6 6 ♗g5 e6 7 f4 ♗e7 8 ♕f3 ♕c7 9 0-0-0 ♘bd7 10 g4 b5 11 ♗xf6 ♘xf6 12 g5 ♘d7 13 f5 ♗xg5+ 14 ♔b1 0-0

14...♘c5 is a sensible alternative.

15 fxe6 ♘b6 16 ♘d5 ♘xd5 17 exd5

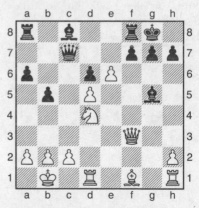

17...♗f6

17...fxe6 looks quite respectable for Black. After 18 ♕g4 he has a choice: 18...♕e7 (18...♗f6 19 dxe6 ♗xd4 20 ♖xd4 ♖e8 21 ♗d3 ♗xe6 22 ♕h5 g6 23 ♖g1 ♗f7 is a robust defence; 18...e5 is probably not best since 19 ♕xg5 exd4 20 ♗d3 gives White

good attacking prospects) 19 dxe6
(19 ♘xe6 ♗xe6) 19...♗b7 (19...♖f4
20 ♕g3) 20 ♖g1 ♗e3 21 ♖g3 ♗f2
22 ♘f5 ♖xf5 23 ♕xf5 ♗xg3 looks
OK for Black.

18 ♗d3 ♗xd4

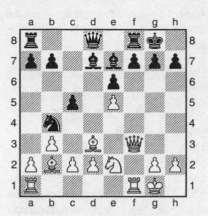

14 ♗xh7+?
14 ♗e4 would seem to be necessary.
14...♔xh7 15 ♕h5+ ♔g8 16 ♖f3
White does not have enough behind
her attack; Black need only side-step
a crude threat or two.
16...g6 17 ♖g3 ♔g7 18 ♖f1
White threatens mate in three with
19 ♖xf7+!.
18...♕e8
Now the consolidation process runs
like clockwork.

**19 ♖f6 ♖h8 20 ♕g5 ♖h6 21 d3 ♕h8
22 ♗c1 ♗e8 23 ♘f4?! ♗xf6 24
exf6+ ♔g8 25 ♗b2 ♕h7 26 ♕xc5
♘c6 27 ♗a3 ♗d7 28 ♕d6 ♖d8 29
♕c7 ♗c8 30 ♘h3 ♕h8 31 ♗e7 ♖e8
32 ♘g5 ♘xe7 33 fxe7 ♕a1+ 34 ♔f2
♕f6+ 35 ♘f3 ♕xe7 36 ♕f4 ♖h5 37
♘g5 e5 38 ♕e3 b6 39 ♔e1 ♖xh2 40
♘f3 ♖h1+ 41 ♔e2 e4 0-1**

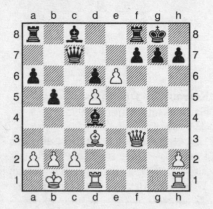

**19 ♗xh7+! ♔xh7 20 ♖xd4 ♔g8 21
♖h4**
White is now winning. The game
concluded as follows:
**21...fxe6 22 ♕h3 ♖f5 23 ♖h8+ ♔f7
24 ♖g1 ♕c4 25 ♖xg7+ ♔f6 26 ♖g1
♕f4 27 ♖f8+ ♔e5 28 ♖e1+ ♔xd5
29 ♕g2+ ♔c5 30 ♖xf5+ ♕xf5 31
♕xa8 e5 32 h4 ♔b6 33 ♕b8+ ♔c6
34 h5 ♗e6 35 ♕e8+ ♗d7 36 ♕g6
♕f3 37 ♕e4+ ♕xe4 38 ♖xe4 1-0**

The next game is a warning example,
and features a failure for our sacrifice.

M. Grigorian – M. Stanković
Zanka U-20 girls Ech 1995

1 e4 c5 2 f4 d5 3 exd5 ♕xd5 4 ♘c3
♕d8 5 ♘f3 ♘f6 6 ♘e5 e6 7 b3 ♗e7
8 ♗b2 0-0 9 ♗d3 ♘fd7 10 ♕f3
♘xe5 11 fxe5 ♘c6 12 ♘e2 ♗d7 13
0-0 ♘b4

Berg Hansen – H. Olafsson
Reykjavik Z 1995

1 d4 ♘f6 2 ♗g5 ♘e4 3 ♗f4 d5 4 f3
♘f6 5 e4 dxe4 6 ♘c3 exf3 7 ♘xf3
♗g4 8 h3 ♗xf3 9 ♕xf3 c6 10 0-0-0
e6 11 ♗c4 ♗e7 12 ♔b1 0-0 13 h4

♘d5 14 ♘e4 b5 15 ♗d3 ♘d7 16
♘g5 ♘7f6 17 ♗e5 a5 18 ♖df1 a4?

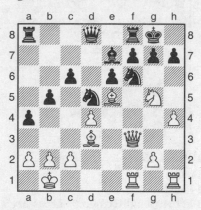

Here the open f-file gives White extra possibilities for the ♗xh7+ sacrifice – it works even though there are two black knights with access to f6!

19 ♗xh7+! ♘xh7

19...♔h8 20 h5 gives White a strong attack for no material deficit. 20...♘xh7 21 h6 is annihilating.

20 ♕h5 1-0

20...♘hf6 21 ♗xf6 ♘xf6 22 ♖xf6 forces mate.

It should always be borne in mind that the ♗xh7+ sacrifice can be declined, and a vigorous follow-up is needed if the opponent is counterattacking.

Oliveira – Silva
Portuguese Ch (Lisbon) 1994

1 e4 c5 2 ♘f3 d6 3 d4 cxd4 4 ♘xd4 ♘f6 5 ♘c3 a6 6 ♗e3 e5 7 ♘b3 ♗e7 8 f3 0-0 9 ♕d2 ♘bd7 10 g4 b5 11 g5 ♘e8 12 0-0-0 ♗b7 13 h4 b4 14 ♘d5 a5 15 ♔b1 a4 16 ♘c1 ♗xd5 17 exd5 ♕b8 18 h5 ♘c5 19 ♗xc5 dxc5 20 ♗d3 ♘d6 21 ♖dg1 c4

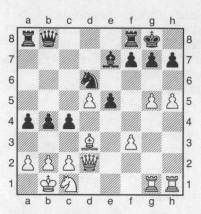

22 ♗xh7+ ♔h8

Black declines the offer, putting his trust in a queenside counterattack, hoping the h7-bishop will get in White's way. Upon acceptance, 22...♔xh7, White would play 23 g6+, with the following possibilities: 23...♔h8? 24 h6; 23...fxg6? 24 hxg6++ ♔g8 25 ♕h2 and mate next move (25 ♖h8+ ♔xh8 26 ♕h2+ would be the way to do it if White had to mate with checks); 23...♔g8 24 h6 c3 25 ♕h2 and White's attack crashes through first.

23 g6 c3 24 ♕g2 cxb2 25 h6 bxc1♕+ 26 ♔xc1 f6 27 ♗g8?

Not the simplest. 27 hxg7+ ♔xg7 28 ♕h3 ♘f5 (else 29 ♕h6+) 29 ♗g8 forces mate.

27...♕b6 28 hxg7++ ♔xg7 29 ♖h7+?

29 ♕h3 was still quite sufficient to win.

29...♔xg8 30 ♖h8+

30 ♕h1! wins.

30...♔g7 31 ♖h7+ ♔g8 32 g7? ♕xg1+ 33 ♕xg1 ♔xh7 34 gxf8♕ ♗xf8 35 ♕g4 ♖a7

35...♘f7 gives Black all the chances.

36 ♕e6 ♔g7 37 ♕g4+ ♔f7 38

♕h5+ ♔g7 39 ♕g4+ ♔f7 40 ♕h5+
♔e7 41 ♕h7+ ♘f7 42 ♕f5 ♘d8 43
♕h7+ ♘f7 44 ♕f5 ♘d8 45 ♕h7+
♘f7 46 ♕f5 ½-½

If Black has a chance for the equivalent ...♗xh2+ sacrifice, then it means something has gone very seriously wrong with White's opening. Nevertheless it does happen, such as the following game, where Black even links it with a destructive rook sacrifice on g2.

Cummins – T. Clarke
Irish Ch (Dublin) 1995

1 e4 e6 2 d4 d5 3 e5 c5 4 c3 ♘c6 5
♘f3 ♗d7 6 ♗e2 ♕b6 7 a3 a5 8 0-0
♘h6 9 b3 cxd4 10 cxd4 ♘f5 11
♗b2 a4 12 b4 ♗e7 13 ♗d3 ♘cxd4
14 ♘xd4 ♘xd4 15 ♕g4 ♘b3 16
♕xg7 0-0-0 17 ♖a2 ♖hg8 18 ♕xf7
♗g5 19 ♕f3 ♖df8 20 ♕e2 ♗f4 21
♗c3 ♘d4 22 ♗xd4 ♕xd4 23 ♘c3

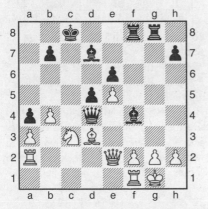

Black has a lot of firepower lined up against the white king, so it's not too surprising that he has a forced win:
23...♗xh2+! 24 ♔xh2 ♕h4+ 25
♔g1 ♖xg2+! 26 ♔xg2 ♖g8+ 27 ♔f3

♕h3+ 28 ♔f4 ♖f8+ 29 ♔g5 ♗e8
This quiet move sets up the threat of 30...h6#.
30 ♗xh7 ♕xh7 31 ♔g4 ♕g6+ 0-1
A pleasing king-hunt.

These ♗xh7+ sacrifices are sometimes very hard to assess. Here is a position where the great Paul Keres feared a sacrifice that wouldn't have worked at all.

Foltys – Keres
Prague 1937

1 d4 e6 2 e4 d5 3 ♘c3 ♘f6 4 ♗g5
♗e7 5 ♗xf6 ♗xf6 6 ♘f3 0-0 7 ♗d3
c5 8 e5 ♗e7

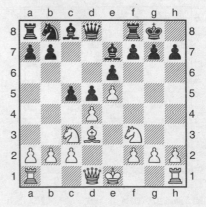

This position shows how it can be very difficult to assess the consequences of a "standard" ♗xh7+ attack. Here Keres, as Black, vastly overestimated the danger his king was in.

The game actually continued as follows: 9 dxc5 ♘d7 10 h4 f5 11 exf6 ♗xf6 12 ♕d2 (12 ♗xh7+ is no good here: 12...♔xh7 13 ♘g5+ ♔g8 14 ♕h5 ♗xc3+ 15 bxc3 ♘f6 – analysis given by Keres) 12...♘xc5

13 0-0-0 ♕a5 14 a3 ♗d7 15 ♖de1
♖ac8 16 ♘e5 ♗xe5 17 ♖xe5 d4 18
♖xc5 ♕xc5 19 ♘e4 ♕d5 20 ♔b1 e5
21 f3 h6 22 b3 ♗e6 23 h5 a5 24 a4
♔h8 25 ♖g1 ♖c6 26 ♗b5 ♖c7 27
♗d3 ♗d7 28 g4 ♖xf3 29 g5 ♗f5 30
gxh6 ♗xe4 31 hxg7+ ♖xg7 32 ♖xg7
♔xg7 33 ♕g5+ ♔f7 0-1.

9 h4 was a move Keres feared,
thinking that he could not play the
natural **9...cxd4** (9...f5 10 exf6 gxf6
11 ♘g5 gives White a dangerous attack – Keres) **10 ♗xh7+ ♔xh7 11
♘g5+ ♔h6** (the critical reply in instances when White has problems
covering the dark squares) **12 ♕d3
g6 13 h5**.

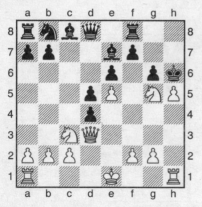

13...♗xg5 (this is perfectly OK, but
13...♔g7 14 hxg6 ♖h8, as indicated
by John Nunn, snuffs out White's
attack completely) **14 hxg6+ ♗h4 15
♕g3 fxg6 16 ♖xh4+ ♔g7 17 ♖g4**
and here, mentioning only 17...♕e8?
18 ♘b5!, Keres terminated his analysis, concluding that White had a
strong attack. However, John Nunn
pointed out the defence **17...♖g8 18
♖xg6+ ♔f7**, when White is a piece
down for not a great deal; perhaps
Keres had missed 19 ♖f6+ ♕xf6.

The Double Bishop Sacrifice

This is an extension of the ♗xh7+
idea, with a further ♗xg7 sacrifice
destroying the rest of the black
king's pawn cover. Obviously there
needs to be a really devastating follow-up, generally involving the white
queen and at least one rook.

Alekhine – Drewitt
Portsmouth 1923

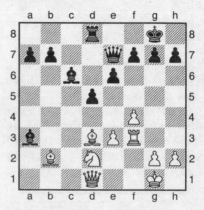

**20 ♗xh7+! ♔xh7 21 ♖h3+ ♔g8 22
♗xg7! 1-0**

22 ♕h5 also wins since after 22...f6
23 ♗xa3 ♕xa3 24 ♕h8+ Black loses
his rook.

Nevertheless, the double bishop
sacrifice, though not absolutely necessary, is a neat and efficient way to
win the position. Black resigned
seeing that his choice was from
22...♔xg7 23 ♕g4+ mating, and
22...f6 23 ♗h6 ♕h7 (23...e5 24
♕h5) 24 ♕h5.

Our next example demonstrates that
this sacrifice can also crop up in
games between strong grandmasters.

Miles – Browne
Lucerne OL 1982

1 ♘f3 c5 2 c4 ♘f6 3 ♘c3 e6 4 e3 ♘c6 5 d4 d5 6 dxc5 ♗xc5 7 a3 a6 8 b4 ♗a7 9 ♗b2 0-0 10 ♖c1 d4 11 exd4 ♘xd4 12 c5 ♘xf3+ 13 ♕xf3

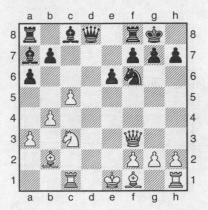

After a fairly quiet opening, it becomes clear that White has a large space advantage and the black bishop is misplaced on a7. White now funnels his pieces towards the black king.

13...♗d7 14 ♗d3 ♗c6 15 ♘e4 ♘xe4 16 ♗xe4 ♕c7

With hindsight one can suggest that Black might have considered exchanging bishops.

17 0-0

17 ♗xh7+ ♔xh7 18 ♕h5+ ♔g8 19 ♗xg7 f6 is unclear since after 20 ♕h8+ ♔f7 21 ♗xf8 Black can throw in the check 21...♕e5+ before capturing the bishop.

17...♖ad8

Now White strikes.

18 ♗xh7+! ♔xh7 19 ♕h5+ ♔g8

Stage one completed. Now it's time for the second unwelcome visitor to arrive in Black's kingside.

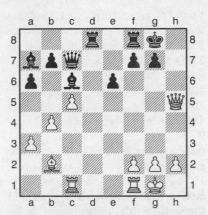

20 ♗xg7! ♔xg7

Now 20...f6 does not work: 21 ♕h8+ ♔f7 22 ♗xf8 wins since 22...♖xf8 23 ♕h7+ picks up the black queen.

21 ♕g5+ ♔h8 22 ♕f6+ ♔g8 23 ♖c4 1-0

Böök – Ingerslev
Gothenburg 1929

1 e4 e6 2 ♘f3 d5 3 ♘c3 ♗b4 4 ♗d3 c5 5 a3 ♗a5 6 b4 cxb4 7 axb4 ♗xb4 8 ♗b2 ♘e7 9 0-0 0-0 10 ♖e1 b6 11 exd5! ♘xd5 12 ♘xd5 exd5 13 ♘d4 ♗b7? 14 ♖e3? ♘d7

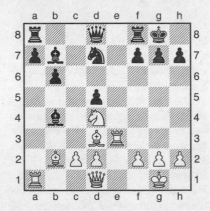

Now White sacrifices not two, but three pieces to strip the defences from the black king.

15 ♘c6!! ♗xc6 16 ♗xh7+! ♔xh7
Or 16...♔h8 17 ♕h5.
17 ♕h5+ ♔g8 18 ♗xg7! ♔xg7
18...f5 19 ♕g6.
19 ♖g3+ ♔f6 20 ♖e1 1-0

Now a game in which the sacrifices should not have meant a knockout.

Kudrin – Machado
Thessaloniki OL 1988

1 e4 e5 2 ♘f3 ♘f6 3 ♘xe5 d6 4 ♘f3 ♘xe4 5 d4 d5 6 ♗d3 ♗d6 7 0-0 0-0 8 c4 c6 9 ♘c3 ♘xc3 10 bxc3 ♗g4 11 cxd5 cxd5 12 ♖b1 ♘d7 13 h3 ♗h5 14 ♖b5 ♘b6 15 c4 ♗xf3 16 ♕xf3 dxc4 17 ♗c2 ♖b8 18 a4 a6 19 ♗g5 ♕c7

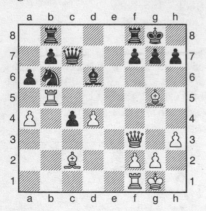

There now follows a textbook series of sacrifices, related to the classic double bishop offer. However, the outcome is far from clear in this case if Black defends accurately.

20 ♗xh7+!
The sacrifice is necessary, since otherwise White would just get pushed

backwards.
20...♔xh7 21 ♕h5+ ♔g8 22 ♗f6! ♗h2+ 23 ♔h1 ♕d6?
Missing White's main idea. A more active defence was essential: 23...♕f4, with the following position:

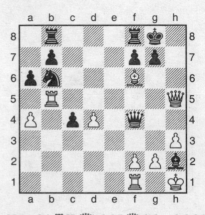

Now 24 ♖f5 ♕h6 25 ♕xh6 gxh6 26 ♔xh2 ♘xa4 is unclear, while after 24 ♗xg7 ♔xg7 25 ♖g5+ ♔f6 26 ♕h6+ ♔e7 27 ♖e5+ ♔d7 28 ♕xb6 ♖fe8! White should probably take a draw: 29 ♖d5+ (29 ♖fe1 ♖xe5 30 ♖xe5 allows Black a perpetual with 30...♕c1+ 31 ♔xh2 ♕f4+, etc.) 29...♔e7 30 ♖e5+ ♔d7 (30...♔f8? 31 ♕c5+ ♔g7 32 ♖g5+, followed by hassling the black king and queen, wins at least the h2-bishop) 31 ♖d5+, etc.

Instead, after the move in the game, White wound things up very quickly.
24 ♗xg7! ♔xg7 25 ♖g5+ ♔f6 26 ♖e1 ♕e6 27 ♖xe6+ fxe6 28 ♖g6+ ♔e7 29 ♖g7+ 1-0

Just to show that Black can sometimes land both bishops on the white king...

Kirillov – Furman
Vilnius 1949

1 e4 e5 2 ♘f3 ♘c6 3 ♗b5 a6 4 ♗a4 ♘f6 5 ♕e2 b5 6 ♗b3 ♗e7 7 a4 b4 8 ♗d5 ♘xd5 9 exd5 ♘d4 10 ♘xd4 exd4 11 0-0 0-0 12 ♕c4 c5 13 dxc6 dxc6 14 ♕xc6 ♖a7

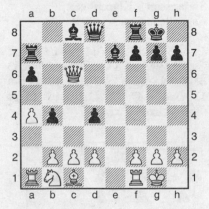

Black has sacrificed a pawn for space, development, and the bishop pair.

15 ♕f3 ♖c7 16 d3 ♗b7
Black is not interested in winning back a pawn on c2; the black rook has greater designs in mind.

17 ♕d1 ♗d6

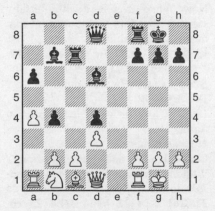

The bishops are aimed at the target, and await the launch codes...

18 ♘d2 ♖e8 19 ♘c4
19 ♘f3 would be an easy move to suggest with the benefit of hindsight, but White's defence would remain difficult.

19...♗xh2+! 20 ♔xh2 ♕h4+ 21 ♔g1 ♗xg2! 22 ♔xg2 ♖c6 23 ♗f4
23 ♕f3 ♖g6+ 24 ♕g3 ♖e2! 25 ♕xg6 fxg6 26 ♗d2 ♖xd2 27 ♘xd2 ♕g5+ is good for Black.

23...♕xf4 24 ♖h1
24 ♖g1 ♖f6 25 f3 ♖g6+ 26 ♔f1 ♖xg1+ 27 ♔xg1 ♖e6 wins: 28 ♕f1 ♖g6+ 29 ♔g2 ♕xf3 30 ♕xg6 hxg6.

24...♖f6 25 ♖h2
25 ♖h3 ♕xf2+ 26 ♔h1 ♖e2 27 ♕g1 ♕f3+!! 28 ♖xf3 ♖h6+ 29 ♕h2 ♖exh2+ 30 ♔g1 ♖h1+ wins the a1-rook, with a decisive advantage, while 25 f3 ♖g6+ 26 ♔f1 ♕g3 gives Black a mating attack.

25...♖g6+ 26 ♔h1 ♖e1+! 0-1
27 ♕xe1 ♕f3+ 28 ♖g2 ♕xg2#.

Strictly speaking the next example is not a double bishop sacrifice, since the initial ♗xh7+ is an exchanging manoeuvre. Nevertheless it fits the theme well, and is perhaps a more typical example of how things work out in practice.

Loef – Gros
Wiesbaden 1993

1 e4 c5 2 ♘f3 ♘c6 3 d4 cxd4 4 ♘xd4 e6 5 ♗e3 a6 6 c4
Putting a clamp on ...d5 ideas.
6...♕c7 7 ♘c3 ♘f6 8 ♗d3 ♗e7 9 0-0 0-0 10 f4 d6 11 ♖c1 ♘xd4 12 ♗xd4 b6 13 e5 ♘d7 14 ♔h1 dxe5 15 fxe5 ♘xe5

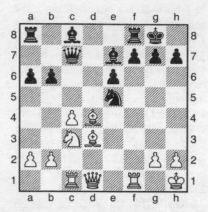

This capture "demonstrates all the good sense of a man parachuting into an alligator farm" as they might put it in the documentation for id software's computer game Quake.

16 ♗xh7+ ♚xh7 17 ♕h5+ ♚g8 18 ♗xe5

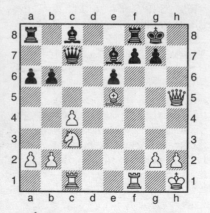

18...♗d6?

18...♕xc4 at least forces White to find 19 ♕f3!, e.g. 19...♗d7 20 ♘e4 ♕b5 21 ♗xg7! ♚xg7 22 ♕g4+ ♚h6 23 ♖f3, winning.

19 ♗xg7

19 ♘e4 also wins on the spot: 19...♗xe5 20 ♘g5 ♖d8 21 ♖xf7, etc.

19...♚xg7

19...f5 prevents immediate mate, but White will have a decisive material plus.

20 ♕g5+ ♚h8 21 ♖f6 1-0

And now a failed attempt at immortality...

Stefansson – Klarenbeek
Cappelle la Grande 1993

1 e4 c5 2 ♘f3 e6 3 d4 cxd4 4 ♘xd4 ♘c6 5 ♘c3 a6 6 ♘xc6 bxc6 7 ♗d3 d5 8 0-0 ♘f6 9 ♕e2 ♗e7 10 b3 0-0 11 ♘a4 ♘d7 12 ♗b2 ♗b7 13 f4 ♘b6 14 exd5 ♘xa4

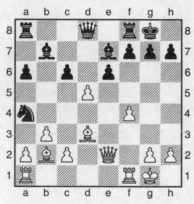

Now White tries a double bishop sacrifice, but this is asking a bit too much of the position.

15 ♗xh7+ ♚xh7 16 ♕h5+ ♚g8 17 ♗xg7 ♚xg7 18 ♖f3 ♗c5+

Black vacates e7 with tempo.

19 ♚h1 ♖g8!

19...♖e8 also provides a fire-escape for the king.

20 dxe6 ♕f6!

Both defending and counterattacking. White has nothing for the pieces, and soon lost, as follows:

21 ♖e1 ♚f8 22 bxa4 ♗b4 23 c3

♗e7 24 ♖ee3 c5 25 ♕xf7+ ♕xf7 26 exf7 ♖xg2 27 ♖xe7 0-1

An important point to remember is that a double bishop sacrifice should not be played just because it is possible. Having sacrificed one bishop on h7, it is wholly conceivable that a second bishop bearing down on g7 might be worth more alive than dead.

D. Lukić – S. Ilić
Arandjelovac 1991

1 e4 c5 2 ♘f3 e6 3 d4 cxd4 4 ♘xd4 ♘f6 5 ♘c3 d6 6 f4 ♘c6 7 ♗e3 ♗e7 8 ♕f3 0-0 9 0-0-0 ♕c7 10 ♖g1 a6 11 g4 ♖e8 12 g5 ♘d7 13 h4 b5 14 ♗d3 ♘xd4 15 ♗xd4 b4 16 ♘e2 a5 17 e5 ♗b7

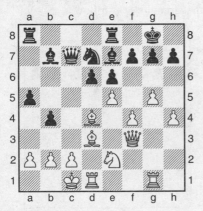

White decides to try a double bishop sacrifice.

18 ♗xh7+!
Bishop number one is good value.
18...♔xh7 19 ♕h5+ ♔g8
Now White should have played a simple attacking move. Instead he opts for a gratuitous second sacrifice, rendering the game highly unclear.
20 exd6?!

It's not clear how bad this is, but there was a clear win by 20 g6! fxg6 21 ♖xg6! ♗f8 (21...dxe5 22 ♖xg7+ ♔xg7 23 ♖g1+ forces mate) 22 exd6 with an overwhelming attack.
20...♗xd6 21 ♗xg7?
Now it is not clear whether White is even better. 21 g6 ♗xf4+ 22 ♘xf4 (not 22 ♔b1? fxg6) 22...♕xf4+ 23 ♔b1 fxg6 24 ♖xg6! is still good for White (and not 24 ♕xg6? ♖e7 25 ♗xg7 ♗e4!, killing the attack).
21...♗xf4+ 22 ♔b1

22 ♘xf4 ♕xf4+ 23 ♔b1 ♔xg7 24 g6 (24 ♖df1 ♖h8) 24...♖h8 25 gxf7+ ♔f6 26 f8♕+ ♖axf8 27 ♖g6+ ♔e7 28 ♖g7+ ♔f6 and now 29 ♖g6+ is a draw. On the other hand, 29 ♕g6+ ♔e5 is messy, though probably good for Black.
22...♔xg7 23 g6 ♖h8 24 gxf7+ ♔f6 25 ♖g6+ ♔e7 26 ♕g4

26 f8♕+ ♖axf8 27 ♖g7+ ♔d8 28 ♖gxd7+ ♕xd7 29 ♕xa5+ ♗c7 30 ♖xd7+ ♔xd7 is good for Black.
26...♘f6 27 ♖xf6 ♔xf6 28 ♘xf4 ♕e5 (forced)

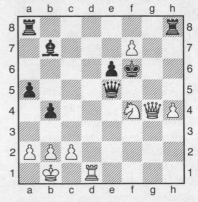

29 ♖f1

Instead 29 ♖d7 ♕e1+ 30 ♖d1 ♕e5 repeats, while after 29 ♕g6+ ♔e7 30

♕g3 ♔f6 (30...♔xf7 31 ♖d7+ ♔e8
32 ♖e7+ ♔xe7 33 ♘g6+ is winning
for White in view of Black's lack of
coordination) 31 ♖d7 (31 ♕g6+ repeats) 31...♔f5 (31...♖h6? 32 f8♕+
♖xf8 33 ♖xb7 is good for White) 32
♕g5+ ♔e4 33 ♕xe5+ ♔xe5 34
♘g6+ ♔f6 35 ♘xh8 ♗d5 the knight
is trapped.

29...♕e4??

29...♕f5.

30 ♘h5++??

White cannot resist the double check,
but in doing so, he misses a simple
win: 30 ♕g5+ ♔xf7 31 ♘d5+ forces
mate.

30...♔e7 31 ♕g5+ ♔d6

The only move.

32 ♘f6

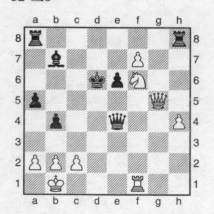

There now follows a comedy of errors, one can only assume in desperate mutual time-trouble.

32...♕xh4??

32...♕e2.

33 ♖d1+

33 ♕xh4 ♖xh4 34 ♘e8+ and White
gets a new queen.

33...♗d5 34 ♘e8+ ♔c6 35 ♕e5??

35 ♕xh4 ♖xh4 36 f8♕ wins simply
enough. Instead the game rolled

along to its illogical conclusion...

35...♕h2??

35...hxe8 wins for Black.

36 ♕d4??

36 ♕xh2 ♖xh2 37 f8♕ was White's
last chance.

**36...hxe8 37 fxe8♕+ ♖xe8 38 ♕a7
♕c7 39 ♕a6+ ♕b6 40 ♕e2 ♖g8 41
♕h5 ♖f8 42 ♕g5 ♕f2 43 ♕e5 ♕c5
44 ♕g7 a4 45 c4 bxc3 0-1**

The Isolated Queen's Pawn (IQP) and the d5 Pawn Sacrifice

An isolated queen's pawn (d-pawn)
can arise from many openings as a
result of two pairs of pawns being
exchanged in the centre. Typically
the structure is as follows:

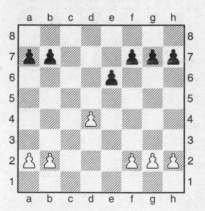

In an ending, the isolated pawn spells
trouble for White, but in a middlegame with the board full of pieces,
the pawn marks out a slight space
advantage and provides support for a
piece (generally a knight) on e5, and
cover for attacking ideas on the b1–
h7 diagonal. Putting a few pieces
onto the board...

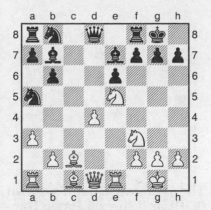

... a typical scenario is for White to put a bishop on c2, play ♕d3, and if Black plays ...g6 in reply, then ♗h6 can be played. For instance, from the diagram (please don't ask me what on earth Black has been doing to reach this position!), White could play **1 ♕d3 g6 2 ♗h6 ♖e8 3 ♘xf7 ♔xf7 4 ♘e5+ ♔g8 5 ♘xg6** with a very strong attack.

The following games demonstrate some rather deeper ideas, you'll be pleased to hear.

Kamsky – Karpov
Elista FIDE Wch (2) 1996

1 e4 c6 2 d4 d5 3 exd5 cxd5 4 c4 ♘f6 5 ♘c3 e6 6 ♘f3 ♗b4 7 cxd5 ♘xd5 8 ♗d2 ♘c6 9 ♗d3 ♗e7 10 0-0 0-0 11 ♕e2 ♘f6 12 ♘e4
Kamsky plays a vigorous pawn sacrifice against his experienced opponent. This was a tense psychological moment to employ such a strategy, with Karpov having won game one. It would be normal in a long match to play quietly in such a situation, rather than play for blood and risk

going two points down at the very start. The standard policy would be to slow things down, as White playing "with the draw in hand", and then blocking as Black before coming out fighting in the next game as White.

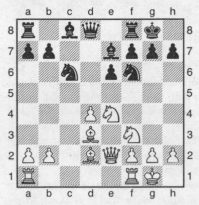

12...♗d7
Let's see what happens if Black grabs the pawn: 12...♘xd4 13 ♘xd4 ♕xd4 14 ♗c3 and now White has some useful open lines and very active pieces:

a) 14...♕d8 tries to cover f6 to hold the kingside structure together: 15 ♘xf6+ ♗xf6 (15...gxf6?? 16 ♕g4+ ♔h8 17 ♕e4) 16 ♖ad1 ♗d7 (16...♕e7 17 ♕e4 g6 18 ♗b4 picks off the exchange) and now White must have some advantageous ways to regain the pawn: 17 ♗xh7+ (17 ♕e4 g6 18 ♗b5 ♗xc3 19 bxc3 ♗xb5 is not so clear) 17...♔xh7 18 ♕e4+ ♔g8 19 ♕xb7 ♗xc3 20 ♖xd7 ♕f6 21 bxc3 ♕xc3 22 ♖xf7.

b) 14...♕d5 15 ♘xf6+ puts the black king under considerable pressure since his pawn cover will be shattered: 15...♗xf6 (15...gxf6 16 ♖ad1) 16 ♗xf6 gxf6.

**13 Rad1 Rc8 14 Rfe1 ♘d5 15 ♘c3
♘f6 16 a3**

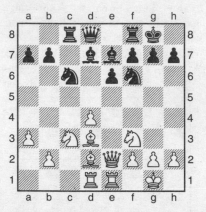

Now we have a fairly normal IQP
position, and Black must choose a
plan carefully. However, his next two
moves create an odd impression; can
he really claim that it is worth losing
a tempo to "lure" White's bishop to
g5?

16...♕c7 17 ♗g5

Threatening 18 d5.

17...♕a5

17...h6 is one attempt to meet the
threat: 18 d5 hxg5 (18...exd5 19
♗xf6 ♗xf6 20 ♘xd5 ♕d8 21 ♗b1
gives Black severe problems on the
centre files; 18...♘xd5 19 ♘xd5
exd5 20 ♗xe7 Rfe8 21 Rc1 ♗g4 22
Rxc6 bxc6 23 ♕e5 ♗xf3 24 gxf3
♕xe5 25 Rxe5 Rc7 26 ♗d6 Rxe5 27
♗xe5 is good for White) 19 dxc6
♗xc6 20 ♘xg5 is not too clear, although Black's king is a cause for
some concern.

18 d5!

This is the standard blow White is
always trying to land in IQP positions. Immediately Black is under
several threats and the coordination
of his pieces comes in for scrutiny.

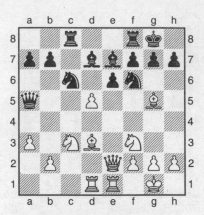

18...exd5 19 ♗xf6 ♗xf6

The scene is set for another, by now
very familiar sacrifice, albeit only a
temporary one.

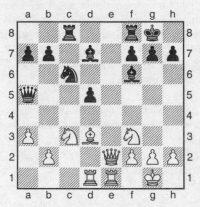

20 ♗xh7+ ♔xh7 21 Rxd5 ♗xc3

Otherwise White regains the piece
with a crushing game, e.g. 21...♕c7
22 ♕d3+ g6 23 Rxd7 gives White an
extra pawn.

22 Rxa5 ♗xa5 23 b4

A key point: White will win a bishop
without shedding the exchange on
e1.

**23...♔g8 24 bxa5 ♗g4 25 a6 bxa6
26 ♕e4 ♗xf3 27 ♕xf3**

White should be winning, but there is

still plenty of work for Kamsky to do.

27...♖fe8 28 ♖a1 ♖e6 29 h3 ♖d8 30 ♕c3 ♖dd6 31 ♖b1 ♖d7 32 ♕c4 a5 33 ♖b5 ♖d1+ 34 ♔h2 ♖d2 35 ♖f5 ♖d4 36 ♕c3 ♖dd6 37 ♖c5 ♖f6 38 ♖c4 ♖fe6 39 ♖c5 ♖f6 40 ♕e3 ♖fe6 41 ♕g3 ♖g6 42 ♕b3 ♖gf6 43 ♕b7 ♖fe6 44 ♕c7 ♖f6 45 f4 g6 46 f5 gxf5 47 ♖xf5 ♖de6 48 ♖h5 ♖h6 49 ♕g3+ ♔f8 50 ♖d5 ♖hg6 51 ♕f2 ♖gf6 52 ♕b2 ♔e7 53 ♖h5 ♖h6 54 ♖b5 ♖hg6 55 ♕c3 ♔f8 56 ♖h5 ♖h6 57 ♖f5 ♖hg6 58 ♕f3 ♖g7 59 ♕f4 ♔g8 60 ♕c7 ♔f8 61 ♕c8+ ♔e7 62 ♖d5 ♔f6 63 ♕h8 ♖e4 64 ♖h5 ♘e7 65 ♖h7 1-0

Dizdar – Am. Rodriguez
Belgrade 1988

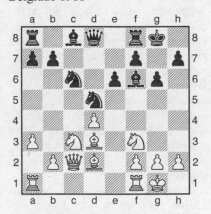

This is a fairly standard type of IQP position, and the game continuation is a good thematic example of the sort of play that can arise.

13 ♗h6 ♖e8 14 ♖ad1 ♘xc3 15 ♕xc3!?

This keeps more pressure on the c6-knight than capturing with the pawn. 15 bxc3 is more obvious, obtaining

the pawn structure (c3 and d4 without pawns on the b- or e-files) that Nimzowitsch dubbed "the isolated pawn couple".

15...♗d7

15...♘xd4 16 ♗b5 is good for White. 15...♗xd4 allows White obvious compensation, but no drastic instant win.

16 ♗e4 ♖c8 17 ♕d2 ♘a5 18 ♕f4 ♗c6 19 ♗xc6 ♘xc6 20 ♘e5!?

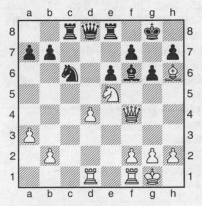

20...♕e7

20...♕xd4!? 21 ♖xd4 ♗xe5 is quite a robust queen sacrifice. Black gets rook, knight and pawn for the queen, and his king is in no particular danger.

21 ♘g4 ♗g7 22 d5!?

22 ♗g5 f6 may just about survive for Black: 23 ♘xf6+ (23 ♗xf6? ♖f8 wins for Black, since after 24 ♗xe7 ♖xf4 two white pieces are attacked) 23...♗xf6 24 ♕xf6 (24 ♗xf6 ♖f8 25 ♗xe7 ♖xf4 26 ♗c5 b6 and Black regains the pawn) 24...♕xf6 25 ♗xf6 ♖f8 26 ♗g5 ♖f5 27 ♗e3 ♖d5 and Black gangs up on the d-pawn.

22...exd5 23 ♗xg7 ♔xg7 24 ♖xd5 f5?!

As a general principle, defensive

pawn moves should only be played when they are absolutely necessary. This is not yet the case here. 24...♖cd8 25 ♖h5 f5 (25...gxh5 26 ♕h6+ and 27 ♘f6(+) wins the black queen) 26 ♘e3 is not very clear at all; is the white rook active, or misplaced on h5?

25 ♕d2!

Threatening both 26 ♖d7 and 26 ♕c3+.

25...♔g8 26 ♖d7 ♕e6 27 ♘h6+ ♔h8 28 ♘f7+ ♔g8 29 ♘h6+ ♔h8 30 ♘f7+ ♔g8

Presumably these rather ugly repetitions were to save clock time, in case complications break out before move 40.

31 ♘g5 ♕b3 32 ♘xh7 ♖ed8?

Black was lost anyway, but now White mates.

33 ♘f6+ 1-0

There will follow 34 ♕h6#.

Steinitz – Von Bardeleben
Hastings 1895 (WGG 6)

1 e4 e5 2 ♘f3 ♘c6 3 ♗c4 ♗c5 4 c3 ♘f6 5 d4 exd4 6 cxd4 ♗b4+ 7 ♘c3 d5

Theory regards 7...♘xe4 as best, when White is struggling for equality in the notorious and thoroughly analysed complications after 8 0-0 ♗xc3 9 d5 ♗f6 10 ♖e1 ♘e7 11 ♖xe4 d6 – see page 120 for further details.

8 exd5 ♘xd5 9 0-0 ♗e6 10 ♗g5

Now White has the initiative in a position with level material.

10...♗e7 11 ♗xd5 ♗xd5 12 ♘xd5 ♕xd5 13 ♗xe7 ♘xe7 14 ♖e1 f6 15 ♕e2 ♕d7

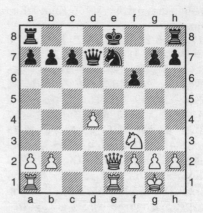

16 ♖ac1

Not the sharpest. 16 d5 is Romanovsky's suggestion, e.g. 16...♔f7 17 ♖ad1 (a vital difference compared to the next note) 17...♖ad8 (17...♘xd5 18 ♘g5+ fxg5 19 ♕f3+) 18 ♕e6+.

16...c6?!

With this move Black underestimates the forthcoming square-vacating pawn sacrifice. 16...♔f7 has been regarded as a major improvement. White has a variety of attempts, but none that gives a serious advantage:

a) 17 ♕xe7+ ♕xe7 18 ♖xe7+ ♔xe7 19 ♖xc7+ ♔d6 20 ♖xg7 ♖hc8 followed by ...♖c7 is good for Black, whose king is very active – this is old analysis by Réti.

b) 17 ♘g5+ (Gufeld and Stetsko) 17...fxg5 18 ♕f3+ ♘f5 19 g4 will regain the material and provides some chance of White keeping an edge, but with his king also now exposed, it will be nothing serious, e.g. 19...c6 20 ♖e5 g6 21 gxf5; 19...♖ae8 20 ♖e5; 19...♖hd8 20 ♖e5 ♔g8 21 ♖xf5.

c) 17 ♘e5+ fxe5 18 dxe5 is Colin Crouch's interesting suggestion in his

book reanalysing the games from great Hastings tournament of 1895.
17 d5!

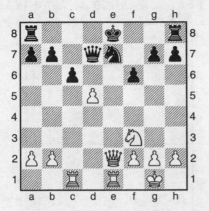

This excellent pawn sacrifice suddenly enlivens the struggle.
17...cxd5 18 ♘d4

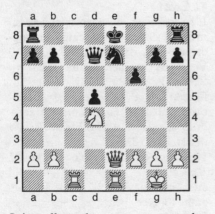

It is well worth a pawn to get such a wonderful square for the knight.
18...♔f7 19 ♘e6

White threatens an invasion on c7.
19...♖hc8 20 ♕g4

Now on g7.
20...g6 21 ♘g5+

The discovered attack on the black queen forces the reply.
21...♔e8 22 ♖xe7+!

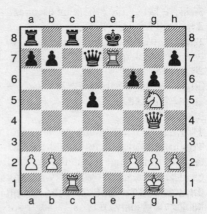

Starting one of the most famous sacrificial sequences in chess history. The rook cannot be taken, but Black has a cunning defensive idea.
22...♔f8

Black suffers a disaster if he touches the rook: 22...♕xe7 23 ♖xc8+ ♖xc8 24 ♕xc8+ leaves White a piece up, while 22...♔xe7 gives White a pleasant choice of winning lines:

a) 23 ♕b4+ ♔e8 (23...♕d6 24 ♕xb7+ ♕d7 25 ♖e1+ ♔d6 26 ♘f7+) 24 ♖e1+ ♔d8 25 ♘e6+ safely wins the queen since White has two pieces covering e1.

b) 23 ♖e1+ ♔d6 24 ♕b4+ ♔c7 (24...♖c5 25 ♖e6+) 25 ♘e6+ ♔b8 26 ♕f4+ wins in view of 26...♖c7 27 ♘xc7 ♕xc7 28 ♖e8#.

After Black's actual choice, 22...♔f8, the black queen cannot be taken due to mate on the back rank. Meanwhile all four of White's pieces are under attack.
23 ♖f7+!

23 ♖xc8+ ♖xc8 24 ♖f7+ ♔g8 25 ♖g7+ ♔h8 26 ♖xh7+ ♔g8 27 ♖g7+ ♔h8 is only a draw, since if White goes in for 28 ♕h4+? ♔xg7 29 ♕h7+ ♔f8 30 ♕h8+ ♔e7 31 ♕g7+

♔d8 32 ♕f8+ ♔c7 the king escapes.

23...♔g8 24 ♖g7+!

Aiming to decoy the black king so that the black queen falls with check.

24...♔h8

24...♔f8 is no better: 25 ♘xh7+ ♔xg7 26 ♕xd7+.

25 ♖xh7+! 1-0

This "1-0" needs some explanation. Von Bardeleben here saw the spectacular finish that awaited him, and elected to "resign" by simply leaving the tournament hall and not coming back. Obviously, this is rather poor sportsmanship.

After this devastating loss he even wanted to withdraw from the tournament. Ironically, this game is now virtually the only thing he is remembered for – perhaps the idea of gaining immortality as a loser is what upset him so much. The key variation is 25...♔g8 26 ♖g7+ ♔h8 27 ♕h4+ ♔xg7 28 ♕h7+ ♔f8 29 ♕h8+ ♔e7 30 ♕g7+ ♔e8 (30...♔d8 allows White to save a couple of moves: 31 ♕f8+) 31 ♕g8+ ♔e7 32 ♕f7+ ♔d8 33 ♕f8+ ♔e8 34 ♘f7+ ♔d7 35 ♕d6#.

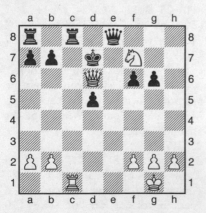

A classic mating finish.

Karpov – Yusupov
USSR Ch (Moscow) 1988

1 c4 e6 2 ♘c3 d5 3 d4 ♗e7 4 ♘f3 ♘f6 5 cxd5 exd5 6 ♗g5 c6 7 ♕c2 g6 8 e4

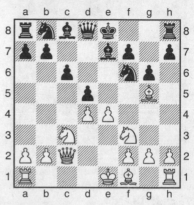

8...♘xe4

It's not clear whether this was an oversight or not; both cases are conceivable. 8...dxe4 9 ♗xf6 ♗xf6 10 ♕xe4+ is considered quite OK.

9 ♗xe7! ♔xe7

Forced since 9...♕xe7 10 ♘xd5! cxd5 (10...♕e6 11 ♘c7+) 11 ♕xc8+ ♕d8 12 ♗b5+ ♔e7 13 ♕xb7+ is a disaster for Black.

10 ♘xe4 dxe4 11 ♕xe4+ ♗e6 12 ♗c4 ♕a5+

12...♖e8 may well hold Black's game together better.

13 ♔f1!

13 ♘d2 ♘d7 14 0-0-0 ♖ae8 enables Black to defend.

13...♕f5 14 ♕e3 ♘d7

14...♔f6? walks into 15 d5! and a deadly queen check on the long diagonal, while 14...♔f8 15 ♗xe6 ♕xe6 16 ♕h6+ ♔g8 17 g3 ♘d7 18 ♔g2 followed by bringing a rook to the e-file, is Karpov's analysis.

15 ♖e1 ♖ae8

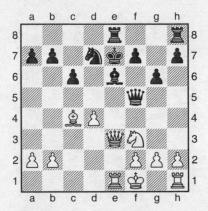

16 d5!!

This pawn sacrifice both gives the white knight an ideal post in the centre and opens several lines for the other white pieces.

16...cxd5 17 ♗b5!

This pin is an essential part of White's plan. Instead 17 ♘d4 ♕e5! is OK for Black.

17...a6

17...♔f8 would be met by 18 ♕c3 and bringing the knight to d4.

18 ♕a3+

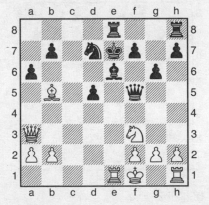

18...♔d8

18...♔f6 loses to 19 ♗xd7 ♗xd7 20

♕c3+; the king has nowhere to run.

19 ♕a5+ ♔e7

19...♔c8 20 ♖c1+ ♔b8 21 ♕c7+ ♔a8 22 ♘d4 ♕f6 23 ♗c6 wins.

20 ♕b4+ ♔f6

20...♔d8 21 ♘d4 ♕f6 22 ♗xa6 bxa6 23 ♖c1! (it's surprising, but the quiet move is best; 23 ♘c6+ ♔c7 24 ♖c1 ♖a8 25 ♘a5+ ♔d8 26 ♕b7 ♔e7 27 ♘c6+ ♔d6 28 ♕b4+ ♔c7 is an amusing way to repeat the position) 23...♖eg8 24 ♖c6 leaves Black with no decent defence against the threat of 25 ♖xa6 and 26 ♖a8+.

21 ♕d4+

21 ♗xd7 is no good in view of 21...♕d3+.

21...♔e7 22 ♗d3! ♕h5

22...♕f6 23 ♕b4+ ♔d8 24 ♕xb7 gives Black an amusing and trappy idea, 24...♕xf3!?, hoping for 25 gxf3?? ♗h3+ 26 ♔g1 ♖xe1+ 27 ♗f1 ♖xf1#, but 25 ♕a8+ ♔e7 26 ♕xe8+ ♖xe8 27 gxf3 wins for White nevertheless.

23 h4!

White starts seizing squares on the kingside.

23...♔d8 24 ♘g5 ♖hf8 25 ♗e2! ♕h6 26 ♗f3

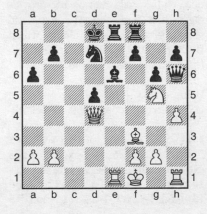

Black's pieces have been systematically pushed back, and White now dominates the centre. A comparison of the last three diagrams eloquently shows the success of Karpov's dynamic strategy.

26...♖e7 27 ♕b4

Threatening both the b7- and d5-pawns.

27...♘f6 28 ♕d6+

28 ♕f4!, threatening both 29 ♘xe6+ and 29 ♕b8+, would bring the game to an end more quickly. However, Karpov's method is quite sufficient to win the game.

28...♖d7 29 ♕f4 ♘g8 30 ♗g4! ♔c8 31 ♗xe6 fxe6 32 ♖c1+ ♔d8 33 ♘xe6+ ♔e7 34 ♕xf8+ ♕xf8 35 ♘xf8 ♔xf8 36 ♖h3 ♘e7 37 h5 ♔g7 38 h6+ ♔f6 39 ♖f3+ ♔e6 40 ♖e1+ ♔d6 41 ♖f6+ ♔c7 42 g4 ♘c6 43 ♖e8 d4 1-0

Having seen some of these d4-d5 pawn sacrifices, you may be wondering whether the d-pawn has to be isolated for it to work. The answer, of course, is no. Even when the d-pawn is supported by a pawn on e4, d4-d5 can be played as a pawn sacrifice, with ...exd5 met by e5, providing White with the d4-square and blocking some lines along which Black might otherwise counterattack. Here is a famous example:

Polugaevsky – Tal

USSR Ch (Moscow) 1969 (WGG 58)

1 d4 ♘f6 2 c4 e6 3 ♘f3 d5 4 ♘c3 c5 5 cxd5 ♘xd5 6 e4 ♘xc3 7 bxc3 cxd4 8 cxd4 ♗b4+ 9 ♗d2 ♗xd2+ 10 ♕xd2 0-0 11 ♗c4 ♘c6 12 0-0 b6 13 ♖ad1! ♗b7 14 ♖fe1 ♘a5 15

♗d3 ♖c8

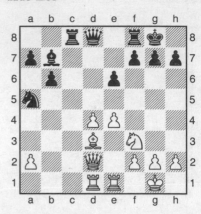

16 d5!

This is a thematic line-opening sacrifice with this central structure.

16...exd5 17 e5!

For the pawn, White has blunted the b7-bishop, gained the d4- and f5-squares and the possibility of e5-e6.

17...♘c4

Black could set up a more stout defence, but Tal wishes to bring the game to an immediate crisis.

18 ♕f4

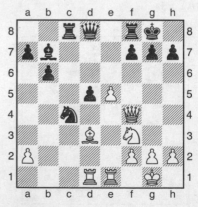

18...♘b2

This allows, and indeed encourages, the familiar bishop sacrifice on h7.

Presumably Tal felt that it ought not to work, otherwise he would have played a more defensive move, e.g. 18...h6 19 e6 (19 ♕f5 g6) 19...fxe6 20 ♕g4 though this gives White some attacking prospects on the light squares. On the other hand, 18...g6 looks ugly, but how should White refute it? 19 h4 is one idea, while 19 ♕h6 is inconclusive:

a) 19...f6 20 ♗xg6 is good for White since 20...hxg6? 21 ♕xg6+ ♔h8 22 ♖d4 wins on the spot.

b) 19...♕d7 20 ♘g5 f5 21 exf6 ♖xf6 22 ♗xc4 ♖xc4 23 ♘xh7 ♖e6 (23...♕xh7 24 ♖e8+ ♔f7 25 ♕f8#) 24 ♖xe6 ♕xe6 25 ♘g5 and White wins easily.

c) 19...f5 is best, e.g. 20 exf6 (probably wrong) 20...♕xf6 21 ♘g5 ♖c7 22 ♘e6 ♕xf2+ 23 ♔h1 ♖e7 isn't too clear, e.g. 24 ♕xf8+ (24 ♖f1 ♕xf1+ 25 ♖xf1 ♖xf1+ 26 ♗xf1 ♖xe6) 24...♕xf8 25 ♘xf8 and then 25...♔xf8 or 25...♖xe1+ 26 ♖xe1 ♔xf8.

19 ♗xh7+! ♔xh7 20 ♘g5+ ♔g6
20...♔g8 21 ♕h4 ♕xg5 22 ♕xg5 ♘xd1 23 ♖xd1 does not give Black enough for his queen.

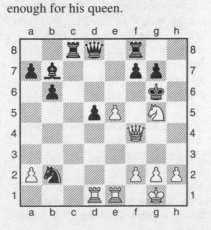

21 h4!
This brilliant move, threatening 22 h5+ ♔xh5 23 g4+ ♔g6 24 ♕f5+, mating, was part of Polugaevsky's and Spassky's preparation.
21...♖c4
21...f5 is met by 22 ♖d4 intending 23 h5+ or 23 ♕g3.

21...♘xd1 is Fritz's initial preference, but there then follows 22 h5+ ♔h6 23 ♘e6+ g5 (23...♔h7 24 ♘xd8) 24 hxg6+ ♔xg6 25 ♕g4+ ♔h6 26 ♕g7+ ♔h5 27 ♘f4+ ♔h4 28 g3#.
22 h5+ ♔h6
22...♔xh5 23 g4+ ♔g6 (23...♔h6 24 ♕h2+ ♔xg5 25 ♕h5+ ♔f4 26 ♕f5#) 24 ♕f5+ ♔h6 25 ♘xf7+ ♖xf7 26 ♕h5#.
23 ♘xf7++
Note that if Black's 21st move had not attacked the white queen, then 23 ♘e6+ would have been decisive.
23...♔h7
23...♔xh5 runs into 24 g4+ ♔g6 25 ♕f5#.
24 ♕f5+ ♔g8

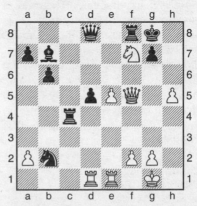

25 e6!
Polugaevsky had been analysing this position before the game, and had

predicted to Grandmaster Efim Geller that it would occur on his board that day! White threatens 26 e7 and 26 ♘xd8. The move is far better than 25 ♘xd8? ♖xf5 26 e6 ♗c8 27 e7 ♗d7, which stops the pawn at the cost of a "mere" bishop.

25...♕f6

25...♕e7 26 h6! wins: 26...♖h4 27 ♖d4 ♖xh6 (27...♖xd4 28 h7#) 28 ♘xh6+ gxh6 29 ♖g4+ ♔h8 30 ♕g6 ♕f6 31 e7.

26 ♕xf6 gxf6 27 ♖d2 ♖c6

27...♖b4 could be a better try.

28 ♖xb2 ♖e8 29 ♘h6+ ♔h7 30 ♘f5 ♖cxe6 31 ♖xe6 ♖xe6 32 ♖c2 ♖c6 33 ♖e2! ♗c8 34 ♖e7+ ♔h8 35 ♘h4 f5 36 ♘g6+ ♔g8 37 ♖xa7 1-0

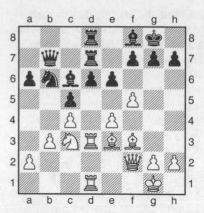

24 ♘d5!

This is a standard idea.

24...exd5 25 exd5 ♗a4 26 ♖c3

The bishop is trapped on a4, so there is no need for 26 bxa4? ♘xc4, when Black would be fully in the game.

26...♘xc4

Black tries to make sense of his queenside pieces, but allows the white rook to transfer triumphantly to the kingside. 26...♗e7 27 bxa4 ♘xa4 28 ♖b3 ♕c7 29 ♖db1 leaves the knight stranded on a4.

27 ♖xc4 ♗b5 28 ♖g4 ♖c7 29 f6 ♗d7

Black is not alert, and allows a pretty, though simple finish. 29...g6 is rather grim for Black, who will find it hard to generate counterplay while White storms the kingside.

30 ♖xg7+! ♗xg7 31 ♕g3 1-0

It will soon be mate.

Next we see a pawn-mass liberated.

The ♘d5 Sacrifice

A white knight landing on d5 (or a black one on d4) eyes a number of key squares, so generally this square is well protected by pieces and pawns. Nevertheless, a common theme is a knight sacrifice on this closely guarded square. There are a number of possible motivations. Perhaps a pawn-mass can be liberated, or else the sacrifice is only temporary: when a pawn recaptures on d5, an enemy piece will be won back, either thanks to a pin, a fork, or an attacked piece simply having no squares – as is the case in the first example.

Landa – Raag
USSR jr Ch (Pinsk) 1989

Black's pieces are congested, which suggests to White a trick to smash through.

Oll – Shabanov
Uzhgorod 1988

1 c4 c6 2 e4 e5 3 ♘f3 d6 4 d4 ♘d7 5 ♘c3 ♘gf6 6 ♗e2 ♗e7 7 0-0 0-0 8

♖b1 ♖e8 9 ♖e1 ♕c7 10 b4 a6 11 ♗g5 h6 12 ♗h4 ♘f8 13 dxe5 dxe5 14 ♗g3 ♘g6 15 c5 a5 16 a3 ♘h5 17 ♗c4 ♘xg3 18 hxg3 ♘f8 19 ♕b3 ♗e6

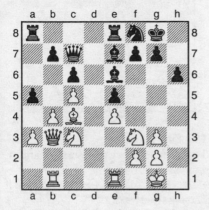

So far, both sides have played fairly methodically, and now it would be all too easy for White to continue by exchanging pieces, his advantage of the first move slowly vanishing. However...

20 ♘d5!

Oll seizes his chance to make something tangible of his space advantage and advanced pawns on the queenside.

20...cxd5

Otherwise the knight enters the black position for free.

21 exd5 ♗f6

21...♗g4? 22 d6 ♗xd6 23 cxd6 is a disaster for Black, since White crashes through to f7.

22 dxe6 ♘xe6

The trade has been very much in White's favour. He now has a mobile queenside pawn majority, a target in the form of the black pawn on e5, and by far the more effective bishop, dominating the light squares.

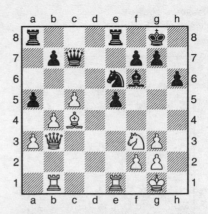

23 ♕e3 axb4 24 axb4 ♘g5 25 ♘xg5 ♗xg5 26 ♕e4 ♗d2 27 ♖ed1 ♗c3 28 ♖d6 ♖ed8 29 ♕b3 ♖xd6 30 cxd6 ♖a1+ 31 ♔h2 ♕xd6 32 ♖xc3 ♕d1

Black has rather desperately sacrificed a piece in the hope of harassing the white king.

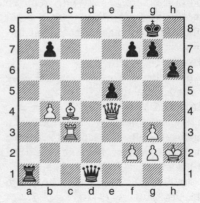

However, White now has a forced mate:

33 ♗xf7+! ♔xf7 34 ♕f5+ ♔e7 35 ♖c7+ ♔d8 36 ♕c8# (1-0)

The next example is far more exciting. The ♘d5 sacrifice is to gain time and some key squares, and to open lines of attack.

Losev – Baikov
Moscow Ch 1989

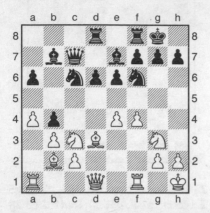

This is a fairly typical position from an Open Sicilian, except for the position of White's bishop on b2. The fact that the bishop indirectly attacks g7 may appear of little importance here, but White realized that he could embark upon a complicated combination based on this precise theme.

16 ♘d5!
After other moves, Black will have quite an easy time.

16...exd5 17 exd5 ♘b8
17...♘xd5 allows White to execute a brilliant, albeit standard, double bishop sacrifice: 18 ♗xh7+! ♔xh7 19 ♕h5+ ♔g8 20 ♗xg7! and now:

a) Not 20...♔xg7? 21 ♘f5+ ♔f6 22 ♕g5+ ♔e6 23 ♘g7+ ♔d7 24 ♕f5#.

b) 20...f6 is the best defence, but 21 ♕h8+ ♔f7 22 ♗xf8 ♗xf8 23 ♕h5+ ♔g7 24 ♕xd5 is good for White in view of Black's exposed king. This is, of course, all familiar ground for readers by now.

18 ♘h5!
Now Black has a tough decision.

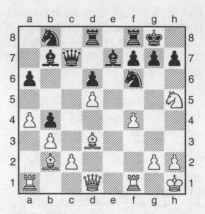

18...♘bd7
The other moves deserve careful analysis:

a) 18...♗xd5 19 ♘xf6+ ♗xf6 20 ♗xf6 gxf6 21 ♕h5.

b) 18...♘e8 19 ♘xg7! ♘xg7 20 ♗xg7 ♔xg7? (20...♕d7 is the best defence, though White is bctter) 21 ♕g4+ ♗g5 (only move) 22 ♕xg5+ ♔h8 23 ♕f6+ ♔g8 24 ♖f3 ♖fe8 25 ♖g3+ ♔f8 26 ♗xh7 and ♖g8#.

c) 18...♘xd5 19 ♘xg7 is murder:

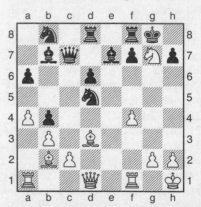

c1) 19...♘c3 20 ♕g4 (20 ♕h5 f5 21 ♗xf5 ♖xf5 22 ♘xf5 is strong too) 20...f5 21 ♗xf5 is awful for Black.

c2) 19...♘f6 20 ♗xf6 ♗xf6 (note

that 20...♕c6 21 ♖g1 changes nothing) 21 ♕h5 wins.

d) 18...♘xh5 19 ♗xh7+ ♔xh7 20 ♕xh5+ ♔g8 21 ♗xg7! ♔xg7 22 ♕g4+ ♔h6 23 ♖f3 ♕c3 (only move) 24 ♖xc3 bxc3 25 ♖e1, "etc." – Krasenkov, but after 25...♗c8 White has no obviously good continuation, e.g. 26 f5 ♗g5 27 ♕h3+ ♔g7 28 ♕xc3+ ♔h7 29 ♕h3+ might possibly offer White something, but not necessarily more than a draw.

19 ♘xg7!! ♔xg7

19...♗xd5 20 ♘f5 ♖fe8 21 ♕e1 ♗f8 22 ♕g3+ ♔h8 23 ♕h4 is good for White.

20 ♕g4+ ♔h8 21 ♕h4

Black is defenceless.

21...♕c3

Or 21...♔g8 22 ♖f3.

22 ♗xc3 bxc3 23 ♗xh7 ♘xh7 24 ♕xe7 ♗xd5 25 ♖ad1 ♘hf6

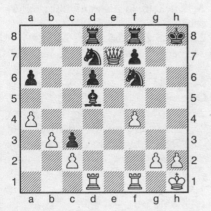

Now White played 26 ♔g1 and White went on to win with his extra material, though **26 ♖xd5** would have been even stronger: 26...♖fe8 27 ♕xf7; 26...♖de8 27 ♖h5+ ♘xh5 28 ♕xd7; or 26...♘xd5 27 ♕h4+ ♔g7 28 ♕g5+, with ♖f3 to follow, forces mate.

Blocked Positions and Pawn Storms

A position that is largely blocked due to interlocking pawn chains may seem to offer little scope for attacking play, but these positions – provided there is at least some lever that can be used to open things up – can lead to some of the most violent attacks. This is because both sides amass their pieces in the part of the board where they have more space and more enemy weaknesses to target. When eventually the position becomes open, both sides will be attacking with their full resources.

Of course, if one side has been unable to manoeuvre their forces in any useful way, the results can be most unfortunate...

Sirota – Tsukerman
Ukrainian/Moldavian Ch 1987/8

1 d4 ♘f6 2 c4 c5 3 d5 e5 4 ♘c3 d6 5 e4 ♗e7

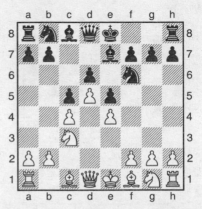

This is the Czech Benoni, a solid, though very passive way for Black to play. To many players it seems an enormous task to make progress against such a solid wall.

6 h3 0-0 7 ⎔f3 ⎔e8

Tony Miles has shown that Black should perhaps leave this knight on f6 for a while, since Black may wish to play ...⎕e8 and ...⎔bd7-f8-g6 if White plays an early g2-g4.

8 ⎕d3 ⎔d7 9 g4 a6 10 a4 ⎕b8 11 ⎕g1 ⎔c7 12 b3 b5 13 a5

Neither of the black knights will find a good square on the queenside.

13...⎔f6 14 ⎔e2 ⎔h8

The idea, presumably, is to play ...⎔g8 and prepare ...f5, but Black never gets the time for this.

15 ⎔g3 g6

Naturally Black wishes to keep the knight out of f5 and h5, but now White's queen's bishop finds a good square.

16 ⎕h6

Note that up to this point, White had not moved this bishop. After all, it would have done little on, for instance, e3, and so putting it there would have merely been stereotyped thinking.

16...⎕e8

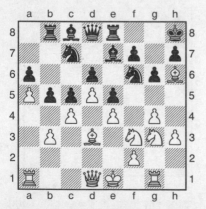

Now White's pieces pile in for the final onslaught.

17 ⎔g5 ⎔g8 18 ⎔f3 bxc4 19 bxc4 ⎕b3 20 ⎔h5!

The knight is invulnerable; the threat is ⎕g7.

20...⎔b5

20...gxh5 21 gxh5 leads to a calamity on the g-file.

21 cxb5 c4 22 ⎕g7

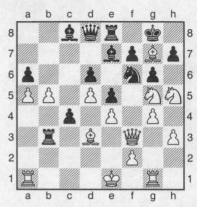

A fianchettoed bishop with a difference!

22...gxh5 23 gxh5 ⎔xg7 24 h6+

24 ⎔e6++ ⎔h8 25 ⎔xd8 is not at all clear.

24...⎔f8?

Otherwise 24...⎔xh6? 25 ⎔xf7#, 24...⎔g6? 25 ⎔e6+ and 24...⎔h8? 25 ⎔xf7# are no use to Black, but 24...⎔g8 is by far the best, and may even keep Black in with a fighting chance, e.g. 25 ⎔e6+ ⎔h8 26 ⎔xd8 ⎕xd8.

25 ⎔h5!! 1-0

25...⎔xh5 26 ⎔xh7# is a beautiful mate.

The King's Indian is well known for its tendency to lead to massive opposite-wing attacks for both sides. In the next example things have gone wrong for White. Black's attack is in full flow, but what has happened to White's queenside penetration?

Starodvorsky – Koniashkin
Naberezhnye Chelny 1988

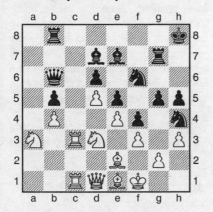

This is a fairly typical King's Indian situation, from which Black launches a virulent attack.

31...♘xg2! 32 ♔xg2 g4 33 fxg4
33 ♗f2 gxf3++ 34 ♔xf3 allows Black a brilliant forced checkmate:

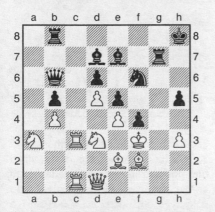

34...♕xf2+!! (34...♖g3+ 35 ♗xg3 ♕e3+ is also good enough) 35 ♔xf2 (35 ♘xf2 ♖g3#) 35...♘xe4+ 36 ♔e1 (36 ♔f3 ♖g3+ 37 ♔xe4 ♖e3#)

36...♗h4+ 37 ♔f1 ♗xh3#.
33...hxg4 34 ♗f2 f3+ 35 ♗xf3 gxf3++ 36 ♔h1
36 ♔xf3 ♕d8 must be an overwhelming attack for Black.
36...♕d8
Black has blown the kingside wide open at minimal material cost, while the white pieces are in no way ready for kingside action. Any King's Indian player should be delighted by this sort of transaction – often well worth heavy material sacrifice.
37 ♕xf3 ♗xh3! 38 ♕xh3+
38 ♖g1 ♖h7 wins; 38 ♘xe5 dxe5 39 ♕xh3+ ♖h7 does not save White either.
38...♖h7 39 ♗h4 ♘d7!
Better than 39...♘xe4 40 ♖c8.
40 ♕g2 ♗xh4 41 ♘xe5 ♘xe5 42 ♖h3 ♕d7 43 ♖cc3 ♖g8 44 ♕f1 ♘g4 45 ♖cf3 ♘f2+ 0-1

Now we see a piece sacrifice smashing through a flimsy carapace that was trying to protect an unhealthy position.

Groszpeter – Mencinger
Belgrade 1988

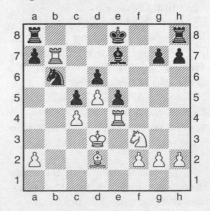

White's position is obviously attractive, but given some time, Black could organize his defences, and even hope to show that White's b7-rook is a liability, rather than a strength. However, White can play an incisive combination to coordinate his rooks and bring the game to a swift conclusion.

21 ♘xe5! dxe5 22 ♖xe5 ♘d7

After 22...♘c8 23 ♗g5 White's task is simpler.

23 ♖e6 0-0-0

It's worth mentioning that some players, including some very strong grandmasters, have made the mistake of thinking that queenside castling is not possible when the b8- (or b1-) square is attacked. This is not the case – it is only the squares to, from, and through which the king moves that matter in this respect. Anyway, castling doesn't help Black here, since there are mating ideas in the air.

24 ♖b5

Threatening mate in one.

24...♖de8 25 ♖c6+ ♔d8 26 ♗a5+ ♘b6 27 ♗xb6+

Again, White's main aim is to get the rooks firing in unison.

27...axb6 28 ♖bxb6 ♖hf8

28...♗f6 would prolong the game, but not change the result, since Black remains paralysed while White's pawns can advance freely.

29 ♖b8+ ♔d7 30 ♖b7+ ♔d8 31 d6 ♖xf2 32 d7! 1-0

It will cost Black all of his pieces to delay mate, even for a short time.

Now for one of the author's humble efforts, in which a handful of sacrifices liven up a blocked position.

A. Martin – Burgess
British League (4NCL) 1995/6

1 e3

An odd first move, but not a bad one, except that it puts Black under far less pressure than normal. When facing such play, it is essential to keep calm as Black, and to view the game as if one were playing with the white pieces, but had somehow lost a tempo along the way, i.e. play to keep the initiative, but don't be too ambitious!

1...g6 2 ♘f3 ♗g7 3 d4 ♘f6 4 c4 0-0 5 ♗e2 d6 6 0-0 ♘bd7 7 ♘c3 e5 8 b4 ♖e8

From the point of view of equalizing, exchanging on d4 might be objectively superior.

9 a4 e4 10 ♘d2

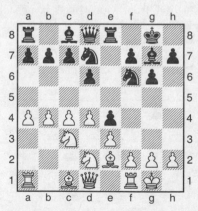

This could well be described as a King's Indian Attack Reversed, since the position is more familiar with colours reversed. For example 1 ♘f3 ♘f6 2 g3 d5 3 ♗g2 e6 4 0-0 ♗e7 5 d3 0-0 6 ♘bd2 c5 7 e4 ♘c6 8 ♖e1 b5 9 e5 ♘d7 10 ♘f1 a5 11 h4 is a typical King's Indian Attack position, which can also be reached via the Sicilian or the French: 1 e4 e6 (1...c5 2 ♘f3 e6 3 d3 d5 4 ♘bd2 is a typical Sicilian move-order) 2 d3 d5 3 ♘d2 c5 4 ♘gf3 ♘c6 5 g3 ♘f6 6 ♗g2 ♗e7 7 0-0 0-0.

10...h5

10...♘f8 is more accurate, since 11 ♕c2 can then be met by 11...♗f5. The move-order I chose has no advantages, and quite possibly some serious drawbacks.

11 ♕c2 ♕e7 12 b5

12 ♘d5?! is ineffective here since 12...♘xd5 13 cxd5 ♘b6 gives White problems defending his d5-pawn.

12...♘f8

This move is essential for Black's plans.

13 a5?!

Not the most relevant move when there is the possibility of some central action. 13 ♘d5 ♘xd5 14 cxd5 is more consistent with White's play. He will then have some pressure on the c-file, while Black will not find it so easy to attack the d5-pawn with his knight on f8, nor to attack on the kingside with one pair of knights off the board.

13...♗f5

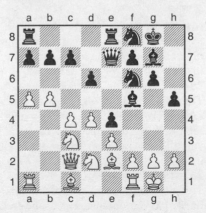

Normality is now restored, and it is far from clear that the queen is well placed on c2, since it is exposed to some tactical tricks, and moving the queen to e1 (a standard resource if Black goes for the ...♘g4, ...♕h4 approach) is no longer feasible.

14 ♗a3

The bishop is not well placed here, but after 14 ♘d5 ♘xd5 15 cxd5 Black can play 15...♗xd4 16 exd4 e3 17 ♗d3 ♗xd3 18 ♕xd3 exd2 19 ♗xd2 ♕e2.

14...♘e6

Black has ...♘xd4, exd4 e3 in mind, but perhaps White should just allow this.

15 ♕b2

Now both queen and bishop are awkwardly placed. It may seem hard to believe if you are new to this type of position, but White soon runs into problems on the long diagonal. 15 ♖fe1 is not good, since f2 is then weak too: 15...♘xd4 16 exd4 e3 17 ♕c1 (17 ♗d3 exf2+! 18 ♔xf2 ♘g4+ 19 ♔f1 ♕e3!! 20 ♖xe3 ♘xe3+ is a fiasco for White; 17 ♕b2 exf2+ 18 ♔xf2 ♕e3+ 19 ♔f1 ♘g4 20 ♗xg4 ♗d3+ wins) 17...exf2+ 18 ♔xf2 ♘g4+ 19 ♗xg4 ♗xd4+ 20 ♔g3 ♕g5 wins for Black.

15...♘g4

A standard attacking move in this set-up. At this point I felt good about my position; almost all my pieces are doing something useful.

16 ♖fe1

16 ♗xg4 hxg4 gives Black the subtle plan of landing his knight on f3 and giving mate on g2 or h2, so White must hurry: 17 ♘dxe4 ♗xe4 18 ♘xe4 ♘xd4 19 exd4 ♕xe4 is quite pleasant for Black, however, in view

of his e-file control and pressure on d4.

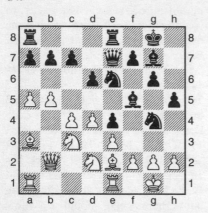

Now I decided that some violence was in order.

16...♘xh2!?

16...♕h4 17 ♗xg4 forces Black to recapture with the queen, rather than the h-pawn, 17...♕xg4 (due to the need to defend e4), and this lessens his attacking potential.

17 ♔xh2 ♘xd4!?

I hadn't actually analysed very much. It felt right, and I'd seen enough to be fairly sure it was at least OK for me.

18 ♔g1

Taking the second knight cannot be recommended, viz. 18 exd4 ♕h4+ 19 ♔g1 ♗xd4 and then:

a) 20 ♖f1 e3! wins for Black.

b) 20 ♘dxe4 ♗xe4 21 ♗d1 ♗xg2!! forces mate, e.g. 22 ♖xe8+ ♖xe8 23 ♔xg2 ♖e1, threatening 24...♕h1+ 25 ♔g3 ♖g1+ 26 ♔f4 ♕h4+ 27 ♔f3 ♕g4#.

18...♕h4 19 ♘f1

After instead 19 g3 ♘e2+ 20 ♘xe2, 20...♗xb2 21 gxh4 ♗xa1 22 ♖xa1 is a messy ending, while 20...♕g5 with ...h4 to follow, is hard to assess.

19...♘xe2+

Note how the pressure on the long diagonal makes it difficult for White to coordinate his defence.

20 ♖xe2 ♗g4

The bishop is heading for f3, but White must attend to the incidental threat to win a whole rook by ...♗xe2, ♕xe2 ♗xc3.

21 ♘g3 ♗f3

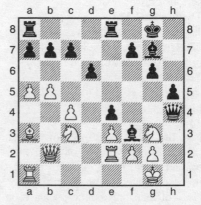

Here the bishop intends to set up some mating nets and also physically prevents White from advancing his f-pawn to provide lateral defence of the kingside.

22 ♖c2 ♕g4 23 ♕c1 h4 24 ♘d5 ♗e5

My main concern was not, of course, to regain material, but to get the king out of the way so the rooks can come to the h-file and give mate!

25 ♗b2 ♔g7

The e5-bishop, having been a true dragon on the long diagonal, is now relegated to the role of "blocker" while Black pours his rooks onto the h-file.

26 gxf3?

This was based on a miscalculation. 26 ♕e1 is the obvious move, and the best practical chance, but Black still has a very powerful attack: 26...hxg3 (26...罝h8 27 奧xe5+ dxe5 28 豐c3 is irritating) 27 fxg3 (27 ②xc7? 罝h8 {threatening mate in three moves by 28...罝h1+ 29 鲁xh1 豐h3+ 30 鲁g1 豐xg2#} 28 fxg3 豐h5 is very good for Black, who has rescued his loose pieces while retaining an attack) 27...罝h8 arrives at a critical position:

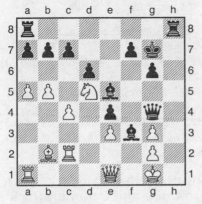

a) 28 ②f4 罝h6 29 gxf3 (29 奧xe5+ dxe5 30 豐c3 f6 is no good for White either) 29...exf3 leaves White defenceless against Black's h-file play.

b) 28 奧xe5+ dxe5 29 豐c3 (29 gxf3 豐h3 wins, e.g. 30 罝g2 exf3) 29...豐xg3 crashes through: 30 ②f4 (White must defend g2) 30...f6 and the house of cards collapses.

26...exf3 27 鲁f1

27 e4 hxg3 28 豐f4 gxf2++ 29 鲁xf2 豐g2+ 30 鲁e3 豐xc2 31 奧xe5+ 罝xe5 32 豐f6+ 鲁g8 is the end of White's "counterattack".

27...hxg3 28 鲁e1 罝h8 29 鲁d2 g2

White is in no position to stop this pawn and save the rest of his position.

30 奧xe5+ dxe5 31 豐b2 豐e4 32 ②xc7

Else Black may play ...c6 and open the d-file free of charge.

32...罝ad8+ 33 ②d5 罝xd5+

Not a difficult sacrifice to play, since various rook-down endings will be easily winning for Black.

34 cxd5 豐xd5+ 35 鲁c3 罝c8+ 36 鲁b4 豐e4+ 37 鲁b3 豐d3+ 38 罝c3 豐xb5+ 39 鲁a2 豐xa5+ 40 罝a3 豐d5+ 41 罝b3

Or 41 豐b3 罝c2+ 42 鲁b1 豐d1#.

41...罝c5 42 罝c1 罝b5 0-1

43 豐c2 罝xb3 (simplest; Black has all sorts of other ways to play) 44 豐xb3 豐xb3+ 45 鲁xb3 g5 intending ...g4-g3, etc.

Next an example with similar themes, but with names that are more difficult to pronounce:

Glianets – Stets
Naberezhnye Chelny 1988

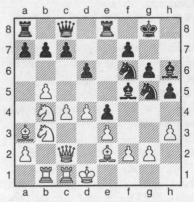

White's king is stuck in the centre (the kingside would be rather too hot for it), but it appears that the position is too closed for this to be a major factor.

21...②f3!

The start of a vigorous, imaginative plan to open avenues of attack.

22 gxf3

If White does not take the knight, then ...♘g1 will follow, exchanging off White's good bishop on e2 – a clear positional gain for Black. 22 ♘d5 is worth considering, though.

22...exf3 23 ♗d3 ♘e4

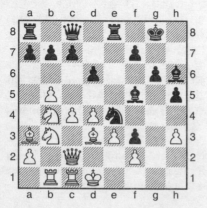

This position is not easy for White, as his major pieces obstruct his king's evacuation. Black will swoop down the kingside, into White's soft underbelly.

24 ♖b2

24 ♘d5, threatening ♗xe4 followed by ♘f6+, can be met by the simple 24...♔g7, with ...c6 to follow.

24...c6

Black prevents ♘d5 before getting on with the attack.

25 h4

White weakens the g4-square, and so allows a trick. 25 ♗xe4 ♗xe4 26 ♕d2 ♕xh3 27 ♕e1 ♕g2 is quite awkward for White though; how does he unravel?

25...♗xe3! 26 fxe3 f2

With the vile threat of 27...♗g4+.

27 ♘d2

27 ♔e2 ♗g4+ 28 ♔f1 ♗h3+ 29 ♔e2 ♕g4#. 27 ♖cb1 is a better try.

27...♗g4+ 28 ♗e2 ♘g3!

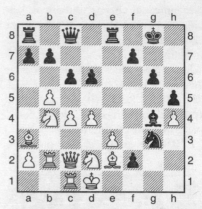

29 ♕d3 ♗xe2+ 30 ♕xe2 ♘xe2 31 ♔xe2 ♕g4+ 32 ♘f3

32 ♔xf2 can be met by 32...♕xh4+ or the more spectacular 32...♖xe3.

32...♕g2 33 ♖f1 ♖xe3+! 34 ♔xe3 ♖e8+ 35 ♘e5 ♕xf1 36 ♖xf2 ♕g1 0-1

Turning the Tables: Active Defence and Counterattack

So far in this section of the book the attackers have had it very much their own way, with the exception of a few warning examples of totally ill-conceived ideas.

Now it's time that the underdogs won a few. Coming under attack is not a death sentence, provided your position is fundamentally sound. Accurate defence should suffice to defuse an attack and either turn the tables or at least survive to some sort of tenable ending.

To be a good defender it is helpful to be a good attacker, since in addition to being able to anticipate the opponent's attacking ideas, the defender should be on the alert for any counterattacking possibilities, maybe by returning sacrificed material to open up the opponent's king, or to disrupt the harmony of his pieces.

The first example sees a little dagger-blow turning the tables on what otherwise looked like a crush.

Tseitlin – Skudnov
Naberezhnye Chelny 1988

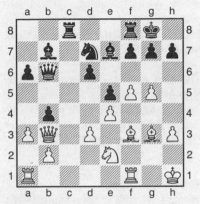

It seems it is time for White, a grandmaster facing a relatively low-rated player, to start forcing matters. However, there is a surprise in store.
23 f6 gxf6 24 &g4 &c5 25 Wxb4 Wxb4 26 axb4

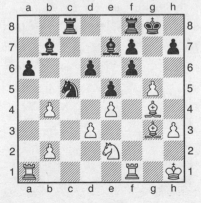

26...f5!

White must have overlooked this move, the main idea of which is simply to prevent White's g-pawn from reaching f6, hitting the black bishop. 26...&e6 27 gxf6 &d8 28 &c3 was the line Tseitlin had probably been anticipating.
27 bxc5
27 &xf5 &xd3 28 &xc8 &xe4+ followed by 29...&xc8 gives Black excellent play for the exchange. 27 &xf5 is met by 27...&xd3.
27...fxg4 28 cxd6 &xd6 29 &f6 &fd8 30 &af1 &d7 31 hxg4 &c2
White's pawns turn out to be very hard to defend.
32 &d4!?
This spirited attempt is met by an exchange sacrifice.
32...exd4 33 &xd6 &xd6 34 &xd6 &d2 35 &c1
35 &f3 gives better drawing chances.
35...&xd3 36 &c7 &xe4+ 37 &h2 &g7
Black has an extra pawn, and went on to win the ending as follows:
38 &e5+ &g6 39 &c8 &xg5 40 &d8 &xg4 41 &xd4 &xd4 42 &xd4 f5 43 b4 h5 44 &c5 h4 45 &f2 f4 46 &e1 h3 47 &d2 &f5 48 &c1 &f3 49 &d2 &c8 50 &c1 &e4 51 &d2 f3 0-1

Viktor Korchnoi is one of the great counter-punchers. Here we see him at his best.

Hübner – Korchnoi
San Francisco 1995

1 e4 e6 2 d4 d5 3 &c3 &f6 4 e5 &fd7 5 f4 c5 6 &f3 &c6 7 &e3 cxd4 8 &xd4 Wb6 9 &cb5
This is a highly committal move.

9...a6

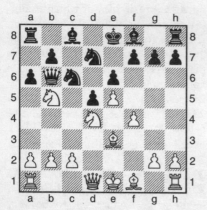

10 ♘f5 ♗c5 11 ♗xc5

Knaak considered this move a blunder, analysing at great length instead the natural 11 ♘bd6+ as leading to a draw after 11...♔f8 12 ♕h5 ♘d8 13 ♘xg7 ♗xe3 14 ♘xe6+ fxe6 15 ♕h6+ ♔e7 16 ♕g5+, a conclusion with which Fritz agrees.

11...♘xc5 12 ♘bd6+ ♔f8 13 ♕h5 ♘d8

Defending f7. Now there is no way for White to hold his queenside together, so he must play all-out for the attack.

14 ♘xg7

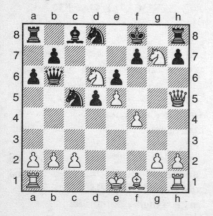

14...♕b4+!

This counterattacking move is a big improvement over 14...♗xg7? 15 ♕g5+ ♔f8 16 ♕h6+ ♔e7 (16...♔g8 17 ♘e8! forces mate) 17 ♕f6+ ♔d7 18 ♕xh8, which was good for White in a game Nunn–Züger, Biel 1990.

15 c3

15 ♔d1 is best met by 15...♕d4+, to which White has no really adequate response.

15...♕xb2 16 ♖d1 ♕xc3+ 17 ♖d2 h6! 18 ♘ge8 ♘e4 0-1

The next example features Vladimir Kramnik in brilliantly resourceful form. White's back rank proves sufficient for him to extract a win after Shirov misplays a good attacking position.

Shirov – Kramnik
Monte Carlo 5th Amber Rapid 1996

1 e4 c5 2 ♘f3 ♘c6 3 d4 cxd4 4 ♘xd4 ♘f6 5 ♘c3 d6 6 ♗g5 e6 7 ♕d2 ♗e7 8 0-0-0 ♘xd4 9 ♕xd4 a6 10 f4 b5 11 ♗xf6 gxf6 12 ♗e2 ♕a5 13 e5 fxe5 14 fxe5 d5

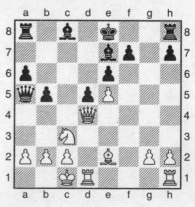

15 ♘xd5!?

15 ♗h5 is a safer way to emphasize the weakness of Black's kingside, but Shirov decided that something rougher was called for.

15...exd5 16 e6 0-0 17 ♖d3 ♗g5+ 18 ♔b1 ♗xe6 19 ♖g3

19 h4 looks quite good. If Black has to reply 19...♕a4, then 20 hxg5 is definitely pleasant for White.

19...h6 20 h4

This looks devastating, but Black has a way to stay in the game. Instead 20 ♕f6 ♕c7 21 ♖xg5+ (21 ♕xh6?? ♕xg3) 21...hxg5 22 ♕xg5+ gives White a draw.

20...♕c7 21 hxg5?

This sacrifice just doesn't work. 21 ♕f2 would keep White well in the game.

21...♕xg3 22 ♖xh6

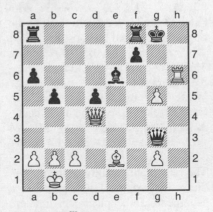

22...f6! 23 ♖g6+

After 23 gxf6 ♖f7 we have a position in which White's back rank buys Black enough time to consolidate; if White's pawn were on b3 rather than b2, then 24 ♗d3 would leave him no worse; as it is, 24...♕e1# would follow.

23...♔h7 24 ♖h6+ ♔g7 25 ♖xf6 ♕e1+ 26 ♗d1 ♖xf6 27 ♕xf6+ ♔g8

28 ♕g6+ ♔f8 29 ♕f6+ ♔e8 0-1

The loose bishop on d1 denies White the time to pick up the a8-rook.

We now see one of the all-time greats defusing an awkward situation.

Marshall – Alekhine
New York 1924

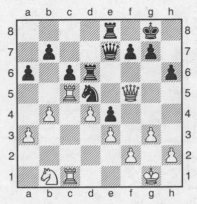

Alekhine, under some pressure, embarks upon a remarkable sequence to force a draw.

21...g6 22 ♕h3 ♕g5

Intending ...f5.

23 ♘c3

The position now explodes in a burst of tactics.

23...b6! 24 ♘xd5

Not 24 ♖c4? ♘xe3!.

24...bxc5 25 ♘c7 cxd4! 26 ♘xe8 dxe3! 27 ♘xd6

27 f4 exf3 28 ♘xd6 f2+ (28...e2? loses to 29 ♕c8+ followed by ♕h8+ and ♘xf7+) 29 ♔f1 e2+ and Black holds the draw: 30 ♔xf2 (30 ♔xe2 ♕xc1 31 ♕f1 ♕b2+ 32 ♔e3 ♕c3+) 30...♕xc1 31 ♕c8+ ♔h7 32 ♔xe2 ♕c2+.

27...exf2+ 28 ♔xf2 ♕d2+ 29 ♔g1 ♕e3+ 30 ♔g2 ♕f3+ 31 ♔g1 ♕e3+ 32 ♔g2 ♕f3+ ½-½

The next game is a strong contender for the award "best blindfold game ever". Believe it or not, the two players sorted through these complications *without seeing the board!*

Kramnik – Ivanchuk
Monte Carlo 5th Amber Blindfold 1996

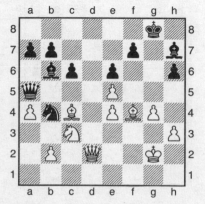

White is in some trouble here. His pawns are ragged and his pieces are not coordinating. Capturing on h6 would allow ...♕xe5, bringing the black queen to a dominant position. Rather than drift into trouble by playing passively, Kramnik finds an imaginative idea:

24 ♗b5!

Now White really threatens 25 ♗xh6 followed by bringing in the queen.

24...cxb5 25 ♗xh6 ♗c5

The only defence.

26 ♕d7

Now the threat is 27 ♕e8+ ♗f8 28 ♕xf8#, so Black must give his king a square.

26...♗g6 27 ♕c8+ ♔h7 28 ♗g5

28 ♕xc5? ♔xh6 is no use to White. After the move played, White has the deadly threat of 29 ♗f6.

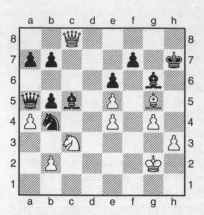

28...♘d5! 29 ♕xc5

29 exd5? ♕b4 allows Black a decisive counterattack.

29...♘xc3 30 ♕xc3

30 bxc3 is possible too.

30...♕xa4

30...♕xc3 31 bxc3 ♗xe4+ 32 ♔g3 bxa4 33 ♗e7 is a draw in view of the opposite-coloured bishops: 33...a5 34 ♔f4 ♗d5 35 h4 b5 (threatening 36...b4 37 cxb4 a3) 36 ♗c5.

31 ♔g3 ♕xe4

White now rekindles his attack to force Black to take perpetual check.

32 ♗f6 b4 33 ♕c8 ♕e1+ 34 ♔f4 ♕f2+ 35 ♔g5 ♕d2+ 36 ♔h4 ♕h6+ 37 ♔g3 ♕e3+ ½-½

The remarkable quality of the play in this blindfold quickplay game is a testament to the phenomenal talent for chess that is possessed by the top players.

The f-pawn Hack

A strategy (if that's the word for it) very popular with club players is to charge the f-pawn up the board towards the opponent's kingside, especially when the king's bishop is fianchettoed. Pieces follow, and the optimum plan is to give mate by move twenty-five. Simplistic, but dangerous.

Tkachev – Alexandria
Biel 1994

1 e4 c5 2 ♘f3 b6 3 d4 cxd4 4 ♘xd4 ♗b7 5 ♘c3 a6 6 ♗d3 d6 7 f4 ♘d7 8 0-0 g6 9 ♕e1 ♗g7 10 ♘f3 b5 11 ♔h1 ♖c8 12 ♗d2 ♘c5 13 a3 ♘f6 14 f5 e6 15 ♖d1 ♘xd3 16 cxd3 0-0

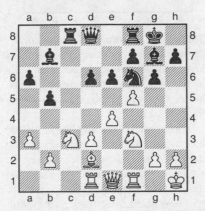

Now we see a standard attacking build-up by White: queen to h4, bishop to g5 or h6, in the latter case with ♘g5 following. Note that an essential prerequisite for this to work is that White can open the f-file and so has the possibility of ♖xf6.

17 ♕h4 exf5 18 ♗g5
Instead 18 exf5 ♘d5! brings about welcome simplifications for Black. Now White intends 19 exf5.

18...h6
An odd move, but it's hard to see how else Black might fight.

19 ♗xh6 fxe4 20 ♘g5
White now has the standard threat of piling in with ♗xg7 and ♖xf6.

20...♖c5

After 20...e3 21 ♗xg7 ♔xg7 22 ♖xf6 ♔xf6 23 ♖f1+ ♔e7 24 ♘h7+ White regains the sacrificed material while keeping the black king on the move.

21 dxe4

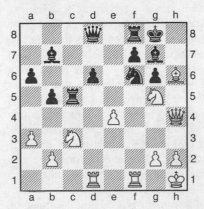

Calmly recapturing. Black is short of defensive or counterattacking plans. The main threat is 22 ♗xg7 ♔xg7 23 ♖xf6 ♖xg5 24 ♖df1.

21...♖e8 22 ♗xg7 ♔xg7 23 ♘xf7!
23 ♖xf6 ♕xf6 24 ♕h7+ is no good since 24...♔f8 is possible thanks to Black's 21st move, but of course the black rook's departure from f8 has its darker side.

23...♔xf7 24 ♕h7+ ♔e6 25 ♕xb7 ♕e7 26 ♕xa6 ♖h8 27 ♖xd6+ 1-0
The black king and queen are overloaded.

I would now like to recommend some ways in which it is possible to defend against this sort of attack. However, once the attacking forces are in place, there is no general method that I have found, so the trick is obviously to stop them getting there in the first place. Ideally, one would like to eliminate White's dark-squared bishop, while retaining the one on g7. Then the black king ought to be very safe. Assuming this is not possible, then if the opponent is limbering up for the big heave-ho, the move ....♗g4 is worth considering. Then it will be possible to eliminate the f3-knight before it can reach g5 and cause the type of destruction that we have seen. But only capture on f3 when you have to; there is no point giving up the bishop pair unless White has invested a fair amount of time into his attack and is developing real threats. More fundamental still, it may be possible to delay kingside castling while the opponent retains the option of this crude scheme. If the centre is still closed, there is no objection to His Majesty staying on e8 until it becomes clear where he should take up more permanent residence.

The h-pawn Hack

Next in the gallery of crudities is another simple but effective plan, popular at all levels of chess. This is particularly directed at a king that is castled on the kingside behind a fianchetto formation. The vital ingredients in White's plan this time are a mobile h-pawn, supported by the king's rook and a queen and bishop lined up on the c1–h6 diagonal, ready to play ♗h6, and exchange off the key defensive bishop. Schematically, the attack is as shown in the next diagram.

From this point, White's idea is simple: exchange pawns on g6, swap bishops on g7, and bring the queen to h6 with check.

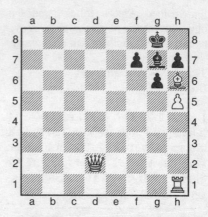

Thereafter it might be instant mate, or there may be more hurdles for White to overcome. In any case, this is a simple plan for bringing some heavy fire-power into the vicinity of the black king.

There will typically be a black knight on f6, which can perhaps be deflected away from defending h7 by means of White playing a knight to d5, or else advancing the g-pawn to g5, and then meeting ...♘h5 with either an exchange sacrifice ♖h1xh5, or else the move ♘g3. Note that the presence of a black knight on f6 rarely discourages White advancing the pawn to h5; the reply ...♘xh5 may only help White to open the h-file at double speed, or be met by a devastating ♖xh5 exchange sacrifice.

If the centre is open, then White may benefit from positioning a bishop on c4 or b3. This is so that when White plays h5 and hxg6, the f7-pawn is pinned, and so the more compromising ...hxg6 is forced. Although in general it is good to keep one's pawns together, and capture towards the centre, this is not the case when the opponent has a queen on h6 just waiting for the chance to drop into h8 and give mate!

Here is a very nice example:

Bläss – Bialas
Bundesliga 1982/3

1 e4 c5 2 ♘f3 ♘c6 3 d4 cxd4 4 ♘xd4 g6 5 ♗e3 ♗g7 6 ♘c3 ♘f6 7 ♗c4 0-0 8 ♗b3 ♕c7 9 f3 a6 10 ♕d2 b5 11 0-0-0 ♗b7 12 h4 ♖ad8 13 h5 e5 14 ♘de2 ♘a5 15 ♗h6

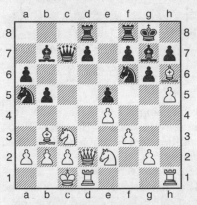

15...♘xb3+ 16 axb3 ♗xh6 17 ♕xh6 d6 18 ♘g3 ♕e7 19 ♖h3 ♘e8 20 ♖dh1 ♖d7

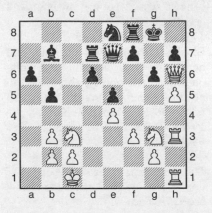

White now has a stunning combination.

21 ♕xh7+!! ♔xh7 22 hxg6++ ♔g7 22...♔g8 23 ♖h8+ ♔g7 24 ♘f5+ ♔f6 25 g7 ♘xg7 26 ♖8h6+ ♔g5 27 ♘xg7! and now mate (28 ♘e2 and 29 ♖1h5#) can only be prevented by great material loss. 22...♔xg6 would be met by 23 ♖h6+ ♔g5 24 ♖1h5+ ♔f4 25 ♘f5 and 26 ♘e2#.

23 ♘f5+ ♔f6 24 g7! ♘xg7 25 ♖h6+ ♔g5 26 ♘xg7! ♗xe4 27 ♘xe4+ ♔f4

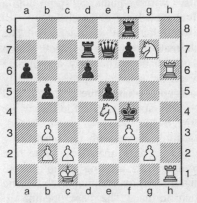

28 ♔d2 1-0

Denying the king its last hope of escape via e3 is the quickest way to force mate, though 28 ♘h5+ ♔e3 29 ♖e1+ ♔d4 30 ♖d1+ ♔e3 31 ♖d3+ ♔e2 32 ♘hg3+ ♔e1 33 ♖d1# would also have been an attractive finish.

When defending against an h-pawn hack, there are principally two approaches: defence and counterattack. This may seem an obvious statement, but here the divide is sharper than normal.

By defence, I specifically mean that Black makes sure that he can recapture on g6 with the f-pawn, and has defence along the second rank lined up for when White threatens to crash in on h7. He will do this with the minimum force required, while pursuing his own counterattacking ideas against the white king, which will either be in the centre or on the queenside. On encountering this stout resistance, White will need to regroup some of his forces for a second wave of attack. Generally, if the centre is closed, this will take some time, so meanwhile Black's own plans with be gathering speed, and a final showdown approaches.

And that is the slow scenario! The alternative response by Black, which tends to be particularly appropriate when the centre is open, is virtually to ignore what White is doing, and go full speed ahead for the white king. This leads to some blood-curdling chess, with the black king either getting mated, or else the counterattack arriving just in time so that his white counterpart bites the dust instead. The best opening to demonstrate this theme is the Yugoslav Attack of the Sicilian Dragon. The assessment remains unclear despite decades of detailed analytical work.

Here are a few examples.

Gunawan – N. Nikolić
Belgrade GMA 1988

1 d4 ♘f6 2 c4 g6 3 ♘c3 ♗g7 4 e4 d6 5 f3 0-0 6 ♗e3 ♘c6 7 ♘ge2 a6 8 ♕d2 ♖b8 9 h4

In this opening, the Sämisch King's Indian, Black generally has no choice but to use the slower, more defensive response to White's h-file attack,

simply because his counterattack takes a little longer to develop than in Sicilian Dragon positions.

9...e5 10 d5 ♘a5 11 ♘g3 c5 12 dxc6 bxc6 13 0-0-0 ♘b7 14 h5 ♗e6 15 ♗h6

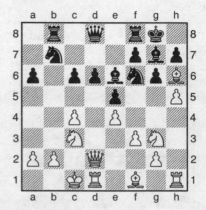

White appears to have some very dangerous threats. However, Black nullifies them with a few accurate moves.

15...♗xh6 16 ♕xh6 ♔h8

This manoeuvre, coupled with the next move, is a standard way to eject the queen from h6. Note that it only works because of the undefended knight on g3; thus 17 hxg6 fxg6 18 ♕xg6? would be met by 18...♖g8 and 19...♖xg3.

17 ♗e2 ♘g8 18 ♕d2 g5

Black's king is now quite safe, and he can set about attacking the white queenside. Obviously, there was no need for Gunawan to self-destruct so fast as he does from here on.

19 c5 ♘xc5 20 ♔b1 ♕a5 21 ♘f1 ♘a4 0-1

The next game takes some beating if you're looking for knife-edge chessboard violence.

Piacentini – Ahn
Belgian Ch 1992

1 e4 c5 2 ♘f3 d6 3 d4 cxd4 4 ♘xd4 ♘f6 5 ♘c3 g6 6 ♗e3 ♗g7 7 f3 0-0 8 ♕d2 ♘c6

White has played the Yugoslav Attack against Black's Dragon Sicilian. This opening, especially when, as here, White puts his king's bishop on c4, often leads to the counterattacking scenario I outlined above. White will attack down the h-file, while Black pins his hopes on the open c-file.

9 ♗c4 ♗d7 10 0-0-0 ♘e5 11 ♗b3 ♖c8 12 h4 ♘c4 13 ♗xc4 ♖xc4 14 g4 ♕a5 15 ♔b1 ♖fc8 16 h5

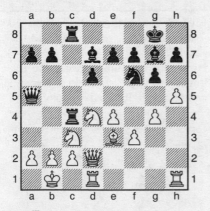

16...♖xc3

This is a standard sacrifice to disrupt White's queenside defences, and prevent the move ♘d5.

17 bxc3 ♗xg4

A surprising move, but the aim is to gain the e4-square for the knight.

18 hxg6

18 fxg4 ♘xe4 is abysmal for White.

18...♗xf3 19 gxh7+ ♔h8 20 ♗h6

20 ♘xf3 ♘xe4 wins for Black.

20...♗xh6 21 ♕xh6 ♘xe4?

21...♗xd1 is better, as White could now hold the draw by 22 ♖hg1!.

22 ♖dg1?

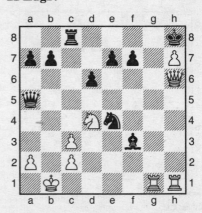

White threatens mate, but Black gets in first.

22...♘xc3+ 23 ♔c1 ♕a3+ 24 ♔d2 ♘e4+ 25 ♔e1 ♕c3+ 26 ♔f1 ♕a1+ 0-1

Pins and Pin-Breaking

Tactics involving pins often lie at the heart of attacks, while breaking a pin can add the impetus to launch an attack.

In the first example we see a straightforward attack by White, in which Black is pinned in various ways.

V. Rasik – Gustafsson
German U-20 open Ch (Hamburg) 1993

1 e4 c5 2 ♘f3 d6 3 d4 cxd4 4 ♘xd4 ♘f6 5 ♘c3 a6 6 ♗e3 e5 7 ♘f3 ♗e7 8 ♗c4 0-0 9 0-0 ♕c7 10 ♕e2 ♗g4 11 ♗b3 h6 12 h3 ♗e6 13 ♘h4 ♔h7 14 ♘f5 ♗xf5 15 exf5 ♘c6 16 ♖ad1

♘a5 17 ♘d5 ♘xd5 18 ♗xd5 ♖ac8
19 ♕h5 ♘c4

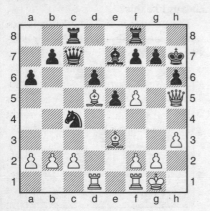

20 ♗c1!

Cunning: a variety of pins will do
Black no end of harm. 20 ♗xf7
♘xe3 21 fxe3 is less effective.

20...♔g8 21 ♕g6 ♕a5 22 ♗xh6 ♗f6
23 ♗xg7! ♖xd5 24 ♕xf6 ♕e4 25
♗h6 1-0

Trabert – Ferkingstad
Gausdal Troll Masters 1995

1 e4 c5 2 c3 ♘c6 3 d4 cxd4 4 cxd4
d5 5 exd5 ♕xd5 6 ♘f3 ♗g4 7 ♘c3
♕a5?! 8 d5 ♘e5?!

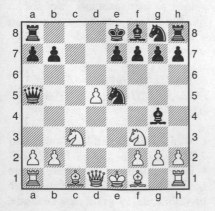

The Norwegian girl's sense of danger lets her down – as it did in the
snowball fight at Tretten station after
this tournament!

9 ♘xe5!

A typical and very strong pin-busting
sacrifice.

9...♗xd1 10 ♗b5+ ♔d8 11 ♘xf7+
♔c8 12 ♔xd1 ♘f6 13 ♗d2 a6 14
♗d3 ♖g8 15 ♘b5 ♕a4+ 16 b3
♕g4+? 17 f3 ♕h5 18 ♖c1+ ♔d7 19
♖c7+ ♔e8 20 ♘bd6+ exd6 21 ♖e1+
♗e7 22 ♖exe7+ ♔f8 23 ♘xd6 1-0

Timman – Kramnik
Riga Tal mem 1995

1 e4 c5 2 ♘f3 ♘c6 3 ♗b5 g6 4 0-0
♗g7 5 ♖e1 ♘f6 6 e5 ♘d5 7 ♘c3
♘c7 8 ♗xc6 dxc6 9 ♘e4 b6 10
♘f6+ ♔f8 11 ♘e4 ♗g4 12 d3
♗xe5!?

I imagine Kramnik foresaw the following tactical "storm in a teacup",
and reckoned it was navigable.

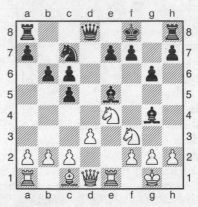

13 ♘xe5!?

Not really a queen sacrifice, but a
very "visual" tactical operation.

13...♗xd1 14 ♗h6+ ♔g8

14...♔e8? is very bad since after 15

♘xc6, in addition to the black queen, White threatens a highly picturesque mate with 16 ♘f6#.

15 ♘xc6

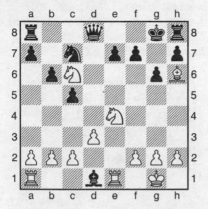

The black queen, strangely enough, is trapped!

15...♗xc2

15...♕d7 16 ♘f6+ exf6 17 ♘e7+ ♕xe7 18 ♖xe7 is good for White in view of Black's severe problems unravelling his kingside.

16 ♘c3

No hurry to take the queen.

16...e6 17 ♘xd8 ♖xd8 18 ♗g5 ♔g7

18...♖xd3 is no good since White can then trap the c2-bishop: 19 ♖ac1. 18...♖d7 allows White to win an exchange with 19 ♗f6.

19 ♗xd8 ♖xd8 20 ♖ac1 ♗xd3 21 ♖ed1 e5 22 ♖e1 ♖e8 23 b3 ♘b5

½-½

Black has two fairly good pawns for the exchange, so a draw is fair.

King-hunt or King-walk?

We have already seen quite a few examples of a series of sacrifices destroying a king's defences, and then the remaining pieces dragging the poor king around the board for a summary mid-board execution. Is it always like this?

The answer is no. The king is not such a weakling that he never survives a mid-board jaunt, even if there is an escort of hostile pieces. Actually mating a king can be a tricky business, and if the attacking forces are not coordinated, the king might even start forking the closest attackers.

The dividing line between a king-hunt and a king-walk is a fine one; sometimes it remains unclear for quite a while whether a king is being pursued to its death, or on its way to safety in some corner of the board.

Kiselev – Dragomaretsky
USSR Central Chess Club Ch 1988

1 d4 d5 2 c4 c6 3 ♘f3 ♘f6 4 ♘c3 e6 5 ♗g5 ♘bd7 6 e3 ♕a5 7 ♘d2 ♗b4 8 ♕c2 c5 9 dxc5 dxc4 10 ♘xc4 ♕xc5 11 ♗f4 ♘d5 12 ♗d6 ♕c6 13 ♗xb4 ♘xb4 14 ♕b3 ♘d5

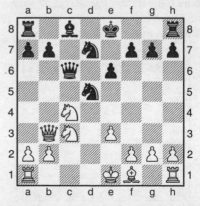

It appears that the position is quite normal, and the main battle will be to bring pieces to good squares, and other such mundane matters. However, White sees a way to prevent Black from castling, and so we now see a thrilling king-hunt; or is it to be a king-walk?

15 ♕a3! ♕c5 16 ♘d6+ ♔e7 17 ♘xd5+

17 ♘f5+ looks better with a lot of hindsight: 17...♔d8 (17...exf5 18 ♘xd5+; 17...♔f6?? is definitely no good here due to 18 ♘e4+) 18 ♕xc5 ♘xc5 19 ♘xd5 exf5 is a little awkward for Black.

17...exd5 18 ♘f5+ ♔f6!? 19 b4 ♕b6 20 ♘d4

This move leads to a position where White is a little better, but Black holds. The game continued 20...♘f8 21 ♕b2 ♔e7 22 ♗e2 ♘g6 23 h4 (23 f4!?) 23...♖d8 24 h5 ♘e5 25 h6 g6 26 ♖c1 ♗e6 27 ♖c5 ♖ac8 28 ♖b5 ♕c7 29 ♖c5 ♕b6 30 ♖xc8 ♖xc8 31 0-0 ♘d7 32 ♖d1 ♘f6 33 ♗f3 ♖c4 34 b5 ♗g4 35 ♕e2 ♗xf3 36 ♕xf3 ♕c7 37 ♘e2 ♖b4 38 ♖c1 ♖c4 39 ♖d1 ♖b4 40 ♖c1 ♖c4 41 ♖d1 ♖b4 ½-½.

On his 20th move White has something more aggressive: **20 e4!?**

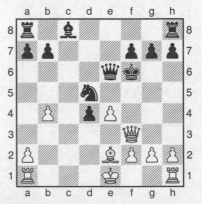

22 f3) 22 ♘e3 is good for White.

21 ♘e3 ♘b6

21...♕xe4 is possible.

22 ♗e2 d4

Else: 22...dxe4 23 ♖d1!; 22...♗d7 23 ♘xd5+ ♘xd5 24 ♕f3+; 22...♕xe4 23 ♗f3 puts pressure on d5.

23 ♘d5+ ♘xd5 24 ♕f3+

This is analysis by Sibiakin, who concludes that White has excellent play, but I think Black can get away with **24...♔e5!?**. Consider: **25 ♕g3+** (25 ♗c4 ♕e7 26 ♗xd5 ♕xb4+ and 27...♕c3; 25 exd5 ♕xd5 26 ♕g3+ ♔f6) **25...♘f4 26 ♕g5+ f5 27 ♕xg7+**.

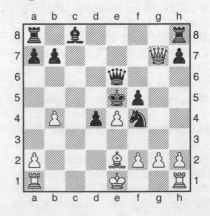

20...♕e6

20...♖e8 21 ♕b2+ ♘e5 (or 21...d4

Now:

a) 27...♔xe4 is surely going too far:

a1) 28 ♕xh8?! is the wrong approach: 28...♔d5 29 ♕d8+ (29 0-0 ♘xe2+ 30 ♔h1) 29...♗d7 30 ♕a5+ b5.

a2) 28 ♗f3+ ♔d3+ (a very far-advanced king taking part in an attack against his opposite number is a wonderful idea, but it doesn't work here) 29 ♔f1 ♖d8 (29...♗d7 30 ♕g3 regains material, while retaining strong attacking prospects) 30 ♕c7 ♕c4 31 ♕xd8 (31 ♖d1+?? ♔c3+ forces the exchange of queens) 31...♔c2+ 32 ♔g1 should be winning for White.

b) 27...♕f6 28 ♕c7+ ♔d6 (but definitely not 28...♔xe4?? 29 ♗f3+ ♔d3 30 0-0-0#) 29 ♕g7+ is a draw.

Now comes a game where the white king walks up to the eighth rank, and lives – more than can be said for his black counterpart...

Den Broeder – De Veij
Dutch Corr. Ch 1980

1 e4 ♘f6 2 e5 ♘d5 3 d4 d6 4 c4 ♘b6 5 f4 dxe5 6 fxe5 ♘c6 7 ♗e3 ♗f5 8 ♘c3 e6 9 ♘f3 ♗e7 10 d5 exd5 11 cxd5 ♘b4 12 ♘d4 ♗d7 13 e6 fxe6 14 dxe6 ♗c6 15 ♕g4 ♗h4+ 16 g3 ♗xh1 17 0-0-0 ♕f6 18 gxh4 0-0

This, a do-or-die system in the Alekhine Defence, is one of the craziest lines in opening theory, which was popular in the 1970s, but is not much seen nowadays, primarily because Black is doing well.

19 ♗g5

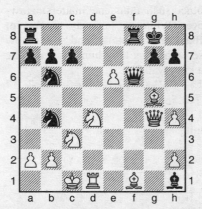

19...♕xf1 20 ♖xf1 ♖xf1+ 21 ♘d1 ♘d3+ 22 ♔c2 ♘e1+ 23 ♔c3

23 ♔c1 gives Black nothing better than 23...♘d3+, repeating.

23...c5

23...♘d5+ is regarded as an improvement.

24 ♘f5 ♘d5+ 25 ♔c4 ♗f3

25...h5!? 26 ♕e2 ♖xf5 27 ♕xe1 may well be fairly good for Black.

26 ♕g3 ♘b6+

Instead 26...♗xd1 is possible, but then 27 ♘h6+ gives White at least a draw. After 27...♔h8 28 ♘f7+ ♔g8 29 ♔xd5, the threat is 30 ♗h6 g6 31 ♕c3.

27 ♔xc5

The king goes on the rampage.

27...♖c8+ 28 ♔d6 ♖c6+ 29 ♔e7 ♘d5+

This forces, or at least encourages, the white king onto its eighth rank, but leaves Black's pieces badly coordinated. Black had to play 29...♖c7+, when White can allow a draw by 30 ♔d6 ♖c6+ or 30 ♔d8 ♖c8+ 31 ♔e7 ♖c7+, with a repetition in both cases. Otherwise he must avoid 30 ♔e8?? ♗c6+ 31 ♔d8 ♖c8+ 32 ♔e7 ♖xf5, but 30 ♕xc7!?

♘d5+ 31 ♔d6 ♘xc7 32 ♘de3 is possible, when the e-pawn may yet cause problems.

30 ♔d8

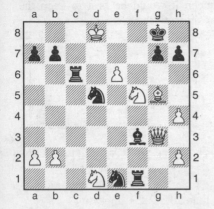

The king has found sanctuary in the most unlikely of places, and it is now White's attack that takes over – and tremendously quickly too...

30...♗h5

30...♖xe6 31 ♘de3 ♘xe3 32 ♗xe3 g6 33 ♘h6+ forces mate, the white king participating by denying his opposite number the e7- and e8-squares: 33...♔f8 34 ♕f4+ ♔g7 35 ♕f7+ ♔h8 36 ♕g8#.

31 ♘de3 ♖xf5

31...♘xe3 32 ♘e7+ wins material.

32 ♘xf5 ♖xe6

32...♘f3 33 ♗h6 g6 34 e7 ♘f6 35 ♗g5 wins.

33 ♘xg7 ♔xg7 34 ♗h6+ ♔xh6 35 ♕g5# (1-0)

Space and Communication

Just as a normal army benefits from the ability to manoeuvre and needs good lines of communication, so it is on the chess board. If one player is able to supply pieces to the important part of the board more quickly than the opponent, then this provides the basis for launching an attack.

Control of the centre and possession of a space advantage are key factors that help a player's pieces to communicate with one another. Here is a good example, from the youngest of the three remarkable Polgar sisters:

J. Polgar – P. Nikolić
Monte Carlo 5th Amber Blindfold 1996

1 e4 e6 2 d4 d5 3 ♘c3 ♗b4 4 e5 c5 5 a3 ♗xc3+ 6 bxc3 ♘e7 7 h4 ♕c7 8 h5 h6 9 ♘f3 ♗d7 10 ♗d3 ♗a4

10...c4 would give Black a very rigid structure and few active prospects. After 11 ♗f1 (the bishop will be more at home on g2 or h3 than f3 or g4), Black would still need to play 11...♗a4 (else a4 and ♗a3) and could expect to come under pressure in all parts of the board.

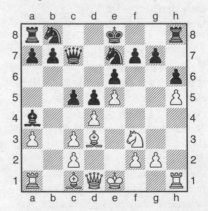

White has been preparing for a massive kingside onslaught in the event of Black's king residing somewhere around g8. The weakening of the g6-square that she has provoked also does much to discourage Black's standard freeing break ...f6. However, Black is by no means committed to kingside castling, so Polgar is sure to keep attacking lines to the queenside open.

11 dxc5!? ♘d7 12 ♖h4!

12 ♗f4 would allow Black more leeway in organizing his position.

12...♗c6

12...♘xc5? 13 ♖xa4 ♘xa4 14 ♗b5+ wins material for White. 12...♕a5!? is possible.

13 ♗f4 0-0-0 14 ♖g4

The idea is to divert a black rook from other duties.

14...♖dg8

14...g5!? could be considered.

15 ♖b1 ♘xc5 16 ♗e3 ♘d7

Taking on d3 would leave Black very passive.

17 ♖gb4

After 17 ♗xa7 a mousetrap would snap shut: 17...b6.

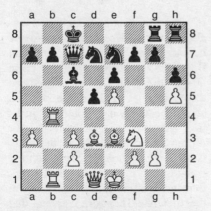

Now all of White's pieces are actively placed and she is threatening in earnest to take the a7-pawn.

17...♔b8 18 ♘d4 ♔a8

I can only assume that Nikolić refrained from 18...♘xe5 because he felt that in the position that arises after the exchange of two rooks for queen it would be best to keep the position closed.

19 ♘xc6 ♘xc6 20 ♖xb7 ♕xb7 21 ♖xb7 ♔xb7 22 ♕b1+ ♔a8 23 ♗b5 ♖c8 24 f4

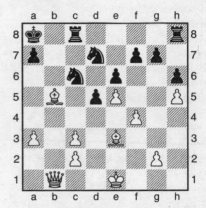

White is now doing rather well, since her queen can achieve more than Black's rooks, which will have difficulty finding much activity.

24...♖c7 25 ♕b3 ♖hc8 26 ♕a4 ♘cb8 27 ♗d3 ♘c5 28 ♗xc5 ♖xc5 29 c4 ♘c6 30 cxd5 exd5 31 ♔f2 ♖c7 32 g4 ♖b7 33 g5 ♖b6 34 f5 hxg5 35 e6 fxe6 36 fxe6 ♔b7 37 ♔g3 ♘e7 38 ♕d4 ♖c7 39 ♕e5 a6 40 ♔g4 ♘g8 41 ♔xg5 ♘h6 42 ♕xd5+ ♔a7 43 c4 ♖e7 44 ♗f5 ♘xf5 45 ♔xf5 ♖c7 46 ♔e5 ♖bc6 47 ♕xc6 ♖xc6 48 e7 ♖c8 49 ♔e6 ♔b7 50 ♔f7 ♖c7 51 ♔f8 1-0

Mikhail Botvinnik (World Champion 1948–57, 58–60, 61–3) did much to develop the modern understanding of space advantages, with games such as the following.

Botvinnik – V. Ragozin
Moscow 1947

1 d4 ♘f6 2 c4 e6 3 ♘c3 ♗b4 4 e3 ♕e7 5 ♘e2 b6 6 a3 ♗xc3+ 7 ♘xc3 ♗b7 8 d5 d6?!
Black should prefer the less compromising 8...0-0 or 8...exd5 9 cxd5 ♕e5. Now White's central superiority becomes hard to challenge.

9 ♗e2 ♘bd7
After 9...exd5 10 cxd5 ♕e5, 11 e4 is possible due to the ♕a4+ idea if Black should take the pawn, and strongly bolsters White's centre.

10 0-0 0-0 11 e4

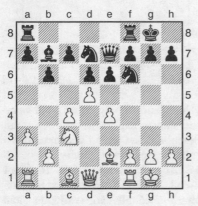

White has the bishop pair and a stable space advantage. How serious are these advantages? Botvinnik makes them look quite sufficient to win the game, but observe how vigorously he has to play.

11...exd5 12 exd5 ♖fe8 13 ♗e3 a6
Else the white knight will manoeuvre, via b5, to the wonderful central square d4.

14 ♕c2 ♘e5?
While the knight looks good on e5, it doesn't actually do a great deal. Other moves:

a) 14...♘e4 15 ♗d3 ♘xc3 16 ♗xh7+ ♔h8 17 bxc3 ♕h4 (17...g6 18 ♗xg6 fxg6 19 ♕xg6 with ♗d4 to follow) 18 ♗f5 ♘e5 19 ♖fd1 looks quite good for White, but Black may have some survival chances.

b) 14...b5 15 cxb5 ♘xd5 (or alternatively, 15...axb5 16 ♗xb5 ties Black up) 16 ♘xd5 ♗xd5 17 bxa6 and, according to Botvinnik, Black has compensation.

15 ♖ae1 ♗c8 16 ♗d4 ♘g6 17 f4 ♗d7

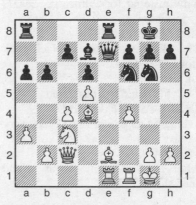

In his book *Planning*, Neil McDonald eloquently described the rationale behind moves such as the one that Botvinnik now plays. The basic point is that the centre is not closed, so therefore one would not expect an action on the wing would be justified. However, the specific reason for refraining from activity on the flank is that the opponent could land a counterblow in the centre. But Black is in no position to land anything in the centre. Therefore, given that White also has no obviously effective central plan, an attack on the wing is fully justified – and as quickly as possible!

18 g4! ♕d8

This fails tactically. Botvinnik analysed two alternatives: 18...h6 19 ♗d3 ♕xe1 20 ♖xe1 ♖xe1+ 21 ♔f2 ♖ae8 22 ♗xf6 gxf6 23 ♗xg6 is hopeless for Black; 18...♘h8 is the best way to save the f6-knight, but then 19 ♕d2 ♕d8 20 h3 preserves a very solid plus.

19 g5 ♘g4 20 ♕d2!

The g4-knight is doomed. It's not clear why Ragozin continued the game any further.

20...h6 21 f5 ♘6e5 22 h3 ♘f6 23 gxf6 ♕xf6 24 ♕f4 ♖e7 25 ♔h1 c5 26 ♗g1 g6 27 fxg6 ♕xf4 28 ♖xf4 fxg6 29 ♖f6 ♗f5 30 ♖xd6 ♘xc4 31 ♖e6!? ♖xe6 32 dxc6 ♗xe6 33 ♗f3 1-0

Discovered Attacks

The side whose pieces are better developed will often be able to discover attacks onto enemy units. A number of threats generated quickly can add up to a lightning initiative.

Ivanchuk – Kamsky
Monte Carlo 5th Amber Rapid 1996

1 e4 c5 2 ♘f3 d6 3 d4 cxd4 4 ♘xd4 ♘f6 5 ♘c3 a6 6 ♗c4 e6 7 0-0 b5 8 ♗b3 ♗e7 9 ♕f3 ♕b6 10 ♗g5!?

Although not actually a novelty, this is a very interesting and almost untested alternative to the normal 10 ♗e3. If the knight doesn't need to be defended by the bishop, why bother? The bishop is more active on g5, while the queen's rook will be used to defend the knight.

John Nunn, a leading authority on the Najdorf Sicilian, the opening

chosen here, confirmed my suspicion that 10 ♗g5 is a very good move.

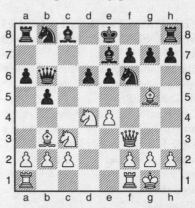

10...♘bd7

Black should probably play 10...0-0 11 ♖ad1 ♗b7 12 ♕g3 ♘c6.

Accepting the gift by 10...♕xd4? 11 e5 gives White a large advantage:

a) 11...♘e4 12 ♗xe7 ♗b7 13 exd6 ♘xd6 allows White the wonderful move 14 ♗d5!! destroying the communication between the black pieces.

b) 11...♕xe5 12 ♗xf6 gxf6 13 ♕xa8 d5 14 ♗xd5! exd5 (14...b4 15 ♗c6+! is a handy check) 15 ♖fe1 ♕d6 16 ♘xd5 ♗e6 17 ♖ad1 ♗xd5 18 ♖xd5 and the two pins and White's active major pieces give him a winning advantage, e.g. 18...♕b6 19 ♖d3 ♔f8 20 ♖xe7 ♕xe7 21 ♕e4+ ♔f8 (21...♕e6 22 ♕b4+ ♔e8 23 ♖e3 wins the queen) 22 ♕b4+ ♔e8 23 ♖e3+ ♔d8 24 ♕e7+ ♔c8 25 ♖c3+ ♘c6 26 ♕xf6, with a decisive material gain.

c) 11...♘d5 12 ♘xd5 exd5 and now 13 ♗e3 ♕xe5 14 ♕xd5 ♕xd5 15 ♗xd5 wins the exchange in simple fashion; instead 13 ♗xd5 ♗xg5 14 ♕xf7+ ♔d8 15 ♗xa8, as in the first game I can find with this line,

Berset–Cesareo, Geneva 1992, is not so clear.

d) 11...d5 12 exf6 gxf6 (12...♗xf6 13 ♖ad1 ♕c5 14 ♗xf6 gxf6 15 ♖fe1 gives White a pulverizing attack) 13 ♗e3 ♕e5 14 ♘xd5! exd5 15 ♕xd5 and White again wins the exchange by trapping the rook in the corner.

11 ♖ad1 ♘c5?

Understandably wanting to cover e6, but Nunn suggests 11...♗b7 with the point that 12 ♗xe6 fxe6 13 ♘xe6 ♘e5 14 ♕h3 ♔f7 15 ♗e3 ♕c6 is unclear.

12 ♗xf6 gxf6

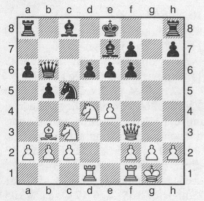

13 ♖fe1

This was White's last chance to use the discovered attack: 13 e5!? ♗b7 14 ♘d5! exd5 15 exf6 ♗f8 16 ♖fe1+ ♔d8 17 ♗xd5 ♖c8 18 ♘f5 ♗xd5 19 ♕xd5, when Nunn considers White to have a powerful attack. For instance: 19...♕b7 20 ♘xd6 ♕xd5 21 ♘xf7+ ♔c7 22 ♖xd5.

13...♖a7

The bishop is quite useful on c8, so Kamsky activates his rook in a slightly unusual way. 13...♗b7 14 ♕h5 would threaten the e6-pawn, so reducing Black's options.

14 ♕h5?

White had two better options:

a) 14 ♘f5!? exf5 15 ♘d5 ♕d8 16 exf5 h5 was indicated by John Nunn. Then 17 ♘xe7 ♖xe7 18 ♖xe7+ looks good to me: 18...♕xe7 19 ♕c6+ ♗d7 (19...♕d7 20 ♖xd6 ♕xc6 21 ♖xc6 forks Black's pieces) 20 ♕a8+ ♕d8 21 ♖e1+ regains the piece; or 18...♔xe7 19 ♕e3+ ♔f8 20 ♕xc5 dxc5 21 ♖xd8+ ♔g7 22 ♖xh8 ♔xh8 23 ♗xf7 gives White a pawn-up ending.

b) 14 ♕g4!, threatening simply ♕g7, is a very awkward move to meet.

14...♘xb3 15 cxb3 ♖c7

15...♕c5, seeking an exchange of queens, is good.

16 b4

Preventing ...♖c5, but the rook finds employment on the c-file nevertheless.

16...♖c4

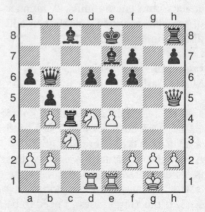

17 ♘f5!? ♖xc3

17...exf5 18 ♘d5 followed by exf5 leaves Black in a terrible mess, so he must eliminate both knights.

18 bxc3

18 ♘g7+ ♔f8 19 ♕h6 ♖c2 does not

give White any sufficiently useful discovered or double checks.

18...exf5 19 exf5 ♕c6

Ivanchuk now decided to kill the game.

20 ♖xe7+ ♔xe7 21 ♖e1+ ♔d8 22 ♕xf7 ♖e8 23 ♕xf6+ ♔c7 24 ♕f7+ ♔d8 25 ♕f6+ ½-½

The Back Rank

Back-rank mates lie at the heart of some great attacking ideas.

E. Adams – C. Torre
New Orleans 1920 (WGG 16)

1 e4 e5 2 ♘f3 d6 3 d4 cxd4 4 ♕xd4 ♘c6 5 ♗b5 ♗d7 6 ♗xc6 ♗xc6 7 ♘c3 ♘f6 8 0-0 ♗e7 9 ♘d5 ♗xd5 10 exd5 0-0 11 ♗g5 c6 12 c4 cxd5

12...♘xd5 13 cxd5 ♗xg5 14 ♘xg5 ♕xg5 15 dxc6 bxc6 16 ♕xd6 gives White the more pleasant pawn structure.

13 cxd5 ♖e8

13...h6, partly with hindsight, could be suggested.

14 ♖fe1

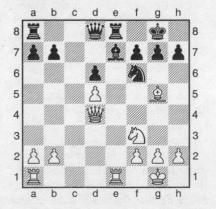

14...a5

This is certainly not the most useful move imaginable, but one idea is to play ...♖a6 and then either ...♖b6 or ...♕b6.

15 ♖e2

Doubling rooks on the e-file is an effective answer to Black's idea. Black now fails to sense the danger.

15...♖c8?

Instead 15...♘d7 16 ♖ae1 f6 followed by ...♘e5 is not too bad for Black.

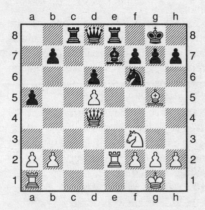

Now everything is set for the great combination.

16 ♖ae1

White threatens 17 ♗xf6, when in reply 17...gxf6, horribly exposing the black king, would be compulsory.

16...♕d7

16...h6 17 ♗xf6 gxf6 18 ♕g4+ ♔h7 gives White a choice of devastating continuations, for instance the simple 19 ♘h4 or 19 ♕h5 ♔g7 20 ♘d4 ♗f8 21 ♘f5+ ♔h8 22 ♘xh6 ♖xe2 23 ♘f5+ ♔g8 24 ♕xe2, but not 19 ♖xe7? ♕xe7! since after 20 ♖xe7? ♖c1+ it is White who is mated on the back rank.

17 ♗xf6 ♗xf6

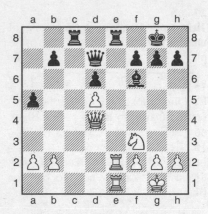

We are now treated to one of the most spectacular sequences in chess history – six consecutive queen offers. Black can never take the queen due to mate on e8.

18 ♕g4!! ♕b5 19 ♕c4!!

Some writers have claimed that 19 ♕a4?? is bad because of 19...♕xe2. This is true, but I'll leave it for the reader to find a simpler answer to White's blunder!

19...♕d7 20 ♕c7!! ♕b5

20...♕d8 is answered by 21 ♕xc8!.

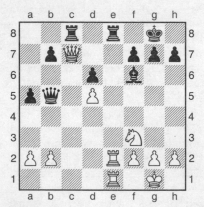

21 a4!! ♕xa4

After 21...♕xe2 22 ♖xe2 neither black rook may move off the back rank.

22 ♖e4!!

White's main threats are now 23 ♕xc8 ♖xc8 24 ♖xa4 and 23 b3 ♕b5 24 ♕xb7.

22...♕b5 23 ♕xb7!! 1-0

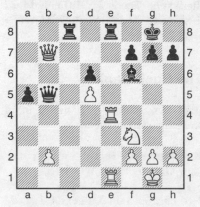

The black queen has finally been run out of squares.

There have been questions asked about whether Torre (the brilliant young Mexican player who was to burst onto the chess scene with his sensational result at the Moscow tournament of 1925) and Adams (his trainer) really played this game, or if it is a composition. There will always be doubts about any brilliant game that was played neither under tournament conditions nor with any eyewitnesses. I do not want to go into details here, but the evidence for this game being fabricated strikes me as circumstantial, and not a compelling reason to assert that the game was definitely not played.

I hope you have enjoyed this chapter. There follow a few puzzle positions, while there are also many more starting on page 428, with attack and defence major themes in most cases.

Test Positions

Here are a handful of positions for you to try. The solutions, in all cases quite detailed, are given immediately afterwards. These are difficult exercises, so take your time, and try to consider all relevant possibilities *for both sides* before making your decision.

2)

Gleizerov – Dragomaretsky
Alushta 1993

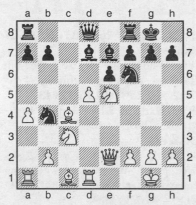

Test 2: White has just played an extremely dangerous d5 advance. As Black (to play), can you analyse your way to equality? (You will need to analyse ahead about six moves.)

1)

Korchnoi – Zsu. Polgar
Prague Women vs Veterans 1995

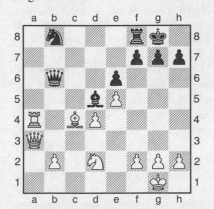

Test 1: It seems that Black (to play) is in some trouble. Calculate carefully an incisive continuation to rescue Black.

3)

De Greef – Seibold
Corr. 1931

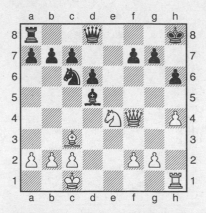

Test 3: Black (to play) is under some pressure here. What should he do and how should play continue?

Solutions to Attack and Defence Tests

1) 25...♕xd4! 26 ♗d3 ♕xe5 27 ♗xh7+

Thus White wins an exchange, but Black's resources are sufficient.

27...♔xh7 28 ♕xf8 ♕g5 29 f3

29 g3 ♕xd2 30 ♖h4+ ♔g6 31 ♖g4+ ♔h5 32 ♖h4+ repeats.

29...♕e3+

29...♕xd2 30 ♖h4+ ♔g6 31 ♖g4+ ♔f6 gives White some winning chances after either 32 h4 or 32 ♕xg7+ ♔e7 33 ♕c3.

30 ♔f1 ♕d3+ ½-½

31 ♔e1 ♕e3+ 32 ♔d1 is the only way to avoid an immediate draw, but in the queen ending after 32...♗b3+ 33 ♘xb3 ♕xb3+ White is in no position to play for a win.

2) 13...♘bxd5 14 ♗xd5 ♘xd5 15 ♘xd5 exd5 16 ♖xd5

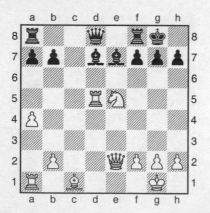

Did you analyse this far and decide Black was lost? He has a spectacular resource:

16...♗g4! 17 ♕d3

17 ♕c4 would be answered in the same manner.

17...♕xd5! 18 ♖xd5 ♖ad8

White's back rank costs him his queen.

19 ♕b3 ♖d1+ 20 ♕xd1 ♗xd1 21 ♗e3 ♗b3 22 a5

22 ♗xa7 ♖a8 regains the pawn.

22...a6

White must even be a little careful here not to be worse.

23 ♘d7 ♖d8 24 ♘c5 ♗d5 25 ♖c1 ♖d6 26 f3 h6 27 ♔f2 ♗h4+ 28 g3 ♗d8 29 ♖d1 ♗e7 30 ♘xa6 bxa6 31 ♗c5 ½-½

3) 18...♘e5!

There are no prizes for other moves: 18...♗xe4?? is met by 19 ♕xh6+ and 20 ♕xg7#; 18...f6? 19 ♗xf6! crashes through; 18...♔g8? 19 ♘f6+ gxf6 20 ♗xf6 gives White a killing attack; 18...♔h7?? 19 ♕f5+ wins the bishop.

19 ♘xd6?!

White goes wrong. The correct path was 19 ♖d1 ♗xe4 (19...c6 20 ♘xd6 ♕xd6 21 ♗xe5 ♕g6 might hold) 20 ♕xe4 (20 ♗xe5 ♗h7) 20...♘c6 21 g4, which gives White attacking chances in return for the pawn.

19...♕xd6

19...cxd6 20 ♖d1! is pleasant for White, but 19...♘d3+! 20 cxd3 ♕xd6 is good for Black, and so a good alternative.

20 ♗xe5 ♕c6 21 ♖d1 ♗e4! with counterplay and a secure position for Black.

Beginning Chess

How do chess players get started? How young does one have to be when starting to have any chance of becoming a master? Are players born with talent for chess, or can it be gained by hard work?

There are no straightforward answers to these questions. Some players pick up the game quickly and easily, while others are slow to learn how the pieces move. Let's take a look at some accounts of how individual players, including some of the all-time greats, became acquainted with the game.

Paul Keres (1916–75; many times candidate for the world championship):

"I made my acquaintance with the game of chess very early, round about the age of 4 to 5 years, when, together with my elder brother, I watched the games my father played with his friends. In this way we learned the moves and the elementary rules of chess, and then naturally there followed the first tries one against the other. How slowly, however, one penetrates into the secrets of the art of chess in this way is shown by the fact that for many a year we were quite unaware that games of chess could be written down. Only after we discovered in the daily papers some mysterious inscriptions together with diagrams did we eventually arrive at the knowledge that these were indeed written games of chess.

"In the small town of Pärnu there were naturally great difficulties in the way of widening and perfecting one's chess knowledge. We had no chess literature at our disposal and, in order to fill this want, I wrote down every possible game I could lay my hands on. In this way I soon had a collection of almost 1,000 games. My first contact with opening theory occurred through the small Dufresne manual, which I succeeded in borrowing from a chess friend for some days. It goes without saying that we let no problem or endgame study that had appeared in the newspapers pass unnoticed without embarking on an attempt to solve it. But my chief chess activity still consisted of the practice games with my brother.

"My chess work only became more varied when new 'rivals' appeared in the shape of school friends and this also led to a gradual increase in my playing strength. I had already achieved very good results against my father and my brother and now wanted to test my strength against other, somewhat stronger, players. The opportunity for this came quite unexpectedly. In the year 1928 Mikenas, already one of Estonia's best players, paid a short visit to Pärnu, and on this occasion he gave a simultaneous display in the town's chess club. Of course, I went, together with my father, to the club for the display, and I even managed to take away a whole point from the master. This success naturally endowed me with fresh courage and self-confidence and spurred me on to further steps." (From *Paul Keres: The Road to the Top*, Batsford 1996.)

This account will probably ring true with many players (except for Keres's remarkable thirst for knowledge, that is): a slow start, and gradual improvement with practice and study.

Then again there are miraculous examples, **José Capablanca** (1888–1942; World Champion 1921–7) for instance:

"I was born in Habana, the capital of the Island of Cuba, on the 19th of November 1888. I was not yet five years old when by accident I came into my father's private office and found him playing with another gentleman. I had never seen a game of chess before; the pieces interested me, and I went the next day to see them play again. The third day, as I looked on, my father, a very poor beginner, moved a Knight from a white square to a white square. His opponent, apparently, not a better player, did not notice it. My father won, and I proceeded to call him a cheat and to laugh. After a little wrangle, during which I was nearly put out of the room, I showed my father what he had done. He asked me how and what I knew about chess? I answered that I could beat him; he said that that was impossible, considering that I could not even set the pieces correctly. We tried conclusions, and I won. That was my beginning. A few

days later, my father took me to the Habana Chess Club, where the strongest players found it impossible to give me a Queen. About that time, the Russian Master, Taubenhaus, visited Habana, and he declared it beyond him to give me such odds. Later, in Paris, in 1911, Mr. Taubenhaus would often say, 'I am the only living master who has given Mr. Capablanca a Queen.'

"Then followed several years in which I played only occasionally at home. The medical men said that it would harm me to go on playing. When eight years old I frequented the club on Sundays, and soon Don Celso Golmayo, the strongest player there, was also unable to give me a Rook. After two or three months I left Habana, and did not play chess again until I returned. I was eleven years old then, and H. N. Pillsbury had just visited the club and left everyone astounded at his enormous talent and genius. Don Celso Golmayo was dead, but there still remained Vasquez and J. Corzo, the latter having just won the Championship from the former. In this atmosphere, in three months I advanced to the first rank. In order to test my strength a series of games was arranged, in which I was to play two games against each of the first-class players. All the strong players took part in the contest except Vasquez, who had just died. The result proved that I stood next to the Champion, J. Corzo, to whom I lost both games." (From *My Chess Career*, 1920.)

Some players learn chess at an early age, but do not develop any strong interest until their teens. For example, **Viktor Korchnoi** (born 1931; Challenger in 1978 and 1981), had this to say in his understandably somewhat embittered autobiography *Chess is My Life*, published in 1977, following his defection in 1976:

"I was born in 1931, during the first Stalin Five-Year Plan. My parents were poor, but there was nothing unusual about this: at that time there were frequent purges, and particular attention was paid to purging the purses of the population – with the aim, of course, of achieving genuine equality for all people. In this respect they were spectacularly successful: on the eve of the war there were tens of millions of people living in poverty.

"I learned to play chess somewhere around the age of six. My father taught me, and I enjoyed playing with him, with his brother and with all members of the family. They sensed my need to play, and I remember my uncle saying to me: 'If you won't speak Polish [Korchnoi was living with his father's relations who were of the Polish nobility], then I won't play chess with you!' But there was as yet no serious interest, we didn't even have one chess book. We followed certain events, and sometimes in a children's magazine we would find a chess section with a game. That was all. I only became interested in chess much later, in adolescence, towards the end of the war."

After surviving the siege of Leningrad, Korchnoi made rapid progress as a teenager, and by age 16 was one of the top juniors in the Soviet Union. Although a top-class GM for a long time, it was not until the 1970s that he fought his way to a world-title match.

Mikhail Botvinnik (1911–95; World Champion 1948–57, 1958–60, 1961–3) did not learn until the age of twelve, but unfortunately his account sheds little light on how he came to make progress, but suggests that hard work was a major ingredient:

"I learned to play chess at the age of twelve, while attending secondary school. My brain was fresh, it could take in an unlimited amount of the information, the elementary knowledge, which is necessary to the perfection of a player's technique and to a master's creative activity at the board. On this preliminary task I had to spend four years, the period from 1923 to 1927. I won the title of Master in 1927, during the U.S.S.R. Fifth Championship tournament, held in Moscow; and one can say that this completed my first period of 'chess development'." (From *One Hundred Selected Games*, 1951)

I find this astonishing: from beginner to master in four years, almost dismissed as though a trivial task! Perhaps the fact that Botvinnik was writing when already a hero of the Soviet Union influenced this. He sheds only a little more light on this period of his development in his autobiographical work *Achieving the Aim*, 1981:

"In the Autumn of 1923 I learned to play chess and everything else receded into the background.

"The chess board was homemade, a square piece of plywood with the squares shaded in ink; the pieces of palm wood, thin and unstable. One white bishop was missing and a lead soldier stood on the f1 square. I calculated badly, and although I was allowed to take moves back I was always blundering something away, including this toy soldier."

A little later we read:

"I played in the school chess championship, but was somewhere in the middle of the table. At the same time the opening textbook by Grekov and Nenarokov started appearing in separate sections, and I greedily took it all in. However, I played a Ruy Lopez according to the book against Vitya Milyutin (he was about five years older than me) and was dismayed as soon as he started playing differently from Nenarokov. Still, in my class I was champion."

Reading between the lines a little, it is clear that Botvinnik's rapid development was due to a lot of hard work and a good deal of enthusiasm, fuelled by the visits to the Soviet Union of great players such as Emanuel Lasker and José Capablanca (whom the young Botvinnik defeated in a simultaneous in 1925).

Vasily Smyslov (born 1921; World Champion 1957–8), one of Botvinnik's main rivals for the world title, gives a more standard account:

"I first became interested in chess as early as 1927 when still a child. My father, Vasily Osipovich Smyslov, was my first teacher. I still have A. A. Alekhine's book *My Best Games*, which my father gave to me in 1928 and which became my constant reference.

"My love for the literature of the game began as soon as I had learnt how to play. I was later to read everything that my father had in his library: Dufresne's handbook, separate numbers of the Soviet magazines *Chess* and *Chess Sheet*, the textbooks of Lasker and Capablanca, and the collections of games of Soviet and international competitions. The games of the great Russian chess master M. I. Chigorin made an indelible impression on me; it was with interest that I read the various declarations on questions of strategy by A. I. Nimzovitch; I studied attentively the genius of prominent Soviet masters.

"During my years as a student my enthusiasm for chess began to take on a serious and systematic character." (From *My Best Games of Chess 1935–1957*, 1958.)

Smyslov made steady progress up to age 17, when he began to rise rapidly towards grandmaster standard.

Sometimes a forced period of inactivity, due maybe to disease or injury, forces a child to pursue sedentary sports. Such was the case with the Danish player **Bent Larsen** (born 1935; considered the leading Western contender for the world title in the late 1960s, before losing to Fischer):

"In January 1947 ... I caught several children's diseases and learnt how to play chess. I recovered from chicken-pox and mumps without any after-effects: with chess it was a little different. My teacher was another boy, by the name of Jørgen. I vaguely remember one of our first games. He captured all my pieces and still had two rooks left, and he very much enjoyed forcing my poor King to the edge of the board and giving mate.

"It appeared that my father knew the game, and we sometimes played. When I was twelve I beat him almost every time; then I entered the chess club. At that time I also began to borrow chess books at the public library. I even found a chess book at home – nobody knew how it had got into the house. Probably the former owner had forgotten it. This book had a certain influence on the development of my play. About the King's Gambit it said that this opening is strong like a storm, nobody can tame it. In the author's opinion modern chess masters were cowards, because they had not the courage to play the King's Gambit. Naturally, I did not like to be a chicken and, until about 1952, the favourite opening of the romantic masters was also mine!

"In the autumn of 1947 the Holstebro Chess Club started a junior section, of which I became a member. I beat the other boys, and by Christmas it was decided to let me play with the grown-ups."

Yasser Seirawan is one of America's top players. He started to play shortly before his teens and "thanks" the beautiful but often wet city of Seattle for this:

"I was born in Damascus in 1960. My father is Syrian and my mother English. When I was two years old we moved to England; in 1967 we moved again, this time to the United States. We settled first in Seattle, Washington, then moved to Virginia Beach, Virginia, and finally settled back in Seattle in 1972.

"While in Virginia Beach, I got used to playing sports on fine, sunny days. The typical cold and rainy days in Seattle made me stir-crazy. When a neighbor offered to teach me chess, I jumped at the chance: anything to relieve the boredom of those long, wet evenings.

"Those first chess lessons soon led me to the legendary Last Exit on Brooklyn coffee house, a chess haven where an unlikely bunch of unusual people congregates to do battle. There, I learned the ropes. When I got used to one player's crazed attacking style, I would sit down with a defensive player and force myself to learn to attack. This training paid off, and I quickly increased my skills." (From *Play Winning Chess* by Seirawan, with Silman.)

Paul Morphy (1837–84), an American, was far and away the strongest player in the middle of the nineteenth century. Löwenthal wrote (in 1860) of his first steps in chess:

"From a recently published Memoir we learn that in 1847, when the boy had completed his first decade, his father taught him the moves, and his uncle gave him a lesson in the art of play. Paul was an apt pupil: in a few months he was able to contest a game with either of his relatives, and soon entered the lists against the stoutest opponents he could meet. In 1849, 1850, and 1851, Mr. Morphy achieved a series of triumphs over the strongest players in the Union, among whom were Mr. Ernest Morphy, Stanley and Rosseau. It is said that out of above fifty games fought during these years with Mr. Ernest Rosseau, his young antagonist won fully nine-tenths.

"We are told that even at that time the boy gave evidence of genius and originality. He did not rest upon precedent, nor pay any great regard to established forms of openings, but used to get rid of his pawns as quickly as possible, regarding them as incumbrances which prevented the free movement of his pieces. A very short experience combined with his rapid insight into the principles of the game, soon corrected that habit without impairing the boldness and decision from which it sprung. When only thirteen years of age he was a really good player." (From *Morphy's Games of Chess* by J. Löwenthal, 1860.)

Bobby Fischer (1943–2008) learned to play at the age of six, as documented by his biographer, Frank Brady:

"Joan [Bobby's sister] and Bobby were close. The story of how she kept him amused with games purchased at the candy store over which they lived – Monopoly, Parcheesi and finally chess – is famous and has been told many times. The two children, six and eleven, figured out the moves from the instructions that went with the set, and for a time considered it as just another diversion. 'At first it was just a game like any other,' Bobby later recalled, 'only a little more complicated.' Even as a baby he had been intensely interested in puzzles. 'He would get those Japanese interlocking rings, and things like that, and take things apart I couldn't figure out at all,' Mrs. Fischer remembered." (From *Bobby Fischer: Profile of a Prodigy* by Frank Brady, 1973.)

What of the player who has dominated chess for the past decade? As might be expected, **Garry Kasparov**'s first encounter with chess was of the "miracle" variety:

"When Garry had just turned six his family reached a decision to teach him music. It is interesting to ponder what he would have contributed to music had the decision been carried through. Would the vacuum in chess have been filled by another genius?

"That same evening of decision Garry's parents set up a position from the local newspaper column run by the old chess master, Suryen Abramian. Their little one, *Garik* (familiar form of Garry), did not raise his eyes from the board; after awaking the next morning – at breakfast – Garry suggested a move to solve the position. This amazed the family; no one had taught him the game. His father, curious, tested him on the notation for the different squares!

"Such skill only called for a partial raising of the eyebrows. After all, Garik had learnt to read and to add up when very young." (From *Garry Kasparov's Fighting Chess* by Garry Kasparov, Jon Speelman and Bob Wade, Batsford, 1995.)

As an aside, Kasparov is not alone

in that a problem (a composed chess position) was his first experience of chess, rather than a game. Indeed Dr Milan Vukcevich's case has become almost legendary. He was initially introduced to chess problems and for years was unaware that chess could actually be played as a game as well. Upon discovering this, he quickly made progress as a player, reaching good master strength.

Apart from providing some fascinating background information about some of the great players, why am I quoting these tales? Quite simply because, with a couple of exceptions, *they are not too extraordinary*. Those who go on to become great players are just ordinary, bright children who are exposed to chess one way or another at some stage of their childhood, and develop a strong interest in the game. No young players should despair of ever mastering chess because they didn't learn before they were ten, or because they found the game difficult at first, or because they can't afford a lot of books. Parental encouragement or discouragement really isn't such a decisive factor – trying to stop a highly motivated enthusiast carries a risk of alienating the child, and on the other hand, pushing a child into chess will not work if the child lacks interest in the game. My experience, both my own and that gained from talking to other players, is that many people are interested in, and play chess at an early age. Most get distracted from the game by other things, and either give it up entirely, or else spend little time on chess for

some years. Otherwise, if, as a young chess enthusiast, you are determined to reach international level, then it ought to be possible.

Then again, getting an early start as a player is no guarantee of superstardom. Consider my own story, which is not unusual.

Some time before or around my fourth birthday I came across a biscuit tin underneath my parents' bed, which contained some strange metal pieces, with green felt on them. I was told it was a chess set, and that I could learn to play when I was a few years older. However, I was fascinated by the unusual pieces, and insisted on being shown what they did. Thus by the time the Fischer–Spassky match was being covered on the television in 1972 (I was born in 1968) I could follow the games, and became part of a generation of players inspired by Fischer's example.

However, progress was slow. I didn't play very often; just occasional games against my father, who, we later discovered on going to a chess club, was of modest club standard, and less frequently against my slightly older sister (our games came to an end after an argument about whether the kings could stand next to each other – I was in the wrong; oops!). About the age of six I acquired my first chess book, and devoured it from cover to cover many times over. For a few years I didn't pursue much of an interest in chess, apart from reading chess columns in newspapers and the occasional book on chess and scribbling down bits of analysis.

When I was nine years old the family moved to Southport (in northwest England), and I found myself at a school with a chess club. There was no real competition there, and I won every game for the school team. Of course, chess in division two of the Southport Primary Schools' league is mainly a case of taking *en prise* pieces, but this experience suggested that I should take a keener interest in chess. My first game with a master came in a simultaneous display given by the local master, Nigel Davies (now a grandmaster). I achieved an advantage, but lost in the end. After this, I simply had to get to the local chess club, and so my father took me along to the Southport Chess Club, a fair-sized club, with something like 40 members. The response was polite enough; there was a junior club, which I was welcome to join, and if I wanted to play at the senior club, could my father also join? It was suggested that I come back in two weeks, since the week after there was to be a lightning tournament, which presumably was not meant to be a good event for a nine-year-old to play in. Undaunted, I played in the lightning tournament, which included two players of international calibre, and came fifth. Attitudes changed somewhat, and I was immediately fully into the world of club chess.

Here are a few tips for an aspiring player (of any age):

1) Try to find someone of a similar age and playing standard to practice against.

2) Every so often, play against someone a good deal stronger than yourself, and ask them to play to win.

3) Play against a computer sometimes, but don't make this your main form of practice.

4) Be ambitious. Remember that Botvinnik went from beginner to master in just four years.

5) Write down ideas that you have, and study them again later. In that way, you will build on your previous work.

6) Read chess columns in newspapers and perhaps some chess books, and material from good online sources, but use these as starting points for your own analysis. Really try to understand why a grandmaster played a particular move, instead of another one. Your chess will improve far more from understanding a few concepts well than from seeing a lot of games briefly.

7) If you have Internet access, have a look around to see what's going on chess-wise. This will most likely be reassuring, since although you'll encounter some really excellent players, you'll find many weaker than yourself!

8) When you think you're ready, visit the local chess club. If they don't make you feel welcome, try a different chess club. It's their loss, not yours!

I have these suggestions for parents of enthusiastic young players:

1) Do not push your youngsters, but encourage their interest. Chess can become something of an obsession, but then there are far worse things youngsters can do in their spare time.

2) If you are buying chess books for your son/daughter, check that the books are being read before buying more.

3) Find out about the chess clubs in your area, and identify those that take an interest in young new members. If you go to a club and get totally ignored for twenty minutes, chances are it's not a good choice!

4) Befriend other chess parents. Only they can fully appreciate what you're going through! Also they may turn out to be of practical help, sharing the burden of transporting the young geniuses to matches and tournaments.

5) If you are at an event where your son/daughter is playing, don't watch over their games, but show interest afterwards when they tell you about how they played, but not to the point of telling them off if they have done badly. They will be angry enough with themselves. Losing at chess can be very painful.

The Chess Clock

Almost all competitive chess, and quite a large proportional of social chess, is played with a time limit of some sort. In lightning chess the players must move every few seconds when a buzzer sounds, whereas even in the more sedate postal chess, with a few days per move, it is surprisingly common for players to lose a game by overstepping the time limit. There are countless ways of timing a chess game, including some that are rather bizarre. In *The Silence of the Lambs*, for example, there is a chess game played with a beetle clock – a live beetle walks from one side of the board to the other; when a player moves, he turns the beetle around and it trundles its way towards the opponent.

However, in the vast majority of games, the time limit is enforced by the use of a chess clock. Traditionally this consists of two standard clocks rigged up so that when one clock is stopped, the other starts, although digital clocks, performing the same function, are becoming increasingly common. When a player moves, he is entitled to stop his clock, so starting the opponent's. Thus the times on the two clocks indicate how much time each player has used in total. When the minute hand is pointing vertically upwards (towards 12), a small "flag" falls. If this indicates that the player's thinking time has elapsed, and he has not completed the specified number of

moves, then he has lost the game of time.

The clock is the most important piece of chess equipment after the board and the set, and a good understanding of how to use it and negotiate the problems of playing under time pressure is essential to anyone wishing to play successful and enjoyable chess. This short chapter is devoted to these topics.

Standard Rates of Play

There are many rates of play in use. Here are the most common:

1. *Blitz chess: five minutes for each player for all of the moves*
This is an extremely popular time limit used by experienced players when playing for fun. There is little time for deep thought; reflexes and intuition count for much in blitz chess. Games often include blunders and are frequently lost on time. Nevertheless, five minutes is not a trivial amount of time, and five-minute games provide wonderful scope for chessboard opportunism. They can be used as a testing ground for ideas, and can be used to develop an understanding of a particular opening scheme – supposing you can find a like-minded opponent of similar strength to yourself, then you will learn a lot more from an hour of blitz games playing either side of an

opening in which you are both interested, than you would from spending the same time reading up on it.

Opinions vary on whether blitz chess is good for your chess generally. Some feel that playing a lot of blitz chess leads to superficial thought-processes, and rushed decision-making. Others point to the increased tactical awareness that it engenders, and argue that the practice at making quick decisions is valuable when in time-trouble in longer games. I feel that for club players, it all depends on your style of play, and in particular whether you tend to play too slowly – if so, then some practice playing quickly might be a good idea.

There's no consensus amongst World Champions on the matter either. Mikhail Botvinnik, an extremely serious man, would never sit down to play a game unless deeply prepared, and never played for fun. There is a story that when the elderly Botvinnik was asked by a young player whether he fancied a five-minute game, his response was that he hadn't played a game of blitz chess for more than fifty years!

On the other hand, Mikhail Tal, charismatic genius and brilliant tactician, would play anyone, anytime, anywhere at blitz chess. He didn't care; he just loved playing chess. In his final weeks, in the grips of his final illness, he would still play many blitz games each day – and to a high standard too.

In some large cities, one can find people willing to play chess in the open air – generally in parks – for money; generally a modest amount

per game. The standard time limit in these games is five minutes for all the moves. It is not unknown for strong players, even of international calibre, expecting to make an easy profit from these hustlers, to get a nasty shock – although they may not be such strong players, their specialism in the five-minute variety of the game can more than compensate for this.

Five minutes is by no means the shortest possible time limit. Three minutes is quite common, while some speed demons try to play entire games in two or even one minute. I must confess to being rather partial to one-minute chess, but could hardly deny that these games have little to do with chess. Still, it's an excellent way to demonstrate, for example at parties, that chess is by no means a slow, boring game!

2. *Rapidplay: 20, 30 or 40 minutes for all the moves*

The chess played at these time limits resembles "real chess" far more. There is time to make proper plans, to avoid blunders and to calculate tactical sequences, rather than relying so heavily on intuition.

These time limits are often used in one-day "quickplay" tournaments; generally six games in one day. These are popular with players and organizers, since there is no need to find overnight accommodation – one of the drawbacks of the traditional two- or three-day weekend tournaments.

Rapidplay may also have a future on television. Intel's series of Grand Prix events brought together the world's top players, battling it out for big money in rapid games. The games made for plenty of excitement and entertained live audiences – ready-made for television. Some of the games were decided by great chess, and others by hideous blunders.

3. *Local league and weekend chess: typically 35 moves in 75 minutes*
Local leagues are generally played in the evenings. Considering that players have to travel to and from the venue, this tends to leave little more than three hours for playing the game. A typical time limit is an hour and a quarter, or an hour and a half, for the first 30 or 35 moves. What happens after those moves varies from league to league, often depending on agreement between the players or the captains. One option, an increasingly popular one, is a blitz finish: an extra 15 or 20 minutes is added to both players' clocks and the game played to a finish – the main drawback being that blunders often decide the game, and local league players then never get a chance to play an ending when they have plenty of time to think. Another possibility is adjudication, but this has always been regarded as a bad way to finish a game – a game should be won by beating the opponent, not by impressing an unseen adjudicator into awarding a full point. In the past, adjourning the game and playing on at a later date was the best option, provided both players found it convenient. However, nowadays upon resumption the result might be determined largely by which player

has the more powerful computer on which to analyse the position.

This sort of time limit is also used for weekend tournaments, in which five or six games are played over a weekend: perhaps one game on Friday evening, two or three on Saturday, and two on Sunday. Clearly with such a rough schedule as this, four hours is a sensible maximum length per game.

4. *International chess: 40 moves in 2 hours*
This is the standard time control in international events. It may sound slow, but for a tough game between two evenly matched experts, it can go very quickly. The players then have a time increment per move and/or an extra hour each to reach move 60. By that point most games are finished, but for those that are not, some sort of quickplay finish is the norm.

Digital Clocks

Electronic chess clocks are becoming increasingly used in chess competitions, so it is well worth acquainting yourself with them. A good example is the Digital Game Timer (DGT 2010 is the current model), which has been endorsed by FIDE, and costs about £60 (c. $100). It is much lighter than a traditional clock, runs off batteries, and features two digital clock displays and various buttons, together with the traditional bar on top. It can time many different modes of play, including: standard blitz or quickplay (all the moves in a certain amount of time); "gong" mode for lightning chess; "Fischer" time controls (in which a certain amount of time is added every time a move is played); and tournament time limits, with several time controls followed by a quickplay finish. I would recommend that competitive players study the instruction book carefully, as there are several sources of confusion related to the use of the clock.

Ten Tips for Successful Play Under the Clock

These tips assume that you are playing competitive chess. If you are just playing informally with a friend, then obviously feel free to do as you please, except that I suggest it is good practice to get into the habit of using the clock properly.

1. *Never forget to press your clock after you have moved!*
This may seem obvious, but at all levels of chess-playing, precious minutes are squandered by players forgetting to press their clock. Even Anatoly Karpov, one of the greatest players of all time, made this fatal error in a critical world championship game against Garry Kasparov. If your opponent forgets to press his clock, you should feel under no compulsion to tell them. It's their fault – enjoy the free time!

2. *Don't forget to check whether your opponent has lost on time*
Under many circumstances, the onus is firmly on the player to point out that the opponent has lost on time. Neither spectators nor team captains have any right to do so.

3. *Press the clock with the same hand with which you have moved the piece*
This is one of the laws of chess, and a player can be warned or penalized for breaking the rule. The reason is clear: otherwise both players could, in a time scramble, have one hand on the clock and the other moving the pieces. The time recorded for each player would have little to do with the time taken for each move.

4. *Do not abuse the clock by hitting it too hard*
Some players really bash the clock, but this is totally unnecessary. A chess clock is a sensitive device, so hitting it too hard might cause a malfunction. You could also be reprimanded, especially if the clock belongs to the arbiter!

5. *If the clock is malfunctioning, draw attention to this immediately, and not after the game*
A clock that is running too fast or slow, or has a flag that falls too early can be replaced, but do not expect the game to be replayed if you make your claim after losing on time!

6. *Never pick up the clock*
This is completely against the rules and can even result in forfeit of the game.

7. *Never stop both clocks without a very good reason*
Stopping both clocks without making a move is a way of resigning, and may well be interpreted as such. There are certain circumstances under which the clocks can be stopped,

but only do so if you are certain you are entitled to do so, or if an arbiter gives permission.

8. *Make sure you know the time limit before you start play!*

This sounds extremely obvious, but there are instances of players losing on time without even realizing it!

9. *Don't get into time-trouble!*

Let's face it, there's no need to get into time-trouble, and while it is sensible to make good use of your clock time, it never does any harm to keep a little in reserve. If you realize you are day-dreaming at the board, or spending a lot of time on an interesting idea that you're sure you won't end up playing, a little self-discipline is required: make a reasonable move, and get on with the game.

10. *Keep score carefully*

Write down each move, as it is played, neatly on your scoresheet. What does this have to do with the clock? There are instances of players believing they have made the time control, only to find upon deciphering the scribble on their scoresheet, that they skipped a move, and so have lost on time.

Here's an example of two top-class GMs playing in time-trouble. It's surprising how some really good moves are played. The fact that they are mixed in with a few blunders is to be expected.

Shirov – Gelfand
Wijk aan Zee 1996

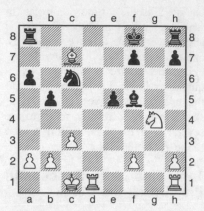

With both players in time-trouble, Shirov found a good move:

30 ♘h6!

Either capture on e5 would give Black time to activate his rook on the g-file, with good drawing chances. Moreover, Black's moves to reach the time-control would then be easy ones.

30...♗g6

30...♗e6 31 ♖hg1 takes the rook off h1, making ♖d6 an unpleasant threat.

31 ♖d6 ♘b4!

An excellent time-trouble move, especially given that Black does not have much to lose. It would be very easy to White to go to pieces totally with just a few minutes – or even worse seconds – to decide on a reply to such a move. Instead 31...♘e7 32 ♖d7 is simply good for White – with easy moves.

32 cxb4

Taking the knight is best. If White had been bluffed into not taking, then Black would have been quite OK.

32...♔g7

Now what does White do? Very few players would be able to find the right continuation in such circumstances.

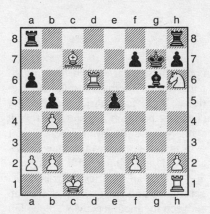

33 h4!

Shirov analysed two alternatives as giving no winning chances:

a) 33 ♘xf7 ♔xf7 34 ♖hd1 ♖hc8 35 ♖d7+ ♔e8 and Black draws.

b) 33 ♘g4 ♖hc8 34 ♖c6 (34 ♘xe5? ♖xc7+ 35 ♔d1 ♖ac8 36 ♖e1 ♖c1+ 37 ♔e2 ♖xe1+ 38 ♔xe1 ♖e8 39 f4 f6 picks off the knight) 34...♗e4 35 ♗xe5+ ♔f8 36 ♗d6+ ♔g7 37 ♗e5+ is a draw by repetition.

33...♖hc8

33...♔xh6 34 h5 wins the bishop while denying Black time to retaliate by rounding up the white bishop.

34 h5!

34 ♖c6 f6! is equal; Black ensures that ♗xe5 will not be check, and will win back one of White's minor pieces.

34...♖xc7+ 35 ♔d2 ♗e4 36 ♖g1+

Gelfand has won back his piece, but Shirov has seen that his attack is now very strong, thanks to his h-pawn covering the g6-square.

36...♔h8

White can cope with 36...♔f8 37 ♖g8+ ♔e7 38 ♖xa8: 38...♔xd6 39 ♖xa6+ should be an endgame win for White; 38...♗xa8 39 ♘f5+ ♔e8 40 ♖xa6 is very good for White.

37 ♔e3

Hounding the bishop yet more to give White's pieces more squares.

37...♗b7 38 ♖gd1!

A good sensible move. "Here I spent a couple of minutes trying to take full advantage of the mating net, but not finding anything special I had to make a move to avoid losing on time." (Shirov).

38...♖e8?

38...♖f8 39 ♘f5 is good for White, but the move played is worse.

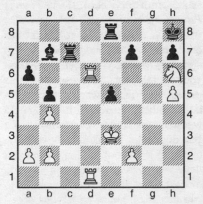

39 ♘f5?

39 ♖d7 wins – it may seem odd that having seen such complicated tactics, Shirov should miss such a simple win of material, but sometimes the mind works that way in time-trouble...

39...♗c8??

This really is a time-trouble blunder. With anything more than a handful of seconds, Gelfand would undoubtedly have played 39...♖c4!, e.g. 40 f3 ♖f4 41 ♖d8 ♖xf3+ 42 ♔e2 ♖xf5 43 ♖xe8+ ♔g7 44 ♖g1+ ♔h6 45 ♖f1 and although Shirov thinks that White should win, the game continues.

40 ♖d8 ♗xf5 41 ♖xe8+ ♔g7 42 ♖xe5 1-0

Competitive Chess

For many chess enthusiasts there comes a time when playing the odd game against friends, relatives, or their computer just isn't enough. They want to test their skills against real opposition, and find out if they are really good or not.

On this point, I quote Steve Davis, snooker champion and chess enthusiast, from his book *Steve Davis Plays Chess*:

"Listen, do you want to get a buzz out of chess? I do, and the best way to do that is to stick your neck out and pit your wits against a stranger who wants to beat you! That's when chess moves into another dimension. It becomes a war, your own private war, where what you do cannot be taken back with the click of a button, or laughed about with your buddy. When you make a mistake in a tournament you have to pay the price, but what if your opponent makes the mistake and it's him squirming on the end of the hook? Now, I know I'm a proven competitive animal but does this scenario not appeal to you? After all, unless you're a Grandmaster, chess is a hobby to you and should be treated as such; winning or losing should come second to the excitement of actually participating."

Are you ready? If so, the first point of call is the local chess club.

Chess Clubs

Chess clubs vary enormously. At best they are warm, cosy places, bursting with life and enthusiasm, with people putting in a great deal of time organizing teams, internal tournaments (serious and for fun) and ideally coaching programmes suitable for all ages. Some clubs even produce their own magazine. At worst, chess clubs are cold and dingy, with confrontational internal politics, slipshod organization and no feeling of kinship between the members. Most clubs fall somewhere in between these two extremes. Venues for clubs to meet and play matches are typically rooms in pubs, libraries, schools, church halls or community centres.

My first experience of chess clubs was in the Merseyside (i.e. Liverpool and surrounding area) League at the end of the 1970s, after I had joined the Southport chess club as a youngster. Some of the clubs where we played away matches were revelations – both positive and negative. A few clubs played in impressive old buildings, dating back to the prosperous days when Liverpool was one of the world's most important shipping ports. The Liverpool Chess Club charged quite a large yearly subscription to its members, and so could afford a very attractive venue, whereas the strongest club, Atticus, charged no membership fee at all, and played in a room with no heating, and broken windows. We once played there in mid-winter, during a blizzard, so it was necessary to keep gloves on during play, taking them off only to play the moves! Working men's clubs, especially those in some of the rougher parts of Liverpool, also provided some excitement, but perhaps these are not typical examples of the chess clubs you will encounter in your local league, so I won't go into details.

When you are trying to choose a chess club to join, my advice is to shop around. Pay a visit to each of the chess clubs in your area and see whether it suits you. If you live in a city, there should be quite a lot of choice, but if you are further from civilization your options will tend to be more restricted.

The first problem, though, is to *find* a chess club. Not all chess clubs publicize themselves very effectively (though some, exceptionally, have their own web site), so you may have to do some searching. Try your local library, especially since it is the better, more active clubs that make the effort to put information in the libraries. Libraries may also have lists of clubs and societies in the area. Otherwise you could try the telephone book or some other advice service. The most definitive information, however, is available from your national chess federation. They will normally have a complete list of clubs in your area, or will be able to put you in touch with someone who does. Here are the details for the federations for the USA, England and Germany:

US Chess Federation
PO Box 3967
Crossville, TN 38557
USA
Tel: 931-787-1234
Fax: 931-787-1200
E-mail: feedback@uschess.org
Web: http://uschess.org

English Chess Federation
The Watch Oak, Chain Lane
Battle
East Sussex TN33 0YD
Tel: 01424 775222
Fax: 01424 775904
E-mail: office@englishchess.org.uk
Web: http://www.englishchess.org.uk

Geschäftsstelle des DSB
Hanns-Braun-Straße
Friesenhaus I
14053 Berlin
Tel: 030/3000780
Fax: 030/30007830
E-mail: info@schachbund.de
Web: http://www.schachbund.de

If you have trouble getting in touch with your national federation, you could try visiting the FIDE web site (**www.fide.com**).

Once you have found and chosen a club, and become a regular, visiting on club nights for friendly games and to compete in internal competitions, you will most likely be invited to play for one of the club's teams in the local league. While this will involve you in a little additional time, travel and expenditure, I would recommend playing local league chess. Otherwise you will eventually get a little bored playing the same people over and over again. Also, you will not feel left out on club nights when everyone else is involved in league matches.

For many players, local league chess is their first taste of *serious* chess. No way can oversights be retracted, and it can be *your* blunder or brilliancy that decides the overall match result. At this point, chess stops being a game and becomes a competitive sport. Depending on the regulations in your country, these games may count for national grading purposes, as will most competitive games; you will be awarded a number (a *grading* or *rating*) that reflects how successfully you have played. Players tend to place great value on these numbers; as Reuben Fine, one of the top players in the 1930s and later a professional psychologist, might have put it, "there is considerable ego involvement".

Once you've got the taste for competitive chess, you may want to try for some individual glory...

Weekend Chess

Weekend chess tournaments are for dedicated enthusiasts: five or six full-length games of chess (typically four hours each) crammed into one weekend! These events are as much a test of stamina as chess skill. In Britain, weekend tournaments are almost always played according to the Swiss system, i.e., in very loose terms, everyone plays someone with the same number of points as themselves, as far as this is possible.

There are usually cash prizes, which tend not to be very large relative to the expenses incurred (entry fee, travel and accommodation). A score of 5/6 or 4½/5 is normally necessary to win a meaningful prize in such a tournament, so specialists in weekend chess develop openings that give them quick-strike potential with both White and Black. The professional approach "win with White, draw with Black" just doesn't work.

In some other countries, players in weekenders are divided into all-play-all sections. Then a score of 75% is quite likely to win a prize, but the prizes are smaller since they are split between more sections.

There are also one-day tournaments, in which five or six quickplay games are played in one day. These are fun, particularly since there is less time to brood over losses.

Unfortunately, it must be said that the weekend chess scene in Britain is not in a good state. The prizes in the 1970s and early 1980s were sufficient for players to hope to make a decent profit from playing in weekenders. As a result the events were keenly contested, and many players became strong and battle-hardened as a result. Masters from overseas would visit Britain to play on the weekend circuit. Now, however, the prizes are still similar in numerical terms. Since all the expenses have been subject to inflation, there's little point in a professional taking part in weekenders. When a GM plays in a weekender in Britain, it is generally for fun and for the sake of keeping in touch with friends in the chess community. It seems an indictment of British chess that a quickplay event with a first prize of only £60 ($100) can attract a few GMs and several IMs. Compare this with the sums that lawyers of similar calibre would expect for a day's work!

The problem is, of course, lack of sponsorship. While in the 1970s many tournaments were able to find a local sponsor, few seem able to do so now – so the prizes are paid for by the entry fees.

Still, if you love playing chess, there can be little better than a weekender. Your chess ought to improve markedly for the experience, you will pick up many ideas to help you win games, and make a lot of friends.

As you become stronger, you will start to enter the upper echelons of the chess world...

Regional and National Events

Beyond local leagues, there are competitions contested by regional teams, and national championships for club teams. Here there is even more pride and sometimes more money at stake than in local events. The ultimate prize for a European club is a place in the prestigious European Clubs Cup. This used to be contested on a knockout basis (away against Moscow, anyone?!), but is now a very attractive Swiss-system event generally played at the end of summer somewhere in the eastern Mediterranean. It resembles a mini-Olympiad, as a fair proportion of the world's best players are recruited by the many teams present.

This brings us on to national leagues. Most European countries have had a national league for many years; in some it is at the heart of their domestic chess, with considerable financial backing, both corporate and from wealthy patrons. In Britain the national league (started in 1993) is now well established, but lacks much corporate backing. The best example of an efficient national league, of great benefit to the entire chess-playing community, is the German Bundesliga. The top division features twenty teams from the whole of Germany. Many of these teams are mighty strong, professional teams, with several top foreign grandmasters, who are flown in specially for the matches and paid well for their efforts. Each Bundesliga weekend is copiously reported in the chess press.

The next level down is the second Bundesliga, which is played on a regional basis. The teams in these divisions tend to be strong, with some of them at least semi-professional, with mercenary GMs and IMs. After all, the teams promoted to the top division are going to need them!

As the divisions become lower, the regions they serve become smaller, until they merge with the local leagues. This is logical: there is no point in travelling several hundred miles when you can get just as good a game in your own city.

It is hard to say precisely what impact the Bundesliga has had on German chess, but the figures speak volumes: in Germany there are more than 95,000 club players, well over 2,000 players on the FIDE rating list and nearly 3,000 chess clubs. Moreover, as any GM who has played a simultaneous at a German chess club will testify, there is a great deal of strength in depth.

You can read more about national championships in the section on women's, veterans', junior and correspondence chess.

International Tournaments

International tournaments are events at which it is possible to gain (or lose) international rating points, and acquire norms towards international titles (IM and GM).

Most players' first experience of international chess is in a large Open tournament. Entry fees normally depend on a player's national or international rating, with concessions for juniors, and free entry or indeed fees for titled players (IMs and GMs). Generally it will not cost too much if you have a very high national rating. The playing schedule is normally one game per day, with the standard international time limit of forty moves in two hours for each player, followed by an additional one hour for the next twenty moves. Thereafter the time limits vary, but an extra half hour to finish the game is typical. That's a maximum of seven hours of nervous tension and quite possibly three time scrambles. Add in a few hours of preparation for each game, and you begin to realize that these events are hard work. Sometimes players go to beautiful foreign cities – and end up seeing little but the inside of the tournament hall and the screen of their notebook computer.

Having said that, many players spend a lot of time after each game in the pub. There are many stories I could tell, but this is a family book...

There are often substantial prizes at stake in international competitions, but still not enough to go around. Typically, a reasonably large Open tournament, lasting a week and a half, might offer ten prizes totalling £10,000 ($16,500). However, there may be ten GMs and forty IMs chasing this money. From a financial viewpoint, most of the IMs would be better off working in their local supermarket!

Much nicer than Open tournaments are all-play-all by-invitation events. The players are then guests of the tournament, with accommodation, meals and sometimes some pocket money provided. The enormity of the difference between the two types of event was brought home to me during the summer of 1990. I had been invited to two small all-play-all events in Denmark. They were wonderful. Everything was provided: excellent food, plenty of beer, blazing sunshine ... it was better than a holiday. I lost rating points, but didn't care. Next were two Open tournaments in Gausdal, Norway. Now Gausdal is a wonderful place, and the organizer, the late Arnold Eikrem, did a marvellous job, his efforts making the small skiing resort into a Mecca for chess players. However, living in a tiny hut and subsisting on cream-cracker sandwiches (since I couldn't afford anything else, having run out of money) left me regretting my career decision to become a chess player.

The situation for professional players in Western Europe worsened considerably when Eastern Europe opened up. This is partly because of the influx of strong players to compete for the prizes, but also since this has tended to put off sponsors – who wants to support an event in their town if a bus-load of unknown Eastern Europeans are going to make off with all the prizes? As a result, the playing standard needed to make a living from chess has increased sharply. In the 1980s, an IM with a rating in the high 2400s could expect to make a living of sorts, while a GM with a rating around 2575 would receive plenty of good invitations, and do quite well from playing chess. By the mid-1990s, invitations had become few and far between for anyone not substantially over 2600, while as for the poor IM, he needed to make a living in other ways.

If you are a good enough player to play international chess, and if you can afford it, do so. The events are fun, highly rewarding and normally provide some scope for sightseeing and socializing.

Drug Testing

In 1999, there were the first signs of a new blight on the lot of the international chess-player. As part of FIDE's doomed campaign to get chess recognized by the International Olympic Committee as a full Olympic sport (which involved FIDE bringing in a new form of "democratic" world championship), chess-players were to have to undergo testing for drugs, with the possibility of severe penalties for players who fell foul of the new rules. This was a truly classic example of finding a solution to a problem that did not exist. It has never been clear which drugs, if any, might enhance chess performance, yet the list of proscribed substances was the same as for athletes, weight-lifters, etc. The list even included caffeine. Even those chess-players who are willing to obey these rules need to monitor their intake of food and drink very carefully, as some substances generate false positives in the tests. Despite being ridiculed by virtually every chess writer and player in the world, FIDE ploughed ahead.

Personally, I would just refuse to take such a test, but those who wish to play international chess on a regular basis may feel it necessary to submit to this humiliation.

A sign of hope came at the 2008 Olympiad, in which Vasily Ivanchuk was selected for a random drug test. This came just after a disastrous loss by the Ukrainian team in a late-round match with medals at stake. Ivanchuk is an emotional character at the best of times, and he was not inclined at that point to pay much attention to the busy-bodies who were chasing after him, clamouring for a sample of his bodily fluids. Failure to provide this sample constituted a positive test, raising the spectre of Ivanchuk being banned (a huge blow to top-level chess) and his results being expunged from the Olympiad, drastically affecting the medal placings. Fortunately, FIDE did not pursue the matter, so perhaps the whole idea of drug testing will be quietly dropped.

Just to put into perspective how absurd this all is, consider that FIDE did very little during this period to counter a much more serious possibility for anyone who actually wants to cheat – see the section "*How to Cheat at Chess* Revisited" in the chapter on Computer Chess. Even nipping off to the toilet to analyse on a pocket set would provide a considerable boost to performance, never mind what is possible with the latest generation of palm-top computers. Note that I am not aware of any cheating of this type; I mention it to illustrate that if there are players seeking an unfair advantage, drug-taking is not the most logical way to do so.

Computer and Internet Chess

It is no exaggeration to say that computers and the Internet have revolutionized almost every aspect of chess. Computers began modestly, as a curiosity more than anything else, as the first playing programs were created. They played terribly, but the wonder was that they could compete at all in a game that was clearly one to which humans were far better suited. Gradually they became more successful, and chess computers appeared in many homes, providing useful playing opponents for children and lower-club players. At the other extreme of the spectrum, endgame number-crunching started to solve endgames with four or five pieces on the board, with perplexing philosophical connotations – a first glimpse of how God might play chess. Then the first game database programs were released, which rapidly changed the way professionals prepared for their games and stored information. This also made research a good deal easier, and the technical aspects of writing about chess – for both amateurs and professionals – became more straightforward. Soon the playing programs became strong enough to assist grandmasters in their analysis, and even to challenge them over-the-board, at least in rapid games. Then the Internet made it possible for everyone to get online chess information from around the world within days of the games being played. Online chess clubs sprang up, so players of all levels could always find opponents of their level, day or night, regardless of their location. By the mid-1990s, the computers had reached grandmaster level, culminating in Kasparov's loss against *Deep Blue* in 1997 – forever changing the general public's view of the game of chess.

Currently, we have analytical engines that play well above grandmaster standard on simple portable computers, and vast numbers of games are played online. Most of the top events are broadcast live on the Internet, with live commentary. The main online chess clubs are lively places, with lectures, guest simuls, broadcasts and training all available. Tournaments need to take the issue of cheating very seriously, given that anyone can have a "grandmaster" in their pocket, and at top level more elaborate possibilities of computer assistance need to be countered – and then there is the issue of false allegations of cheating that have blighted some high-profile events. Meanwhile, computer-assisted analysis has had an extraordinary effect on the way chess is played. Working with the machines has led players to consider "crazy" ideas that somehow work, and gradually this has changed their move selection when sitting at the chessboard. Modern chess is almost seeing a return to the good old Romantic times of the 19th century, with a dramatic increase in outlandish gambits and sacrifices – but now backed up by a lot of concrete analysis. Lively chess sites on the Internet provide a wealth of free and entertaining material for chess enthusiasts. Data overload is the main problem, whereas in the past it was hard to come by good chess information at all. Grandmasters of ever younger ages are appearing, and many of them from developing nations, or ones without a strong chess tradition. In terms of opportunities for up-and-coming players, computers and the Internet have levelled the playing field.

So we have mostly positives, together with a few negatives. Each subtopic could be the subject of a book in itself, so in this chapter we shall take a breathless whistlestop tour of the highlights.

Computers as Playing Opponents

There's something special about the battle between a human and a computer over the chessboard that fires the human imagination. Will human intuition and creativity triumph? Or will iron logic and brute-force calculation snuff out the challenge of the carbon lifeform? There are even elements of "can we create a machine that can replace us?", a question prevalent in science fiction writing, and in general it is a metaphor for much greater questions about humanity's place in the cosmos. Human vs machine over the chessboard is a popular theme in films. HAL's chess victory in *2001:*

A Space Odyssey symbolizes that this soft-spoken machine has ultimate control over the fate of its human cargo (and is the error in its chess notation a sign that HAL is malfunctioning? Let's leave that question to one side, and assume it is an error on the part of the film makers, given how many errors are normally made in chess scenes). Captain Kirk would often play 3D chess with computer-like Spock in *Star Trek*, and the battle between logic and intuition was an ever-present backdrop, as it also has been in many other references to chess in popular culture. As early as the late 18th century, the world took note when a chess-playing machine, *The Turk*, made headlines. Of course, it was a hoax – there was a human player concealed within this large mechanical device – but the visual spectacle of a machine apparently playing chess proved irresistible, and public demand led to a match being contested against the top player of the day – Philidor. In that case, the human came out on top.

So it was then that in 1997, when Kasparov lost against *Deep Blue*, to the wider non-chess-playing world this was a sign of human frailty – that yet another human bastion had fallen to the relentless machines. Meanwhile, chess-players were simply perplexed, wondering why on earth Kasparov had played so suicidally in the decisive final game...

But the computers had made a long and remarkable journey to reach that point. The Deep Blue programmers were able to draw upon decades of experience and techniques developed by computer chess experts, and

IBM had created highly sophisticated chess-specific hardware just for the matches against Kasparov. The journey has not ended there, of course; 12 years on, the best modern programs play much stronger chess than Deep Blue did – and running on an ordinary PC.

Let's go right back to the start. The first computer chess scientists had enough problems creating a program that could play a competent game of even human-beginner standard. Some of the earliest experiments were done without a computer, in the days before the hardware was available, or powerful enough to perform the necessary calculations. Instead human beings, including the legendary computing visionary Alan Turing, tried out algorithms for deciding upon chess moves, making the computations manually. Turing had been involved in the code-breaking activities during World War II at Bletchley Park, together with a number of the best British chess-players of the day. And the code-breaking culminated in the secret development of the computer *Colossus*. So chess and computers were together from the start, and it is no surprise that a chess-playing program was high on the agenda once the war was over.

The first task is for the computer to be able to play a legal game of chess. This is simply a case of competent programming to encode the rules of the game without forgetting any of the subtleties of the rules – a talented child could do it. This part of the program is known as the move generator – given a chess position as input (including information on castling rights, *en passant* possibilities and the player to move), it generates a list of all the legal moves. The next step is less clear, and is a question of programming philosophy. How is the program to seek the best move? Should the aim be to mimic human thought, or should it just calculate as much as it can? Arguably, the former is conceptually more interesting, but the latter has proved clearly the more effective – not a surprise with hindsight, as it plays to the computer's strengths. Nevertheless, some computer scientists persisted with a more AI (Artificial Intelligence) approach, notably former World Champion Mikhail Botvinnik after retiring from competitive play in 1970. While some progress has been made in this direction, AI-based chess engines still lag far behind their faster-searching brethren.

The brute-force method has been the clearly preferred method for a long time, albeit with more and more "pruning" and chess "knowledge" built into the process. In its basic form, the computer just calculates as many variations as possible, terminating them with a very crudely-based assessment. A minimax is performed on the assessments of these terminal positions, and this enables the machine to choose which move gives it the best position, assuming the opponent chooses the best responses at each point. Of course, "best" here is in terms of these very crude assessments, which may turn out not to reflect reality at all. But with a deep search, and a slightly more sophisticated assessment function than just counting material, the machine can play a vaguely decent game of chess in this manner.

Let's see a computer game from the early days, between computers from the Institute for Theoretical and Experimental Physics (Moscow) and Stanford University (California):

ITEP computer – Kotek-McCarthy computer
ITEP – Stanford, March 1967

1 e4 e5 2 ♘f3 ♘c6 3 ♘c3 ♗c5 4 ♘xe5

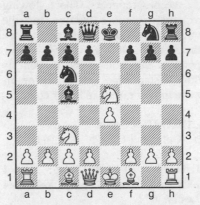

A standard trick, which some writers have presumed came from the computer's opening "**book**" – a set of opening sequences provided by the programmers from which the computer looks up the move to play, rather than working it out by analysing the position. However, it doesn't take much computing power to see that White is not really sacrificing a piece, and accounts from Russian sources confirm that this good move was a result of the program thinking for itself – in fact, the program did not have an opening book at all. The Russians themselves were surprised by the move, given that they had made the computer highly value castling rights, which would be lost if Black replied 4...♗xf2+ 5 ♔xf2 ♘xe5, but in return White has the bishop-pair and a strong centre, which the ITEP machine must have been factoring in to its assessment.

4...♘xe5 5 d4 ♗d6 6 dxe5 ♗xe5 7 f4 ♗xc3+ 8 bxc3 ♘f6?!

Now the knight gets kicked around. 8...d6 is safer and preferable.

9 e5 ♘e4

9...♕e7 10 ♗e2 still leaves Black needing to make an awkward knight move.

10 ♕d3?!

10 ♕d5 is better, as it rules out the ...d5 defence. After 10...f5 11 ♗d3 Black faces a difficult defence, but this may involve White being a pawn down for some time, so a computer might reject it for that reason. In fact, the ITEP team tested this, and found that if their creation had been analysing half a move deeper, it would indeed have played 10 ♕d5. The line in question was simply 10...♘xc3 11 ♕c4, when the otherwise pointless check 11...♕h4+ 12 g3 pushes the loss of the knight further into the analytical distance.

10...♘c5

10...d5 is clearly correct and gives Black a more-or-less playable game.

11 ♕d5 ♘e6?

The knight is not stable here. Black should dig in with 11...d6.

12 f5 ♘g5?

Now the knight is lost. 12...c6 is necessary, but 13 ♕c4 (better than 13 ♕d6?!, as given in some sources, due to 13...♕h4+ followed by a queen check and ...♕xf5) 13...♘c7 14 ♕g4 leaves Black under enormous pressure. Possibly the idea of White playing moves like h4 was given a low priority by the American program (in an effort to prune the variation tree), as there is no question of analytical depth being the reason for it losing the knight here.

13 h4 f6 14 hxg5 fxg5 15 ♖xh7!

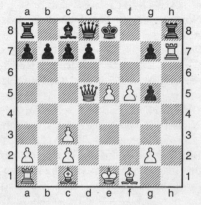

"Historic. Probably the first real sacrifice made by a computer." wrote Gerald Abrahams in *The Chess Mind*. It's mate in two if Black accepts (15...♖xh7 16 ♕g8+ ♚e7 17 ♗xg5#), so not exactly deep, but it's a significant achievement.

15...♖f8 16 ♖xg7 c6 17 ♕d6 ♖xf5 18 ♖g8+ ♖f8 19 ♕xf8# (1-0)

Given how little computing power was available at the time, the play is rather impressive. The Russian program featured a technique that has become standard in chess programming: **alpha-beta** pruning to speed up the minimax; the basic idea is that one refutation is enough, and so there is no need to look at all branches of the analytical tree once a move is

established as bad. A later Russian program, *Kaissa*, added a further pruning technique, **null move**, by which lines are cut short if one side cannot even make good use of a pure extra move, and the **killer move heuristic**, which prioritizes moves that have been effective in other variations. Kaissa also used **search extensions**, whereby variations are analysed further if they feature material exchanges or checks.

However, a lot of lessons were learnt the hard and embarrassing way by the programmers. The following example is most famous for the tragic episode at the end, but let's see the game in full to get a sense of how crudely the computers played in those distant times and to set the bizarre turn of events in better context.

COKO III – Genie
US Computer Ch, Chicago 1971

1 d4 d5 2 ♘f3 ♘f6 3 ♗g5 ♗g4 4 ♘c3 ♘e4 5 ♘e5 ♗e6 6 ♘xe4 dxe4 7 c4? ♘d7?

7...f6 wins a piece.

8 ♘xd7 ♗xd7 9 e3 f6 10 ♗f4?

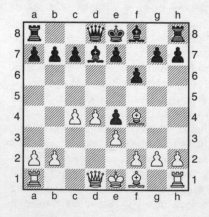

10...♗e6?

10...e5 followed by ...♗b4+ causes White some problems.

11 ♕h5+ ♔d7?

Probably the computer played this to avoid losing the b7-pawn, but there are more important factors than that. 11...g6 12 ♕b5+ ♗d7 13 ♕xb7?! e5 14 dxe5? (Black is more or less OK after other moves; e.g., 14 ♗g3 ♖b8 15 ♕xe4 ♖xb2) 14...♖b8 gives Black a winning counterattack (obvious at a glance to an experienced human or a modern computer), but it was way beyond the capabilities of the computers back then to "see" far enough into the variations to realize this.

12 d5 ♗g8 13 ♕f5+ e6 14 dxe6+ ♗xe6 15 ♕xe4? c6??

15...♗b4+ limits the damage to a pawn (for nothing). Now it is just a wipe-out.

16 ♖d1+ ♔e8 17 ♖xd8+ ♔xd8 18 ♕xe6 ♗b4+ 19 ♔e2 ♖e8 20 ♕g4 g6 21 ♕h4 g5 22 ♕xh7 ♗e7 23 ♕d3+ ♔c8 24 ♗d6 ♔d7 25 ♗xe7+ ♔xe7 26 ♕h7+ ♔e6 27 ♕e4+ ♔d6 28 c5+ ♔xc5 29 ♕d4+ ♔b5

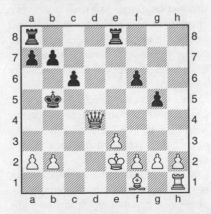

Already, White has a choice of forced mates in just a few moves. It

would seem a triviality to choose one of them (after all, the moves are natural and forcing enough), but something turns out to be very wrong in COKO's program.

30 ♔d1+ ♔a5 31 b4+ ♔a4 32 ♕c3

Now ♕b3# will follow. All Black can do is delay this by giving away his rooks.

32...♖ad8+ 33 ♔c2 ♖d2+ 34 ♔xd2 ♖d8+ 35 ♔c2 ♖d2+ 36 ♕xd2

With hindsight, the first sign that things are wrong. Why wouldn't a computer – *a computer!* – choose 36 ♔xd2 with mate next move by 37 ♕b3#? It turns out that COKO had not been programmed with a way to choose between a mate in 1, a mate in 2, or a mate in 3, etc. Here it chooses a mate in 4 over a mate in 2. Much worse is to follow.

36...♔a3 37 ♕c3+ ♔xa2

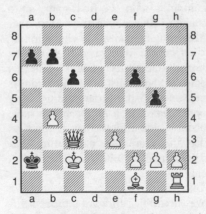

This is the position where the game is normally quoted from. White has a choice of two ways to give mate in 1, and many ways to give mate in 2, 3 or more. But in this overwhelming position, it nevertheless plays the classic role of the rabbit caught in the headlights, or indeed the Adélie penguin in front of the icebreaker. No human could ever do what COKO does now. The worst a total beginner would do is accidentally give stalemate.

38 ♔c1 f5 39 ♔c2 f4 40 ♔c1 g4 41 ♔c2 f3 42 ♔c1 fxg2 43 ♔c2 gxh1♕

Throughout this last sequence, COKO has been choosing a move that leads to mate in 2 rather than giving mate in 1.

44 ♔c1??

But now, unable to choose between two moves that give mate in 1 (and still ways to give mate in 2 or move), COKO opts for a move that doesn't even win.

44...♕xf1+ 45 ♔d2 ♕xf2+ 46 ♔c1 ♕g1+ 47 ♔c2 ♕xh2+ 48 ♔c1 ♕h1+ 49 ♔c2 ♕b1+ 50 ♔d2 g3 51 ♕c4+ ♕b3 52 ♕xb3+ ♔xb3 53 e4 ♔xb4 54 e5 g2 0-1

And a quarter of a century later, a computer won its first game at a standard tournament time-limit over a reigning human world champion...

Of course, individual bugs can be ironed out easily enough, but this episode shows just how much care is needed with the programming. Any optimization in a program can have bizarre side-effects that remind us that these are just calculating machines, and definitely not intelligent entities.

We should fast-forward a little at this point, since without major advances in hardware, no chess program would ever have reached human grandmaster standard, or even come remotely close. The necessary computing power just didn't exist in the early 1970s. Back then, an electronic calculator was a sophisticated piece of office equipment, and computer video games had not evolved beyond the level of "bat and ball". And as the common meme has it, NASA used less computing power to send men to the moon than can be found in *[insert small handheld device here]* nowadays.

And playing chess without using human intuition and judgement *does* require a lot of calculation. In the initial position White has 20 moves, and Black has 20 moves in reply. That gives 400 possible positions after move 1. Going just a few moves further, we quickly get to millions and billions of possibilities, and the numbers keep multiplying until the figures soon become astronomical. Even the most sophisticated pruning and prioritizing can only help up to a point. As the 1970s wore on, hardware advanced rapidly, and computers started to become interesting opponents for club players at least, and clearly would be progressing quickly to higher levels. And as miniaturization and mass-production was starting to make computers available to the general public, it would not be long before chess enthusiasts would be able to have a silicon opponent of their very own.

But some club-level players were destined to face the machines earlier than that. In 1977, the sensational report came from Minnesota that a computer had achieved close to a master performance in a tournament playing against human opponents. However, a statement from the tournament director suggests that it was somewhat less impressive a display –

the opponents were mostly very rusty from lack of practice, and played well below their nominal ratings (especially in the unexpected situation of facing a machine), and an average club player could well have achieved a similar result against them. In a later event also in Minnesota, the computer struggled to score many points against a group of players with a similar average rating – but these were more active players who had also seen the computer's earlier games.

This highlights a couple of problems, from a human viewpoint, with computers as opponents. Firstly, until the 1990s, it was very hard to get a reliable indication of the computer's playing strength. The quoted figure would generally come from the manufacturer rather than an independent source, and be based on a small sample against unprepared opponents. Many players in the 1980s would order a highly-rated chess computer, only to find that, once the novelty of a machine actually playing chess in their living room wore off, turned out to be a rather tedious opponent who put up little resistance. The machine would gather dust and the player would once more need to seek out his local chess club. The second issue is that players would sometimes turn up at a tournament only to find that they were paired against a computer, which many of them resented. Why should a computer be involved in a contest between humans, especially when it might impact the battle for prize money or trophies? Also, playing a computer would often mean a long and unnecessarily tiring game, as

the computer will play out almost any position long after the result is clear. Moreover, one knew that any loss against the machine would do the rounds of the computer chess journals or advertising materials for the machine.

Anyway, back to the late 1970s, where one of the first chess microcomputers was making a name for itself. Here is a sample of its play.

Microchess – Human player
1977

1 d4 ♘f6 2 c4 e6 3 ♘f3 b6 4 g3 ♗b7 5 ♗g2 ♗e7 6 0-0 0-0 7 ♘c3 ♘e4 8 ♕c2 ♘xc3 9 ♕xc3 d6
The machine was now out of its opening book. From here on it plays at about 1-3 minutes per move.
10 e4?
Simply giving a pawn away for next to nothing. The evaluation function must have been very heavily weighted towards open lines, attacks on central squares and piece activity.
10...♗xe4 11 ♖e1 d5 12 ♗f4 ♘d7?

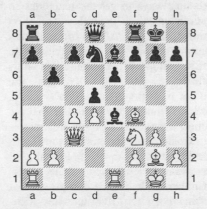

We can see that Black is a weak player, missing the attack on c7.

Why the machine decides not to take the pawn is not clear, but perhaps the programmers built in an endgame-avoidance factor, knowing that the computer's play in almost any endgame would be lamentable.

13 cxd5 exd5 14 ♕c6!? ♘f6 15 ♘g5?! ♖e8? 16 ♗h3?

16 ♗xc7 is simple and very good for White.

16...♗b4?! 17 ♖e2?! ♖e7 18 ♖c1 ♕f8

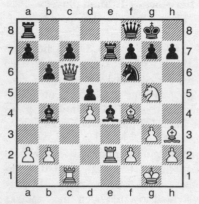

19 ♖a1?

It took many years for programmers to find ways to get the machines to avoid making pointless, planless moves like this. All too often, if they could not see any concrete way to make progress, they would just shuffle pieces aimlessly. Of course, the point is that computers don't plan at all, so finding algorithms to make a chess engine play purposeful moves in quiet positions is a very difficult task indeed. As an aside, I recall that in the early 1980s, my Fidelity Chess Challenger had some odd glitches of this type. Often it would play a Sicilian Dragon, but if you got it out of book before it had castled, then it

would start shuffling its rook between h8 and g8.

19...♖ae8 20 ♖c1 ♗d3 21 ♖xe7 ♖xe7 22 ♖d1? ♖e1+?

22...♗e2 followed by ...h6 wins a piece.

23 ♖xe1 ♗xe1 24 ♗xc7 g6?? 25 ♕xf6

Computers have always been good at taking *en prise* pieces!

25...♗d2 26 ♘f3

But this computer also experiences problems giving mate: 26 ♗e5 forces mate next move.

26...♕b4 27 ♕d8+ ♔g7 28 ♗e5+ ♔h6 29 ♕h4# (1-0)

In fairness, there were many later programs that played much more crudely, and players nowadays might well wish that computers would make more oversights! Clearly, for entry-level club-players and below, Microchess could be a fun opponent.

At the other end of the scale, an MIT team felt their program was ready for testing against the world elite. Unexpectedly, this testing came against none other than Bobby Fischer, who had not played competitive chess since his 1972 world championship victory over Boris Spassky. Fischer won all three games with great ease, emphasizing the vast gulf of understanding that still lay between the machines and grandmasters.

Greenblatt MIT – Fischer
Cambridge (USA) 1977

1 e4 c5 2 ♘f3 d6 3 d4 cxd4 4 ♘xd4 ♘f6 5 ♘c3 a6 6 ♗e2 e5 7 ♘b3 ♗e7 8 ♗e3 0-0 9 ♕d3

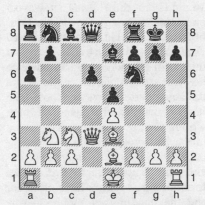

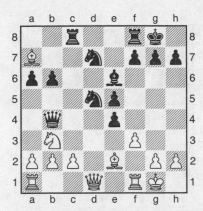

This looks like the computer's first non-book move, but it's not too bad.

9...♗e6 10 0-0 ♘bd7 11 ♘d5 ♖c8

In modern practice 11...♗xd5 is preferred (and has scored well), as the text-move is strongly met by 12 c4!.

12 ♘xe7+? ♕xe7

White has spent time exchanging off a good knight for a bad bishop. That's not necessarily a bad thing in all cases, but there needs to be a good reason. Here it just gives Black a Sicilian player's dream.

13 f3 d5 14 ♘d2 ♕b4 15 ♘b3?!

White's game is poor whatever he plays, but 15 ♕b3 at least avoids immediate material loss, and gives White some grovelling chances.

15...dxe4 16 ♕d1 ♘d5 17 ♗a7 b6

Now the bishop is trapped. Computers typically have problems understanding that such a piece cannot escape, as there are often ways to push the loss of the piece further into the analytical distance, and so beyond the "horizon". This problem still afflicts modern computers, but their massively greater analytical capability lessens the problems in most cases.

18 c3 ♕e7 19 fxe4 ♘e3 20 ♕d3 ♘xf1 21 ♕xa6 ♘e3 22 ♗xb6 ♕g5 23 g3 ♖a8 24 ♗a7

Black can win however he pleases. Fischer targets the white king.

24...h5 25 ♕b7 h4 26 ♔f2 hxg3+ 27 hxg3 f5 28 exf5 ♖xf5+ 29 ♔e1 ♖af8 30 ♔d2 ♘c4++ 31 ♔c2 ♕g6 32 ♕e4 ♘d6 33 ♕c6 ♖f2+ 34 ♔d1 ♗g4 35 ♗xf2 ♕d3+ 36 ♔c1 ♗xe2 37 ♘d2 ♖xf2 38 ♕xd7 ♖f1+ 39 ♘xf1 ♕d1# (0-1)

But clearly the computers were making great strides forward, The following 1979 game was described by Karpov and Gik as an "absolutely human-like game". That's overstating it, as we shall see, but the computers were clearly becoming real players, rather than a curiosity.

Belle – Chess
USA Computer Ch, Detroit 1979

1 d4 ♘f6 2 c4 c5 3 d5 e6 4 ♘c3 exd5 5 cxd5 d6 6 e4 g6 7 ♘f3 ♗g7 8 ♗e2 0-0 9 0-0 ♖e8 10 ♘d2 ♘a6 11 f3 ♘c7 12 a4 b6 13 ♘c4 ♗a6 14 ♗g5

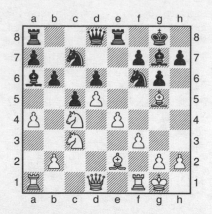

No doubt the play up to here came straight from the computers' opening books, and they were now (or very soon) on their own. They have "played" a sophisticated line of the Modern Benoni, with many of the moves based on subtle plans of which the computers have no concept and are unlikely to follow. The upshot of this approach to the opening book – putting in a mass of lines from human grandmaster chess – is that when both machines are thrown into battle, it is almost a lottery as to which has a position that it handles better. It was not until the 1990s that the programs started to have opening books that were at least tweaked to produce positions that the machines would handle well – generally this means avoiding blocked positions and ones based on long-term plans, though engines differ in their specific strengths and weaknesses. Nowadays the best engines have a book that is specially prepared to suit them, with weightings based on engine vs engine games, and that the engine – via computer-assisted analysis – has had a hand in developing.

14...h6

14...♕d7 15 ♕d2 ♗xc4 (it was to make this exchange for the powerful blockading knight that the bishop went to a6) 16 ♗xc4 a6 is a typical line, with Black seeking to advance his queenside majority, while White has a number of ways to oppose this. It's noteworthy that as I sit here writing this, Rybka is working away in the background (with no opening book loaded), quietly indicating precisely this as its preferred line of play for both sides! Times have changed, and the handling of mobile pawn-majorities doesn't seem to be such a mystery to modern analysis engines. The text-move is also known, as a way to avoid White getting a grip on the c1-h6 diagonal, but Black normally follows it up with a similar plan with ...♗xc4.

15 ♗h4 g5 16 ♗f2 ♘h5 17 ♘e3

An exchange of light-squared bishops would suit White, and leave f5 weak.

17...♗c8 18 ♕c2

White now starts to "drift". A typical plan would be to stabilize the queenside with ♕d2, ♖ab1, b4, and with Black's counterplay neutralized, to set about squashing Black on either the kingside or queenside, depending on how Black responds.

18...♘f4 19 ♗c4 ♗d7 20 ♖fd1 ♕f6 21 ♗g3 ♘h5 22 ♗e1 ♘f4 23 ♔h1 a6 24 ♗g3

White's shuffling has not improved his position, and allowed Black to achieve his strategic aim. That's how a human would see it – "Chess" was perhaps more focused on ways to win material, but in any case it now plays the right move.

24...b5 25 axb5 axb5 26 ♖xa8 ♖xa8

27 ♗f1 b4 28 ♘e2

Now White is getting pushed around in dismal fashion. 28 e5 at least gives White some activity and squares for his knights.

28...b3 29 ♕b1

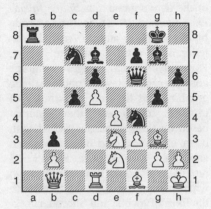

29...♘h5?

An odd choice. Presumably "Chess" was unable to assess 29...♘xe2 30 ♗xe2 ♕xb2 31 ♕xb2 ♗xb2 32 ♗xd6 clearly (it is very good for Black, as Rybka can assist me in judging, 30 years on), and its assessment function didn't value its passed pawns highly enough to choose this line on "general" grounds. Modern analysis engines tend to award large bonuses for far-advanced passed pawns, especially connected ones, given that there are very often tactical means to shepherd them through to promotion, even if these are too far away to be seen when analysing the position from afar.

30 ♗f2?!

30 ♘c4 keeps White in the game.

30...♘f4?! 31 ♘c4 ♘xe2 32 ♗xe2 ♗b5 33 ♗g3 ♖a4 34 ♕c1 ♗f8?!

Few Benoni players would go passive like this, and most would be

more willing to exchange bishop for knight on c4. 34...♗xc4 35 ♗xc4 ♕xb2 36 ♕xb2 ♗xb2 37 ♗xb3 ♖b4 38 ♗xd6 ♘b5 39 ♗xc5 ♖xb3 40 d6 ♗f6 is a logical continuation.

35 ♖d2 ♕d8 36 ♗f1 h5 37 ♔g1 h4 38 ♗f2 ♗g7 39 ♘e3 ♖xe2 40 ♕xe2 ♖a1+ 41 ♖d1 ♖a2 42 ♕d3 ♖xb2 43 ♘c4 ♖c2 44 e5!

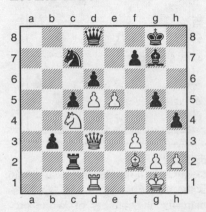

This attractive move is a definite glimmer of human-like chess, as White executes the central pawn-break that is latent in most Modern Benoni positions.

44...♗xe5

44...♖xc4 45 ♕xc4 b2 46 exd6 ♕xd6 47 ♗xc5 is good for White.

45 ♘xe5 dxe5 46 ♕xb3 ♖e2 47 ♔f1 c4 48 ♕b7

There's an old saying, "the pawn you decide not to take is the one that costs you the game". Had Belle been human, you might have expected to hear that in the bar after the game. 48 ♕xc4 is simple and strong.

48...♖a2 49 ♗b6 h3?!

This has a "swindle mode" feel about it. 49...♕a8 avoids immediate material loss, but White's d-pawn remains an unsolved problem.

50 ♕xc7
Good enough, but 50 d6! is the *quietus*.
50...♕f6 51 ♕d8+ ♕xd8 52 ♗xd8 ♖xg2

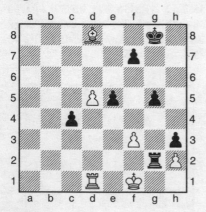

53 ♖e1?
Going after an irrelevant pawn. 53 d6 is the simplest way to win. To a human, the inevitability of White promoting his pawn, and the fact that this is more important than any other factor in the position, is obvious, but a machine has to calculate it, and it is still several moves away, and Black can make it further away by throwing in checks or advancing his c-pawn.
53...c3 54 ♖xe5 c2
Now Black's c-pawn is a major threat, and White is fighting to save the game.
55 ♖e8+
55 ♖xg5+? fails because Black does not exchange rooks, but instead just moves his king.
55...♔g7 56 ♗xg5 ♖xg5 57 ♖c8 ♖g2 58 d6 ♖xh2 59 d7 ♖d2 60 ♔g1 ♖xd7 61 ♖xc2 ♖d3 62 ♖f2 ♔f6 63 ♔h2 ½-½
Still, this is a remarkably impressive performance for two computers in the 1970s. To put things in perspective, we can compare advances in computer games, another field that is critically dependent on hardware capabilities and the programmers' ingenuity. The latest craze at the time of the above game was *Space Invaders* (released 1978), featuring crude blocky graphics and no Artificial Intelligence worthy of the name. Nowadays we have hugely complex computer games with photorealistic graphics and lighting, multitudes of in-game characters that interact based on their own specific AI with other characters and human players, and plots worthy of a Hollywood movie. We should bear this in mind when comparing Belle and co. with the likes of Rybka and Shredder!

The 1980s was truly the decade when humanity came face to face with computers. They started appearing in our homes, offices and schools. By the end of the decade, even quite simple devices often featured some sort of silicon chip that controlled their functions. The children of the 1980s were the first true computer generation, as home computers became cheap enough for everyone to own one. These machines were not very powerful or compatible with one another, and not a great deal of useful work could be done with them, but a generation gained a firm foundation for proficient computer use in later years. This had a profound effect on many fields, including chess. However, chess programs for personal computers were quite weak to start with, so most chess-players' first encounter with a silicon opponent came in the form of dedicated chess computer – a computer built to play chess, and only to play chess. These had names like Fidelity Chess Challenger, Novag and Mephisto, etc. At first they were rather weak, despite some impressive-sounding claims of their ability, but had fantastic novelty value. Christian Kongsted wrote:

"I have been interested in computer chess since 1982, when I was ten years old and my father gave me my first chess computer. It was a Fidelity Chess Challenger about the size of a pocket chessboard, and it had two diodes, one for 'Check' and one for 'I lose'. While it was thinking, the light was switching between these two diodes until it finally made a move, and I remember being fascinated by looking at the diodes. One move before being checkmated the computer would usually realize that it was losing and light up the 'I lose' diode. By modern standards the Chess Challenger was laughably weak, and within a year it had stopped being a challenging opponent for a 10-year-old boy."

Indeed, in this decade one could have some fun wiping these computers off the board. No special strategy was needed, but it was entertaining to use some anti-computer strategies, playing against their weaknesses and getting them to play dreadfully in positions where their lack of understanding became painful. (As an aside, if you are looking to enjoy a similar experience nowadays, I have noticed that the in-flight entertainment systems of some airlines have programs of this standard.)

But the machines had their appeal. You could have an opponent whenever you wanted, and they had various analytical features (find the mate, overnight analysis, etc.), an opening book and a variety of other features, such as hints and some rudimentary teaching functions. For a child they were fantastic. Many of the models included a rather nice built-in chess set, which could prove useful even after the user had outgrown the computer (or it had broken down). Some had voice capabilities, and a few could even move the pieces on their own. Towards the end of the 1980s, sensory boards started to appear, so that you just made your move on the board without needing to key anything in or press the chessboard squares as if they were buttons. This led on to the technology for the sensory boards used nowadays in many tournaments, which allows the games to be recorded automatically and transmitted live online.

By the end of the 1980s, these machines, especially the top-end models, were becoming strong enough to beat most club players. For instance, the Mephisto Portorose 68020, released in October 1989, claimed a playing strength at a tournament time-limit of about 2320 Elo, with a range of playing styles available, an opening book of 10,000 lines, and a typical search depth of 11 plies (half-moves – i.e. 6 moves by one side and 5 by the other), or up to 31 in simplified positions. The Portorose would make search extensions if a position was "tactically rich" according to its algorithms. It came with a beautiful sensory board and a rather less lovely price-tag of about £1500 (c. US$2500). But this machine had beaten Deep Thought, the machine that would later become the world-famous Deep Blue, which would have cost rather more to buy, even if it had been on sale.

Let's see an example of the Portorose at work.

Mephisto Portorose – Sharp
Cambridge University "Olympiad" 1990

I had competed in this team rapid-play event myself the previous year. Then the computer team had won, but the University's best players (Elo 2100+) had mostly been able to cope with the computers. My game the previous year (as White) had gone something like 1 d4 ♘f6 2 c4 e6 3 ♘f3 b6 4 a3 d5 5 ♘c3 dxc4 6 e4 c5 7 d5 ♗a6, with the computer clearly having trouble grasping the dynamics of the position, and losing rather badly.

A year on, and the humans stood little chance, as the computers' ability to keep making decent moves made them almost impossible opponents in games with a short time-limit. Its opponent here, Jeremy Sharp, was a solid and experienced 2250+ player.

1 d4 d5 2 ♘f3 ♘f6 3 c4 e6 4 ♗g5 ♗e7 5 ♘c3 0-0 6 e3 h6 7 ♗xf6 ♗xf6 8 ♖c1 c6 9 ♗d3 ♘d7 10 0-0 dxc4 11 ♗xc4 e5 12 ♘e4 exd4 13 ♘xf6+

Mephisto had been working from its opening book so far.

13...♕xf6 14 ♕xd4

One might expect a computer to want to keep the queens on the board, but this is the move that has been favoured by human grandmasters, and is the best way to put some pressure on Black.

14...♕xd4 15 ♘xd4

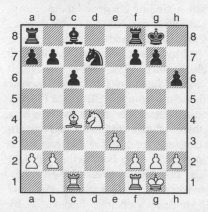

Black has some development problems to solve in this queenless middlegame, but I am sure that Jeremy would have been confident of handling this simplified position better than a computer. For a while, he does.

15...♘b6 16 ♗b3 a5

16...♖e8 17 ♖c3 a5 18 a3 a4 19 ♗a2 ♖a5 20 ♖fc1 may give White a tiny edge; in any case, he ground out a win in Andersson–A.Lawson, European Union Ch, Liverpool 2008.

17 a4

17 a3 is probably better, avoiding a weakness, as in the Andersson game.

17...♖d8 18 g3

A peculiar move, and while not a blunder of course, it is hard to explain what might have attracted Mephisto to the move, unless it was belatedly trying to put its pawns on dark squares (not a very relevant consideration unless the pawns are likely to become fixed). It's not even in Rybka's top ten moves in this position.

18...♗h3 19 ♖fd1 ♘d5

Heading for the nice safe outpost on b4.

20 ♖c5 ♘b4 21 ♖d2 b6 22 ♖c3 c5 23 ♘f3 ♖xd2 24 ♘xd2 ♖b8

Now it's the human's turn to play an odd move. He was thinking of ...b5, but never gets around to playing it. 24...♖d8 is natural, when White finds it hard to do very much, 25 ♘c4?? ♘a2! being an important point. If there is one thing we have learnt from computers, it's that tactics are present in *every* position!

25 ♘c4 ♗e6 26 ♔g2 ♗d5+ 27 ♔h3 ♔f8 28 ♔g4 ♔e7 29 h4 f6 30 ♔f5

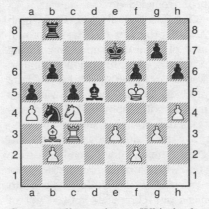

Conceptually at least, White's last few moves have been along the right lines – activating his king in preparation for a pawn advance. This is a far cry from the days when computer programmers wanted the games adjudicated at move 40 to avoid the embarrassment of their machines having to play an endgame!

30...♗f7! 31 e4

But this gives Black the d4-square. White should manoeuvre and stabilize the kingside structure.

31...♘c6 32 ♔f4 ♘d4 33 ♗d1 g5+ 34 ♔e3 ♗xc4 35 ♖xc4 ♖d8 36 ♗g4 ♘c6?! 37 f4 gxh4 38 gxh4 ♖g8 39 ♗f3 ♘d4 40 ♔f2 ♔d6?! 41 ♖c3 ♘xf3?! 42 ♔xf3 ♖g1 43 ♖d3+! ♔c7 44 e5

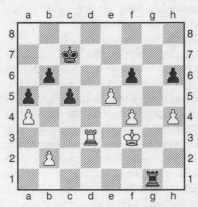

The human has made all the running, but with scant reward: he must be careful in this rook ending.

44...fxe5 45 fxe5 ♖e1?

45...h5 is better.

46 ♔f4 ♖e2 47 b3 ♖h2 48 ♔g4 ♖f2 49 e6?

49 h5 and 49 ♔h5 are both good.

49...♔c6?

49...♖f6 should draw: 50 e7 ♖e6 or 50 ♖e3 ♔d8 51 e7+ ♔e8.

50 ♖e3 ♖f8 51 e7 ♖e8 52 ♔f5 ♔d7 53 ♔f6 ♖h8 54 ♖d3+ ♔c7 55 ♔f7 1-0

By no means a masterpiece, but a game where you'd have great difficulty judging from the bare gamescore who was the computer and who was the human. Significantly, areas of the game that were previously "human domain" were becoming less clearly so.

But the days of the dedicated chess-playing computers were already numbered. The rise of the multi-purpose PC, and the standardization of their operating systems, meant that the next generation of programs used by the typical player would be supplied as software-only. This greatly reduced the cost to the user (assuming they already had a PC), and meant that upgrades could be supplied much more easily and cheaply. The first of these PC-based programs to make a major impact were Fritz and Chess Genius. Initially, Fritz was promoted by Chess-Base primarily as an analytical engine to be used within its flagship database program. It was designed to sit in the background, quietly giving its assessment of the current position and a suggested line of play. Its ability to find tactical ideas made it a favourite with professionals working on their opening preparation, and before long, grandmaster games were being decided (or at least impacted) by "Fritzy" opening novelties. It was particularly strong at finding forcing lines, as moves that created a strong threat were heavily favoured in its search. It also had an odd tendency to give assessments of a position that jumped around chaotically, giving the impression of an overexcited child genius with a very short attention span! This endeared the engine to some, but drove others mad. (To this day, Fritz still has notoriously jumpy assessments compared to other top engines such as Rybka.)

Chess Genius was always much more of a chess-playing program, and shot to fame with victories over some the best human players in rapidplay events in the early 1990s. ChessBase also produced a standalone program for Fritz, designed primarily for playing games (featuring a 3D board, sounds and sometimes cheeky messages), but also with database and analytical capabilities. The Fritz program allows other engines to be used, and the ChessBase "family" was extended to include several other of the best and brightest chess engines of the day; including Hiarcs and Junior. These engines were all roughly similar in overall playing ability, but each with their own sets of strengths and weaknesses, so the general advice was to use several different ones, for variety when playing, or to get a better-rounded view in analysis.

The user-friendly ChessMaster series of programs also had a prominent place in the market for playing programs, but the engine supplied was never in the same class as Fritz or Chess Genius, and so it was more popular with hobby players than professionals or higher-end club players.

By the mid-1990s, the best engines running on a good PC were somewhere around grandmaster standard, and so the battle between humans and computers moved out of the living room and onto the world stage. For ordinary mortals, handicap levels were offered, in which the machine would attempt to play at a rating of the user's choosing, but these tended not to be too satisfying: in its crudest form, the machine would blunder a piece at some point, and then resume playing like a grandmaster for the next few moves. To this day, no programmer seems to have achieved a truly human-style handicap level. In those times, it was still possible for top-end club players to have a fair chance against the best computers by resorting to extreme anti-computer chess, but as the years wore on, this became harder and harder. Trying to keep control in a quiet position against a machine with a phenomenal tactical ability is very hard work indeed.

Let's take a look at an example of anti-computer strategy from the 1990s:

Ki. Georgiev – Fritz 3
Munich (5 minute) 1994

1 g3 e5 2 ♗g2 d5 3 b3 ♘f6 4 ♗b2 ♗d6 5 d3 0-0 6 ♘d2 c5 7 e3 ♘c6 8 ♘e2

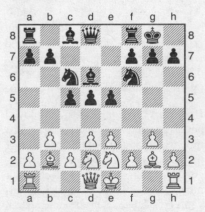

Georgiev has set up the solid but highly passive "Hippopotamus" position (the name is reasonably self-explanatory). This gets the computer out of its book, and into a position where it should form a plan. Since the computer doesn't know how to plan, White expects to make

steady inroads into the position in the middlegame.
8...♕b6 9 0-0 ♗g4 10 h3 ♗e6 11 ♔h2 ♖fe8 12 a3 ♖e7
Black's last few moves have been somewhat disjointed.
13 c4 dxc4
13...d4 would be met by 14 e4 and then a gradual kingside pawn-storm – an excellent position against a computer, since it is unlikely to perceive, until it is far too late, the scale of White's kingside threats.
14 dxc4 ♖d8 15 ♕c2 ♖ed7 16 ♖ad1 ♗c7 17 ♘c3 a6 18 ♘de4 ♘xe4 19 ♗xe4

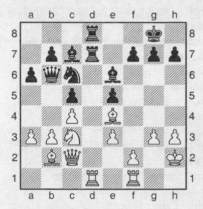

Now White is establishing firm control over the d5-square, and still Black has no targets for counterplay.
19...♖xd1 20 ♖xd1!
20 ♗xh7+ ♔h8 21 ♖xd1 ♖xd1 22 ♘xd1 ♘a5! sharpens the game for no good reason. Instead, Georgiev sticks to his plan. He was finding the game extremely easy, and had time to smile at the audience and play around, peering at the underside of the computer's keyboard, and so on. Georgiev gave every indication that he could score a massive percentage

against computers using the type of strategy demonstrated in this game. Note that it is not a specific plan or sequence of moves that he was using, but rather a computer-hostile way of thinking.

20...罝xd1 21 豐xd1 ②a5 22 ②d5 盒xd5

22...豐d6 might be a better try; e.g., 23 豐h5 h6 24 ②xc7 豐xc7 25 盒xe5 豐d7 26 盒c3 ②xb3 27 豐e5 f6 28 豐b8+ 含f7 29 盒xb7 盒xc4 30 盒xa6 盒xa6 31 豐xb3+ c4 and White's king gives Black some counterchances.

23 豐xd5

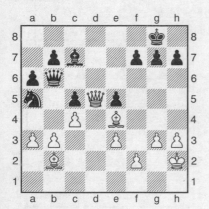

23...豐d6

Black falls under a decisive attack if he grabs the b3-pawn: 23...豐xb3 24 豐d7 g6 25 盒d5 forces mate; 23...②xb3 24 豐d7 g6 (24...豐d6? loses the queen: 25 豐e8+ 含f8 26 盒xh7+) 25 盒d5 豐f6 26 含g2 and now something black must drop off; e.g., 26...盒d6 27 豐xb7 ②d2 28 盒c3 and White wins the knight.

24 豐xd6 盒xd6 25 盒c3

White has several pluses here, but most importantly, Black has no play.

25...②c6

25...②xb3 26 盒xb7 a5 27 盒c6 盒c7

(else the a-pawn falls) 28 盒a4 ②c1 29 盒c2 leaves the knight in grave danger.

26 g4 f6 27 含g2 含f7 28 含f3 h6 29 盒d5+ 含g6 30 盒e4+ 含f7 31 h4 盒c7 32 h5

Gaining yet more squares.

32...含e6 33 盒d5+ 含d7 34 含e4 b6

Now for an excellent liquidation.

35 盒xc6+

White has delayed exchanging until his king's penetration is guaranteed.

35...含xc6 36 含f5

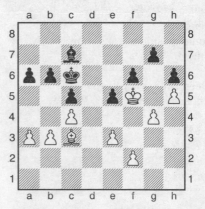

And White won very easily.

However, the methods employed here are not of much use against modern computer programs. Some of the underlying failings are still present, but submerged too deeply for most humans to be able to take advantage of them. On the other hand, they can certainly raise their head when we use computers as analytical assistants, so we shall be returning to these shortcomings later in this chapter.

The best-known man vs machine chessboard battles occurred in the second half of the 1990s, and will no doubt be recorded in history as the point at which the humans were forced to surrender this bastion of the intellect to the machines. To chess-players, the story isn't as clear-cut as that, given that Kasparov's loss in the 1997 rematch against Deep Blue probably said more about Kasparov the man than about the relative strengths of the players. We shall examine the first and the last games from the 1996 Deep Blue–Kasparov match, which indicate how well computers could at the time play in some positions, and how badly in others.

Deep Blue – Kasparov
Philadelphia (1) 1996 (WGG 96)

1 e4 c5
Even Kasparov's first move came in for criticism from some commentators, on the basis that it leads to open positions of the type that are to the liking of computers. However, if a player with White wishes to obtain an open position, and chooses his openings wisely, then this aim can generally be realized. Those same commentators were later to criticize his choice of overtly anti-computer openings the following year, when that failed to give Kasparov the type of positions where his abilities could shine.

2 c3
A good choice. A main-line Sicilian, although sharp and tactical, would walk into Kasparov's lifetime of specialist knowledge and understanding.

2...d5 3 exd5 ♛xd5 4 d4 ♞f6 5 ♞f3 ♗g4 6 ♗e2 e6 7 h3 ♗h5 8 0-0 ♞c6

9 ♗e3 cxd4 10 cxd4 ♗b4
This is the start of a somewhat unusual manoeuvre, but one that Kasparov believed in.

11 a3 ♗a5 12 ♞c3 ♛d6 13 ♞b5

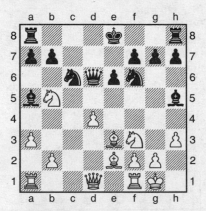

13...♛e7?!
This gets Black into some trouble. 13...♛d5 was Kasparov's planned improvement when he repeated the same opening line in game 3. Maybe he saw this move during this game, but avoided it on the grounds that a draw by repetition could arise after 14 ♞c3 ♛d6 15 ♞b5. Instead, 14 ♗c4?! (hoping for 14...♛xc4?? 15 ♞d6+) is well met by 14...♗xf3! 15 gxf3 ♛d7, so if White wants to make anything of the position, he/it must try the pawn offer 14 b4 ♗xf3 15 ♗xf3 ♛xb5 16 bxa5 ♞xa5 17 ♛e1, which could give White compensation.

14 ♞e5 ♗xe2 15 ♛xe2 0-0 16 ♖ac1 ♖ac8 17 ♗g5
Black is now under considerable pressure, and will have problems dealing with the pin on the f6-knight.

17...♗b6
17...♖fd8 is a possible alternative; after 18 ♗xf6 gxf6 (after 18...♛xf6

19 ♘xc6 ♖xc6 20 ♖xc6 bxc6 21 ♘xa7 White wins a pawn) 19 ♘c4, besides putting the bishop on b6 Black can choose between 19...♗c7 and 19...a6 20 ♘xa5 ♘xa5.

18 ♗xf6 gxf6

18...♕xf6? 19 ♘d7 picks up an exchange.

19 ♘c4 ♖fd8 20 ♘xb6 axb6 21 ♖fd1 f5 22 ♕e3!

As we are about to see, the queen is superbly placed on e3. It is hard to give Black good advice. His pawns are weak and White's d4-d5 advance will shatter them completely.

22...♕f6 23 d5!

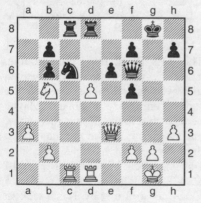

In an article in *Time* magazine entitled "The Day that I Sensed a New Kind of Intelligence", Kasparov wrote of this move:

"I got my first glimpse of artificial intelligence on Feb. 10, 1996, at 4:45 p.m. EST, when in the first game of my match with Deep Blue, the computer nudged a pawn forward to a square where it could easily be captured. It was a wonderful and extremely human move. If I had been playing White. I might have offered this pawn sacrifice. It fractured Black's pawn structure and opened up the board.

"Although there did not appear to be a forced line of play that would allow recovery of the pawn, my instincts told me that with so many 'loose' black pawns and a somewhat exposed black king, White could probably recover the material, with a better overall position to boot.

"But a computer, I thought, would never make such a move. A computer can't 'see' the long-term consequences of structural changes in the position or understand how changes in pawn formations may be good or bad."

However, when various people tried the position on far more primitive computers than Deep Blue, they were more than a little surprised by the results. Jouni Uski from Finland posted a message on the Internet: "I think the move Kasparov is talking about is 23 d5! – it's found in couple of seconds by Genius4!!"

Robert Hyatt from the University of Alabama at Birmingham followed up with: "I've tried it on a couple of programs. My old Fidelity Mach III finds it, Crafty finds it (takes about a minute, though, because Crafty likes other moves better, although if you make it search only that move it only requires 1 ply [half-move] to see it doesn't sacrifice anything). No idea what in the world Garry thought he saw here, or maybe this is the wrong game entirely. In any case, d5 doesn't sacrifice a pawn or anything ... hmmm ..."

23...♖xd5 24 ♖xd5 exd5 25 b3

A calm move. Black's weaknesses cannot be solved in one free tempo.

25...♔h8?
This move is the final straw. Black's counterattack will just not work – no great surprise really.

Black had to try to grovel to an ending: 25...♘e7 26 ♖xc8+ (or 26 ♕g3+ ♔h8 27 ♖xc8+ ♘xc8 28 ♕b8 ♔g7) 26...♘xc8 27 ♕e8+ ♔g7 28 ♕xc8 ♕a1+ 29 ♔h2 ♕e5+ 30 g3 ♕e2 regains the knight in view of the threat of perpetual check, but White will have a good queen ending in view of Black's shattered pawns.

Deep Blue now wins the position in not quite the way a human would, allowing a lot of optical counterplay, but having accurately calculated that it does not work.

26 ♕xb6 ♖g8 27 ♕c5 d4 28 ♘d6 f4 29 ♘xb7 ♘e5 30 ♕d5 f3 31 g3 ♘d3 32 ♖c7 ♖e8 33 ♘d6 ♖e1+ 34 ♔h2 ♘xf2 35 ♘xf7+ ♔g7 36 ♘g5+ ♔h6 37 ♖xh7+ 1-0

At the time, Frederic Friedel, one of the key men at ChessBase, put forward an interesting view of the computers vs humans battle. His feeling was that in a certain percentage of chess positions that are liable to arise in practice – maybe 20% – the computer was already far stronger than the best humans, and would win practically the whole time. Equally, there is a percentage of positions where the computers will stand no chance against the top players – also perhaps 20% at that time. While the game is in the no-man's-land in the middle, things are very finely balanced, and the human's task is to reach the good 20% rather than stumble into the bad 20%. The computer, of course, is oblivious to this struggle, though the programmers may try to bias it toward playing human-hostile chess.

Frederic's view, therefore, was that while these percentages would become worse for the humans as computers got faster (they may now – in 2009 – be more like 80% and 5%), there will still be scope for humans to steer the game into the positions where the computer has no chance, while avoiding those where the computer rules supreme. At some point, though, this will cease to be possible, as the slightest, most imperceptible inaccuracy (in the sense of allowing a computer-friendly position) will throw the player into the abyss.

If Frederic's view is right, we have just seen an example of the computer's domain. Now for the human's. It's just as ugly.

Kasparov – Deep Blue
Philadelphia (6) 1996

1 ♘f3 d5 2 d4 c6 3 c4 e6 4 ♘bd2 ♘f6 5 e3 c5
This looks odd, but Black reckons that the d2-knight is not well placed to battle for central control.

6 b3 ♘c6 7 ♗b2 cxd4 8 exd4 ♗e7 9 ♖c1 0-0 10 ♗d3 ♗d7 11 0-0
The opening has been a success for White. He has good central control, and prospects of a gradual queenside advance. More importantly, there is no direct plan for Black, so the computer drifts for a few moves, with disastrous consequences. The bishop is already a little clumsy on d7; I suspect a strong human player would have sunk into thought at move 10,

and devised a plan for liberating his game.

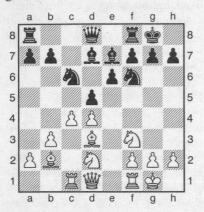

11...♘h5?

This over-ambitious idea met with strong disapproval from most human commentators. However, Yasser Seirawan told me that, oddly enough, one well-known chess computer scientist suggested that the move may well be OK, but it might need a highly advanced computer in a few years' time to justify this view. I suspect that this is a case in point of someone believing that a strong chess-playing program is doing something profound, when in fact it is just crunching numbers. Few GMs felt that ...♘h5 was anything other than a bad move. Thirteen years on, Rybka would certainly not play 11...♘h5, though it isn't very far down its list of preferences, surprisingly enough. The basic problem is that Black's position is already difficult, and so good moves are hard to come by.

12 ♖e1 ♘f4 13 ♗b1 ♗d6 14 g3 ♘g6 15 ♘e5 ♖c8 16 ♘xd7 ♕xd7 17 ♘f3 ♗b4 18 ♖e3 ♖fd8 19 h4 ♘ge7

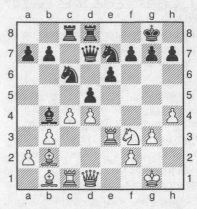

Here White has a very interesting combinative opportunity in 20 ♗xh7+ ♔xh7 21 ♘g5+. However, Kasparov made the correct *practical* decision by keeping things simple against the supercomputer, for it would only require the slightest hole in the combination to cost White the game.

20 a3 ♗a5 21 b4 ♗c7 22 c5 ♖e8 23 ♕d3 g6 24 ♖e2

White is much better, still in a simple position. With his plan of rolling Black up on the queenside, Kasparov must have been at least 90% sure of winning.

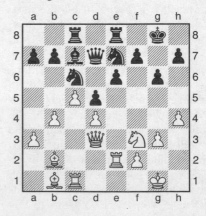

24...♘f5 25 ♗c3 h5 26 b5 ♘ce7 27 ♗d2

The bishop has far more scope on d2 than it had on b2.

27...♔g7 28 a4 ♖a8 29 a5 a6 30 b6 ♗b8

The a8-rook cannot be too happy with life! Black might be able to erect some sort of defence based on control of c6, but White will place his bishop on a4 and taunt Black with ideas of ♘e5 or infiltration on the kingside dark squares – or else a massive kingside onslaught if Black goes into a queenside huddle.

31 ♗c2 ♘c6 32 ♗a4 ♖e7 33 ♗c3 ♘e5

The computer spots a freeing tactic, but it is to no avail.

34 dxe5 ♕xa4 35 ♘d4 ♘xd4 36 ♕xd4 ♕d7 37 ♗d2 ♖e8 38 ♗g5 ♖c8 39 ♗f6+ ♔h7

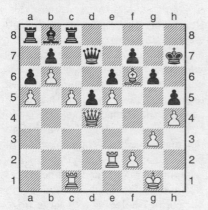

Black's position is a complete disaster. Kasparov now executes a tactical breakthrough.

40 c6! bxc6

Black cannot avoid giving White a passed b-pawn, since 40...♖xc6 41 ♖ec2 ♖xc2 42 ♖xc2 leaves Black completely helpless.

41 ♕c5 ♔h6 42 ♖b2 ♕b7 43 ♖b4 1-0

Black has no moves apart from shuffling his king, while White has all the time in the world to walk in to finish the rout.

The rest is history. Kasparov lost in 1997, after playing suicidally in the decisive final game, and accused IBM of cheating, after which Deep Blue was dismantled and there were no further matches of this type. There was to be no scope for objectively testing Deep Blue against other computers or other humans, and torch was again to be carried by the familiar analysis engines running on PCs. For the next few years, the top engines were Fritz and Junior. A number of matches were contested between top GMs and the latest versions of these and other leading engines running on ever more powerful hardware, with generally mixed results – these programs were at least holding their own with the top players. Of course, these were also the engines that the players were working with day in day out in the course of their preparation and analysis, so there was not the same element of surprise as when Kasparov faced IBM's supercomputer.

The next "monster" in the Deep Blue mould was to emerge some years later. Called Hydra, and boasting powerful custom hardware and the latest refinements in chess computer algorithms, this machine claimed to have more computing power than Deep Blue and to be able to analyse far deeper – typically 18 half-moves when playing at tournament speed.

After some resounding successes by Hydra in tournament play, Britain's top player, Michael Adams, a world-class grandmaster, bravely stepped up to face the machine. The result was a sobering ½–5½ loss for humanity's representative. To his credit, Adams played normal chess, rather than resorting to anti-computer strategies. However, it was clear that man vs machine chess was fast becoming a non-event. Here is one of the games:

Hydra – Adams
London (3) 2005

1 e4 e5 2 ♘f3 ♘c6 3 ♗b5 a6 4 ♗a4 ♘f6 5 0-0 ♗e7 6 ♖e1 b5 7 ♗b3 d6 8 c3 0-0 9 d4 ♗g4 10 d5 ♘a5 11 ♗c2 c6 12 h3 ♗c8 13 dxc6 ♕c7 14 ♘bd2 ♕xc6 15 ♘f1 ♗e6 16 ♘g5 ♗d8 17 ♘e3 ♗d7 18 a4 h6 19 ♘f3 ♖c8 20 axb5 axb5 21 ♘h4 ♘c4 22 ♘xc4 bxc4 23 ♗a4 ♕c7 24 ♗xd7 ♕xd7 25 ♘f5 d5 26 ♖a6 ♕b7 27 ♖d6 ♗e7

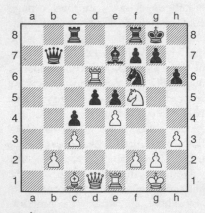

28 ♗xh6 1-0

2005 was also a year when "normal" chess engines made great strides

forward. The engine Fruit (it is now freeware and open source) successfully implemented a technique known as **Late Move Reductions**, which has subsequently been adopted by many other engines. From 2006 onwards, the engine Rybka has occupied top spot in the computer rating lists, often by a very large margin, with old Rybka versions among the contenders for the no. 2 ranking. It has also earned high praise from many grandmasters for its relatively reliable assessments and good all-round play. Rybka has in recent years been playing matches at odds (e.g., pawn and move, or more) against titled players.

What the future may hold for human vs computer events is not so clear, but in order to make it at all interesting, there will need to be some measures taken to even the odds. Removing the opening book and endgame tablebases is one step (after all, the human doesn't have these advantages), while it has already become standard for the human to have been able to prepare by having a copy of the engine in advance (with only minor tweaks allowed before the match). But the human will still need to adopt a really good anti-computer strategy, and that needs effort and dedication that is unlikely to be worth it unless a very large prize fund is offered. And the end result will be ugly chess in any case. Probably the time has come to draw a veil over the issue of human vs computer at the chessboard and to focus on cooperation instead.

Freestyle and advanced chess are two forms of the game that involve just such cooperation, as does correspondence chess. Advanced chess features a human and a computer working together, while freestyle chess allows any sort of consulting team, but the most successful teams will naturally involve a computer, and it has repeatedly been shown that teams that work interactively with their computer are at a considerable advantage over those where the computer is primarily or solely in charge of choosing each move. Perhaps the final blow in the humans vs computer struggle will be struck when the humans aren't even of any use in this capacity, and computers perform better without any human intervention. But currently, that seems a long way off. We shall return to this theme later in the chapter, in the section on "Analytical Engines and Assisted Analysis".

Endgame Databases and Tablebases

In parallel with programmers' efforts to create playing engines, a wholly different approach was being used to solve chess, or rather a limited segment of the game. This was the creation of endgame databases, by which complete information about a certain type of endgame with only a few pieces on the board is calculated. This is stored as a data file, which can then be accessed to discover the assessment of any position of the relevant type. For instance, if you have a position with ♖+♙ vs ♖, then the endgame database for this material balance will be able to tell you if the position is won, and if so how many moves it will take.

This is an interesting process from a philosophical viewpoint, as it is the start of a process which, in principle, could solve chess completely. Playing against the database is also akin to "playing chess against God".

To create an endgame database, the computer starts with all "terminal positions" – those where the game has ended with checkmate or transition to another ending (by a capture or pawn promotion), and then works back from these positions, creating lists of positions that are one move from mate, two moves from mate, etc. For this process to be possible, all the databases for the "simpler" endings need to exist already. Thus one starts with ♔+♕ vs ♔, ♔+♖ vs ♔ before one can create ♔+♙ vs ♔. Then the work on four-man databases can begin. This is a very time-consuming process, demanding huge amounts of processing power, and as more pieces are added, the size of the files becomes enormous too. At the time of writing, all important six-man endings (i.e. those with six pieces, including the two kings, on the board) have been completed, with work on seven-man endings in an early stage. A subset containing just the most important of these is more than 100 gigabytes, while the full set is more than half a terabyte. The most common data format of modern endgame databases is that devised by Eugene Nalimov, and consequently they are called Nalimov tablebases, or "tablebases" for short.

As the databases started to be made available, it became clear that many new secrets about endgame theory were to be uncovered in this way. One of the earliest was that ♕ vs ♖ is not such a simple endgame as had been assumed. GM Walter Browne, for instance, had some trouble defeating the database. However, this did not fundamentally change the theory: the ending remained a theoretical win, and the defender's chances in practice (between two humans) remain minimal, as it is just as hard to defend optimally with the rook as it is to attack with the queen against perfect defence. The first major surprise was that 2♗ vs ♘ turned out to be a win, albeit with some positions requiring many moves. But this is more a curiosity than anything else, whereas the later five-man databases covered some more major endings, with ♖+♙ vs ♖ and ♕+♙ vs ♕ both major areas of endgame theory that were heavily affected. They also made it possible to assess objectively how well humans handled these endings, or – if you like – how "close to God" the best human players had come.

Initially, the results of this process were of interest mainly to computer scientists and endgame theoreticians – and to FIDE, who made drastic changes to the fifty-move rule for some of the endings featuring longer wins. In practice, this only had the effect of allowing players to torture their opponents longer in ♖+♗ vs ♖ (a generally drawn but tricky ending to defend), as the 50+ move wins are way beyond human comprehension. Once a few 200+ move wins were uncovered in some six-man endings, sanity prevailed, and the fifty-move rule was restored – meaning that some of the theoretical wins are now practical draws. Or does that mean they are now theoretical draws after all? Take

your pick – it doesn't affect practical chess very much either way. But for the purpose of endgame studies, the convention has been adopted that the fifty-move rule does not apply for endings where there is a longer win.

Nowadays, anyone seriously examining any endgame position needs to take the tablebases into account. They are readily available, and can be accessed by all good modern chess engines. Note that they access them during their normal search, not just when the current position has six pieces or fewer. Thus if there are many pieces on the board and the engine sees a simplifying line that reaches, e.g., ♔+2♙ vs ♔+2♙, it will use the tablebase to look up the result of this pawn ending, with a huge increase in its effective search depth and accuracy of assessment. However, accessing tablebases is also relatively slow, so if the tablebase look-ups are not of great importance (e.g. the position is clearly won on a normal assessment basis), then accessing the tablebase can actually make the search *less* efficient, as the time could have been used to analyse many more relevant positions instead. Programmers therefore try to reduce the frequency of tablebase look-ups in the search process, without of course preventing the engine from gaining the vital information it needs to assess critical lines correctly. Those doing endgame research may therefore wish to look at any optional settings that their engine has, if they wish the engine to use the tablebases more frequently.

Tablebases can be downloaded freely from the Internet, but the files are truly enormous, as mentioned above. Several companies (including ChessBase and Convekta) sell sets of DVDs packed with the most important of the tablebases, which you may find a convenient solution if you don't have a very high speed Internet connection (or if you have a download limit). There are also websites that allow you to look up tablebase results online, but these are just for finding the result of a given position; they cannot be used by your chess engine in the same way that tablebases stored on your own computer can be.

If you have a large collection of tablebases, there is then the practical issue of how to manage this mass of data. Unless your hard disk is colossal, you will probably want to keep the full set on an external hard-disk, and only have a subset of the most important ones (all five-man and less, and some six-man) on your hard-disk. You can freely choose which tablebases to include at any one time; the engine won't complain about finding some tablebases and not others – it will use any tablebases that it finds, and make "normal" assessments in any endings for which it doesn't find one. Note that your engine can be slow to start up if it is accessing a huge set of tablebases, especially if they are on an external device with which communication is at all sluggish.

Game Database Programs

The most indispensable piece of software for all chess professionals, writers and any remotely serious chess enthusiast is the game database. This is a program that stores, accesses and organizes a mass of chess games past and present. The user can search the database in a great variety of ways to search for specific material for study, training or general interest. He can also create his own databases on whatever topic he likes, and enter games or annotations of his own. The most common uses of the game database program are to prepare for a particular opponent or to work on one's opening repertoire in more general terms. Various search features (for players, for positions, etc.) are vital for finding the relevant information, and once you have obtained it, a user-friendly graphical interface is necessary to get the most value out of the data. You will want to be able to use an analytical engine "on the fly", while getting statistical info about the current position, a list of games that have reached the position, and perhaps also to see the contents of a "tree", such as the opening book of a major chess engine. With all this information conveniently at your fingertips, it is possible to appraise very quickly what the main ideas are in a position, and if there are any new developments or major problems facing one side or the other.

The main database program is **ChessBase**, as it has been since its introduction in 1987. **Chess Assistant** is an alternative program, but it has a smaller following, and works rather differently. You can also try **Scid**, which is free (scid.sf.net). ChessBase has all the features described in the previous paragraph, and many, many more. It is so feature-rich that even highly experienced users will be surprised every so often to discover some useful feature that they never knew existed. It is often worth right-clicking to get context-sensitive options, and a look through the menu options in each of the main views can be illuminating too. Some familiarity with general Windows techniques is very useful, as Copy, Cut and Paste can be used in many contexts to move data around between databases and game windows. Games can be merged together into trees or into a single game (with annotations), and opening reports can be generated for any position of your choosing; likewise for player reports. A huge player encyclopedia comes with the ChessBase program, with a wealth of information about, and pictures of, players past and present. The search feature is immensely powerful, with the ability to search for manoeuvres, sacrifices, structures, etc., in addition to more obvious things like player names, dates, ratings and position. And all these search methods can be combined. Vaguely remember a game from Kasparov's early career where he sacrificed a knight on f5 with a blocked King's Indian-type centre? Yes, you can search for that.

Remember, however, that even with these powerful tools at your fingertips, the answers it comes up with are only as accurate, complete, or as up-to-date, as the data that it is referring to. I'd suggest keeping low-quality data separate from high-quality data, rather than throwing everything into one big melting pot. ChessBase offer large databases for sale, with Mega Database their flagship product. There is a cheaper version of this available, with the same data quality, but without annotations.

For up-to-date information each week, you will want to download The Week in Chess, and add the games from that to a copy of Mega Database, and use this as your Reference Database – i.e. the one ChessBase uses by default for searches or when providing data on the current position in the Reference Search pane. Depending on your interests, you might also want to add databases of correspondence or computer games. You can also get *Informator* on disk, which is a good source of annotated material.

Like any piece of software, Chess-Base is not without its bugs and annoyances, but generally speaking, recent versions have fewer such issues than earlier versions did. You can still get the occasional crash, especially when trying out one of the less-often-used features, so be sure to save your work if you have been entering a lot of information or comments of your own. And you will from time to time find some odd behaviour – don't be too shocked; this is not a Microsoft product!

Steve Lopez of ChessBase USA writes regular "ChessBase Workshop" articles on getting the most out of ChessBase (and the Fritz interface). Generally, his articles are aimed at non-expert users, but always include tips and ideas that anyone might find useful. These articles can be found on the ChessBase web site (www.chessbase.com).

Analytical Engines and Assisted Analysis

So far in this chapter I have written much about analytical engines, but in this section we are going to focus on how we can use them to our own benefit, as analytical assistants. This is a tremendously important aspect of computer chess, and I do not think it is an exaggeration to say that it has revolutionized modern chess. Firstly, it has changed the style of openings that people play. Some ideas that would have been simply too risky and chaotic are now played quite routinely because it is possible to prepare them to the point where the risk seems acceptable. Certain speculative opening lines have dropped out of fashion because the easy availability of good analysis engines means that any opponent could come to the board armed with a refutation. Generally speaking, players nowadays adopt a broader opening repertoire than in the past, since hard-hitting preparation (and this can be done very quickly before the game if one is sure what the opponent will play) renders it too easy to strike a stationary target, outweighing the benefits of even a great deal of prior experience – which used to be the principal argument in favour of adopting a narrow repertoire.

But most important of all, working with chess engines has changed the way people understand chess, and with the current generation of players who have grown up with the engines, this process can be expected to accelerate. Anyone who has worked with an analysis engine will have seen the computer repeatedly suggesting bizarre-looking moves. At first one might dismiss them as the product of a lack of understanding, but after a while you take a closer look, and perhaps attempt to refute them with good solid replies. Sometimes you'll be right, and the computer will reverse its assessment after a while, but on other occasions, the idea will turn out to be good. In due course, the human starts to anticipate these ideas, and so considers a much broader selection of candidate moves when at the board and when preparing. I think we can also attribute the modern trend towards long-term unclear material sacrifices to players working closely with computers. Rather than being the relentlessly materialistic machines that we tend to view them as (especially when they have just beaten us by taking our loose pieces), a computer's assessment function factors in *all* elements in a position, often encouraging us to take a closer look at sacrifices that we would otherwise have considered too speculative. If we can't defend the position against the computer, then maybe we should try it against our next opponent, especially if we are armed with a mass of specific variations prepared together with the machine.

Getting down to specifics, the first point to make is that analysing with the computer does **not** mean just turning the engine on, and passively watching its assessments. While even this can lead to useful conclusions, far better results can be achieved by working together with the machine, using human intuition and pattern recognition in harmony with the computer's tactical prowess and deeply searching analysis. There are plenty of different methods for doing so, but as long as the skills are used together in some way, the result should be good reliable analysis that is of a far higher standard than either party working in isolation. Note that you should be working hard during the whole process, as otherwise you won't be bringing your skills to the analysis. You are standing on the machine's shoulders, not being carried by it!

Even those players who feel they are simply unable to think independently when the engine is running have some options. You can analyse on your own, creating a variation tree that you feel represents the critical lines in the position, and then have your engine perform a blundercheck on the whole of this analysis. Most likely this will at least throw up some interesting points that you will wish to investigate further. A blundercheck is an immensely powerful method, as the computer starts at the end of each variation, and spends a while analysing each position before stepping back to analyse the previous position. The conclusions of the previous analysis will still be available to the engine via its **hash tables**, giving it a greatly enhanced effective search depth.

But a more interactive approach will lead to better results, and also avoid the human spending a lot of time working on variations that the computer might be able to shoot down in seconds. Here is a suggested method.

1) From the initial position you have chosen to analyse, give the computer a while to reach some sort of assessment. Firstly, it may find a

devastating resource; secondly, if it is a situation with a material imbalance, with one side enjoying obvious compensation, then the computer's assessment indicates whether it "sees" the compensation. If the computer does not recognize the compensation, then, unless the compensation truly is not there, the computer's assessments and suggestions will be somewhat skewed by this. For instance, in an excellent position from a gambit, the computer may be looking for ways to regain the pawn and reach a tenable ending, simply not seeing the long-term attacking ideas it should be pursuing. In such cases you need to lead the analysis with a firmer hand.

2) If the computer has suggested something very interesting, then pursue that path. Otherwise, enter a move that you consider logical and sensible. If there are several such moves, then enter one as the main line and the others as variations. If you are at a loss even for a choice of candidate moves, then go with the computer's suggestion, or leave the computer analysing for a while. It may well be that you have already reached the critical moment to hand the position over to the computer to sort out the tactics.

3) At each point give the computer a little time to make a suggestion and assessment. If the assessment suddenly changes, or is widely at odds with what you would expect, then stop and investigate. It may have found something important. If a new and vital idea has been spotted, then it is useful to back up through the variations leading to the position and

any related lines, as having seen the key idea (which will therefore now be present in the hash tables), its assessment of these positions may now be radically different.

4) Continue in this way while you have a fair idea what is going on in the variations. How long you leave the computer thinking on each position that arises is a matter for your judgement. Where there is no chance of short-term tactics, there is little point leaving the computer thinking for a long time. If you are looking for the computer to find a defence against an attack, for instance, then you must take into account how deep the threats are. If they are no more than two or three moves deep, then the computer will see them very quickly, and find a defence if it exists. On the other hand, a mating plan that takes eight moves to achieve anything may not be seen quickly, and if you want the computer to suggest anything sensible (unless it is able to find a counterattack that crashes through before the eight moves are up), you must make sure it has time for its search depth to extend to eight moves by both sides. This may not be practicable, and so it may be necessary to input plausible-looking defences to advance the computer nearer the problem, but the drawback then is that a hidden defence may be overlooked.

5) When you have decided to let the computer lead the analysis, there are ways in which you can make it more efficient. Firstly, if its analysis is indicating that there is only one move worth considering, execute this move and let it move on to analysing the best reply. If its analysis is pointing to one move that is probably the only viable option, but there may be some tempting alternatives, activate the "analyse second best option" (if available) to take a look at other moves. If there seem to be some viable alternatives, then make these into variations and push the computer on to looking deeper into the main variations.

6) When the position ceases to be heavily tactical, either resume full manual control of the analysis (with the computer continuing to comment on the positions arising in your analysis) or conclude with an assessment, when this becomes clear enough to be stated with confidence.

7) Go back over the analysis and round up any loose ends.

8) Once the analysis is complete (in so far as it can be), you may wish to consider running a blundercheck over the complete tree of analysis you have generated. (Blundercheck is a powerful feature available in the Fritz interface, and you can naturally use any compatible engine, Rybka included.) This will often generate some very interesting ideas or improvements, despite the fact that the computer has already "seen" every position, and it seems that you have incorporated anything of value that it has to say. This is because, as described above, a blundercheck works in a totally different way from normal analysis, starting at the end of each variation and working backwards. Via the analysis stored in its hash tables, it comes better prepared to assess each position, and ideas of extraordinary depth can thus be produced. A blundercheck can be run

overnight, for instance, and to make best use of the time available, give it a number of seconds on each position that means it will be working most of the night. If you have less time, you might want to run a quicker blundercheck – even a few seconds per move can produce some useful corrections (set a higher threshold for a quicker blundercheck). But be sure to verify the blundercheck results with a critical eye (working with the engine, and/or a different engine perhaps), as it often suggests some nonsense, or at least non-improvements, especially as there can be glitches in the hash tables.

This procedure can take a long time in a really messy position, and there is a danger that the analysis will throw up many other complex positions for analysis – indeed this is inevitable in a genuinely unclear position. So be selective in the positions you subject to really searching analysis.

I could go into further details, but to a large extent it's a case of using your common sense and bearing in mind that a computer analyses by looking progressively deeper and deeper into a tree of variations. For instance, if the computer has been looking twelve plies (half-moves) ahead, and you move ahead three plies and set it thinking again, you can only expect any refinement of its previous assessment once it is looking ahead at least nine plies!

It is high time to show some examples of assisted analysis, as this is much more a practical skill than a theoretical concept.

Canal Variation – assisted analysis

1 e4 e5 2 ♘f3 ♘c6 3 ♗c4 ♘f6 4 d4 exd4 5 0-0 ♘xe4 6 ♖e1 d5 7 ♘c3
This move defines the Canal Variation of the Two Knights Defence, which has generally been regarded as of similar merit to the main line, 7 ♗xd5 ♕xd5 8 ♘c3.

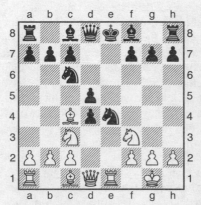

Now 7...dxc4 8 ♖xe4+ ♗e6 9 ♘xd4 ♘xd4 10 ♖xd4 ♕f6 is a good line for Black, but a Rybka blundercheck indicated a different line, with a claim that Black is winning:
7...dxc3 8 ♗xd5 f5
This clearly needs attention – it is a whole piece at stake after all, and surely someone must have looked at this at some point. The Canal Variation has been in the theory books for a long time and played a fair amount in practice, and this is an obvious try for Black. The standard line is 8...♗e6, when White has nothing better than 9 ♗xe4 ♕xd1 10 ♖xd1 cxb2 11 ♗xb2 f6, when White might perhaps have enough compensation.

Checking in the specialist literature, I found that 8...f5 is normally given a "?", based on old analysis by Tartakower. This continued...

9 ♞g5

Now, 9...♝e7?? loses to 10 ♖xe4 fxe4 11 ♕h5+, while the old Tartakower line ran 9...cxb2(?) 10 ♞xe4 fxe4 11 ♖xe4+ ♞e7 12 ♝xb2 ♝f5 13 ♕f3, with advantage to White.

9...♝d6!

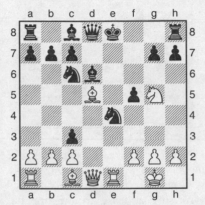

This was Rybka's follow-up, and wasn't mentioned at all in the old theory. So we might be on to something valuable here. The first thing to check is what happens after the consistent 10 ♞f7. However, it is quite simple: 10...♝xh2+! (we immediately see one reason for putting the bishop on d6) 11 ♔xh2 ♕h4+ 12 ♔g1 ♕xf2+ 13 ♔h1 and Black has a choice of straightforward ways to keep a winning game. So if White is to justify his play, he needs to be more cunning.

10 bxc3

This looks slow, but is probably the best try. Black still has some issues to solve with his king and the e-file pin. To be honest, I didn't really believe White had anything here, and on my own I would have given it up as completely lost for White. And Rybka too,

sitting there working on the current board position, wasn't very optimistic either. But nothing ventured nothing gained, so I pushed Rybka closer to what looked like some sort of critical positions, basically just to see it demonstrate a win for Black.

10...♞e5

10...♕e7 11 ♞xe4 (11 f3? ♕e5) 11...fxe4 12 ♖xe4 ♞e5 13 ♝f4 (13 f4? ♝f5 14 ♖e1 ♝g4 15 ♕d2 0-0-0) 13...♝f5 14 ♖e1 isn't so clear, as 14...0-0-0? (14...♔f8 is better, but Black isn't getting untangled any time soon then) 15 ♝xe5 ♝xe5 16 ♕f3 ♝xh2+ 17 ♔f1 ♕c5 18 ♝xb7+ ♔b8 19 ♖ab1 c6 20 ♝xc6+ ♔c8 21 ♝b5! gives White a strong attack.

11 ♝f4

11 ♝xe4 fxe4 12 ♕d5 ♕e7! 13 ♝f4 ♖f8 (13...♝d7 14 ♝xe5 ♕xg5 15 ♕xb7 ♖d8 16 h4 ♕f5 17 ♝xd6 cxd6 18 ♖xe4+ and White is fighting) 14 ♝xe5 ♕xg5 15 ♖xe4 ♝e7 16 ♖ae1 ♖f7 and White doesn't seem to have enough for the piece.

11...♕f6

11...♕e7 12 ♞xe4 fxe4 13 ♖xe4 transposes to the 10...♕e7 line.

12 ♞xe4 fxe4 13 ♖xe4

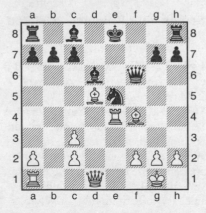

Again, having pushed Rybka to this position, I took a breather and made a nice pot of coffee, and waited for the computer to demonstrate the clearest win for Black. However, its assessment was not so unequivocal once it had chugged through its calculations.

13...♗f5 14 ♖xe5+ ♗xe5 15 ♕e2 ♗g4

15...0-0-0 16 ♗xe5 ♕b6 should also be good for Black, but there is more potential danger with the queens on the board.

16 ♕xe5+ ♕xe5 17 ♗xe5 0-0-0 18 ♗xg7 ♖he8 19 ♗b3 ♗d1

Although White has two pawns for the exchange, the activity of Black's rooks means that White has problems. So we can see that the combined work by computer and human has enabled us to refine the assessment beyond what would have been achieved by either of them working in isolation. While not a completely clear-cut refutation of the Canal Variation, 8...f5 9 ♘g5 ♗d6 is very close to being one; at the very least it leaves White struggling to keep some chances in murky and highly dubious circumstances.

Scotch Four Knights – assisted analysis

1 e4 e5 2 ♘f3 ♘c6 3 ♘c3 ♘f6 4 d4 exd4 5 ♘xd4 ♗b4 6 ♘xc6 bxc6 7 ♗d3 d5

This is a standard position in the Scotch Four Knights Game, an old opening that is not reckoned to give White a great deal, but is quite popular as the moves leading to it are very natural, and it is a rather safe and easy-to-learn option for White.

8 e5

This is a rare move. 8 exd5 cxd5 9 0-0 0-0 10 ♗g5 is the main line, with Black at least very close to equality.

8...♘g4 9 ♗f4

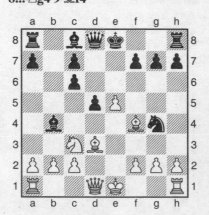

In another Rybka blundercheck, the move **9...d4** was thrown up here as a possible win for Black. This seemed surprising at least, as the line has been played in quite a few high-level games, and 9...f6 recommended by the theory books as Black's best (with at most a slight plus for Black; e.g., 10 h3 ♘xe5 11 ♗xe5 fxe5 12 ♕h5+ ♔f8 13 ♕xe5 ♗d6). The move 9...d4 is not unknown, but after **10 ♕f3** Rybka's idea was the astonishing **10...g5**. When a computer advocates a move such as this, it is important to try to understand what the point of it is – otherwise you won't be able to assist very much in the analytical process. Once the idea is grasped, you should be able to see what might be an argument against it, and then confront the computer with this argument (which might of course be shot down in flames).

Instead, Black has always played 10...dxc3, but this is probably very good for White after 11 0-0-0. We shall return to the reason why this is so later.

OK, let's start (after 10...g5) with the natural **11 ♗g3**.

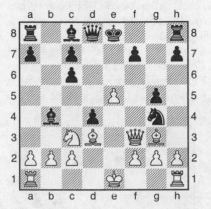

Why might Black then have gained from the gross weakening of his kingside that ...g5 entails? The idea is **11...dxc3**. Therefore we should now take a closer look at what happens after 10...dxc3 11 0-0-0, to see what the difference might be, as this is not obvious at a glance. The key variations are as follows:

a) 11...cxb2+ 12 ♔b1 and now 12...♕d5? walks into 13 ♗e4, while 12...♘xf2?! 13 ♗b5 ♘xd1 14 ♗xc6+ ♔f8 15 ♖xd1 is not in Black's interest either. 12...♖b8 occurred in a game with GM Savon, a USSR Champion, as Black, but 13 ♗g6! ♕e7 14 ♗g5 is good for White.

b) 11...♕d5 leads to spectacular and forcing play: 12 ♗e4 ♕xa2 13 ♗xc6+ and now:

b1) 13...♔f8 14 ♖d8+ ♔e7 15 ♗g5+ f6 16 exf6+ gxf6 17 ♖e1+ ♗e6 18 ♖xe6+ ♕xe6 19 ♖d7+ ♔f8 20 ♕xg4 ♕xg4 21 ♗h6+ ♔e8 22

♖g7+ ♔d8 23 ♖xg4 is good for White.

b2) 13...♔e7 14 ♗g5+ f6 15 exf6+ gxf6 16 ♖he1+ ♗e6 17 ♖xe6+! (interestingly, Rybka only realized the strength of this move *after* analysing the analogous 13...♔f8 line, where the rook came from d8; the assessment of that line was still in the hash table, so it spotted the idea here too; instead 17 ♖d7+ ♔f8 18 ♗h6+ ♘xh6 19 ♕xf6+ ♘f7 20 ♖xf7+ ♗xf7 21 ♕xh8+ ♗g8 22 ♕f6+ ♗f7 {not 22...♕f7?? 23 ♕h6+ ♔g7 24 ♕f4+ and ♕xb4+} 23 ♕h8+ only leads to perpetual check) 17...♕xe6 18 ♖d7+ transposes to the 13...♔f8 line.

Anyway, the precise evaluation of this line isn't central to our quest to discover what the idea behind 10...g5 might be. But the fact that the black king ran short of squares is very much to the point: Black intends to play the same way, but with his king able to run to safety. So we can go back to our main position and everything will be clear.

12 0-0-0 ♕d5! 13 ♗e4 ♕xa2 14 ♗xc6+

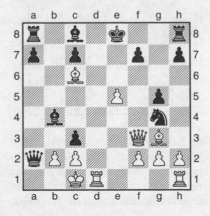

Now either king move is simply winning for Black: 14...♔e7 and White doesn't even have the bishop check on g5, while after 14...♔f8 15 ♖d8+ ♔g7 White achieves nothing. So Black's principal idea works like a dream. We just need to go back and see if it gives White any extra possibilities. If not, then this line can be labelled "Busted".

So we return to the position after 7 ♗d3 d5 8 e5 ♘g4 9 ♗f4 d4, and scour the ground for attempts to deviate for White:

10 ♕f3
10 a3 dxc3 11 axb4 ♕d4 12 ♕f3 (12 ♗g3 cxb2 13 ♖b1 h5!?) 12...cxb2 13 ♖b1 leaves White struggling to draw.
10...g5 11 ♗g3
After 11 ♕xc6+ ♗d7 12 ♕e4 neither 12...dxc3 13 ♕xb4 gxf4 nor 12...gxf4 13 ♕xd4 will give White enough for the piece.
11...dxc3 12 0-0

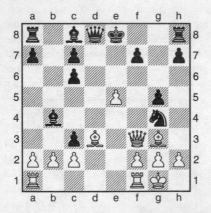

We have already seen that 12 0-0-0 fails to 12...♕d5, but with Black's kingside weakened, perhaps this less drastic approach is viable. The only move Rybka likes here is **12...cxb2**,

so let's push the analysis forward to get a better view: **13 ♖ad1 ♖b8**. Now it isn't clear how White should try to knock Black out, especially with Rybka indicating defences for Black. After **14 c3** (14 h3 can be met by 14...h5) **14...♗a3** (odd-looking, but most other squares have specific drawbacks) **15 h3 h5 16 hxg4 ♗xg4 17 ♕xc6+ ♕d7 18 ♕f6**, you are perhaps already sensing that the game is far from clear. Some possible lines:

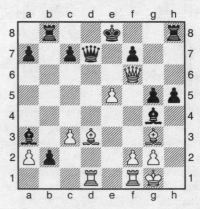

a) 18...♖h6 can lead to crazy "computer-style" play: 19 ♕xh6 ♗xd1 20 ♗b1 ♗e2 (20...h4 21 e6 ♕xe6 22 ♕h8+ ♗f8 23 ♗xc7 ♖b7 24 ♗a5 ♗g4 25 ♗b4 ♕h6 26 ♕e5+) 21 ♖e1 ♖b6 22 ♕xg5 ♗e7 23 ♕g8+ ♗f8 is another fine mess.

b) 18...♖g8 19 e6 (otherwise Black consolidates with moves like ...♖b6) 19...♗xe6 20 ♖fe1 ♕e7 21 ♕h6 ♗d6 (preventing ♗e5-f6) 22 ♗e5 ♗xe5 (22...♕f8 23 ♕f6) 23 ♖xe5 ♖b6 24 ♗c2 is one rather murky sample line (amongst many possible).

Thus one cannot really talk of this being a refutation of White's opening play – it is just an unclear mess.

10...g5 is a really neat idea, but the human bias against such moves does have some basis. Objectively, it may or may not be better than Black's standard approach in this line with 9...f6.

G. Jones – L'Ami
Staunton Memorial, London 2009

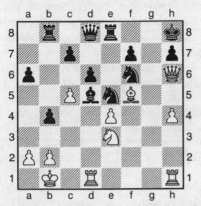

This is an extremely complex position. Before reading further, you may like to analyse (together with your computer) 31 ♖hg1, 31 ♘xd5 and 31 ♖xd5, and try to determine for yourself which is best.

The position is very messy, so I won't claim that what follows necessarily represents the whole and complete truth. Let's start with the move played in the game:

31 ♖hg1 ♘g6 32 ♘xd5 ♘xd5 33 h5 ♘c3+?

33...♕h4 is better:

a) 34 ♖xd5 ♕f4.

b) 34 ♖h1 ♘c3+! (now that Black has the ...♕f4 defence, this is basically a desperado) 35 ♔c2 ♕f4 36 hxg6 ♕xh6 37 ♖xh6 fxg6 38 ♖dh1 (White needs to attend to the attack

on his rook) 38...gxf5 39 ♖xh.. ♔g8 40 bxc3 is roughly equal.

c) 34 ♖df1 ♘de7 35 ♖h1 ♘xf5 36 exf5 ♕e4+ 37 ♔a1 ♕e3 doesn't give White much.

d) 34 exd5 might be best, but 34...b3 35 ♔a1 ♖e2 gives Black counterplay.

34 bxc3

34 ♔a1! is good for White; e.g., 34...♕h4 (34...♘xd1 35 hxg6 fxg6 36 ♗xg6 ♖e7 37 ♗e8!!, mating) 35 ♖df1 threatening ♗xg6 and ♖f7.

34...bxc3+ 35 ♔c1 c2?

35...♕h4 is again correct; e.g., 36 ♗xg6 fxg6 37 ♖xg6 ♖e7 38 ♖f6 ♖g7 39 ♖df1 ♔g8.

36 ♔xc2?

36 hxg6 cxd1♕+ 37 ♖xd1 fxg6 38 ♖h1 ♖e7 39 ♕xg6 ♕g8 40 ♕f6+ ♖g7 41 ♖xh7+ ♕xh7 42 ♗xh7 ♔xh7 leads to a draw.

36...♕h4 37 ♖d2 ♖xe4 38 ♗xe4 ♕xe4+ 39 ♖d3 ♕c4+ 40 ♔d2 ♖b2+ 41 ♔e3 ♕e6+ 0-1

But our conclusion (from the 33...♕h4 analysis) is that 31 ♖hg1 is, with best play, at most a touch better for White. We need to look for other moves, drawing ideas from our own imagination and the computer's suggestions. Two moves catch the eye:

a) 31 ♘xd5 ♘eg4 (forced) 32 ♕f4 ♘e5 (32...♘xd5? 33 ♖xd5! ♘f6 34 ♕h6 threatening e5 followed by ♖g1) 33 ♖dg1 ♘g6 34 ♗xg6 ♘xd5 35 ♕xf7 ♕e7 36 exd5 hxg6 37 ♕xe7 ♖xe7 38 cxd6 cxd6 39 ♖xg6 gives White an extra pawn and some decent winning chances in the double-rook ending. This line was not too difficult – quite forcing and not many significant alternatives for either side, so

...assistance, we can be ...ent that we haven't ...hing important here. It's not ... option for White, but our intuition (and the engine) should be telling us that White can hope for more.

b) **31 ♖xd5** threatens 32 ♖xe5 followed by ♘d5 or ♘g4, removing the knight that defends h7. This is probably the move that your engine is advocating, and a little encouragement – i.e. playing Black's most stubborn-looking reply and waiting for it to come up with something good – will tease the main idea out of it. 31...♘g6 (31...♕e7 32 ♖xe5 ♕xe5 33 ♘d5 and White wins) 32 h5! (this and the follow-up queen sacrifice are the big idea) 32...♘g8 (nothing else puts up much resistance, so we play this and move forwards to a critical position – if there is one, and White's concept isn't simply pulverizing) 33 ♕xh7+!! ♔xh7 34 hxg6++ ♔g7 35 ♖h7+ ♔f6 (not 35...♔f8? 36 ♖xf7#).

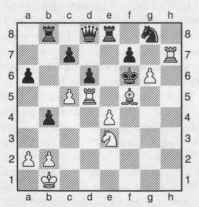

Here we hit a slight roadbump. The engine is still giving a very positive assessment for White, but isn't offering a very clear main line, and to the human eye it isn't obvious that this ought to be winning for White. So we need to look at all moves that are getting a favourable assessment and push ahead to reach some conclusions about them, and then if necessary peel back to examine any alternatives along the way. 36 gxf7 (36 ♘g4+ ♔g5 37 gxf7 and we see that Black's king is moving into relatively open space, while White is playing gxf7 in any case; it makes sense to focus on the immediate gxf7 and only return here if we see a good reason) 36...♘e7 (the engine's main choice, but 36...♖f8 is ranked high enough to merit attention; then 37 ♘g4+ ♔g5 38 ♖d1 threatening 39 ♖g7+ ♔f4 40 ♖f1+, mating, appears as winning after a while, which is convincing to the human mind too, so we can focus on our main line) 37 cxd6.

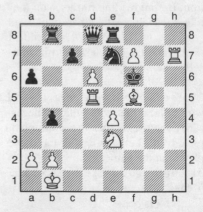

It seems odd to throw in a pawn exchange with so much else going on, but the engine likes it, so let's go with it and see what the computer is up to; using the "show threat" function after this move, we see that 38

e5+ would lead to mate, so Black must react.

b1) 37...cxd6 isn't even one of the engine's top choices, but of course we are curious to see what happens – the answer is 38 fxe8♕ ♕xe8 39 ♖xd6+ ♔g5 (after 39...♔e5 40 ♖e6+ followed by taking on e7, we can readily accept that White is winning) 40 ♖g7+ ♔f4 41 ♘g2+ ♔f3 42 ♖d3+ ♔f2 (42...♔e2 43 ♘f4+ mates) 43 ♖d2+ ♔f3 44 ♗g4+ ♔xe4 45 ♖xe7+ ♕xe7 46 ♖e2+. That's convincing enough, so let's go back to Black's other options on move 37.

b2) 37...♘xf5 38 ♖xf5+ ♔g6 39 fxe8♕+ ♕xe8 40 ♖e7 ♕h8 (40...♕g8 41 ♖f2 ♖b5 42 e5 and White wins the queen) 41 ♖f1 cxd6 42 ♖g1+ and the only move to save the queen, 42...♔f6, loses the king: 43 ♘d5#.

So our conclusion is that 31 ♖hg1 is more or less equal, 31 ♘xd5 is quite good for White, but that 31 ♖xd5 would have forced a win.

We shall now look at a couple of examples of how computer-assisted analysis can be employed in opening repertoire maintenance.

Avoiding the Portuguese Gambit

We suppose here that White is generally happy to face the regular lines of the Scandinavian Defence, but is concerned about the Portuguese Gambit, a sharp and chaotic line which has seen a number of short and violent victories by Black.

1 e4 d5 2 exd5 ♘f6

As noted, we're assuming White is happy to face 2...♕xd5 3 ♘c3, when

3...♕a5 and 3...♕d6 are the standard moves.

After 2...♘f6, the line we are trying to avoid is 3 d4 ♗g4!? (rather than the standard 3...♘xd5). Then:

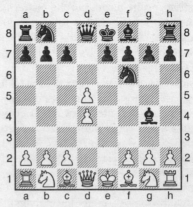

a) 4 ♗e2 ♗xe2 doesn't offer White much after 5 ♘xe2 ♕xd5 6 0-0 ♘c6 or 5 ♕xe2 ♕xd5 6 ♘f3 e6 7 c4 ♕f5.

b) 4 ♘f3 ♕xd5 5 ♗e2 ♘c6 looks superficially similar to the 2...♕xd5 line, but here Black has additional options for where to put his queen, with f5 and h5 now notable possibilities. After 6 ♘c3 ♕h5 7 h3 0-0-0 8 0-0 ♘xd4 we see that White's d4-pawn has become a target for a nasty piece of tactics. The lines following 6 c4 may hold more promise for White, but these are also sharp, with a number of variations elaborated in some detail, and a Portuguese Gambit devotee will no doubt have some surprises ready for us here too:

b1) 6...♕f5 7 ♗e3 0-0-0 8 ♘bd2 e5 9 d5 and now 9...♘b4 10 ♖c1 e4 11 ♘d4 ♕g6 12 0-0 is far from clear, while after 9...♗xf3 10 ♗xf3 we would need to deal with both 10...♘b4 and 10...♘d4.

b2) 6...♕h5 7 ♗e3 (7 0-0 0-0-0 8 ♗e3 e5 9 h3 exd4 10 hxg4 ♘xg4) 7...0-0-0 8 ♘bd2! e5 9 d5 ♘d4 10 ♘xd4 exd4 and on the face of it 11 ♗xd4 denies Black enough compensation for the pawn, but the matter is far from settled, as it is following 11 ♗xg4+ ♘xg4 12 ♗xd4 ♖e8+ 13 ♔f1 ♘xh2+ 14 ♔g1 ♕xd1+ 15 ♖xd1 ♘g4.

c) The scary line runs 4 f3 ♗f5 5 c4 (5 ♗b5+ ♘bd7 6 c4 is probably better, but definitely not just a cosy extra pawn for White) 5...e6 6 dxe6 ♘c6; e.g., 7 exf7+? ♔xf7 8 ♗e3 ♗b4+ 9 ♔f2 ♖e8 10 ♘e2 ♖xe3!! (see Dimitrov–Rivera on page 173).

OK, so the lines where the d4-pawn becomes a target have given us an idea...

3 ♘f3!?

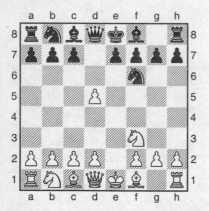

This is our move-order trick to side-step the Portuguese Gambit, and we shall be using computer assistance to help assess whether it works and if it has some real bite.

3...♗g4

3...♕xd5 is met by 4 ♘c3, when after 4...♕a5 5 d4 we have achieved our goal: a normal line of the

2...♕xd5 Scandinavian. If Black persists with 4...♕h5 5 ♗e2 ♗g4 6 0-0 ♘c6 7 h3, then he has far less counterplay. Searching our database, we see that, because anything else is just dismal, Black has generally tried the piece sacrifice 7...0-0-0 8 hxg4 ♘xg4.

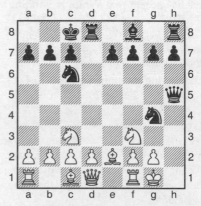

While this gives Black more play than you might expect, it doesn't really come to anything much, and there isn't even too much scope for White to go badly wrong; e.g., 9 d3 (9 ♘e4 ♘d4 10 ♘eg5 is also possible) 9...e5 10 ♘e4 ♘d4 11 ♖e1 (hey, it's only a check on h2 – no need to panic!) 11...f5 12 ♘g3 ♘xf3+ 13 ♗xf3 ♕h2+ 14 ♔f1 ♘xf2 15 ♕e2.

4 ♗b5+

We can now play this bishop check in better circumstances than after 3 d4 ♗g4!? 4 f3 ♗f5, as we haven't weakened our pawn-structure with f3, and can hope for an advantage in a quieter positional struggle. We shall only hang on to the extra pawn if Black makes it really attractive to do so.

We can quite quickly work out some likely continuations by a combination of the Database Reference facility in ChessBase and by using our own common sense together with the watchful eye of our analysis engine:

4...♘bd7 5 h3 ♗h5

5...a6 6 ♗e2 ♗h5 gives White the extra option of 7 c4, which looks like a fairly solid extra pawn now that the bishop is not stuck out at a4.

6 ♘c3

6 c4 a6 7 ♗a4 b5 gives Black the kind of chaos he is seeking.

6...a6 7 ♗e2!

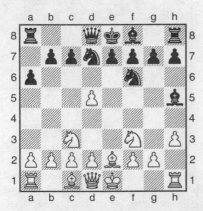

As we have noted, White is not determined to hang on to his extra pawn; he just wants a straightforward advantage.

7...♘b6 8 d4 ♘fxd5

8...♘bxd5 9 ♘xd5 ♕xd5 (9...♘xd5 10 c4 ♘f6 transposes) 10 c4 ♕d8 11 ♕b3 ♖b8 12 d5 is quite a depressing position for Black, with no active prospects.

9 ♘xd5 ♕xd5 10 0-0 e6 11 b3 ♗e7 12 c4 ♕d8 13 ♗e3 0-0 14 ♘e5 ♗xe2 15 ♕xe2 ♗f6 16 ♖ad1

White has a very useful spatial plus, whereas Black has very limited prospects for counterplay – it's like an Alekhine Defence gone wrong.

Assessing an Incoming New Idea

Suppose the Scotch forms part of our repertoire with either Black or White, and the following game catches our eye as we scan through recent games in "our" lines.

G. Jones – Smeets
Staunton Memorial, London 2009

1 e4 e5 2 d4 exd4 3 ♘f3 ♘c6 4 ♘xd4 ♘f6 5 ♘xc6 bxc6 6 e5 ♕e7 7 ♕e2 ♘d5 8 g3 g6 9 c4 ♗a6 10 b3 ♗g7 11 ♗b2 0-0 12 ♘d2 d6 13 ♕e4

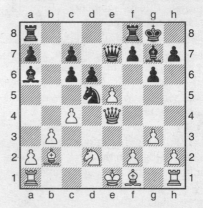

13...♘b4 14 a3 d5 15 cxd5 ♗xf1 16 ♔xf1 ♘xd5 17 ♔g2

White has a very pleasant position, as it will be hard for Black in the long run to defend his queenside pawns.

17...f6 18 exf6 ♗xf6 19 ♕xe7 ♗xe7 20 ♖he1 ♖fd8 21 ♘c4 a5 22 ♖ad1 ♗f8 23 ♔g1 a4 24 b4 c5 25 bxc5 ♗xc5 26 ♖e5 c6 27 ♖e6 ♘b6 28 ♖c1 ♘xc4 29 ♖xc4 ♗xf2+?? 30 ♔xf2 1-0

OK, the game was ended by a blunder, but Black had clearly been under some pressure, and at face value,

White's handling of the opening looks attractive. But before we modify our repertoire, we should check that the concept is really as good as it looks.

The first sign of trouble is that any good modern analytical engine will suggest **13...♗xe5!**, possibly with a very positive assessment. We simply need to have the thing turned on, and notice its assessment (and give it a little time to reach it – all too often one hears the claim "the computer didn't see it!", based on giving the computer just a second at the one and only critical moment). But this should not be the end of the story – computers quite often give mistaken assessments, especially in odd or strategically complex positions such as we have here. And a grandmaster *was* playing White – perhaps he had a sneaky reply ready.

We must verify the assessment by carefully looking through all the key lines, using both the work of our own mind and the computer's assistance to reach a more definitive verdict. In particular, if there are any computer assessments that don't make sense to us (a simple rule is that if you can't explain the assessment in your own words, you don't truly understand it), then we should investigate them more deeply until we do understand them (or to avoid insanity, up to the point where we admit "this is beyond me!").

14 cxd5

White must respond to the threat of ...♗xb2 somehow. 14 ♗xe5 is another way, but the computer quickly shows us 14...f5! (the only good

move), when the queen has no good square. You may wish to try out a few possible squares for the queen to see what refutation the computer has in mind, but none of it is very deep, and with a bit of thought should be readily comprehensible to the unaided human mind.

14...cxd5! 15 ♕e3 ♗xb2!

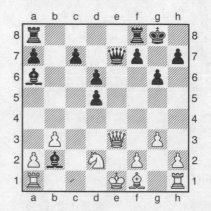

A key point – the e-file pin means that Black will regain the queen. However, we shouldn't stop our analysis here, as it isn't clear that Black will be getting all of his material back.

16 ♕xe7 ♖fe8 17 ♕e3

17 ♕xe8+ ♖xe8+ 18 ♔d1 ♗xf1 (the only move) 19 ♖b1 (otherwise Black emerges simply with two extra pawns) 19...♗e2+ 20 ♔c2 ♗d4 and it is hard to see White surviving as the two bishops are a very powerful force here; note that 21 f4? allows 21...♖e3 and ...♖c3+.

17...d4!

Another "only" move; would you have seen this over the board – and from a few moves in advance, as you would have needed to in order to choose this line? Black loses material after 17...♗xf1? 18 ♔xf1 ♖xe3 19 ♖b1 or 17...♗xa1? 18 ♗xa6.

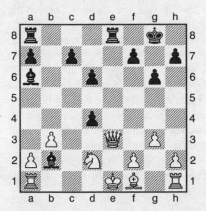

18 ♖b1

18 ♗xa6 dxe3 19 ♖b1 is the same, while 18 ♕xe8+ ♖xe8+ 19 ♔d1 ♗xf1 20 ♖b1 ♗e2+ 21 ♔c2 is a slight modification of a position we saw after 17 ♕xe8+. Now the pawn on d4 denies the bishop this square, but after 21...♗a3 Black still has two pawns for the exchange, and the idea of ...d3+ helps the two bishops do their evil work.

18...dxe3 19 ♗xa6

Seeking opposite-coloured bishops; after 19 ♖xb2 exd2++ 20 ♔xd2 Black's extra pawn should be enough to win.

19...exd2++ 20 ♔xd2 ♗a3

This prevents ♖e1 and allows Black to activate his rooks. While pure opposite-coloured bishops are notoriously drawish, when there are also rooks on the board, it can be far easier to exploit an advantage, as the old adage "opposite bishops favour the attacker" often comes into play. Black has good winning chances here.

By this point we have looked at what appear to be the key variations, and reduced them down to positions where the assessment is reasonably clear in human terms. So we may conclude that White's 13 ♕e4? idea is refuted by 13...♗xe5! and that we should neither add it to our repertoire as White, nor be worried by it as Black.

In fact, the true story of this game is that White fluffed his moves, and that Black had been tricked by White's 1 e4 e5 2 d4 exd4 3 ♘f3 move-order into an opening that he wouldn't normally play (Smeets prefers the Petroff, 1 e4 e5 2 ♘f3 ♘f6). But there is also a notable point here, concerning the importance of simply being alert at the board: if Black had been more tactically sharp at the critical moment, he would have won a crisp and attractive game, no matter that he had been tricked outside his repertoire. So never get despondent at the board; the precise moment when you are feeling sorry for yourself might be a chance for glory!

In the next chapter, you will find a number of puzzle positions designed with computer-assisted analysis in mind.

Choosing and Comparing Analysis Engines

There are a great many analysis engines available, some free, some not, with all sorts of odd names, and their playing strength is constantly increasing as hardware becomes faster and the algorithms are refined with each new release. It is very hard to keep track of all this, and to decide when and if it is worth paying for a new engine or an upgrade. The computer vs computer events that gain the most publicity are the Computer World Championships, but these, like human tournaments, are based on only one game between each pair of engines, and the hardware they are running on can vary significantly. Given that computers can be set to play for hours on end without complaint or an appearance fee, more rigorous testing is clearly possible.

Fortunately, there is a website that provides helpful and objective information. The Swedish Computer Chess Association (SSDF) carries out extensive testing in the form of lengthy matches between the various engines, using standardized hardware and settings to provide a level playing field (upgraded periodically, so each engine may have several entries in the list, according to the hardware being used). SSDF's website is at ssdf.bosjo.net. This provides their computer rating list, together with game downloads and information about the statistical reliability of the ratings in the list. At the time of writing (in September 2009), the mighty Rybka 3 heads the list (as various Rybka versions have done since 2006), with the little-known Naum 4 in second place, 90 Elo points behind. Next we have Zappa Mexico II, a further 60 points below. All these three are running on the current hardware standard, a powerful multiprocessor system, and based on enough games (500-800) for the rating order to be statistically reliable. Then we come to some more familiar names like Fritz, Shredder and Hiarcs, intermingled with a copy

of Rybka running on slower hardware and an older version of Naum.

So if you are thinking of paying money for an analysis engine, Rybka and Naum are the obvious candidates to start with, though you might also consider Shredder if you like its opening and endgame features (opening advisor and Shredderbases). Here are a couple of games between Rybka and Naum (two of the more entertaining ones from their 40-game SSDF match), the best current chess players in the world, one could say:

Naum 4 MP – Deep Rybka 3
SSDF match (17), Sundsvall 2009

1 d4 ♘f6 2 c4 g6 3 ♘f3 ♗g7 4 ♘c3 d5 5 cxd5 ♘xd5 6 e4 ♘xc3 7 bxc3 c5 8 ♖b1 0-0 9 ♗e2 cxd4 10 cxd4 ♕a5+ 11 ♗d2 ♕xa2 12 0-0 ♗g4 13 ♗g5 h6 14 ♗e3 ♘c6 15 d5 ♗xf3 16 ♗xf3 ♘e5 17 ♖xb7 a5 18 ♗e2 ♘c4 19 ♖xe7 ♕a3 20 ♗xc4 ♕xe7 21 ♕d3 ♕e5 22 d6 ♖fd8 23 ♖d1 g5

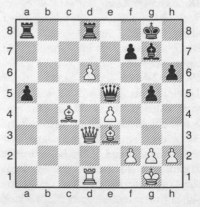

24 g3 ♖ab8 25 ♗d5 a4 26 ♕a6 ♖xd6 27 ♕xa4 ♖dd8 28 ♗a7 ♖bc8 29 ♗b6 ♖e8 30 ♗e3 ♕e7 31 ♔g2

罩b8 32 曾c6 罩ed8 33 罩d2 曲h8 34
罩a2 罩d7 35 曾c4 罩b4 36 曾c8+
曾d8 37 曾c5 罩b8 38 罩a6 罩c7 39
曾a5 曾c8 40 罩d6 罩d7 41 罩c6 曾d8
42 曾c5 曾e7 43 曾c4 曲h7 44 曾e2
罩c7 45 罩a6 曾d7 46 曾f3 罩b5 47 h3
曾c8 48 罩a8 罩b8 49 罩a3 罩b5 50
罩a4 罩b8 51 罩a5 曾d7 52 罩a6 罩e8
53 罩b6 罩e7 54 h4 gxh4 55 曾f4 罩e5
56 罩xh6+ 曲g8 57 罩xh4 罩xd5 58
exd5 曾xd5+ 59 曲h2 罩b7 60 曲c1
罩b6 61 曾g4 曾e6 62 曾f3 曾c8 63
曾d5 罩g6 64 罩c4 曾e8 65 曲e3 罩e6
66 罩g4 曾c8 67 曾h5 曾a6 68 曾g5
罩g6 69 曾d8+ 曲f8 70 罩h4 曾c6 71
曲g1 曾d6 72 曾a8 曾e7 73 曲h2 曾d6
74 罩h5 曾d1 75 罩e5 曾d6 76 罩e8
曲g7 77 罩d8 曾e7 78 曲d4+ f6 79
曲e3 曾f7 80 曾c8 曲e7 81 罩d7 [...]
1-0

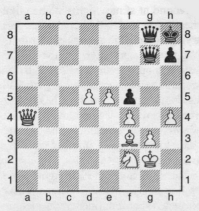

53 ⌅h1 曾c8 54 d6 曾f7 55 ⌅f2
曲g7 56 曲c6 曾g8 57 d7 曾e6 58
⌅d3 曲h8 59 ⌅b4 曾d8 60 ⌅d5 h6
61 ⌅f6 曾f7 62 曲d5 曾f8 63 曾c2
曾g7 64 曾c6 曾gf8 65 ⌅e8 曲h7 66
h5 曾b8 67 曾c8 **1-0**

Deep Rybka 3 – Naum 4 MP
SSDF match (32), Sundsvall 2009

1 e4 e6 2 d4 d5 3 ⌅c3 ⌅f6 4 e5
⌅fd7 5 f4 c5 6 ⌅f3 ⌅c6 7 曲e3
曾b6 8 ⌅a4 曾a5+ 9 c3 c4 10 b4
曾c7 11 曲e2 曲e7 12 0-0 f5 13 ⌅g5
⌅d8 14 曾e1 曾c6 15 ⌅c5 0-0 16
⌅xd7 曲xd7 17 a4 曲e8 18 曲f2
曾d7 19 曲h4 ⌅c6 20 ⌅h3 曲f7 21
曲xe7 ⌅xe7 22 曲f3 罩fc8 23 a5 b6
24 曾d2 ⌅c6 25 g3 bxa5 26 b5
⌅d8 27 罩xa5 罩cb8 28 罩b1 曲e8 29
⌅f2 罩b6 30 罩b4 罩ab8 31 曾a2
罩6b7 32 罩ba4 曾c8 33 罩xa7 罩xb5
34 ⌅d1 ⌅c6 35 罩7a6 ⌅xd4 36
cxd4 c3 37 罩xe6 曲f7 38 罩e7 c2 39
罩aa7 c1曾 40 罩xf7 曲h8 41 罩xg7
罩5b7 42 罩gxb7 罩xb7 43 罩a8 罩b8
44 罩xb8 曾xb8 45 曾xd5 曾b6 46
曲h1 曾a3 47 曲g2 曾f8 48 曾d7
曾a6 49 h4 曾a5 50 ⌅f2 曾ad8 51
曾a4 曾g7 52 d5 曾dg8

But before you part with your hard-earned cash, what about free engines? It is definitely worth trying a few to see if they meet your requirements. The best free engines are certainly good enough to beat most human players and to assist admirably with analysis. However, note that to get the most out of an engine, you will still need a good user interface, so you might want to buy a copy of one of the ChessBase engines to get this program – the ChessBase "stable" includes Rybka, Fritz, Junior, Shredder and Hiarcs. Rybka also offers its own interface, called Aquarium (see www.chessok.com for details).

One of the best known free engines is the open-source Fruit, which has also spawned a number of projects developed from its codebase, including Grapefruit (the project can

et) – with names like
411 n tell that they're not
these engines! Fruit is
not very high on the SSDF
list (it's outside the top 20), but the
testing has been done with an old
hardware set-up, and there is a newer
version of the engine available at
www.superchessengine.com, a site
that also features a number of other
free engines.

But probably the strongest free
engine is... Rybka 2. It seems Vasik
Rajlich is so confident that people
will want the stronger Rybka 3 that
he is allowing the previous version to
be downloaded for free from
rybkachess.com, together with a
simple (but also free) user interface
called Tarrasch.

In the previous edition of this book, I
tested the performance of a number
of the top engines of late 1999 (Fritz
6, Junior 6, Hiarcs 7.32 and Crafty
17.04) in a number of tricky positions. Here I shall revisit a few of
these positions and compare how
Rybka 3 (programmed by Vasik
Rajlich) and **Naum 4** (by Alexander
Naumov) acquit themselves in comparison with the engines and hardware of one decade earlier.

All testing was done with the engines running within ChessBase 9
running on Windows Vista, on a 1.2
GHz Centrino Duo with 2 GB RAM,
and 128 MB for hash tables (an appropriate amount given that a lot of
the testing is to see what the engines
produce in seconds or minutes; only
for longer testing or blunderchecks
are much larger hash tables very useful). If you have the older edition of

this book and want to compare, then
for the positions that are not included
here, the newer engines achieved
similar results to the older ones, apart
from reaching their conclusions
much faster and with greater certainty.

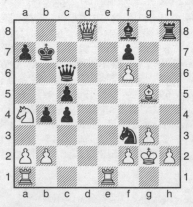

This first position, from a line of the
Botvinnik System of the Semi-Slav,
is a little embarrassing. I had published some analysis claiming a win
for White, and concluded in the previous edition "While it was human
suspicion that led to a search for
something good for White here, it
was only thanks to computerized assistance that I felt confident enough
to assess the position as +– (winning
for White)." and "Any of the engines
would provide useful assistance in
finding these variations." Given that
the position is in fact *not* winning for
White, the question ten years on has
to be "would the current engines
have helped me avoid making this
erroneous claim?"

Yes, they would. Both Rybka and
Naum assess 22 ♖e8 highly for a
while, but within a minute or so they

see the problem that eluded me and the engines a decade earlier: Black holds a draw by 22...♖xh2+! 23 ♔f1 ♘d2+!, with perpetual check resulting soon. After 22 ♔f1 the right reply is 22...♘d4, when a number of lines lead to repetition, but White appears to have nothing better than that (after 23 f3 ♖xh2 24 ♖e7+ ♔a6 25 ♘xc5+ ♕xc5 the main question is whether *White* can draw).

Karpov – Kasparov
Moscow Wch (9) 1984/5 (WGG 77)

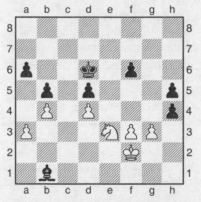

This is a famous position. Kasparov has just taken a pawn on h4, in the expectation that he would be able to set up an impregnable position after White recaptures.
47 ♘g2!!
47 gxh4 is the "automatic" move, and the one favoured by all the analysis engines, both old and new, though they do not assess the position as greatly in White's favour. 47 ♘g2 is the second preference, and while not considered bad for White, there is no way any of the engines would have played it with a tournament time-limit. After analysing overnight, Naum 4

still assessed 47 gxh4 as a hundredth of a pawn better than 47 ♘g2.

To a human, the problem here is detecting the idea of 47 ♘g2 *at all*. Once we have seen and understood the move, it is clear that this is the right way to proceed: White wins his pawn back and will surely be able to make further progress eventually. A computer sees the move very easily, but finds it difficult to choose between the more blocked position after 47 gxh4 and the more open one following 47 ♘g2 – it may even be tending to favour the bishop because it has been programmed with the knowledge that bishops like open positions. It doesn't see that progress is virtually impossible without opening the game, nor is it able to calculate far enough after 47 ♘g2 to reach the (intuitively obvious) conclusion that White will end up winning material.

The game ended:
47...hxg3+ 48 ♔xg3 ♔e6 49 ♘f4+ ♔f5 50 ♘xh5 ♔e6 51 ♘f4+ ♔d6 52 ♔g4 ♗c2 53 ♔h5 ♗d1 54 ♔g6 ♔e7 55 ♘xd5+? ♔e6?! 56 ♘c7+ ♔d7?! 57 ♘xa6 ♗xf3 58 ♔xf6 ♔d6 59 ♔f5 ♔d5 60 ♔f4 ♗h1 61 ♔e3 ♔c4 62 ♘c5 ♗c6 63 ♘d3 ♗g2 64 ♘e5+ ♔c3 65 ♘g6 ♔c4 66 ♘e7 ♗b7 67 ♘f5 ♗g2?! 68 ♘d6+ ♔b3 69 ♘xb5 ♔a4 70 ♘d6 1-0

The next example is a very beautiful study (White to play and win) by D.Gurgenidze and L.Mitrofanov (First Prize, *Molodoi Leninets*, 1982).

It is a very difficult position for a human solver, who would be best advised to tackle the position by considering what Black's defensive ideas might be. Otherwise, White's winning procedure doesn't really make sense. The computer cannot think this way, and has to rely on calculation. Unfortunately, the standard algorithms to prune the variation tree are very likely to prune out the winning line, as the moves only make sense when you have seen to the end of the line.

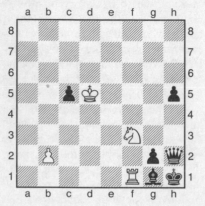

Black's plan is to play ...c4, ...h4, ...h3, give up his c-pawn, sacrifice his queen (by checking the white king) and then to play ...h2, when White would have no good way to lift the stalemate.

The older engines didn't get very far with this study, either considering the position drawn, or claiming that a number of rook moves win for White (whereas only one of them does). Only Fritz 6 with selectivity set to zero (i.e. less pruning) found the solution, but I only knew to activate this option because I already knew what the position involved – and the normal reason for using an analysis engine is to tell you something you don't already know!

As for the new engines, Rybka was making no obvious progress after 15 minutes. Naum, on the other

hand, identified the right move, 1 ♖b1!, in about a minute, and within a further 20 seconds was assessing it as winning. Bravo! (Note: that was with tablebases loaded; without tablebases, it took about 3 minutes.) Let's now see the solution.

1 ♖b1! c4

1...h4 2 ♔c6 h3 3 ♔b7 c4 comes to the same thing.

2 ♔c6! h4 3 ♔b7! h3 4 ♔a8!

Only when this position was reached did most of the older engines' assessments jump dramatically in White's favour.

4...c3 5 bxc3 ♕b8+

White's king-walk to the corner square has made sure this is Black's only queen check; his odd-looking decision to put the rook on b1 means that he can now take with the rook, which can then switch to the h-file.

6 ♖xb8 h2 7 ♖h8 and mate next move.

The next two positions feature the world's most famous chess computer.

Deep Blue – Kasparov
New York (2) 1997

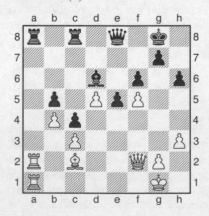

37 ♗e4! was Deep Blue's choice here – by no means a typical computer move, and one that prompted Kasparov to allege that there must have been human involvement in the computer's move selection behind the scenes. 37 ♕b6 was preferred by the older chess engines, even after a lot of analysis, or with the settings adjusted in a way that ought to have favoured a more cautious approach. There may not be a great deal actually wrong with 37 ♕b6 – it's just that Black retains the hope of counterplay with ...e4, whereas 37 ♗e4 is a lot more unpleasant to face, especially from a human viewpoint.

What of the new engines? Both Rybka and Naum very quickly prefer 37 ♗e4!, and rank it well above 37 ♕b6 in their assessments from then on. So this is indeed a move a computer can come up with.

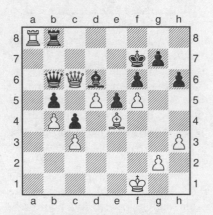

This position occurred later in the same game. Here Deep Blue went wrong with **45 ♖a6?** (45 ♕xb6 is good for White), whereupon Kasparov resigned, missing that he could seize a draw by **45...♕e3!**. The old

engines also preferred 45 ♖a6?, even after a lot of analysis, and despite regarding 45...♕e3 as Black's best reply, though without seeing that it was a draw.

Our two modern engines fare a lot better. Although Rybka favours 45 ♖a6? for about a minute, it is soon ranking 45 ♕d7+ (e.g., 45...♔g8 46 ♖a7 ♗f8 47 ♕e6+) and 45 ♕xb6 as its top two choices. Thus, at a tournament time-limit, it would **not** have thrown away the win. Rybka is unable to assess 45 ♖a6? ♕e3! as a clear draw, but can analyse enough of the relevant lines to give White no more than a small plus. Naum reaches similar conclusions, but in more than twice the time.

Kasparov – Topalov
Wijk aan Zee 1999 (WGG 105)

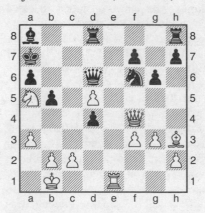

This is from near the start of a great king-hunt by Kasparov. Kasparov himself did not see the variations to the end, but used the safety-net of perpetual check to proceed a few moves ahead, before looking to see whether he could play for a win (and if not, then he could still take the draw). Here, I wanted to see which engines would find the continuation **25 ♖e7+! ♔b6 26 ♕xd4+ ♔xa5 27 b4+ ♔a4 28 ♕c3** (or 28 ♖a7, which is also good). Most of the older engines did so fairly readily, but assessed it as equal. After the forced move **28...♕xd5** comes the next test: does the engine take a draw, or play for a win? After a little over three minutes, Fritz 6 found the correct **29 ♖a7!** (29 ♕c7 is one of several ways to draw) **29...♗b7 30 ♖xb7!**, assessing it as +0.06 – a minute plus, presumably because it keeps the draw in hand in some lines, rather than the position being a cut-and-dried draw. Thus, without seeing the lines to anything like a finish, Fritz 6 would have played the correct move. The other old engines would have taken a draw at tournament time-limits. The game concluded **30...♕c4 31 ♕xf6 ♔xa3 32 ♕xa6+ ♔xb4 33 c3+! ♔xc3 34 ♕a1+ ♔d2 35 ♕b2+ ♔d1 36 ♗f1!! ♖d2 37 ♖d7!! ♖xd7 38 ♗xc4 bxc4 39 ♕xh8 ♖d3 40 ♕a8 c3 41 ♕a4+ ♔e1 42 f4 f5 43 ♔c1 ♖d2 44 ♕a7 1-0**.

The new engines, very surprisingly, do less well. They see 25 ♖e7+ as the best move, but assess it as good for Black. They also take quite a while to rank 27 b4+ at all high in their list of moves. Rybka struggles to find 28 ♖a7 or 29 ♖a7, or the critical ideas behind these moves, and assesses 29 ♖a7 as a draw – which it would take at a tournament time-limit, like most of the old engines. Naum performs better once the key position at move 28 is reached, and is quicker to see both possible ♖a7 ideas and to assess them as good for White.

Note that their performance in a blundercheck would be drastically better, as they would already have seen and assessed the key positions before deciding whether to enter them, rather than needing to find them from scratch themselves.

Bad tablebase implementation

If the use of tablebases leads to play that is bad from a practical viewpoint, then something has gone wrong.

Consider this position. A queen has excellent practical winning chances against two knights, though in general the endgame is a theoretical draw. This was one of the discoveries made by the use of endgame databases, which overturned the prevailing view of endgame theory that the queen should win.

This is indeed a position where Black is able to hold the draw. Some of the old engines made a poor practical choice, by just giving away the queen. While this doesn't change the result from a technical viewpoint, it is not something you would associate with a very strong player. Of our current stars, Rybka falls flat on its face, with the absurd 1 ♕f4 and 1 ♕xf6+ as its top choices. Naum will play more naturally, even though it knows the objective assessment is drawn in any case. Against another engine (with tablebases loaded) this will make no difference to the result, but against a human it will yield good winning chances.

Playing Chess Online

Not everyone has a local chess club, or is able to attend regularly. Others would simply prefer to play from home. For them the only alternatives to playing social chess used to be to play against computers or to play correspondence chess. The Internet has changed all that. It is now possible to find opponents around the world, day or night, for real-time games of chess.

The best-known place for playing real-time chess on the Internet is the **Internet Chess Club** (ICC), which boasts a great many members worldwide and many thousands of games played online every day. For GMs and IMs the membership is free, but everyone else must pay. There is a free trial membership, and as far as I know there is nothing to stop you using this repeatedly, but if you find yourself spending a lot of time there, you will definitely want a proper account, as this offers extra features and means you can maintain a rating based on all your games at ICC. The ICC offers a vast wealth of features besides playing games; there are broadcasts (such as John Watson's excellent weekly show which features an interview with a chess VIP

of some sort), lectures, simuls, live commentary and many titled players offering online training (for a fee, of course). The main alternative to ICC is the **PlayChess** server provided by ChessBase. This is also very lively, with many strong players from around the world online at all times (Garry Kasparov visits from time to time too), and lectures, etc. Again, there is a membership fee, but various ChessBase products come with a free one-year membership, and there is a free trial membership too. Try both ICC and PlayChess and see which you like best. As with almost any websites, you can find them using a search engine, but the URLs at present are www.chessclub.com and www.playchess.com. Note that at both sites, many players like to play at extremely fast time-limits, with just three minutes (or less) for all the moves. So you'd better be quick with your mouse, and give some thought to whether this highly addictive form of the game is really going to benefit your tournament play. You can play slower games, but may have to wait longer for an opponent of a suitable level.

However, not everyone wants to play in real-time at all. Just as some players prefer correspondence chess to the over-the-board variety of the game, so some of those who play online prefer a slower game. For them, e-mail is an ideal medium. This saves the delays and uncertainties of using the traditional post, and provides scope for playing a relatively fast form of correspondence chess. Some of the traditional correspondence chess organizations have

now switched over to online trans-
mission of moves, with **ICCF**'s
World Correspondence Championship now played via a server. See
www.iccf.com for information and
downloads.

Chess News on the Internet

There is a great deal of chess news
and information available online, and
as with anything on the Internet, the
best way to find what you're looking
for is to search online – any attempt
to list the most important sites is liable to go out of date quickly; besides, typing in long URLs is a pain,
whereas a search for a few keywords
will find the right page more quickly
and with less risk of error. So in this
section I shall just mention a few of
the more important resources.

The liveliest and also one of the
best places for news is the **Chess-
Base** site (www.chessbase.com). It is
updated most days, often with several new stories or articles. There are
always plenty of photos, and most
aspects of chess are represented. Reports on events will always include
the basics, such as a crosstable and
downloadable games, and often annotated games and interviews. Con-
tentious issues of the day are
frequently aired, with feedback from
readers included with little or no
censorship, making it a good forum
for debate. Word has it that Kirsan
Iliumzhinov reads the ChessBase site
regularly, so this is the place to send
your views if you want them read by
the FIDE President. Frederic Friedel
is in charge of the website – a man
with a good sense of humour and

who knows everyone who is anyone
in the chess world – so contributions
and opinions from the best players
and most colourful characters in the
chess world can be found here.
Frederic also knows his audience
well, and makes sure that there are
pictures of attractive female chess-
players as often as possible, which
has led to some allegations of sexism
("Ukrainian Chess Babes in Biki-
nis!"), but also to an increase in the
readership, no doubt. The ChessBase
site also offers a large online game
database and product support for the
company's software and data products, and demo versions including
ChessBase Lite.

The most essential site for those
looking for hard chess information is
The Week in Chess (which has the
unfortunately   cumbersome   URL
www.chesscenter.com/twic/twic.html
– surely the final "twic.html" should
be dispensed with, at least). Every
week since 1994, Mark Crowther has
been producing his online chess
magazine, which as I write in September 2009 has just reached issue
number 775. The jewel in TWIC's
crown is the game file, which includes
most of the important games from the
week in question from around the
world, often running into the thousands. It is neatly packaged each
Monday evening (UK time) in PGN
or ChessBase format ready to be
loaded into a database program, with
nicely standardized event and player
data (rather than the inconsistent jum-
ble that free data often suffers from).
Crowther has a network of people
who feed games from their region
through to him, and he exercises a

remarkable degree of quality control over the data, given the time constraints. TWIC also includes brief reports on the events covered, with full results and crosstables in text or html format. There are also links to sites for events and a wealth of other information about forthcoming events and news from the chess world. TWIC has so far provided chess enthusiasts with more than a million downloadable chess games – and all for free.

A different style of chess site can be found at www.chesscafe.com. Since 1996, **ChessCafe** has been providing a variety of monthly columns by noted chess writers, with two or three appearing each Wednesday, together with a weekly book review (or a review of a chess product of some other sort). The mainstays include the famous trainer Mark Dvoretsky and the renowned endgame theoretician Karsten Müller. ChessCafe also features an archive of previous columns, and an excellent collection of links to other chess sites of many types.

It is also worth mentioning that **Wikipedia**'s chess pages have had some solid work put into them – the main chess page can be found at en.wikipedia.org/wiki/Chess, but there are individual pages for many aspects of chess and individual players. Additionally, there are individual wiki projects for some specialized topics, such as chessprogramming.wikispaces.com, which is recommended to anyone seeking more advanced information on the details of programming computers to play chess than I have felt appropriate to include in this chapter.

Pitfalls

In this section, I shall be pointing out some of the possible problems that may be encountered when using computers to assist with analysis, odd glitches in their play, and issues with data quality and sloppy analysis presented online.

Misassessment of Repetitions

In recent versions of ChessBase and the Fritz interface, moves that repeat a position from earlier in the game or variation are given an assessment of "0.00" – the same as a completely drawn position. This is regardless of the actual assessment of the position, and is for any repetition (not just threefold), whether forced or not, and there is no way to disable this behaviour. This can be extremely misleading, not to mention annoying. You can find yourself staring at a position trying to work out what spectacular drawing idea the machine has spotted before realizing there is none. Normally the assessment changes to the "real" one after the move has been executed, in which case it is merely a major irritation. But in a position where the opponent then has a move that brings about a position from earlier, this will also be reported as 0.00. In cases where a lot of the similar positions have arisen already, the only way to get a real assessment of the position is to cut off the earlier moves and have the engine analyse the position without any move history (or else use a different program entirely). Note that this is not an engine bug – it happens regardless of the engine being used – it is the interface that is at fault. Of course, it is possible to construct examples where the analysis is made into total gibberish by this bug (or rather misguided feature), but here is a typical example:

Huang Qian – Gunina
Russia–China (women), Sochi 2009

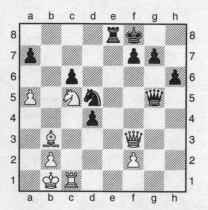

36...♕g6+ 37 ♗c2 ♕d6 38 ♗b3 ♘f6

Here a blundercheck gave the move 38...♕g6+ as apparently drawing. And an engine running in the position before this move will also be made to report this same evaluation. The position is clearly much too unbalanced for this to be anything other than a perpetual check, if the assessment really is correct, but a glance at the position suggests this cannot be so. Sure enough, when the "drawing" move is executed, the assessment jumps to "very good for White". Whether this assessment is correct is another matter, but at least the engine is now being allowed to provide its assessment based on its own analysis. So bear in mind that when you see the 0.00 assessment, it might not be all that it seems.

Assisted Analysis Failure

Yakovenko – Kramnik
Dortmund 2009

1 e4 e5 2 ♘f3 ♘f6 3 ♘xe5 d6 4 ♘f3 ♘xe4 5 d4 d5 6 ♗d3 ♗d6 7 0-0 0-0 8 c4 c6 9 ♕c2 ♘a6 10 a3 ♗g4 11 ♘e5 ♗xe5 12 dxe5 ♘ac5 13 f3 ♘xd3 14 ♕xd3 ♘c5 15 ♕d4 ♘b3 16 ♕xg4 ♘xa1 17 ♗h6 g6 18 ♘c3 ♕b6+ 19 ♔h1 ♕xb2 20 ♕f4

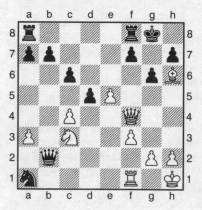

20...f6?

It has been pointed out that this move is probably losing, and due to an idea that had already occurred in a correspondence game. However, Yakovenko chose 21 ♘a4? and the struggle eventually ended in a draw. The whole line, up to and including Black's 18th move, had also occurred in a number of earlier high-level over-the-board games (including one with Kramnik as Black just two days earlier), so this looks like an error in both players' preparation, during which they no doubt used computer assistance.

So how did both players fail to find the right line in their preparation? This seems to be a case of them just letting the computer ineffectually analyse the current position, rather than pushing it down any critical-looking lines. If left to its own devices analysing the position after 20...f6?, even Rybka will take a very long time to rate the winning **21 e6!** as anything above equal. However, it will list the move among its top choices (true for Rybka at least, and you'd certainly expect the top players to be using the best engines), and a human looking alertly at both the position and the engine's output may well notice that this move ought to be considered "interesting" at least – it leaves a piece *en prise*, after all! The thing you need to do then is to execute the move, and then leave the computer to think about the position after the move. Once the assessments of the various possibilities in the new position have stabilized, you should then push the analysis forwards to any new critical positions. By these means, one very quickly finds that 21 e6! does indeed win. (20...f5 appears necessary, but that's a story for another day.)

After 21 e6! the computer will very quickly show that **21...♕xc3** is the only critical reply.

Once we are convin
nothing important being
can soon push the compu
analyse the position after this
Now that it can concentrate all
forts on this position (rather tha.. .
being one of many possibilities and so getting a fraction of its attention), it soon gets to the core of the issue, viz. **22 ♕d6!** (22 ♕c7? f5 doesn't give White much). This is a move that the computer took a very long time to find if starting its analysis in the position after 20...f6?, but now uncovers in less than a minute (I should mention that the current no. 2 engine, Naum, struggles a little more with this). Having found 22 ♕d6, the lines are fairly straightforward: 22...f5 23 e7; 22...♖fe8 23 ♕d7 f5 24 ♕f7+ ♔h8 25 e7 and ♗g5; 22...♘b3 23 ♕d7 f5 24 e7 ♘c5 25 exf8♕+ ♖xf8 26 ♕e7; 22...dxc4 23 ♕d7 f5 24 e7 ♖fe8 25 ♕e6+ ♔h8 26 ♗f4; or 22...♕xc4 23 ♖xa1 ♕c3 24 ♖g1.

Data Errors and Opening Books
Human error can result in odd problems for the computers. Play over the following sequence:

Tiviakov – Galliamova
President's Cup, Elista 1998

1 e4 c5 2 ♘f3 d6 3 d4 cxd4 4 ♘xd4 ♘f6 5 ♘c3 a6 6 ♗g5 b5 7 ♕d2 e6 8 0-0-0 ♘c6 9 f4 ♗d7 10 ♗xf6 gxf6 11 ♔b1 ♕b6 12 ♘xc6 ♗xc6 13 ♕e1 h6 14 ♗d3 h5 15 ♘d5
This is the course of the game as cited in both *ChessBase Magazine* and *The Week in Chess*. Given that this was a game between two strong human players, one realizes that there have

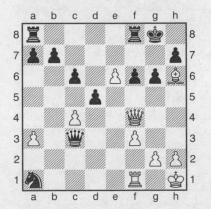

...eral gross data errors, and detective work might determine ... Black's 13th move was really .3...♕c5. The game as given in the databases continued absurdly too:

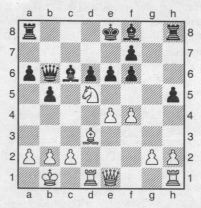

15...0-0-0 16 ♘b4 ♗b7 17 c3 ♖g8 18 ♕e2 f5 19 ♖hg1 fxe4 20 ♗xe4 d5 21 ♗f3 h4 22 ♘d3 ♕c7 (½-½, 66)

However, once such an error has entered the databases, it will tend to crop up again and again in unexpected ways. It skews the statistics that the game database reports, and it may also get dumped into computers' opening books. Thus in the game Nimzo–Fritz, Microcomputers blitz Wch 2000, the diagram position occurred for real, together with the blunder-laden follow-up: Black's queen was left *en prise* and White didn't take it. Both computers were slavishly following their opening book (after all, 13...h6 and the later queen blunder had a 50% score according to the data!), and were not allowed to think for themselves.

Hash-Table Woes

I have already said much in this chapter about the value of the engine using hash tables. However, even

this feature is not always trouble-free, as sometimes there is a glitch, and the engine reads garbage from its hash tables, rather than useful information.

Lafuente – Shredder 9
Olivos 2005

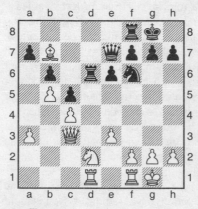

19...♖fd8??
This otherwise inexplicable move, failing to recapture a piece for no good reason, was the result of a hash-table error.

The Authority of the Digitized Word
The last example in this section relates to electronic data. Just like the printed word having an exaggerated authority, so it is easy to imagine that information presented in electronic format will have been checked using electronic tools. This is not necessarily so. Indeed, ChessBase's own printed magazine has been known to suffer from errors in chess notation that the use of their own software should minimize, and that their programs can be used to detect in chess documents. The following comes from an online site, where a "prolific" chess writer

recommended for White (in a set of three articles) a line against the Caro-Kann that has a dubious reputation.

Ker – L. Jones
Warwick (Fiji) Z 2002

1 e4 c6 2 d4 d5 3 exd5 cxd5 4 c4 ♘f6 5 c5?!

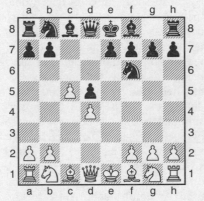

This is the Gunderam Attack, a line that tends to give well-prepared Caro-Kann players some rather easy wins. Indeed, as a junior in Britain in the 1980s, the fact that this had been recommended for White in a popular repertoire book was a good reason for choosing this opening! Naturally, I was curious to see what new development could possibly have rejuvenated this line – after all, computer analysis has in recent years resurrected some apparently very rustic opening lines.

5...e5! 6 ♘c3 exd4 7 ♕xd4 ♘c6 8 ♗b5 ♗e7!

This is a well-known improvement over Gunderam's original analysis, which continued with the "cooperative" 8...♗d7?, which just spends time misplacing the bishop.

9 ♗e3 0-0 10 ♗xc6 bxc6 11 ♕a4

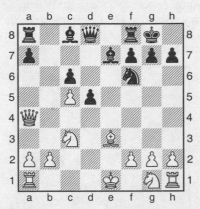

This manoeuvre, played in just this one game won by White, was the basis for the recommendation. White's position looks shaky, but if one uses annotation by result, then the conclusion might be rosy for White. But it is nowadays the easiest thing in the world to avoid this pitfall, as the analysis engine is just a keypress away. But in this case, the key was not pressed...

11...♖b8 12 b4 ♘g4 13 ♗f4 ♗f6 14 ♖c1 ♗xc3+

This is certainly convincing, though if Black wants a simpler alternative, then 14...♗e5 is rather good.

15 ♖xc3 ♕f6 16 ♘e2

The comment given at this point in the online article is "Phew! Holding everything. I leave it to you to judge whether this was luck or logic." The rest of the game is presented as if White is at least OK, and the line is difficult for Black in practice. In fact, White is dead lost.

16...♖e8 17 0-0 ♖xe2 18 ♗xb8 ♕xc3??

Now the game becomes less clear, though it takes several more poor decisions to lose the game. As any good analytical engine will indicate in a second or so, 18...♖xf2! wins by force:

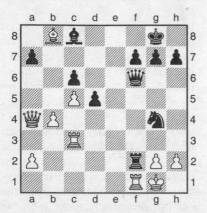

a) 19 ♕d1 ♖xf1+ 20 ♕xf1 ♕xc3 is hopeless for White.

b) 19 ♖fc1 ♖e2 20 ♗g3 ♕d4+ 21 ♔f1 (21 ♔h1 ♘f2+ mates) 21...♖f2+ 22 ♔g1 ♖xa2+ wins heavy material.

c) 19 ♖f3 ♖xf3 20 ♖xf3 (20 gxf3 ♕d4+ 21 ♔h1 {21 ♔g2 ♘e3+ 22 ♔h1 ♕d2 23 ♖g1 ♗h3} 21...♕d3 22 ♕d1 ♘f2+) 20...♕a1+ 21 ♖f1 ♕d4+ 22 ♔h1 ♘f2+ 23 ♔g1 ♘h3++ 24 ♔h1 ♕g1+ 25 ♖xg1 ♘f2#.

That's pretty conclusive. So it is clear that a line that has long been considered very dubious for White has here been recommended on the basis of a single non-GM game without even a cursory computer check of the critical positions.

19 ♕xc6 ♗f5 20 ♕xd5 ♕f6 21 ♗xa7 ♖e8?! 22 c6 ♖d8 23 ♕c5 ♕e5? 24 f4 ♕xc5+?! 25 ♗xc5 ♖c8 26 ♖d1 h6 27 b5 ♘f6 28 b6 ♘e8 29 b7 1-0

In conclusion, while there is a lot of good free chess information available online, sometimes the quality is equal to what you are paying.

How to Cheat at Chess Revisited

When Bill Hartston published a book of chess humour in the 1970s, his choice of the title *How to Cheat at Chess* was all part of the joke. How could anyone cheat at chess? The idea it conjured up was of a player trying to sneak an extra queen onto their board, much like a card sharp might have the ace of spades hidden up his sleeve. Adding to the sense of the whole notion of cheating at chess being a joke was the notorious protest delivered by the Korchnoi team during the 1978 World Championship match. The gist of it was that the blueberry yoghurt that was brought to Karpov during the game was a signal to play a particular move. A different flavour could have been used to imply another instruction and, e.g., a marinated quail's egg being delivered to the Champion might be an instruction to offer a draw immediately. The whole thing was really just a joke (but also a psychological ploy in this tense match), and the press loved it of course, and it was dealt with seriously – any change in the flavour from then on had to be notified in advance. Of course, back then, it is hard to say who exactly would have been expert enough to be able to give Karpov advice, in real time, on what he should play. Anyone who has been in the GM analysis room during a World Championship match (before the computer era) will probably have seen for themselves that the players at the board tend to have a much better idea of what is going on than the analysts, even though they are able to move the pieces around.

Nowadays, those days of innocence seem a long way off. There have been allegations of cheating even at the very highest level, and proven cases of blatant cheating at lower levels. Quite apart from the notion that computer-based cheating could actually be going on, the ease with which allegations can be made – and ones that may seem quite plausible to journalists, for instance – is a major issue in itself.

The temptation to cheat, and the suspicion that opponents might be cheating, is only natural. Hand-held devices can play to a very high standard (indeed, as I write these words in September 2009, there is a news story that Pocket Fritz has just shredded an IM/GM field at a tournament in South America, dropping only half a point). Miniaturization technology has also made transmitting and receiving devices all too easy to conceal.

The earliest targets, in the 1990s, were the lower sections of big open tournaments – some of these have a large first prize. The *modus operandi* would be for a player with a suitably low rating to enter, and then play all his games wearing a hooded jacket, or voluminous hair, or simply headphones (ostensibly to listen to quiet music during the game, which sounds absurd, but I have known players who genuinely did this). The idea was that they had a small receiver hidden somewhere on their person, linked to a tiny ear piece. At this level of play, all that was needed was a way to communicate, say,

Fritz's choice of move (after a few seconds) to the player, and tournament victory would be quite probable. So one accomplice would be sufficient, and just a way for this accomplice to discover the move that had been played would have to be devised. After a few instances of such schemes being uncovered, there does not seem to have been much recurrence. Most tournament directors would now be quick to intervene in the case of any suspicious behaviour, and even with further miniaturization of the devices, they could not be completely concealed. Big-money events nowadays may also sweep the area for electronic devices, and the penalty for a mobile phone ringing during a game is instant loss. Basically, the cost-risk analysis does not favour this type of cheating nowadays.

But in higher-level chess, the great increase in strength of the engines could potentially make cheating of a less blatant form effective. First we should note that in games at top level, the players do not *need* a lot of assistance in order to achieve a large increase in effective playing strength. For instance, World Champion Vishy Anand stated that, if he were told at just three points in each game that he had a strong possibility in the current position (not what it is – only that one exists), then his results would improve to the tune of 100 Elo rating points – that's the difference between a World Championship Candidate and a dominant World Champion. And to convey *that* information to the player would require just a nod or a wink – no need for any electronics in the playing hall. And three times a game would not arouse suspicion. One possible method for providing much more than that level of assistance is as follows. This has in fact been claimed to have been employed at top level, but not proven in terms of documented, publicly-presented evidence.

Three people are needed, at least two of them very strong grandmasters. The first is of course the player at the board. The second is some distance away, and not in a public location (possibly in a hotel room). He is working with a computer the whole time, looking at possibilities in the current position of the game going on in the tournament hall (the moves may be available online). The third man is the go-between, who spends some time in the tournament hall, and some time outside the playing area, communicating with the computer man (e.g. by mobile phone). The go-between may need to tell the computer man the moves that have been played, in case the online coverage is unreliable. The computer man is an expert in computer-assisted analysis, who has also worked closely with the player at the board, and is therefore familiar with his playing style. At crucial moments, the go-between will signal to the player at the board based on the conclusions of the computer man's assisted analysis.

Does this sound far-fetched? I don't think so. Would it be easy to stamp out? Yes, but not without fairly draconian restrictions on the players and/or spectators. In a World Championship match, you can employ methods to defeat this type of scheme (making sure the players can never see the spectators, for instance, while jamming all telecommunications in the area is another possibility), but that depends on the organizers (and often the match will be held in the home country of one of the players, so allegations of partiality can come into play).

But as I mentioned earlier, *allegations* of cheating are as much of a problem as the possibility of cheating itself. Most readers will no doubt remember "Toiletgate", which nearly overshadowed the Kramnik-Topalov World Championship reunification match in 2006, and came within an inch of sinking the entire reunification process. After a bad start to the match, the Topalov team made some obviously absurd allegations against Kramnik, based on the fact that he was visiting the toilet fairly often. How exactly this enabled him to cheat, given that the players and whole area had been swept for electronic devices, was never fully explained. But the match officials gave the allegations credence when they responded by putting restrictions on Kramnik for further games. Naturally incensed by this, Kramnik refused to start the next game. The whole sorry tale is recounted elsewhere, so I'll spare my readers a blow-by-blow account, except to mention that the Topalov team later used a common ploy in allegations of cheating. They compared Kramnik's choices of move with those of a top engine, and found that they often agreed. Some journalists even found this quite compelling.

However, in many positions there is a clearly best move, and any strong player is likely to choose it, whether they be carbon- or silicon-based. If you ran such a comparison on the Capablanca-Alekhine match games from 1927, you'd also find a fair degree of correlation. If you are determined to make such a claim, then you can bias the figures even more by a little trick. Rather than giving the computer a set amount of time on each move, and then seeing how many of its choices match, you can instead set the computer thinking, and as soon as, at any point within the next, say, ten minutes, the computer agrees with the human's choice, mark this down as "success" and move on to the next move. Or you could just make the results up in fact, since no one will be able to replicate your set-up exactly and so disprove your "analysis".

Another type of false allegation of cheating can arise when a player is disgruntled after a bad loss. All chess-players know how rotten it can feel to lose a game, and how it takes some self-control to react gracefully. Sadly, some players see fit to strike back with a farcical allegation. One recent example involved one of the world's finest young grandmasters, who claimed his opponent (also a grandmaster) must have used computer assistance during the game. His opponent had introduced a new move in this game, in an opening that he had played before and so was well-prepared for. The novelty proved successful, and led to a very quick victory. In the course of these few remaining moves (none of them very complex for grandmasters), the player who was being accused of cheating had in fact missed a much stronger possibility that any engine would have pointed out very quickly. Sadly, the accuser did not withdraw his allegation once he had got over his loss, but even added to it by the familiar method of comparing his opponent's earlier games with a computer's choices. The clinching argument, apparently, was that the player then went on to perform badly in the following rounds. No wonder – he had been called a cheat in front of the whole chess world, and knowing that some mud will always stick, was no doubt concerned about the effect this would have on his future career.

It would be a sad state of affairs if chess tournaments in the future are to require airport-style security checks, but this might be what is needed to protect the innocent.

Puzzles

This selection of 60 puzzle positions is completely new for this third edition of *The Mammoth Book of Chess*. Most of the positions are taken from recent events, and none have appeared as puzzle positions anywhere before, so you can be confident that you won't be recognizing the solutions rather than needing to work them out – unless you follow current chess events extremely avidly!

None of these puzzles are novice-level, although the first 11 should be accessible to just about all chess-players. After that, the difficulty level rises, with the "Tricky" puzzles all involving a harder-to-see concept or involving more complex analysis. If you do find them too tough to solve, then please view them as additional examples, as I have tried to pack a good deal of instructive comments into the solutions. But at least think about the puzzle position before turning to the solution, as you will learn a lot more that way. Note also that the solutions are often lengthy; I do not expect you to have analysed everything – the detail is there in case you need it, and also to make them work better as instructive examples.

The final section features puzzles that are designed for computer-assisted analysis, a technique described in the previous chapter.

Fairly Easy Puzzles

These first 11 positions should be solvable by almost all chess-players.

1) A. David – Yakovich
Kavala (open) 2009

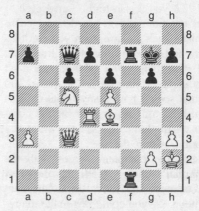

White is clearly doing well here, but can you see a way to smash through and win immediately?

2) Bosiočić – C. Bauer
Jubilee Open, Zurich 2009

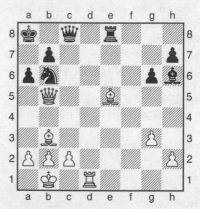

White has a large advantage, but now rejected 27 ♕xb6, presumably due to the back-ranker 27...♖xe5 28 ♖d8?? ♖e1+. Was this the right decision?

3) Based on Motoc – Anon, Queenstown blitz 2009

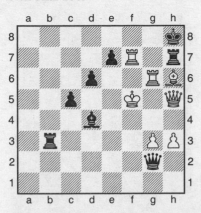

This is based on a blitz game with Alina Motoc as White played at Queenstown 2009. Black has many ways to win here; is 1...♖xf7+ one of them?

5) **Le Roux – S. Feller**
French Ch, Nîmes 2009

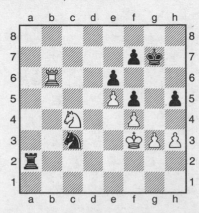

What are your thoughts on possible plans by which Black might try to win this ending?

4) **Dzhumabaev – Ismagambetov**
Tashkent Zonal 2009

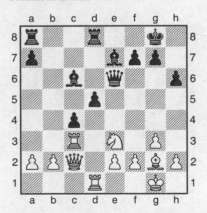

Black has just played 22...♕c8-e6?. How could White have made him regret this careless move?

6) **Dzagnidze – Sandipan**
Kavala (open) 2009

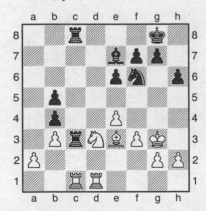

If White could neutralize Black's domination of the c-file, he could look forward to targeting the weak b-pawns. Thus he played 27 ♗d2, based on 27...♖xd3?? being ruled out by 28 ♖xc8+. Was this a good idea?

7) G. Jones – I. Sokolov
Staunton Memorial, London 2009

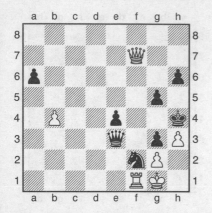

What is the quickest and most elegant way for Black to win?

9) Yakovich – E. Danielian
Kavala (open) 2009

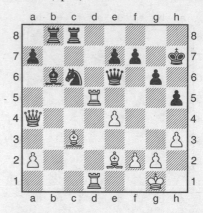

Black is clearly under some pressure, but can you see a shortcoming of the black position that allows White now to bring about an immediate collapse?

8) E. Pähtz – K. Arakhamia
Baltic Queen, St Petersburg 2009

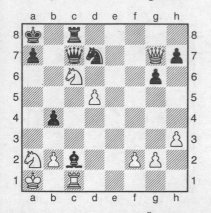

White has just played 32 ♘a5-c6, attacking the b4-pawn and c2-bishop, so Black replied 32...b3, and went on to win many moves later after a struggle in which both sides had their chances. Did Black have anything better?

10) Mamedov – Yilmaz
Acropolis Open, Khalkida 2009

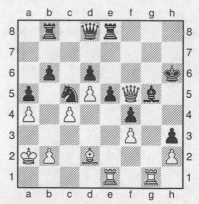

White has sacrificed a piece for an attack. Is it good enough? White to play.

11) Duchess – Kaissa (variation)
World Computer Ch, Toronto 1977

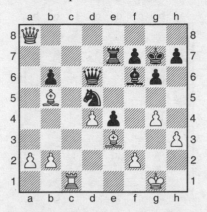

This position could have occurred in a game between two of the top computers of the late 1970s. Black had avoided this position by giving up a whole rook, and apparently none of the human players present could see why. Can you do better and find the forced mate at White's disposal?

Tricky Puzzles

The next 40 puzzles should prove quite a challenge even for strong players. Players of more modest abilities can be happy if they have seen the main idea, even if they have missed some of the details.

However, in most cases the analysis involved is not enormously complicated; the difficulty is instead due to an idea that is counter-intuitive, or hard to see for some other reason. Once you have got to the heart of the puzzle, the analysis should fall into place quite neatly. Where the position does contain some complex possibilities, I have sought to limit your task by asking a specific question.

12) Smerdon – V. Mikhalevski
Queenstown 2009

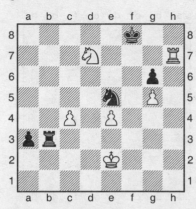

The game now ended in a draw after the moves 39...♔g8 40 ♘f6+ ♔f8 41 ♘d7+ ½-½. Can you work out how Black could have won?

13) A. Rychagov – Grishchuk
Russian Ch, Moscow 2007

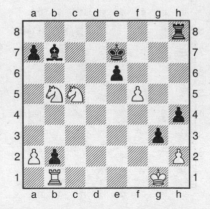

Black now had at his disposal a clear-cut win. Can you find it?

14) **E. Korbut – Tairova**
Russian Women's Ch, Moscow 2007

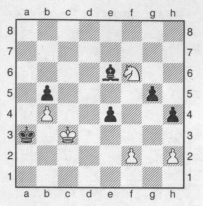

Can Black (to play) make progress?

16) **Girya – Gunina**
Russian Women's Ch, Moscow 2007

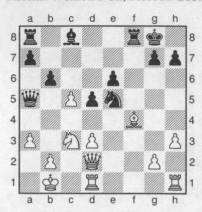

Is it a good idea for Black to try to win a pawn by 21...♘xd3 here?

15) **Matveeva – E. Korbut**
Russian Women's Ch, Moscow 2007

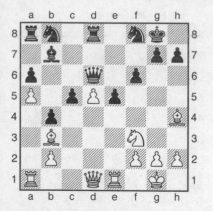

Black's position is fragile, but given a respite to catch up in development, that could quickly change. The iron is certainly hot, but how should White now strike?

17) **Khamrakulov – Rodshtein**
Pamplona 2007

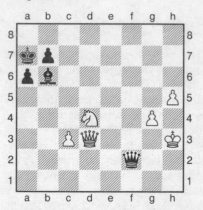

White now played 51 h6 and won quickly. Should he have done?

18) **Beliavsky – Khamrakulov**
Pamplona 2007

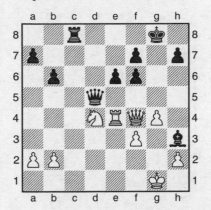

Should White play 27 ♕xf6 or 27 ♕h6 here? As a more difficult exercise, try to assess the position after the correct move.

19) **Salgado Lopez – San Segundo**
Pamplona 2007

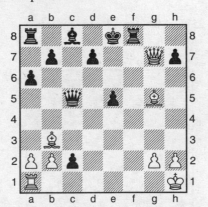

White is on the brink of victory. Is 22 ♖e1 the right way to press home his huge advantage?

20) **Huerga Leache – Rubio Mejia**
Pamplona 2007

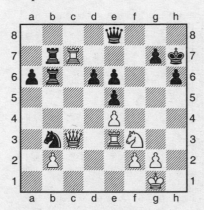

In what had been a highly advantageous position, Black has just played a careless move, 40...♖b8-b7. How serious an error was this?

21) **Pieri – C. Bernard**
French open Ch, Paris 1994

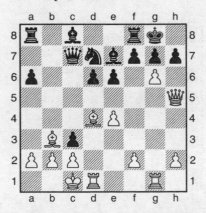

The game now concluded 16...cxb2+ 17 ♔b1 fxg6 18 ♗xe6+ ♔h8 19 ♖xg6 ♘e5 20 ♖xg7 ♔xg7 21 ♖g1+ ♔h8 22 ♕h6 1-0. Could Black have saved himself by avoiding ...cxb2+ but otherwise playing the same way?

22) **Botvinnik – Gligorić**
Moscow Olympiad 1956

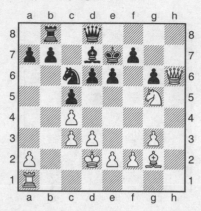

Black played the passive 16...♗e8? and lost quickly, while 16...♕h8?! 17 ♖h1 ♕xh6 18 ♖xh6 ♘d8 has been claimed to be Black's best defensive try. Adopt a more positive frame of mind, and show that Black can launch an immediate counterattack that puts him fully in the game.

23) **I. Nikolaidis – Chadaev**
Kavala (open) 2009

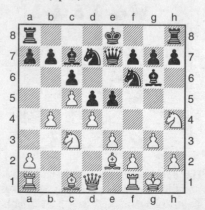

White now played 12 f3. Was this a good idea?

24) **S. Williams – D. Howell**
British Ch, Torquay 2009

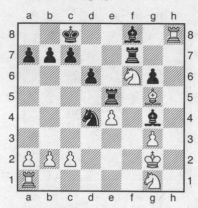

White now played 19 ♗h6 ♖xf6 20 ♗xf8. Does this:
a) Win material by discovered check and a skewer on the long diagonal; or
b) Lose material because of Black's counterattack?

25) **Dzhumaev – Ismagambetov**
Tashkent Zonal 2009

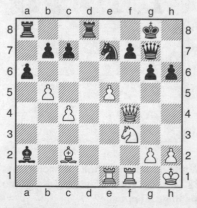

Black's position looks a little fragile, but what aspect of it should White target, and how?

26) A. Filippov – Dzhumabaev
Tashkent Zonal 2009

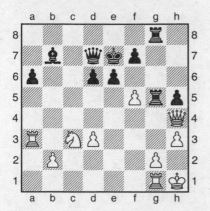

Black decided to break the pin by 31...♔f8 and the game was later drawn. What opportunity did he thereby miss?

28) Ivanchuk – Alekseev
FIDE Grand Prix, Jermuk 2009

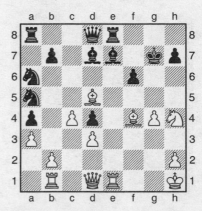

White has sacrificed a piece for an interesting attack. How would you continue the onslaught, and how confident are you of success?

27) Inarkiev – Cheparinov
FIDE Grand Prix, Jermuk 2009

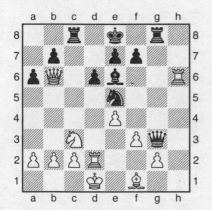

Black is a pawn down and seems to be under pressure. How can he secure counterplay, with an idea based on line-blocking?

29) Ivanchuk – Kamsky
FIDE Grand Prix, Jermuk 2009

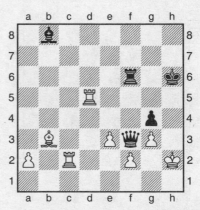

It seems extraordinary that Black should have any problems winning this position in any way that he feels like, but there are fortress possibilities to be considered. How can Black (to play) win immediately?

30) R. Hess – Areshchenko
Jubilee Open, Zurich 2009

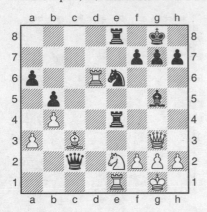

White now played 28 f4, no doubt aware that the e-file pin could be a problem, but perhaps reckoning on the threats against g7 and Black's back rank weighing as heavily. Is this so?

32) Gopal – Hobuss
Jubilee Open, Zurich 2009

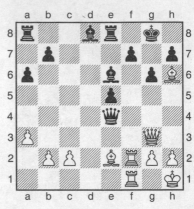

White now played the surprising move 21 ♗g4. Should Black take this bishop, and if so, how?

31) Heimann – Sandipan
Jubilee Open, Zurich 2009

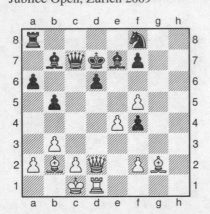

White has just sacrificed a piece for an attack, so he must follow up vigorously if he is to have anything like enough compensation. Is 25 e5 ♗xg2 26 exd6 the right way forward, or would you play something else?

33) Malakhatko – Sutovsky
Jubilee Open, Zurich 2009

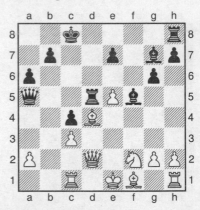

In a sharp opening line, Black (to play) has sacrificed a piece – probably as a prepared novelty. Can you see Black's strong and surprising follow-up idea?

34) **Fedorchuk – Carron**
Jubilee Open, Zurich 2009

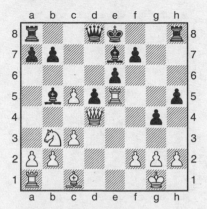

How should Black defend against White's threat of 16 ♖xe6 here? Be careful, as the obvious move might run into a very nasty reply.

36) **L'Ami – D. Howell**
Staunton Memorial, London 2009

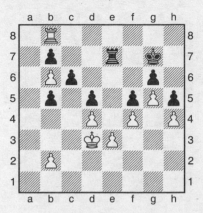

Can you see a clear-cut and effective way for White (to play) to press home his advantage?

35) **Malaniuk – Mikhalevski**
Jubilee Open, Zurich 2009

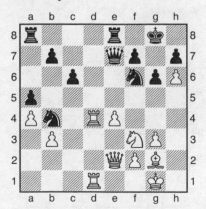

Here White chose 25 ♗h3? but after 25...♕f8 26 e5 ♕xh6 27 ♖h4 ♕f8 28 ♕c4 ♘fd5 he had lost control of the game and succumbed within a few moves. Can you suggest a strong and fairly simple improvement?

37) **Werle – G. Jones**
Staunton Memorial, London 2009

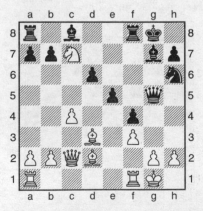

In the game, Black (to play) found the next move (a thematic King's Indian thrust) successfully, but failed to play the decisive follow-up after White took the a8-rook. Armed with this information, can you do better?

38) **Korchnoi – S. Williams**
Staunton Memorial, London 2009

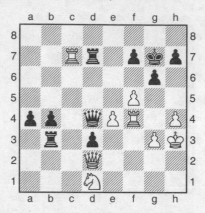

White simply has to be winning here, but after 44 e5 ♕d5 45 f6+ ♔g8 46 ♖c8+ ♖d8 47 ♖xd8+ ♕xd8 48 e6 ♕c8 it wasn't even clear if he was better any more. How could he have made life easier for himself?

40) **Cornette – Edouard**
French Ch, Nîmes 2009

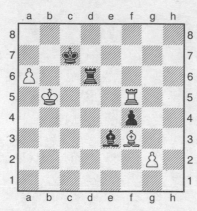

White terminated his opponent's resistance with a very elegant move based on some simple but nice tactical points. Can you find it?

39) **Vachier Lagrave – Degraeve**
French Ch, Nîmes 2009

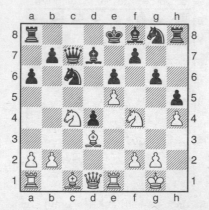

How did White, by means of a very attractive idea, now launch an overwhelming attack?

41) **Z. Almasi – Ruck**
Hungarian Ch, Szeged 2009

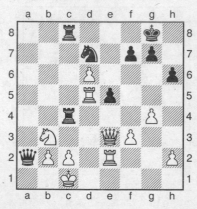

Black can create threats on the b-file by 28...♖b8 or 28...♖b4. Does it matter which he chooses, or are the two moves equivalent?

42) **Kolev – Yilmaz**
Acropolis Open, Khalkida 2009

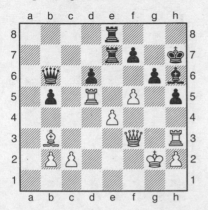

The game now ended 33...罝xe4 34 fxg6+ fxg6 35 豈f7+ 堂h8 36 豈f6+ 堂h7 37 豈f7+ 堂h8 38 豈f6+ ½-½. Was this a correct and logical end to proceedings? Did White have anything better than repeating?

43) **Ris – M. Gurevich**
Acropolis Open, Khalkida 2009

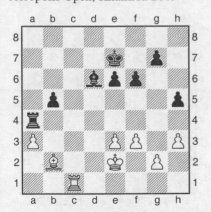

How should White parry the attack on his a3-pawn? Beware – there are some hidden perils in this inoffensive-looking position.

44) **Smirin – A. David**
Acropolis Open, Khalkida 2009

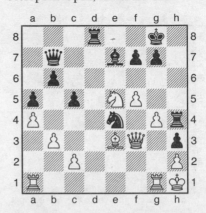

White has got himself into a somewhat sticky situation and decided to fight his way out by pressing forward on the kingside by 28 g5, which has the merit of preventing ....全f6 and threatening f6. Was this a good idea?

45) **Aroshidze – Papaioannou**
Acropolis Open, Khalkida 2009

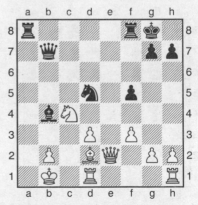

Black has played vigorously, sacrificing pawns as necessary to open lines for his attack. Your task now is to find a crisp way to round off a nice victory.

46) Melia – Aroshidze
Acropolis Open, Khalkida 2009

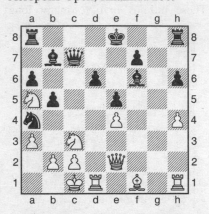

White now played 20 ♘xb7 and a draw was agreed (presumably due to the variation 20...♘xc3 21 ♘xd6+ ♛xd6 22 ♖xd6 ♘xe2+ 23 ♗xe2 ♔e7). What would you have played in the diagram position?

47) Nadezhdin – Gritsenko
Peterhof 2009

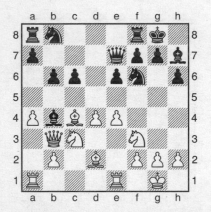

This Slav has not gone well for Black. How would you blast your way through, 15 e5 or 15 d5?

48) Obregon – Valerga
Villa Martelli 2009

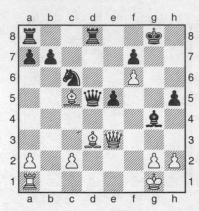

White is a rook down but threatens both 26 ♛g5+ and 26 ♛h6, mating quickly in both cases. Identify how Black can defend against these threats and make your choice for Black.

49) Deepan – Rathnakaran
New Delhi Zonal 2009

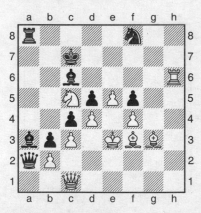

Hack Attack! White (to play) can blast his way through with a couple of sacrifices, but then needs to follow up accurately to bring his remaining forces into the onslaught.

50) **Vescovi – Barrientos**
Pan-American Team Ch, Mendes 2009

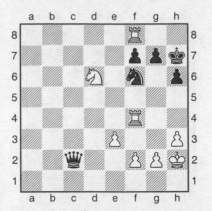

Is Black's position hopeless, or can he save himself by choosing just the right square for his queen? There are some pins possible, after all...

51) **Bruzon – Barrientos**
Pan-American Team Ch, Mendes 2009

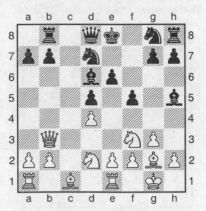

White now played the dramatic central thrust 11 e4. Was this:
a) A superb idea that shatters Black's position; or
b) An absurd move that fails completely?

Complex Puzzles

These puzzles involve many long and difficult variations; you may wish to use computer assistance.

52) **Malakhov – Ni Hua**
Russia-China match, Sochi 2009

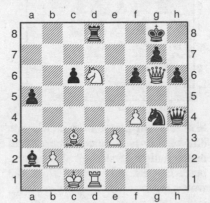

The natural 29 ♖g1 ♕f2 30 ♕xg4 ♕xe3+ 31 ♗d2 ♕c5+ is a draw, so White played **29 b3**. Good idea?

53) **Degraeve – Cossin**
French Ch, Nîmes 2009

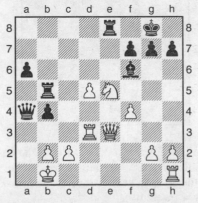

Should White (to play) be thinking in terms of attacking or defending?

54) **Schekachev – Safarli**
Jubilee Open, Zurich 2009

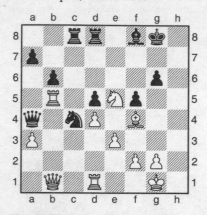

Should White play for the attack with 35 ♘xg6 or is he just losing a lot of material after 35...♘xa3? (As a computer-assisted task, try to work out what happens after other moves too.)

55) **Gajewski – Mastrovasilis**
Kavala (open) 2009

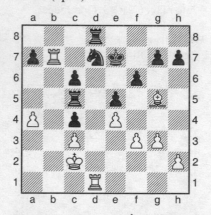

White now played 26 ♗xf6+. Had he fallen victim to the "touch-move" rule, or was his move deliberate, and if so, what was the idea?

56) **Sandipan – Morozevich**
Jubilee Open, Zurich 2009

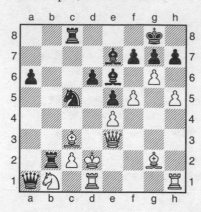

Morozevich uncharacteristically rejected a tempting and very strong tactical possibility here. Can you see what it is, and can you assess enough of the lines to believe it is a good idea?

57) **Chatalbashev – Nestorović**
Macedonian Team Ch, Struga 2009

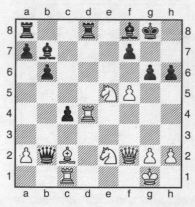

Black is under attack, but White's pieces are a little loose. Decide what your next move would be as Black. If you wish, using computer assistance, try to work things out more or less to a finish in the critical lines.

Computer-Assisted Analysis Puzzles

These last three positions are extremely complicated, and most suitable to tackling by combining your efforts with those of a powerful computer. For some suggestions and examples of how best to carry out this type of work, please see the previous chapter.

Without computerized assistance, all it is feasible to do within a puzzle-solving framework is to identify the main idea. Alternatively, you could view them as analytical projects, to be tackled by moving pieces on the board and working with a chess-playing friend.

58) **Classical French analysis**

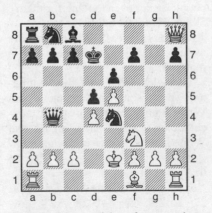

This position, arising from a sharp sideline of the Classical French, was condemned as bad for Black by Leinier Dominguez in analysis in *Informator 80*. Do you see a glimmer of hope for Black (to play) here? By means of computer-assisted analysis, come to a conclusion on how the position should be assessed.

59) **Zhigalko – Gopal**
Enschede 2009

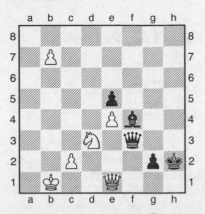

Here Black played 68...g1♕ and the game was agreed drawn without further play. Your computer, however, is insisting that 68...♗g3 is good for Black. Investigate, by interactive analysis with your computer, if this is true.

60) **R. Hess – Recuero Guerra**
Jubilee Open, Zurich 2009

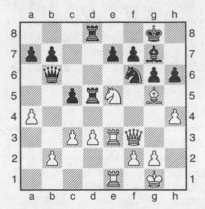

Here White opted for 24 ♘xf7!?. Choose at least two critical-looking replies for Black and try to determine what the outcome should be.

Solutions to Puzzles

Fairly Easy Puzzles

1)

30 ♖xd7! 1-0

After 30...♖xd7, 31 ♘xe6+ wins the black queen.

2)

No. After 27 ♕xb6 ♖xe5 White has the much stronger **28 ♗d5**, threatening 29 ♗xb7+ ♕xb7 30 ♖d8+, and Black has no good defence. After 28...♔b8? 29 ♗xb7, the best Black can do is the completely hopeless 29...♖b5 30 ♕xb5 axb5 31 ♗xc8, while 28...♖e7 allows 29 ♕xa6+ ♔b8, when White is two pawns up without even having lost the initiative.

His actual choice, **27 ♕a5?! ♕g4 28 ♖e1?!**, was unfortunate, as Black replied **28...♕d7**, giving White more significant back-rank issues. After **29 ♗f4?! ♖xe1+ 30 ♕xe1 ♗xf4 31 gxf4 ♕d4 32 ♕f1 ♘d7** it wasn't even clear if his advantage should be enough to win, and the game was eventually drawn after tenacious defence by Black.

3)

No, 1...♖xf7+?? loses. After 2 ♔e6 White threatens 3 ♗g7++, forcing mate, and the apparently solid defence 2...♖h7 allows mate in two by 3 ♖g8+! ♔xg8 4 ♕e8#.

4)

23 ♘xd5! ♗xd5 24 ♖e3 overloads the black queen, and therefore wins a good pawn.

In the game, White preferred the good positional move **23 ♘f5 ♗f6 24 ♘d4**, when the only way to avoid material loss would have been the ugly 24...♗xd4. Instead Black preferred **24...♕d6**, when White could once more have won a pawn, this time by 25 ♘xc6 ♕xc6 26 ♖cd3!, although here Black can expect rather more counterplay, and the opposite-coloured bishops *might* help him survive.

5)

Well of course, he just gives mate! Endgames are full of tactics; the main reason they are missed is that people aren't even looking for them.

59...♘d1! 60 g4 h4! 0-1

After 61 gxf5 exf5 White can only avoid ...♖f2# at a catastrophic cost in material.

I should clarify that this mating-net wasn't some random tactic that White blundered into; it was a tactical defence for a pawn on b6 that White had just (unwisely!) captured.

6)

No, it was a terrible blunder. After 27 ♗d2?? ♘xe4+! 28 fxe4, now 28...♖xd3+ comes with check. White resigned because he loses not just a pawn, but a piece as well following 29...♖xc1.

7)

That's right – he employs the idea known as Philidor's Legacy, normally used to deliver a smothered mate.

49...♘xh3++ 50 ♔h1 ♕g1+ 51 ♖xg1 ♘f2+

Not mate here, but it creates a pair of unstoppable connected passed pawns.

52 ♕xf2 gxf2 53 g3+ ♔h3 54 ♖a1 e3 0-1

8)

I hope you said "yes"! **32...♘c5!** wins on the spot, because 33...♘b3# is threatened, and White has no way to defend against this that doesn't leave her queen *en prise*.

9)

Black's queen is short of squares, and White wins by targeting it:

23 ♗c4!

It's as simple as that. The queen has nowhere to run, and the position of the black king means there is no time to prepare an escape-route either.

23...♘b4

A desperate try which might cause momentary confusion, but it doesn't prevent White's main threat. 23...♔g8 can be met by just moving the rook from d5 (there's not even any need for 24 ♖xh5), winning the black queen. 23...♖c7 gives the queen the c8-square but allows 24 ♖xh5+ gxh5 25 ♗xe6. 23...♕xe4 is the closest thing to a critical line, but White wins by 24 ♖xh5+ gxh5 25 ♗d3.

24 ♖xh5+

Not: 24 ♕xb4?? ♗xf2+; 24 ♗xb4?? ♖xc4.

24...gxh5 25 ♗xe6 ♖xc3 26 ♗xf7 ♖c2 27 ♖f1 ♖f8 28 ♕b3

and White won shortly.

10)

Yes, absolutely, because he has the crushing blow **36 ♗xf4!**, to which

Black has no viable reply.

36...♘e6

36...♗xf4 allows 37 ♕g6#, while 36...exf4 37 ♖xe8 diverts the black queen from the defence of the g5-bishop, so White mates or wins most of Black's pieces.

37 dxe6 exf4 38 e7 1-0

Even the noble self-sacrifice of the black knight has not saved the king-dom from ruin. 'Tis not but a scratch.

11)

White wins by **35 ♕f8+!** ♔xf8 36 ♗h6+ ♔g7 (or 36...♔g8 37 ♖c8+) 37 ♖c8+, mating.

35 ♖c6 also wins easily enough, while 35 g5 has been given in some sources to be bad for White due to 35...♘xe3, but as long as he now plays 36 ♖c6!, he still wins com-fortably (not 36 gxf6+?? ♕xf6 37 fxe3 ♕g5+ and ...♕xb5, which is good for Black).

Tricky Puzzles

12)

The solution is as straightforward as it is surprising: **39...♘xd7!** 40 ♖xd7 a2.

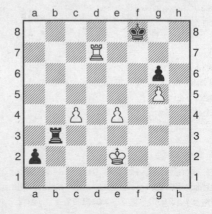

White can't stop the pawn promoting, despite apparently being in plenty of time to do so: 41 ♖a7 (41 ♖d1 is met by 41...♖b1) 41...h3! intending ....♖h1 and ...a1♕, and there is nothing White can do about it. e2 is precisely the wrong square for White's king to be on, and h3 precisely the right square for Black's rook (cutting off the white king from advancing to the third rank). If White could play either ♔c2 or ♔g2 in this position, he would be fine. As it is, he loses his rook for the a-pawn: 42 ♔d2 ♖h1 43 ♖xa2 ♖h2+, 42 ♔f1 ♖h1+ 43 ♔g2 a1♕, 42 ♔d1 ♖h1+ 43 ♔c2 a1♕ or 42 ♔f2 ♖h1 43 ♖xa2 ♖h2+.

13)

In the game Black played 32...♗d5? but this natural consolidating move gives Black little. **32...♖c8!** is a surprising switch by the black rook to the queenside, but it coordinates with the pawns on both flanks and penetrates to the heart of White's position:

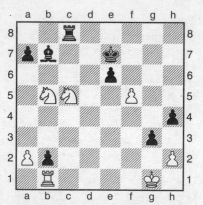

a) 33 ♘xb7 loses to 33...♖c1+.

b) 33 ♘d3 ♖c2 34 hxg3 (34 h3 ♖h2 threatening ...♖h1#) 34...h3 and ...h2+.

c) 33 ♘b3 is also met by 33...♖c2.

d) 33 ♖xb2 ♖xc5 threatens mate, and 34 ♘c3 (34 hxg3 ♖c1+ 35 ♔f2 h3 36 ♔e3 ♗g2) 34...♗f3 35 ♘e2 ♖e5 doesn't help White much.

e) 33 f6+ ♔xf6 (only move) 34 ♖f1+ ♔g6 35 ♘xb7 ♖c1 36 ♘a3 gxh2+ overloads the white king, and so the rook drops off.

14)

In the game 56...♗f5? allowed White to dig in: 57 ♘d5 ♗g4 58 ♘e3 ♗f3 59 ♘c2+ ♔a4 60 ♘e3 g4 61 ♘f5 h3 and White had a fortress and should now have held the draw without incident (in fact it was drawn only after further mistakes by both sides).

56...e3! wins; the main idea is naturally to create a passed g- or h-pawn that the knight cannot stop, while there are also themes of zugzwang and diverting the white king from the defence of the b4-pawn.

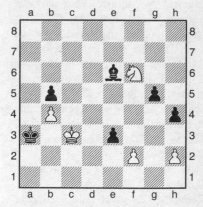

The main lines are as follows:

a) 57 f3 e2 58 ♔d2 ♗c4 is a win for Black; e.g., 59 ♘e4 ♔xb4 60 ♘xg5 ♔a3 61 ♘e4 b4 62 ♔e1 b3 63 ♘d2 ♔b4 64 f4 ♔c3 65 f5 ♔d3 66 f6 b2.

b) 57 fxe3 ♗f5 (57...g4 gives White the extra option of 58 ♘e4 ♗f5 59 ♘d2) and now:

b1) 58 ♔d2 g4 59 ♔e2 ♔xb4 60 e4 ♗e6 and Black wins; e.g., 61 ♔e3 ♔c4 62 ♘e8 b4 63 ♘d6+ ♔c5 64 e5 ♔d5 65 ♔f4 g3 66 hxg3 h3.

b2) 58 ♘h5 g4 59 ♔d4 (59 ♘f4 g3 60 hxg3 h3) 59...g3 60 hxg3 h3 61 g4 ♗xg4 62 ♘g3 ♔xb4.

b3) 58 e4 g4! 59 exf5 g3 60 hxg3 hxg3 and the g-pawn promotes.

15)
20 ♖xe5!
20 ♘xe5!? fxe5 21 ♗e7 ♕d7 22 ♖xe5 is also promising, but less forcing.
20...♘g6
Black accepts an inferior position. 20...fxe5 loses to 21 ♗xd8 (21 ♗e7 ♕xe7 22 d6+ ♘e6 23 dxe7 ♖xd1+ 24 ♖xd1 ♔f7 is less clear-cut) 21...♕xd8 22 d6+ ♔h8 23 ♘xe5.

20...g5 is the critical line, but Black goes down in flames:

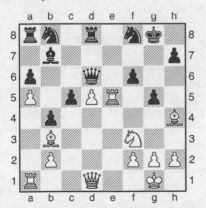

21 ♖e7! (21 ♗xg5 is promising, but murkier after either 21...fxg5 22 ♖xg5+ ♘g6 or 21...fxe5 22 ♗xd8 ♕xd8) 21...♗xd5 22 ♖e8!! – a stunning geometrical move!

21 ♖e6 ♕f8 22 ♗g3 ♘d7 23 ♖c1 ♔h8 24 d6 ♖ac8 25 ♕e2 ♗xf3 26 ♕xf3 ♘de5 27 ♕d5 c4 28 ♗xc4 ♖c6 29 h4 ♖cxd6 30 ♖xd6 ♖xd6 31 ♕b7 ♖c6 32 b3 ♖c8

Now White squandered most of her advantage by 33 ♕xc8+? and the game was eventually drawn. Instead, 33 ♖d1! exploits Black's back rank in elegant fashion and should lead to a comfortable victory.

16)
No, it is a blunder; after 21...♘f7 Black is still in the game.
21...♘xd3? 22 ♕xd3 ♖xf4

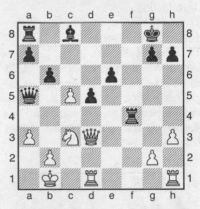

White now landed a devastating blow:
23 ♘xd5! ♖f8
This attempt to bail out with a safe move leads to a total calamity. 23...exd5 is met by 24 ♕xd5+ and ♕xa8(+). 23...♗a6 is relatively the best try, but dismal after 24 ♘e7+ ♔h8 25 ♕e3.
24 ♘e7+ ♔h8 25 ♖hf1 ♖e8 26 ♖f4!
Threatening 27 ♕xh7+ ♔xh7 28 ♖h4#.
26...h6 27 ♕g6 ♗a6 28 ♖f7 ♖g8 29 ♘xg8 ♖xg8 30 ♖xg7 1-0

17)

No, 51 h6? is a serious error. **51...♗c7!** threatens 52...♕h2#, and White has no good way to avoid this that doesn't allow perpetual check: 52 g5 ♕h2+ 53 ♔g4 ♕f4+ 54 ♔h5 ♕h2+ 55 ♔g6 ♕d6+ or 52 ♘c6+ bxc6 53 ♕d4+ ♕xd4 54 cxd4 ♗d8 (perhaps this is what one or both players missed).

Instead the game ended 51...♕f6? 52 h7 ♕h6+ 53 ♔g2 ♕g7 54 ♕f5 1-0.

18)

Let's first take a look at the game continuation:

27 ♕xf6??

This is a terrible blunder.

27...♕xe4! 0-1

Ouch! White resigned in view of 28 fxe4 ♖c1+ 29 ♔f2 ♖f1+ and ...♖xf6.

27 ♕h6! (attacking the h3-bishop and guarding the entry square on c1) is correct, and should probably lead to a draw.

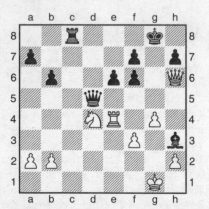

If you tried to work this out to a finish, here are some lines: 27...e5 (27...f5 will lead to perpetual check by one side or the other) 28 ♘f5

♕c5+! (28...♕d1+? 29 ♔f2 ♖c2+ 30 ♔g3 ♕g1+ 31 ♔h4! ♕f2+ 32 ♔h5 and White mates) 29 ♖e3! ♕c1+ 30 ♔f2 ♖c2+! 31 ♖e2! (31 ♔g3? now loses due to the difference in the position of the white rook: 31...♕g1+ 32 ♔h4 ♕f2+ 33 ♔h5 ♗xg4+! 34 fxg4 ♕xf5+ 35 gxf5 ♖xh2+ 36 ♔g4 ♖xh6) 31...♖xe2+ 32 ♔xe2 ♕xh6 (Black could take a perpetual check instead, of course) 33 ♘xh6+ ♔g7 34 ♘f5+ ♔g6 35 ♔f2 (35 ♘g3?! h5) 35...h5 36 ♔g3 and Black's extra pawn should not afford him winning chances.

19)

No, it certainly isn't:

22 ♖e1??

22 ♗xc2! is simplest, and wins on the spot. Black can do very little, while White can choose between moves like ♖e1 or ♗xh7, with too many threats in either case. Then White's position is every bit as won as it looks.

22 h4?! is also good, removing the danger of back-rank mate, but far less incisive. After 22...♖f5 Black can at least try to put up some resistance.

22...c1♕

Black's only move, but at a glance it is hard to believe that it is any more than a distraction for White. In fact, it rescues Black.

23 ♗xc1

Not 23 ♖xc1?? ♕xc1+ 24 ♗xc1 ♖f1#.

23...♕e7

White must now take a step backwards, which gives Black time to put his house in order. White must even be careful not to end up worse.

24 ♕h6

24 ♖xe5?? ♖f1#; 24 ♕xe5?? ♖f1+.

24...♖f5 25 ♗c2

25 g4 is well met by 25...♕b4.

25...♖f7 26 ♕h5 d6 27 ♗g5 ♕e6 28 ♗b3 ♕g6 29 ♗xf7+ ♕xf7 30 ♕d1 ♕g6 31 ♖xe5+ dxe5 32 ♕d8+ ♔f7 33 ♕e7+ ♔g8 34 ♕d8+ ♔f7 35 ♕e7+ ½-½

20)

Very serious indeed, as White wins outright by **41 ♘g5+!**. It's hard to believe that Black can't avoid a total catastrophe, but chess can be a cruel game.

41...♔g6

41...hxg5 42 ♖h3+ and Black loses his queen: 42...♔g6 (42...♔g8 43 ♖c8) 43 ♕f3 ♖xc7 44 ♕h5+ ♔f6 45 ♕xe8; 41...♔g8 is ruled out by the simple 42 ♖c8.

42 ♘xe6!

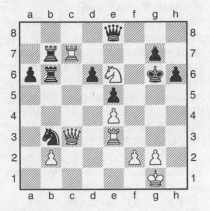

White's pieces seem to be hanging in mid-air, but they stay alive long enough to cause a total collapse on g7.

42...♔h7

Alternatively:

a) 42...♕xe6 43 ♖g3+ ♔h7 (or: 43...♔f6 44 ♕f3+; 43...♔h5 44

♕f3+ ♔h4 45 ♖gxg7 ♖xc7 46 g3+ ♔h3 47 ♕h1#) 44 ♖gxg7+ ♔h8 45 ♖h7+ ♔g8 46 ♕g3+ mating.

b) 42...♖xc7 43 ♖g3+ ♔f6 (or 43...♔h7 44 ♕xc7) 44 ♘xc7 and ♘d5+ will be devastating.

43 ♖g3 1-0

Black only has a choice of losing lines that we saw in the previous note.

21)

It looks that way: 16...fxg6 17 ♗xe6+ ♔h8 18 ♖xg6 ♘e5 19 ♖xg7 ♔xg7 20 ♖g1+ ♔h8 21 ♕h6 can now be met by 21...♗g5+ (check!) followed by 22...♗xe6 with a lot of extra material and without being checkmated.

22)

I hope you found **16...♕b6!**, as there aren't many other active moves for Black.

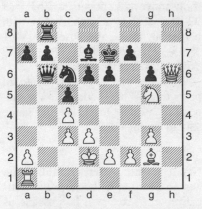

The problem is that at first it doesn't look like a major inconvenience for White; you need to have seen Black's follow-up idea – ...♘d4(+) – in addition to the obvious ...♕b2(+) – to assess the idea correctly.

a) 17 ♔c2? is obvious, but unexpectedly loses to 17...♘d4+! 18 cxd4 ♗a4+ 19 ♔c1 ♕b4 20 ♘e4 ♕a3+ 21 ♔d2 (21 ♔b1 b5 and Black's rook joins in the action, with decisive effect) 21...♕b2+ 22 ♔e3 ♕xd4+ and ...♕xa1 with a decisive material advantage.

b) 17 ♔c1 is also met by 17...♘d4!, although now this is now a draw rather than a win: 18 cxd4 ♕b4 19 ♘e4 ♕e1+ 20 ♔b2 ♕b4+ 21 ♔c1, etc.

c) 17 ♖c1 doesn't stop the idea either: 17...♘d4 18 cxd4 and now Black even has a choice:

c1) 18...♕b4+ 19 ♔e3 (forced) 19...♕b2 20 ♖e1 ♕xd4+ 21 ♔f3 ♕f6+ 22 ♔e3 ♕d4+ with a draw.

c2) 18...♕a5+ 19 ♔c2 (forced; 19 ♔e3? cxd4+ mates) 19...♕b4 (19...♗a4+? 20 ♔b1 b5 21 ♕g7 bxc4+ 22 ♔a1 ♗e8 23 ♘h7 gives White a decisive attack) 20 ♖b1 (only move) 20...♗a4+ 21 ♖b3 ♕a3 22 ♕g7 ♗xb3+ 23 axb3 ♕a2+ with perpetual check because 24 ♔c1 ♕a1+ 25 ♔d2 ♕b2+ 26 ♔e3?? ♕c1+ picks off the g5-knight.

Thus all the ways for White to parry the ...♕b2(+) idea allow a successful ...♘d4(+), and so the game should end in a draw.

23)

No, it wasn't. After **12...a5!** White has no good reply, because the tactical blow ...♘xc5 will be possible as soon as the c5-pawn loses its support from the b-pawn.
13 b5?!
13 ♗a3 exd4 forces 14 ♕xd4 ♗e5 15 ♕d2 axb4 16 ♗xb4, when White's position is looking a bit silly.

13 bxa5 is certainly not what White had in mind with his queenside advance, and not much of a bailout either: 13...exd4 (13...♗xa5 is very healthy for Black) 14 exd4 ♘xc5 15 a6 bxa6 16 ♗a3 is very similar to the game:

a) 16...♕e3+?! 17 ♔h1 ♘e6 (17...♗a5 18 ♖c1; 17...♘d3 18 ♕a4 ♔d7 19 ♖ad1 ♘f2+ 20 ♖xf2 ♕xf2 21 ♖c1) 18 ♕a4 gives White too much play against the stranded black king.

b) 16...♗d6 and Black keeps an extra pawn without too much drama.
13...exd4 14 exd4 ♘xc5
This is the main tactical point, and the reason why f3 was such a bad move. If you saw this, then you have basically solved the exercise.

15 bxc6
15 dxc5 ♕xc5+ exploits the loose knight on c3.
15...bxc6 16 ♗a3 ♗d6!
Simple and strong. Your analysis engine might scream out 16...♕e3+, but if you press it for a justification, it will come up empty-handed and quite soon start to become enthusiastic about White's chances following 17 ♔h1; e.g., 17...♘d3 (17...♘e6 18 ♕a4; 17...♕xc3 18 ♗xc5) 18 ♘xg6 (18 ♕a4 ♔d7 19 ♖ad1 ♘b4!?) 18...hxg6 (18...♘f2+ 19 ♖xf2 hxg6 20 ♖g2 ♕xc3 21 ♗c5) 19 ♕xd3 ♕h6 20 h4 ♗xg3 21 ♔g2.
17 ♕c1 ♘d3 18 ♗xd6 ♘xc1 19 ♗xe7 ♘xe2+ 20 ♘xe2 ♔xe7
and Black duly won with his extra pawn in the endgame.

24)

It was a bad idea, and loses material. After **19 ♗h6? ♖xf6 20 ♗xf8 ♖e8**

21 &g7 &xh8 22 &xh8 White is indeed skewering Black's pieces, but he never gets to enjoy the feast:

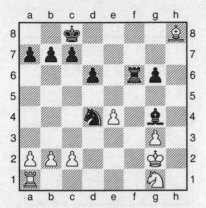

22...&xc2 23 &xf6

23 &c1? &e3+ (making good use of Black's control of the f-file) 24 &h1 &f7 and not only are the black pieces safe, but White loses a piece due to the threat on the h-file: 25 &c3 &h7+ 26 &h3 &xh3+ 27 &g1.

23...&xa1

Black is a pawn up with good winning chances, but the game was drawn in the end.

White should have played **19 &e3!** &xc2 (19...&xf6 20 &xd4 and now the skewer *does* win an exchange) 20 &xg4 &xe4 (20...&xa1 21 &xe5 dxe5 22 &h6 and now the back-rank pin *does* cost Black a piece) 21 &f1! (the key point: Black loses his grip on the f-file) 21...&xf1 (or 21...&xe3+ 22 &xe3 &xf1 23 &xf1) 22 &xf1 &xg4 23 &xf8+.

25)

The key feature is the a2-bishop's lack of squares, and White needs to cut off Black's way to support it. Seeing that 26 &a1? is well met by

26...axb5, we need to find a way to keep the a-file closed, and this is provided by **26 b6!**:

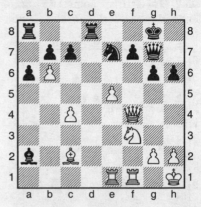

a) 26...&c6 27 &a1 &b4 28 bxc7 &dc8 and now 29 &d2 a5 (29...&xc4 30 &xb4 is similar) 30 &e4 &xc7 31 &xa2 &xa2 32 &xa2 is very good for White, since attempts by Black to coordinate his forces will be severely hampered by White's pressure on f7.

b) 26...cxb6 27 &a1 and the bishop is trapped. Black will have three pawns for the piece, but they are insufficiently mobile, and White's pieces will have too many weaknesses to target.

In the game, White blew his chance:

26 e6? f5 27 bxa6

Now 27 b6? fails to 27...cxb6 28 &a1 g5 and White can't defend c4.

27...&xa6 28 &xc7 &c8 29 &xb7 &xc4

and Black was OK.

26)

It is very easy to miss **31...&xg2+!** because White can simply reply 32 &xg2. However, White then has no reply to 32...♕c6! (it must be to precisely this square, because 32...♕b7?? loses to 33 ♘e4) 33 ♘e4 ♕c1+ 34 ♔h2 ♕f4+! (the point) 35 ♕xf4 ♖xg2+ 36 ♔h1 ♖g1+ 37 ♔h2 ♖8g2#.

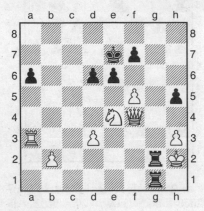

Nice idea, isn't it?

32 ♔h2 avoids this immediate collapse, but gives Black a number of very good options, including 32...♕c6 33 fxe6 (33 ♘e4? ♕c2) 33...f6 34 ♕a4 ♕xa4 35 ♖xa4 ♗f3.

27)
25...♖c5!

Threatening 26...♘xf3 27 gxf3 ♕xf3+, when 28 ♗e2 would allow 28...♖g1#, now that the white queen isn't covering this square.

26 ♗e2

26 ♖xe6 (getting rid of the rook, which is rather loose on h6, and eliminating the useful black bishop) 26...fxe6 27 ♕xb7 ♘xf3 28 gxf3 ♕xf3+ 29 ♔e1 and if nothing else, Black can take a draw by perpetual check.

26...♗c4?!

This is based on a nice idea, but might not be best. 26...♕xg2? loses to 27 ♗b5+ ♖xb5 28 ♖xg2 ♖xb6 29

♖xg8+, but 26...♗d7! is again a line-blocking idea, this time with the point that White playing ♗b5 won't be check.

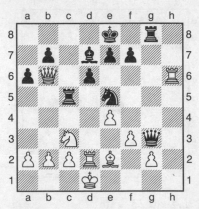

This shows up after 27 ♕xb7 ♕xg2, when the black queen is safe. After 28 ♔c1 ♘xf3 29 ♗xf3 ♕xf3 Black has at least enough play, including threats against the loose h6-rook as well as the white king.

27 ♕xb7 ♘xf3! 28 ♗xf3 ♕xf3+! 29 ♔c1

Not 29 gxf3?? ♖g1#.

29...♕f1+ 30 ♘d1

30 ♖d1 ♕f4+ 31 ♔b1 ♕xh6 32 ♕b8+ ♔d7 33 ♕xg8 also favours White.

30...♗e6 31 e5 ♕f4 32 exd6 exd6 33 ♕b8+ ♔d7 34 ♕a7+ ♔e8 35 ♖h1 ♖d5

Now 36 ♕e3 would have kept White's extra pawn.

28)

If you said **24 g5!**, and that you are winning, well done. The game ended within a few moves:

24...♔h8

The critical point is that 24...fxg5 loses to 25 ♕h5! (after 25 ♗e5+?

♗f6 White gets nowhere) 25...♖f8
(25...gxf4 26 ♖xe7+ ♕xe7 27 ♖g1+)
26 ♗e5+ ♗f6 27 ♕xg5+ ♔h8 28
♘g6+, etc.

25 ♕h5 ♖g8 26 ♗xg8 ♔xg8

White has a wide choice of ways to
win here. Typically, Ivanchuk finds
the neatest way, which leads quickly
to a forced mate.

**27 g6 ♗c6+ 28 ♖e4 ♗xe4+ 29 dxe4
hxg6 30 ♕xg6+ ♔h8 31 ♕h5+ 1-0**

29)

**44...♗xg3+! 45 fxg3 ♕f1 46 ♖g2
♖f2!.**

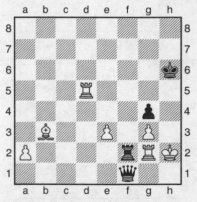

The point is really to gain time for
the rook to slip in via the h-file: 47
♖d6+ (47 ♖xf2 ♕xf2+ 48 ♔h1
♕f1+ 49 ♔h2 ♕h3+ 50 ♔g1 ♕xg3+
and the g-pawn will win) 47...♔g5
48 ♗d5 and now the advertised
switch to the h-file: 48...♖f8! and
...♖h8+, winning.

We should take a look at the game
continuation to see why Black did
actually need to be accurate, and find
a concrete winning idea, if not immediately then before White has
been able to erect a solid defensive
wall:

44...♗d6 45 ♖cd2 ♗b4

45...♗xg3+ again wins.

**46 ♗d1 ♕e4 47 ♖5d4 ♕b1 48 ♖c2
♗a5 49 ♔g2 ♗b6 50 ♖d3 ♕b5 51
♖cd2 ♕b4 52 ♔g1 ♗a5 53 ♖c2
♕b5 54 ♖d4 ♗b6 55 ♖dc4 ♕b1 56
♖c1 ♕xa2 57 ♖1c2 ♕a5 58 ♖c6
♖xc6 59 ♖xc6+ ♔g5 60 ♖e6**

60 ♖d6 is met by the nice geometric
idea 60...♗e3 61 fxe3 ♕e5.

60...♗c7 61 ♗e2 ♕a2

61...♗xg3! 62 fxg3 ♕a2 and now
White has nothing resembling a fortress. After Black's actual choice, the
position is becoming very marginal.

**62 ♖e7 ♗xg3 63 ♖g7+ ♔f6 64 ♖xg4
♗e5**

64...♕xe2 65 ♖xg3 is a clear draw –
and would be even without the e3-
pawn.

65 ♗f3

and White had a fortress (or at least a
quasi-fortress) that Black failed to
break down before the 50-move rule
kicked in.

30)

No, White never has time to play his
trump-cards, and the obvious capture
28...♘xf4 is winning for Black: **29
♖d2** (29 ♕xg5 ♘xe2+ 30 ♔h1
♘xc3 is terminal) **29...♘xe2+ 30
♖exe2 ♕c1+ 31 ♔f2 ♕xd2** (not the
only winning move, but a very clear-
cut one; not 31...♗h4?? 32 ♕xh4
♕xd2 {32...♖xh4 33 ♖xe8#} 33
♕xe4) **32 ♖xd2 ♗h4 0-1**.

31)

No, **25 e5??** loses: **25...♗xg2 26
exd6 ♕xd6!** (Black walks into a pin,
but White cannot exploit it – this is
the key point that I wanted you to
find, as it is conceptually hard but

analytically simple; 26...♗xd6? is much worse, although after 27 ♗a3 ♖d8 28 ♕xd6+ ♕xd6 29 ♖xd6+ ♚c7 30 ♖xd8 ♚xd8 31 ♗xf8 Black should hold the draw thanks to the opposite-coloured bishops) **27 ♕xf4 ♗d5 28 ♕g4 f6 0-1**.

There are various other ways for White to play, none of them devastating, but **25 f6** looks the healthiest: 25...♗d8 26 ♗h3+ (26 ♗e5 ♚e8 27 ♗xd6 ♕a5 is another line where Black's defences are just about holding White at bay) 26...♘e6 (after 26...♚e8 27 ♗f5, preventing ...♘g6 ideas, it is hard for Black to free his game versus White's slightly slower attacking plans) 27 ♗e5 ♗xe4 28 ♗xd6 ♕xc2+ 29 ♕xc2 ♗xc2 30 ♚xc2 ♗xf6 31 ♗xf4+ and White should have the better side of a likely draw. 25 ♕xf4 is also possible, but less forcing.

32)
He shouldn't take it at all. In the game he chose **21...♗xg4?** and lost as follows:
22 ♖xf7
White has mating threats with both ♖f8+ and ♕b3. Black lacks any good defence.
22...♗g5
22...♗f6 is the most resilient defence, but will not save Black. The problemists among you might have spotted 22...♗f3, which prevents both threats by intersecting both critical lines. This doesn't save Black here (White hasn't sacrificed so much that the mere act of avoiding mate is enough in itself!), but an ability to spot defences like this can save or even win games.

23 ♕b3!
23 ♗xg5 ♗e6 defends.
1-0
The main point is 23...♗e6 24 ♕xe6! ♖xe6 25 ♖f8+ ♖xf8 26 ♖xf8#.

So what should Black have played? 21...♕xg4? also loses: 22 ♕xe5 f6 23 ♖xf6 and White mates; e.g., 23...♗f7 24 ♕xe8+ ♗xe8 25 ♖f8#.

21...♗c4 looks like the best defence, although **21...f6** is possible too.

33)
18...h5!

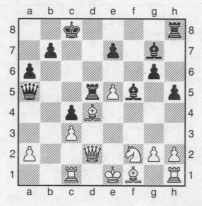

This looks at first sight too slow for a blood-and-guts position, but the idea of ...♗h6 is impossible to parry and highlights all the defective aspects of White's position (vulnerable pieces on c1 and d2, pin on the a5-e1 diagonal, exposed white king). His pieces must flee like ants from the floodwaters, but they have nowhere good to run.
19 g4
Or:
  a) 19 ♖a1 ♗h6 20 ♕d1 ♖hd8 and a disaster on d4 follows.

b) 19 ♗xc4 ♗h6 20 ♕d1 ♖xd4 21 ♕xd4 ♖d8 22 ♗d5 and White will manage to castle, but he will have lost too much of his army in the process.

c) 19 ♖d1 ♗h6 20 ♕e2 (20 ♕b2 is the only way to protect c3, but 20...♖hd8 adds another attacker, causing a total collapse) 20...♖xd4 21 ♖xd4 ♕xc3+ 22 ♖d2 ♗xd2+ (22...♖d8?? 23 ♕xc4+) 23 ♕xd2 ♕xe5+ 24 ♗e2 (or 24 ♕e2? ♕a5+ and now 25 ♕d2 c3 or 25 ♔d1 ♖d8+) 24...c3 25 ♕c1 ♖d8 26 ♘d1 c2 and now 27 0-0 is the move White would like to play, but it allows 27...♕xe2. Instead, 27 ♘e3 ♕c3+ 28 ♔f2 ♗e4 29 ♖e1 ♖d2 leaves White hopelessly tied up.

19...hxg4

There will be no escaping the ...♗h6 idea.

20 ♖d1 ♗h6 21 ♕b2 ♖hd8 22 ♗g2

White's g-pawn has bought him this extra idea, but it doesn't help.

22...♖b5 23 ♕a1 ♖xd4 24 ♖xd4 ♖b1+ 25 ♕xb1 ♕xc3+!

25...♗xb1? 26 ♖xc4+ ♔b8 27 0-0 allows White to fight on.

26 ♔e2 ♗xb1 27 ♗xb7+ ♔c7 0-1

34)

Let's see the game first:

15...♗f6?

Either Black saw no solution, or his sense of danger had malfunctioned. When a strong player has apparently allowed a very strong move, it pays to be a little suspicious. That's not to say you should allow yourself to be bluffed though; if you're sure the opponent has blundered, then take advantage!

16 ♗g5!

Ouch! A nice geometrical move.

16...♗xg5 17 ♖xg5

Now White has a strong attack.

17...f6 18 ♖g7 ♔f8 19 ♖xb7 ♗c6 20 ♖b4 ♔f7 21 ♕d3 e5 22 ♖f1 d4 23 cxd4 ♕d5 24 f3 ♖ag8

Black has drummed up some activity, but it is insufficient.

25 ♘d2 a5 26 ♖b6 gxf3 27 ♘xf3 e4 28 ♘e5+ ♔e8 29 ♖b8+ ♔e7 30 ♘xc6+ ♕xc6 31 ♕b5 ♕d5 32 ♖b7+ ♔d8 33 ♕xa5+ 1-0

So did Black have a way out? Yes, **15...♕d7!** is best.

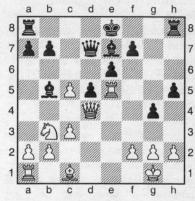

This is because 16 ♖xd5 (16 ♖xe6?? ♕xe6 17 ♕xh8+ ♔d7) 16...♕xd5 17 ♕xh8+ ♗f8 (17...♔d7 is also possible) leaves White dealing with a mate threat on d1, and some ideas coming up against g2 too. 18 ♕d4 (18 ♗h6? 0-0-0! and Black wins: 19 ♗xf8 ♕d1+ 20 ♖xd1 ♖xd1# or 19 ♘d4 ♗c6 20 f3 ♗xc5) 18...0-0-0 19 ♕xd5 ♖xd5 is completely OK for Black.

35)

25 ♕b2! threatens ♖d7, based on the possible mate on g7. Black has no good response to this; e.g.:

a) 25...♕f8 leaves the f6-knight undefended, and so fails to 26 ♖xb4 axb4 27 ♕xf6.

b) 25...♘g4 exposes g7 and also loses to 26 ♖xb4.

c) 25...♖ad8 26 ♖d7 ♖xd7 (or 26...♘h5 27 ♖xe7 ♖xd1+ 28 ♔h2 ♖xe7 29 g4) 27 ♖xd7 ♕xd7 28 ♕xf6 ♔f8 29 ♘g5 ♖d8 30 ♗h3 annihilates Black's defences.

36)
48 ♔c3!
White activates his king, seeking to enter Black's position via d6.
48...♔f7
The black king rushes over to deny access to his white counterpart. 48...♖xe3+ 49 ♔b4 ♖e7 50 ♔c5 ♔f7 51 ♔d6 is clearly hopeless for Black.
49 ♔b4 ♖d7 50 ♔c5 ♔e7
What now?
51 ♖xb7!
Of course! Black is so short of space that even with an extra rook he cannot defend his position once White has a passed b-pawn. 51 ♖h8 ♔f7 52 ♖h7+ ♔e6 53 ♖xd7 ♔xd7 is just a drawn pawn ending.
1-0
51...♖xb7 52 ♔xc6 ♖b8 53 ♔c7 ♖d8 54 b7 ♖d7+ 55 ♔b6 ♖d8 56 ♔a7 ♔d6 57 b8♕+ ♖xb8 58 ♔xb8 ♔c6 (or 58...b4 59 ♔b7) 59 b4 is clearly hopeless for Black.

37)
Play continued **18...e4! 19 ♘xa8**, but now Black went astray with 19...exd3? 20 ♕xd3 ♗e6 21 ♕e4 ♕c5+ 22 ♔h1 ♗e5 23 g3! and the game had become highly messy. Instead, the natural **19...♗d4+!** is devastating:

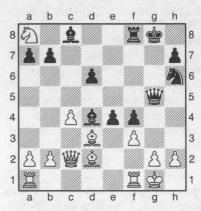

a) 20 ♖f2 gives Black many good options, including 20...♗h3 21 ♔h1 (21 ♗f1 ♗xf2+ 22 ♔xf2 e3+ 23 ♔g1 e2) 21...♗xf2.

b) 20 ♔h1 ♘f5! and the threat of 21...♘g3+ 22 hxg3 ♕h5# is decisive. Even 21 ♗e1 is no defence: 21...♘g3+! (21...♘e3 is also good, but Black should be going for the jugular here) 22 ♗xg3 fxg3 23 h3 ♕h4 and ...♗xh3.

38)
44 f6+! is a clear win:

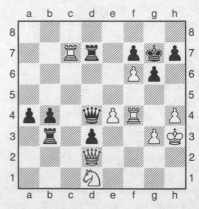

a) 44...♔f8 45 ♕e3! (this move overloads the black queen) 45...♕d6

(45...♕xe3 46 ♖c8+ ♖d8 47 ♖xd8#) 46 ♖c8+ ♖d8 47 ♕c5.

b) 44...♔g8 45 e5 ♕d5 transposes to the game, with 46 ♖d4! winning.

White also had some strong possibilities later in the quoted sequence of moves, which you may have spotted:

44 e5?! ♕d5 45 f6+ ♔g8?!

45...♔f8 is more resilient, though White is still winning.

46 ♖c8+?!

46 ♖d4! wins on the spot, as Black faces mate on g7 or his back rank no matter what he does: 46...♕h1+ (46...♕xd4 47 ♕h6; 46...♕e6+ 47 ♔g2! ♖xd4 48 ♕h6) 47 ♕h2! ♕f1+ 48 ♕g2.

46...♖d8 47 ♖xd8+ ♕xd8 48 e6?

48 ♖c4, threatening ♕h6, wins: 48...♕f8 (48...♕a8 49 ♕h6 ♕h1+ 50 ♔g4 ♕xd1+ 51 ♔g5 ♕d2+ 52 ♖f4) 49 ♕c1 intending ♖c8.

48...♕c8

and White only won after a messy struggle in which Black went astray.

39)
14 ♘d5!

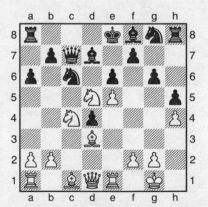

Sacrifices on empty squares can be notoriously hard to spot, even when the calculation needed to support them is well within our capabilities. The problem is that the move simply doesn't come onto our "radar". With a black pawn on d5, the sacrifice would be much easier to spot.

14...♕b8

The main point is that 14...exd5 is crushed by 15 ♘d6+:

a) 15...♗xd6?? 16 exd6+ opens up an attack on the black queen.

b) 15...♔e7 loses to 16 ♗g5+ f6 (16...♔e6 17 ♕f3 f6 and the funniest of many wins is 18 ♗f5+!? ♔e7 19 exf6++ ♔d8 20 ♖e8+ ♗xe8 21 f7+) 17 exf6++ ♔xd6 18 ♗f4+.

c) 15...♔d8 16 ♘xf7+ ♔c8 17 ♘xh8 is winning for White because there is not even any question of the knight failing to escape from the corner.

15 ♘db6 ♖a7 16 ♗g5

White has a wonderful position, whereas Black is virtually paralysed. The end was mercifully swift:

16...♘h6 17 ♕f3 ♖h7 18 ♖ad1 ♘g4 19 ♕f4 ♗c5 20 f3 ♘e3 1-0

Black resigned without waiting for White to choose among the many ways to win.

40)
91 ♗c6!

White creates the threat of ♖f7+, while the bishop proves untouchable: 91...♖xc6 is met by 92 ♖f7+ ♔d6 93 ♖f6+.

91...♖d2 92 ♖f7+ ♔b8 93 a7+! ♗xa7 94 ♖b7+ 1-0

Black loses his bishop since 94...♔a8 allows 95 ♖b6#.

41)
Yes, it does matter.

28...♖b4?

28...♖b8! is far better, as 29 ♖xe5? now loses to 29...♖xb3, while White must also avoid 29 ♖a5? ♕xb3 30 ♕xb3 ♖xb3 31 ♖a7 ♘c5. Therefore 29 ♖d3 looks best, when one possibility is 29...♘c5!? 30 d7 ♘xb3+ (not 30...♖xb3? 31 d8♕+ ♔h7 32 ♕xe5 ♘xd3+ 33 ♕xd3+ ♖xd3 34 ♕f5+ and White mates; 30...♘xd7 31 ♖c3 looks more comfortable for White) 31 ♖xb3 ♕a1+ 32 ♔d2 ♖d8 33 ♖d3 ♕xb2 and the outcome is not yet decided.

29 ♖xe5 ♘xe5

29...♖xb3?! 30 ♖e8+ ♔h7 and the difference is that White now has 31 ♕e4+ g6 32 ♖xc8, winning.

30 ♕xe5 ♖bb8?!

This effectively squanders a piece, but 30...♖xb3 31 d7 ♕a1+ 32 ♔d2 ♖bb8 33 dxc8♕+ ♖xc8 isn't exactly attractive for Black.

31 d7 ♖d8 32 ♕xb8! ♖xb8 33 ♖e8+ ♔h7 34 ♖xb8 1-0

42)

No, it was not correct, and probably one or both players were in time-trouble. **33...♖xe4?** is a mistake, and should lose (33...♕c7 is better). Possibly this was a "calculated risk" in White's time-trouble, but Black's position isn't desperate enough to justify this.

34 fxg6+ fxg6 35 ♕f7+ ♔h8

35...♗g7? allows 36 ♖dxh5+ gxh5 37 ♖xh5#.

36 ♕f6+ ♔h7 37 ♕f7+?!

37 ♖g3! is the winning move. White threatens mate in two, so I hope this move came onto your "radar"! At the board, one might be instinctively concerned by Black's possible checks, but they come to nothing at all.

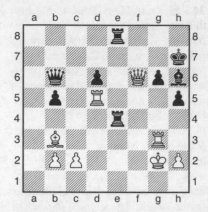

a) 37...♖e2+ 38 ♔h3 and any further checks will come at a large cost in material.

b) 37...♖g8 38 ♖xd6 is a massacre, as White has threats everywhere.

c) 37...♖4e6 38 ♕f7+ ♔h8 39 ♖xh5 gxh5 40 ♗xe6 and Black is defenceless.

d) 37...♖8e6 38 ♕f7+ ♔h8 (or 38...♗g7 39 ♖xh5+) 39 ♖xh5 is no improvement.

e) The main point is that 37...♖g4 leaves the e8-rook unprotected, so 38 ♕f7+ ♗g7 39 ♕xe8 is a simple win.

37...♔h8 38 ♕f6+ ½-½?

43)

First off, we need to identify what Black is threatening. ...b4 is in fact a more dangerous idea than the obvious ...♗xa3, but White need not allow either, of course. **34 ♖b1** is a safe move; e.g., 34...♔d7 (34...♗xa3 35 ♗xa3+ ♖xa3 36 ♖xb5 ♖a2+ 37 ♔f1 isn't a major problem for White; 34...b4 35 axb4 ♖xb4 36 ♔d2 and White is in plenty to time to defend against the ...♗e5 idea) 35 ♗c1 ♔c6 36 ♖b3 leaves Black slightly more active, but White's position is solid.

34 ♖a1 is a passive defence, but even this isn't bad since Black has no very pressing threats. White will need to reactivate his rook soon though, probably after bringing his king to b3. Instead, the game continued:

34 ♖c3?

If you have only seen one of Black's threats – ...♗xa3 – this active move seems ideal, as ♖b3 follows. But...

34...b4!

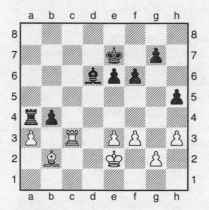

35 ♖c4

35 axb4 ♖a2 36 ♖c2 ♗e5 costs White a piece, while after 35 ♖b3 bxa3 36 ♗a1 Black's extra pawn is too strong for White even to mount a sturdy blockade: 36...♗e5 37 ♗xe5 fxe5 38 ♖b1 a2 39 ♖a1 and Black wins as if it were a pawn ending with an infinite supply of reserve tempi, as White will never have time to bring his king over to round up the a2-pawn without allowing a decisive penetration by the black king.

35...♖a8 0-1

36 a4 ♖xa4 is dismal for White, while his other options are the same as in the previous note. White's resignation was arguably a touch premature, but quite understandable.

44)

No, it certainly wasn't, and Black has a choice of immediate wins, one of them particularly striking. White's pieces are hopelessly overworked.

28...♗d6?!

This wins, so the marking is harsh, but it is a shame to miss 28...♖f4!!.

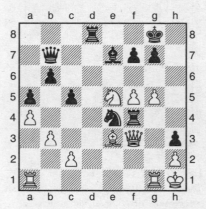

Mate follows after 29 ♕xf4 ♘f2# or 29 ♗xf4 ♘f2#.

29 ♖ad1

29 ♘g4 unprotects the queen and so allows 29...♘f2+, winning the queen and mating. 29 ♗f4 allows the immediate 29...♘f2#.

29...♖e8

This move wins neatly, by emphasizing the fact that White's knight is overloaded. Of course, we know that 29...♖f4! is still possible.

30 ♖xd6 ♘xd6 0-1

White is a whole exchange down with negative compensation.

45)

27...♖fe8!

Black has various other promising options, but this cuts to the heart of the matter, as the rook breaks into White's position by force.

28 ♕f2 ♗xd2 29 ♕xd2
29 ♖xd2 ♕b3 is hopeless for White, as ...♘c3+ is threatened and 30 ♖c2 ♘b4 is a wipe-out.

29...♖e2!

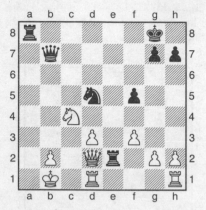

This is the point. The rook is defended tactically, so all Black's pieces will now be in the attack.

30 ♕c1 ♕b3 0-1

After 31 ♖d2 ♘b4 White's king will be mated in his bed.

46)

I hope you would have considered **20 ♘xb5!**, as it is good for White and risks nothing:

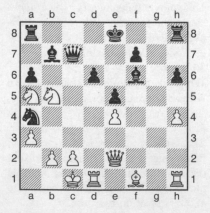

a) 20...♖xa5 21 ♘xd6+ ♔f8 22 ♕c4 (22 ♕f2 is also possible) 22...♖h7 23 ♘xb7 is very good for White.

b) 20...axb5 21 ♕xb5+ ♔e7 (21...♔f8 22 ♘xb7 and now Black's best appears to be 22...♘c3 {desperado} 23 bxc3 ♖b8, but this will leave him two pawns down and relying on White's pawn weaknesses and the opposite bishops to provide some hope of salvation) 22 ♕xb7 ♕xb7 23 ♘xb7 and it is clear that Black is struggling; e.g.:

b1) 23...♖hb8 24 ♘xd6 ♘xb2 (or 24...♖xb2 25 ♗c4 ♖b6 26 ♘f5+) 25 ♘f5+ allows White to whip up an attack.

b2) 23...♘xb2 24 ♖d5! ♘a4 (24...♖hb8 25 ♘xd6 ♖xa3 26 ♘b5) 25 ♖h3 ♖hg8 26 ♘xd6 ♖g1 27 ♖f3 with continuing problems for Black.

47)

It is almost a general principle that if a pawn-break can be made on a heavily fortified square, it will damage the opponent's position more than one made against a softer target. On that basis, the d5 thrust would be preferred over the e5 advance in this structure. But normally in these Slav positions, d5 is so well fortified that d5 can't be forced through without a number of additional tactical justifications. Black's peculiar development provides a clue that we should be adopting the maximalist approach here.

And indeed, **15 d5!** is very strong:

a) 15...cxd5 16 exd5 only brings White's e1-rook into the assault on e6, as Black does not have enough support for the ...e5 advance (what is that knight still doing on b8?!).

b) 15...exd5 fails to 16 ♘xd5!, taking advantage of the loose bishop on b4.

c) 15...e5 fails because of Black's inadequate control over b4 *and* e5: 16 ♘xe5 ♕xe5 (16...♗xc3 17 ♗xc3) 17 ♕xb4.

d) 15...♗xc3 16 ♗xc3 ♘xe4 (consistent, at least) 17 dxe6 fxe6 and now, rather than simply recapturing with the bishop on e6, 18 ♘d4! is very strong, as after ♘xe6, the g7-pawn comes under attack. Black will not survive this storm.

In the game, White chose the stereotyped **15 e5?!** either through not considering the other advance, or missing a tactical point. After **15...♘fd7 16 ♘e4 ♗xd2 17 ♘fxd2 c5 18 dxc5 ♘xc5 19 ♘xc5 bxc5** White couldn't claim a structural advantage (it often happens in the Slav main lines that a- and c-pawns for Black are no weaker than White's a4- and b2-pawns, which are technically one pawn-island, but behave more like split pawns), and couldn't make his extra mobility count. A draw soon resulted: **20 ♕f3 ♘d7 21 ♗b5 ♘b6 22 ♘e4 ♗xe4 23 ♕xe4 ½-½.**

48)
The game continued with **25...♖d6?**, which is an adequate defence against the mating threats as it grants the king f8 as a flight-square, but allows White to escape with a draw by 26 ♕h6! ♕xc5+ 27 ♔h1. Black's only way to avoid mate on g7 is now 27...♖xf6, when White salvages a perpetual check with the well-known mechanism 28 ♗h7+ ♔h8 29 ♗g6+ ♔g8 30 ♗h7+, etc. However, White

missed his chance, and after **26 h3?** (26 ♕g5+? ♔f8 also gives White nothing) **26...♖xf6 27 hxg4 e4 28 ♗xe4 ♕e5** Black won shortly.

But there is a way out. **25...e4!** provides a defence against both queen moves.

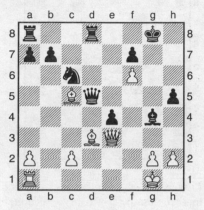

The black queen now covers g5, so 26 ♕h6 is the only try, but this fails to 26...♕xc5+ 27 ♔h1 ♕f8 now that White's access to h7 has been blocked off for one critical moment. If White tries to play more slowly by 26 ♗xe4, then 26...♕d2 is convincing enough, with 27 ♕g3 ♘d4 28 ♔h1 ♖ac8 29 ♗xa7 ♕c3 one way to rule out any accidents.

49)
First the two demolition sacrifices: **46 ♖xc6+! ♔xc6 47 ♗xd5+! ♔c7** 47...♔xd5? allows 48 ♕h1#, so White is only sacrificing an exchange to blast open a path to Black's king. I hope you saw this far. But Black has serious counterplay on the queenside, so White must find the most accurate way to launch his queen into the battle.
48 ♕f1?!

This move, as played in the game, lets Black off the hook. **48 ♕h1!** is best, as the queen can come into play with check on either the h-file or the long diagonal in some key variations.

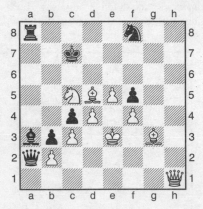

If you had an intuitive feeling that this was the right square, well done. Here are some variations to back it up: 48...♕xb2 (48...♗xc5? now fails to 49 ♗xa8, when ♕b7+ is a threat) 49 ♕h6! leaves Black defenceless: 49...♕xc3+ 50 ♔e2! ♕c2+ 51 ♔f3 ♕d1+ 52 ♔g2 ♕e2+ 53 ♔g1 ♕d1+ 54 ♔h2 ♕e2+ 55 ♗g2 ♘g6 56 ♕g7+ (56 ♕xg6?? ♖h8+ draws) 56...♔b6 57 ♕b7+ ♔a5 58 ♕xa8+ ♔b4 59 ♕a4+ ♔c3 60 ♕xa3.

48...♗xc5

48...♕xb2? 49 ♕xc4 shows a positive side of the queen's placement on f1.

49 ♕xc4 ♖a5! 50 dxc5

White's last winning try might be 50 ♕xb3 ♕xb3 51 ♗xb3, when White's swathe of pawns might give Black some anxious moments, despite his extra rook.

50...♕xb2 51 ♕xb3 ♕xb3 52 ♗xb3 ♖a3 53 ♗c4 ♖xc3+ 54 ♗d3 ♘e6 55 ♔d2 ♖a3 56 ♗f2 ♘xf4 57 ♗xf5 ♖f3 ½-½

50)

It's the pin on the a3-f8 diagonal that matters most! After **56...♕c5!** it turns out that White has no advantage.

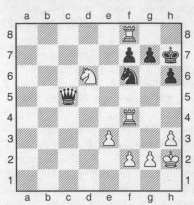

57 ♖xf6 gxf6 58 ♖xf7+ ♔g8 59 ♖d7 gives White nothing, while the attempt to take a step back and regroup by 57 ♖d4 is disrupted by 57...♘d5! 58 ♖d8 ♕c7!.

In the game, Black instead played **56...♕c7??**, but this alluring move, seeking to exploit the pin on the b8-h2 diagonal, has a fatal tactical flaw: **57 ♖xf6!**

Not: 57 ♘xf7? ♘d5; 57 ♖xf7? ♕xd6 and 58 ♖4xf6 is illegal; 57 ♘c4? ♘d5 58 ♖8xf7 ♕b8.

1-0

Black resigned seeing that 57...gxf6 58 ♖xf7+ costs him his queen.

51)

11 e4! is an excellent move. It's also a typical and thematic idea that anyone who plays this structure (especially as Black!) needs to be aware of.

11...fxe4

11...dxe4? 12 ♕xe6+ is obviously no good for Black.

12 ♘g5!

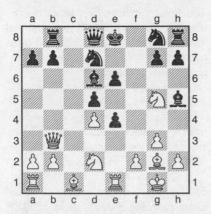

12...♗f7

On the face of it, this looks relatively solid, so it is again a bit surprising that White has more than one way to come out well on top. 12...♘xg5 13 ♘xe4 ♕e7 14 ♘xd6+ ♕xd6 15 ♗f4 and Black's position disintegrates; e.g., 15...♕b6 (15...♕e7 16 ♗xb8 ♘xb8 17 ♗xd5 ♗f7 18 ♗xe6) 16 ♕xd5 ♗f7 17 ♗xb8 ♘xb8 18 ♕e5 ♕d8 (18...♘d7 19 ♕xg7) 19 d5. It's surprising that these lines turn out *quite* so badly for Black.

13 ♗xe4

13 ♘xf7 ♔xf7 14 ♗xe4 dxe4?! 15 ♘xe4 ♗e7 16 ♘d6+ (or 16 ♗f4) is also very good for White.

13...♕xg5

13...dxe4?! 14 ♘dxe4 ♗e7 15 ♘xf7 ♔xf7 is a line we have already seen via 13 ♘xf7.

14 ♗xd5 ♔f8 15 ♗xe6 ♖e8?! 16 ♘e4 ♗xe6 17 ♘xd6 ♕e7

17...♗xb3 allows 18 ♖xe8#.

18 ♕f3+ ♘gf6 19 ♘xe8 ♔xe8 20 ♗d2

White has rook and two pawns for two pieces together with far better coordination and is in complete control. Black now blundered, but this just saved him some suffering.

20...♘b6? 21 ♖xe6 ♕xe6 22 ♖e1 ♕xe1+ 23 ♗xe1 ♘bd5 24 ♕b3 1-0

Complex Puzzles

52)

Yes and no. Yes, because White *did* go on to win the game, but no because **29...♕f2!** leaves White in trouble:

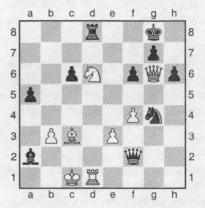

a) 30 ♕xg4 ♗xb3 31 ♖d2 ♕f1+ 32 ♔b2 ♖b8 gives Black a devastating counterattack – this is a key line.

b) 30 ♘e8 ♖xd1+ 31 ♔xd1 ♗xb3+ 32 ♔c1 ♔f8 and Black comes out on top; e.g., 33 ♕xg7+ ♔xe8 and White's checks run out quickly, or 33 ♘d6 ♕xe3+ 34 ♔b2 ♘f2!? 35 ♔xb3 ♕e6+ 36 ♘c4 a4+ 37 ♔b4 ♘e4 with too many threats.

c) 30 ♖d2 ♕xe3 31 ♕xg7+ (31 ♔b2 ♗xb3 32 ♔xb3 ♖b8+ 33 ♔c2 ♕g1! 34 ♕f7+ ♔h7 35 ♕a2 ♘e3+ 36 ♔d3 ♘d5 with a strong attack, not to mention the four pawns for the piece) 31...♔xg7 32 ♘f5+ ♔g6 33 ♘xe3 ♖xd2 and Black will win, opposite bishops notwithstanding.

Let's see the game continuation: **29 b3? ♗xb3? 30 ♖g1! ♖xd6?**

30...♕f2 31 ♖xg4 is now good for White (in the analogous line after 29 ♖g1, Black would have had the deadly ...♕f1+ followed by ...♖xd6+ or ...♗b1+). However, this was Black's best try, as 31...♖d7 32 ♕e8+ ♔h7 33 ♕e4+ ♔h8 34 ♖g2 ♕f1+ 35 ♔b2 is not completely clear-cut.

31 ♖xg4 ♕h1+ 32 ♔b2 ♔f8 33 ♖g1 ♕f3 34 ♕xg7+ ♔e8 35 ♔xb3 ♕d5+ 36 ♔b2 1-0

53)

Often it pays to have an eye on both defence *and* attack. In the game, White sought to defend by direct means with **25 b3?** but after **25...♕a3 26 ♕d4 ♖a5** he had a problem as 27 ♕b2? fails because 27...♕xb2+ 28 ♔xb2 ♖xe5! 29 fxe5 ♗xe5+ is very good for Black. He therefore chose **27 ♖e1 ♖d8 28 ♕b2** (28 d6 ♖xd6 forces 29 ♕b2 anyway) **28...♕xb2+ 29 ♔xb2 ♖axd5 30 ♖ed1 ♖xd3 31 ♖xd3 ♖e8 32 ♖d5 g5** and Black was no worse in the ending.

Things would have been different if he had chosen the apparently empty attacking gesture **25 ♕a7!**.

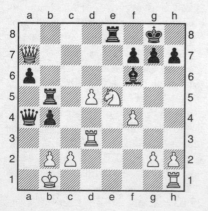

The threat against f7 cannot be ignored, and Black's only ways to attend to it mean that White can then return to defensive measures in improved circumstances:

a) 25...♖a5?? is mated by 26 ♕xf7+ ♔h8 27 ♘g6+! hxg6 28 ♖h3+.

b) 25...♗e7? removes the bishop from its attacking duties, and fails to, amongst other things, 26 b3 ♕a3 27 ♘c4 (now that ...♕a1# is impossible).

c) 25...♗xe5? 26 ♕d7! (an important point: White creates a threat while parrying Black's deadly ...♖a5 idea; 26 fxe5?? loses to 26...♖a5) 26...♖a5 27 ♕xa4 ♖xa4 28 fxe5 and Black can't recapture because of 28...♖xe5? 29 d6 ♖e8 30 d7 ♖d8 31 ♖e1 ♔f8 32 ♖de3, when Black's back rank costs him the game.

d) Therefore 25...♖f8 appears to be forced, but this removes the rook from its active post and so leaves Black a vital tempo down compared to the game continuation: 26 b3 (26 ♕d7 is possible, but maybe messier after 26...b3 27 ♖xb3 ♕xf4) 26...♕a3 (Black can play 26...♖a5, but where is his counterattack then?) 27 ♕d4 and now White is in time to meet 27...♖a5 by 28 ♕b2, unlike in the game, while neither 27...♖d8 28 ♖hd1 nor 27...♖e8 28 ♖e1 changes the basic picture. Therefore Black's counterplay lacks potency, and White can seek to exploit his extra d-pawn.

54)

White is right to play for the attack. After 35 ♘xg6 ♘xa3?, **36 ♕xf5!** wins, as Black is mated after **36...♕xd1+ 37 ♔h2 ♘xb5**. The game ended 38 ♕e6+ ♔h7 39 ♘xf8+ ♖xf8 40 ♕h6+ 1-0, but 38

♘e7+ is an alternative, and slightly quicker, mate: 38...♗xe7 39 ♕g6+ ♔f8 (39...♔h8 40 ♗e5+) 40 ♗h6#.

The computer-assisted analysts among you will no doubt have focused on the following two moves, and hopefully come to the conclusion that White wins after the former, and is (at least) a lot better in case of the latter:

a) **35...♖c6?** 36 ♘xf8 ♘xa3 (36...♖xf8 37 ♖xd5) 37 ♕xf5 ♕xd1+ 38 ♔h2 ♕c2 (38...♘xb5 39 ♘e6! and 38...♖xf8 39 ♕g5+ are also winning for White) 39 ♕g5+ ♔f7 40 ♖b2!? (a nice desperado to draw the black queen out of position) 40...♕xb2 41 ♕xd8 ♕c2 42 ♗g5 ♕f5 43 ♘d7 and White wins; e.g., 43...♘c4 44 ♕f8+ ♔g6 45 ♕g8+ ♔h5 46 ♗f6!? ♖xf6 47 g4+.

b) **35...♗xa3** 36 ♕xf5!? (the simpler 36 ♘h4 is also very strong) and now:

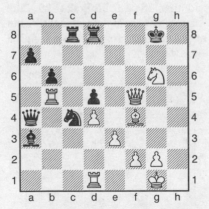

b1) 36...♕xb5? 37 ♕e6+ ♔g7 38 ♗h6+ ♔h7 39 ♕f7+ ♔xh6 40 ♘h4! ♖c6 (40...♕c6 is met in the same way) 41 ♘f5+ ♔g5 42 f4+ ♔g4 43 ♘h4 ♘xe3 44 ♕g7+ ♔xf4 45 g3+ ♔e4 46 ♕e5#.

b2) 36...♕xd1+ 37 ♔h2 ♖c6 (37...♔g7 38 ♘h4) 38 ♖xd5 ♖xd5 39 ♕xd5+ ♔g7 40 ♘h4 and then:

b21) 40...♘a5? 41 ♕d7+ ♔g8 (41...♔f8 42 ♕d8+ ♔g7 43 d5) 42 ♕e8+ ♗f8 (42...♔g7 43 ♗e5+ ♖f6 44 ♘f5+) 43 ♘f5!, threatening ♘e7+, and White wins.

b22) 40...♖f6 41 ♕xc4 is good for White.

55)

It was certainly deliberate. While Gajewski's concept may not objectively give him the advantage, it is very interesting, and forced Black to solve some concrete problems at the board.

26 ♗xf6+!?

26 ♗e3 ♖a5 27 ♗xa7 ♔e8 doesn't give White much, if anything.

26 ♖xa7 has a similar idea to the move played, but doesn't work because White doesn't have enough tempo moves on the kingside with this formation; e.g., 26...fxg5 27 ♔b2 ♔e6 28 ♔a3 h6 and it is White who is in zugzwang after 29 ♖axd7? ♖xd7 30 ♖xd7 ♔xd7 31 ♔b4 ♔d6 32 h3 g6 33 g4 h5.

26...gxf6 27 ♖xa7

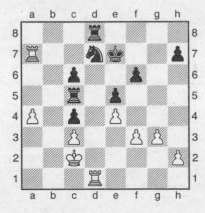

White's idea is to target the c5-rook, which now has no flight-squares.

27...♔e8

Black can't afford to wait, as White has a plan: 27...♔e6 28 g4 ♔e7 29 ♔b2 ♔e6 30 ♔a3 ♔e7 31 ♖axd7+ ♖xd7 32 ♖xd7+ ♔xd7 33 ♔b4 ♔d6 34 h4.

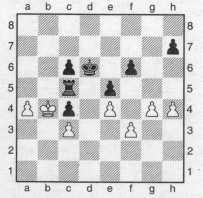

White wins thanks to zugzwang. If you had more or less seen this idea, and that it wasn't easy for Black to avoid it in an obviously advantageous way, then you can consider the exercise solved. But I'm sure you want to see how the drama unfolded.

28 g4 h6

28...♘b6!? 29 ♖xd8+ (29 ♖b1!?) 29...♔xd8 30 ♔b2 ♔c8 (30...♘c8 31 ♖a8 ♔c7 32 ♔a3 ♘b6 33 ♖a7+ ♔b8 is the same) 31 ♔a3 ♔b8 32 ♖xh7 ♖a5 33 ♔b4 ♖xa4+ 34 ♔c5 ♖a6 35 ♔xc6 with a rather unclear ending.

29 ♖b1

29 ♔b2 ♖b8+ 30 ♔a2 ♘b6 gives Black counterplay, or at least renders it hard for White to make progress.

29 h4 ♘b6 is an improved version of the previous note for Black, as the pawn is no longer *en prise* on h7.

29...♘f8

29...♔e7 30 h4 ♔e6 31 ♖d1 ♔e7 32 ♔b2 is a line we already know Black can't afford to enter.

30 ♖bb7 ♖d7

30...♘d7? 31 ♔b2 ♖b8 (what else?) 32 ♖xb8+ ♘xb8 33 ♔a3 is hopeless for Black.

31 ♖xd7 ♘xd7 32 ♔b2 ♘b6 33 ♔a3 ♘xa4 34 ♖xa4 ♔d7 35 ♖a7+ ♔d6 36 ♔b2

Now Black was able to set up a robust defence. 36 ♔b4!? might be a better try; e.g., 36...♖b5+ 37 ♔xc4 ♖b2 38 h4 ♖f2 39 ♖f7 ♔e6 40 ♖h7 ♖xf3 41 ♖xh6 ♔e7 42 g5 fxg5 43 hxg5 and it will not be trivial for Black to hold this rook ending.

36...♖b5+ 37 ♔c2 ♖b8 38 ♖h7 ♖a8 39 ♖xh6 ♔e7 40 ♔b2 ♖b8+ 41 ♔c1 ♖d8

and Black held the draw.

56)

Morozevich no doubt saw **27...♖xc2+!**, and that 28 ♔xc2? ♕a2+ 29 ♗b2 ♘xe4+ is a complete slaughter, but may have had problems assessing **28 ♔e1**. Then:

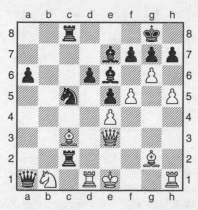

a) **28...♕a2** is the most obvious move; then 29 fxe6 ♖xg2 30 exf7+

♚h8 31 ♝d2 appears messy, but is probably still good for Black.

b) 28...♛a4! seems Black's best:

b1) 29 ♝f3 ♝c4 leaves White's pieces too tied up to support his kingside advance; e.g., 30 h6 fxg6 31 fxg6 hxg6 32 hxg7 ♛b3 (32...♚f7 is also good) 33 ♜h8+ ♚f7 and White can't even play 34 ♜xc8 because of 34...♝h4+ and mate next move.

b2) 29 fxe6 ♜xg2 30 exf7+ ♚h8 and the possibility of ....♛xe4 enables Black to neutralize White's kingside demonstration, and remain a few pawns up with excellently placed pieces.

Morozevich instead chose **27...h6** and after **28 ♚e1 ♝d7 29 gxf7+ ♚f8** the game was a lot murkier than it could have been, but Morozevich went on to win in the end.

I hope you got at least somewhere with this tricky example, not because I believe my readers are better tacticians than Morozevich, but because you had the major clue that the idea worked, and you didn't have the additional task of evaluating (with the clock ticking) whether it was a better practical option than other lines at Black's disposal.

57)

Let's first take a look at the game continuation:

24...g5?

After this passive move, White can put his house in order. 24...♝c5?! is also inadvisable, as White makes rapid progress by 25 fxg6 ♝xd4 26 gxf7+ ♚f8 (or 26...♚h8 27 f8♛+) 27 ♘g6+ ♚g7 28 f8♛+ ♜xf8 29 ♛xd4+ ♛xd4+ 30 ♘xd4 ♜f6, when White has a small but significant

material advantage, and all the winning chances.

25 ♘xc4 ♛b5

25...♛xc1+ 26 ♘xc1 ♜xd4 gives White the choice between 27 ♘e3 and 27 ♛xd4 ♝c5 28 ♛xc5 bxc5, in both cases with an unbalanced situation where White has good winning chances.

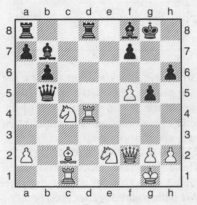

26 ♘c3?!

Now White faces heightened dangers on the a7-g1 diagonal once more. After 26 ♜b1 or 26 a4 it is easier for White to consolidate his material advantage.

26...♛b4 27 ♘e4?! ♝xe4 28 ♜xe4 ♝c5 29 ♘e3 ♛c3?

Black misses his chance: 29...♜d4!, based on the remarkable idea 30 ♜e5 ♛b2! 31 ♛e1 (or 31 ♜b1 ♜d1+!) 31...♜d1!, keeps Black in the fight.

30 ♛e1

White went on to win, albeit not without some adventures along the way.

Clearly it is wrong to give White any respite, especially as his position in the puzzle position did appear visibly loose. **24...♜xd4!** initiates a forcing sequence with an unclear outcome.

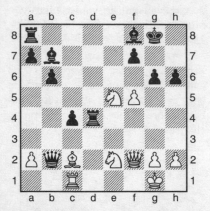

Given that Black's other options are unappealing, this is the move Black should try. If you saw enough of the likely possibilities to make that judgement, well done!

25 fxg6 f6 26 ♕xf6 ♗d5 27 ♗f5

These last few moves have been forced for both sides. If you analysed this with your computer, you perhaps reached the conclusion that the game should end in a draw, based on lines something like the following. White threatens to win by 28 ♗e6+, so Black's choice is limited:

27...♖d1+!

This dramatic move seems better than 27...♖d2?! 28 ♗e6+ ♗xe6 29 ♕xe6+ ♔h8 30 ♕f6+ ♗g7 31 ♘f7+ ♔g8 32 ♘xh6+ ♔h8 33 ♕h4 (White could take the immediate draw, of course) 33...♗d4+ 34 ♔f1 ♕xc1+! 35 ♘xc1 ♖f2+ 36 ♕xf2 (36 ♔e1 ♖e8+ 37 ♔d1 ♖f1+ 38 ♔c2 ♖f2+ is a draw) 36...♗xf2 37 ♔xf2, when White has excellent winning chances in a tricky ending.

28 ♔f2

Now we get one of those wonderful lines where White advances his king up the board and uses it in an attack

on its opposite number. However, Black's resources are sufficient to keep the game in the balance (at least).

After the safer 28 ♖xd1 ♗c5+ 29 ♔h1 ♗xg2+ 30 ♔xg2 ♕xe2+ Black gives perpetual check, as neither side may dare deviate; e.g., 31 ♔h3 ♕e3+ 32 ♔g4 ♕e2+, etc.

28...♗c5+ 29 ♔g3 ♖d3+ 30 ♔h4

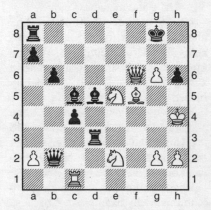

Now Black has a choice:

a) 30...♖e8 31 ♘g4 ♕d2 32 ♔h5 ♗f8 33 ♗xd3 (33 ♖c2 ♕xc2 34 ♘f4 ♗g7 35 ♘xh6+ ♔h8 36 ♘f7+ ♔g8 37 ♘h6+ is an immediate draw) 33...♗g7 (33...cxd3? 34 ♘f4 ♗g7 35 ♘xh6+ ♔h8 36 ♖c7!) and then:

a1) 34 ♕f4 ♕xd3 35 ♘g3 ♔h8 (35...♖f8 36 ♘xh6+ ♗xh6 37 ♕xh6 ♗f3+ 38 gxf3 ♕xf3+ is another draw) 36 ♘xh6 ♖f8 37 ♘hf5 is unclear.

a2) 34 ♕f5 cxd3 (34...♕xd3 35 ♕xd3 cxd3 36 ♘f4) 35 ♖c8 ♖xc8 36 ♕xc8+ ♗f8 37 h4 ♕xe2 38 ♕d7 ♕e7 39 ♕xd5+ ♔h8 40 ♘e5 d2 and the d-pawn provides enough counterplay: 41 ♘f3 d1♕ 42 ♕xd1 ♕c5+ 43 ♔g4 h5+ 44 ♔f4 ♗d6+ 45 ♔e4 ♕c6+ 46 ♕d5 (46 ♔f5 ♕d7+ 47 ♔f6 ♗e7+ 48 ♔f7 ♗d6+ 49 ♔f6 ♗e7+ is a funny perpetual) 46...♕c2+ 47 ♔e3 ♕c3+.

b) 30...♖f8(!) 31 ♗e6+ ♗xe6 32 ♕xe6+ ♔g7 33 ♘xd3 cxd3 34 ♕d7+ ♔xg6 35 ♕xd3+ ♔g7 36 ♖c4 ♕f6+ 37 ♔h3 ♕f5+ 38 ♖g4+ and a draw is likely, though it is White who will be more anxious about achieving it.

Computer-Assisted Analysis Puzzles

58)
11...♘c6!
Black's threat of ...♘xd4+ forces the pace. 11...♕xb2? (the only move given in *Informator*) 12 ♔e3 ♕xc2 13 ♗b5+ c6 and now Dominguez gave 14 ♗e2, but 14 ♖hf1! looks better still, as 14...cxb5? loses to 15 ♖ac1.

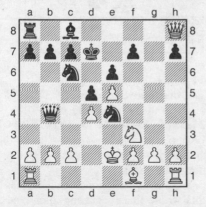

12 ♔e3
12 c3? now loses to 12...♕xb2+ 13 ♔e3 ♕xa1 because ♗b5 is not check.

12 ♖d1 ♕xb2 13 ♔e3 (13 ♕xh7 ♕xc2+ 14 ♔e3 transposes) 13...♕xc2 14 ♕xh7 (14 ♗b5? ♘c3! 15 ♗xc6+ bxc6 16 ♖de1 ♗a6! 17 ♕xa8 ♕e4+ 18 ♔d2 ♕d3+ 19 ♔c1 ♗c4 gives Black a winning attack) 14...♕xd1 15 ♕xf7+ ♔d8 and White has nothing better than giving perpetual check.
12...♘xd4!

This elegant sacrifice is the only way to justify Black's play. 12...♕xb2? 13 ♗d3 leaves Black empty-handed.

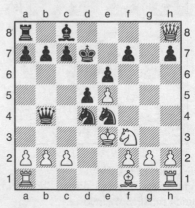

13 ♗d3
White covers c2. 13 ♘xd4? ♕d2+ 14 ♔f3 ♕xd4 is good for Black; e.g., 15 g3 (15 ♕g7 h5!) 15...♕xf2+ 16 ♔g4 ♕f5+ 17 ♔h4 ♕g6! (threatening ...f5) 18 ♕f8 and now:

a) 18...f5? 19 exf6 ♕g5+ 20 ♔h3 ♔c6 (20...e5?? 21 ♗b5+) 21 ♕e8+ ♗d7 22 ♗b5+ and Black will not succeed in giving the cherished killer check on the c8-h3 diagonal. After 22...♔b6 23 ♕xd7 ♕f5+ 24 ♔g2 ♕f2+ 25 ♔h3 ♘g5+ 26 ♔h4 ♕xf6 attack and counterattack are in balance and a draw will result.

b) 18...♘f2 19 ♗b5+ c6 20 ♗e2 h6 21 g4 ♕g5+ 22 ♔g3 ♘xh1+ and Black emerges with a significant material advantage.

13...♘f5+ 14 ♔e2
14 ♔f4?? is suicide: 14...♘xf2+.

14...♘d4+ 15 ♔f1
Now White has started to organize his position and is still material up. 15 ♔e3 repeats the position – so the first conclusion we can firmly draw is that White is not worse in this line.

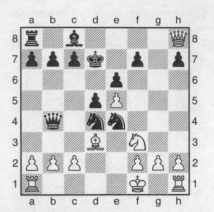

15...♕xb2 16 ♖d1

White has several threats here, so Black must reply in kind.

16...♘c3 17 ♘xd4

Fleeing by 17 ♖e1?! is futile since 17...♘xc2 corners the rook, and 18 ♗xc2 ♕xc2 leaves Black with two pawns and good play against the white king for the exchange. White should bail out with perpetual check by 18 ♕f8! ♘xe1 19 ♘d4 ♘xd3 20 ♕xf7+.

17...♘xd1 18 ♘b3

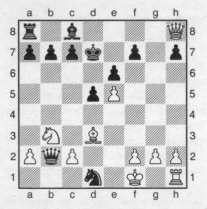

It seems like White's play against the black king is about to become the most relevant factor, but Black's thread of counterplay holds firm:

18...♕b1 19 g3 ♘e3++

19...♘xf2+ 20 ♔xf2 ♕xh1 21 ♘c5+ ♔e7 (21...♔c6?? 22 ♕e8+ ♔xc5 23 ♕b5+ ♔d4 24 ♕b4+ ♔xe5 25 ♕f4#) 22 ♕f6+ with a draw by perpetual check.

20 ♔e2 ♕xh1 21 ♘c5+ ♔c6

Or 21...♔e7 22 ♕f6+, etc.

22 ♕e8+ ♔xc5 23 ♕b5+ ♔d4

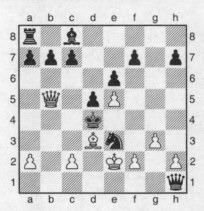

24 ♕b2+

The only move to draw. 24 ♕b4+?? ♘c4; 24 fxe3+? ♔xe5 25 ♕b2+ ♔d6.

24...♔c5 25 ♕a3+ ♔c6 26 ♕a4+ ♔c5

and neither side can avoid a draw by perpetual check.

So the overall conclusion is that this whole line (occurring after 1 e4 e6 2 d4 d5 3 ♘c3 ♘f6 4 ♗g5 ♗e7 5 e5 ♘e4 6 ♗xe7 ♘xc3 7 ♕g4 ♕xe7 8 ♕xg7 ♕b4 9 ♕xh8+ ♔d7 10 ♘f3 ♘e4+ 11 ♔e2) should be a draw, and neither side has any particularly appealing ways to avoid it.

59)

Basically, White holds the draw against all Black's tries, albeit by a fine thread in many lines. I'll give the critical lines without much verbal commentary, as it is all down to specifics, and the reasoning at each point should be clear enough if you are looking at the screen with a good engine running. 68...♗g3 69 ♕d2 ♕f8 70 ♕e2 and now:

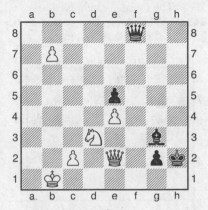

a) 70...♔h3 71 ♕e3!.

b) 70...♔h1 is met by 71 ♕h5+ ♗h2 72 ♕a2! g1♕ (72...♕g8+ 73 ♔b2 g1♕ 74 ♕f3+ ♕1g2 75 ♕d1+ ♗g1 76 ♕h5+ ♕h2 77 ♕f3+ and Black cannot escape the checks) 73 b8♕ ♕ff1 (73...♕xb8 74 ♕f3+ is the familiar perpetual check idea; 73...♕gg8+? 74 ♕b3 {only move} is good for White) and both 74 ♕b2 and 74 ♕bxe5 are adequate.

c) 70...♗h4 71 ♔b2! (avoiding 71 ♔a2? ♕f7+) 71...♕d8 (71...♔h3? 72 ♕e3+ ♔h2 73 ♕a7; 71...♔h1 72 ♕h5; 71...♕b8 72 ♘c5) 72 ♘c5 ♕b6+ and now:

c1) 73 ♔a1 ♕xc5 (73...♕b4 74 ♔a2 – compare line "c2") 74 b8♕ ♕a3+ 75 ♔b1 ♔h1 76 ♕d1+ g1♕ 77 ♕xg1+ ♔xg1 78 ♕xe5 and Black has achieved only a "symbolic advantage" as ♕+♗ vs ♕ is a draw.

c2) 73 ♔a2 ♕b4 is a kind of reciprocal zugzwang position – except

that the concession White must make isn't fatal.

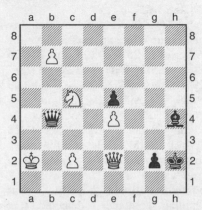

74 ♕h5 ♕a5+ (74...g1♕ 75 ♕xh4+ ♔g2 76 ♕g4+ and Black must stay on the h-file and allow a perpetual, since 76...♔f1?? loses to 77 ♕f3+ ♕f2 78 ♕xf2+ ♔xf2 79 ♘d3+) 75 ♔b2 ♕b5+ 76 ♔a2 g1♕ 77 ♕xh4+ ♔g2 78 ♕g4+ ♔f1 79 ♕d1+ ♔f2 80 ♘d3+ ♔g2 81 ♕g4+ ♔h2 82 ♕h4+ once more with perpetual check.

So our conclusion is that White would have had to find some accurate moves, but 68...♗g3 only leads to a draw.

60)

It's surprising what subtleties lurk in this position. You'd expect something like this sacrifice to be either very good or very bad.

a) **24...hxg5?** was the move played in the game, but, working with the computer, should not have occupied too much of your time. White wins: **25 ♘xd8 ♕xd8 26 hxg5 ♖xg5 27 ♖xe7 ♕d5 28 ♕xd5+ ♖xd5 29 ♖xb7** (Black cannot coordinate his pieces, whilst White's a-pawn proves strong) **29...♖xd3 30 ♖xa7 ♖d2 31**

♖b7 c4 32 a5 ♗f8 33 a6 ♗c5 34 a7 ♗xf2+ 35 ♔f1 ♗xa7 36 ♖xa7 ♖xb2 37 ♖e6 1-0.

b) 24...♖f5 leads to an almighty mess, but White appears to have the better of it: 25 ♕e2 (25 ♗f4 ♖f8 26 ♘e5 ♘h5 27 ♘d7 ♕b3 28 g3 ♖8f7 29 ♖xe7 ♘xf4 30 gxf4 ♖xf4 and Black's position is hanging together) 25...♔xf7 (25...hxg5 26 ♘xd8 ♕xd8 27 ♖xe7 gxh4 28 ♖xb7) 26 a5! (a clever little move that would be easy to ignore as an irrelevance or a "horizon effect" computer glitch; hopefully your "human computer" detected that there may be a real idea behind the move and you felt it was worth pursuing; instead 26 ♖xe7+ ♔g8 gives White little) and now:

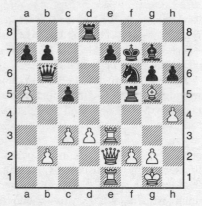

b1) 26...♕d6 27 ♖e6! (27 ♖xe7+? ♔g8 leaves White with nothing) 27...♕xd3 28 ♖xe7+ ♔f8 (28...♔g8 29 ♖xg7+ ♔xg7 30 ♕e7+ is similar) 29 ♕e6 ♕d5 30 ♖f7+ ♔g8 31 ♖xg7++ ♔xg7 32 ♕e7+ ♔g8 33 ♗xf6 and White wins.

b2) 26...♕c6 27 ♖xe7+ ♔f8 (the point of White playing 26 a5 is shown by 27...♔g8 28 ♖xg7+ ♔xg7

29 ♕e7+ ♔h8 30 ♕xd8+) 28 ♖xg7 ♖e8 (the only move) 29 ♗xh6 ♖xe2 30 ♖xe2 ♖h5 31 ♖c7+ ♖xh6 32 ♖xc6 bxc6 33 ♖e6 and White's pawns should be worth more than the knight in this ending.

c) The most obvious move is 24...♔xf7!, which also seems to be best. 25 ♖xe7+ ♔f8 and then:

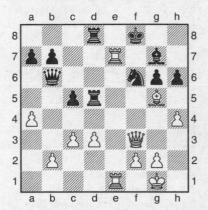

c1) 26 ♗xh6 ♗xh6 27 a5 (this move again; 27 ♖1e6? ♖f5 28 ♕g3 ♕xb2 gives Black a decisive counterattack) 27...♕c6 28 ♖1e6 ♖f5 29 ♕g3 ♕xe6 30 ♖xe6 ♔f7 31 ♖c7+ ♖d7 32 ♖xf6+ ♔e7! with a rather unclear ending in prospect.

c2) 26 a5 ♕c6 gives White nothing better than 27 ♗xh6 ♗xh6 transposing to line "c1".

c3) 26 ♖7e6 ♖xd3 27 ♗xf6 ♕xe6 (27...♖xf3 28 ♗e7+ ♔f7 29 ♖xb6 ♖d7 30 ♖be6 leaves White a pawn up) 28 ♖xe6 ♖xf3 29 ♗xd8 ♖f7 keeps the game unclear because the white bishop is short of squares.

So, the sacrifice should lead to one of a number of messy, unbalanced endings. Further analysis might clarify that assessment further, perhaps to "drawn".

Women's, Veterans', Junior and Correspondence Chess

These are four types of chess events in which the essential rules of chess remain the same, but are nevertheless a little different from standard chess events. In the first three there are restrictions on who can play, while in correspondence chess the time limit is wholly different. In this short chapter we shall be looking at the special features of each.

Women's Chess

Unfortunately, relatively few women play chess – maybe no more than 5% of all chess players. This is despite the proportion being far higher among young juniors, many girls tending to give up the game in their pre-teen years. I do not propose to speculate here why this is. Social conditioning must be a contributing factor, while just about every other reason has been advanced, from a supposed genetic "inferiority" to the view that women are far too sensible to waste their time playing chess. One thing that does seem clear: women players are not on average weaker chess players than their male counterparts; they are distributed throughout the rating lists very much as one would expect a small random sample to be.

Rightly or wrongly, plenty of women-only events are organized. These include women's tournaments, a women's world championship, a women's Olympiad, and women's prizes in open tournaments. There are women's titles (WGM, WIM and WFM), which can be gained in much the same way as the corresponding titles GM, IM and FM, but do not require the same level of competitive success; additionally, to gain the women's titles, a certain proportion of the games have to be against other women. Note that there are no men-only events, so it is completely wrong to talk of the "men's" Olympiad, "men's" titles, or the "men's" world championship. There are a handful of WGMs (the title is roughly equivalent to FM in terms of minimum playing standard) who also have the GM title, and quite a lot with the IM title. Women's national championships are often contested by the women playing in the overall championship, with whoever scores the most points being declared champion. The danger with this is that by rewarding a low standard of achievement (in junior events the girls' prizes often go to those who scrape the most draws), the players' full development is not encouraged.

Does all this help to encourage more women to play chess? Opinion is sharply divided on this point. One view is that it is patronizing and counterproductive to award titles and prizes to women who play at a level for which a man would receive no such accolades, and that this is the main reason why so few women play chess, and why there are only a handful of women in the world's top thousand players. An alternative view is that everything should be done to encourage the women who are interested in the game to continue playing, and that to have high-profile women's events is good for chess generally, not least from a marketing viewpoint. I suspect that from a long-term perspective the former view is right, but in the short term the latter. If women's events and women's prizes were all of a sudden halted, women's chess would become very low-key. Many women who currently can justify a career in chess would have to give up. In time, though, the strength of the top women would increase, since those who had ambitions would need to aim higher than is currently the case.

For sponsors, women's and girls' chess is very attractive. It is interesting for newspapers and presents a good image for chess and the sponsor. The yearly Women vs Veterans tournaments, sponsored by the millionaire Dutch chess patron, Joop van Oosterom were a good example. Although Van Oosterom did not aim to get massive exposure for his tournaments, events such as this are highly marketable.

Veterans' Chess

The fact that there are special veterans' tournaments comes as rather a surprise to those who imagine that chess is a game played by old men. Experience counts for a lot in chess, but speed of thought and physical stamina are even more vital over the board, so a player's strength tends to decline gradually from about the age of 40 onwards. Many elderly players therefore prefer to play in veterans' tournaments, where they can play interesting games against their peers. Although there can be an interesting clash of styles when a young lion meets an old warrior, the types of games that result can be unsatisfying for both: for instance the elder might outplay the younger, only to be swindled in a time-scramble; or else the young player, more highly motivated to study chess theory, might blow away his older adversary with some new idea in the opening.

However, there is certainly no segregation of chess along ageist lines, but veterans events and prizes are a growing area. Since they do not affect the development of up-and-coming players, they cause no real controversy. If it means that players of the calibre of Smyslov, Portisch and Spassky, with their deep understanding of chess, continue to play in high-profile events, rather than be lost in the midst of huge Swiss-system events, then it is no bad thing.

Junior Chess

There is little doubt that juniors should be encouraged to play chess, and that events organized specifically for juniors are a good thing.

This in no way holds back the strongest of the juniors, who will take part in "senior" events from an early age, normally in addition to playing junior chess. Note that I am thinking mainly of ages 8 to 18, though many of the comments in this section apply to student chess (ages 19 to 21) too.

Junior chess activities fall into the following areas in roughly ascending order of playing level: school chess clubs, junior chess clubs, inter-schools chess, inter-regional junior team events, junior coaching, international junior tournaments, and junior championships (both national and international).

School Chess Clubs

Many schools have a chess club, but the organization is often haphazard, depending mainly on a teacher (or a parent, or a trusted older pupil) being sufficiently interested to run the club. With this in mind, school chess clubs vary greatly in the range of activities they provide.

At worst, they are just a handful of players gathering around a chess board every now and then, or a place to go to get out of the rain; at best a thriving environment for chess, with a variety of internal competitions and regular matches against other school teams, or against senior chess clubs in a local league. This, then, is effectively a "real" chess club that just happens to be in a school, and draws its members exclusively from its students.

Also, there are a few schools – few and far between – that specialize in chess, and actively seek chess players as students. In England, Oakham School has had close links with chess, in particular with the series of biennial junior internationals from 1984 to 1992, which became the most important junior event in the world, after the World and European junior championships. In Denmark, Tjele Efterskole provides chess tuition alongside the more traditional subjects. Many Danish juniors are educated at Tjele, and as far as I can gather they enjoy the experience of being at school with so many other chess enthusiasts, and emerge as better players.

Discovering which schools in your area have a good chess club is not necessarily very easy. I would suggest speaking to someone at the local chess club, or contacting your national federation, who might be able to put you in touch with an organization that could advise.

Junior Chess Clubs

Junior clubs provide an ideal alternative to a school club (which is not available to many children) and full membership of a predominantly adult chess club. However, this is an area where far more could be done. There are very few junior chess leagues, apart from schools' leagues. Although it seems natural for any chess club to want to have a thriving junior section, relatively few actually do. Like most things that go wrong in the world of chess, this is not due to any failure to see that the concept is good, but rather the lack of the necessary personnel. Running a junior club requires a lot of time and a regular commitment and involves a great deal of responsibility. Collecting small amounts of money from the children each week will hardly cover the costs of the equipment. At a chess club AGM it is hard to imagine the members agreeing to a higher annual subscription to pay someone to run a junior club; at that point it seems a better idea that the juniors just become members of the senior club – as the best of them will.

Inter-schools Chess

In some cities there are leagues in which school chess teams compete against one another on a regular basis, but in many places it is more problematic for school teams to meet, with just occasional matches being played. A strong school chess team in this situation should definitely consider entering a team in the local chess league.

Most countries have a national schools chess competition. In Britain, this is sponsored by *The Times*, and is a very well established event. The initial stages are played on a regional basis with winners of the regional qualifiers going on to the national stages. Age handicaps are used, a little crudely, to give schools with a low age range a chance against those that can field a team of experienced players in their late teens. The main problems with the event are that very much the same set of teams tends to emerge as the winners in each of the regions every year, and that a big chunk of the sponsorship money is spent on the finals in London, in which only four teams are involved, of the hundreds originally entering the competition.

Inter-regional Junior Team Events

From a British viewpoint, this means county chess. Almost all counties have a junior team, and many of the larger counties have several. Junior county matches are great fun for the players: a day out, and, since they tend to be played over many boards, a chance for the less experienced players to see some big names in junior chess in action.

Junior Coaching

In the former Soviet Union, promising players were identified at an early age and given expert tuition in chess. Many of them went on to become grandmasters. In the USA and Western Europe, the situation has always been far more random. Most Western players who have become successful professionals have needed to work a lot on their own, and still suffer from gaps in their technical knowledge of chess. The strength of the English national team in recent decades owes much to the coaching programme set up mainly by Bob Wade and Leonard Barden in the late 1960s and early 1970s. From that era emerged players such as Miles, Keene, Speelman, Mestel and Nunn. In turn this provided the competitive background from which a younger generation, including Short, Adams and Sadler, could emerge.

Coaching can take many forms, but the central part has to be an experienced player sitting across the board from the junior and giving one-to-one tuition on the game, both general and specific. Good coaching can correct general flaws in chess thinking that might otherwise fester and damage the player's understanding of chess for ever more. Good coaching can also inspire the pupils to work on their game in the most profitable way in their own time. For instance, the Dvoretsky/Yusupov school only met occasionally, but in the few days they had at the school, the pupils were encouraged to think in new ways about the game. As a result, they tended to become resilient, self-sufficient masters, who returned for the next session of the school as stronger players than they were on their previous visit.

Most national chess federations will organize some coaching for the strongest of their juniors, but there is generally a limited budget for this, and the all-important one-on-one coaching is rare. For instance, as a junior I was invited to just one coaching weekend, at which an IM or GM would go through games on a demonstration board. It was interesting, but not inspirational. The best things about the weekend were the flick-chess games against Michael Adams. He was good too.

There are a great many people offering private chess tuition, especially in major cities. I'm far from convinced that all these people offer good value for money. If you are unsure, it is best to check with your national federation, who may have a register of approved chess teachers, or a local chess expert, if you can find one (try your local chess club). However, the federation will not necessarily have a clear idea of who is any good. There is no examination chess teachers need to take, and an international chess title is no

guarantee that a player has any aptitude for teaching. Chess teaching is often used as a way to scrape an existence by those who would like to make a living as chess players or writers, but aren't good enough.

As a rough guide to how much one can expect to pay, in major cities the going rate tends to be £30 ($50) per hour for IM tuition. If this price seems high, then consider the travelling involved, the various overheads and the preparation necessary. Prices elsewhere, and for non-IM tuition, tend to be somewhat lower. Some GMs charge premium rates, but unless the pupil is really talented, this seems inappropriate. The most important thing is that the teacher is strong enough as a player to perceive the ways in which the pupil can improve, and good enough as a teacher to explain how to do so.

International Junior Tournaments
This is quite a new phenomenon, as in the past there were few junior IMs, let alone GMs, and so, while juniors frequently played in international events, their titled opponents were, for the most part, adults. Now that there are generally a handful of teenage grandmasters and dozens of teenage IMs at any time, sponsors see junior international tournaments as attractive events that are not too difficult to arrange.

These events are fun for the players, and tend to feature highly enterprising, aggressive chess, and little of the "halving out" (i.e. those out of the running for prizes drawing lots of short games) that can plague events featuring more mature players.

Junior Championships (National and International)

The highest level of junior competition are the world junior championships, with the European championships not far behind. They are held each year, often at exotic venues. They are very strong events, even in the lower age groups. The top-scoring players in each age group would typically have ratings such as the following:

	Open	Girls
U-20	2650	2475
U-18	2575	2400
U-16	2475	2300
U-14	2375	2200
U-12	2250	2100

As you can see, junior chess at world championship level is tough, with some really good players fighting it out for the medals.

National championships take various forms. In some countries they are played at the same time and place as the senior national championship in the particular country. While this makes it a wonderful get-together for the players, the drawback is that the very best of the juniors will play in the senior championship, thus devaluing the junior events by depriving them of the strongest competitors. An alternative is to combine the junior championships with the senior events, as, for instance, was done with the British Under-21 Championship some decades ago. However, it then ceases to be a real event, and more of an afterthought when the prize is awarded. Certainly, when I played in the British Championship in 1988 and 1989, it never crossed my mind that I was competing in the Under-21 championship! Also, if players need to qualify to play in the senior championship, then this denies many players the chance to participate at all.

In some countries the junior championships are held as a separate event in their own right. The problem then is that it is not such an exciting tournament to play in. The children get little chance to see the top players in their country in action – an inspirational influence that should not be underestimated. One popular way to pep up a junior championship is to make entry open to foreign junior players, with the championships of course awarded only to home players, but with prizes and the title of "Open Champion" to attract strong foreign juniors. This formula is popular in mainland Europe, and seems to work well.

Correspondence Chess

To many people, regular "over-the-board" chess players included, the idea of playing chess by sending a move, and waiting days for the reply to arrive from the opponent, is rather odd. Nevertheless, correspondence players enjoy their variety of chess and make a good case for it. The main benefits of playing by post (or following a similar regime, but transmitting the moves by e-mail or server) may be summarized as follows.

- Brilliant games need never be ruined by blunders made through sheer panic in time-trouble.
- No travelling is involved; you play from the comfort of your home.

- You can work on your postal games at any time of day or night.
- There is no need to memorize large amounts of opening theory, since it is possible to refer to books and databases during the games.
- Correspondence chess provides excellent motivation to analyse positions and openings in depth, which is useful training if you also play over-the-board chess.
- Players with good positional understanding but who are weak on tactics have a chance to shine in correspondence play, where the time to think and the ability to move the pieces on the board and use a computer allows one to sort through the most opaque tactical mess.

There are many levels at which correspondence chess is played, ranging, as in standard over-the-board chess, from simple club events (correspondence clubs do not, of course, need to have a narrow geographical focus) through national leagues to national championships (both team and individual) to Olympiads and individual world championships. In high-level correspondence chess, the use of computerized assistance goes without saying.

In the past, the length of games used to depend heavily on the geographical locations of the players and the speed and reliability of the postal service between them. In domestic events the games tended to last only a few months, whereas at international level, individual games could last several years. Nowadays, games are increasingly being played by e-mail or via a server, so the main factor is the time-limit that is being used.

Traditionally, players have normally specialized in either over-the-board chess or in correspondence play, with few simultaneously playing at a high level in both disciplines. The names of the top correspondence players have tended to be unknown outside the world of correspondence chess. The exceptions are players who took up correspondence chess after a successful over-the-board career – notably Jonathan Penrose, for many years Britain's leading player, who established himself as one of the world's best correspondence players. Also, there are some players who played correspondence chess when they were young as a way of practising their analytical skills before concentrating on the over-the-board game in later life. Paul Keres is the outstanding example here, though in his case this was partly due to the difficulty finding tough opposition closer to home. However, there is now a trend for players to compete in both disciplines simultaneously. Swedish grandmaster Ulf Andersson has tried his hand, with great success, at correspondence chess, while the Scottish Correspondence Chess Association has been remarkably successful at recruiting members of the regular national team, with the result that Scotland now possesses one of the world's finest correspondence teams.

It is no surprise that the larger, more sparsely populated countries are strong in correspondence chess: Scandinavia has many of the top players, as does Russia. Canada and Australia are more significant forces in correspondence chess than in the over-the-board game. But, in line with the situation for over-the-board chess, it is Germany that has the largest number of internationally rated correspondence players.

If you are wondering whether correspondence chess is for you, a revealing comment was made to me by one very strong player, Peter Millican, when I asked whether the fear of being attacked, or the elation of playing a brilliant attack, was at all like the sensations experienced at the board. His view was that the emotions were just the same, and just as strong, except that they last for *months*, rather than minutes or hours!

Here are two games from the most recent world championship:

Marcinkiewicz – Winckelmann
23rd Corr. Wch 2007–

1 e4 c5 2 ♘f3 d6 3 d4 cxd4 4 ♘xd4
♘f6 5 ♘c3 a6 6 ♗e3 e5 7 ♘b3 ♗e7
8 ♕d2 ♗e6 9 0-0-0 ♘bd7 10 f4 ♘g4
11 g3 ♘xe3 12 ♕xe3 b5 13 ♔b1 ♕b6
14 ♕e2 ♘f6 15 ♘d5 ♗xd5 16 exd5
exf4 17 gxf4 0-0 18 ♕g2 ♕e3 19 ♖g1
g6 20 f5 ♘h5 21 ♖d4 ♗f6 22 ♖e4
♕h6 23 ♗d3 ♖ae8 24 ♖g4 ♗g7 25
fxg6 fxg6 26 ♗xg6 hxg6 27 ♖xg6
♕h7 28 ♘d4 ♔h8 29 ♘e6 ♖g8 30
♖g4 ♗f6 31 h3 a5 32 a3 b4 33 axb4
axb4 34 ♕f3 ♖xg4 35 hxg4 b3 36
♕xb3 ♕a7 37 ♖h1 ♖b8 38 ♕f3
♖xb2+ 39 ♔c1 ♕a1+ 40 ♔d2 ♕a5+
41 ♔d1 ♕a1+ 42 ♔d2 ♕a5+ ½-½

Geenen – Hoeven
23rd Corr. Wch 2007–

1 e4 c5 2 ♘f3 d6 3 d4 cxd4 4 ♘xd4
♘f6 5 ♘c3 a6 6 ♗g5 e6 7 f4 ♕b6 8

♕d2 ♕xb2 9 ♖b1 ♕a3 10 e5 h6 11
♗h4 dxe5 12 fxe5 ♘fd7 13 ♘e4
♕xa2 14 ♖d1 ♕d5 15 ♕e3 ♕xe5 16
♗e2 ♗c5 17 ♗g3 ♗xd4 18 ♖xd4
♕a5+ 19 ♖d2 0-0 20 ♗d6 f5 21 ♗xf8
♘xf8 22 ♘d6 ♘bd7 23 0-0 ♕c5 24
♕d4 b5 25 ♖b1 ♖b8 26 ♖b3 ♕xd4+
27 ♖xd4 ♘f6 28 ♖d1 ♗d7 29 ♖a3
♖b6 30 ♗f3 b4 31 ♘c4 ♖b5 32 ♖xa6
♖c5 33 ♘e3 ♖c3 34 ♖d3 ♖xd3 35
cxd3 ♗b5 36 ♖d6 ♔f7 37 d4 ♘8d7
38 ♗c6 ♗xc6 39 ♖xc6 f4 40 ♘c4
♘d5 41 ♖a6 ♔f6 42 ♖a7 ♘7b6 43
♘xb6 ♘xb6 44 ♔f2 g5 45 ♔f3 ♘d5
½-½

Winners of the Correspondence World Championships

1st Ch, 1950–3: Cecil Purdy
2nd Ch, 1956–8: Viacheslav Ragozin
3rd Ch, 1959–62: Alberic O'Kelly de Galway
4th Ch, 1962–5: Vladimir Zagorovsky
5th Ch, 1965–8: Hans Berliner
6th Ch, 1968–71: Horst Rittner
7th Ch, 1972–5: Yakov Estrin
8th Ch, 1975–80: Jørn Sloth
9th Ch, 1977–83: Tõnu Õim
10th Ch, 1978–84: Vytas Palciauskas
11th Ch, 1983–8: Fritz Baumbach
12th Ch, 1984–91: Grigory Sanakoev
13th Ch, 1989–95: Mikhail Umansky
14th Ch, 1994–9: Tõnu Õim
15th Ch, 1996–2002: Gert Jan Timmerman
16th Ch, 1999–2004: Tunç Hamarat
17th Ch, 2002–7: Ivar Bern
18th Ch, 2003–5: Joop van Oosterom
19th Ch, 2004–7: Christophe Léotard
20th Ch, 2004–: unfinished
21st Ch, 2005–8: Joop van Oosterom
22nd Ch, 2007–: unfinished
23rd Ch, 2007–: Thomas Winckelmann

Endgame Studies

Endgame studies are composed positions where the solver is required to find a specific line of play achieving either a win or a draw. They may be regarded as puzzles, but are a good deal deeper than that.

Most study composers regard their work as an art form. Awards are given for those that display the most originality, achieve the best effects and have the most aesthetic appeal.

Studies have their roots in two fields of chess activity. Firstly, in the primitive chess puzzles that passers-by might have been challenged to try, with a sum of money riding on whether they could find the key winning (or drawing) move. From this comes the requirement that there should be a unique solution, which is not trivial to find. Secondly, in manuals for those wishing to improve their endgame play it is quite normal for the author to compose instructive positions to illustrate specific themes and ideas (for instance the positions on pages 89–97). As these positions become more and more complex, they become very difficult to solve and require precise analysis.

The boundaries between these activities became blurred. From them evolved three areas that are now actively pursued: work on the theory of practical endgames; the composition of artistic endgame positions; and chess problems, in which a clear-cut mate is normally the target.

Here is a small selection of studies that have impressed me. In each case, before the diagram you will find the composer's name, followed by the source, i.e. where it was first published, and an indication of any awards the study received.

M. Gromov
"Shakhmaty v SSSR" 1989

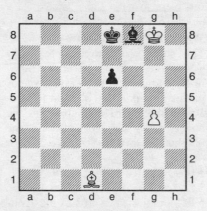

White to Play and Win
It seems a tall order for White to win here: he must win the black bishop and keep the white pawn alive.
1 ♗a4+ ♔e7 2 g5 e5 3 ♗c2!
3 ♗d1 e4 and the e-pawn proves a nuisance to White.
3...♔e8 4 ♗g6+ ♔e7
Compare this position with that after White's ninth move. The point of White's manoeuvre is just to transfer the move to Black.
5 ♗e4! ♔e8 6 ♗c6+ ♔e7 7 ♗d5!
♔e8 8 ♗f7+ ♔e7 9 ♗g6! and wins. Black is caught in a zugzwang.

A. Troitsky
"Shakhmaty v SSSR" 1941
2nd Hon. Mention

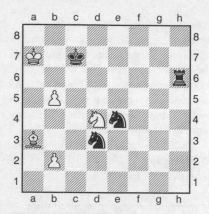

White to Play and Draw

This study was composed by Troitsky to illustrate the "Troitsky Line" in the endgame of two knights versus pawn. This is a line of eight squares across the board behind which the pawn must be blockaded if the knights are to win. See page 537 for details.

1 b6+! ♖xb6 2 ♗d6+! ♘xd6

2...♖xd6 3 ♘b5+ ♔c6 4 ♘xd6 ♘xd6 5 b4! and the pawn crosses the Troitsky Line: a knight's pawn need only reach the fourth rank to be safe.

3 ♘e6+ ♔c6 4 ♘d4+ ♔c5 5 ♘e6+ ♔b5 6 ♘d4+ ♔a5 7 b4+! ♘xb4

7...♖xb4 8 ♘c6+.

8 ♘b3+ ♔b5 9 ♘d4+ ♔c5 10 ♘e6+ ♔c6 11 ♘d4+ ♔c7 12 ♘e6+

With perpetual check, and a draw.

G. Nadareishvili and V. Smyslov
"64" 1986

This is a fine study by a well-known composer and a world champion. White's method is far from obvious.

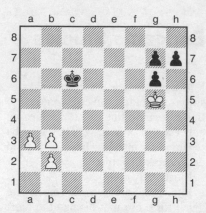

White to Play and Win

1 b4 ♔b5 2 b3 ♔b6 3 a4 ♔c6 4 b5+ ♔c5 5 b4+ ♔b6

White's pawns cannot advance further without being lost. So White transfers the move to Black.

6 ♔g4 h6 7 ♔f4 g5+ 8 ♔f5 g6+ 9 ♔g4

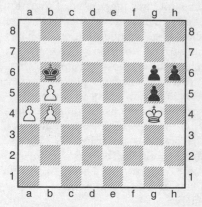

Now Black's pawns are stymied just as White's were. The manoeuvre now repeats on both sides of the board, and since White's pawns are one rank further advanced, it is he who comes out on top.

9...♔b7 10 a5 ♔c7 11 b6+ ♔c6 12 b5+ ♔b7 13 ♔f3 h5 14 ♔g3 g4 15

♔f4 g5+ 16 ♔g3 ♚b8 17 a6 ♚c8 18 b7+ ♚c7 19 b6+ ♚b8 20 ♔g2 h4 21 ♔f2 g3+ 22 ♔f3 g4+ 23 ♔g2

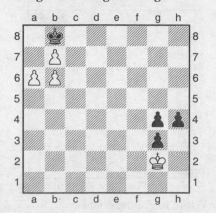

Black is now in total zugzwang and must start shedding pawns. The study finishes at this point, since the win for White is now very clear-cut (though after 23...h3+ 24 ♔xg3 h2 25 ♔xh2 g3+, White must avoid 26 ♔g2?? which is stalemate, and play 26 ♔g1 g2 27 a7+ ♚xb7 28 ♔xg2).

J. Beasley
"The Problemist" 1980–1
Hon. Mention

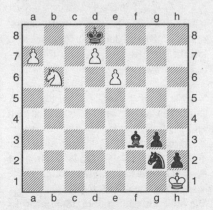

White to Play and Draw

This looks impossible, since it seems only a matter of time before Black can move his knight, giving mate.
1 a8♕+! ♗xa8 2 ♘d5!
Not 2 ♘xa8? ♘e3 aiming for f2.
2...♗c6!
2...♗xd5 3 e7+ ♔xe7 4 d8♕+ ♔xd8 is stalemate – White's key idea.
3 e7+!
Attacking the bishop is inadequate: 3 ♘b4? ♗xd7 4 exd7 ♘e3 (heading for f2) 5 ♘c6+ ♔xd7 6 ♘e5+ ♔d6 7 ♘f3 ♔d5 8 ♘xh2 ♔e4 gives Black a won ending: 9 ♔g1 ♔f4 10 ♔h1 (10 ♘f1 ♘xf1 11 ♔xf1 ♔f3) 10...g2+ 11 ♔g1 ♔g3 12 ♘g4 ♔xg4. A study composer must check lines such as this very carefully, since if there is an alternative way to draw, then the study is unsound and worthless.
3...♗xd7 4 e8♕+ ♔xe8 5 ♘f6+ ♔f7 6 ♘e4!
Now Black must either give stalemate by taking the knight, or else allow the capture of both of his pawns, with a draw.

J. Nunn
"EG" 1978

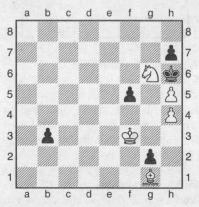

White to Play and Win

1 ♗e3+ f4!

1...♔g7 2 ♔xg2 hxg6 3 h6+ ♔h7 4 ♗c1 f4 5 ♔f3 ♔xh6 6 ♔g4.

2 ♘xf4! g1♕ 3 ♗xg1 b2 4 ♗c5! ♔g7

4...b1♕ 5 ♗f8#.

5 ♗d4+ ♔h6! 6 ♘e6

6 ♗xb2 is stalemate.

6...b1♕ 7 ♗g7+ ♔xh5 8 ♘f4+ ♔xh4 9 ♗f6#

This is what is known as a model mate: each square in the black king's field is covered only once, and all the white pieces participate in the mate. The economy of forces creates a powerful aesthetic effect.

J. Speelman
"EG" 1979

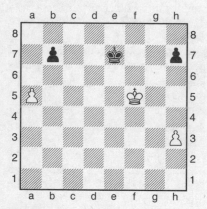

White to Play and Win

1 ♔g5!

1 ♔e5 ♔d7! is sufficient for Black.

1...♔f7 2 ♔h6 ♔g8 3 h4 ♔h8 4 ♔h5! ♔g8 5 ♔g4! ♔f8 6 ♔f4! ♔e8 7 ♔g5! ♔f7 8 ♔f5 ♔e7 9 ♔e5 ♔d7 10 ♔f6 ♔c6 11 h5 ♔b5 12 h6 ♔xa5 13 ♔g7 b5 14 ♔xh7 b4 15 ♔g7 b3 16 h7 b2 17 h8♕ b1♕ 18 ♕a8+ ♔b4 19 ♕b8+

White wins the black queen.

A. Sevilanov
"Shakhmaty v SSSR" 1990

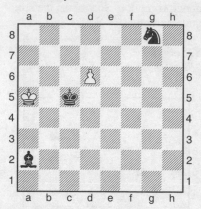

White to Play and Draw

1 d7 ♘e7

Otherwise White makes a queen.

2 d8♘

White must underpromote, since 2 d8♕ ♘c6+ is a win for Black.

2...♔d6

Bishop and knight versus knight is in general a draw, but if Black can trap and win the knight, then he wins; he has two main ways to try to do so. The alternative line runs 2...♗d5 3 ♔a6 ♘c8 4 ♘b7+ ♔c6 5 ♘a5+ ♔c5 6 ♘b7+ ♔b4 7 ♘a5 ♔a4 8 ♘c6 (8 ♘b7?? ♗c4#) 8...♗xc6 with stalemate; if Black does not capture the knight, then it escapes, and the position is drawn.

3 ♔b6!

Not 3 ♘b7+? ♔c6 4 ♔a6 ♗c4+ 5 ♔a7 ♔c7 6 ♘c5 ♘c8+ 7 ♔a8 ♗d5+ and mate.

3...♘c8+ 4 ♔b7!

4 ♔b5? ♗d5 5 ♔b4 ♘a7 and 6...♔d7 wins the knight.

4...♔d7 5 ♘c6 ♗d5 6 ♔b8! ♗xc6

We have another stalemate, similar to that which occurred in the line after

2...♗d5. These are thematically linked variations – together with the underpromotion, they make the study quite attractive.

Y. Soloviev
"Shakhmaty v SSSR" 1989

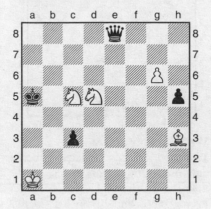

White to Play and Win
Here we see minor pieces cornering not one, but two queens in highly surprising fashion.

1 ♘b3+!
Not 1 ♘b7+? ♔a4 2 ♗d7+ ♔a3! 3 ♗xe8 c2 4 ♘c3 c1♕+ 5 ♘b1+ ♔b4 6 ♘d8 ♕c8 7 g7 ♕a8+ 8 ♔b2 ♕g2+.

1...♔a4
Otherwise the king and queen will be forked.

2 ♗d7+! ♕xd7
2...♔xb3 3 ♗xe8 c2 4 ♗a4+!.

3 ♘c5+ ♔a3 4 ♘e3!!
White threatens 5 ♘c2#. Instead 4 ♘xd7? c2 is no good.

4...♕d1+!? 5 ♘xd1 c2 6 ♘c3! c1♕+ 7 ♘b1+ ♔b4 8 ♘d3+
White wins the new queen too.

P. Shulezhko
"Shakhmaty v SSSR" 1990
White to Play and Win

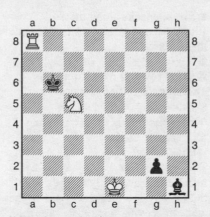

How can White keep his pieces while preventing a promotion on g1?

1 ♘d7+!
1 ♘a4+? ♔b5 2 ♘c3+ ♔b4 3 ♘d5+ (3 ♘a2+ ♔b3 4 ♘c1+ ♔b2 5 ♘d3+ ♔c2) 3...♔c5! 4 ♖a5+ ♔d4 5 ♔f2 g1♕+ 6 ♔xg1 ♗xd5 is a draw.

1...♔c6!
The best chance, since 1...♔c7 2 ♖a7+ followed by 3 ♔f2 snuffs Black out quite simply.

2 ♘e5+ ♔d6
2...♔d5 3 ♖a5+ is again hopeless for Black.

3 ♘c4+!
3 ♘f7+? ♔e6 4 ♘g5+ ♔f6 5 ♘e4+ ♔e5! 6 ♖e8+ ♔d4 7 ♔f2 g1♕+ 8 ♔xg1 ♗xe4 is OK for Black this time.

3...♔d5 4 ♘e3+ ♔d4
4...♔e4 5 ♔f2 wins for White since the position of the black king prevents ....♗h1xa8.

5 ♘f5+ ♔e4 6 ♘g3+ ♔f4 7 ♘e2+
White has managed to cover the queening square, g1, without his rook or knight going astray in the process, and so wins without further difficulty. The repeated gyrations of the knight, together with the idea of

the rook checks along the a-file, constitute what is known as a systematic manoeuvre.

B. Kozyrev and M. Gromov
"Kommunist" 1988, 1st prize

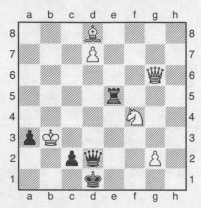

White to Play and Win

This study is an excellent demonstration of effects occurring in studies that could never be achieved in over-the-board play.

1 ♕g4+ ♔c1 2 ♔a2 ♕c3 3 ♘d3+

3 ♘e2+ ♖xe2 4 ♗g5+ ♖d2 5 ♗xd2+ ♕xd2 draws; e.g., 6 ♕f5 (6 ♔xa3 ♕a5+ 7 ♔b3 ♕b5+ 8 ♔a3 ♕a5+ repeats the position) 6...♕d5+ 7 ♕xd5 is stalemate.

3...♕xd3 4 ♗g5+

Now there are two lines, both with underpromotions by the d-pawn:

4...♖xg5

4...♖e3 5 ♗xe3+ ♕xe3 6 d8♗! (6 d8♕? ♕e6+! 7 ♕xe6 is stalemate) 6...♕d2 7 ♗g5 c1♕ 8 ♗xe3+ ♔xe3 9 ♕g5+ wins the second queen too.

5 ♕xg5+ ♔d1 6 d8♖!

6 d8♕? c1♘+! 7 ♕xc1+ ♔xc1 8 ♕xd3 is stalemate.

6...c1♘+ 7 ♕xc1+ ♔xc1 8 ♖xd3

White wins.

O. Pervakov
"Shakhmaty v SSSR" 1986, 1st Prize

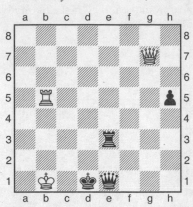

White to Play and Win

With both kings completely exposed and plenty of major pieces on the board, it's often a case of "whoever moves first, wins" – so it is in this wonderfully subtle study, but not, as generally is the case, by a barrage of checks.

1 ♕g2!

Here it is more important to stop Black checking than to give a check immediately. 1 ♖d5+ ♔e2+ 2 ♔c2 ♕g3! allows the black king to safety on the kingside.

1...♖e2

1...♕c3 2 ♕f1+ ♔d2 (2...♖e1 3 ♖d5+) 3 ♖b2+ wins the queen. 1...♕g3 2 ♕f1+ ♔d2 3 ♖d5+ ♔c3 4 ♖c5+ ♔b3 5 ♕c4+ ♔a3 6 ♖a5#.

2 ♖d5+ ♖d2

Now White's winning idea is simply to move the rook somewhere on the d-file. The point is that the black rook must stay on d2 (it is pinned both against the king, and the c2-square), while Black's queen is tied to defending the rook and to parrying checks from the white queen.

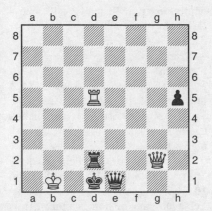

3 ♖d8!!

It turns out that only this one square will do for the rook. Consider:

a) 3 ♖d6 ♕e2 4 ♕h1+ ♕e1 5 ♕f3+ ♕e2 6 ♕b3+ ♔e1 is only a perpetual for White, since 7 ♖e6? loses to 7...♖d1+.

b) 3 ♕f3+ ♕e2.

c) 3 ♖d4 h4! (3...♕e2 4 ♕c6! ♕e3 5 ♕a4+ and 6 ♖e4 wins the queen) 4 ♕f3+ ♕e2 5 ♕c6 ♕e1 6 ♕h1+ ♕f1 7 ♕xf1+ ♔xf1 8 ♖xd2 ♔g1 and now the h-pawn is far enough up the board for Black to hold the draw!

3...h4 4 ♕g4+! ♕e2 5 ♕a4+

Now the rook does not get in the way of the queen, but will be supported by it on e8.

5...♔e1 6 ♕xh4+ ♔d1

6...♕f2 7 ♕h1+ ♔e2 (7...♕f1 8 ♕xf1+ ♔xf1 9 ♖xd2) 8 ♖e8+ wins.

7 ♕h1+ ♕e1 8 ♕f3+ ♕e2 9 ♕c6! ♕e3

9...♔e1 10 ♕h1+ ♔f2 11 ♖f8+ wins in short order.

10 ♕a4+ ♔e2 11 ♖e8

White forces the won ending of queen vs rook, since now **11...♖d1+** does not work: **12 ♕xd1+ ♔xd1 13 ♖xe3**

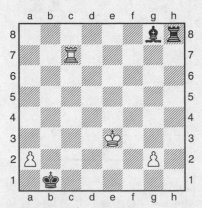

White to Play and Win

White obviously isn't going to win this position by normal means – his pawns simply aren't far enough advanced. So he must rest his hopes on the badly placed black pieces.

1 ♖c8!

As Dr Nunn might put it, the sign "Beware of Reciprocal Zugzwangs" is hanging over the board. 1 ♖b7+ ♔a1! (1...♔xa2 2 ♖b8 is the same as the main line) 2 ♖b8 ♔xa2 reaches the zugzwang position with White to move, and so Black draws: 3 g3 ♔a3 4 ♔f4 ♔a4 5 g4 ♔a5 6 g5 ♖h4+ 7 ♔g3 ♖h8 8 g6 ♗f7! 9 ♖xh8 ♗xg6 and with rook vs bishop White cannot win provided Black, if forced into a corner, chooses one where the bishop is not on the same colour as the corner square.

1...♔xa2

There is no choice now that Black's bishop is pinned; after 1...♔a1, 2 a4 followed by the simple advance of the pawn would win trivially.

2 ♖b8

Restricting the king to the a-file.

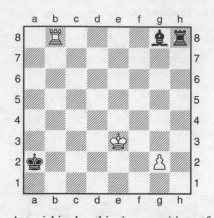

Astonishingly, this is a position of reciprocal zugzwang: if White is to play, then he can only draw, but if Black is to play, he loses. In other words, any move by either side weakens his position to the extent of worsening the result of the game! Let us consider why this should be so. The white rook needs to stay on the eighth rank to pin the black pieces. It also needs to stay on the b-file to stop the black king returning to the action on the kingside. The white king dare not move onto a light square, since then a check from the black bishop would mean loss of the rook for White. White must also look out for a check from the black rook, if this liberates the bishop too. But why should moving the black king lose?

2...♚a3

2...♗d5 would be OK, were it not for 3 ♖xh8 ♗xg2 4 ♖h2, exploiting the king's position on a2.

3 g3!

White will play in such a way as to leave the pawn undefended only when it is on a dark square, or on the same rank as the black king, and the white king not. Instead 3 g4? ♗e6 4 ♖xh8 ♗xg4 draws.

3...♗a4 4 ♚f4 ♗a5

4...♗a3 5 g4.

5 g4! ♚a6

5...♗a4 6 ♚e5 ♗e6 (6...♚a5 7 g5 intending 8 ♚f6, 9 g6 and 10 ♚g7) 7 ♖xh8 ♗xg4 8 ♖h4 pins the bishop again.

6 g5 ♖h4+

6...♚a7 7 ♖f8 does not help Black.

7 ♚g3 ♖h8 8 g6 ♗f7 9 ♖xh8 ♗xg6 10 ♖h6

Yet again the bishop is pinned, this time with terminal effect.

Next a rook vs pawns situation that is, as so often, very hard to assess.

M. Gromov
"Shakhmaty v SSSR" 1986

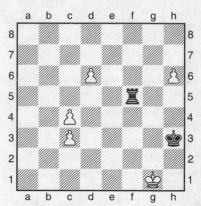

White to Play and Win
Here's a real puzzler. Which pawn should White push?

1 c5!

This turns out to be the only way. Other moves draw or even lose:

a) 1 h7? ♖f8 2 c5 ♚g4 3 c6 ♚f5 4 c4 ♚e6 5 c5 ♚d5 6 c7 ♚c6 7 ♚g2 and White will scrape a draw.

b) 1 d7? ♖f8 2 c5 (2 h7 ♔g4, etc.) 2...♔g3 3 c6 ♖a8 4 ♔f1 ♔f3 5 ♔e1 ♔e3 6 ♔d1 ♔d3 7 ♔c1 ♔xc3 8 ♔b1 ♖b8+ 9 ♔a2 ♖a8+ 10 ♔b1 ♖b8+ draws.

1...♔g3

1...♖xc5 2 d7 ♖g5+ (2...♖d5 3 h7 ♔g3 4 ♔f1 ♖f5+ 5 ♔e2 ♖f8 6 ♔e3 ♔g4 7 ♔e4) 3 ♔f2 ♖g8 4 ♔f3 and the king will come up and support the pawns, winning.

2 h7 ♖f8 3 c6 ♖a8!

This is the best try.

4 ♔f1 ♔f3 5 ♔e1 ♔e3

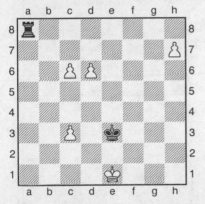

6 ♔d1 ♔d3 7 ♔c1 ♔xc3 8 ♔d1! ♔d3 9 ♔e1 ♔e3 10 ♔f1 ♔f3 11 ♔g1 ♔g3 12 h8♕!

We now see the reason for the kings dancing over to the queenside – the c3-pawn, which Black was obliged to capture, is no longer obstructing the long diagonal. Therefore the new-born queen is covering the a1-square, and the rook must take the new queen.

12...♖xh8 13 c7!

It must be this pawn, since the b8-square is vital for Black's defence.

13...♖a8 14 ♔f1 ♔f3 15 ♔e1 ♔e3 16 ♔d1 ♔d3 17 ♔c1 ♔c3 18 ♔b1

Now there is no check on b8, so

White wins. There will follow 19 d7 and the birth of a queen.

R. Tavariani
"Shakhmaty v SSSR" 1989

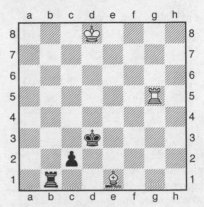

White to Play and Draw

1 ♖g3+ ♔e4! 2 ♖g4+!

Instead 2 ♖c3? does not work since after 2...♖d1+! 3 ♔e8 (3 ♔c8 c1♕ 4 ♖xc1 ♖xc1+ is also a deadly check) 3...♖xe1 4 ♖xc2 ♔d3+ Black picks off the rook.

2...♔f3!

2...♔f5 3 ♖c4 ♖d1+ 4 ♗d2! ♖xd2+ 5 ♔c7! ♔e5 6 ♔c6 ♖f2 7 ♔c5 ♖f8 8 ♔b5 is a theoretical draw.

3 ♖g3+ ♔f4 4 ♖c3 ♖d1+ 5 ♔c8! c1♕ 6 ♗g3+ ♔g4 7 ♖xc1 ♖xc1+ 8 ♔c7

Now we see why the king had to go to c8! The position is drawn.

I have decided not to investigate chess problems (such as "White to play and mate in 3") in depth in this book, feeling the subject is too specialized, and that to do it justice would require a detailed coverage. However, here is a position from the grey area between studies and problems.

A. Lobusov
"Vecherny Kharkov" 1985

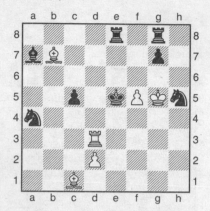

The task here is White to play and force mate in 16 moves! Unbelievable? Here's the solution:

1 ℤd5+ ♔e4 2 ℤd7+ ♔e5 3 ♗a3

The threat is 4 d4+ cxd4 5 ♗d6#.

3...c4

3...ℤe6 4 d4+ cxd4 5 ♗d6+ ℤxd6 6 ℤe7+ ℤe6 7 ℤxe6#.

4 ♗d6+ ♔d4 5 ♗f8+ ♔e5 6 ℤd5+ ♔e4

We are now almost back where we started, except that White's bishop has moved from c1 to f8, and the pawn is now on c4.

7 ℤd8+ ♔e5 8 ℤxe8+ ♔d4 9 ℤd8+ ♔e5 10 ℤd5+ ♔e4 11 ℤd7+

The rook needs to be able to give a check on the e-file after the bishop has moved from f8.

11...♔e5 12 ♗d6+ ♔d4 13 ♗b4+ ♔e5 14 d4+ cxd3

14...♗xd4 15 ♗d6#.

15 ℤe7+ ♔d4 16 ℤe4#

If you have enjoyed these positions, I recommend that you consult some of the specialist literature and periodicals on studies and problems.

Here are a couple of chess problems, both "White to play and force checkmate in two moves". They were the mates-in-two in the 5th International Solving Contest (ISC), held globally on 25th January 2009.

1)

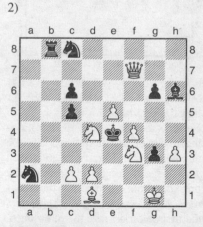

2)

The solutions are given on page 497. If you found these manageable, you may have what it takes to be a competitive solver. But be warned: the other contest problems were longer mates or had other stipulations.

Chess in the Media

Back in the late 1960s, one man started a revolution in the world's view of chess. His name was Bobby Fischer.

Bobby was brash, charismatic, spoke his mind and stuck to his principles. He was also a winner. He beat the whole Soviet "machine" single-handed, at a time when, politically, that was a very good thing for an American to do.

Bobby's success and notoriety brought unprecedented publicity to chess and greatly increased the prizes typical at chess tournaments. As Bill Hartston pithily put it, it was the start of the Financial Age.

Suddenly chess was a game for the young and for the rebellious. Chess was sexy.

The general media, however, has always seemed a little uneasy about chess. All too often the line taken is how weird chess players are, or how boring the game is (to those who don't understand anything about it). Either that or they are "trying to make chess exciting" (as if it isn't already).

In the case of Bobby Fischer, the press coverage had a most unfortunate effect, and he developed a deep distrust of the media. Since he didn't give interviews, reporters had free rein to make up whatever they liked about him. So far as the non-chess-playing world was concerned, the image the media created *was* Fischer. The subject of Fischer is too big to

discuss in detail here, but for a sympathetic, chess-player's view of the great man, I refer you to Frank Brady's biography *Profile of a Prodigy* (if you can get hold of a copy) and Yasser Seirawan's *No Regrets*, which is an account of Fischer's 1992 return match against Spassky and recounts Seirawan's conversations with Fischer.

Chess experienced an explosion of interest in 1972 when Fischer beat Boris Spassky in their world championship match in Reykjavik. Chess was in the news! Television news bulletins recounted the latest stories from Reykjavik, whether on or off the board. Sales of chess books and equipment sky-rocketed and chess club membership increased dramatically.

Unfortunately, Fischer played no competitive chess in the years after winning the title, and as it became clear that the king would not return, media interest in chess began to wane.

Occasionally there is a blip in media interest, but nothing that causes a really large increase in the popularity of chess. For instance, one might have expected the Kasparov vs Short match in London in 1993 to have a major long-term effect on the popularity of chess in Britain. As one would expect, sixty hours of chess on television, albeit largely of low quality, and chess motifs splashed on the sides of

London buses had a dramatic short-term effect. Chess book sales went up by between 300% and 500% and chess club membership reportedly rose by a quarter. However, Nigel Short was no Bobby Fischer, and after he lost the match, everything quickly returned to normal – or indeed worse than before the match. Sponsorship of chess in Britain has fallen to an almost non-existent level since 1993. The reason for such a negative effect is hard to pin-point: perhaps it was Nigel's poor performance in television interviews, the largely superficial coverage on television, or the hyping of Nigel's chances prior to the match causing what was an extremely valiant effort to be viewed as a dismally poor showing. Or perhaps potential sponsors for chess heard the stories that ticket sales for the match were very poor, and so decided that sponsoring chess was a bad option.

If chess is to become more popular, really good television coverage is essential. How to present chess well on television effectively is no mystery. The best approach was refined and perfected in Britain by BBC2 with their *Master Game* series. The programmes were cheap to make and got excellent viewing figures. The series was produced as follows. First, a knock-out chess tournament was played. One of the merits of this format is that it discourages draws. Although each game was to form the basis of a half-hour programme, the time limit was similar to that used in normal tournament games. (Why not play good chess, and then show it accelerated, rather than show bad chess in real-time?) Then the players went to the studio, were given plenty of wine and recounted their thoughts during the game. They were not allowed to cite lengthy variations, but had to describe their ideas in words. A re-enactment of critical moments of the game was then filmed. What the viewer saw on screen was a large clear diagram of the board position, with any squares or pieces that were mentioned in the commentary highlighted. The two players were shown by the side of the board, with their thoughts and commentaries dubbed in.

For club players this provided wonderful insights into how grandmasters and international masters think. The viewing figures were unusually large for the slot when the programme was broadcast – so large that a good proportion of the viewers must have had only a rudimentary knowledge of the game. Yet they stayed tuned.

To me, this is the way forward for chess on television. *The Master Game* did not "try to make chess exciting", but rather portrayed the excitement of chess.

Unfortunately, *The Master Game* was axed in the early 1980s, and has not since been reinstated. This is apparently due to no one in a position of sufficient power at BBC2 believing in the potential for chess on television – in spite of the evidence provided by the viewing figures. Perhaps I am being cynical, but I believe that those who have no experience of chess are all too willing to cling to a preconceived notion of chess and the people who enjoy the game, rather than believe the hard evidence.

Perhaps someone who can change things is reading this. If so, please look at the demographics of chess-players, and investigate the idea of chess on television further.

Until some visionary brings chess back to our television screens, we will have to make do with online coverage, books, magazines and the traditional newspaper columns. Most quality newspapers feature a chess column. Some columns feature up-to-the-minute chess news, while others focus on features of more general chess interest, for instance games by great players. Regrettably, some columns are occasionally used to political effect too.

Incidentally, if your favourite newspaper doesn't cover chess, or does not cover it well, write to the editor and tell him. A few well-written letters making the point can have a very considerable effect. By all means write to television companies too!

Marathon Chess World Record

My closest encounter with the general media came in 1994, when I set a new chess world record.

I was involved in this rather unusual event from Wednesday 18th May to Saturday 21st May at the London Chess Centre – a successful attempt on the World Record for marathon blitz chess playing. My task was to play more than 500 five-minute games, more or less non-stop, with just short rest breaks (how long and how many depending mainly on how quickly I played – clearly 500 five-minute games would take more than 80 hours if both players used all of their clock time). Just to make it more of a challenge, I had to score at least 75%, and my opponents had to have an average grading of 150 ECF (1800 Elo), with ungradeds counting only as 125 ECF (1600 Elo).

Those who agreed to play against me fell into two main groups:

1) inexperienced, aspiring players who viewed it as a learning experience – a chance to play someone who knows a bit about chess;

2) strong players (often friends of mine I'd managed to rope in) who viewed it as a bit of fun, or were going to be at the Chess Centre anyway.

My policy was clear – blow away players of type 1 using about half a minute on my clock, so I could afford a bit of time to think against the good players. My experience at my club in Denmark came in handy here, since there I often played with a one-to-five minute time handicap.

The event went pretty smoothly, though with plenty of excitement and amusing incidents along the way. Naturally, at times I did feel a bit lousy, though nothing like as bad as I'd expected. I certainly didn't come close to hallucinating, or throwing fits or anything. My ...♗c8-f5 (over a pawn on d7), in game number 498 was my only illegal move in the course of the event.

The whole event was rather hectic, with a couple of radio interviews to be slotted in on top of everything else. I turned up at LBC Radio at 6.30 a.m. on the 18th and was interviewed by two people who were obviously so famous that no one bothered to tell me their names! My inexperience let me down somewhat, and unfortunately I failed to dive in when there was a fleeting chance to work in a plug for my latest book. By Saturday morning, I'd had time to work out just what was involved in these interviews, so when another radio station, GLR, spoke to me, I was sure to mention everything I could think of.

The following are a few of the memorable games from the event. Firstly, one against Natasha Regan, a member of the England women's team.

Burgess – N. Regan
London blitz (Game 466) 1994

1 e4 ♘f6 2 e5 ♘d5 3 d4 d6 4 c4 ♘b6 5 f4 dxe5 6 fxe5 ♘c6 7 ♗e3 ♗f5 8 ♘c3 e6 9 ♘f3 ♗g4 10 ♗e2 ♗xf3 11 gxf3 ♕h4+ 12 ♗f2 ♕f4 13 c5 ♘d7 14 ♘e4

I tried 14 ♗b5 in a few games, but Natasha had found something decent there in the end; either 14...f6 or 14...♗e7 followed by ...f6.

14...f6 15 ♕a4 0-0-0 16 ♖d1

Natasha has played a suggestion from my book *The Complete Alekhine*, but at the time I did not realize it was a bad one. Instead of the move played, 16 d5 ♘cxe5 17 c6! is extremely good for White.

16...fxe5 17 ♗g3 ♕h6 18 ♖d3

I'd spent the previous game grinding

down someone who had played 2 ♘c3 against my Alekhine Defence and gone all-out for the draw, so such blatant violence is perhaps forgivable.

18...exd4 19 ♖b3 ♗xc5 20 ♖xb7 ♔xb7 21 ♗a6+ ♔b8 22 ♕xc6 ♕c1+ 23 ♔f2

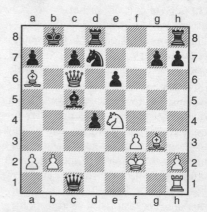

23...♕xb2+

Oh no!! A few moves back I'd only reckoned on 23...d3+? (discovered checks are the first things one looks at, and with such a time limit, second things don't tend to get looked at!) 24 ♔g2 ♕xb2+ 25 ♔h3 when it seems that White does in fact win as spectacularly as I had hoped when launching my kamikaze rook:

a) 25...♗d6 26 ♘xd6 ♕b6 27 ♖b1 ♕xb1 28 ♘e8 ♕f1+ 29 ♔h4 g5+ 30 ♔xg5 and Black will be mated soon.

b) 25...e5 26 ♘c3 with the rather horrible threats of ♖b1 and ♘b5.

24 ♔f1 ♕b6 0-1

After I had broken the record, Grandmaster John Nunn was kind enough to give me a few games. I lost three and won one – a score I would have been happy with under any conditions! Here are the first two games:

Burgess – Nunn
London blitz (Game 504) 1994

**1 d4 ♘f6 2 c4 g6 3 ♘c3 ♗g7 4 e4 d6
5 ♘f3 0-0 6 ♗e2 e5 7 0-0 ♘c6 8 d5
♘e7 9 ♗g5 ♘h5 10 ♘e1 ♘f4 11
♘d3 ♘xe2+ 12 ♕xe2 h6 13 ♗d2 f5
14 f4 fxe4**

A good alternative is 14...c6, as played in Burgess–S.Pedersen, Assens 1990.

15 ♘xe4 ♘f5

15...exf4 is possible, but a little obliging; indeed Neil McDonald played this against me in game number 321 (but with the pawn still on h7, having played the less accurate move 12...f6) and he had slightly the worse of a draw.

16 fxe5 dxe5 17 ♗c3 c6 18 dxc6

"Extra pawn" is Fritz's perceptive comment on 18 ♘xe5 cxd5 19 cxd5.

**18...♘d4 19 ♗xd4 ♕xd4+ 20 ♔h1
♖xf1+ 21 ♖xf1 bxc6 22 ♘f6+**

22 ♘dc5 is possible.

**22...♗xf6 23 ♖xf6 ♗f5 24 ♘f2 ♖b8
25 b3**

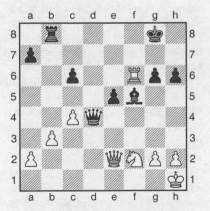

My position's beginning to creak.

25...♖d8

John Nunn provided the variation 25...e4 26 ♖xc6 e3 27 ♘d1 ♖d8 28

♘xe3 ♖e8, winning for Black. At the time John just couldn't believe that after his actual choice, 26 g4 was possible, but in fact things now become unclear again.

26 g4 ♔g7 27 ♖xc6 ♗d7 28 ♖c7 ♕d6

The rest of the game was played without much time on my clock. Black's compensation is not utterly clear, but had my flag not fallen, I imagine I would have dropped a piece somehow.

**29 ♖xa7 ♔g8 30 ♖d7 ♖xd7 31 ♘e4
0-1 (time)**

Nunn – Burgess
London blitz (Game 505) 1994

**1 e4 ♘f6 2 e5 ♘d5 3 d4 d6 4 ♘f3
♗g4 5 ♗e2 c6 6 c4 ♘b6 7 ♘bd2**

7 exd6 exd6 8 ♘bd2 gives Black more options since the b8-knight can often come to a6. But 7 ♘g5 is a more critical test of Black's opening play, and possibly a reason to consider putting the knight on c7 instead of b6.

7...♘8d7

7...dxe5 8 ♘xe5 is good for White.

8 exd6

I believe this is White's best way to play an exchange line here. Now 8 ♘g5 ♗xe2 9 e6 f6 is just unclear.

8...exd6 9 0-0 ♗e7 10 h3

10 ♖e1 0-0 transposes to a game Yudasin–Timoshenko, which continued 11 a4 a5 12 ♖a3 with advantage for White.

10...♗h5 11 b3 0-0 12 ♗b2 a5

This is a debatable decision, holding up White on the queenside at the cost of some weaknesses.

13 a4

This is possibly not necessary.

13...d5 14 c5 ♘c8 15 ♖e1

White could try 15 ♗d3.

15...♗f6

Threatening ...♘xc5.

16 ♖c1 ♖e8 17 ♘f1

17 ♕c2 could be considered.

17...♘f8 18 ♘g3 ♗g6

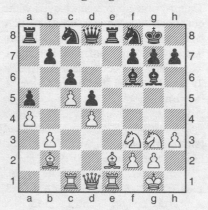

A fairly standard type of position for the opening line as a whole. Black's counterplay springs from the vulnerability of the d4-pawn and the f4-square (and if White *really* asks for it, ...b6 at the right moment), whereas White may look to the weak(?) a5-pawn, b6-square, e-file domination and maybe some kingside play.

19 ♗f1

All the other legal moves are possible, perhaps most notably 19 ♕d2 ♘e6 20 ♗d3 and 19 ♗d3 ♖xe1+ 20 ♘xe1 ♘e7.

19...♘e7

Again not the only move; 19...♘e6 is plausible, as is 19...♖xe1 20 ♕xe1 ♘e6 21 ♘e5 ♘e7 22 ♘xg6 ♘xg6 when Black's grip on f4 gives him counterplay.

20 ♘e5 ♘f5

I am not entirely sure about the sequence in which the next four moves occurred; what follows looks the most

plausible, but John assures me that it was really 20...♘e6 21 ♕d2? (21 ♘xg6 ♘xg6 22 ♗d3 ♘gf4 is probably critical) 21...♘f5 22 ♘xf5 ♗xf5, i.e. that he allowed me to win an exchange with 21...♗g5, and I missed it. Strange, but I *do* recollect playing ...♘e6 somewhere around here. Oops?!

21 ♘xf5 ♗xf5 22 ♕d2 ♘e6 23 g3?

This loses a pawn, but the alternative would be to retreat either the queen or the knight.

23...♘g5

White cannot defend his h-pawn and prevent a capture on e5 followed by a killing fork on f3.

24 ♕f4 ♗xh3 25 ♔h2 ♗e6

25...♗xf1 is somewhat clearer.

26 f3 h6 27 ♗d3 ♘h7 28 ♕d2 ♕c8

Black has a sound extra pawn with a good position.

29 ♕g2 ♗f5 30 ♗xf5 ♕xf5 31 ♖e3 h5

This was intended as a random attacking gesture (a better idea than losing on time), but turns out to be appropriate and quite strong.

32 ♕f2 ♘g5 33 f4 ♕h3+ 34 ♔g1 ♘e4 35 ♕g2 ♕xg2+ 36 ♔xg2 ♗e5 37 dxe5 f5

Again, rather a good idea, played mainly by instinct.

38 ♗d4 ♖e6

Thankfully, a plan.

39 ♔h3 ♔f7 40 ♖ee1 ♖g6 41 ♖e3 ♖e8 42 ♖f1 ♖g4 43 ♖c1 ♖e6 0-1

On time, but White's kingside is in trouble in any case. With or without a few more preparatory moves, ...h5-h4 will cause devastation. Rather an aesthetically pleasing way to use the extra pawn – if White had an h-pawn, this wouldn't be such a big deal.

Here are a few statistics from the event.

- Games played: 510 (431 wins; 25 draws; 54 losses)
- Score vs 2200 and higher: 40½ out of 72
- Score vs 2100–2199: 65½/84
- Score vs players rated below 2100: 337½/354
- Most consecutive victories: 35

During the periods when I was at the board, I averaged 8½ games an hour. This suggests that on average I spent less than two minutes of my clock time on each game.

As a rough estimate, I played about 20,000 moves: one every ten seconds for the whole of three days, with an average of less than three seconds thinking time per move.

Solutions to Mate-in-Two Chess Problems

Given that chess problems are one of the features that have traditionally appeared in newspaper chess columns, it is appropriate to give the solutions to the two "White to play and checkmate in two moves" problems (from page 490) in this chapter. Note that in a chess problem, the task is not merely to win the game, but to achieve the stated task; thus, a way to give mate in three moves, while good in a game situation or in a study, is of no use in a mate-in-two problem.

1) **A.F. Mackenzie**, 1st Prize, *Mirror of American Sports*, 1886: **1 ♘b7!**.

2) **O. Wielgos**, *Die Schwalbe*, 1962: **1 ♘f5!**.

Glossary of Chess Terms

This glossary is intended to be dipped into, and read, rather than just used for reference. I have made it as lively as possible, and often given far more than just a definition of each term. SMALL CAPITALS are used to show that a term used can be found elsewhere in the glossary, but note that not all occurrences of these words are highlighted in this way, but only when the definition may be enhanced by reference to the highlighted term.

The glossary also provides a grounding in the main concepts of chess strategy.

Accept
To capture SACRIFICED MATERIAL and hang on to it, at least temporarily.

Active
An idea or move that furthers one's own PLANS, or a piece that is well placed to ATTACK. Compare PASSIVE.

Advantage
Some aspect of the position that justifies a player in aiming for victory.

Algebraic notation
The modern form of writing down chess moves. In many countries it has been the standard for a long time, though in English- and Spanish-speaking countries it has only taken over from the older descriptive notation in the last two decades. See Appendix B for a detailed description of chess notation.

Analysis
A process by which a chess player considers what are the most logical moves in a position, the best replies to them, etc., and so builds up a "tree" of variations which are possible from the starting position. Note that the choice of moves to analyse is based largely on intuition. Also refers to the VARIATIONS produced by the process of analysis.

Analytical engine
A computer module that takes a chess POSITION as its input and analyses possible lines of play from that position, and provides as output a numerical assessment of the position and a best line of play.

Annotation
Comments about a chess move or position, discussing possible alternatives, PLANS for both sides, explaining the method by which the move may have been decided upon, or anything else the writer feels it appropriate to mention at that point.

Assessment
A player's feeling as to who has the ADVANTAGE in a position, and why. An initial assessment is largely intuitive, but subsequent ANALYSIS refines the assessment, but it is still based on the player's intuitive assessments at the end of the variations he analyses. Blumenfeld wrote eloquently on the intuitive aspect: "assessment is linked

with the perception of a position and is a fundamentally subconscious act in the sense that its intermediate links, to a considerable, if not the whole extent, do not work through the consciousness."

Attack

A concerted action by one player, with the aim of forcing concessions from the opponent. It is also used to refer to an opening variation played (generally) by White of one of two types: a system that launches a direct attack; or is analogous to a set-up played more often by Black, e.g. the King's Indian Attack features White placing his pieces in much the same way that Black does in the King's Indian Defence.

Back-ranker

A simple mating idea, in which a rook or queen checks a king along its first RANK, and, thanks to the presence of a row of pawns along the second rank, it is also mate. This is often a rather random finish to games between novices, but the idea is relevant at all levels.

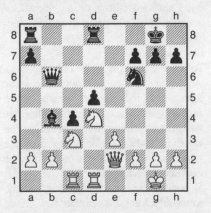

Consider this very famous example (O.Bernstein–Capablanca, Moscow 1914 – WGG 13), in which it turns out that Capablanca's position is supported by a back-rank idea. Black's pawns may not look wonderful, but his pieces provide good support for them. Due to some tactical points, Black is well in the game, but Bernstein still tries to exploit the pawns' weakness.

18 b3?! ℤac8 19 bxc4 dxc4 20 ℤc2 ♗xc3 21 ℤxc3 ♘d5! 22 ℤc2

The first clever point is that 22 ℤxc4 ♘c3 wins the exchange.

22...c3

Now White gangs up on the c-pawn.

23 ℤdc1 ℤc5 24 ♘b3 ℤc6 25 ♘d4 ℤc7 26 ♘b5

It appears that White has succeeded in his aim.

26...ℤc5 27 ♘xc3? ♘xc3 28 ℤxc3 ℤxc3 29 ℤxc3

Now what?

29...♕b2!! 0-1

Black wins a rook due to back-rank mate ideas: 30 ♕xb2 ℤd1# or 30 ♕e1 ♕xc3 31 ♕xc3 ℤd1+ 32 ♕e1 ℤxe1#.

Backward pawn

A pawn that, although not ISOLATED, cannot be supported by either neighbouring pawn because they have advanced ahead of it. If the backward pawn cannot easily advance, then it may well turn out to be a WEAKNESS.

Bad bishop

A bishop that is obstructed by pawns fixed on the same coloured squares as those on which it moves. Note that this does not mean that it is not necessarily an effective *piece*, if it can find some good squares. With this in mind, Peter

Wells coined these helpful terms: good "bad" bishop, good "good" bishop, bad "good" bishop and bad "bad" bishop; the first adjective refers to whether the piece is effective, while the latter is the formal description based on the pawn structure. Nevertheless, his descriptions do remind me of two small Danish towns whose names translate to New Newtown and Old Newtown.

Barry
An alliterative term, sometimes used by chess players to refer to an ATTACK that is UNSOUND but dangerous.

Battery
A situation whereby a player prepares a shielded strong THREAT. Consider the following position:

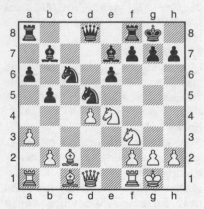

Now 1 ♕d3 sets up a battery on the b1–h7 diagonal. If the e4-knight vanished, White would have the threat of ♕xh7#, so Black must be careful not to allow this knight to move away with devastating effect. The main threats are 2 ♘c5 and 2 ♘d6, winning a piece. 1...g6 would be concession, since 2 ♗h6 could follow.

Bind
A situation in which aims to prevent the other from undertaking any ACTIVE PLAN, or making any good PAWN BREAKS. The idea then is gradually to increase the PRESSURE. Also a name for opening systems that aim to exert a bind, e.g. the Maroczy Bind.

Bishop pair
In open positions it is often a tangible advantage to have two bishops against some other combination of two MINOR PIECES. This is because the main drawback of the bishop is that it can only operate on squares of one colour, so if it can be operating in unison with another bishop that can reach these inaccessible squares, you have a strong team. However, the idea must not be taken to extremes; in many positions the bishops are no better than knights, or may even be relatively clumsy. One major idea that can be employed when playing with the bishop pair against bishop and knight is to *place pawns on the same colour squares as the opponent's bishop*. This limits the scope of the enemy bishop, and means that if an exchange of bishops occurs, it is one's GOOD BISHOP that remains.

Blockade
To place a piece in front of a pawn to prevent its further advance. The concept of the blockade was an important part of Nimzowitsch's teachings on POSITIONAL chess, as expounded at length in his famous book *My System*.

Blocked position
A position in which there are many pawns blocking one another.

Blunder
A dreadful move which turns a reasonable position into a lost one, or throws away a large ADVANTAGE.

Blundercheck
A powerful analysis feature available in CHESSBASE's FRITZ GUI (any compatible engine can be used). It examines an existing game annotation or piece of analysis, and works back from the end of each line in turn. It thus draws upon previous assessments stored in hash tables to increase the effective depth of the analysis, and can discover ideas and tactics that would be too deep to find in normal analysis.

Book
In chess computing terms, a collection of opening lines from which the computer looks up which move to play, rather than working it out by analysing the position. Normally the data structure is a tree of positions, with weightings based on the book's author's ideas of what suits the machine, and also on the results of games (by human and/or computers).

Break
See PAWN BREAK.

Breakthrough
A device, often requiring a SACRIFICE, to make progress through a defensive wall. Typically, this may take the form of a piece sacrifice for a few pawns, or a line-opening pawn sacrifice.

Brilliancy
A spectacular game of chess, featuring SACRIFICES and slashing ATTACKS. In some tournaments there are special prizes for brilliancies. Note that this is not the same as a best game prize, which is awarded for a game featuring accurate play, and at least plausible play from the loser, if the game is not a draw. A brilliancy may contain errors aplenty, provided there are also fantastic moves and ideas.

Calculation
One of the key aspects of ANALYSIS of a chess position. It is allied with intuition, and involves working out sequences of likely moves from the current position to reach others in which ASSESSMENTS are made.

Castling
A special move in chess, involving a king and a rook of the same colour. It is very often a useful move, as it takes the king away from the CENTRE and brings the rook into play. However, one must be careful not to castle into an attack, or reduce one's options by castling too early, as this may help clarify the opponent's choice of plan.

CC
Short for CORRESPONDENCE CHESS.

Centralization
Since pieces are generally most effective and mobile when placed in the CENTRE of the board, it is often a wise policy to amass forces in the centre. This is known as centralization. Often, and somewhat paradoxically to newcomers to chess, the best way to repulse an ATTACK on the WING is to centralize, so as to cut the lines of communication that a successful attack needs.

Centre

The squares in the middle of the board (d4, e4, d5 and e5), which forms the main strategic battleground, especially in the early part of the game. However, note that the word "centre" can be used in other ways too; for instance when one talks of a king left "stuck in the centre", it generally means that the king is not able to CASTLE, and is still somewhere near his starting square, and not that the king has been hunted into mid-board.

Checkmate

The ultimate aim in the game of chess, by which the enemy king is checked (threatened with capture), and has no means of escape. Checkmate ends the game immediately; the king is not actually captured.

Chess Assistant

A Russian chess database program, which became quite fashionable in the mid-1990s. Although it is less sophisticated than the main rival product, CHESSBASE, it is cheaper and has powerful indexing and searching facilities that enable the desired data to be found quickly, even on relatively slow computers.

ChessBase

A popular chess database program. It has grown from a little program that Matthias Wüllenweber wrote to run on his Atari computer while he was at university in Edinburgh into a powerful, multi-purpose chess study tool with tens of thousands of users world-wide. ChessBase is based in Hamburg. Wüllenweber was joined by Mathias Feist, who, amongst other programming tasks, converted ChessBase for different computer platforms (most notably Windows), Frederic Friedel (who now runs the lively ChessBase news website), a well-known figure in the chess world, and Gisbert Jacoby, who edited *ChessBase Magazine*, the first major electronic chess magazine. Garry Kasparov endorsed ChessBase in 1987, having used it to prepare for his games, most notably a simultaneous match against the strong Hamburg chess team in February 1987, against whom he had lost a similar match at the end of 1985. It is no exaggeration to say that ChessBase has revolutionized the way professional players study chess and prepare for their games.

Classical

A school of chess thought that dictates that it is vital to OCCUPY the CENTRE. Compare HYPERMODERN – the modern view is that neither school is entirely right or wrong, and that a flexible approach to the centre is essential.

Clearance

A simple device: by exchanging, sacrificing, or simply moving a piece, a line is cleared to the benefit of other pieces.

Closed Games

General term for all openings, apart from the Indian Defences, that begin with 1 d4. Overwhelmingly the most important is the Queen's Gambit, 1 d4 d5 2 c4. Note that closed games do not at all necessarily lead to CLOSED POSITIONS.

Closed position

One in which there are many pawns blocking the free movement of the pieces.

Combination

A forcing sequence of moves of benefit to the player initiating it.

Compensation

Strategic or tactical benefits, either short- or long-term, for the sake of which MATERIAL is offered.

Connected pawns

Pawns that are on adjacent FILES and are capable of defending one another.

Control

A square or line is controlled if enough pieces are attacking it so that the opponent's pieces cannot safely move onto it.

Correspondence chess

A general term for chess played by post, telephone, fax, e-mail, server, etc., when not played in real-time (i.e. time in correspondence chess games is measured discretely rather than continuously). Jonathan Berry, writing in his book *Diamond Dust* (ICE, 1991) put forward an ecological case for playing by correspondence: "In principle, chess is kind to the ecology. All you need is a chess set which could be made of wood, or even if it is made of plastic, its useful life can be decades. However, chess players must travel if they don't find nearby the level of competition they crave. As we know, travelling by car or plane is hard on the planet, releasing into the atmosphere carbon that has been locked away for millions of years. The fuel used to transport 2 kg of postcards (plenty for a 14-game CC tournament) is less than that required for 80 kg live weight."

Counterattack

The ideal response to an ATTACK: the defender attacks the attacker!

Countergambit

A GAMBIT by Black, not necessarily as a direct response to a gambit by White.

Counterplay

Life-saving activity for a player under PRESSURE or ATTACK.

Cramp

A player without sufficient room to arrange his pieces conveniently suffers from cramp.

Critical position

A point at which the result of the game hangs by a thread, and a player failing to make the right decision will land in deep trouble.

Cross-check

A move in response to a check which itself gives check. This is a particularly useful device in queen and pawn endings as a way to end a barrage of checks from the opposing queen. Consider the position on the next page, which comes from the game Botvinnik–Minev, Amsterdam OL 1954. Botvinnik played 91 ♔c5!!. No matter how Black chooses to give check, a cross-check in reply will force off the queens.

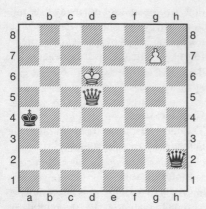

For instance: 91...♕g1+ 92 ♕d4+; 91...♕f2+ 92 ♕d4+; 91...♕c2+ 92 ♕c4+; or 91...♕c7+ 92 ♕c6+. Minev therefore resigned.

Decline

To refuse to capture some SACRIFICED MATERIAL.

Decoy

A tactical idea in which an enemy piece is obliged to move to a particular square or line, with catastrophic consequences.

Defence

Responding to and parrying the opponent's THREATS and organizing one's pieces to be able to prevent the opponent's ATTACK from breaking through. The defender's aim must be eventually to break out and launch a COUNTER-ATTACK, or else exchange off the attacking units.

Deflection

A tactical device by which an enemy piece is obliged to leave a particular square or line, with fatal consequences.

Development

One of the most important concepts in chess is that it is essential to bring pieces into play quickly at the start of the game. This process is called development. If one player is ahead in the race to bring pieces to good squares, he is said to have a development advantage, and should be looking for concrete ways to benefit from this, perhaps by launching an ATTACK.

Diagonal opposition

A related idea to OPPOSITION, except that the kings are on the same diagonal, separated by an odd number of squares. The king to move must either give ground or else allow the opponent to gain the normal opposition on a rank or file.

Discovered attack

A simple tactical theme: a piece moves, and in so-doing opens a line of attack from one on its own side onto an enemy unit. How strong the move is, tends to depend on what the piece that moves can achieve.

Discovered check

The same idea as DISCOVERED ATTACK, except that it is the enemy king onto which the attack is "discovered".

Distant opposition

A endgame situation in which two kings stand on the same line with three or five squares between them, and need to battle for position. The player who is not to move is said to have the distant opposition, since if the opponent's king advances, he will be able to gain the OPPOSITION.

Distractions

Although the laws of chess state that a player may not distract his opponent in any way, and that spectators also have an obligation not to disturb the players, at virtually any chess event there will be some factors that will prevent full concentration on the game. In extreme cases one must complain, but for routine things it is best somehow to ignore the disturbance. Botvinnik, an extremely determined man, even trained himself specifically to cope with cigarette smoke over the board, conducting training games in which he asked to be bombarded throughout with a constant "smokescreen". (Smoking is not allowed nowadays at many chess events, but the problem persists at some events, and in certain countries.)

Some of the most commonly encountered forms of distraction are:

1) Spectators' "whispered" conversations that can be heard loud and clear by anyone trying to concentrate.

2) "Quiet" POST-MORTEM analysis sessions in among other boards where games are still in progress.

3) Table shakers – some players translate nervous tension into vibrating their table or chair.

4) Fidgets – nervous tension again.

5) Coin janglers – I cannot understand why, but some spectators seem to shake a pocketful of coins when watching other games.

6) Spectators who press their bodies just a bit too close to the players whose game they are watching. Particularly unpleasant on a hot day!

7) Noisy fans – on hot days an alarming number of venues offer a choice between baking heat, traffic noise from opening the windows or listening to the rhythmic rattling of a faulty fan or air-conditioning system.

8) Silent distractions – an opponent who reads the newspaper when waiting for your move, screws their moves into the board, or stands up by the board or behind your shoulder.

Double (or Multiple) attack

A simple tactical idea, by which two (or more) enemy units are threatened simultaneously. Since there is only one move in which to save them, this is often a way in which material can be won. When a single piece attacks the enemy units, it is called a FORK.

Double check

When giving a DISCOVERED CHECK, it is sometimes possible for the piece that moves also to give check – thus putting the enemy king is check twice. This is one of the most potent ideas in chess, since in reply a king move is forced – it is not possible to take both checking pieces simultaneously, nor to block both lines along which they may be attacking. Here's an extreme example:

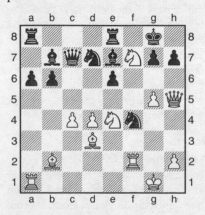

In this position, from the famous game Moser–Underwood, Corr. 1962, White launched a mating attack with the spectacular queen sacrifice 22 ♕xh7+!!, the key point being that 22...♔xh7 allows 23 ♘f6# – there is no way to escape from both checks. It does not matter that either checking piece can be captured – this would do nothing about the check from the other piece. (For the full game, see *The King-Hunt* by John Nunn and William Cozens, Batsford, 1996.)

Doubled pawns

Two (or more) pawns of the same colour on the same file (following a capture). In themselves, doubled pawns can be strong (provided they are not also isolated), but not especially mobile. The concentration of pawns in one place may leave other areas a little bare.

Draw

A game that ends in victory for neither player, and the point is shared. The most common way for a game to be drawn is by agreement between the two players (see DRAW OFFER), while if the players fight until they have little or no material left, a draw by INSUFFICIENT MATERIAL can arise. Other ways in which a game can be drawn are THREE-FOLD REPETITION, FIFTY-MOVE RULE, STALEMATE or by a player running out of time on the clock when the opponent does not have enough material to give mate.

Draw offer

A draw may be offered by a player after making his move, and, when playing with a chess clock, before starting the opponent's clock. If the opponent accepts, then each player receives half a point. A draw offer only stands for one move; it cannot be accepted on the next turn. There are several points of etiquette that must be observed:

1) A player should not make repeated draw offers. If one offer has been declined, then unless the position changes substantially, it is for the opponent to offer a draw, should he choose to.

2) A draw must not be offered when the opponent's clock is ticking.

3) A draw should not be offered by a player who obviously has no winning chances at all, when there may still be chances for the opponent.

4) A draw should not be offered without first making a move. The opponent then has every right (and generally should) ask for a move to be made before considering the draw offer (which cannot be retracted).

Severe breaches of etiquette, especially when the opponent is short of time, may be punishable, e.g. by a time penalty.

Dynamic play

Play based on the temporary and potential features of the position overriding its static characteristics.

Edge

A small advantage.

Elastic band

A name that may be given to a type of COMBINATION that apparently puts a piece *EN PRISE*, but does not lose material, since an attack is also opened onto an enemy piece. The vital point is that the opponent, in dealing with this attack, must allow the originally moved piece to be rescued. Like almost all tactical ideas, the definition makes it sound far more complicated than it is, so here are a couple of examples:

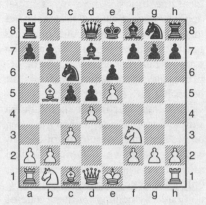

White has just played 6 &f1-b5?. This allows Black to win a pawn with the elastic-band move 6...&xe5!. White does not win a piece by 7 dxe5 or 7 &xe5 since Black then plays 7...&xb5. Nor can White exchange bishops, 7 &xd7+, before winning the knight, since then 7...&xd7 rescues the knight. This is the sort of tactic that quite often decides games at lower club level. Although the analysis is simple, the idea is a little paradoxical, and easily missed – White may not bother to analyse Black's capture on e5, since the pawn is securely defended. The moral is always to think carefully before leaving a piece undefended, especially in enemy territory. Succinctly put: loose pieces drop off.

When combined with other ideas, the elastic band can decide top-level games. Here's an example, from the game Hübner–Nunn, Skellefteå World Cup 1989.

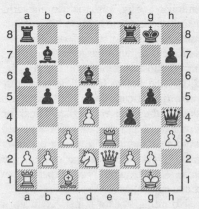

Black has just played 18...f5-f4 – he has already sacrificed a pawn so some aggression is necessary. It seems as though the rook must move, but Hübner found a magnificent sequence: 19 &f3! &h5 20 &xg5!. The black queen is attacked, so there is still no time to take the rook, while 20...&xe2 is answered by 21 &xe2, saving the piece in question, and leaving White two pawns up. 20...&xg5 21 &g3 wins the queen thanks to two pins – 21...fxg3 allows 22 &xg5. The final point of the combination – a fork – was seen in the game itself: 20...&g6 21 &e6 &xg5 22 &xd6. Although Black actually managed to regain one of his pawns, his position was wrecked: 22...&ae8 23 &e6 &f7 24 &e5 &xe5 25 dxe5 &e6 26 &d2 &xe5 27 &d3 and White went on to win the game without undue difficulty.

Elo rating

Contrary to popular belief, Elo is a man's name, and not an acronym. Professor Arpad Elo (1903–1992) was the founder of the United States Chess Federation and creator of the rating system used by FIDE and most national rating systems. In the Elo rating system, each player is given a numerical rating, based on their results to date, with the most recent figuring most prominently. It is the difference between two players' ratings that determines the expected score if they play each other. Thus, for instance, a player rated 1500 would expect to score 25% against a player rated 1700, which is the same score that a 2500 would be expected to make against a 2700.

No rating system is perfect; from a mathematical viewpoint the Elo rating system is both deflationary and unstable. Nevertheless on the whole it works well, and has been adopted by other sports, including table tennis.

Professor Elo continually refined his system to maintain its accuracy and integrity. He discouraged the tendency, natural though it is, for ambitious players to view increasing their Elo as a primary aim: "It is a measuring tool, not a device of reward or punishment; it is a means to compare performances, assess relative strength, not a carrot waved before a rabbit or a piece of candy given to a child for good behavior." Inevitably, players' Elo ratings have taken on considerable financial significance – at international level, the higher the Elo, the better the invitations and conditions, while players without an Elo rating tend to be charged large sums simply to play in major international open tournaments.

En passant

This is one of the laws of chess that seems particularly odd to non-players or hard to grasp for social players. One of the worst things for an experienced player to hear when playing a casual opponent (especially if playing for money, in a park for instance) is "I've never heard of *en passant*, and I don't like cheaters neither!" The rule was introduced at the same time as the pawn's initial double move when it was realized that otherwise one could obtain a passed pawn by moving a pawn two squares past an enemy pawn on its fifth rank. Since a passed pawn can be such a powerful force, it was considered improper that it should be so simple to create one, and so the pawn on the fifth rank should be enabled to capture the pawn just as if it had moved one square. *En passant* is the only case in chess where a capture is not made by occupying the square of the piece being captured.

En prise

Able to be captured by an enemy piece. Generally used when the piece has been accidentally left in a position to be captured, as a BLUNDER.

Endgame

The last possible phase of a game of chess, although quite often games end in the middlegame or even in the opening. Many attempts have been made to classify just when the middlegame finishes and the endgame starts. Considerable simplification is necessary, but the queens being exchanged is certainly not a sufficient (or necessary) criterion. The key concept is that in an ending the king ceases to be primarily a liability to be guarded, but becomes a fighting unit, and the main battle revolves around the creation and advancing of passed pawns. This does not mean that the king is not subject to any attack, or that complex tactics cannot occur, however, but just that the need to activate the king overrides the dangers.

Endgame databases
Powerful computers have made it possible to analyse certain endgames exhaustively, so rather than an assessment such as "White is better", one can now say with certainty, e.g. "White wins in at most 24 moves". Currently (2009) databases exist for all endgames with five pieces or fewer (including kings) on the board and almost all six-man endings. Work has begun on the seven-man databases. The term "tablebases" is often used, referring to Nalimov tablebases, a data format that enables the data to be read by a chess engine.

Constructing the database is no simple matter, nor does it involve any positional understanding of chess being programmed into the machine. The computer generates all possible "final" positions which are winning for the stronger side. This may be mate or transition to another ending (after a capture of a piece, or promotion of a pawn) that is already known to be a win. The computer then works backwards from these positions, assigning numbers to positions, denoting how many moves are needed to win from the given position.

The result of this complicated procedure is a list of all the winning positions with the particular material balance, and the maximum number of moves needed to win them. If a position is not in the list, this means the attacker cannot force a win.

In view of the colossal amount of computer time needed to construct these databases, they might have remained merely a theoretical possibility, were it not for one man: Ken Thompson of Bell Laboratories. Apparently, his "serious" computing work has been of such value, that in return he is allowed *carte blanche* to use their powerful mainframes however he pleases!

In the 1990s, John Nunn took on the task of interpreting the results to the chess world, distilling general principles out of the mass of data.

Equality
A state in which neither side has an ADVANTAGE. This does not necessarily mean that the game will inevitably result in a draw, but rather that the chances are equal. There are considered to be two varieties of equality: sterile equality, in which there is little or no imbalance in the position, and dynamic equality, where both sides have advantages and weaknesses, which should cancel each other out. In practice dynamic equality provides scope for the more skilful player to outplay the opponent, whereas in a position of sterile equality, it takes considerable grinding and/or a gross error for either side to make progress.

Evergreen Game
The name given to the following spectacular and famous game:

Anderssen – Dufresne
Berlin 1852 (WGG 3)

1 e4 e5 2 ♘f3 ♘c6 3 ♗c4 ♗c5 4 b4 ♗xb4 5 c3 ♗a5 6 d4 exd4 7 0-0 d3

**8 ♕b3 ♕f6 9 e5 ♕g6 10 ♖e1 ♘ge7
11 ♗a3 b5 12 ♕xb5 ♖b8 13 ♕a4
♗b6 14 ♘bd2 ♗b7 15 ♘e4 ♕f5 16
♗xd3 ♕h5 17 ♘f6+ gxf6 18 exf6
♖g8 19 ♖ad1 ♕xf3 20 ♖xe7+ ♘xe7**

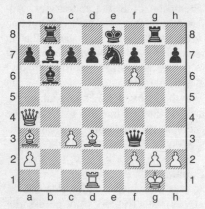

**21 ♕xd7+ ♔xd7 22 ♗f5++ ♔e8 23
♗d7+ ♔f8 24 ♗xe7# (1-0)**

Exchange

To capture an enemy piece in the
knowledge that the opponent will recapture.

Knowing which pieces to exchange
off is one of the thorniest problems in
practical chess. Strong players can win
games almost effortlessly by virtue of
a greater feel than their opponent for
which pieces they should retain in
certain types of positions. As one Soviet trainer put it: "If you are playing
against a weaker opponent, exchange
off some pieces. He will almost certainly not understand which pieces he
should exchange, and which he needs
to keep on the board."

Exchange Chess

A popular chess variant, played by
four players (two teams of two players) using two boards. One player in
each partnership takes White, and the
other Black. When either player captures an enemy piece, he passes it to
his partner, who, subject to various
rules, may, instead of playing an ordinary move, drop it onto an empty
square on his board. Exchange Chess
has various alternative names, and in
particular when played over the Internet it generally goes under the name of
Bughouse.

Exchange sacrifice

A SACRIFICE of a rook for a MINOR
PIECE. The motivation for an exchange
sacrifice may be far more subtle and
long-term than for most sacrifices.
This is because in certain circumstances, the minor piece in question
may simply be a more effective piece
than the rook. If so, then rather than
the line of thought being "I can expect
to give mate or win back the material",
it is "here my pieces are worth more
than those of my opponent – if he
wishes to change that situation, he will
have to make some concession or another." Here's an example of what Seirawan called a "text-book exchange
sacrifice":

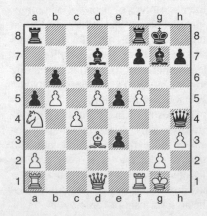

Perhaps he was hoping that someone writing a book such as this would recall his comment. The position comes from Seirawan–Kožul, Wijk aan Zee 1991. Seirawan now played 19 ♕g4! ♕xg4 20 hxg4 e4 21 ♗e2! (White's idea is to keep lines for Black's rooks closed, so he avoids taking on e4) 21...♗xa1 22 ♖xa1 ♖ab8 23 ♔h2. The point here is that there is simply no way for the black rooks to do anything, apart from protect weak pawns. There are no open lines for them, so they are worse than White's minor pieces. White's plan is to bring his king to f4, and rook to h6, and there's not much Black can do about it – but try telling your computer that Black isn't better!

Excuses

Excuses for losing at chess are probably as old as the game itself. Few ambitious players will readily admit that they lost because the opponent simply played better. Illness, of course, is often a genuine mitigating circumstance, but I am yet to hear someone saying after a win that they were too ill to play well, and that they were lucky that the opponent was even more out-of-sorts. I particularly like the following comment by Johann Löwenthal, writing in *Morphy's Games of Chess* (1860), about a loss of his own to the young Morphy: "When only thirteen years of age he was a really good player. At that early age he was victorious in one or two games against the Editor of this work, who was then paying a short visit to New Orleans, and though the latter was at that time depressed in mind and suffering in body, and was also prostrated by the climate, yet the achievement of the young Paul argues a degree of skill to which it is wonderful that a child could have attained." As if one needed any excuse to lose against Morphy at any age!

Fianchetto

The flank development of a bishop, achieved by advancing the knight's pawn and placing the bishop in the square it has vacated.

FIDE

Much maligned, but still the official world governing body for chess, the *Federation Internationale Des Echecs* (International Chess Federation) boasts the third-largest world-wide membership of all sporting bodies. FIDE organizes the international rating system and titles, the biennial chess Olympiad, World Junior Championships and the World Championship itself once more, following the reunification process of 2005–8.

FIDE Master (FM)

The third highest permanent title that a chess player can achieve. Like the higher titles, grandmaster and international master, there is a FIDE rating requirement, 2300, but there is no need to achieve norms. There are about 5,000 FIDE masters in the world.

FIDE rating

The name for the rating system used and maintained by FIDE. It is run according to the mathematical system devised by Prof. Arpad Elo, and so FIDE rating is virtually synonymous with ELO RATING.

Fifty-move Rule

One of the ways in which a game can be drawn. If fifty moves have been played without a pawn move or a capture, then a draw may be claimed. The player making the claim must have an up-to-date scoresheet. Note that the player hoping to claim a draw in this manner should not count the moves aloud (for some reason, many young juniors seem to do this).

Files

The lettered lines of squares running from White's side of the board over to Black's. One refers to the a-file, b-file, etc.

Flank

A general term for the KINGSIDE or QUEENSIDE. One talks of "play on the WINGS".

Flank Openings

Openings in which one player or the other (or both) follow HYPERMODERN principles, and do not occupy the CENTRE of the board in the initial stages of the game, but rather aim to CONTROL it with pieces. Flank openings by their nature involve at least one FIANCHETTO.

Fluid position

One in which the PAWN STRUCTURES are not yet determined – either because the two sides' pawns have not come into contact, or because the TENSION is being maintained.

Fool's Mate

The name given to the shortest possible checkmate from the starting position, which runs as follows:

1 f3 e5 2 g4 ♛h4#.

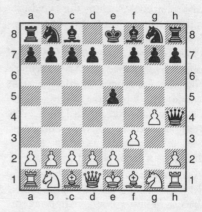

Clearly, one is not likely ever to find an opponent cooperative enough to play like that as White, so Fool's Mate is a curiosity, with no real practical importance – there is no point sitting down to play as Black aiming for Fool's Mate – it is White who does all the "work". In the early days of modern chess, when the powers of the queen had been extended, Fool's Mate was used as an example of the new possibilities opened up: what a fast-moving game chess now was, if the game could finish with mate in just two moves. Nowadays it is just a stark example that gratuitous pawn advances exposing one's king are to be avoided, especially early in the opening. Compare SCHOLAR'S MATE, which does have practical importance, at least at novice level.

Force

One of the main components in evaluating a chess position is the amount of MATERIAL both sides possess. If the material is equal, then other factors must be considered. If one side has an advantage in force (i.e. more material), then unless the opponent has sufficient COMPEN-SATION, the player with the extra material should expect to win.

Most chess games are decided by one player gaining an advantage in force, reaching an ENDGAME and then PROMOTING a pawn and giving mate – or rather the opponent resigning in the face of inevitable loss in this manner.

Forced

A move or sequence of moves for which there are no viable alternatives for one or both players.

Fork

A simple tactical device, in which one piece attacks two (or more) enemy pieces simultaneously.

Fortress

An endgame position which, despite the opponent having an apparently overwhelming material advantage, cannot be broken down. This is a type of positional draw. Here is a typical example:

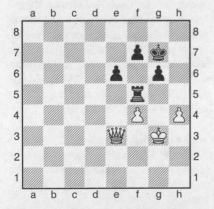

There is simply no way for White to make any progress here. The black

rook will oscillate between f5 and h5 (or d5), while the black king cannot be eked out. White's king cannot penetrate, since the black rook cuts it off along the fifth rank, there is no good way for White to sacrifice his queen for the rook, and pawn advances to f5 or h5 will just be gobbled up by the black rook.

Free Internet Chess Servers (FICS)

There are many chess servers on the Internet which allow chess players to play against opponents in Cyberspace. Although there are not the same possibilities for meeting really strong players or for watching GM commentaries as exist on the Internet Chess Club, as the name suggests, FICS are free to use.

Fritz

One of the strongest PC-based chess-playing programs on the market. It is sold by ChessBase and was designed from the outset to be compatible with their products. For instance, it is possible to be using CHESSBASE and to have Fritz running in the background, constantly giving an assessment of the position and a suggested line of play. Starting with version 2, the main programmer was the Dutchman Frans Morsch. "Fritz" also refers to the graphical user interface (GUI), which can be used with other engines too.

Gambit

A pawn SACRIFICE in the OPENING for some tangible COMPENSATION.

Game reference

In chess literature there is a standard convention for mentioning a specific game: the name of the player with White is given first, followed by a dash and then the name of the player with Black. Next a comma and a description of the event, generally just a place name, followed by the year. Thus Armstrong–Aldrin, Sea of Tranquility 1969 would refer to a game played by the two astronauts when on the moon, in which Neil Armstrong had the white pieces.

General principles

Sometimes a player chooses a move based purely on working out all the variations to a finish, or by calculating a lot of lines. Very often, however, his choice is guided (in both selection of candidate moves and assessments) by rules of thumb that have been built up from generations of chess players' experience. These are known as general principles. Typical of these principles are that it is a good idea to control the centre, to put pressure on the opponent's king or to strengthen control of certain key squares in the position, e.g. the square in front of a backward pawn. Blindly following general principles can lead to bad choices of move, as chess is too complex a game to be reduced to a set of rules, and so modern GMs primarily rely on concrete considerations and analysis – a phenomenon for which John Watson has coined the term "rule independence".

Good bishop

A bishop that is unobstructed by pawns fixed on the same colour squares as those on which it moves. In view of its MOBILITY, and provided there is work for it to do, it should be an effective piece. See BAD BISHOP.

Grandmaster (GM)

The highest permanent title that a chess player can be awarded. Currently there are about 1,200 grandmasters in the world, so it is still a very exclusive title, despite the claims of some notable players who feel that the title is being devalued. To obtain the grandmaster title, a player must achieve a FIDE RATING of at least 2500 and achieve grandmaster norms in a number of tournaments making up a total of at least 24 games. There are several criteria that determine whether a result is a norm (e.g. the opponents must include a certain proportion of titled players), but the basic principle is that the rating performance should be over 2600.

Grandmaster draw

A somewhat derogatory term for a short draw, normally without any particular content or interest. Sometimes the games are prearranged in advance, but on other occasions the players simply do not wish to take any risks. Note that the players do not need to be grandmasters! Ordinary players should not imagine that they are being clever by agreeing quick draws: for professional players, with a living to make, a short draw may serve their purposes well, but for someone trying to improve, or playing for fun, there is no point in avoiding a sharp battle.

Half-open file

A file on which there are no friendly pawns, but at least one enemy pawn.

Hang

A piece "hangs" if it is undefended. A player must be very careful about leaving pieces hanging, as they can easily become targets for COMBIN-ATIONS.

Hanging pawns

Two pawns that stand abreast, often c- and d-pawns on their fourth rank, without pawns on adjacent files. Thus they cannot receive support from other pawns.

Hole

A WEAKNESS in the PAWN STRUCTURE that provides an ideal potential home for enemy pieces.

Horizon

How far a computer is able to analyse from a particular position in a certain amount of time. For instance, if the computer is playing at a rate of five minutes per move, and as a result of this restriction in the particular position is able to analyse ahead only six moves, then it will be unable to anticipate a THREAT that is seven moves deep. The threat would then be said to be "beyond the computer's horizon". A SELECTIVE SEARCH helps the computer to see a little deeper, but may cause it to miss some shorter-term ideas, especially where ZUGZWANG or heavy SACRIFICES are involved.

Horse

Unofficial and slightly childish but nevertheless popular alternative name for the knight. After all, the piece does look like a horse. Some beginners' guides imply that one should never call the knight a horse for fear of being laughed at in learned chess-playing company. However, there are plenty of strong players who call them horses.

Nevertheless, I doubt that H will become the symbol used for the knight when writing down chess moves, although a young pupil of mine in a school in Denmark used it persistently.

Hypermodern

A school of chess thought which argues that it is essential to CONTROL the CENTRE, but that actually occupying the centre is often a double-edged venture. Compare CLASSICAL.

Immortal Game

The name given to one of the most famous games on record, featuring a cascade of sacrifices:

Anderssen – Kieseritzky
London 1851 (WGG 2)

1 e4 e5 2 f4 exf4 3 ♗c4 ♕h4+ 4 ♔f1 b5 5 ♗xb5 ♘f6 6 ♘f3 ♕h6 7 d3 ♘h5 8 ♘h4 ♕g5 9 ♘f5 c6 10 g4 ♘f6 11 ♖g1 cxb5 12 h4 ♕g6 13 h5 ♕g5 14 ♕f3 ♘g8 15 ♗xf4 ♕f6 16 ♘c3 ♗c5 17 ♘d5 ♕xb2 18 ♗d6 ♕xa1+ 19 ♔e2 ♗xg1 20 e5 ♘a6 21 ♘xg7+ ♔d8

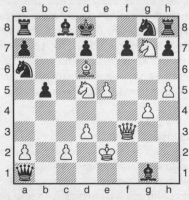

22 ♕f6+ ♘xf6 23 ♗e7# (1-0)

Initiative

The ability to create THREATS. One of the key concepts in chess is that both players must battle for the initiative, since although a prolonged initiative may not be enough to force a win, it makes it far more difficult for the opponent to stay afloat. In positions where both sides have WEAKNESSES, seizing the initiative tends to prove decisive, since a player who can only respond to threats against his own weaknesses is in no condition to exploit those of his opponent.

Innovation

A prepared new move in the opening. An innovation may also be called a novelty or a theoretical novelty. For top-class players innovations are vital weapons, used to surprise their opponents and seize the INITIATIVE at the board. As Yasser Seirawan puts it in *Five Crowns* (ICE, 1991) "An opening novelty is to the chess Grandmaster what a slick draw was to the gun fighter. You gotta have one or you're gonna die!" Ideally an innovation such be an improvement over the moves that have previously been played, but any tricky new move can have a powerful psychological effect. Note that the *Informator* symbol "N" (claimed to mean "novelty") does not imply that the move is genuinely new, but just that it is new to the *Informator* database.

Insufficient material

One of the ways in which a game can end in a draw. It occurs when neither side has enough material to be able, even with highly cooperative play, to mate the other. Specifically, they are:

a) king against king;

b) king against king and bishop or knight;

c) king and bishop against king and bishop, with both bishops on diagonals of the same colour.

Note that this rule does not cover endings such as knight vs bishop or rook vs rook or even two knights vs bare king. Mates are possible, so the draw must be made in another way.

International Master (IM)

The second highest permanent title that a chess player can attain. The way in which a player qualifies for the title is very similar to that for GRANDMASTER, except that the qualifying FIDE RATING is 2400 and the rating performance for a norm is 2450. There are about 3,000 international masters in the world.

Internet Chess Club (ICC)

In return for a yearly fee, ICC provides its members with facilities for playing real-time chess games on-line with opponents around the world. It is also possible to view and comment upon other games in progress. ICC also provides grandmaster commentaries on games from major events.

Interpose

To block an attack or a check by placing a piece in between an enemy piece and the unit it is attacking.

Intuition

A chess player's feeling, based on experience, about the ASSESSMENT of a position, and what is the best move, or the selection of plausible moves from which to choose.

IQP
An isolated queen's pawn (d-pawn). Also called an isolani.

Isolated Pawn
A pawn with no "friendly" pawns on adjacent files. In itself a WEAKNESS, but this can easily be outweighed by DYNAMIC factors.

Keeping score
In tournament games and matches not played at a quickplay or faster time limit, both players must write down each move as it is played, generally on a score-sheet provided for this purpose. This is known as "keeping score". Failure to do so, especially when the opponent is in time-trouble, may be punished, generally by a time penalty. The compulsion to keep score is waived for a player with less than five minutes to reach the next time control, though once a player's flag has fallen, the players must update their score-sheets, reconstructing the game if ncither was keeping score. A complete and up-to-date score-sheet is essential if one needs to make a claim for a draw by THREE-FOLD REPETITION or FIFTY-MOVE RULE.

Kingside
The e-, f-, g- and h-FILES. Often used more specifically ("playing on the kingside rather than in the CENTRE") to refer to the f-, g- and h-files.

Liquidation
The process of exchanging pieces in order to clarify a position, perhaps to reach a winning ending from a favourable position, or to reach a tenable ending from an awkward situation.

Lobster
See OCTOPUS.

Luft
A flight square made for a king to protect it from a possible BACK-RANKER.

Major piece
A rook or queen.

Manoeuvring
Improving the positions of one's pieces so that they will be better placed when the forces meet. Generally undertaken in QUIET or BLOCKED POSITIONS.

Master
A description for a strong chess player. "Master" is often used as a way to refer to an INTERNATIONAL MASTER, while in some countries there are domestic master titles, which may imply a skill level no greater than that of a good club player.

Mate
A common abbreviation for the word CHECKMATE. The standard symbol for mate in chess notation is "#".

Material
Some quantity of pieces and/or pawns.

An advantage in material is one of the easiest concepts to grasp: if you have extra pieces, then other things being equal, you can expect to win. Also if your pieces are more valuable than the opponent's (e.g. a rook for a knight), then you also have a material advantage. All beginners are taught a very approximate scale for the values of the pieces:

Pawn	1 point
Knight	3 points
Bishop	3 points
Rook	5 points
Queen	9 points
King	Infinite

(Apologies to my fellow mathematicians for using the word "infinite" in this way, but you know what I mean!) Sometimes people try to refine the scale (e.g. bishop = $3\frac{1}{4}$ points, etc.), but there is no point doing this. The scale is only meant to be a very rough guide. When there are slight material imbalances, the assessment has to be based on the specifics of the position. Chess is not a game of point-counting. Successful chess players do not lose their queen for a knight, but neither do they have any qualms about sacrificing a pawn, piece or whatever to gain other advantages in position.

Mating attack

A direct ATTACK against the enemy king, the aim of which is to deliver CHECKMATE. This aim outweighs all others, so it is well worth SACRIFICING any amount of MATERIAL to bring a mating attack to a successful finish. When pursuing a mating attack, one should not be utterly single-minded; if the opponent gives up a lot of material to break the attack, by all means take it and coast to victory.

Middlegame

The phase of the game between the OPENING and the ENDGAME. The middlegame begins when the sides are more or less fully developed and lasts until king safety ceases to be a vital and central aspect of the game. The middlegame is the stage of the game

that gives the most scope for creativity and fighting chess. TACTICS and STRATEGY are two of the fundamental ingredients in successful middlegame play, and should be used hand in hand to devise and execute appropriate PLANS.

Minor piece

A bishop or knight.

Minority attack

A subtle form of positional attack, arising from the nature of imbalances in the pawn structure. The aim is not to force mate, or large gain of material, but to weaken the opponent's pawn structure. The idea is best explained by a diagram.

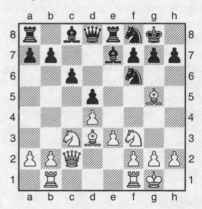

Here White is ready to advance his queenside pawns (b2-b4-b5) to create weaknesses in Black's queenside. The fact that White does not have a c-pawn provides him with a line along which to attack. Black will seek piece play on the kingside to compensate, and may do well to dominate the e-file and establish a rook on the third rank (e.g. on g6 or h6), where it is useful both for defence and attack.

Mobility
The ability of pieces to move freely around the board.

Mutual Zugzwang
See RECIPROCAL ZUGZWANG.

Nalimov tablebases
See ENDGAME DATABASES.

Novelty
See INNOVATION.

Occupy
To place a piece or pieces on a square or line.

Octopus
A term sometimes used to denote a knight on an extremely powerful square, its eight "tentacles" exerting a grip on key squares in the opponent's position. The black knight on d3 in the following position, from Karpov–Kasparov, Moscow Wch (16) 1985 (WGG 79), could well be described as an octopus:

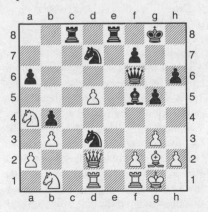

The knight prevents White from playing a rook to c1 or e1 or bringing his wayward a4-knight back into play.

In fact, White is very short of moves that do not lose on the spot!

When interviewed once on German television, Kasparov was asked about a knight that he had apparently described as a "lobster". Something had obviously been lost (or added) in translation. After some bewilderment, he corrected the interviewer, who nevertheless proceeded to ask him again about this "lobster"!

Open
Describes a position in which there are few pawns blocking the CENTRE of the board, and so the pieces are able to move freely around the board. In an open position the play is very critical, as even one badly placed piece can quickly become a fatal WEAKNESS, whereas by comparison in a CLOSED POSITION it is difficult to initiate direct action quickly enough to crash through before a bad piece can be recycled.

Open file
A FILE on which there are no pawns of either colour.

Open Games
A group of openings that begin with the moves 1 e4 e5. Naturally this does not necessarily lead to OPEN positions, though the moves d4 and ...d5 are only needed to blow open the CENTRE completely.

Opening
The first stage of a chess game, during which both players aim to activate all their pieces, and fight for CONTROL of the CENTRE and to seize the INITIATIVE.

Openings
Named sequences of moves from the start position of the game. Well-known openings include the Sicilian Defence, King's Indian and Queen's Gambit. See the section on openings.

Opposite-coloured bishops
A situation in which both sides have one bishop, and one player's bishop moves on dark squares, while the other's operates on light squares. The traditional wisdom is that simple endings with opposite-coloured bishops are drawish since even when material down, a player can hope to set up a BLOCKADE on the colour squares that the opponent's bishop cannot reach. However, in the middlegame, opposite-coloured bishops tend to favour whichever player is attacking, since the defender's bishop will be unable to defend squares attacked by its opposite number.

Opposition
The opposition is a vitally important concept in ENDGAME play. It refers to a stand-off between the two kings, such as the following.

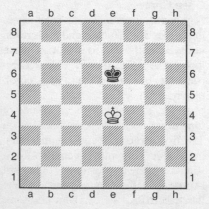

One side has the opposition if the opposing king must give ground. In some positions having the opposition makes the difference between winning and drawing, holding a draw or losing – or in extreme cases between winning and losing. Sometimes it simply doesn't matter very much. In the diagram, whoever is *not* to move has the opposition. If Black is to move, then if he plays 1...♚d6, White can reply 2 ♚f5, while 1...♚f6 may be met by 2 ♚d5 – in both cases the white king has gained ground. If Black simply retreats his king, then White's may advance, while keeping the opposition (1...♚d7 2 ♚d5; 1...♚e7 2 ♚e5; 1...♚f7 2 ♚f5) and so gaining more ground next move.

As explained in the section in the Endgames chapter on king and pawn vs king, if we add a white pawn on e3 in this diagram, then the opposition ceases to be a theoretical abstraction: if White is to play he can only draw, while Black loses if the burden falls upon him.

See also DISTANT OPPOSITION and DIAGONAL OPPOSITION.

Outpost
An ideal square for a piece (typically a knight) in the opponent's half of the board. An outpost is generally supported by a friendly pawn, and is immediately in front of an enemy BACKWARD PAWN on a HALF-OPEN FILE. Occupying the outpost will not only put a piece on a good square, but also ensure that the backward pawn cannot advance, and so remains weak, and ripe for later plucking. However, beware that if exchanges occur and you have to recapture on the outpost square

with the supporting pawn, you will no longer have an outpost.

Overextension

This problem can occur when a player has seized too much space and lacks the army necessary to hold a large territory. The just retribution for such megalomania is normally an invasion by enemy pieces or the far-advanced pawns becoming targets for attack.

Overload

When a piece is required to carry out two functions, then it is said to be overloaded if the opponent can force the piece to execute one of its functions (recapturing a piece, for instance) and then cause a calamity since the piece in question is unable to perform its other function (e.g. parrying a killing check).

Overprotection

One of the concepts that Nimzowitsch systematized was that strategically important points should be afforded abundant protection. One idea is that if the opponent challenges, for instance, a pawn on the key square then the pieces that have been overprotecting it will be able to make good use of the square after it has been liquidated.

Overworked

A piece is overworked if it has too many jobs to perform, and although this may not be instantly tactically disastrous, leads to some inflexibility in the position.

Passed pawn

A pawn which has no enemy pawns either blocking its path, or able to capture it, on its way to PROMOTION. Generally an asset!

Passive

A move or idea that hinders the opponent's plans, or a piece that is defensively placed. Compare ACTIVE.

Pawn break

A pawn move that forces a change in the structure of the position. An important strategic device, especially in BLOCKED POSITIONS.

Pawn centre

A mass of a player's pawns in the middle of the board. In the ideal case a pawn centre will be mobile and flexible, cramping the opponent and providing cover for piece manoeuvres behind the pawns. However, a pawn centre is not always strong, and if the pawns become fixed, and subject to so much attack that they need to be defended passively, then the player attacking the pawn centre can confidently expect to undermine the pawns, and reduce them to rubble.

Pawn chain

The pawn is unique amongst chess pieces in that it moves and captures in different ways. As a result, a white pawn can be blocked by a black pawn standing directly in its path. Both pawns are unable to advance. It is thus a common sight for linking chains of pawns to build up on the board, each pawn obstructed by its counterpart, and some providing defence for a friendly pawn diagonally forward from them. Such pawn chains form the strategic backbone of chess positions, and experienced players know a wealth of typical plans for both sides. The optimal plan is to attack the "base" of a pawn chain; that is, a pawn that defends others in the chain, but is not protected by a pawn itself. Remove that pawn and the new base(s) will become subject to attack. However, dynamic considerations, or the inaccessibility of a base to attack, often dictate alternative plans. Attacking the head of a pawn chain can lead to pawn exchanges and gain some breathing room. Another common idea is a massive pawn advance against the enemy king.

Pawn island

This was a term coined by Capablanca for a group of connected pawns that have no friendly pawns on adjacent files. Thus an ISOLATED PAWN is one island, while an arrangement of pawns, one each on the a-, b-, d-, e- and g-files and two on the h-file, constitutes three pawn islands. In general, other things being equal, the fewer the pawns islands one has the better, since the pawns will then be better able to look after one another.

Pawn structure

The arrangement of pawns on the board. From the pawn structure flows everything else in a game of chess. The pawns mark out each side's territory, suggest the side of the board on which each player should attack, and provide squares for pieces – both one's own, by protecting key squares and for the opponent if there are gaps in the structure. One simply cannot play chess without an understanding of pawn structure, and pawn structures

figure in almost all the positions discussed in this book.

Pearl of Wijk aan Zee

This name has been given to one of the most brilliant games of the 1990s. I'll leave it to the reader to judge how this ranks alongside ancient brilliancies such as the IMMORTAL GAME and the EVERGREEN GAME.

Cifuentes – Zviagintsev
Wijk aan Zee 1995 (WGG 92)

1 d4 e6 2 ♘f3 d5 3 c4 ♘f6 4 ♘c3 c6 5 e3 ♘bd7 6 ♕c2 b6 7 ♗e2 ♗b7 8 0-0 ♗e7 9 ♖d1 0-0 10 e4 dxe4 11 ♘xe4 ♕c7 12 ♘c3 c5 13 d5 exd5 14 cxd5 a6 15 ♘h4 g6 16 ♗h6 ♖fe8 17 ♕d2 ♗d6 18 g3 b5 19 ♗f3 b4 20 ♘e2 ♘e4 21 ♕c2 ♘df6 22 ♘g2 ♕d7 23 ♘e3 ♖ad8 24 ♗g2 ♘xf2 25 ♔xf2 ♖xe3 26 ♗xe3 ♘g4+ 27 ♔f3 ♘xh2+ 28 ♔f2 ♘g4+ 29 ♔f3 ♕e6 30 ♗f4 ♖e8 31 ♕c4

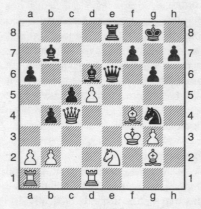

Now for the queen sacrifice that made this game famous...
31...♕e3+ 32 ♗xe3 ♖xe3+ 33 ♔xg4 ♗c8+ 34 ♔g5 h6+ 35 ♔xh6 ♖e5 0-1
It is mate next move.

Perpetual check

If one side can give checks indefinitely, and chooses to do so, then the game will be drawn. Note that there is no special provision in the laws of chess for this, so normally the players will simply agree the DRAW, or else one of them will claim the draw by THREE-FOLD REPETITION.

Piece

Can be used to signify *either* any chess piece, *or* a MINOR or MAJOR PIECE, as opposed to a pawn. Generally the context makes the meaning clear.

Pig

According to Yasser Seirawan, this is a word sometimes used to refer to rooks in especially powerful positions. Based on the idea of "blind swine".

Pin

A tactical device in which a bishop, rook or queen attacks an enemy piece, which dare not (or cannot) move for fear of exposing a more important piece behind.

Plan

A player's intended means of achieving his aims in a position.

Poisoned pawn

A pawn deliberately left *EN PRISE*, often to the enemy queen, with the idea that if the pawn is snatched, the time lost will prove catastrophic, with a direct attack the standard form of retribution. Often the pawn in question is a knight's (b- or g-) pawn, which is the case in two named Poisoned Pawn variations, in the Sicilian Najdorf and the French Winawer.

Position

A particular arrangement of pieces on a chessboard, together with an indication as to who is to move, and whether CASTLING or *EN PASSANT* is possible. Note that under the laws of chess, two positions are not regarded as identical unless they match in all these respects.

Positional

Positional play is based on a consideration of permanent and semi-permanent features of the position. It goes beyond STRATEGY and TACTICS; positional considerations dictate strategy, which in turn dictates tactics. Thus, when offering a positional sacrifice (e.g. an EXCHANGE SACRIFICE that shatters the opponent's PAWN STRUCTURE), one may not have a specific tactical follow-up in mind, or a specific PLAN, but may have judged that in time it will be possible, by one strategy or another, to exploit the WEAKNESSES created. Positional play is a rather deep part of a chess player's understanding, and the ability to think in this way is built up over the years. There are many rules of thumb that have been gathered from the experiences of chess players over the centuries. To have to reinvent this body of understanding would be too much, so reading the works of the great players is an excellent way to build up positional understanding.

Post-mortem

The analysis session immediately following the conclusion of a game. The two players are the main participants, though spectators and other participants in the event, if they have finished playing, may also take part, sometimes wanted, sometimes not. The post-mortem may be seen as a search for truth in the game that has just finished, but often is a continuation of the clash of egos!

Premature
An action that is best delayed until the circumstances are more appropriate.

Preparation
In a chess sense, preparation refers either to moves to pave the way for a particular move or idea, or to a player's study and analysis prior to a game against a specific opponent, deciding which opening line to play. In a more general sense, preparation is the work a player does to improve his prospects of competitive success.

Pressure
A player under pressure, although not necessarily subject to any immediate THREAT, will find his choice of moves limited, and have difficulty finding any ACTIVE PLAN.

Promotion
The changing of a pawn into a queen (or knight, bishop or rook) of the same colour when it reaches the eighth rank. This is often described as QUEENING, when a queen is chosen.

Prophylaxis
A term coined by Nimzowitsch, and a key concept of chess STRATEGY. The importance of prophylactic thinking is stressed by Mark Dvoretsky, a well-known chess trainer. The idea is that it is just as important in chess to prevent the opponent's PLANS as it is to execute your own.

Thus in any position it is worth considering what plans the opponent may have, and look for ways to prevent them from coming to fruition. It may well be best, rather than playing an ACTIVE move, to play one that completely frustrates the opponent's intentions while enhancing your own position, if only very slightly. Karpov's games provide many superb examples. John Nunn once told me of the problems of playing against Karpov, which are often overlooked by those who have never played the man, and write superficial notes to his games. Repeatedly Karpov will keep the opponent's ideas at bay, calculating a great many tactical variations. The opponent will be looking for ways to make progress, but find them frustrated for the subtlest of reasons. Meanwhile Karpov's position will have improved by just the slightest amount.

Protected passed pawn
A PASSED PAWN that is defended by another pawn. This is especially important in pure king and pawn endings, as a king cannot capture the defender without letting the protected pawn run through to become a queen.

Punt
Slang term, referring to an ambitious move or idea tried out without much analysis or preparation.

Queening
See PROMOTION.

Queenside
The a-, b-, c- and d-FILES. Compare KINGSIDE.

Quiet move

A move that involves neither a check nor a capture. It may, however, contain a THREAT.

Quiet position

A position in which there are few imminent TACTICS.

Rank

The numbered rows of squares running across the board. For notation purposes the first rank is at White's side of the board, and the eighth is at Black's side. However, it is common to refer to Black's first rank (meaning White's eighth), and so on.

Rating

A number based on a player's previous results, which to some extent represents that player's strength. Various systems are employed by national federations, but it is the ELO RATING system that has been adopted by the international bodies and most national federations.

Reciprocal zugzwang

A position in which whoever is to move is in ZUGZWANG. This can be most pithily expressed as "whoever is to move must weaken their position" and most precisely as "a situation in which the stronger side cannot force a win if he is to move, while the weaker side loses if he must move". It is implicit in the definition that there is no way for either side to lose a move, and pass the burden to the opponent.

The concept is quite difficult to grasp, since normally the right to move in chess is of enormous value, with both players fighting to make full use of every TEMPO – but here it becomes a catastrophic burden!

It may seem that a reciprocal zugzwang is an infrequently occurring oddity, of little general importance to chess as a whole. However, this is not the case at all. Many of the most fundamental endgames hinge upon positions of reciprocal zugzwang, the following being the simplest:

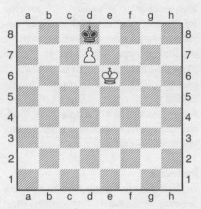

If White is to play, then he has no way to win. 1 ♔d6 is stalemate, whereas any other king move allows 1...♔xd7.

If Black is to move, then he loses: 1...♔c7 2 ♔e7 followed by 3 d8♕. Note that if Black were able to "pass", this ending would be a draw, and *any* position with king and pawn vs king would be a draw provided the defending king could get in front of the pawn.

The construction of ENDGAME DATABASES, and study and interpretation of the information in them, has shown that reciprocal zugzwangs occur surprisingly frequently, and have a significance way beyond their numbers.

Refutation

A clear analytical demonstration that a move or idea is UNSOUND.

Resignation

When a player feels he has no realistic chance of avoiding eventual defeat, he may choose to resign. Traditionally this involves turning the king on its side, but it is more normal simply to stop the clock, possibly say "I resign", and shake hands. While it is bad etiquette to refuse to resign in a completely hopeless position, if you are in any doubt as to whether your position is hopeless, play on. Perhaps your opponent won't be sure how to win the position either; and if he is, you'll learn something.

Roller

A pawn roller is a mass of pawns advancing up the board, sweeping enemy pieces from their path.

Romantic

In the style of the nineteenth century players, with sacrifices aplenty, and little thought for DEFENCE or PAWN STRUCTURE.

Russian dynamism

This concept was developed by Russian players around the middle of the twentieth century. The idea was that it is often worth accepting WEAKNESSES in return for ACTIVE play. This led to the development of whole new opening systems such as the King's Indian and Sicilian lines with ...e5.

For instance, consider the Boleslavsky Variation of the Sicilian. After 1 e4 c5 2 ♘f3 ♘c6 3 d4 cxd4 4 ♘xd4 ♘f6 5 ♘c3 d6 (the Classical Sicilian) 6 ♗e2 Boleslavsky's idea was to play 6...e5, gaining time by attacking the white knight and staking a territorial claim in the centre.

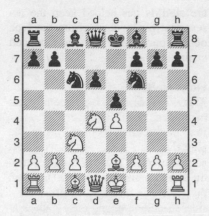

Structurally it appears to be a concession since the d-pawn is now BACKWARD, and the d5-square a potential OUTPOST for a white piece. However, DYNAMIC considerations are more relevant. Black will attack the e4-pawn, and CONTROL the d5-square with his pieces, and can often execute the ...d6-d5 advance, liquidating the "weak" pawn. White will never have time to occupy d5 with a piece without it being instantly challenged or exchanged. Nowadays the Boleslavsky Variation is considered so satisfactory for Black that White rarely plays 6 ♗e2 against the Classical Sicilian. Moreover, in other variations in which Black has already played ...e7-e6, one of the key strategic ideas at his disposal is at some moment to play ...e6-e5 – these positions can be satisfactory even with Black a whole move down!

Rybka

The leading ANALYTICAL ENGINE from 2006 to the time of writing. It tends to be a good partner for assisted analysis, as its assessments are less "jumpy" than other engines, and the fact that the Rybka team (led by Vasik Rajlich) are all IMs has helped keep the assessment function free from the type of misconceptions that have dogged engines written by weaker players.

Saavedra Position

This is one of the most famous of all composed positions. There are just four pieces on the board, yet in the play there are twists and turns, tricks and countertricks. It was published in the *Glasgow Weekly Citizen*, in 1895.

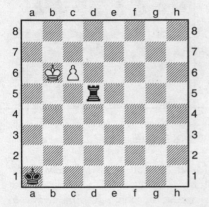

This is the sort of position that might very well occur in a game – perhaps White has just sacrificed his last piece for a black pawn that promoted on a1.

1 c7

The first surprise is that the rook has difficulty stopping the pawn.

1...♖d6+ 2 ♔b5!

2 ♔c5? is a draw: after 2...♖d2 and a check on c2 Black stops the pawn.

2...♖d5+ 3 ♔b4 ♖d4+ 4 ♔b3 ♖d3+ 5 ♔c2

It looks like the end of the road for Black, since the rook has run out of squares on which it might SKEWER the king and soon-to-be-crowned queen. However, he has a last throw:

5...♖d4!

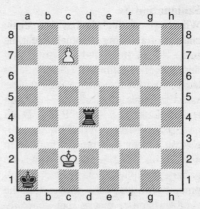

The idea is that if White promotes to a queen, Black can force a draw by STALEMATE: 6 c8♕? ♖c4+! 7 ♕xc4 and Black has no moves. This had been the original composer's idea; it had previously been published with colours reversed as a "White to play and draw" position. Saavedra's contribution, a single move, but a great one, has earned him immortality:

6 c8♖!

Now material is level, but the unfortunate positions of Black's king and rook doom him to loss.

6...♖a4

Else 7 ♖a8+ wins, while 6...♖c4+ 7 ♖xc4 is no longer stalemate, so it is checkmate next move.

7 ♔b3

White threatens both the rook with capture and ♖c1#. There is no defence, so White wins.

This position has inspired many composers to think, "If you can achieve that with just four pieces, think what is possible with a full set!"

Sacrifice

An offer of some quantity of MATERIAL, with a specific aim in mind.

Scholar's Mate

"Give two of the uninitiated a chess-board, a set of chessmen, a list of rules and a lot of time, and you may well observe the following process: the brighter of the two will quickly understand the idea of checkmate and win some games by P-K4, B-B4, Q-R5 and QxKBP mate. When the less observant of our brethren learns how to defend his KB2 square in time, the games will grow longer and it will gradually occur to the players that the side with more pieces will generally *per se* be able to force an eventual checkmate." – Michael Stean, in *Simple Chess*, 1978.

The mate to which he refers is known as Scholar's Mate. In the standard algebraic notation, the moves involved are (by White) e4, ♗c4, ♕h5 and ♕xf7# or (by Black) ...e5, ...♗c5, ...♕h4, ...♕xf2#. The queen moves right next to the enemy king, supported by the bishop. Unless some precautions have been taken, it is instant mate – game over. To lose a game this way is humiliating, and obviously gives no scope for demonstrating any endgame techniques that you might have mastered. Countless games between novices have started this way, and all too many of them ended that way too! However, no one need ever lose a game to Scholar's Mate. Every chess player needs a defence to brush aside Scholar's Mate, and punish those who doggedly play for the snap mate. Let's consider a typical sequence:

1 e4 e5 2 ♗c4 ♗c5 3 ♕h5

Phase one completed. White threatens mate, and incidentally the e5-pawn.

3...♘c6??

Black develops a piece, controls central squares and defends the e5-pawn. A great move, except that it loses on the spot! I suppose it is easier for a novice to see the threat to the e5-pawn (attacked once, and not defended) than to the f7-pawn (attacked twice, defended once).

4 ♕xf7#

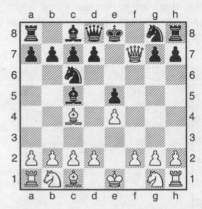

Mate. Yes, chess is definitely an art form.

Let's run through some ways to avoid this nightmare.

On move one: Black does not have to play 1...e5. This move is perfectly good, of course, but if you are facing opponents whose only plan is to attack the f7-pawn, one of the Semi-open defences detailed in the section on openings might prove highly effective. For instance the French: 1 e4 e6 2 ♗c4 d5 leaves White having to relocate his bishop – in the Caro-Kann, 1 e4 c6 2 ♗c4 d5 is similar. Obviously the Alekhine, 1 e4 ♘f6, makes White's idea infeasible too, though I have had the pleasure of playing the black side of 2 ♗c4 ♘xe4 3 ♕f3? d5 in casual games. The Sicilian was my choice when up against ten-year-olds with only one plan, and the game tended to proceed 1 e4 c5 2 ♗c4 e6 (no mates on f7 now; Black intends 3...d5, attacking the bishop) 3 ♘c3 a6 4 a4 (else 4...b5) 4...♘c6 5 ♘f3 ♘f6.

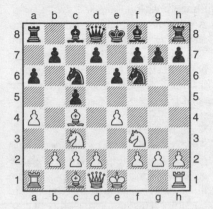

Black has a comfortable game, and plans to advance in the centre with ...d5, pushing White back and seizing the initiative.

Naturally, one's choice of opening should not be dictated by a cheap trap the opponent might try, but if you are playing a lot of chess against novices, you will find that when they have graduated from the routine of ♗c4, ♕h5 and hammer f7, they may have moved on only to the new routine of ♘f3, ♗c4, and ♘g5 (if appropriate) and hammer f7.

On move two: Black could play 2...♘f6, which is a move with an excellent reputation. This prevents ♕h5.

On move three: Last chance! Black needs a move that stops ♕xf7 being mate. 3...g6 stops the mate, but loses the e5-pawn and the rook in the corner: 4 ♕xe5+ and 5 ♕xh8. Not good. The queen is needed, and e7 is the best square:

3...♕e7

Black plans 4...♘f6, forcing the white queen into a disorderly retreat.

4 ♘f3

White threatens the e5-pawn.

4...♘c6

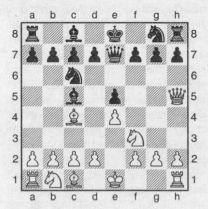

Defending the pawn, and again threatening 5...♘f6.

5 ♘g5 ♘h6

Defending f7 once more. White has no way to increase the pressure and will soon have to back-pedal.

White will regret his crude opening. There is much more to chess than mate on f7!

Scorched earth policy

As applied to chess, this refers to a plan of exchanging pieces whenever possible to empty the board as much as possible, the aim being to reduce the risk of loss. Normally employed when facing a stronger player, though sometimes players who feel they are very strong in simplified positions may adopt this approach. Since exchanging without a good reason is generally a concession, playing in this way can hardly be recommended, although it may sometimes work.

Selective search

A process used by most chess computer programs to enable them to calculate more deeply. The idea is to cut off the analysis of obviously inferior continuations, to leave more processor time to analyse the critical variations. Precisely how this is done is one of the main tests of the programmer's skill. The criteria cannot be purely materialistic – the program should not miss a winning queen sacrifice because it throws out any continuations in which the material balance temporarily shows a deficit of nine points! How the computer's analytical tree is pruned is a major factor in determining its style. For instance, two of the top 1990s engines had very different approaches. Fritz prioritized moves that carried a strong threat, making it very effective when there were forcing variations, but relatively weak in slower positions. Chess Genius, on the other hand, used an armoury of chess understanding provided by its programmer, Richard Lang. The result was that it could come up with some subtle ideas, but at the expense of some raw power in tactical shoot-outs.

Semi-open games

The group of openings in which White opens 1 e4 but Black does not reply with the symmetrical 1...e5. Far and away the most important of the semi-open games is the Sicilian Defence, 1...c5. Others include the French Defence (1...e6), Caro-Kann (1...c6), Pirc (1...d6), Modern (1...g6), Alekhine (1...♘f6), Scandinavian (1...d5), Nimzowitsch ('...♘c6), Owen's Defence (1...b6) and the St George (1...a6). Other moves are a bit silly (e.g. 1...♘a6, the Lemming; 1...g5, the Basmanic Defence) or suicidal, e.g. the Fred (1...f5), which loses a pawn and exposes the black king! (Don't try this at home.)

Sharp position

A position in which TACTICS predominate – essentially a pure shoot-out. The ASSESSMENT hinges principally on how effectively both sides can exploit the other's WEAKNESSES in the short term.

Sight of the board

An expression used to signify a chess player's ability to perceive at a glance at a position where the pieces can move, and what tactical devices are possible. This intuitive ability is developed through experience, especially efficiently by young players.

Simplification

A reduction in the amount of FORCE and/or TENSION on the chessboard. For a player with a clear advantage, it is a useful step towards victory, since it reduces the opponent's possibilities for muddying the waters.

Skewer

A tactical device, by which an attack is made along a line that contains two valuable units, one behind the other. If the piece in front moves, the one behind is subject to possible capture.

Smothered mate

A checkmate delivered by a sole knight, based upon many or all of the king's flight squares being occupied by pieces of its own colour. Here is a nice example:

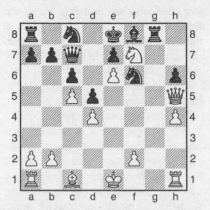

This position comes from the game Nigmadzhanov–Kaplin, USSR 1977. White finished off as follows:

20 ♘d6++ ♔d8 21 ♕e8+!! ♘xe8 22 ♘f7# (1-0)

Four black pieces block in the king. Note that for a pure smothered mate, there ought to be a black unit on d7.

Sound

Correct; for sufficient COMPENSATION.

Space

The idea of a space advantage is not an easy one to grasp in chess. Determining who has more space is not difficult, e.g. by counting the number of squares attacked in the opposing half of the board, but experienced players can sense at a glance who has more space. However, simply seizing territory does not necessarily imply obtaining an advantage. Just as in war, a large territory demands a large and well-organized army to defend it. Besides, chess is not a territorial game; the aim is to destroy a single enemy unit. If controlling space is desirable, it is only as a means to the end of delivering mate.

How is controlling space useful?

1) Extra space makes it easier to MANOEUVRE, and switch an ATTACK between various enemy WEAKNESSES.

2) In a cramped position, pieces may get in each other's way, reducing their effectiveness and MOBILITY.

3) A player with more space is likely to have his pieces nearer the enemy king, and have more options for defending his own king.

4) If pawns stake out the territorial advantage, as is normally the case, then they are only a few moves from queening, and so there are greater possibilities for combinations based on rushing a pawn through.

So far, so good, but how do we assess when a restricted position is viable? Michael Stean put forward the concept of the "capacity" of a position: the number of places in the structure from which pieces can operate. Thus if a player has more pieces than the capacity of his position allows, then this is a problem, and some freeing exchanges, or a change in the structure, are desirable. However, if the structure provides ample scope for all the pieces, then there is no problem, and it is well worth wondering if the opponent might be a little overextended, and have problems defending some key squares.

Let's now consider a few positions where questions of "capacity" are relevant.

The first diagram on the next page shows a position from the Modern Benoni. Black has spent some time exchanging off bishop for knight, but it was worth it, because now Black has pieces that suit the capacity of his position.

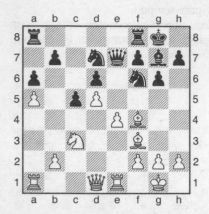

Here, Lev Psakhis's excellent idea 14...h5 makes sure of some squares for knights on the kingside (...♞h7-g5 is in the offing) and gives Black good play.

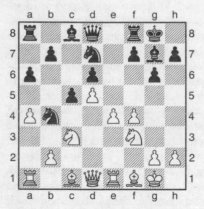

This is another Modern Benoni, but a different picture entirely. Black has great difficulties finding squares for his pieces, especially with an e4-e5 thrust hanging over him. There is not even the possibility of unloading the c8-bishop by ...♝g4xf3, since White will be able to rule this out with h3 when necessary. In fact, it was when discussing this position that John Nunn wrote, in 1982, "Black needs a

new idea against 8 ♝b5+ *[the key move leading to this position]* to keep the Benoni in business." He meant it too: later that year he unsuccessfully tried his last idea against Kasparov, and subsequently took up the King's Indian (obtaining draws with it in two later games against Kasparov).

But I digress. Here is another specific instance, from the game Spielmann–Nimzowitsch, Niendorf 1927, with an illuminating quote from Richard Réti, writing shortly before his death in 1929, in his classic book *Masters of the Chessboard*:

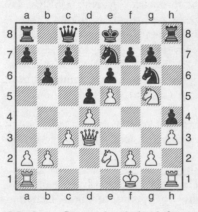

"Much profit can be derived from a study of this position. White is in control of more territory, and so one might think he has the advantage. But that is not the case. The real criterion by which to appraise close positions is the possibility of breaking through. In general, the player who can move freely over a greater area can probably place his pieces more advantageously for a possible breakthrough than his opponent, who is restricted in his movements.... Nimzowitsch ... now shows that one may be in a restricted position and yet have every possibility of breaking through. Thus, in the present position, the possibilities of White's breaking through obviously lie in c4, and f4-f5. The first is scarcely a strong move, for White dominates more territory in the middle and on the kingside, but not on the queenside. In the present case it is a particularly doubtful move, since White's d-pawn would become backward. The liberating move dictated by the position would therefore be f4-f5.

"But there can be no question of making those moves, as White will obviously never be able to dominate the f5-square. Furthermore, Black has made a very good provision for the future in his seemingly artificial but really very profound manoeuvres (...♘g6, ...h5-h4, ...♘ce7, but above all in the exchange against White's king's bishop).

"Thus, while White has no possibilities of breaking through, and is therefore limited to making waiting moves behind the wall of his pawns, Black has at his disposal the possibilities of breaking through afforded him by ...f6 and ...c5. Black alone, therefore, is able to take the initiative, and consequently he is in a superior position, in spite of his limited territory."

Play continued 15 ♔g1 f6 16 ♘f3 ♕d7 17 ♔h2 c5 18 c4 (the fact that White feels obliged to play this move speaks volumes about his inability to use his extra space) 18...♕c7 19 cxd5 c4 (Black nevertheless gains ground on the queenside) 20 ♕c2 exd5 21 ♖he1 0-0 22 ♘c3 fxe5 23 ♘xe5 ♘xe5 24 dxe5 d4. Clearly there is no question of Black suffering from a lack of space any more.

Spare tempo

An important concept in ENDGAME play, when ZUGZWANG is relevant. Consider the following position:

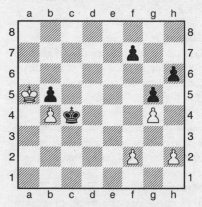

The position of the kings and the b-pawns is a familiar situation of reciprocal zugzwang. Whoever's king must move first, will lose the b-pawn and the game. Thus the ability to play a harmless pawn move, changing nothing vital in the position, is extremely useful. This ability is called "having a spare tempo". After such a move, the burden to play a move falls upon the opponent. We see that in this position, White has two spare tempi at his disposal, f2-f3 and h2-h3, whereas Black has only one, ...f7-f6. Thus White plays 1 h3 f6 2 f3, whereupon Black must make fatal concessions. Note that if in the diagram, the black pawn were on h7 rather than h6, it would be White in a terminal zugzwang after 1 h3 f6 2 f3 h6.

Speculative

Said of an ATTACK or SACRIFICE that cannot be calculated to a finish and constitutes deliberate risk-taking by the player choosing to play it.

Speed of thought
As applied to chess, the speed at which a player can analyse variations from a position. See SIGHT OF THE BOARD and TACTICS.

Stalemate
If a player has no legal moves, but is not in check, then it is stalemate and the game is drawn immediately. Note that the word "stalemate" should only be used to describe this situation – it is not a general term for a drawn game. Many categories of endgame are only drawn due to stalemate possibilities.

Strategy
The chess player's craft of making, adapting and adjusting PLANS as the game develops. While there are many rules of thumb that have been developed over the years to help with the process of strategic decision-making, there is enormous scope for creative strategy in chess. Each situation must be assessed on its merits, with small differences in position able to dictate wholly different strategies. The bottom line is that a player must design his strategy to be in line with what is tactically feasible in the position. Chess strategy is a vast subject, discussed in many places throughout this book.

Studies
These are composed positions (also known as endgame studies) in which there is the stipulation "White to play and win" or "White to play and draw". They may be regarded either as puzzles, instructive examples or an art form. There should be only one solution, no wasted pieces, and an attractive, crisp idea demonstrated.

Style
There is plenty of scope in chess for individual style. In some positions there is only correct move, and of course a strong player will choose this move regardless of individual taste, there are many situations where there are many different approaches, from which it is impossible to select an objectively best course of action. In these instances, it is the player's style that will dictate his choice. A world champion's style is a multi-faceted entity, but at the risk of presenting stereotypes, the styles of world champions and challengers from the last forty years could be seen as follows:
Anand: activity-oriented, with a preference for launching attacks that do not burn his boats;
Topalov: dynamic attacker, confident in highly unbalanced positions;
Kramnik: all-rounder, with a fine feel for structure and positional nuances;
Kasparov: ultra-dynamic, scientific attacker;
Short: a straight attacking player who favours piece activity to structural considerations;
Karpov: structurally minded minimalist, a specialist in prophylaxis;
Korchnoi: a materialist especially adept in defence and counterattack;
Fischer: an all-rounder, especially skilled in transforming advantages from one type to another;
Spassky: a classical attacker;
Petrosian: specialized in deep prophylaxis and messy positions.

Swindle
An unjustified win or draw scored by a player by deceiving his opponent in some way. This is a major facet of

practical chess, and often involves laying tactical traps, or gunning straight for the opponent's king to give him the maximum headaches on the road to exploiting an advantage.

Symmetry

Some positions from the opening remain fully symmetrical for some moves. Occasionally this leads to a tenable game for Black, but in the majority of cases it spells trouble, since in most cases when White gives a check, or plays, e.g., ♕x♕, the symmetry is broken and White will be left with any advantages that there are in the position. Clearly Black should seek a good moment to break the symmetry.

A more common use for the term symmetry in chess is to refer to pawn structures, which are described as symmetrical if both players have the same number of pawns as the opponent on each file. This makes it difficult for either side to achieve much by pawn play alone, while the OPEN FILES provide scope for exchanging off the MAJOR PIECES.

Tactics

The interplay of the pieces. A player's ability to handle tactics well hinges on his SPEED OF THOUGHT and his SIGHT OF THE BOARD.

Tempo

The time taken for a useful move – not on the clock, but on the board. The plural is tempi.

Tension

When referring to pawn structures, this is a state in which either side could exchange pawns, or possibly advance a pawn ("resolving the tension"), but both instead prefer to leave them where they are for the time being. This is known as "maintaining the tension". Resolving the tension often uses time and clarifies the opponent's plan, so strong players will generally maintain tension unless there is a specific reason not to do so.

The text

The move actually played in a game, or given as the main line in a book (and convenient jargon for writers on chess!).

Theory

The constantly evolving body of opening analysis and master practice that has built up over the years. Massive tomes explain and add to this body of knowledge each year, while for the true enthusiast, enormous databases of games are available, which can be classified according to opening variations.

Threat

A strong continuation that would be played if it were not the opponent's turn to move – and will be played if the opponent does not prevent it in some way.

Three-fold repetition

Apart from mutual agreement, this is the most common way in which chess games are drawn. When a POSITION has been repeated three times, with the same possibilities open to both sides on each occurrence (including CASTLING and EN PASSANT possibilities), then the player to move may claim a DRAW. Alternatively, when a player intends to play a move that will bring about the third such repetition, then he may write down the move on his scoresheet and then, without actually playing it on the board, claim the draw. An up-to-date scoresheet is necessary to claim a draw by three-fold repetition. Note that the repetitions do not have to be consecutive (they could be several moves apart) and that it is the *position* that matters – individual moves do not need to be repeated. There are time penalties for incorrect claims, so only make a claim if you are certain!

Through check

A simple tactical device, identical to a SKEWER, except that the piece immediately attacked is the king. The term is not often used, however.

Time

When not referring to time on the chess clock, "time" is one of the key chessboard factors. It is the time needed to move pieces, not measured in seconds, but in tempi, e.g. it takes four tempi to play ♘f3, g3, ♗g2 and 0-0. If you use two moves to accomplish something that could have been done in one move, then you have "lost a tempo".

The power to move is generally extremely valuable in chess; think how big an advantage it would be to be able to make two moves to the opponent's one, even at just one moment in a game! To gain time, it is therefore often well worth sacrificing material. As an extreme example, in a sharp position, it might even be worth giving up a whole queen just to gain a move to bring a key piece into the attack.

Emanuel Lasker devised, in his magnum opus *Lasker's Chess Manual*, a very approximate system for reckoning how much material a tempo was worth *in the early stages of the game*. Generally I would rebel against any point-counting system, but then Lasker was world champion for 27 years!

1st move	1 point
2nd move	$^4/_5$
3rd move	$^3/_4$
4th move	$^2/_3$
5th move	$^1/_2$
e- or d-pawn	2
f- or c-pawn	$1^1/_2$
g- or b-pawn	$1^1/_4$
h- or a-pawn	$^1/_2$
knight	$4^1/_2$
king's bishop	5
queen's bishop	$4^1/_2$
king's rook	7
queen's rook	6
queen	11

Obviously this must not be used as a look-up table to determine whether to play a particular gambit or sacrifice, but if knowing that one of the all-time greats valued the early moves to this extent helps give you the courage to play good sacrifices, then all good and well. On the basis of Lasker's table, the well-known gambit in the Torre Attack, 1 d4 ♘f6 2 ♘f3 e6 3 ♗g5 c5 4 e3 ♛b6 5 ♘bd2 ♛xb2, would be considered to give roughly enough for the pawn (the b-pawn in exchange for Black's 4th and 5th moves), whereas the Morra Gambit (1 e4 c5 2 d4 cxd4 3 c3 dxc3 4 ♘xc3) could be regarded as Black's 2nd and 3rd moves in exchange for White's d-pawn – not a good bargain for White, but by no means appalling.

Time control

A specified number of moves that must be made before the time on a player's clock has elapsed. When the required number of moves has been played inside the allotted time, a player is said to have "made" (or "reached") the time control.

Time pressure

When shortage of time on the clock causes a player to hurry some of his decisions.

Time-trouble

When the lack of time on the clock is so acute that a player must play his moves very quickly.

Transposition

Reaching the same POSITION via a different sequence of moves.

Trap

A situation in which a plausible move leads to disaster.

Troitsky Line

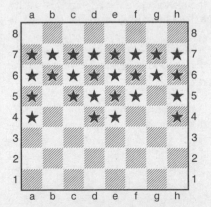

Named after Alexei Troitsky, the great Russian endgame analyst and study composer, this is the key concept in the ending of two knights versus pawn. The knights win if the pawn is behind the Troitsky Line and is blockaded by a knight (i.e. it stands on the square in front of the pawn, and cannot be ejected by the enemy king). Two white knights vs one black pawn win if the pawn is blockaded on a marked square in the previous diagram.

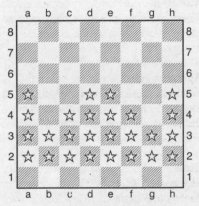

These are the squares where a white pawn loses versus two black knights.

Troitsky performed his work at the start of the twentieth century, but his conclusions have been confirmed by modern ENDGAME DATABASES.

Unclear

A situation that is difficult to assess, generally since both sides have play, and to come to any better ASSESSMENT would involve a great deal of ANALYSIS. In a genuinely unclear position, even a lot of analysis will tend to throw up yet more unclear positions, so there is often justification for a writer giving "unclear" assessments. Nevertheless, it is all too often used as a cop-out by a lazy annotator.

Underpromotion

To choose either a rook, bishop or knight when promoting a pawn.

Unsound

This has several meanings: incorrect (of a COMBINATION); for insufficient COMPENSATION (of a SACRIFICE); should not achieve its goal if the opponent responds well (of an ATTACK).

Variation

A sequence of moves, which may or may not have occurred in a game.

W-manoeuvre

A W-shaped knight manoeuvre that is needed to force mate with bishop and knight versus a bare king. Since mate can only be forced near a corner square that can be attacked by the bishop, the defender will aim, when forced to the edge of the board, for a safe corner. Then the W-manoeuvre is the way to drive the king to a corner where it can be mated.

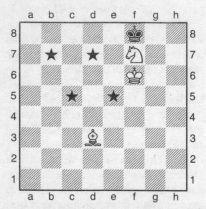

The black king has just been checked out of the safe corner.

1 ♗h7

Stopping the king returning to g8.

1...♚e8 2 ♘e5

The first step of the W. The knight is headed for d7, where it will stop the king getting back to f8. The point of the W-manoeuvre is not the shape itself, but rather that the knight must cover key squares the bishop cannot reach, i.e. h8, f8, d8, c5 and b6, as the king is driven across to a8. The W enables the knight to cover these squares in quick enough succession.

2...♚f8

2...♚d8 3 ♚e6 ♚c7 4 ♘d7! (the next step of the W covers all the right squares) 4...♚c6 5 ♗d3 just traps the king in the "right" corner.

3 ♚e6 ♚e8 4 ♘d7 ♚d8 5 ♚d6

The king covers any possible escape squares on the second rank.

5...♚e8 6 ♗g6+

Ejecting the king from e8, and neatly covering f7, which the white king no longer guards.

6...♚d8 7 ♘c5

Setting off to cover d8, now that e8 is sealed off.

7...♚c8 8 ♗f7

Simply losing a move, while keeping the bishop covering e8.

8...♚d8 9 ♘b7+

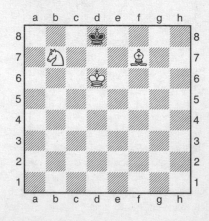

9...♔c8 10 ♔c6 ♔b8 11 ♔b6

Again the king prevents his opposite number from reaching the second rank.

11...♔c8 12 ♗e6+

And again the bishop drives back the king.

12...♔b8

Now White can relax a little. The king and bishop confine the black king to two squares, and it's just a case of manoeuvring the knight in such a way as to give checkmate, rather than stalemate!

13 ♗f5

Just losing a move, so that when the knight arrives on a6, it will be with check. Any sensible square on the h3-c8 diagonal would do just as well.

13...♔a8 14 ♘c5 ♔b8 15 ♘a6+ ♔a8 16 ♗e4#

If you understand this manoeuvre, mating with bishop and knight is routine. Without knowing this manoeuvre, it can be an extremely difficult ending to finish off. To extend a little chess rhyme (referring to how various pieces cooperate together):

Queen and knight, they're all right;
Rook and knight, not too bright;
Bishop and knight, takes all night!

Weak pawn

A pawn which is able to be attacked, is not easy to defend and cannot easily move forward in such a way as to escape from its difficulties.

Weak square

A square in one's territory that is hard to CONTROL and which is liable to be used or occupied to good effect by the opponent's pieces.

Weakness

A facet of a chess position that can be exploited by the opponent. Typical types of weakness are: an exposed king; a sensitive square in which the opponent can lodge a piece; a pawn that is easily attacked and difficult to defend, etc.

Wrong Rook's Pawn

A rook's pawn whose potential queening square cannot be covered by one's only remaining bishop. This becomes significant if the opponent can eliminate all material apart from these pieces, since he can then draw by getting his king to the queening square.

Wings

General term for the KINGSIDE and the QUEENSIDE, as opposed to the CENTRE. Play on the wings becomes the main feature of play when the centre is BLOCKED.

Zugzwang

A situation in which a player, although under no actual threat, is obliged to weaken his own position due to the need to make a move. See also RECIPROCAL ZUGZWANG and SPARE TEMPO.

Zwischenzug

An "in-between" move, often a check, before playing what seemed like an obligatory move – a recapture for instance. Very easily overlooked, even by strong players.

A Brief History of the World Chess Championship

Unofficial Champions

Prior to 1886, there was no universally recognized title of World Champion, though there were individual players acclaimed as the greatest of their time.

François-André Danican **Philidor** (1726–95), a French operatic composer, was regarded as the world's leading player in the mid-eighteenth century. His *L'analyze des échecs* (1748) was an enormously influential book, introducing many concepts that have become part of the modern understanding of chess. His was the famous aphorism, "the pawn is the soul of chess".

Louis-Charles Mahé **de la Bourdonnais** (1795–1840) developed his chess at the Café de la Régence in Paris, and quickly became recognized as the leading player. He defended his status in a series of marathon matches against the Englishman, McDonnell, in 1834. These matches were the precursor of world championship matches, not only due to their gladiatorial aspect, but because the games were widely published and analysed.

Howard **Staunton** (1810–74) was the leading English player of the nineteenth century, and the top player in the 1840s, beating the Frenchman, Saint-Amant in a match in Paris in 1843. He organized the first ever chess tournament, in London in 1851, and wrote extensively on the game. He also prepared an annotated edition of the complete works of Shakespeare, work on which prevented him from meeting Morphy in a match.

Paul Charles **Morphy** (1837–84) was the first great American player. He burst onto the chess scene in 1850, like Fischer a century later, as already one of the best players in America at the age of thirteen. He visited Europe in 1858, and decisively beat the leading European players. However, after returning to America he hardly played at all, but such had been his superiority that no other player dared to claim to be World Champion while Morphy was still alive. His dashing attacks were based on firm logic, and demonstrated that chess was far from properly understood at the time.

Official Champions

Wilhelm **Steinitz** (1836–1900; 1st World Champion, 1886–94) set about developing a "theory" of chess, and bequeathed to the world the basis for the modern understanding of the game. He won a series of matches in the 1860s, and remained the strongest player into the 1890s. In 1886 he met

Zukertort in the first match at which the title of World Champion was at stake.

Emanuel **Lasker** (1868–1941; 2nd World Champion, 1894–1921) beat the ageing Steinitz and brushed aside several challenges in subsequent years. He was a superb all-round player who developed and, in his profound writings, popularized Steinitz's theories.

José Raúl **Capablanca** (1888–1942; 3rd World Champion, 1921–7) is widely regarded as the greatest natural talent in chess history. At the age of twelve he won a match against the champion of his native Cuba, and later, despite hardly reading anything about the game, established himself as the natural successor to Lasker, whom he eventually met in a title match after the First World War. There was general astonishment when he lost his title six years later. Those who met Capablanca were impressed by his personal charm, and his ability to assess chess positions accurately at a glance.

Alexander Alexandrovich **Alekhine** (1892–1946; 4th World Champion, 1927–35; 1937–46) was the antithesis of Capablanca in many ways: industrious, devious and a heavy drinker. He carefully scrutinized the "invincible" Capablanca's style, and successfully played against weaknesses that few thought existed. His chess was often spectacular, and he wrote well to describe his chessboard battles. He avoided a rematch against Capablanca – an understandable reluctance perhaps, but a great shame for the chess world.

Machgielis (Max) **Euwe** (1901–81; 5th World Champion, 1935–7) seized the title briefly from Alekhine, who undoubtedly underestimated him at first. Euwe was a fine tactician and an erudite theoretician, who later put these talents to great use in his writings. He did much to popularize chess both in his native Holland and, as FIDE President, around the world.

Mikhail Moiseevich **Botvinnik** (1911–95; 6th World Champion, 1948–57; 1958–60; 1961–3) was the first of the Soviet World Champions. He was probably already the strongest player in the late 1930s, but it was not until the match-tournament in 1948 that he could claim the title left vacant by Alekhine's death. He quickly became a hero of Soviet society. A tremendously serious man, he never played for fun, and gave up playing in 1970 in order to concentrate on computer chess.

Vasily Vasilievich **Smyslov** (1921–; 7th World Champion, 1957–8) played three tense matches with Botvinnik in the 1950s, emerging victorious in one. An opera singer away from the board, he has stressed the importance of harmony in chess. He has enjoyed a long career, reaching the Candidates final in 1983.

Mikhail Nekhemievich **Tal** (1936–1992; 8th World Champion, 1960–1), was one of the greatest attacking geniuses in chess history. His attacks seemed like pure magic, and his contemporaries were baffled as he swept aside the opposition on his way to becoming the youngest world champion up to that time. This led to a reappraisal of defensive technique, and a better understanding of chess generally. Tal was plagued by ill-health for the whole of his life; otherwise he might have been champion for longer.

Tigran Vartanovich **Petrosian** (1929–84; 9th World Champion, 1963–9), was a champion whose play was far from accessible to the public. His games featured a great deal of manoeuvring, yet his handling of messy positions and his understanding of exchange sacrifices was unequalled.

Boris Vasilievich **Spassky** (1937–; 10th World Champion, 1969–72) is best known to the general public as "the man who lost to Fischer", which is a shame since he is a great player. His direct, classical style led to two fascinating matches against Petrosian.

Robert James (Bobby) **Fischer** (1943–2008; 11th World Champion, 1972–75) did more than anyone else to popularize chess in the western world. He brought a new professionalism to chess, both in his preparation for games, and his insistence on good playing conditions and decent pay for the top players. Most of all, he inspired a generation of players by showing that one man could take on the Soviet chess establishment, and win.

Anatoly Evgenievich **Karpov** (1951–; 12th World Champion, 1975–85; FIDE Champion 1993–9) became World Champion when Fischer did not agree terms with FIDE (World Chess Federation)

under which he would defend his title. A small, unassuming man from the Ural mountains, Karpov immediately set about proving to the world that he was a worthy champion by completely dominating tournament chess in the subsequent years. For a decade he stood head and shoulders above all others, and he continued to be a top player into the late 1990s. In 1993 he regained the FIDE World Championship, following the PCA break-away, and successfully defended it in 1996 against Kamsky, and against Anand in a very short match in 1998, following FIDE's new knockout system. He did not compete in FIDE's 1999 Championship, which was won by Alexander Khalifman.

Garry Kimovich **Kasparov** (1963–; 13th World Champion, 1985–2000) is widely regarded as the greatest chess player the world has ever seen. His chess was a synthesis of raw talent, scientific research and grim determination. Opponents found his physical presence at the board intimidating, and his powerful personality is ideally suited to television. He was not content just to dominate the chessboard; he was also heavily involved in the rough-and-tumble of chess politics. In 1993, he helped to establish the PCA (the Professional Chess Association), under whose auspices title matches against Short and Anand were played. This organization since ceased to exist, and Kasparov's subsequent attempts to organize a new title defence were plagued by difficulties. Eventually, he arranged a match with Kramnik in 2000, which he lost to the surprise of many. However, he remained clearly World No. 1 up until his retirement from professional chess in 2005. He has since turned to Russian politics, in which he is seen internationally as the main opposition figure. He is still involved in chess, occasionally playing exhibition events and kibitzing online. He is also coaching Magnus Carlsen.

Vladimir Borisovich **Kramnik** (1975-; 14th World Champion, 2000–7) is from Tuapse, in the south of Russia. He has an all-round style, with a particular emphasis on solidity and a feel for positional nuances, which has become increasingly pronounced as his career has progressed. He was tipped by Kasparov for stardom from an early age, and indeed he assisted Kasparov in his 1995 match against Anand. Kramnik was already one of the leading players from his late teens, and he was the only player who consistently managed to score fairly well against Kasparov, from whom he won the title in 2000, without a single loss. After two successful defences (Leko 2004, Topalov 2006), he lost the world championship in the 2007 Mexico City tournament, and subsequently failed to win the "return match" against Anand the following year.

Viswanathan (Vishy) **Anand** (1969-; 15th World Champion, 2007-; FIDE Champion 2000–2) is a chess sensation from Chennai (Madras), India. One of the world's top players since the early 1990s, he plays lively attacking chess and sees variations and tactics at an astonishing speed – in his early years, he would complete tournament games with barely minutes used on his clock. However, he was always in the shadow of Garry Kasparov, the one player against whom he failed to score well. Anand seized his chance at the 2007 World Championship tournament, a format that suited his style perfectly. His imperious victory over Kramnik in the 2008 title defence confirmed his place in history as a great champion.

Looking to the future, the heir apparent in the view of many is Magnus **Carlsen** (born 1990) from Norway. A very strong player from a tender age, Magnus appears to find chess very easy. His games feature both highly creative preparation and inventive play at the board, and he seems to be at home in all types of positions and in playing a very broad repertoire of openings. At the time of writing (September 2009), it has just become public knowledge that Garry Kasparov is training Carlsen, whom he sees as the most talented of the current generation of players.

FIDE Champions

FIDE's alternate lineage in the period 1993–2006 was as follows:

1993–9 Anatoly Karpov
1999–00 Alexander Khalifman
2000–2 Viswanathan Anand
2002–4 Ruslan Ponomariov
2004–5 Rustam Kasimdzhanov
2005–6 Veselin Topalov

Appendix A: How to Play Chess

In this book I have largely assumed in this book that the reader knows how to play chess. This appendix is for those who are starting from scratch, or else are a little unsure on some of the details.

You doubtless know that chess is a game for two players, referred to as "White" and "Black". The game is played on a square board, called not surprisingly a "chessboard", of 64 light and dark squares. The empty board looks like this (though some do not have the numbers and letters):

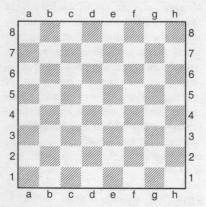

Each player possesses an army of chess pieces, sometimes called "chessmen". A piece occupies one square on the board; no square can contain more than one piece. Pieces can move between squares on the board according to a strict set of rules.

The pieces are as follows:

♙   the white king
♚   the black king
♕   the white queen

    the black queen
    two white rooks
    two black rooks
    two white bishops
    two black bishops
    two white knights
    two black knights
    eight white pawns

    eight black pawns

These pieces are arranged at the start of the game as follows:

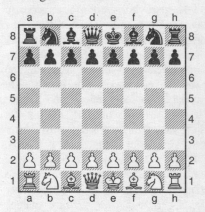

In a game of chess, White and Black take it in turns to play a single move using their pieces. White always makes the first move of the game.

We must now look at how each of the pieces moves.

The King
The king moves one square at a time, to a square adjacent to that which it occupies, horizontally, vertically or diagonally.

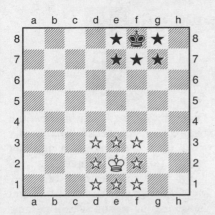

In the diagram, the white king can move to those squares marked with a white star, and the black king to those on which a black star is shown. The king is not a very powerful piece, but is the most valuable, since a player who is unable to save his king loses the game. There are some special rules involving the king: see the items on castling (page 551), and check and checkmate (page 550).

The Queen

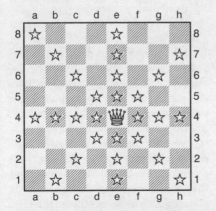

The queen is the most mobile and therefore the most powerful piece. A queen can move any number of squares diagonally, vertically or horizontally, provided the intervening squares are not obstructed (it cannot jump over other pieces).

The Rook

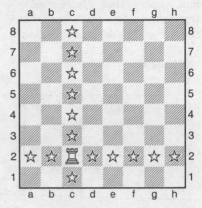

The rook moves horizontally or vertically, any number of squares, provided that there are no pieces in the way. It is the second most powerful piece after the queen. There is one special move involving the rook – see the item on castling (page 551).

The Bishop

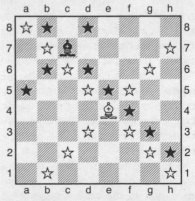

The bishop can move any number of

squares diagonally, provided the intervening squares are not occupied. Note that this means that a bishop that starts off on a light square can only ever move to other light squares (similarly for one that starts on a dark square). Thus a bishop may be described as either a "light-squared bishop" or a "dark-squared bishop".

The Knight

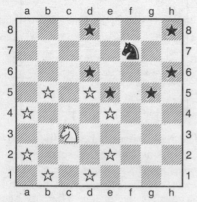

The knight's move is the one that causes the most confusion to those new to chess, but there is no need for this. Rather than start talking about "jumping", "moving between", "one move orthogonally and one diagonally" or any of the other nonsense that is generally used in beginner's books, I'll explain the simple method that my father used to explain the knight's move to me when I was three years old. I understood it easily then, and it has stayed in my memory for nearly four decades, so it must be effective!

Consider the "six" on a die or a domino. Depending on how you are looking at it, the dots are displayed as either:

or:

Quite simply, the knight moves from one corner to the furthest corner from it. It doesn't matter if other squares (dots!) are occupied.

I'm sure that learning this easy way of understanding how the knight moves is one reason why it became my favourite piece: winning the opponent's queen with a knight fork was simply a matter of visualizing three dominoes!

For those of you seeking a really technical definition of the knight's move, to impress your friends perhaps, it is a "root five leaper". The distance between the centre of the square the knight leaves and the square where it arrives is the square root of five (approx. 2.236) times the width of the squares – but don't get a ruler out during a serious game!

Capturing

Before moving on to discuss how the pawns move, I should introduce the concept of capturing, and show how the pieces we have looked at so far make captures.

Firstly, a piece cannot capture a piece of its own colour, though normally, of course, one would not want to make such a capture! Likewise, at the risk of stating the obvious, a piece cannot move off the board.

All the pieces we have so far seen capture simply by moving in their normal way onto the square occupied by an enemy piece. The enemy piece is removed from the board, its square taken by the piece making the capture. The captured piece takes no further part in the game. There is no restriction on what pieces may be captured by another piece. A queen being more powerful than a knight does nothing to stop the knight making a capture if it can legally move to the square occupied by the enemy queen.

The only piece that can never actually be taken is the king, but as we shall see this is because of the rules of the game: a player cannot allow his king to be captured.

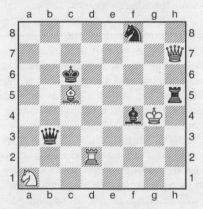

There are many captures possible in the above diagram:

By White:
the king can take the black rook;
the king can take the black bishop;
the queen can take the black rook;
the bishop can take the black knight;
the knight can take the black queen.

By Black:
the king can take the white bishop;
the rook can take the white queen;
the bishop can take the white rook;
the knight can take the white queen.

The Pawn

The pawn is the only piece that cannot move backwards. It is also the only piece that does not move in the same way when capturing as when moving otherwise. There are also three special rules involving the pawn: the initial double move, promotion and *en passant*. I shall explain them in that order, once we have dealt with its normal way of moving and capturing.

Firstly this is the standard move of the pawn:

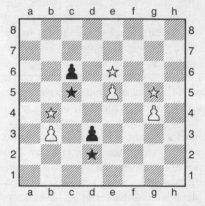

The pawn simply moves one square forward (i.e. towards the side of the board where the opponent's pieces started the game) provided the square is unoccupied.

However, the pawn does not *capture* by moving one square forward. If anything stands on the square in front of a pawn, it cannot move to that square.

The pawn captures by moving one square *diagonally forward*. Note that it can only move in this way when making a capture.

In the following diagram, a variety of pawn captures are possible.

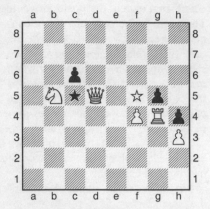

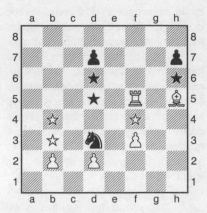

The black pawn on c6 (using the self-explanatory coordinate system displayed around the diagram) has a choice between capturing the white knight or white queen, or moving forward one square. The white pawn on f4 has two possible moves: one square directly forward, or capturing the black pawn on the square g5. The black pawn on g5 can in turn take the white pawn, but otherwise has no possible moves. The remaining pair of pawns, the white one on h3 and its black counterpart on h4, are completely immobilized at the moment.

The pawn's initial double move

On its first move in a game, a pawn has a choice: it can move either one or two squares forward, provided there is no obstruction.

In the following diagram White's pawn on b2 is on the square where it started the game. Both b3 and b4 are unoccupied, so it could move to either of these squares in a single leap. On the other hand, the white pawn on d2 has no moves at all; it cannot jump over a piece to make its double move.

The white pawn on f3 has clearly already moved, and so can only make its normal single-square move to f4.

As for Black's pawns, the one on d7 has a free choice between moving one square or two, while that on h7 can move as normal one square forward, but cannot move two squares, since its path is blocked by the white bishop. The pawn's initial double move, like its normal move, cannot capture a piece.

Just to remove a possible point of confusion, an unmoved pawn only has the normal power to capture by moving one square diagonally forwards. There is no two-square diagonal capture, and so neither black pawn can capture the rook on f5!

Pawn promotion

Thinking about it, it would be pretty pointless for a pawn to make the journey to the far side of the board only to find that it could make no further moves, its path blocked by the edge of the board. Something special *must* happen.

The reward for getting a pawn to the end of the board is a great one: it becomes a queen (or a rook, bishop or knight, should the player prefer) of the same colour. This rule provides the hidden strength of the pawn, and is the reason why an advantage of a single pawn is quite enough to win a game (as we shall see in Appendix B, king and queen easily win against a lone king).

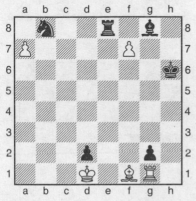

In this position, there are four pawns one square from promotion. The white pawn on a7 could promote by advancing to a8 or else by taking the knight on b8. The pawn on f7 has three choices of square on which to promote: e8 (taking the rook), f8, or g8 (taking the bishop).

The black pawns in this diagram do not have such luxuries of choice. The pawn on d2 cannot promote at all, its path blocked by the white king, but the pawn on g2 can promote on f1 by capturing the white bishop.

In each case, the promoting pawn could become a queen, rook, bishop or knight.

Supposing White were to promote on b8 to a queen, and then Black on f1, taking a knight, and then White

on g8 to a queen, the position would be as follows:

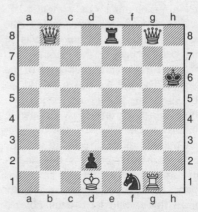

Note that there is no problem with having two queens on the board. There is nothing in the rules of chess to prevent there from being as many as nine queens, or ten knights, on the board, though this would be overkill!

The en passant *rule*

This is the least well known of the basic rules of chess, and was introduced to compensate for the pawn's double move. Consider the following situation:

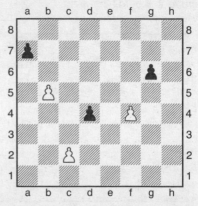

First, look at the pawns on f4 and g6.

If either pawn moves forward, it can be captured. Pawns situated like this restrain each other's movement.

The reason for introducing the pawn's initial double move was to quicken the pace of the game, not to change fundamental properties of the pieces. The double move would allow the white pawn on c2 to get past the black pawn on d4, by advancing directly to c4. Likewise the black a-pawn could move directly to a5. The *en passant* rule corrects this anomaly: immediately after the pawn has made its double move, an enemy pawn that would have been able to capture the pawn if it had moved only one square, *may capture it as though it had done precisely that*. It seems bizarre at first, but the capturing pawn moves diagonally forward to the square behind the pawn that has just moved two squares, removing it from the board.

Supposing White were to play his pawn from c2 to c4, and Black captured *en passant*, and Black's pawn went from a7 to a5, and White also made an *en passant* capture, the new situation would be like this:

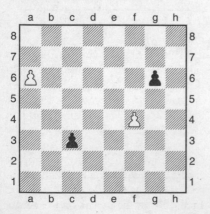

Check and Checkmate

If a king is threatened with capture, it is said to be "in check". The rules of chess require a player who is in check to get out of check immediately. If this is impossible, the king is said to be "checkmated" or "in checkmate" and the game is over, with the side delivering checkmate the winner.

Here is a typical situation of a king in check:

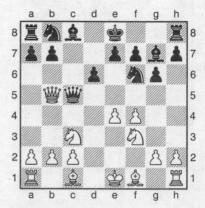

The black king is in check from the white queen. In general, there are three possible ways to get out of check:

1) *Capturing the piece giving check*. Here, this could be accomplished by the black queen taking the white queen.

2) *Putting a piece in the way of the check*. Here, two of Black's pieces could go to c6, while three black units could block the check by going to d7.

3) *Moving the king to a square where it is not attacked*. In this case d8 or f8 would fit the bill.

If none of these methods is feasible, then it is checkmate.

It goes almost without saying that the rules of chess prohibit any move that puts one's own king in check.

Castling

Now that I have defined "check", I can present the final special move, which involves the king and the rook. Consider this part-diagram:

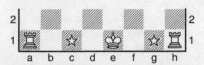

To castle, the king moves two squares towards a rook (either of the marked squares). Thus:

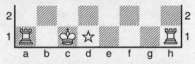

or:

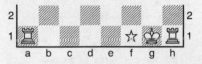

Then *as part of the same move*, the rook jumps over the king, landing on the square immediately next to His Majesty. The final situation is as follows:

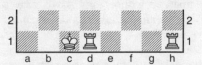

or:

Castling with the a-rook is described as castling queenside, or castling long, while using the h-rook instead is known as castling kingside or castling short.

The situation is exactly analogous for Black, viz.

becomes either:

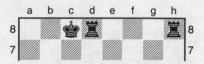

or:

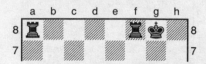

There are some restrictions on castling, however:

1) There must be no pieces between the king and the rook.

2) Both the king and rook must be previously unmoved in any way.

3) The king may not castle at a moment when it is in check.

4) While it is obviously illegal to castle into check, it is also impossible to castle if the king *moves through check*, i.e. would be in check if it instead moved a single square towards the rook.

To clarify one point that often causes confusion: it does not prevent castling if the rook is attacked, or, in the case of queenside castling, if the square b1 (or b8 for Black) is under attack. Note this well, for there are even cases of grandmasters getting this wrong.

Stalemate

One curious rule of chess, totally at odds with any real-life battle scenario, is that if a player has no legal moves at his disposal, but is not in check, then the game is an immediate draw.

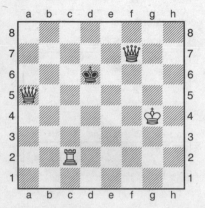

Despite White's enormous material advantage, and variety of ways to give mate in one move, if it is Black to play in this position, the game is drawn.

The stalemate rule is no bad thing though, since it gives a little hope to a player in trouble, and adds a great deal of subtlety in some finely balanced endgames, as we see elsewhere in this book.

The End of the Game

There are three possible results to a game: a win for White, a win for Black, or a draw. The winner receives one point, and the loser none. In the event of a draw, both players receive half a point.

The game is won for a player if:
- he has checkmated his opponent's king; or
- his opponent has resigned the game; or
- his opponent has lost on time (see the chapter on the chess clock, page 354).

The game is drawn if one of the following applies:
- The player to move is stalemated.
- A position arises in which it is impossible for either side to give mate (even if both sides cooperate); generally this means king vs king, king and bishop vs king or king and knight vs king.
- A player runs out of time on his clock, but the opponent does not have sufficient pieces left to be able to deliver mate.
- The players agree to a draw.
- The exact same position has occurred three times, with the same player to move, and one player claims a draw.
- Fifty moves by both players have passed without any pawn moves or captures, and one player claims a draw.

For further details of these last four eventualities, please refer to the Glossary, page 506.

Appendix B: Chess Notation

One of the reasons why chess has such an extensive literature is the ease with which chess games and analysis can be written down. In turn, this means that chess is ideally placed to become increasingly important in the information age, since the symbols used to record chess moves are normal letters and numbers. The moves of thousands of games can be downloaded in seconds, and the only constraint on playing chess online is the connection time – the few bytes needed to convey a chess move can be transmitted in a tiny fraction of a second.

The form of notation used in this book is called figurine algebraic notation. I have largely assumed that readers will already be familiar with this notation, since it is the standard in chess books and newspaper columns, and computers use algebraic, or at least a modified form of it. Moreover, it is very easy to learn algebraic notation.

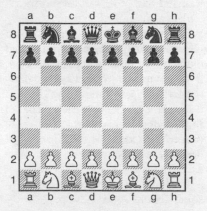

In this familiar diagram, each square has a unique name, defined by the two coordinates shown around the edge of the diagram. Thus in the initial position, as shown, the white king is on e1, and the black queen's knight on b8. In every diagram in this book (for maximum ease of reference) and on many chess boards these coordinates are given. However, in most books they are not given, so it is worth committing them to memory.

The conventions by which moves are defined are not complicated, and it is possible to get by if you just know the first two, and otherwise use common sense.

1) A move is indicated simply by the figurine for the piece that is moving, followed by the square on which it arrives. Example: ♘e4 denotes a knight moving to e4.

2) If a pawn moves, then only the arrival square is given. Example: e4 denotes a pawn moving to e4.

3) A check is indicated by a plus sign (+) after the move. Example: ♕e5+ denotes a queen moving to e5, and giving check.

4) A capture is indicated by a multiplication sign (or simply a letter x) before the arrival square. Example: ♗xb5 denotes a bishop making a capture on b5.

5) When more than one piece of the same type can move to a particular square, the file is given if this is sufficient to identify the piece that is moving. The additional letter is

always placed immediately after the figurine, before any capture symbol. Examples: ♘de4 denotes a knight moving from a square on the d-file to e4, when there is a knight on a different file that could also move to e4; ♘dxe4 would be the notation if a capture took place on e4.

6) When more than one piece of the same type *on the same file* can move to a particular square, the number of the rank is given if this is sufficient to identify the piece that is moving. The additional number is placed immediately after the figurine, before any capture symbol. Example: ♖1d5 denotes a rook moving from d1 to d5, when there is another rook on the d-file that could move to d5. Note: in exceptionally rare circumstances, both the rank and file are needed to specify which piece is moving. In this case the letter for the file is given before the number for the rank, e.g. ♕a8xd5.

7) Pawn captures are shown by giving the file on which the pawn starts, followed by the capture sign, and finally the square on which the capture is made. Example: exf5 denotes a pawn from the e-file making a capture on f5.

8) Odds and ends: checkmate is shown by # after the move; *en passant* capture is shown just as if it were a normal pawn capture on the square where the pawn arrives; promotion by putting the new piece after the pawn's move, e.g. exd8♕+ signifies a pawn from the e-file capturing on d8, promoting to a queen and giving check; castling is shown by 0-0 for the kingside version or 0-0-0 for queenside castling.

When the moves of a game are written down, there is a number placed before each move by White. The move by Black follows the one by White. Example: 1 e4 e5 2 ♘f3 ♘c6 3 ♗b5 a6 4 ♗a4 ♘f6 is a possible sequence of four moves by each side from the start position, resulting in the following position:

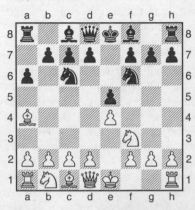

If a move by Black is given without the move by White preceding it, then three dots are placed before the move by Black to signify the missing move by White. Thus one would say that Black's second move in this example was 2...♘c6.

When one needs to **write down chess moves by hand**, such as when playing a game of competitive chess, it is obviously impractical to draw out little shapes of the pieces. Instead a simple letter denotes each piece. In English the letters are: K (king), Q (queen), R (rook), B (bishop) and N (knight). In the past Kt was once used for knight, but this is obsolete.

In **long algebraic**, as used in some books and newspaper columns, the square from which the piece is departing is always given in full, and a dash placed between the departure and arrival squares (unless it is a capture, in which case the standard "x" is used).

Descriptive Notation

For several centuries algebraic was not universally used by chess players, since another form of chess notation was prevalent in English-speaking countries. This was the so-called "descriptive notation", which is used by some players to this day.

In descriptive notation, each file has a unique name, just as in algebraic, but the name is given by the piece that starts the game on that file. Thus:

a-file   = QR-file
b-file   = QN-file
c-file   = QB-file
d-file   = Q-file
e-file   = K-file
f-file   = KB-file
g-file   = KN-file
h-file   = KR-file

However, the number attached to this to give a coordinate for a particular square is different depending on whose viewpoint is being taken. The square on the queen's file that is closest to White (d1) is known as Q1 to White, but for Black is called Q8, since it is the eighth square from him. Likewise, White's KB3 is Black's KB6, and so on. Moves are denoted according to the following method:

1) First the name of the piece in question (in full, e.g. QN, KBP) is written, followed by a hyphen, followed by the square to which the piece is moving, as seen by the player making the move. Example: QN-KB4 denotes *either* White's queen's knight (the one that started life on b1) moving to the fourth square from White's side of the board on the KB-file (i.e. f4 in algebraic) *or* Black's queen's knight (the one that started life on b8) moving to the fourth square from Black's side of the board on the KB-file (i.e. f5 in algebraic).

2) If the move is a capture, then the move is given as the piece moving, followed by the captures symbol (x) and then the piece that is being captured. Example: KRxQNP denotes *either* White's king's rook (the one that started life on h1) capturing a black pawn on the QN-file (b-file) *or* Black's king's rook (the one that started life on h8) capturing a white pawn on the QN-file (b-file).

3) Checks are denoted in the same way as for algebraic notation.

4) Obviously, this scheme leads to a lot of redundancies in the notation, so any really excessive clarification is omitted. Thus the move KRxQBP would be written simply RxP if there are no other moves by which a rook can capture a pawn, or RxBP if there are several pawns that can be captured by a rook, but only one way in which it can be a bishop's pawn.

It is this omission of redundant codes, so necessary if the notation is to be even vaguely concise, that leads to confusions with the notation. Firstly, there are often several equally valid ways in which a move can be written (e.g. KN-B4 and N-KB4 might be one and the same move, and equally efficient ways of expressing it), and, since deciding how to write down a move requires some thought and alertness, it is very easy to forget to give enough clarification.

Appendix C: The Basic Mates

Having learned how to play chess, the next step, before studying some simple tactics, is to become familiar with a few of the basic procedures for finishing off the game. This is useful not only from a direct practical viewpoint, but also since it helps get a feel for how the various pieces work together.

Here I shall explain how to mate with king and queen vs king, king and two rooks vs king, king and rook vs king and king and two bishops vs king.

Note that I do not cover king, bishop and knight vs king, since this is too difficult to be regarded as a basic mate. Please refer to the entry for the W-manoeuvre in the Glossary (page 538) if you are really interested. If you are wondering how optional it is to study this procedure, I had beaten a few grandmasters and several dozen international masters before bothering to commit it to memory! Still, I was quite relieved one day in 1983 when I had two games which could have come down to this rare ending – but both opponents chose to resign instead.

King and Queen vs King

This one is quite easy. The king and queen push the lone king quickly to the edge of the board, and give mate.

The main danger is that since the queen covers so many squares, it is quite easy to give an accidental stalemate, as shown in the following two part-diagrams:

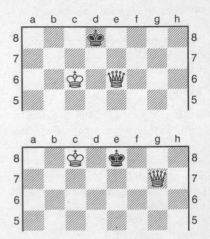

With Black to play, both of these positions are drawn by stalemate.

Typical checkmating positions for which to aim are as follows:

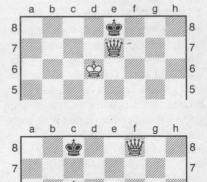

In driving the king to the edge of the board, the main idea is to use the queen to restrict the defending king to ever-smaller portions of the board, and to use the attacking king to push it further to the edge. Checks are not necessary, though are sometimes useful. Here is a typical sequence:

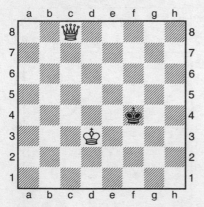

1 ♕e6

Restricting the black king to the f-, g- and h-files. The choice of e6 is not random, since if the black king wishes to remain on the f-file, it must now go opposite the white king.

1...♔f3 2 ♕f5+

Pushing the king back a further rank, since the white king covers all the flight squares on the e-file.

2...♔g3 3 ♔e2

This puts the black king in the same predicament again: either it voluntarily goes to the edge or will be checked there next move.

3...♔g2

Or 3...♔h4 4 ♕g6 ♔h3 5 ♔f3 ♔h2 6 ♕g2#.

4 ♕g4+ ♔h2 5 ♔f2 ♔h1 6 ♕h3#

King and Two Rooks vs King

You may have thought king and queen vs king was simple, but this one is even easier. The two rooks

mate on their own, mostly with checks; the king is not even needed, so tuck it away somewhere and let the rooks do the rest. The only danger is that one might carelessly leave a rook where the king can take it; stalemate is implausible, since the method involves check after check.

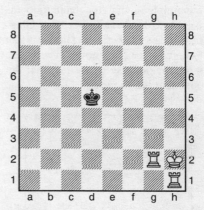

1 ♖d2+ ♔c4

All the king can do is choose where it is to be mated. 1...♔e4 2 ♖e1+ ♔f5 3 ♖f2+ ♔g5 4 ♖g1+ ♔h4 5 ♖f8 ♔h5 6 ♖h8# is another possibility.

2 ♖c1+ ♔b3

Preventing ♖b2+, but rooks can run far faster than kings...

3 ♖c8 ♔b4 4 ♖b2+ ♔a3 5 ♖b7 ♔a4 6 ♖a8#

King and Rook vs King

This one is important and very useful. Quite often in quickplay games or blitz finishes, your opponents will want to see whether you can mate quickly with king and rook. Even the simple hand and eye coordination to deliver the mate (which may require about twenty moves) with less than twenty seconds on the clock can be tricky.

Like the mating technique with king and queen, the idea is to use the combined powers of the king and rook to force the lone king to the edge of the board, where it is to be mated. However, the rook being far less powerful than the queen, more subtlety is needed; indeed a vitally important part of the technique involves "zugzwang". See the Glossary, page 539 for details on this technical term; for now I'll rephrase it to "making use of the fact that the opponent has to move".

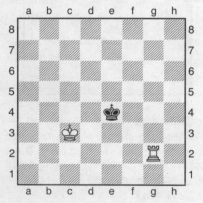

First, decide which edge of the board you are going to force the king towards – generally the side it's closest to.

1 ♖d2

Confining the king to the e-, f-, g- and h-files. The rook will now remain on the d-file until it is possible to give a check on the e-file that forces the king to the f-file.

1...♔e3

1...♔e5 2 ♔c4 ♔e6 3 ♔c5 ♔e7 4 ♔c6 allows White to push back the king more quickly.

2 ♖d8 ♔e4

2...♔e2 3 ♖d7 is a typical tempo

loss, in order to achieve the desired arrangement: kings a knight-move apart on opposite sides of the line controlled by the rook, with the rook at a distance, but closer to its own king.

3 ♖d1

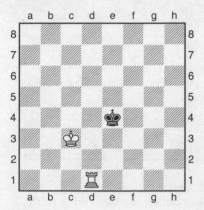

This is a key concept, as described in the last note. The black king must now either give ground or walk into a check that knocks it back onto the f-file.

3...♔e5

3...♔e3 4 ♖e1+ and the king must go closer to the edge of the board; after 4...♔f2 5 ♖e8 ♔f3 6 ♔d4 the process repeats itself.

4 ♔c4

"Efter ham!" as I used to say to my pupils at a small school in Herrested, Denmark. The king pursues its counterpart up the board, staying a knight-move away.

4...♔e6

4...♔e4 5 ♖e1+ is the familiar tale.

5 ♔c5 ♔e7 6 ♔c6 ♔e6

6...♔e8 would be a bad idea, since rather than continuing systematically, White would shorten the procedure considerably by 7 ♖d7 and mating the black king on the eighth rank, rather than the h-file.

7 ♖e1+

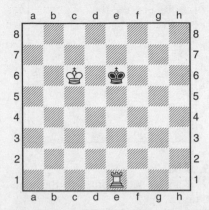

Finally the king is forced to the f-file. Remember: the rook only gives check when the kings oppose each other like this.

7...♔f5 8 ♔d5

On the next move, the white rook will choose a square on the e-file as far as possible from the black king.

8...♔f4

8...♔f6 9 ♖e2 is the old "kings a knight-move apart" routine.

9 ♖e8 ♔f3 10 ♔d4 ♔f2 11 ♔d3 ♔f3 12 ♖f8+

I hope you can anticipate the next few moves by now.

12...♔g4 13 ♔e4 ♔g5

13...♔g3 14 ♖f7, etc.

14 ♖f1 ♔g6 15 ♔e5 ♔g7 16 ♔e6 ♔g6 17 ♖g1+

Forcing the king to the edge. The next time there is a check such as this, it will be mate.

17...♔h5 18 ♔f5 ♔h4

Or 18...♔h6 19 ♖g2 ♔h7 20 ♔f6 ♔h8 21 ♔f7 ♔h7 22 ♖h2#.

19 ♖g8 ♔h3 20 ♔f4 ♔h2 21 ♔f3 ♔h1 22 ♔f2 ♔h2 23 ♖h8#

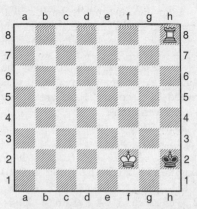

I would suggest studying this mating procedure carefully, and practising it with friends or a computer until it becomes absolutely routine. You will then have learnt a systematic manoeuvre, and a practical use of zugzwang. Even if that doesn't impress your friends, mating with king and rook vs king in less than twenty seconds should do the trick!

King and Two Bishops vs King

You will be relieved to hear that this is a good deal easier than king and rook vs king, but this ending isn't of much practical importance.

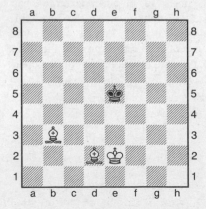

I won't give detailed commentary, since no great precision is needed to give mate. The bishops work well together to restrict the king to an area of the board and then constrict the king to a yet smaller area, until it is mated in a corner. Here are a few typical variations.

1 ♗c3+ ♚d6

Or 1...♚e4 2 ♗c4 ♚f4 3 ♗d3 ♚g4 4 ♗e5 ♚g5 5 ♚f3 ♚h5 6 ♗f4 ♚h4 7 ♗g6 ♚h3 8 ♚g5 ♚h2 9 ♚f2 ♚h3 10 ♗f5+ ♚h2 11 ♗f4+ ♚h1 12 ♗e4#.

2 ♚e3 ♚c5 3 ♚e4 ♚d6 4 ♗b4+ ♚c6 5 ♗a4+ ♚c7 6 ♚d5

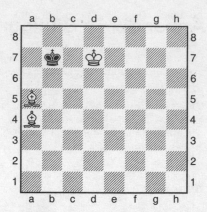

9...♚b8

9...♚a6 10 ♗c7 comes to the same thing.

10 ♗c7+ ♚b7 11 ♗b5 ♚a7 12 ♚c8 ♚a8

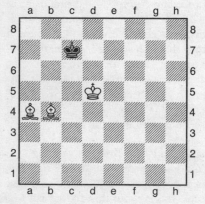

The two bishops work perfectly together to set up an impenetrable barrier on their own, so the restricting process is easy. Precise manoeuvres are not required to prevent the black king from breaking out into the open.

6...♚d8 7 ♚d6 ♚c8 8 ♗a5 ♚b7 9 ♚d7

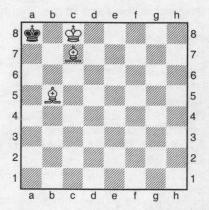

White to play and mate in three (several solutions). Just don't stalemate!

13 ♗d6 ♚a7 14 ♗c5+ ♚a8 15 ♗c6#

Appendix D: Bibliography

I referred to a great deal of books, magazines, electronic data and websites while working on this book. The following were the most significant sources:

Electronic: ChessBase Magazine
Online and Internet: CompuServe Chess Forum, The Week in Chess
Magazines: Inside Chess, British Chess Magazine, New in Chess Magazine, Bulletin of the Central Chess Club of the USSR, Shakhmatny v SSSR
Periodicals: Informator, New in Chess Yearbook
Books:
Play Winning Chess (Seirawan and Silman), Microsoft Press, 1990
The Oxford Companion to Chess, Second Edition (Hooper and Whyld), Oxford University Press, 1992
Encyclopedia of Chess Openings, vols. A–E, (Ed. Matanović), Šahovski Informator, various years
Chess Personalia: A Biobibliography (Gaige), McFarland, 1987
Steve Davis Plays Chess (Davis and Norwood), Batsford, 1995
How to Use Computers to Improve Your Chess (Kongsted), Gambit, 2003

Suggestions for Further Reading

An immense number of books have been published on chess, covering every aspect of the game. Some are good; some are bad. How is one to choose which to buy? If you find a reviewer whose opinions you value, then that is a starting point, but note that a lot of chess-book reviews are somewhat shallow and non-critical.

A good way to choose chess books is by author. Once you have found some authors whose work you enjoy and have found useful, then chances are that their other works will appeal, if they are on subjects of interest to you. Likewise, you might also look out for other books by the same publishers, as the degree of quality control they exert is likely to be maintained across their list. Two of the authors who inspired me to become a chess writer were John Watson and John Nunn, and it has been my privilege to work with both of these gentlemen. They both continue to produce work of a very high standard. Everything they write can be recommended, and bought unseen with a knowledge that it will be conscientious and interesting work. Other reliable authors include Yasser Seirawan, Jeremy Silman, John Donaldson, Joe Gallagher, John Emms, Igor Stohl, Mihail Marin, Peter Wells and Viktor Bologan. Garry Kasparov's work is obviously of interest, but check the reviews to see how much effort he has put into each particular volume, while Mark Dvoretsky's books are top quality, but note that some are reissues of earlier works, with new titles.

If you are looking for good general works on the opening, then I can suggest Paul van der Sterren's comprehensive *Fundamental Chess Openings* (Gambit, 2009), and John Watson's *Mastering the Chess Openings* series (four volumes), which goes into much greater depth on a selection of opening topics. These books all have plenty of verbal commentary. For a concise endgame guide, there is John Nunn's *Understanding Chess Endgames* (Gambit, 2009); for further ideas on computer-assisted analysis, Robin Smith's *Modern Chess Analysis* (Gambit, 2004) is the masterwork.

Index of Games and Part Games

Key: The second-named player is Black if his/her/its name appears in **bold**. Otherwise the first-named player was Black. Computers are shown in *italic*. All numbers refer to pages.

Index of Openings

All numbers refer to pages. The main entry for an opening is given in **bold**.